February 11–13, 2013
Monterey, California, USA

**Association for
Computing Machinery**

*Advancing Computing as a Science & Profession*

# FPGA'13

Proceedings of the 2013 ACM/SIGDA International Symposium on
## Field Programmable Gate Arrays

*Sponsored by:*
**ACM SIGDA**

*Supported by:*
**Altera, Microsemi, Microsoft Research, Xilinx, Atomic Rules,
Algo-Logic, and BEEcube**

*With logistical support from:*
**The Trimberger Family Foundation**

**Association for
Computing Machinery**

*Advancing Computing as a Science & Profession*

**The Association for Computing Machinery**
2 Penn Plaza, Suite 701
New York, New York 10121-0701

**Notice to Past Authors of ACM-Published Articles**
ACM intends to create a complete electronic archive of all articles and/or other material previously published by ACM. If you have written a work that has been previously published by ACM in any journal or conference proceedings prior to 1978, or any SIG Newsletter at any time, and you do NOT want this work to appear in the ACM Digital Library, please inform permissions@acm.org, stating the title of the work, the author(s), and where and when published.

**ISBN:** 978-1-4503-1887-7

Additional copies may be ordered prepaid from:

**ACM Order Department**
PO Box 30777
New York, NY 10087-0777, USA

Phone: 1-800-342-6626 (USA and Canada)
+1-212-626-0500 (Global)
Fax: +1-212-944-1318
E-mail: acmhelp@acm.org
Hours of Operation: 8:30 am – 4:30 pm ET

**ACM Order Number:** 420130

Printed in the USA

# Foreword

It is our great pleasure to welcome you to the *2013 ACM International Symposium on FPGAs (FPGA 2013)*. This year's symposium continues its tradition of being a premier forum for the presentation of FPGA-related research across a wide variety of topics: new FPGA architectures and circuit designs, enhancements to Computer-Aided Design (CAD) algorithms and flows, applications well-suited to FPGAs, and design studies. In addition to facilitating the sharing of research results through the paper and poster presentations, FPGA provides an excellent opportunity for researchers from around the world to mingle and discuss research results and ideas.

This year we received 106 submissions from twenty-one countries. The program committee accepted 24 full (ten page) and 4 short (four page) papers, each of which are published in the proceedings, for an acceptance rate of 26%. Full papers will each also have a twenty-minute oral presentation, while short papers will have a five-minute oral presentation, followed by a poster presentation at which attendees can further discuss the work with the authors. Finally we will have four poster sessions in which a total of 37 additional research projects will be displayed on posters, and at which you may ask detailed questions of the authors.

This year the symposium begins with a day of tutorials related to high-level synthesis and design flows for FPGAs. A total of four tutorials will be presented in two parallel tracks, and the three-hour length of each tutorial allows an in-depth presentation on each of the four design flows and tools. The symposium also includes an evening panel moderated by Jason Cong of UCLA on the question of "Are FPGAs Suffering from the Innovator's Dilemna?" Bring your questions for our panel of industry experts, and enjoy a lively discussion on whether the barriers to entry to the FPGA industry are helping or harming innovation.

Putting together *FPGA 2013* was a team effort. We first thank the authors and tutorial presenters for providing the content of the program. We are grateful to the program committee who worked very hard to review the papers and provide detailed feedback to authors. We are in debt to all the members of the program committee who took on additional responsibility as finance, publicity, webmaster, tutorial, panel and session chairs, and to Lisa Tolles and Marie Efinger of Sheridan Communications for assembling the proceedings. Last, but certainly not least, we greatly appreciate the support of our sponsor, ACM SIGDA, and our corporate supporters Algo-Logic, Altera, Atomic Rules, BEEcube, Microsemi, Microsoft Research, and Xilinx. We also thank the Trimberger Family Foundation for additional logistical support.

Welcome to FPGA 2013!

**Brad Hutchings**      **Vaughn Betz**
*FPGA 2013 General Chair*      *FPGA 2013 Program Chair*
*Brigham Young University*      *University of Toronto*

# Table of Contents

## Tutorials

## Session 1: CAD for High-Level Synthesis and Debug
Session Chair: Kia Bazargan *(University of Minnesota)*

## Session 2: Applications I
Session Chair: Miriam Leeser *(Northeastern University)*

## Session 3: FPGA Circuitry and Security
Session Chair: Lei He *(University of California, Los Angeles)*

## Session 4: Computer-Aided Design Tools
Session Chair: Deming Chen *(University of Illinois, Urbana-Champaign)*

## Evening Panel: Are FPGAs Suffering from the Innovator's Dilemna?
Session Chair: Jason Cong *(University of California, Los Angeles)*

## Session 5: FPGA Architecture
Session Chair: Peter Cheung *(Imperial College)*

## Session 6: Design Studies and Design Methodologies

Session Chair: James Hoe *(Carnegie-Mellon University)*

## Session 7: High-Level Abstractions and Tools

Session Chair: Mike Hutton *(Altera Corporation)*

## Session 8: Applications II

## Poster Session 1

## Poster Session 3

## Poster Session 4

# FPGA 2013 Symposium Organization

**General Chair:** Brad Hutchings *(Brigham Young University, USA)*

**Program Chair:** Vaughn Betz *(University of Toronto, Canada)*

**Publicity Chair:** Derek Chiou *(University of Texas at Austin, USA)*

**Finance Chair:** Katherine Morrow *(University of Wisconsin at Madison, USA)*

**Webmaster:** John Lockwood *(Algo-Logic Systems, USA)*

**Tutorial Chairs:** Jason Anderson *(University of Toronto, Canada)*
James Hoe *(Carnegie-Mellon University, USA)*

**Panel Organizers:** Jason Cong *(University of California at Los Angeles, USA)*
Vaughn Betz *(University of Toronto, Canada)*

**Program Committee:** Jason Anderson *(University of Toronto, Canada)*
Kia Bazargan *(University of Minnesota)*
Vaughn Betz *(University of Toronto, Canada)*
Chen Chang *(BEEcube, USA)*
Deming Chen *(University of Illinois at Urbana-Champaign, USA)*
Peter Cheung *(Imperial College London, UK)*
Derek Chiou *(University of Texas, Austin, USA)*
Paul Chow *(University of Toronto, Canada)*
Katherine Morrow *(University of Wisconsin at Madison, USA)*
Jason Cong *(University of California at Los Angeles, USA)*
George Constantinides *(Imperial College London, UK)*
Carl Ebeling *(University of Washington, USA)*
Jonathan Greene *(Actel, USA)*
Scott Hauck *(University of Washington, USA)*
Lei He *(University of California at Los Angeles, USA)*
James Hoe *(Carnegie-Mellon University, USA)*
Brad Hutchings *(Brigham Young University, USA)*
Mike Hutton *(Altera, UK)*
Ryan Kastner *(University of California, Santa Barbara, USA)*
Martin Langhammer *(Altera, UK)*
Miriam Leeser *(Northeastern University, USA)*
Guy Lemieux *(University of British Columbia, Canada)*
Philip Leong *(University of Sydney, Australia)*
David Lewis *(Altera, Canada)*
Mingjie Lin *(University of Central Florida, USA)*
John Lockwood *(Algo-Logic Systems, USA)*
Wayne Luk *(Imperial College London, UK)*
Patrick Lysaght *(Xilinx, USA)*
Stephen Neuendorffer *(Xilinx, USA)*

# FPGA 2013 Sponsor & Supporters

**Sponsor:**

**Supporters:**

**Also with the support of:**

**With additional logistics from:**

# Building Zynq®Accelerators with Vivado®High Level Synthesis

Stephen Neuendorffer
stephen.neuendorffer@xilinx.com

Fernando Martinez-Vallina
vallina@xilinx.com

Xilinx Inc.
2100 Logic Drive
San Jose, CA

## ABSTRACT

Engineering complex systems inevitably requires a designer to balance many conflicting design requirements including performance, cost, power, and design time. In many cases, FPGAs enable engineers to balance these design requirements in ways not possible with other technologies like ASICs, ASSPs, GPUs or general purpose processors. This tutorial will focus on two of the newest commercial FPGA-related technologies, High Level Synthesis (HLS) and Programmable Logic integrated tightly with high performance embedded processors. In particular, we will present a detailed introduction to Vivado® HLS, which is capable of synthesizing optimized FPGA circuits from algorithmic descriptions in C, C++ and SystemC. We will also present an introduction to the architecture of Zynq® devices and show how interesting system architectures can be constructed using High Level Synthesis and the programmable logic portion of these devices.

The tutorial will focus on the practical application of HLS and Zynq® to build real systems. It will demonstrate both HLS and system-level optimization techniques and ways to identify and eliminate bottlenecks in computation and communication. In addition, the tutorial will draw from a number of application areas including video, wireless communications, and medical imaging.

Vivado® HLS can be downloaded as a part of the Vivado® Design Suite. Evaluation licenses are available with a xilinx.com website account. Academic licenses can be requested through the Xilinx® University Program. Multiple Zynq® boards are available, including the ZC702, ZC706, and the community zedboard.

For more information see:
http://www.xilinx.com/hls
http://www.xilinx.com/support/download/index.htm
http://www.xilinx.com/getlicense
http://www.xilinx.com/university
http://www.xilinx.com/zc702
http://www.xilinx.com/zc706
http://www.zedboard.org/

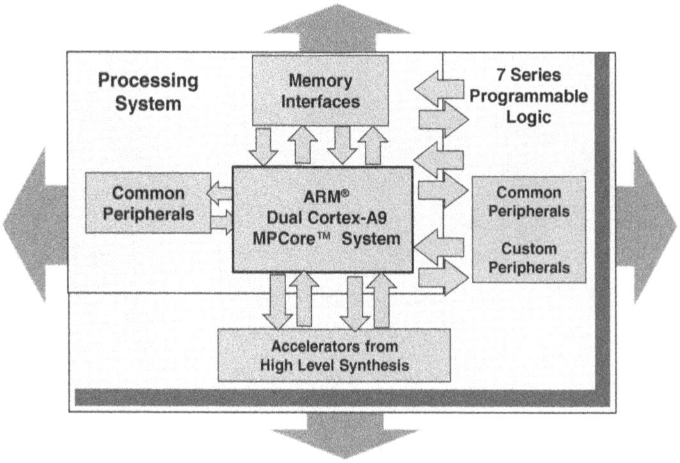

Figure 1: Simplified Block Diagram of a Zynq® design.

## Categories and Subject Descriptors

B.6.3 [**Logic Design**]: Design Aids—*Automatic synthesis*

## Keywords

Field Programmable Gate Array, High Level Synthesis

*FPGA'13*, February 11–13, 2013, Monterey, California, USA.
ACM 978-1-4503-1887-7/13/02.

# Cross-Platform FPGA Accelerator Development Using CoRAM and CONNECT

Eric S. Chung
Microsoft Research Silicon Valley
Mountain View, CA
erchung@microsoft.com

Michael K. Papamichael, Gabriel Weisz,
James C. Hoe
Carnegie Mellon University
Pittsburgh, PA
{papamix, gweisz}@cs.cmu.edu,
jhoe@ece.cmu.edu

## ABSTRACT

The CoRAM memory architecture is an easy-to-use and portable abstraction for FPGA accelerator development [1, 2]. Using the CoRAM framework, FPGA developers can write their applications once and re-target them automatically to different FPGA platforms and devices (e.g., Xilinx ML605, Altera DE4, ZYNQ-702, etc). In this tutorial, participants will learn the key concepts of the CoRAM Virtual Architecture and the underlying CONNECT Network-on-Chip generation framework [3]. The tutorial is organized into three parts. The first part will provide an overview of the CoRAM Virtual Architecture and include a hands-on section where participants will work on a small example to get first-hand experience with the CoRAM development flow. The second part of the tutorial will provide a beneath-the-hood look at CoRAM and cover more advanced topics. These topics include memory loading, user I/O, debugging, as well as a segment on the CONNECT NoC generation framework which serves as the on-chip interconnect for CoRAM. The final part of the tutorial will be devoted to more advanced exercises and demos, as well as a Q&A session for CoRAM and CONNECT. The tutorial assumes a basic understanding of RTL design and C programming. To join in on the hands-on exercise, the attendees need laptops with 15GB of free space and VirtualBox installed. Please visit http://www.ece.cmu.edu/~coram for information about CoRAM and updates on this tutorial.

## Categories and Subject Descriptors

C.0 [**Computer System Organization**]: System Architectures

## Keywords

FPGA computing, memory architecture, Network-on-Chip

## REFERENCES

[1] E. S. Chung, J. C. Hoe, and K. Mai. CoRAM: An in-fabric memory architecture for FPGA-based computing. In Proceedings of the 19th ACM/SIGDA International Symposium on Field Programmable Gate Arrays, FPGA'11, pages 97-106, New York, NY, USA, 2011.

[2] E. S. Chung, M. K. Papamichael, G. Weisz, J. C. Hoe, and K. Mai. Prototype and evaluation of the CoRAM memory architecture for FPGA-based computing. In Proceedings of the ACM/SIGDA International Symposium on Field Programmable Gate Arrays, FPGA '12, pages 139-142, New York, NY, USA, 2012.

[3] M. K. Papamichael and J. C. Hoe. CONNECT: Re-examining conventional wisdom for designing NOCS in the context of FPGAs. In Proceedings of the ACM/SIGDA International Symposium on Field Programmable Gate Arrays, FPGA '12, pages 37-46, New York, NY, USA, 2012.

# Harnessing the Power of FPGAs using Altera's OpenCL Compiler

Deshanand P. Singh
Altera Corporation
150 Bloor Street West, Suite 400
Toronto, Ontario, Canada
dsingh@altera.com

Tomasz S. Czajkowski
Altera Corporation
150 Bloor Street West, Suite 400
Toronto, Ontario, Canada
tczajkow@altera.com

Andrew Ling
Altera Corporation
150 Bloor Street West, Suite 400
Toronto, Ontario, Canada
aling@altera.com

## ABSTRACT

In recent years, Field-Programmable Gate Arrays have become extremely powerful computational platforms that can efficiently solve many complex problems. The most modern FPGAs comprise effectively millions of programmable elements, signal processing elements and high-speed interfaces, all of which are necessary to deliver a complete solution. The power of FPGAs is unlocked via low-level programming languages such as VHDL and Verilog, which allow designers to explicitly specify the behavior of each programmable element. While these languages provide a means to create highly efficient logic circuits, they are akin to "assembly language" programming for modern processors. This is a serious limiting factor for both productivity and the adoption of FPGAs on a wider scale.

In this talk, we use the OpenCL language to explore techniques that allow us to program FPGAs at a level of abstraction closer to traditional software-centric approaches. OpenCL is an industry standard parallel language based on 'C' that offers numerous advantages that enable designers to take full advantage of the capabilities offered by FPGAs, while providing a high-level design entry language that is familiar to a wide range of programmers.

To demonstrate the advantages a high-level programming language can offer, we demonstrate how to use Altera's OpenCL Compiler on a set of case studies. The first application is single-precision general-element matrix multiplication (SGEMM). It is an example of a highly-parallel algorithm for which an efficient circuit structures are well known. We show how this application can be implemented in OpenCL and how the high-level description can be optimized to generate the most efficient circuit in hardware. The second application is a Fast Fourier Transform (FFT), which is a classical FPGA benchmark that is known to have a good implementation on FPGAs. We show how we can implement the FFT algorithm, while exploring the many different possible architectural choices that lead to an optimized implementation for a given FPGA. Finally, we discuss a Monte-Carlo Black-Scholes simulation, which demonstrates the computational power of FPGAs. We describe how a random number generator in conjunction with computationally intensive operations can be harnessed on an FPGA to generate a high-speed benchmark, which also consumes far less power than the same benchmark running on a comparable GPU. We conclude the tutorial with a set of live demonstrations.

Through this tutorial we show the benefits high-level languages offer for system-level design and productivity. In particular, Altera's OpenCL compiler is shown to enable high-performance application design that fully utilizes capabilities of modern FPGAs.

## Categories and Subject Descriptors

B.6.1 [**Logic Design**]: Design Styles – *Parallel Circuits*

## Keywords

FPGAs, OpenCL

*FPGA'13*, February 11–13, 2013, Monterey, California, USA.
ACM 978-1-4503-1887-7/13/02.

# High-Level Synthesis With LegUp:
# A Crash Course for Users and Researchers

Jason H. Anderson, Stephen D. Brown, Andrew Canis, and Jongsok Choi
Department of Electrical and Computer Engineering
University of Toronto
legup@eecg.toronto.edu

## ABSTRACT

High-level synthesis (HLS) has been gaining traction recently as a design methodology for FPGAs, with the promise of raising the productivity of FPGA hardware designers, and ultimately, opening the door to the use of FPGAs as computing devices targetable by software engineers. In this tutorial, we introduce LegUp [1], an open-source HLS tool for FPGAs developed at the University of Toronto. With LegUp, a user can compile a C program completely to hardware, or alternately, he/she can choose to compile the program to a hybrid hardware/software system comprising a processor along with one or more accelerators. LegUp supports the synthesis of most of the C language to hardware, including loops, structs, multi-dimensional arrays, pointer arithmetic, and floating point operations. The LegUp distribution includes the CHStone HLS benchmark suite [2], as well as a test suite and associated infrastructure for measuring quality of results, and for verifying the functionality of LegUp-generated circuits. LegUp is freely downloadable at www.legup.org, providing a powerful platform that can be leveraged for new high-level synthesis research.

## Categories and Subject Descriptors

B.7 [**Integrated Circuits**]: Design Aids

## Keywords

High-level synthesis, FPGAs, hardware/software co-design

## 1. OVERVIEW

This tutorial is a crash course on LegUp, both as an HLS tool for designing hardware, and as a framework for new research on HLS algorithms and methodologies for hardware/software co-design. While understanding any new large software system can be a daunting task, this tutorial will lower the learning curve for LegUp and provide hands-on experience in using and modifying the tool.

We will begin with a general overview of the main HLS steps (allocation, scheduling, binding and HDL code generation) and then discuss the particular HLS algorithms used within LegUp. We will also overview the key compiler concepts needed to understand the LegUp implementation, such as the control dataflow graph. We then demonstrate the use of LegUp as a tool for the HLS of hardware-only and hybrid hardware/software systems, and describe the current capabilities and limitations of the tool. The HLS-generated hardware will be simulated with ModelSim and synthesized to an Altera FPGA. We will show how TCL parameters can be used to influence the HLS results, for example, by disabling or enabling resource sharing or the chaining together of computations in a single hardware clock cycle. TCL parameters that define the architecture of the hybrid processor/accelerator system will also be described.

The second part of the tutorial deals with the implementation of LegUp itself, and should be of interest to HLS researchers wishing to modify the tool. LegUp is implemented within the open-source LLVM compiler framework [3]. We will explain the key concepts of LLVM's intermediate representation (IR) of a software program and go over the basic LLVM programming idioms necessary for extending the LegUp codebase. We will describe the software architecture of LegUp, how it fits into LLVM, its internal data structures, and the software modules in which the key pieces of HLS functionality reside.

The last part of the tutorial will consist of demonstrations/labs that illustrate how LegUp can be modified on several fronts: 1) we will change the scheduling algorithm, which assigns operations from the C code to specific FSM states; 2) we will alter LegUp's approach to binding, which saves area by mapping several operations from the C to a single hardware functional unit; and 3) we will illustrate the steps needed to add support for new FPGA device architectures. Participants who have LegUp pre-installed on their laptops will be able to follow along with the demonstrations and try them out themselves during the tutorial.

## 2. REFERENCES

[1] A. Canis, J. Choi, M. Aldham, V. Zhang, A. Kammoona, J. Anderson, S. Brown, and T. Czajkowski. LegUp: High-level synthesis for FPGA-based processor/accelerator systems. In *ACM FPGA*, pages 33–36, 2011.

[2] Y. Hara, H. Tomiyama, S. Honda, and H. Takada. Proposal and quantitative analysis of the CHStone benchmark program suite for practical C-based high-level synthesis. *J. of Information Processing*, 17:242–254, 2009.

[3] LLVM. *The LLVM Compiler Infrastructure Project (http://www.llvm.org)*, 2013.

# Improving High Level Synthesis Optimization Opportunity Through Polyhedral Transformations

Wei Zuo[2,5], Yun Liang[1] *, Peng Li[1], Kyle Rupnow[3], Deming Chen[2,3] and Jason Cong[1,4]
[1]Center for Energy-Efficient Computing and Applications, School of EECS, Peking University, China
[2]University of Illinois, Urbana-Champaign, USA
[3]Advanced Digital Science Center, Singapore
[4]Computer Science Department, University of California, Los Angeles, USA
[5]School of Information and Electronics, Beijing Institute of technology,China
{weizuo,dchen}@illinois.edu,{ericlyun,peng.li}@pku.edu.cn
k.rupnow@adsc.com.sg,cong@cs.ucla.edu

## ABSTRACT

High level synthesis (HLS) is an important enabling technology for the adoption of hardware accelerator technologies. It promises the performance and energy efficiency of hardware designs with a lower barrier to entry in design expertise, and shorter design time. State-of-the-art high level synthesis now includes a wide variety of powerful optimizations that implement efficient hardware. These optimizations can implement some of the most important features generally performed in manual designs including parallel hardware units, pipelining of execution both within a hardware unit and between units, and fine-grained data communication. We may generally classify the optimizations as those that optimize hardware implementation within a code block (intra-block) and those that optimize communication and pipelining between code blocks (inter-block). However, both optimizations are in practice difficult to apply. Real-world applications contain data-dependent blocks of code and communicate through complex data access patterns. Existing high level synthesis tools cannot apply these powerful optimizations unless the code is inherently compatible, severely limiting the optimization opportunity.

In this paper we present an integrated framework to model and enable both intra- and inter-block optimizations. This integrated technique substantially improves the opportunity to use the powerful HLS optimizations that implement parallelism, pipelining, and fine-grained communication. Our polyhedral model-based technique systematically defines a set of data access patterns, identifies effective data access patterns, and performs the loop transformations to enable the intra- and inter-block optimizations. Our framework automatically explores transformation options, performs code transformations, and inserts the appropriate HLS directives to implement the HLS optimizations. Furthermore, our framework can automatically generate the optimized communication blocks for fine-grained communication between hardware blocks. Experimental evaluation demonstrates that we can achieve an average of 6.04X speedup over the high level synthesis solution without our transformations to enable intra- and inter-block optimizations.

## Categories and Subject Descriptors

B.5.2 [**Hardware**]: [Design Aids] — automatic synthesis

## General Terms

Algorithm, Design, Performance

## Keywords

Polyhedral, High Level Synthesis, FPGA

## 1. INTRODUCTION

FPGAs have long been adopted for computation acceleration, especially in domains that also demand power and energy efficient computing. Their highly flexible architecture enables significant optimization opportunities. Designers can implement fine-grained computation units, highly parallel architectures, fine-grained pipelining of computation units, efficient communication structures and customized memory and compute unit partitioning. However, the flexibility that is a strength for optimization opportunities is also a challenge for efficient programmability. FPGA implementation remains a significant challenge for prospective users — manual design at register transfer level (RTL) is error-prone and difficult to debug. Such manual design often takes weeks and months in comparison to the hours or days to implement an algorithm in software. Furthermore, efficient manual design typically requires significant specialized knowledge — efficient FPGA implementations must consider architecture-specific parameters and implement functions for efficient mapping to the FPGAs' fixed-size allocation quota (LUT, BRAM, DSP, ...).

High level synthesis (HLS) seeks to address these problems. HLS offers automated translation from high level languages (e.g., C,C++, SystemC, Haskell and CUDA) to register transfer level (RTL) implementations to reduce the design effort, automated optimization to reduce the requirement of design knowledge, and FPGA-specific mapping to automate low-level optimization choices. Thus, HLS promises to be a critical bridging technology that offers the latency and power/energy benefits of FPGA-based hardware acceleration at the design effort (and expertise) of software development. State-of-the-art HLS tools cover a wide range of input source code and achieve high-quality results [8].

---

*Corresponding Author

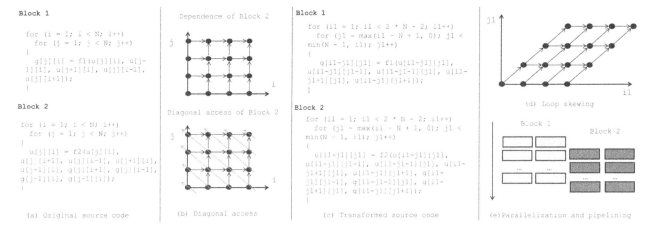

**Figure 1:** An example of two data-dependent blocks. In sub-figure (e), we assume the parallelization degree is 2.

These tools have achieved significant improvement; however, recent studies show that although these tools can offer high quality designs for small kernels, there is still a significant performance gap between HLS and manual design for real-world complex applications [23, 17, 10]. For example, [23, 17] demonstrated a 40X difference between HLS and the manual design for a high-definition stereo matching implementation. Small kernels (often used as simple HLS benchmarks) contain a single block (a loop nest), but real-world applications often contain many data-dependent blocks that communicate through complex data access patterns. Whereas a video processing kernel may be a single nested loop performing a median filter, a real application would employ a sequence of data-dependent blocks, including blocks such as image up/down sampling, cost aggregation, and energy minimization. Video processing applications are often structured so that each processing step is a loop nest (block) that operates on array inputs and produces array outputs such that block $i + 1$ reads the array variables written by block $i$. As seen in efficient manual RTL implementations of these algorithms, it is crucial to minimize the communication granularity, pipeline the data-dependent blocks, and duplicate compute units to improve both throughput and latency. However, existing HLS tools fail to enable intra-block parallelization and inter-block pipelining when the data access patterns are complex [23, 17] — and although advanced commercial tools *support* these optimizations, they are not always able to efficiently identify the opportunity and transform source code to enable such optimizations.

Code transformations to enable these important and powerful optimizations are thus critical for HLS tools. One of the primary goals of HLS is to reduce design effort; thus, HLS tools must efficiently support a variety of code — including source code written by software engineers with little hardware expertise, and software not written for use with HLS. Software programmers choose data access patterns based on properties such as intuitive ordering, cache locality, and code modularity. Even software written for HLS may still contain loops that demand transformation; efficient inter-block optimization may demand non-intuitive iteration ordering such that even experienced hardware designers may have difficulty seeing an intuitive ordering of blocks that enables optimization. Thus, it is quite natural that the default data access pattern does not support intra-block parallelization or inter-block pipelining. Nevertheless, data access patterns can be altered via loop transformations such as permutation, reverse, and skewing [24]. Using these transformations, we can enable intra-block parallelization by reordering loop iterations so that successive iterations are independent; similarly, we can enable inter-block pipelining by ensuring that block $i$ pro-

duces data in the order that block $i + 1$ consumes data (by transforming block $i$, block $i + 1$ or both). Both intra-block parallelization and inter-block pipelining are currently supported by existing HLS tools. The problem is rather that these optimizations cannot always be enabled with the default data access patterns. Thus, the goal of this work is to enable efficient integrated use of intra- and inter-block optimizations through loop transformation.

**Motivating Example.** We illustrate the concept of intra- and inter-block optimization using the *Denoise* [11] application in medical imaging (Figure 1). The source code in Figure 1 (a) is modified to highlight the data access pattern, with computation arithmetic omitted for clarity. The application is composed of two blocks (loop nests), where the first block writes to the $g$ array that is subsequently read by the second block. Both blocks are representative of stencil codes where the array update operation follows a fixed input dependence pattern that reads neighboring elements. In this example, only the second block has data-dependence between loop iterations, as shown in Figure 1 (b), and the first block writes the data array $g$ in the same order that the second block consumes array $g$ (column order). Thus, in this example, intra-block parallelization is available in the first block and inter-block pipelining is available by default between the blocks, but a transform is required to enable parallelization in the second block. However, note that if the second block is transformed to enable parallelization, then the first block must also be transformed in order to retain the opportunity for inter-block pipelining.[1]

**Table 1: Comparison of different implementations**

| | Implementation | Cycles | Frequency | Speedup |
|---|---|---|---|---|
| 1 | w/o transform, w/o opt | 5408 | 160MHz | 1 |
| 2 | w/o transform, w/ opt | 1809 | 182MHz | 3.40 |
| 3 | w/ transform, w/ opt | 250 | 230MHz | 31.09 |

In Table 1 we can see the performance in cycles and speedup over the original source for this example. By default, the original source code supports some optimization, as seen in the second implementation — inter-block pipelining improves the performance, but the latency of the individual blocks become the performance bottleneck. Note that in the second implementation, we do not perform partial parallelization (e.g., parallelize the first block only) because if the throughputs are not matched, the buffering between

---

[1]For efficient implementation of inter-block pipelining, we also implement memory partition optimization and customized communication blocks which will be discussed in section 3.3.

the blocks would not be feasible. In the third implementation, the loop transformation is used to alleviate the dependence problem and retain the opportunity for inter-block pipelining. In Figure 1 (c) and (d), we perform loop skewing on both blocks to traverse the loop in a diagonal fashion from the bottom-right to top-left, as shown in Figure 1 (b). This loop skewing both preserves the data dependence and enables parallelization of the inner loop because the iterations on the same diagonal line are independent. The first block can also use the loop skewing transformation safely because it does not have any data dependencies. The optimized execution schedule is shown in Figure 1 (e). This transformation significantly improves the speedup opportunity from about 3X to 31X speedup. In this case, some optimizations were supported by default, but there was still significant speedup opportunity by ensuring that both optimizations were enabled. In the experiments section, we will demonstrate that some source codes support neither parallelization nor pipelining by default, but loop transformations can enable both intra-block parallelization and inter-block pipelining.

As this brief motivation discussion demonstrates, real-world applications commonly contain multiple data-dependent blocks with communication through complex data access patterns. For such applications, the powerful optimization functions of existing high level synthesis tools may not be supported by default due to the data access patterns. In this paper we develop an integrated method to model, analyze, and transform block data access patterns to support these important and powerful optimizations. Using polyhedral models [24, 13, 20, 6, 5], we represent the loop iteration space, dependencies, data access patterns, and loop transformations in a linear algebraic form. For loops amenable to this algebraic representation, the polyhedral model allows us to analytically determine valid loop transformations that best support both intra-block parallelization and inter-block pipelining. This paper advances the state-of-the-art of high level synthesis with

- An automated polyhedral model-based framework that systematically identifies effective access patterns and applies appropriate loop transformations that enable intra- and inter-block optimizations.

- An automated framework to generate communication interfaces between blocks.

We demonstrate that our automated framework achieves an average of 6.04X speedup over HLS with all available optimizations but without transformations to enable.

This paper is organized as follows. Section 2 briefly provides the background of the polyhedral model and introduces the useful notation. Section 3 presents our framework, which defines data access patterns, identifies data access patterns for effective optimizations, and discusses the implementation of fine-grained data communication modules. Section 4 presents experimental results. Section 5 discusses related work, and conclusions are presented in Section 6.

## 2. BACKGROUND AND NOTATION

In this section we briefly introduce the polyhedral model and the notation that we will use in this paper. A detailed description of polyhedral models can be found in [5, 6, 13, 20]. In this work we are using the polyhedral model to consider data access patterns for communication between sets of loop nests, and to optimize this communication ordering in order to perform fine-grained communication and enable parallelization within a loop nest and pipelining between loop nests through loop transformation. In particular, in this work we consider programs that consist of a sequence of data-dependent blocks, where each block is a loop nest containing mul-

tiple statements, and each statement may have multiple accesses to data arrays.

### 2.1 Polyhedral Model

Polyhedral models can be used to represent execution information of a program's loop nests, such as the loop iteration domain, statement/iteration dependencies, array access functions, and scheduling functions (execution order).

DEFINITION 1 (**Polyhedron**). *The set of all vectors $\vec{x} \in Z^n$ such that $A\vec{x} + \vec{b} \geq 0$, where $A \in Z^{m \times n}$ and $\vec{b} \in Z^m$.*

Each row of $A$ represents a half-space that limits $A\vec{x} + \vec{b}$ to non-negative values, and the *polyhedron* is the intersection of the $m$ half-spaces represented by the $m$ rows of $A$. A bounded *polyhedron* is a *polytope*.

DEFINITION 2 (**Iteration Vector and Domain**). *The iteration vector $\vec{i}$ of a loop nest represents an execution instance of the loop nest. $\vec{i}$ contains the values of the loop indices of all the surrounding loops. The iteration domain $D_L$ of loop nest $L$ is the set of all iteration vectors that satisfy the loop-bound constraints. Because an iteration domain is bounded by these loop-bound constraints, it is a polytope.*

DEFINITION 3 (**Schedule Function**). *Given a $m$-dimensional loop nest, a $d$-dimensional ($1 \leq d \leq m$) schedule $\boldsymbol{F}(\vec{i})$ is defined as*

$$
\begin{aligned}
\boldsymbol{F}(\vec{i}) &= \mathrm{S}\vec{i} + \vec{o} \\
&= \begin{pmatrix} C_{11} & C_{12} & \dots & C_{1m} \\ C_{21} & C_{22} & \dots & C_{2m} \\ \vdots & \vdots & \vdots & \vdots \\ C_{d1} & C_{d2} & \dots & C_{dm} \end{pmatrix} \vec{i} + \begin{pmatrix} C_{10} \\ C_{20} \\ \vdots \\ C_{d0} \end{pmatrix}
\end{aligned}
$$

*where $\mathrm{S} \in Z^{d \times m}$, $\vec{o} \in Z^d$, and $C_{ij} \in Z$. The schedule function takes the iteration vector $\vec{i}$ as input and produces an ordering of the loop iterations using the matrix $\mathrm{S}$ and an offset vector ($\vec{o}$).*

Thus, the schedule function creates a particular ordering of iterations by mapping each iteration in the domain to a timestamp, where mapping $m$ dimensions into fewer ($d$) timestamps implies that some of the iterations can be performed in parallel. The schedule function has the additional benefit that the timestamp ordering also corresponds to a lexicographic ordering. For example, for iteration vectors $\vec{i_1}$ and $\vec{i_2}$, $\vec{i_1}$ is scheduled before $\vec{i_2}$ if $\mathbf{F}(\vec{i_1}) < \mathbf{F}(\vec{i_2})$.

DEFINITION 4 (**Transformation Function**). *In the polyhedral model, the transformation function is represented as a sequence of schedules applied to perform the transformation.*

In theory, any loop transformation can be represented in the polyhedral model. In this paper we focus on a set of uni-modular loop transformations [24], including loop reverse (e.g., reverses the traverse direction), loop permutation (e.g., interchange two loops), and skewing (e.g., make the inner-loop bounds dependent on the outer-loop bounds) and their composite transformations. The schedule function/execution order of iterations of a loop nest can be altered through loop transformations.

Figure 2 illustrates the polyhedral model using a concrete example. The original source code that consists of two data-dependent blocks (loop nests) is shown in Figure 2 (a). The first block writes to array $B$, and the second block subsequently reads from it. Without transformation, each individual block can be parallelized, but

```
for (i1 = N - 1; i1 >=0;  i1--)
   for (j1 = 0; j1 < N; j1++)
     S1 : B[i1][j1] = B[i1][j1] + A[i1][j1];
```
$$\begin{pmatrix} 1 & 0 & 0 & 0 \\ -1 & 0 & 1 & -1 \\ 0 & 1 & 0 & 0 \\ 0 & -1 & 1 & -1 \end{pmatrix} \begin{pmatrix} i1 \\ j1 \\ N \\ 1 \end{pmatrix} \geq \vec{0}$$
$$F_{s1}(\vec{i}) = \begin{pmatrix} -1 & 0 \\ 0 & 1 \end{pmatrix} \vec{i} + \begin{pmatrix} N-1 \\ 0 \end{pmatrix}, \ \vec{i} = \begin{pmatrix} i1 \\ j1 \end{pmatrix}$$

```
for (i2 = 0; i2 < N; i2++)
   for( j2 = 0; j2 < N; j2++)
     S2: D[i2] = D[i2] + B[i2][j2] * C[j2];
```
$$\begin{pmatrix} 1 & 0 & 0 & 0 \\ -1 & 0 & 1 & -1 \\ 0 & 1 & 0 & 0 \\ 0 & -1 & 1 & -1 \end{pmatrix} \begin{pmatrix} i2 \\ j2 \\ N \\ 1 \end{pmatrix} \geq \vec{0}$$
$$F_{s2}(\vec{i}) = \begin{pmatrix} 1 & 0 \\ 0 & 1 \end{pmatrix} \vec{i} + \begin{pmatrix} 0 \\ 0 \end{pmatrix}, \ \vec{i} = \begin{pmatrix} i2 \\ j2 \end{pmatrix}$$

(a) Original source code      (b) Iteration domain      (c) Schedule function

**Figure 2: An example of polyhedral representation.**

their execution can not be overlapped through pipelining as they access array $B$ in different order. In Figure 2 (b), we show the iteration domain (polytope) of the two blocks which establishes the lower- and upper-bounds for each loop dimension. In Figure 2 (c), we show the scheduling function that corresponds to the original source code for each of the loop nests. In order to transform the original scheduling function to achieve a desired data access pattern, we can define a desired data access pattern and derive the necessary loop transformations; a proof that this derivation is always possible is shown in Section 3.

As described above, the polyhedral model (including iteration domain, iteration vector, scheduling function and transformation function) describes the iteration domain and order for any loop nest that has all array accesses as affine expressions of loop indices. In addition, dependency relations between iterations in the program can be represented in the polyhedral model. Two iterations of a loop nest (or two instances of blocks) are dependent if they access the same array locations, and at least one of the accesses is a write operation. These dependencies can be represented by additional rows in the iteration domain to establish constraints between the loop iterations. Loop transformations are valid only if they also preserve the additional program dependency constraints.

## 3. METHODOLOGY

Our integrated intra- and inter-block optimization framework takes a data-dependent multi-block program as input, and performs three steps, as shown in Figure 3. The goal of our optimization is to minimize the overall latency (maximize the performance speedup). First, we systematically define a set of data access patterns, classify them, and derive the associated loop transformations (Section 3.1). Next, for each loop transformation that validly preserves data-dependencies, we estimate the performance improvement (Section 3.2) and choose the best estimated performance. The performance estimation models both intra- and inter-block speedup and associated implementation overheads. The intra-block parallelization degree is determined by the resource usage of the program and the available resource on the implementation platform. Finally, for the chosen transformation, we automatically perform the loop transformations, insert high level synthesis directives, and generate the communication blocks that interface the data-dependent blocks. If the communication block is a simple FIFO, we automatically insert FIFO high level synthesis directives; when the communication interface requires multiple reads or a stencil pattern, we automatically customize the communication blocks (Section 3.3). The final output of the flow is an optimized RTL design.

Note that in prior works [5, 6, 13, 18, 20, 24], polyhedral models consider data access patterns for external memory accesses and loop transformations in order to optimize data localities and maximize parallelism for CPUs. Optimizations for CPU code attempt to minimize memory bandwidth and improve cache behavior. In ad-

dition, the transformed CPU code often has complex control flow that is not suitable for efficient FPGA implementation. Thus, the transformation chosen for optimization on CPU platform may be the wrong decision for our HLS optimization.

In this work, we use polyhedral model to define data access patterns for a different objective. We aim to optimize the inter-block communication and enable intra-block parallelization and inter-block pipelining through loop transformation for FPGAs using HLS. For our objective, we model the FPGA-specific features. Therefore, although the candidate data access patterns might be the same as prior work, we apply different transformations in different combinations in order to meet our optimization objective. Although the underlying techniques are all based on polyhedral models, different objectives lead to different ways to select data access patterns and loop transformations.

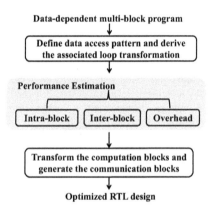

**Figure 3: Optimization Framework.**

## 3.1 Classification of Array Access Patterns

We model the array access patterns using the polyhedral model, thus we assume that all array accesses are affine expressions of loop indices and constants. The program inputs are composed of multiple data-dependent blocks where each block contains a single multi-dimensional loop nest. Let us consider a loop nest of dimensionality $D$ that accesses an $N$-dimensional array. The array access pattern is defined by matrix $\mathbf{M}$ whose size is $N \times D$, where the rows ($i$) represent the data access pattern in dimension $i$ of the data array, and columns ($j$) represent the access pattern in the loop level $j$.

Given the array access pattern $\mathbf{M}$, loop iteration vector $\vec{i}$, and constant offset vector $\vec{o}$, the array access vector $\vec{s}$ is defined as

$$\vec{s} = \mathbf{M}\vec{i} + \vec{o}$$

$\vec{s}$ is column vector of size $N$, where each row ($i$) represents array accesses in dimension $i$, and the offset vector is a constant offset into that dimension. Figure 4 shows an example of array access pattern and vector for the writes to array $B$; similar access patterns and vectors could be derived for the reads from array $A$.

```
for(i =0; i < N; i++)
  for(j=0; j < N; j++)
    B[i][j] = A[i][j] + A[i - 1][j];
```

$$M = \begin{bmatrix} 1 & 0 \\ 0 & 1 \end{bmatrix}, \qquad \vec{s} = \begin{bmatrix} 1 & 0 \\ 0 & 1 \end{bmatrix}\begin{bmatrix} i \\ j \end{bmatrix} + \begin{bmatrix} 0 \\ 0 \end{bmatrix}$$

**Figure 4: An example of array access pattern.**

In the following, we demonstrate the data access patterns for 2-dimensional arrays and 2-dimensional loop-nests. For ease of illustration, we classify the access patterns below; although, the polyhedral framework treats these access patterns in a uniform way. In the framework, we need to define the candidate access patterns that can be evaluated for the program; in this work we limit the access patterns to the simple set of access patterns below. The polyhedral model can be easily extended to handle a wide variety of additional access patterns, and our work can use any additional access patterns to estimate the performance benefit. We leave the extension to future work.

Now we will describe how to define the array access patterns using $\mathbf{M}$. Let

$$\mathbf{M} = \begin{pmatrix} a_1 & b_1 \\ a_2 & b_2 \end{pmatrix}$$

We classify the array access patterns based on the values of $a_1$, $a_2$, $b_1$ and $b_2$. For array accesses with non-unit loop strides, we perform loop normalization as a preprocessing step so that our analysis can assume unit loop stride.

**Column and Reverse Column.**

$$\begin{pmatrix} \pm 1 & 0 \\ 0 & \pm 1 \end{pmatrix}$$

The array access vector can be obtained by $M\vec{i}$. Figure 5 shows the four patterns in this category, where the signs of $a_1$ and $b_2$ determine traversal direction. For example, with outer loop index $i$ and inner loop index $j$, if $a_1 = 1$ and $b_2 = 1$, then the outer loop traverses increasing values of $i$, and the inner loop traverses increasing values of $j$.

**Row and Reverse Row.**

$$\begin{pmatrix} 0 & \pm 1 \\ \pm 1 & 0 \end{pmatrix}$$

Similar to column and reverse column, there are four patterns in this category, and the signs of $b_1$ and $a_2$ determine the traversal directions.

**Diagonal Access.** In this category, the loop traverses in a diagonal line fashion. We further divide this into two cases based on the slopes of the diagonal lines.

- $slope \geq 1$.

$$\begin{pmatrix} \pm 1 & N > b_1 \geq 1 \\ 0 & \pm 1 \end{pmatrix}$$

The array access vector can be obtained by $M\vec{i}$. The slope of the diagonal line is determined by $b_1$, and the signs of $a_1$ and $b_2$ determine the traversal directions. When $b_1 \geq N$, the traversal order reduces to one of the column access orders. Figure 6 shows the four data access patterns for $slope = 1$.

- $slope < 1$.

$$\begin{pmatrix} N > a_1 > 1 & \pm 1 \\ \pm 1 & 0 \end{pmatrix}$$

The slope of the diagonal line is determined by $\frac{1}{a_1}$, and the signs of $a_2$ and $b_1$ determine the traversal directions. When $a_1 \geq N$, the traversal order reduces to one of the row access orders.

All of the array access patterns defined above are unimodular matrices where $|a_1 \times b_2 - a_2 \times b_1| = 1$. Thus, all of these access patterns can be achieved by unimodular loop transformations of the block(s) [24].

**Loop Transformation.** Loop transformations can change the schedule (e.g., execution order) of loop iterations such that the data access pattern can be changed. Thus, here we derive the loop transformation given a desired data access pattern.

THEOREM 3.1. *The transformation function $T$ required for the desired data access pattern $M_{des}$ can be obtained by*

$$T = M_{des}^{-1} M_{ori} F_{ori}^{-1}$$

*where $M_{ori}$ and $F_{ori}$ are the data access pattern and schedule function of the source code without transformation.*

PROOF. Let $\vec{i'}$ be the loop iterator vector after transformation. Thus, the desired array access vector after transformation is $M_{des}\vec{i'}$. Let us assume the schedule function and data access pattern of the original code are $\mathbf{F}_{ori}$ and $\mathbf{M}_{ori}$, respectively. Thus, the schedule function after transformation is $\mathbf{TF}_{ori}$. Schedule function maps the original loop iterations to a new ordering of the loop iterations. Thus,

$$\mathbf{TF}_{ori}\vec{i} = \vec{i'}$$

Thus,

$$\vec{i} = \mathbf{F}_{ori}^{-1}\mathbf{T}^{-1}\vec{i'}$$

The data accessed by the iterations before and after transformation is the same

$$\mathbf{M}_{ori}\mathbf{F}_{ori}^{-1}\mathbf{T}^{-1}\vec{i'} = \mathbf{M}_{des}\vec{i'}$$

Thus,

$$\mathbf{T} = \mathbf{M}_{des}^{-1}\mathbf{M}_{ori}\mathbf{F}_{ori}^{-1}$$

□

The data access pattern and loop transformations are all unimodular matrix. For unimodular matrix, we can always derive its reverse matrix.

## 3.2 Performance Metric

In the previous subsection we defined a set of data access patterns that include row, column, and diagonal access with different slopes and directions. We also described how to derive the required loop transformation for a given data access pattern. Our design objective is to maximize the performance speedup. Now, we will discuss the process of evaluating all of the candidate data access patterns and choosing the candidate that maximizes application speedup. To perform this evaluation, we develop a performance metric that combines modeling of both intra- and inter-block speedup and their associated implementation overhead. We define that a program is a sequence of $K$ blocks $\{b_1, b_2, \ldots, b_K\}$, and

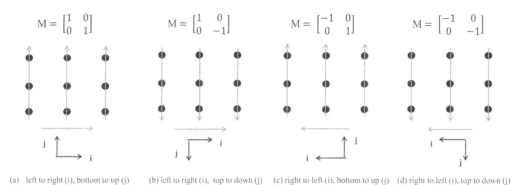

Figure 5: An example of column access pattern. There are 4 patterns with different traverse directions.

$$M = \begin{bmatrix} 1 & 0 \\ 0 & 1 \end{bmatrix} \qquad M = \begin{bmatrix} 1 & 0 \\ 0 & -1 \end{bmatrix} \qquad M = \begin{bmatrix} -1 & 0 \\ 0 & 1 \end{bmatrix} \qquad M = \begin{bmatrix} -1 & 0 \\ 0 & -1 \end{bmatrix}$$

(a)  left to right (i), bottom to up (j)   (b) left to right (i), top to down (j)   (c) right to left (i), bottom to up (j)   (d) right to left (i), top to down (j)

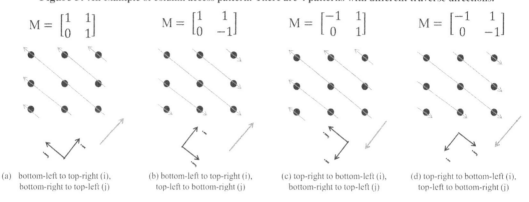

$$M = \begin{bmatrix} 1 & 1 \\ 0 & 1 \end{bmatrix} \qquad M = \begin{bmatrix} 1 & 1 \\ 0 & -1 \end{bmatrix} \qquad M = \begin{bmatrix} -1 & 1 \\ 0 & 1 \end{bmatrix} \qquad M = \begin{bmatrix} -1 & 1 \\ 0 & -1 \end{bmatrix}$$

(a)  bottom-left to top-right (i), bottom-right to top-left (j)   (b) bottom-left to top-right (i), top-left to bottom-right (j)   (c) top-right to bottom-left (i), bottom-right to top-left (j)   (d) top-right to bottom-left (i), top-left to bottom-right (j)

Figure 6: An example of diagonal access pattern with $slope = 1$. There are 4 patterns with different traverse directions.

each block $b_i$ has a $d_i$ dimensional loop nest that accesses an $n_i$ dimensional data array. In this work we restrict that the loop nest dimensionality and data-array dimensionality are equal for all sets of communicating blocks in the program, so we denote the loop nest dimensions and data array dimensions as $N$. The latency in clock cycles of each block $b_i$ without intra-block optimization is $lat_i$. If there is any control flow between the blocks, we consider the worst-case path; thus, the total baseline program latency in clock cycles (without any optimization) is the simple sum of the blocks' latencies

$$lat_{base} = \sum_{i=1}^{i=K} lat_i$$

$lat_i$ for each block is estimated by performing block-wise high level synthesis, and using the HLS-generated performance estimates[2]. When no optimizations are applied, we have verified that these estimates are accurate by comparing them with post-synthesis simulations. However, the HLS performance estimates can be inaccurate for modeling the parallelism, especially because the inter-block pipelining hides execution latency. Therefore, we develop an alternative performance metric that can estimate this optimization effect. Note that our performance estimation is based on clock cycles only. By default, we apply intra-block pipelining (e.g., loop pipelining within a block by setting initiation interval (II)) for all the blocks and set the same target period for all the implementations. Thus, the clock period tends to be similar across different implementations, and we ignore the effect of clock period in our estimation.

Let **P** be the set of all candidate data access patterns. Given $p \in \mathbf{P}$, we can estimate the performance of each block by the intra-block parallelization factor, and then the performance of the entire

<hr>

[2] We use the commercial AutoPilot [25] HLS tool to estimate $lat_i$.

program with the inter-block pipelining that overlaps the blocks' execution. In this work, we target inter-block pipelining, and correspondingly, it always makes sense to parallelize each block to the same factor to match the blocks' throughput and minimize inter-block buffering. Thus, we can simplify the program performance estimate in clock cycles as follows

$$lat_p = \frac{lat_{base}}{S_p^{intra} \times S_p^{inter}} + cost_p$$

where $S_p^{intra}$ and $S_p^{inter}$ represent the intra- and inter-block speedup (discussed next), respectively and $cost_p$ represents the implementation overhead.

For each block, we can fit multiple data processing pipelines for parallel processing. In high level synthesis, duplicate data processing pipelines are implemented by unrolling the inner loop. As we discussed above, we want to match the blocks' parallelism degree; therefore we search for the maximum unrolling factor where all blocks in the program can be unrolled to the same factor. For block $b_i$, we use $R_i$ to denote its resource usage. $R_i$ is a 4-tuple that represents its resource usage in *FFs, LUTs, BRAMs*, and *DSPs*. Then the total communication cost (in resources) between block $i$ and block $i + 1$ is estimated as another 4-tuple $Comm_i$, where we use the HLS estimates for $R_i$ and $Comm_i$. We have observed and experimentally validated that the HLS resource usage estimates correlate with actual resource after logic synthesis, although they tend to be conservatively high estimates. In particular, the HLS estimates for FF resource use and LUT resource use tend to be high. As we scale the unroll factor, this overestimate is compounded due to underestimation of resource sharing and LUT/FF packing into Slices. Therefore, we empirically determined another correlation factor tuple $\alpha$ that represents this scaling; unlike the communication factor, we use the same $\alpha$ factor for all blocks in a design and for all designs in our benchmark set. In total, we predict the actual resource usage as follows

$$(\sum_{i=1}^{i=K} R_i + Comm_i) \times \alpha \times par$$

where $par$ represents the intra-block parallelization degree.

Then, given the fixed resource budget of the FPGA, we can derive the maximally allowed parallelization degree, $Max_{par}$. We define $S_p^{intra}$ as follows

$$S_p^{intra} = \begin{cases} Max_{par} & \text{pattern } p \text{ enables parallelization} \\ & \text{for all the blocks} \\ 1 & \text{otherwise} \end{cases}$$

Similarly, for the inter-block pipelining factor $S_p^{inter}$, if we can transform all of the blocks to follow the same data access pattern for inter-block communication, then we can fully enable inter-block pipelining. Therefore, we define $S_p^{inter}$ as follows

$$S_p^{inter} = \begin{cases} K & \text{pattern } p \text{ enables pipelining} \\ 1 & \text{otherwise} \end{cases}$$

where $K$ is the number of blocks in the program. Note that we ignore the pipelining fill and drain overhead in the above estimation.

Finally, the implementation of the access patterns may incur additional overhead, which can significantly affect the program's performance estimate. Both row ($slope = 0$), column ($slope = \infty$) and their reverses are easy to implement without any overhead, but diagonal access patterns require loop skewing, as shown in Figure 1. Therefore, the inner-loop iteration domains are a function of outer-loop index values. When $slope = 1$, we can use $min$ and $max$ operations to bound the inner-loop iteration domains, as shown in Figure 1 (c); but with $1 < slope < N$ or $0 < slope < 1$, we must use a combination of $min$, $max$, $ceil$ and $floor$ functions to bound the inner-loop iteration domains. As discussed previously, we apply intra-block pipelining (e.g., loop pipelining within a block) for all the blocks by default to improve the performance. However, to enable intra-block pipelining, the inner-loop bounds have to be constants for HLS tools. Thus, for diagonal access patterns, we use the maximum loop bound ($N$) for the inner loop but add extra if-else conditions to filter out the false loop iterations. The if-else statement compares the current inner-loop index with its domain and executes the loop body only if the condition is true. The if-else comparison to filter out false loop iterations takes extra cycle and the number of false iterations depends on the domain of the outer loop. When $slope > 1$, the domain of the outer loop increases linearly with the $slope$; when $slope < 1$, the domain of the outer loop increases linearly with $\frac{1}{slope}$. Hence, the performance overhead $cost_p$ is defined as follows

$$cost_p = \begin{cases} 0 & slope = 0 \text{ or } slope = \infty \\ C \times slope & 1 \leq slope < N \\ C \times \frac{1}{slope} & 0 < slope < 1 \end{cases}$$

where $C$ is a constant.

In our formulation, the intra-block parallelization and inter-block pipelining are performed globally as a coarse-grained optimization. It is possible that a fine-grained optimization that selects different parallelization and pipelining parameters among different sets of blocks and/or communication paths could yield better performance. We expect that this could be implemented by applying this technique separately to subsets of program blocks with additional refinement to the performance model and buffers between the blocks; we leave these tasks for future work.

**Pattern Selection.** As shown previously, there are multiple data access patterns that include row, column and diagonal patterns with a variety of slopes and traversal directions. With high-dimension loop nests, this can be a large number of candidate patterns; however, we can easily prune the search space using the data dependencies to prune candidates that would violate dependencies. For stencil applications, the update of one data item depends on its neighbors in the surrounding stencil window, which is usually small compared to the size of the entire array. For diagonal access, we only need to focus on the data access pattern with $\frac{1}{n} \leq slope \leq n$, where $n$ is the stencil window dimension. For all remaining slope values ($n < slope < N$ and $\frac{1}{N} < slope < \frac{1}{n}$), they are equivalent to $slope = n$ or $slope = \frac{1}{n}$ in terms of the traversal order of data items in the stencil window, except that they incur additional overhead in implementing the loop bounds. This traversal order is the only factor that affects the ability to apply intra-block parallelization and inter-block pipelining. Using these dependencies to prune the list, it is in practice feasible to estimate performance for each of the candidates and choose the best.

Note that we only explore a subset of legal polyhedral transformations in this work. In theory, it is also possible to select the optimal pattern following the polyhedral optimization flow in [20] where all the FPGA-specific features discussed above including resource modeling and performance metrics have to be encoded as constraints and cost functions for the optimization problem. In practice, our pattern selection solution runs very fast for all the tested benchmarks.

## 3.3 Implementation

Our framework is an automatic flow consisting of three logical steps: we automatically transform source code, use HLS tools to enable optimizations and synthesis, and generate FIFO interfaces between computation and communication blocks. If the communication block requires a large communication buffer and a complex multi-read communication interface, we automatically insert customized communication blocks.

For the first step, we integrate our framework into PoCC polyhedral framework [1]. Our framework defines data access patterns, estimates performance, selects desired patterns based on performance metrics and performs loop transformations. The PoCC framework is at the C-code source level; we have also modified the framework to automatically produce source code compatible with our chosen HLS tool, AutoPilot [25][3].

Next, we use the AutoPilot HLS tool to enable optimizations and synthesize the computation blocks. AutoPilot provides a set of directives for optimization, including $loop\_unrolling$ and $pipeline$ for the intra-block parallelization and pipelining, and the $dataflow$ and $AP\_FIFO$ directives for inter-block pipelining (with communication through a FIFO interface). AutoPilot will execute unrolled loop iterations in parallel if there are no data dependencies between the iterations. Similarly, AutoPilot will overlap execution of data-dependent blocks if they use the same access pattern and can thus communicate through a FIFO interface. However, for the blocks that have multiple accesses to an array, either due to algorithm (e.g., stencil codes read a pattern of neighboring data) or parallelization (e.g., multiple iterations execute and access data in parallel), memory bandwidth bottleneck often prevents the design from reaching the expected intra-block parallelism and inter-block pipelining. To alleviate the memory bottleneck, we implement the memory partition technique [16] that partitions the arrays into several banks and enables more array accesses per clock cycle.

---

[3] AutoESL was acquired by Xilinx; AutoPilot is now part of Vivado HLS.

It is important to emphasize again that although AutoPilot provides these directives for intra- and inter-block optimizations, these optimizations can not always be applied with the default data access patterns and AutoPilot is unable to identify the optimization opportunities to enable them through transformations. Thus, the importance of this work is not just that we generate the AutoPilot directives that are already available, but that we automatically improve the number of situations in which the directives can be used.

In the first two steps, we can handle applications with simple inter-block communication patterns that can be transformed to use the FIFO interface automatically. However, some communication patterns are more complex; a block may perform multiple data reads per inner-loop iteration. In these situations, we need an optimized communication block. Particularly, we automatically insert a reuse buffer [15] that stores data that will be temporally reused. The implementation of the reuse buffer can use multi-port BRAMs or registers depending on resource and buffer sizes, as shown in Figure 7.

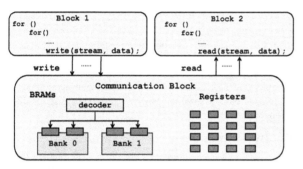

**Figure 7: Communication block.**

## 4. EXPERIMENTAL EVALUATION

In this section, we present our experimental results using a set of real-world applications that contain multiple data-dependent blocks and communicate through complex data access patterns. We first discuss the experiments setup and evaluated benchmarks. Then, we show the performance improvement of our proposed framework.

### 4.1 Experiments Setup

For our experiments, we use a set of benchmarks from Poly-Bench 3.0 [1] and some real-world applications from [11]. Table 2 describes the benchmark details.

Our framework is based on the polyhedral compiler infrastructure PoCC 1.1 [1]. PoCC is a source-to-source compiler that includes a set of tools for polyhedral compilation. It extracts the polyhedral intermediate representation at source code level. We modify PoCC to define data access patterns, evaluate FPGA architecture-specific performance, perform loop transformations and code generation. Finally, PoCC also provides libraries for program dependencies checking.

The output of our modified PoCC is transformed C code with AutoPilot pragmas to enable the HLS optimizations. Then, we use the AutoPilot HLS tool version 2011.3 to synthesize the transformed C code into Verilog RTL. As previously discussed, AutoPilot supports intra- and inter-block optimizations. We automatically insert directives into the configuration file to enable these optimizations. The target FPGA platform is Xilinx-Virtex-6 LX75T. We synthesize the RTL generated from AutoPilot using Xilinx ISE 13.1 and gather area and clock period data. To compute the operating frequency, we round down the operating frequency determined by the synthesis report's achievable clock period to an inte-

ger. The clock cycles are collected through simulation using Modelsim 6.1. Finally, we compute latency using the operating frequency and clock cycles and compute speedup using the latency value.

**Table 2: Benchmarks**

| Benchmark | Description |
|---|---|
| Deconv | Image Rician Deconvolution [11] |
| Denoise | Image Rician Denoising [11] |
| Seg | Image Segmentation [11] |
| Seidel | Seidel stencil computation [1] |
| Jacobi | Jacobi stencil computation [1] |

### 4.2 Performance Improvement

We compare the performance of three different implementations. The first implementation is the baseline — it is the original source code without using intra-block parallelization or inter-block pipelining optimization. The second implementation is an improved version — it applies the intra-block parallelization and inter-block pipelining optimizations to the original source code when supported without code transformation. The first and second implementations do not require source code transformation. Although the second implementation tries to use optimizations, they cannot be enabled if the default data access pattern does not support it. The third implementation is our proposed implementation — it transforms the source code and then enables the intra- and inter-block optimizations. Note that by default, we apply intra-block pipelining within each individual block for all the implementations and benchmarks.

**Performance Comparison.** Table 3 describes the clock cycles, resources and achieved frequencies of the three implementations for all the benchmarks. Table 4 presents the details of the chosen data access patterns and enabled optimizations with and without transformation for all the benchmarks.

Compared to the baseline design, the second and third implementations improve the latency in clock cycles at the expense of more resource usage using the pipelining and parallelization optimizations. This demonstrates that with greater opportunity for intra-block parallelization and inter-block pipelining, HLS tools can effectively use additional FPGA resources. The latency speedup is shown in Figure 8. The speedup is normalized to the baseline implementation. Compared to the baseline, the second implementation (without transformation, with optimization) achieves an average of 4.89X speedup. Our proposed implementation (with transformation, with optimization) achieves further speedup by enabling more optimizations through polyhedral transformations. Our proposed implementation achieves an average of 29.59X speedup over the non-optimized source code and 6.04X speedup over code that is optimized but not transformed to enable optimizations. The average speedup is computed using geometric mean.

The performance improvement is from three-fold: first, the intra-block parallelization improves computation latency within blocks; second, the inter-block pipelining improves computation latency by overlapping the execution of blocks; and third, our memory and communication block optimization improves the memory bandwidth. We again use the example of the *Denoise* benchmark to demonstrate these points; the second implementation employs inter-block pipelining in conjunction with memory partition. These two optimizations improve clock cycles by overlapping the execution of two blocks and allowing multiple memory accesses per clock cycle. Without code transformation, the intra-block parallelization is available for the first block but not the second block as shown in Figure 1. We do not perform partial parallelization (e.g., parallelizing the first block only) together with inter-block pipelining

**Table 3: Performance and resource comparison of different implementations**

| Benchmark | Implementation | Cycles | LUT | FF | DSP | BRAM | Frequency(MHz) |
|---|---|---|---|---|---|---|---|
| Deconv | w/o trans, w/o opt | 5408 | 3234 | 948 | 24 | 48 | 151 |
| | w/o trans, w/ opt | 1809 | 6433 | 2650 | 24 | 5 | 182 |
| | w/ trans, w/ opt | 257 | 13819 | 13826 | 108 | 17 | 182 |
| Denoise | w/o trans, w/o opt | 5408 | 3266 | 948 | 24 | 5 | 160 |
| | w/o trans, w/ opt | 1809 | 6503 | 2672 | 24 | 5 | 182 |
| | w/ trans, w/ opt | 250 | 13817 | 13824 | 108 | 17 | 230 |
| Seg | w/o trans, w/o opt | 9864 | 3735 | 1202 | 30 | 24 | 117 |
| | w/o trans, w/ opt | 9864 | 3735 | 1202 | 30 | 24 | 117 |
| | w/ trans, w/ opt | 500 | 48796 | 9560 | 216 | 34 | 156 |
| Seidel | w/o trans, w/o opt | 64803 | 1400 | 891 | 2 | 2 | 103 |
| | w/o trans, w/ opt | 1818 | 13375 | 6626 | 32 | 6 | 134 |
| | w/ trans, w/ opt | 1130 | 47402 | 20040 | 96 | 14 | 134 |
| Jacobi | w/o trans, w/o opt | 5373 | 5563 | 1890 | 3 | 16 | 101 |
| | w/o trans, w/ opt | 1439 | 39430 | 18832 | 64 | 10 | 134 |
| | w/ trans, w/ opt | 482 | 38877 | 18664 | 64 | 10 | 133 |

**Table 4: Details of optimizations and data access pattern**

| Benchmark | Optimizations | | Selected Data Access Pattern |
|---|---|---|---|
| | w/o trans | w/ trans | |
| Deconv | inter-block pipeline | inter-block pipeline & intra-block parallel | diagonal (slope = 1) |
| Denoise | inter-block pipeline | inter-block pipeline & intra-block parallel | diagonal (slope = 1) |
| Seg | none | inter-block pipeline & intra-block parallel | diagonal (slope = 1) |
| Seidel | inter-block pipeline | inter-block pipeline & intra-block parallel | diagonal (slope = 2) |
| Jacobi | intra-block parallel | inter-block pipeline & intra-block parallel | row |

because if the throughputs are not matched then it would require a buffer size proportional to the total data size which is not feasible in general. The third implementation transforms the code to a diagonal access pattern. Then, in addition to inter-block pipelining and memory customization, it enables intra-block parallelization for both blocks that allows multiple iterations to execute simultaneously. The third implementation maximizes resource use such that each block is parallelized to the same degree and fits in the Virtex 6 LX75T, which has 46240 LUTs, 92480 FFs, 288 DSPs, and 312 18Kb BRAMs. For *Denoise*, the intra-block parallelization degree is 9, given the resources on FPGA. As a result, our implementation achieves 31.09X and 9.14X speedup over the first and second implementations, respectively.

In addition, our optimization produces a side-benefit of improved operating frequency. As stated earlier, we assume that the clock period is not affected by our transformations and make no specific effort to improve clock period. However, because our technique implements simplified memory and communication interfaces, we also have the benefit of reducing the complexity of addressing and communication structures. Therefore, we also improve the design's critical path and get a corresponding modest improvement in operating frequency as shown in Table 3.

**Data Access Pattern and Optimization.** For benchmarks *Denoise*, *Deconv* and *Seidel*, without transformations inter-block pipeline can be enabled as different blocks communicate in the same order; but intra-block parallelization cannot be enabled with the default data access order. Our implementation transforms them into diagonal access order with different slopes, which enables both intra- and inter-block optimization. The slope of the data access order is chosen based on the performance metric we developed in section 3.2. In particular, we choose $slope = 2$ for *Seidel* as it allows simultaneous execution of the iterations on the same diagonal line and retain inter-block pipelining. For benchmark *Seg*, without transformation neither intra-block parallelization nor inter-block pipelining can be enabled. Thus, the first and second implementation are the same as shown in Table 3. Our implementation transforms it into diagonal access pattern ($slope = 1$), which enables both intra- and inter-block optimization. For benchmarks *Jacobi*, without transformation intra-block parallelization is available as there are no dependencies among iterations, but inter-block pipelining cannot be enabled as two blocks produce and consume data in different orders. Our implementation transforms it to enable both intra- and inter-block optimization. For all the benchmarks, our implementation successfully enables both intra-block parallelization and inter-block pipelining optimizations.

# 5. RELATED WORK

High level synthesis has seen significant advances in recent years, improving the quality of input source languages. There are many currently active HLS tools in both industry and academia, such as [8, 25, 4, 7, 19, 14]. Leading HLS tools support various intra-block and inter-block optimizations, including pipelining and parallelization. With such powerful optimizations, HLS offers increased productivity with lower design effort; however, in practice these transformations are difficult to apply — only certain data access

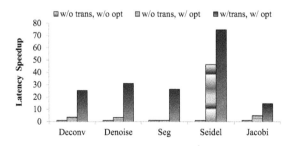

**Figure 8: Latency speedup comparison.**

patterns are supported, limiting the applicability of an important HLS feature. Recent studies show that there is still a significant performance gap between manual design and HLS-generated designs [23, 17, 10], and the inability to apply these optimizations is one of the causes of this gap.

Real-world applications contain multiple data-dependent blocks that communicate through complex data access patterns, with source code that was not originally intended for HLS. These applications commonly have original data access patterns that do not support the HLS optimizations; thus, it is critical to transform the source code to enable these optimizations. Prior work in optimization opportunities for data-dependent blocks individually worked on pipelining and communication techniques [26, 22, 9]. Ziegler et al. developed coarse-grained pipelining for data-dependent loops that find efficient communication schemes [26], but they assume that the data access order is already identical between the communicating loops. Cong et al. developed a resource constrained scheduling formulation for the communication problem that can find the optimal communication order [9], but the technique requires completely unrolled loops, and additional storage and computation overhead for communication reordering. Similarly, Rodrigues et al. presented a fine-grained synchronization technique with hardware inter-stage buffers to manage the communication [22]. Prior works retain the original execution order but apply techniques to reorder communication; however, these techniques may require large inter-stage buffers in order to handle the reordering, which limits the feasible problem sizes they can support. Furthermore, these works manually optimize communication interfaces, rather than automated optimization such as that performed for high level synthesis.

In our technique, we instead rely on loop transformations to convert the execution order so that the communication order is optimized, while simultaneously minimizing the need for inter-stage buffers. The polyhedral model based loop transformations are based on a mathematical model that can represent any composition of loop transformations using affine transformations [24, 20, 13]. In the past, polyhedral models have been used for maximizing parallelism while minimizing communcation for parallel computing [18, 2]. Recently, polyhedral models have been used in high level synthesis for FPGAs to optimize on-chip memory bandwidth [12, 21], or to optimize the SDRAM bandwidth [3]. In contrast, our approach is to optimize multiple data-dependent blocks simultaneously in order to match their data access patterns and thus simultaneously optimize both intra-block parallelism and inter-block pipelining.

# 6. CONCLUSION

High level synthesis is a critical technology to ease the adoption of hardware accelerator resources. However, although current high level synthesis offers a variety of powerful optimizations, the implementation constraints limit the applicability and thus impact of the optimizations. Input source codes commonly have complex data access patterns that do not inherently support important high level synthesis optimization techniques, but polyhedral models can model the data access patterns and find loop transformations that enable these important parallelization and pipelining optimizations.

We have presented an integrated technique using polyhedral models to model and enable both intra- and inter-block optimizations. This integrated technique substantially improves the opportunity to use HLS optimizations for parallelism, pipelining, and fine-grained communication. Our framework automatically identifies data access patterns and candidate loop transformations, evaluates the performance benefit of each candidate to select the best option, performs the code transformations, and inserts the HLS code directives

and communication structures to implement the optimized hardware. Experimental evaluation demonstrates an average of 6.04X speedup over high level synthesis without our transformations to enable intra- and inter-block optimizations.

# 7. ACKNOWLEDGMENTS

This work was partially supported by National High Technology Research and Development Program of China 2012AA010902 and A*STAR Singapore under the Human Sixth Sense Project.

# 8. REFERENCES

[1] Pocc. The polyhedral compiler collection. http://www.cse.ohio-state.edu/~pouchet/software/pocc/.

[2] Nawaaz Ahmed, Nikolay Mateev, and Keshav Pingali. Synthesizing transformations for locality enhancement of imperfectly-nested loop nests. *Int. J. Parallel Program.*, 29(5):493–544, 2001.

[3] Samuel Bayliss and George A. Constantinides. Optimizing SDRAM bandwidth for custom FPGA loop accelerators. In *FPGA*, pages 195–204, 2012.

[4] Thomas Bollaert. *High-Level Synthesis: From Algorithm to Digital Circuit*, chapter Catapult synthesis: A practical introduction to interactive C syntheis. Springer, 2008.

[5] Uday Bondhugula et al. Automatic transformations for communication-minimized parallelization and locality optimization in the polyhedral model. In *CC*, pages 132–146, 2008.

[6] Uday Bondhugula, Albert Hartono, J. Ramanujam, and P. Sadayappan. A practical automatic polyhedral parallelizer and locality optimizer. In *PLDI*, pages 101–113, 2008.

[7] Andrew Canis et al. Legup: high-level synthesis for FPGA-based processor/accelerator systems. In *FPGA*, pages 33–36, 2011.

[8] Jason Cong et al. High-level synthesis for FPGAs: From prototyping to deployment. *IEEE TCAD*, pages 473–491, 2011.

[9] Jason Cong, Yiping Fan, Guoling Han, Wei Jiang, and Zhiru Zhang. Behavior and communication co-optimization for systems with sequential communication media. In *DAC*, pages 675–678, 2006.

[10] Jason Cong, Muhuan Huang, and Yi Zou. Accelerating fluid registration algorithm on multi-FPGA platforms. In *FPL*, pages 50–57, 2011.

[11] Jason Cong, Vivek Sarkar, Glenn Reinman, and Alex Bui. Customizable domain-specific computing. *IEEE Des. Test*, 28(2):6–15.

[12] Jason Cong, Peng Zhang, and Yi Zou. Optimizing memory hierarchy allocation with loop transformations for high-level synthesis. In *DAC*, pages 1233–1238, 2012.

[13] Paul Feautrier. Some efficient solutions to the affine scheduling problem: I. one-dimensional time. *Int. J. Parallel Program.*, 21(5):313–348, 1992.

[14] Swathi T. Gurumani et al. High-level synthesis of multiple dependent CUDA kernels on FPGA. In *ASPDAC*, 2013.

[15] Ilya Issenin, Erik Brockmeyer, Miguel Miranda, and Nikil Dutt. DRDU: A data reuse analysis technique for efficient scratch-pad memory management. *ACM Trans. Des. Autom. Electron. Syst.*, 12(2), 2007.

[16] Peng Li et al. Memory partitioning and scheduling co-optimization in behavioral synthesis. In *ICCAD*, pages 488–495, 2012.

[17] Yun Liang et al. High-level synthesis: Productivity, performance, and software constraints. *J. Electrical and Computer Engineering*, 2012.

[18] Amy W. Lim, Gerald I. Cheong, and Monica S. Lam. An affine partitioning algorithm to maximize parallelism and minimize communication. In *ICS*, pages 228–237, 1999.

[19] Alex Papakonstantinou et al. Multilevel granularity parallelism synthesis on FPGAs. In *FCCM*, pages 178–185. IEEE, 2011.

[20] Louis-Noël Pouchet et al. Loop transformations: convexity, pruning and optimization. In *POPL*, pages 549–562, 2011.

[21] Louis-Noël Pouchet, Peng Zhang, P. Sadayappan, and Jason Cong. Polyhedral-based data reuse optimization for configurable computing. In *FPGA*, 2013.

[22] Rui Rodrigues, Joao M. P. Cardoso, and Pedro C. Diniz. A data-driven approach for pipelining sequences of data-dependent loops. In *FCCM*, pages 219–228, 2007.

[23] Kyle Rupnow et al. High level synthesis of stereo matching: Productivity, performance, and software constraints. In *FPT*, pages 1–8, 2011.

[24] Michael. E. Wolf and Monica. S. Lam. A loop transformation theory and an algorithm to maximize parallelism. *IEEE Trans. Parallel Distrib. Syst.*, 2(4):452–471, 1991.

[25] Zhiru Zhang et al. *High-Level Synthesis: From Algorithm to Digital Circuit*, chapter AutoPilot: a platform-based ESL synthesis system. Springer, 2008.

[26] Heidi E. Ziegler, Mary W. Hall, and Pedro C. Diniz. Compiler-generated communication for pipelined FPGA applications. In *DAC*, pages 610–615, 2003.

# Towards Simulator-like Observability for FPGAs:
# A Virtual Overlay Network for Trace-Buffers

Eddie Hung
Dept. of Electrical and Computer Engineering
University of British Columbia
Vancouver, B.C., Canada
eddieh@ece.ubc.ca

Steven J. E. Wilton
Dept. of Electrical and Computer Engineering
University of British Columbia
Vancouver, B.C., Canada
stevew@ece.ubc.ca

## ABSTRACT

The rising complexity of verification has led to an increase in the use of FPGA prototyping, which can run at significantly higher operating frequencies and achieve much higher coverage than logic simulations. However, a key challenge is observability into these devices, which can be solved by embedding trace-buffers to record on-chip signal values. Rather than connecting a predetermined subset of circuits signals to dedicated trace-buffer inputs at compile-time, in this work we propose that a virtual overlay network is built to multiplex all on-chip signals to all on-chip trace-buffers. Subsequently, at debug-time, the designer can choose a signal subset for observation. To minimize its overhead, we build this network out of unused routing multiplexers, and by using optimal bipartite graph matching techniques, we show that any subset of on-chip signals can be connected to 80–90% of the maximum trace-buffer capacity in less than 50 seconds.

## Categories and Subject Descriptors

B.7 [**Integrated Circuits**]: Design Aids—*Verification*

## Keywords

FPGA Debug; FPGA Prototyping; Verification; Trace-Buffers; Overlay Network

## 1. INTRODUCTION

As the achievable capacities of digital integrated circuits grow, the verification and debugging tasks are becoming increasingly difficult. A Mentor Graphics study found that whilst silicon density doubles every 18 months, designer productivity only doubled every 39 months, and that half of all designer effort was spent performing functional verification [5]. Designers make extensive use of simulation to verify that their designs operate as expected and to hunt for the cause of incorrect behaviour, however, simulation is slow; IBM engineers reported that software simulation was only able to reach 10Hz while their custom ASIC had a target frequency of 1.6GHz — a difference of over 8 orders in magnitude [2].

A growing number of designers are now opting to prototype their design using one or more Field-Programmable Gate Arrays (FPGAs). The same Mentor study found that 55% of industry employed FPGA prototyping techniques in 2010, an increase from 41% in 2007 [5]. FPGA prototyping enables significantly higher verification coverage compared to simulation, allowing designers to exercise their design using realistic scenarios (e.g. booting an operating system).

The primary challenge during FPGA prototyping is one of visibility. Unlike software simulation, in which the designer can view the behaviour of any signal in the design at any time step, in prototyping only those signals which drive output pins can be observed. This significantly limits debug productivity, since it is often difficult to deduce internal behaviour by only observing output signals. Providing *simulator-like visibility* to an FPGA platform is seen as one of the key technologies required as FPGAs scale to larger and larger capacities [18]. This paper is a step in this direction.

A common technique for increasing visibility is to insert trace-buffers into a circuit, and use these trace-buffers to record a history of a subset of internal signals during normal device operation. Altera and Xilinx provide tools enabling this [24, 1] and third-party solutions are also available [19, 17]. A key constraint of this method, however, is that the signals that a designer wishes to observe must be predetermined at compile-time, before the circuit is operational, and often, before the exact nature of the bug is known. As a result, a designer wishing to change the set of signals that are recorded would have to recompile his or her design. Recompiling and/or reconfiguring the design to observe different signals is referred to as a *turn* in [22]; often many turns are required during debug to narrow down the cause of unexpected behaviour. References [8, 6, 1] all show how incremental routing can be used to connect signals to trace-buffers or output pins without a complete recompile, however, these techniques are still slow (in [8], a re-route time of 2,000 seconds for a 100,000 LUT circuit is reported).

In this paper, we propose a method which accelerates the debug process by significantly reducing the amount of time required to perform a turn. We do this by allowing the designer to change which signals are to be connected to the trace-buffer without recompiling the design, and without requiring a re-route of signals between debug iterations. We achieve this by, at compile-time, embedding a flexible overlay network which multiplexes almost all combinational and sequential signals of the gate-level circuit into these trace-buffers. Unlike [19], the network is not built using the normal soft FPGA logic. Instead, we *reclaim unused routing multiplexers within the FPGA fabric* and use them to implement this network. As a result, the area overhead due to this network is essentially zero. At debug time, we then configure this network by setting a small number of routing bits to connect selected signals to the trace-buffers. Using our technique, we can forward any signal selection of a designer's choosing to 80–90% of the on-chip trace capacity.

Although our approach falls short of a software simulator in that we can only observe a limited number of signals and for a limited number of clock cycles as constrained by trace-buffer capacity, crucially, we will show that our technique allows the designer to defer the selection of which signals to observe to debug-time. This negates the need to recompile the circuit whenever the signal selection is changed, greatly accelerating debug productivity.

## 2. RELATED WORK

On-chip observability can be enhanced using either scan- or trace-based techniques. Scan-based techniques involve connecting internal flip-flops sequentially; in FPGAs, this can be achieved using general-purpose soft-logic as in [21], where the area and delay costs can be prohibitive, or through dedicated device readback support [9]. Scan techniques can provide complete visibility into the state of all flip-flops in the design, but typically require that the circuit is halted before scan-out. This can greatly slow down their use for real-time debugging; reference [9] reported that viewing one flip-flop using device readback can take between 2 to 8 seconds.

Trace-based techniques operate by utilizing a portion of the FPGA's embedded memory resources to record a small subset of internal circuit values during continued device operation. Examples of trace IP offerings include Xilinx ChipScope Pro, Altera SignalTap II and Synopsys Identify [24, 1, 17]. For these products, the subset of signals that are connected to trace-buffers must be determined by the designer ahead of time, before the circuit is compiled. Once trace instrumentation has been inserted, if a designer wishes to modify the observed signals, the circuit would often need to be recompiled. To combat this, commercial tools support general purpose incremental-compilation techniques whilst researchers have also proposed a trace-specific procedure in [8].

Most similar to our work is Tektronix Certus [19], which allows designers to specify a large subset of signals to connect to a proprietary Observation Network during compilation, from which they can select a smaller subset to trace at runtime. A related product is Altera SignalProbe [1], which uses incremental ECO techniques to multiplex up to 256 circuit signals to each reserved I/O pin for external analysis. Our work differs in that we do not require the designer to predetermine which signals they can observe — we aim to provide the designer with complete visibility, nor do we use general-purpose logic to provide this runtime flexibility.

Authors have also proposed exploiting an FPGA's unique reconfiguration capabilities for debug. Reference [7] describes a method to reclaim spare FPGA resources for debug by speculatively inserting trace-buffer logic connected to a set of "influential" signals without any user intervention. Signals used for this purpose are determined using automated selection techniques such as those presented in [11, 10]. In a proposal similar to our approach, Moctar et al. [13] reuse the local routing multiplexers present inside each FPGA logic cluster to implement the programmable shift operation

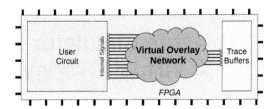

Figure 1: Virtual overlay network for multiplexing a large set of circuit signals to a small number of trace-buffer inputs

in floating-point computation, freeing up valuable soft-logic resources to be more efficiently used elsewhere.

Similar to [8], one important aspect that enables this proposed work is the realization that circuit signals can be connected to *any* free trace-buffer input for it to be observable. Instead of using a fully-populated crossbar where every network input can be forwarded to any network output, this flexibility can be exploited by using a sparse $(n, m)$ concentrator network [14], which guarantees that any size-$m$ combination of the size-$n$ input set can be routed through to its outputs in an arbitrary order. However, because we intend to connect all circuit signals to our overlay network, and allow all of them to access as many trace-buffer inputs as possible, even a concentrator may add too much routing pressure to the FPGA. In this paper, we pursue a blocking network which sacrifices the absolute guarantee of any-$m$-of-$n$, but as the results later show, approximately 80–90% of full connectivity can still be achieved.

## 3. OUR APPROACH: OBSERVATION WITHOUT RECOMPILATION

We propose a method to allow the set of signals connected to on-chip trace-buffers to be modified without requiring the circuit to be recompiled. These techniques can be used to greatly reduce the time between debug turns, and hence rapidly accelerate the debugging flow. The key enabling component to this work is that, instead of building a custom FPGA mapping to connect each signal to one dedicated trace-buffer input as in existing IP [24, 1], we insert a virtual overlay network which allows multiple signals to be multiplexed to each trace-input; this is illustrated in Figure 1. Subsequently, changing the signals that are forwarded over this network will require only the virtual network to be reconfigured, rather than a new place-and-route solution.

Existing work pursue a debug flow similar to that shown in Figure 2a, in which the instrumentation procedure requires a new FPGA mapping to be constructed for each new set of observed signals at each debug turn. Whilst incremental compilation techniques can be used to accelerate this procedure [8], it still requires the entire circuit to be loaded into the memory of a CAD tool and some amount of additional routing (and perhaps placement) operations to be performed. Figure 2b describes our proposed debug flow. This debug flow consists of two phases: compile-time and debug-time. During compile-time, the uninstrumented circuit is fully compiled as normal, and the resulting mapping is then *completely* fixed. Next, the virtual overlay network is then added incrementally, using only the FPGA resources that were leftover from the initial mapping — this is described in Section 7. It is also possible to insert the overlay network during the original full compile, though this option is not explored here.

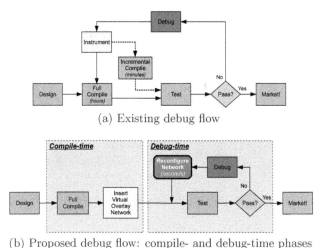

(a) Existing debug flow

(b) Proposed debug flow: compile- and debug-time phases

Figure 2: Existing and proposed debug flows

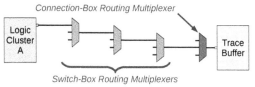

(a) Prior work: single trace connections

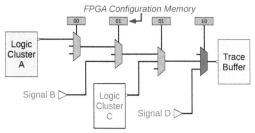

(b) Proposed: overlay network with multiple connections

Figure 3: Trace-buffer connectivity

At debug-time, this overlay network is then repeatedly configured with the signals that a designer wishes to observe, and the device tested at each turn in order to record the desired signal values, until the root-cause of the bug is located. By eliminating all forms of recompilation from the inner loop, each debug turn can now be completed in a matter of seconds.

A number of key technical challenges have to be overcome in order to realize such a proposed flow, and these will be described as follows: Section 4 presents the details of our virtual overlay network, which seeks to connect all combinational and sequential signals of the user-circuit to the available trace-buffers. Section 5 describes the graph-based method we employ for computing a valid network configuration Lastly, Section 6 describes how this configuration can be programmed into the device.

## 4. VIRTUAL OVERLAY NETWORK

In this section, we will describe the details of our virtual overlay network. The key purpose of this network is to multiplex *all* on-chip signals to *all* trace-buffer inputs. With previous work, it is necessary to compile a custom point-to-point network for each new signal selection, generating a mapping such as that illustrated by Figure 3a where each observed signal is connected exclusively to a single trace-buffer input via a set of dedicated routing multiplexers. Instead, we propose that an overlay network is created out of these routing multiplexers, as shown in Fig. 3b, where a total of 4 signals: A, B, C and D are now connected to the same trace-input. The select-lines to each of these routing multiplexers are driven by the FPGA configuration memory — methods to reprogram their values are covered in a subsequent section. The reconfigurable nature of FPGAs arises from the abundance of multiplexers inside, and by utilizing routing multiplexers to build this overlay network instead of general-purpose user-logic, this network can be built much more efficiently. The feasibility of this proposal is supported by analysis that in mapping our set of uninstrumented benchmark circuits to a minimum array size FPGA with a small amount of routing slack, only 32–51% of the total interconnect capacity (geomean at 41%) was utilized.

We note that our approach of instrumenting the circuit after compilation means that only gate-level signals are ac-

cessible; but due to the effects of optimization or technology-mapping, such signals may not posses a direct one-to-one correspondence to those at the RTL or HDL-level signals that a designer is most familiar with. We believe several approaches exist to alleviate this mismatch: first, unless register re-timing is performed, both commercial and academic CAD tools preserve the names of all sequential signals in the design, which designers can use as fixed points of reference. With sufficient visibility into the sequential signals that affect it, any intermediate combinational signals can then be re-computed using offline simulation.

Second, designers are able to manually specify additional points of reference by using synthesis attributes to prevent combinational signals from being optimized away — the "`syn_keep`" attribute is available in Quartus II, and Synplify, whilst the "`S`" (SAVE_NET) attribute in ISE. Trace IP which instrument at the RTL or HDL-level (SignalTap II, ChipScope, Certus) implicitly do this. During prototyping, large circuits are likely to be I/O-bound due to the need to partition the circuit amongst multiple FPGAs — in those cases, it would be feasible to optimize the circuit less aggressively so that more combinational signals can be preserved. This approach is not dissimilar to debugging software applications, where speed is traded for visibility; in fact, the upcoming version of GCC 4.8 supports a new "`-Og`" optimization level to address this.

Building the virtual overlay network is essentially a routing problem. This routing problem can be represented as a routing resource graph $G(V, E)$. We define $V = V_{signals} \cup V_{routing} \cup V_{trace}$ where $V_{signals}$ is the set of all circuit signals that can be traced, $V_{routing}$ the set of unused routing multiplexers, and $V_{trace}$ the set of trace-buffer inputs. $E$ is the set of unused routing tracks that exist between these resources. Example routing resource graphs are shown in Figure 4 where $V_{signals}$ is indicated by ▷ triangles, $V_{routing}$ as ∘ circles, and $V_{trace}$ as ◁ triangles. Fig. 4a illustrates an example point-to-point network that would be created by prior work for observing signals B and D. Here, each routing multiplexer would be used to carry only one signal.

Figure 4b shows a routing solution for the same resource graph in which all five circuit signals are connected to either of

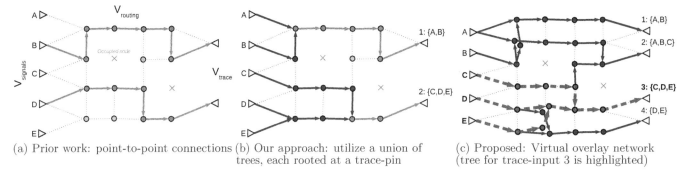

(a) Prior work: point-to-point connections    (b) Our approach: utilize a union of trees, each rooted at a trace-pin    (c) Proposed: Virtual overlay network (tree for trace-input 3 is highlighted)

Figure 4: Routing Resource Graphs $G(V,E)$: ▷ indicate circuit signals, ○ for routing multiplexers and ◁ are trace-buffer inputs

the two trace-buffer pins available. Each routing multiplexer can have a fan-in of more than one. At debug-time, a designer can now configure the routing multiplexers in such a way as to forward just one signal to each trace-input. For this particular solution, designers can observe any single signal in their circuit, and a limited selection of any two signals simultaneously, as defined by the Cartesian product of the two signal sets {A,B} × {C,D,E}: {AC,AD,AE,BC ...}.

The key feature of this routing solution is that it is made up of a disjoint union of trees, each rooted at a trace-buffer input, with the leaves of each tree being the circuit signals that it connects. We use a disjoint union of such trees, to allow signal selections to be made for each trace-buffer input *independently* of other trace inputs; it is this constraint which differentiates and abstracts our virtual overlay network from the more general routing problem faced when building point-to-point networks. Whilst each trace-buffer input in the general routing resource graph $G$ can be considered the root of a much larger tree which touches all the signals in its fan-in cone, the union of such trees will not be disjoint and hence signals for each trace-input cannot be selected independently.

Our virtual overlay network can be described as a graph $G'(V', E')$ where $V'$ now consists of $V_{signals} \cup V_{trace}$, and $E'$ the set of edges that describe connectivity between a circuit signal and a trace-pin. Furthermore, rather than connecting each signal in the circuit to a trace-buffer input just once as in Fig. 4b, it is possible for a signal to be a leaf of multiple trees. A valid routing solution for a network where this is the case is shown in Figure 4c; here, by occupying a few more routing resources, each of the five signals can now be connected to two of the four trace-buffer inputs. The increased flexibility of this overlay network can now guarantee that any combination of two signals can be selected for observation, but in practice, many more signals are possible.

## 5. NETWORK MATCHING

So far, we have assumed that at debug-time, the designer chooses which signal they wish to connect to every input pin of every trace-buffer in their circuit. Once this decision is made, a simple algorithm can be used to determine the select bits for each of the $V_{routing}$ multiplexers that make up the overlay network. This algorithm follows a greedy strategy: starting at the leaf node of the desired $V_{signal}$, move through all $V_{routing}$ multiplexers in the routing resource graph $G$ belonging to the signal tree towards its root, $V_{trace}$. At each $V_{routing}$ multiplexer encountered, set it to forward the output from the previous node. However, making the choice

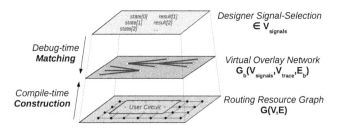

Figure 5: Virtual overlay network abstraction

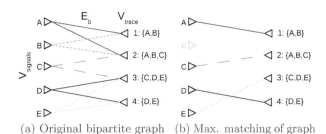

(a) Original bipartite graph    (b) Max. matching of graph

Figure 6: Bipartite graph $G_b(V_{signals}, V_{trace}, E_b)$ capturing signal/trace-input connectivity of virtual overlay network

of which signal to forward to which trace-input is not trivial. Consider the network in Figure 4c: although the designer can select any combination of two signals, they can only select a limited combination of three signals — defined by the Cartesian product of all sets. Given that each signal can be connected to one of two trace-buffer pins, there exists a problem of deciding which signals to connect to which pin. As an example, suppose that a designer wishes to observe the signals ACD; A can only be forwarded to trace-input 1 or 2, C to 2 or 3, whilst D can be forwarded to 3 or 4. From this list of constraints, a feasible assignment must be found: A→1, C→2, D→3 would be one valid solution, as would A→2, C→3, and D→4. However, assigning A→2 and D→3 would prevent signal C from reaching any trace-buffer input. Although this example was easy to compute by hand, it may not be so simple for circuits containing 10,000s of signals, connected to 1,000s of trace-inputs, from which 100s of signals are selected.

To solve this assignment problem, we utilize matching techniques for bipartite graphs. A bipartite graph can be described as $G_b(U_b, V_b, E_b)$, where $U_b$ and $V_b$ represent two disjoint sets of vertices, and $E_b$ the set of edges that connect between them. Edges must not exist between elements in the same set: from $U_b$ to $U_b$, nor from $V_b$ to $V_b$. The definition for our virtual overlay network fits this pattern, when substituting $U_b = V_{signals}$, the set of all circuit signals, $V_b = V_{trace}$, the set of all trace-buffer inputs, and $E_b = E'$ — the set of edges which describe the network connectivity between the two. The relationship between the virtual overlay network $G_b$ and the general routing resource graph $G$ is shown in Figure 5. The bipartite graph capturing the connectivity of the overlay network from Fig. 4c is shown in Figure 6a.

A maximum matching in a bipartite graph can be computed in polynomial time. A matching of graph $G_b$ represents a subgraph of $G_b$ in which none of its edges share a common vertex; a maximum matching is the largest such subgraph that can be formed. This is a very convenient property for computing which signal to forward to each trace-pin: given that each pin can only support one such connection, therefore, each node in $V_{trace}$ must have at most one edge. The maximum matching solution for selecting signals ACDE from its bipartite graph is shown in Figure 6b, which returns the solution: $A \rightarrow 1$, $C \rightarrow 2$, $D \rightarrow 4$ and $E \rightarrow 3$. The maximum number of edges that can exist in a maximum matching is the minimum value of $|V_{signals}|$ and $|V_{trace}|$. In typical circuits, we would expect that more circuit signals exist than trace-inputs, and hence $|V_{signals}| >> |V_{trace}|$.

An additional useful characteristic of the maximum matching algorithm is that it not only returns a pass-fail result, for cases where a complete match is not possible, it will return a best-effort partial assignment. Because the virtual overlay network that we build is blocking, a maximum match can be used to return partial, but optimal, result where the maximum number of signals possible are forwarded over the network. In cases where not all requested signals can be forwarded, more than one maximum partial-match may exist — currently, only an arbitrary match is returned. Similarly, the solution may not capture designer intent in situations where higher emphasis is placed on certain signals — they may prefer one high-value signal to be selected over multiple, lower-value ones. This is a scenario we plan to address in future work using maximum weighted matching techniques.

# 6. NETWORK RECONFIGURATION

Once the select bits for each of the $V_{routing}$ multiplexers in the overlay network have been computed, the final task is to program these bits into the FPGA. For this we propose two different approaches: one which requires the FPGA to be powered down and fully reprogrammed, and an alternative which, with the correct architectural support, would allow the signal selection of a live FPGA to be changed on-the-fly.

## 6.1 Static Reconfiguration

The flow employed in existing work [24, 1, 8] is to create a new point-to-point circuit mapping for each new signal selection. The resulting bitstream would then be used to fully reprogram the all of the configuration memory on the FPGA device. This static reconfiguration procedure is identical to that which is undertaken during the initial power-on of the FPGA, and is also responsible for resetting all flip-flop and memory contents to a known value, destroying any existing user-state. For this reason, after reprogramming each new trace configuration, designers must then rerun their tests from scratch to collect their new signal trace.

In our proposed flow, because we do not recompile the circuit between each debug turn, we do not automatically generate a new bitstream. However, with exact knowledge of where the configuration bits for each routing multiplexer is located within this bitstream, it would be possible to directly modify only those bits necessary for configuring our overlay network. Then, when the FPGA device is statically reprogrammed, the desired signal selection is forwarded for observation. Graham et al. [6] adopt this bitstream modification approach for creating point-to-point trace networks.

## 6.2 Dynamic Reconfiguration

Alternatively, it may be possible for the overlay network to be changed for a new signal selection without losing user-state or interrupting live FPGA operation by using dynamic, partial reconfiguration. This feature allows circuit designers to dynamically reprogram only a portion of their FPGA during runtime, whilst the rest of the device continues functioning as normal.

Major FPGA vendors support dynamic reconfiguration in their high-end parts, and provide fine-grained, non-glitching support [25, 3] which does not corrupt user-state, showing the feasibility and viability of our application. Altera states that individual routing multiplexers in their fabric can be reconfigured; Vansteenkiste et al. [20] have also proposed that FPGA circuit-specialization be created using such fine-grained reconfiguration support.

Interestingly, current architectural support for reconfiguration goes beyond the needs of our transparent, observe-only trace-buffer network, as it enables all aspects of the FPGA to be reconfigured, including logic elements and lookup-tables, logic clusters, memory and DSP blocks, as well as their associated routing resources. Our network requires only the latter (specifically, only the configuration cells for all routing switch-boxes, as well as all connection-boxes for just the memory resources as shown in Fig 3b). Unfortunately, due to the proprietary nature of commercial FPGAs, we are unable to quantify what savings can be made here, nor to test our techniques on a physical device.

# 7. METHODOLOGY

To evaluate the feasibility of our virtual overlay network, we implemented our techniques using the FPGA CAD tool VPR, which forms part of the Verilog-To-Routing academic project [15]. Using VPR 6.0, we packed, placed and routed a set of benchmark circuits as normal onto the default VPR architecture (given in Table 2, but with an increased Fc_out of 0.2 as done in [8]) to generate the baseline data outlined in Table 1. In this flow, packing is performed with the objective of minimizing logic cluster usage, and placement is subsequently performed onto the minimum-sized FPGA array that will fit the circuit. The minimum channel width, $W_{min}$, is a measure for the routing efficiency of the CAD tools and FPGA architecture involved, and describes the absolute minimum number of routing tracks that is possible to implement the circuit on the given FPGA.

We make the same assumptions as in [8] that any free memory-block in the FPGA can be transformed into a trace-buffer for zero overhead, its contents can be extracted for free (using device readback techniques, or built in JTAG logic) and that triggering to control when to start and stop tracing is specified by the designer manually, or driven externally from a global pin. We do not believe these to be unrealistic

| Circuit | 6LUTs | Flip-Flops | FPGA Size | $W_{min}$ | I/O | Logic Clusters | Multipliers | Memories |
|---|---|---|---|---|---|---|---|---|
| or1200 | 2963 | 691 | 25x25 | 72 | **779/800** | 298/475 | 1/18 | 2/12 |
| mkDelayWorker32B | 5580 | 2491 | 42x42 | 76 | 1064/1344 | 560/1302 | 0/50 | **41/42** |
| stereovision1 | 10366 | 11789 | 43x43 | 70 | 278/1376 | **1365/1376** | 38/50 | 0/42 |
| stereovision0 | 11462 | 13405 | 45x45 | 44 | 354/1485 | **1479/1485** | 0/66 | 0/42 |
| LU8PEEng | 21954 | 6630 | 59x59 | 86 | 216/1888 | **2583/2596** | 8/98 | 45/72 |
| stereovision2 | 29849 | 18416 | 84x84 | 118 | 331/2688 | 3635/5208 | **213/231** | 0/154 |
| bgm | 30089 | 5362 | 69x69 | 88 | 289/2208 | **3419/3519** | 11/153 | 0/99 |
| LU32PEEng | 75530 | 20898 | 110x110 | 130 | 216/3520 | **8861/9020** | 32/378 | 150/252 |
| mcml | 99700 | 53736 | 119x119 | 86 | 69/3808 | **10436/10591** | 30/435 | 38/285 |

Table 1: Benchmark summary (values in bold indicate the limiting resource)

| FPGA Architecture Parameter | | Value |
|---|---|---|
| Logic Cluster Size | N | 10 |
| Lookup Table Size *(non-fracturable)* | K | 6 |
| Inputs per Cluster | I | 33 |
| Channel Segment Length | L | 4 |
| Cluster Input Flexibility | Fc_in | 0.15 |
| Cluster Output Flexibility *(default: 0.10)* | Fc_out | 0.20 |

Table 2: FPGA architecture used, based on Altera Stratix IV

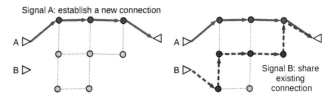

Figure 7: Circuit signals can either establish new trace connections (signal A) or share existing connections (signal B)

assumptions, given that the memory blocks inside the Xilinx Virtex family have built-in hard logic to implement FIFO functionality [23] with which we can build a ring-buffer to constantly record signal samples until halted by the trigger. In the FPGA architecture used, the widest configuration for each memory block is 72 bits (by 2048 entries) — this is adopted for our trace-buffers.

Rather than operating on each circuit at their minimum channel width, we inflate this value by a small amount, 30%, in order to reflect a realistic commercial architecture in which routing resources have been over-provisioned above the very best-case; this is a common approach also taken by other researchers such as [16]. To perform our experiments, we use our custom version of VPR to install our trace-buffer network incrementally — using only the spare resources not used in the original mapping — in a similar manner to [8]. However, instead of employing these techniques to build a custom point-to-point network, we have modified them to build our overlay network whilst preserving the guarantee that no existing circuit blocks nor routing are moved or re-routed. We then sweep each circuit to find the maximum number of times that all circuit signals can be connected to a different trace-buffer pin, a parameter we refer to as network connectivity. Once a feasible overlay network is found, we record the signals connected to each trace-pin into a text file which is subsequently used for matching at debug-time.

Currently, the VTR flow supports mapping circuits with only a single clock-domain. However, we believe that our approach can be extended to those with multiple clock-domains — given that each trace-buffer can only record signals from a single domain, we can also build an separate virtual overlay network to support all trace-buffers from each clock.

## 7.1 Compile-Time Construction

At compile-time, the virtual overlay network is constructed once per circuit. The primary challenge in constructing this overlay network using normal CAD tools is that these tools are designed to build a circuit mapping where each and every routing resource can, at most, be used once to connect one net source to one (or more) net sinks. The proposed network

requires the reverse of this — we require multiple net sources to feed (multiplexed) a single trace-buffer sink.

Within VPR 6.0's routing stage, the PathFinder algorithm is employed to iteratively resolve routing resources that become overused, by slowly increasing their costs so that only the most critical nets can afford them, through a process known as negotiated congestion [12]. The goal of our algorithms is to attempt to connect all circuit signals — both combination and sequential — to the requested number of trace-buffer inputs, using a directed-search strategy which terminates whenever any input is found. However, rather than directing each net towards its nearest trace-buffer so that its routing wirelength, and hence any routing congestion, is minimized, we have found experimentally that higher network connectivity is possible if each circuit signal was directed towards a randomly chosen trace-buffer. We believe this is because it is beneficial to establish connections to trace-buffers that circuit signals would not normally prefer in order to fully utilize the flexibility provided by as many trace-pins as possible; this also has the added benefit that because signals are randomly distributed, higher quality signal to trace-pin matches, which are explained in the next section, can be achieved.

Instead of building point-to-point trace connections, where each routing resource can be used only once, we allow all $V_{routing}$ multiplexers to be overused, with the understanding that their select bits can be determined at debug-time. During network insertion, circuit signals have two options: either they can establish new connection to a new trace-input (signal A in Fig. 7), or they can branch onto an existing connection (signal B). A naïve approach would be to force all signals to always take the latter option whenever a used $V_{routing}$ node is encountered. However, we found that this made the solution sensitive to the order in which nets were routed: those processed first would be able to consume all the resources that suited itself most, with no regard for other nets, and hence causing all subsequent nets to work-around those connections. This is not desirable; we need to allow existing connections to be ripped up and relocated if it will lead to a globally better solution.

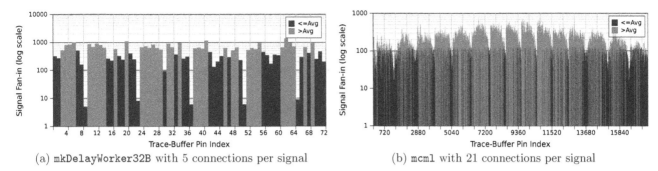

(a) `mkDelayWorker32B` with 5 connections per signal      (b) `mcml` with 21 connections per signal

Figure 8: Signal fan-in for overlay network — histogram of the number of signals connecting to each input

This is accomplished by modifying the routing cost function used by the neighbour expansion procedure in the directed search routing algorithm used to build the network. Although we do not wish to force nets, when encountering a $V_{routing}$ node that is part of a different connection, to connect to the same trace-pin, we do wish to make it preferential to do so in order to minimize the routing search space and hence runtime. By default, the routing cost function used for all nodes inside VPR is:

$$cost = back\_cost + this\_cost + astar \times expected\_cost \quad (1)$$

where $back\_cost$ is the congestion cost up to the current node, plus the $this\_cost$ of the node under consideration, and then the expected cost to the target scaled by an aggressiveness factor. Instead, for $V_{routing}$ nodes that are already part of another connection, we omit the $expected\_cost$ and discount $this\_cost$ by the occupancy of the new node, which indicates how many nets are already using it:

$$cost' = back\_cost + \frac{this\_cost}{node\_occupancy} \quad (2)$$

The intuition here is that the more nets that already pass through this node, the less likely it will be moved in subsequent routing iterations, and the more seriously the routing algorithm should consider it. A lower cost causes the preferred node to be removed from the heap much sooner than it would be otherwise, allowing the routing algorithm to follow the established connection to the trace-pin, yet does not force the router to take only this path. It must be noted that the new cost of a node must not take a value less than its predecessor (by discounting $back\_cost$ or using a negative value for $this\_cost$) otherwise the tool will enter an infinite loop in which the cost of each node is endlessly reduced.

### 7.2 Debug-Time Matching

Given a designer-specified signal selection, we then process the text file describing the overlay network to build a custom bipartite graph containing only the desired signals, before applying the Hopcroft-Karp algorithm (as implemented in [4]) to find a maximum matching. A downstream tool can then be used to determine which signals to connect to which trace-pins, and thus compute the routing multiplexer bits required using a simple greedy algorithm. Subsequently, these bits can then be statically or dynamically reconfigured onto the FPGA.

In the absence of a large collection of realistic signal selections for each of our benchmark circuits, we have evaluated the feasibility of our work using random signal selections.

| Circuit | Max Conn. | Comb&Seq. $\lvert V_{signals} \rvert$ | Excl. | $\lvert V_{trace} \rvert$ Pins |
|---|---|---|---|---|
| or1200 | 15 | 3483 | 2 | 720 |
| mkDelayWorker32B | 5 | 7439 | 1 | 72 |
| stereovision1 | 19 | 16211 | 11 | 3024 |
| stereovision0 | 20 | 14937 | 12 | 3024 |
| LU8PEEng | 8 | 27657 | 3 | 1944 |
| stereovision2 | 23 | 46646 | - | 11088 |
| bgm | 22 | 34966 | 66 | 7128 |
| LU32PEEng | 11 | 95026 | 1 | 7344 |
| mcml | 25 | 106555 | 4 | 17784 |

Table 3: Maximum network connectivity results

Although automated signal selection as proposed by [11, 10] may be used, these would only generate a handful of data-points. Instead, we would like to understand how the trace-buffer network fares for any signal that a designer may wish to select by using a sufficiently large sample size. For our experiments, we generated 100,000 signal selections randomly each at a different fraction of the trace-buffer network's capacity: from 0.1 to 1.0 in 0.1 increments. For example, if the trace-buffer network had a total of 720 input pins as for the `or1200` benchmark, then we randomly generated selections of 72 signals, 144, up to the full 720 for a total of 1,000,000 signal selections per circuit.

## 8. RESULTS

### 8.1 Maximum Network Connectivity

Table 3 shows the maximum network connectivity — the maximum number of trace-input trees that each signal belongs to, the number of circuit signals and trace-buffer inputs that exist for each circuit. For all but one of the nine benchmarks, not every internal signal could be incrementally connected to the trace-buffer network due to routing congestion. Upon further investigation, we found that only nets absorbed locally within a logic cluster suffered from this difficulty, caused by an inability to exit the cluster due to a lack of free resources in its vicinity. Unlike those nets that already had a presence on the global interconnect, for these local nets a new global route needed to be made from scratch using only the resources leftover from the original mapping. In very rare cases, this would be impossible. The number of signals that did fail in this manner are shown in the Excl. column, and represents at most 0.2% of all available combinational and sequential circuit signals. The number of trace-buffer inputs that exist for each circuit are also shown.

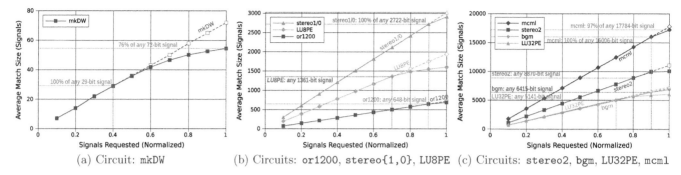

(a) Circuit: `mkDW`    (b) Circuits: `or1200`, `stereo{1,0}`, `LU8PE`    (c) Circuits: `stereo2`, `bgm`, `LU32PE`, `mcml`

Figure 9: Average match size — number of arbitrary signals that can be simultaneously forwarded by the overlay network to trace-buffers; dotted lines indicate the requested number of signals, solid lines indicate the average number of signals matched

As described earlier, this network connectivity parameter represents the guaranteed minimum number of signals for which a designer can observe *any* combination of, though in practice many more can be selected.

Figure 8a shows a histogram of the signal density at each trace-buffer input for the `mkDelayWorker32B` benchmark circuit, which contains only a single free memory-block to be reclaimed as a trace-buffer. In this circuit, all but five combinational and sequential signals can each be connected to 5 different trace-inputs. It would be expected that, on average, each input-pin would be connected to $\frac{7438 \times 5}{72} \approx 517$ signals, though in this particular instance 35 trace-pins exist which connect less than this value (with a minimum number of 5) leaving 37 pins which connect 517 or more signals (including a maximum of 1393 signals — almost 20% of all on-chip signals). A histogram for the largest circuit at our disposal, `mcml`, is produced in Fig. 8b, where it would be expected that each trace-input would be the target of approximately 126 signals. Here, a smaller proportion (40%) of trace-inputs are connected to by more than this value, indicating that there are some trace-buffers which are easier to access (i.e. more centrally located, as indicated in the histogram which shows a vertical scan-line ordering across the chip) than others, or that a tipping point is reached whereby it is cheaper for the routing tool to create new branches onto existing trees than to create entirely new trees.

If full observability into all circuits signals was strictly necessary, it may be possible to achieve this by increasing the channel width or the cluster output flexibility (Fc_out). We have observed that although increasing the channel width slack from $W_{min}+30\%$ to $+50\%$ had only a minimal effect on its network connectivity, in five of the nine benchmarks, all circuit signals can now be connected to the overlay network, whilst of the remaining four circuits, at most only 5 signals were impossible in the worst-case: `bgm`.

## 8.2 Average Match Size

Figure 9 shows the average match size returned by the maximum matching algorithm, where each data-point represents a sample size of 100,000 randomly-generated signal selections. This figure represents the average number of signals that can be simultaneously forwarded across the overlay network. The dotted lines of this graph show the number of signals requested by a designer, whilst the solid lines represent the average number of signals that can be forwarded across the network for observation. Where the lines coincide indicate

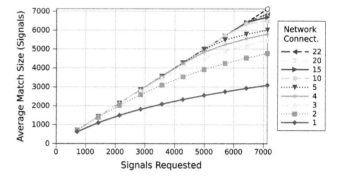

Figure 10: Network connectivity and match quality for `bgm`

that a complete-match was made, where the lines diverge indicate that only partial-match was possible.

In Figure 9a, which corresponds to the `mkDelayWorker32B` benchmark, it can be seen that the probability of observing all of the desired signals decreases after approximately 40% of the network capacity — that is, after 29 signals are selected from a total capacity of 72. At full capacity, on average only 54 of the 72 signals requested can be matched. This is not a surprising result given the memory-constrained nature of this circuit, which contains only one free memory-block available for use as a trace-buffer. As stated in the previous section, the average number of signals that each trace-pin is expected to support for the `mkDelayWorker32B` circuit is 517 of the total 7439 signals; each time a trace-pin is used, 516 other signals are blocked from using this same pin, drastically reducing the flexibility of the overlay network. In contrast, the remaining non memory-limited circuits presented in Figures 9b and 9c show much more promising results: in most cases, the network can fully connect up to 80–90% of the trace-buffer capacity before conceding.

Figure 10 graphs how the number of signals observable through the overlay network varies with the network connectivity parameter, when applied to the `bgm` circuit. Intuitively, the more times that each signal is connected to a trace-buffer input, the less likely it will be blocked when a different signal is picked. However, these results show that it may not be necessary to connect each signal as many pins as possible — reducing this network connectivity parameter to 10 or 15 has no effect on the signals observable when requesting 90% trace capacity, and only a 2 or 5% reduction at 100% capacity when compared with the maximum connectivity value of 22.

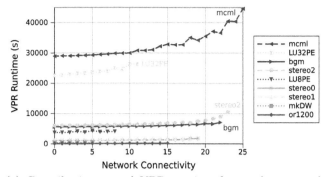

(a) Compile-time: total VPR runtime for overlay network insertion at various connectivities; connectivity=0 represents baseline with no network or instrumentation

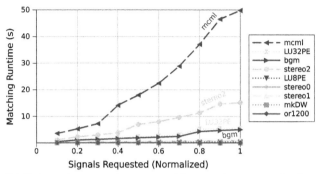

(b) Debug-time: maximum matching runtime, per selection

Figure 11: Runtime overhead

## 8.3 Runtime

Figure 11a shows the total VPR runtime for building the overlay network, for each connectivity parameter possible, averaged over 10 tries. An X value of zero indicates the baseline measurement, which does not include any trace-buffers nor an overlay network. X values greater than zero specify the total runtime for the standard CAD stages: packing, placement, routing, as well as the additional stage of incremental-routing to embed our overlay network. The difference in runtime represents the additional overhead of our overlay network; on average this is a 34% increase on the baseline, and in the worst-case this reaches 76% for stereovision2. As expected, runtime increases with the network connectivity value, with the gradient increasing more rapidly towards the tail-end of each circuit as it reaches its breaking point. However, it may not be necessary to push each circuit to this point as Figure 10 from the previous subsection showed. We anticipate that with greater focus on optimizing the CAD algorithms, we can further reduce this overhead.

The runtime for finding a maximum signal to trace-pin match is charted in Figure 11b — this is the average time required to recompute a matching network assignment to support new signal selections. In the worst case, for the largest mcml benchmark where the full trace-buffer capacity is requested, a solution can be returned in less than 50 seconds, with the relationship between runtime and the number of signals requested appearing to be linear. This contrasts with the time required to either fully or incrementally recompile the circuit to create a new point-to-point trace-buffer configuration: in the previous figure we observed 30,000 sec-

| Circuit | Original T_cpd (ns) | Instrum'ed T_cpd (ns) | Change |
|---|---|---|---|
| or1200 | 21.6 | 21.9 | +1.4% |
| mkDelayWorker32B | 7.4 | 7.6 | +2.7% |
| stereovision1 | 5.1 | 6.1 | +19.6% |
| stereovision0 | 4.1 | 5.8 | +41.4% |
| LU8PEEng | 134.0 | 136.0 | +1.5% |
| stereovision2 | 15.0 | 16.6 | +10.7% |
| bgm | 25.8 | 27.1 | +5.0% |
| LU32PEEng | 134.2 | 137.4 | +2.4% |
| mcml | 96.7 | 98.7 | +2.1% |
| Geomean | 23.6 | 25.7 | +9.0% |

Table 4: Effect of overlay network on critical-path delay

onds to fully compile an uninstrumented instance of mcml, whilst reference [8] stated that approximately 2,000 seconds was required to incrementally utilize 75% of the on-chip trace capacity. Matching runtime can be improved further by implementing our techniques in a more efficient programming language instead of Python.

## 8.4 Circuit Delay

A comparison of the critical-path delay before and after inserting our virtual overlay network on each of our benchmark circuits is shown in Table 4. Currently, because our CAD algorithms are routability-driven rather than timing-driven, on average the network incurs a 9.0% penalty to the critical delay, with a worst-case of 41.4% for stereovision0 which has the shortest critical-path. We believe that these results may be a little on the conservative side due to the nature of the circuits and CAD tools involved, where the majority of the critical-path delay — between 53% and 89% (geomean at 72%) — is made up of logic delay rather than routing delay.

Given that we add our overlay network incrementally, that is, only after the original user circuit is fully-compiled, the critical-path delay of the newly instrumented design is due entirely to the connections added by this network. If the observability that the trace infrastructure provides is not required, the circuit can revert to operating at its original, uninstrumented, clock frequency. During prototyping, however, it is unlikely that circuits will be operated at this maximum frequency, perhaps limited by off-chip (inter-FPGA) communication and hence timing degradation may not be a critical issue. Despite this, one promising direction for future work is to apply pipelining techniques to the overlay network in order to reduce its effect on delay — a technique particularly relevant for this application because any increase in signal latency will not affect its observability.

## 9. CONCLUSION

FPGAs are increasingly being used as prototyping platforms. Compared to software simulators, these prototypes can achieve significantly higher operating frequencies allowing designers to increase their verification coverage by several orders of magnitude. When unexpected or erroneous circuit behaviour is detected, designers begin a debugging procedure so that they may understand the root cause of their anomaly. However, the key challenge with debugging FPGA prototypes is their lack of built-in observability; unlike simulation, designers cannot simply probe any signal of their choice. One common solution to this problem is to insert trace-buffer instrumentation; these blocks seek to record a small, predetermined subset of signals into on-chip memory for subsequent analysis.

Existing academic work [8, 6], and many of the current commercial offerings [24, 1] require a designer to preselect the signals they wish to observe at compile-time, after which point-to-point connections are made for each signal to a trace-buffer. In this work, we have proposed a method which aims to allow designers to look at *any* subset of combinational or sequential signals in their circuit at debug-time, relieving them of the need to predetermine a selection beforehand. Due to on-chip memory constraints, it is not possible to make a dedicated trace connection for each signal; hence, we pass each signal through an overlay network which multiplexes these connections between the available trace-buffers, thus allowing this signal selection to be deferred to debug-time. Unlike a similar approach adopted in [19], we do not use soft-logic for this purpose, opting instead to utilize switch- and connection-box routing multiplexers that form part of the FPGA fabric. Because we reclaim these routing multiplexers from those that were leftover in the original circuit mapping, the area overhead of our work is essentially zero.

Due to routing requirements, it would be impractical to build a fully-populated crossbar network in which all inputs can be forwarded to all outputs; hence we build a blocking network in which only a reduced amount of connectivity exists. To decide which of the input signals to connect to the output trace-pins, we apply a maximum matching algorithm to the bipartite graph that represents our network to find the optimal solution with the highest number of observed signals. Once this assignment has been determined, the configuration memory of those routing multiplexers are reconfigured using either static or dynamic techniques. Our experiments have shown that for the majority of the benchmark circuits that were investigated, we were able to build an overlay network connecting to over 99.8% of all circuits signals whilst increasing initial CAD runtime by an average of 34%. However, once this network has been built, it can be reconfigured as many times as necessary to forward any set of signals through the overlay network to approximately 80–90% of the on-chip trace capacity, in no more than 50 seconds.

## Acknowledgements

The authors are grateful to Altera for supporting this work, and would also like to acknowledge Wayne Luk and the Department of Computing at Imperial College London, where most of this research was conducted over the summer of 2012.

## 10. REFERENCES

[1] Altera. Quartus II Handbook Version 12.0 Volume 3: Verification. http://www.altera.com/literature/hb/qts/qts_qii5v3.pdf, June 2012.

[2] S. Asaad, R. Bellofatto, B. Brezzo, C. Haymes, M. Kapur, B. Parker, T. Roewer, P. Saha, T. Takken, and J. Tierno. A Cycle-Accurate, Cycle-Reproducible Multi-FPGA System for Accelerating Multi-core Processor Simulation. In *Proceedings of the ACM/SIGDA International Symposium on Field Programmable Gate Arrays*, FPGA '12, pages 153–162, 2012.

[3] M. Bourgeault. Altera's Partial Reconfiguration Flow. http://www.eecg.utoronto.ca/~jayar/FPGAseminar/FPGA_Bourgeault_June23_2011.pdf, June 2011.

[4] D. Eppstein. Hopcroft-Karp Bipartite Max-Cardinality Matching and Max Independent Set (Python Recipe). http://code.activestate.com/recipes/123641-hopcroft-karp-bipartite-matching/, April 2002.

[5] H. Foster. Challenges of Design and Verification in the SoC Era. http://testandverification.com/files/DVConference2011/2_Harry_Foster.pdf.

[6] P. Graham, B. Nelson, and B. Hutchings. Instrumenting Bitstreams for Debugging FPGA Circuits. In *Field-Programmable Custom Computing Machines, FCCM'01. The 9th Annual IEEE Symp. on*, pages 41–50, March 2001.

[7] E. Hung and S. J. E. Wilton. Speculative Debug Insertion for FPGAs. In *FPL 2011, International Conference on Field Programmable Logic and Applications; Chania, Greece*, pages 524–531, September 2011.

[8] E. Hung and S. J. E. Wilton. Limitations of Incremental Signal-Tracing for FPGA Debug. In *FPL 2012, International Conference on Field Programmable Logic and Applications; Oslo, Norway*, pages 49–56, August 2012.

[9] Y. S. Iskander, C. D. Patterson, and S. D. Craven. Improved Abstractions and Turnaround Time for FPGA Design Validation and Debug. In *FPL'11, Proceedings of the 2011 21st International Conference on Field Programmable Logic and Applications*, pages 518–523, 2011.

[10] H. F. Ko and N. Nicolici. Algorithms for State Restoration and Trace-Signal Selection for Data Acquisition in Silicon Debug. *Computer-Aided Design of Integrated Circuits and Systems, IEEE Transactions on*, 28(2):285–297, 2009.

[11] X. Liu and Q. Xu. On Signal Selection for Visibility Enhancement in Trace-Based Post-Silicon Validation. *Computer-Aided Design of Integrated Circuits and Systems, IEEE Transactions on*, 31(8):1263–1274, Aug. 2012.

[12] L. McMurchie and C. Ebeling. PathFinder: A Negotiation-Based Performance-Driven Router for FPGAs. In *Proceedings of the 1995 ACM Third Int'l Symp. on Field-Programmable Gate Arrays*, FPGA '95, pages 111–117, 1995.

[13] Y. O. M. Moctar, N. George, H. Parandeh-Afshar, P. Ienne, G. G. Lemieux, and P. Brisk. Reducing the Cost of Floating-Point Mantissa Alignment and Normalization in FPGAs. In *Proceedings of the 20th ACM/SIGDA Int'l Symp. on Field-Programmable Gate Arrays*, FPGA '12, pages 255–264, 2012.

[14] B. Quinton and S. Wilton. Concentrator Access Networks for Programmable Logic Cores on SoCs. In *Circuits and Systems, 2005. ISCAS 2005. IEEE International Symposium on*, pages 45–48 Vol. 1, May 2005.

[15] J. Rose, J. Luu, C. W. Yu, O. Densmore, J. Goeders, A. Somerville, K. B. Kent, P. Jamieson, and J. Anderson. The VTR Project: Architecture and CAD for FPGAs from Verilog to Routing. In *Proceedings of the 20th ACM/SIGDA International Symposium on Field Programmable Gate Arrays*, FPGA'12, pages 77–86, February 2012.

[16] N. Shah and J. Rose. On the Difficulty of Pin-to-Wire Routing in FPGAs. In *FPL 2012, International Conference on Field Programmable Logic and Applications; Oslo, Norway*, pages 83–90, August 2012.

[17] Synopsys. Identify: Simulator-like Visibility into Hardware Debug. http://www.synopsys.com/Tools/Implementation/FPGAImplementation/CapsuleModule/identify_ds.pdf, Aug. 2010.

[18] S. Teig. Programmable logic devices in 2032? (FPGA2012 Pre-Conference Workshop). http://tcfpga.org/fpga2012/SteveTeig.pdf, February 2012.

[19] Tektronix. Certus Debug Suite. http://www.tek.com/sites/tek.com/files/media/media/resources/Certus_Debug_Suite_Datasheet_54W-28030-1_4.pdf, July 2012.

[20] E. Vansteenkiste, K. Bruneel, and D. Stroobandt. Maximizing the Reuse of Routing Resources in a Reconfiguration-Aware Connection Router. In *FPL 2012, International Conference on Field Programmable Logic and Applications; Oslo, Norway*, August 2012.

[21] T. Wheeler, P. Graham, B. E. Nelson, and B. Hutchings. Using Design-Level Scan to Improve FPGA Design Observability and Controllability for Functional Verification. In *FPL '01: Proceedings of the 11th International Conference on Field-Programmable Logic and Applications*, pages 483–492, 2001.

[22] M. Wirthlin, B. Nelson, B. Hutchings, P. Athanas, and S. Bohner. FPGA Design Productivity: Existing Limitations and Root Causes. http://www.chrec.org/ftsw/FDP_Session1_Posted.pdf, June 2008.

[23] Xilinx. Virtex-6 FPGA Memory Resources: User Guide (UG363 v1.6). http://www.xilinx.com/support/documentation/user_guides/ug363.pdf, April 2011.

[24] Xilinx. ChipScope Pro Software and Cores, User Guide. http://www.xilinx.com/support/documentation/sw_manuals/xilinx14_2/chipscope_pro_sw_cores_ug029.pdf, July 2012.

[25] Xilinx. Partial Reconfiguration of Xilinx FPGAs Using ISE Design Suite (WP374 v1.2). http://www.xilinx.com/support/documentation/white_papers/wp374_Partial_Reconfig_Xilinx_FPGAs.pdf, May 2012.

# Polyhedral-Based Data Reuse Optimization for Configurable Computing

Louis-Noël Pouchet,[1] Peng Zhang,[1] P. Sadayappan,[2] Jason Cong[1]
[1] University of California, Los Angeles {pouchet,pengzh,cong}@cs.ucla.edu
[2] Ohio State University saday@cse.ohio-state.edu

## ABSTRACT

Many applications, such as medical imaging, generate intensive data traffic between the FPGA and off-chip memory. Significant improvements in the execution time can be achieved with effective utilization of on-chip (scratchpad) memories, associated with careful software-based data reuse and communication scheduling techniques.

We present a fully automated C-to-FPGA framework to address this problem. Our framework effectively implements data reuse through aggressive loop transformation-based program restructuring. In addition, our proposed framework automatically implements critical optimizations for performance such as task-level parallelization, loop pipelining, and data prefetching. We leverage the power and expressiveness of the polyhedral compilation model to develop a multi-objective optimization system for off-chip communications management. Our technique can satisfy hardware resource constraints (scratchpad size) while aggressively exploiting data reuse. Our approach can also be used to reduce the on-chip buffer size subject to bandwidth constraint. We also implement a fast design space exploration technique for effective optimization of program performance using the Xilinx high-level synthesis tool.

## Categories and Subject Descriptors

B.5.2 [**Hardware**]: Design Aids — optimization; D 3.4 [**Programming languages**]: Processor — Compilers; Optimization

## Keywords

Program Optimization; High-Level Synthesis; Data Reuse

## 1. INTRODUCTION

High level synthesis (HLS) tools for synthesizing designs specified in a behavioral programming language like C/C++ can dramatically reduce the design time especially for embedded systems. While the state-of-art HLS tools have made it possible to achieve QoR close to hand coded RTL designs from designs specified completely in C/C++ [5], considerable manual design optimization is still often required from the designer [17]. To get a HLS friendly C/C++ specification, the user often needs to perform a number of

explicit source-code transformations addressing several key issues such as on-chip buffer management, choice of degree of parallelism / pipelining, attention to prefetching, avoidance of memory port conflicts etc., before designs rivaling hand coded RTL can be synthesized by the HLS tool.

Our objective is to develop automated compiler support based on the latest advances in polyhedral frameworks (e.g., [12, 38]) to greatly reduce the human design effort currently required to create effectively synthesizable specification of designs using HLS tools. In particular, we develop compiler support for source-to-source transformations to optimize critical resources such as memory bandwidth to off-chip memory and on-chip buffer capacity. We present in this article algorithms and tools to automatically perform the needed loop/data transformations as well as effective design space exploration techniques. Specifically, we make the following contributions.

1. A full implementation of a complete and automated technique to optimize data reuse for a class of programs, for FPGAs. This includes complete technique for dedicated on-chip buffer management, that exploits the data reuse in the transformed program.

2. A compile-time technique to automatically find communication schedules and on-chip buffer allocations to minimize the communication volume under maximal buffer size constraint.

3. A framework for fast design space exploration of transformation candidates based on an available high-level synthesis tool and leveraging the specifics of the optimization framework we use.

The rest of the paper is organized as follows. Section 2 covers the related work. Section 3 presents our automated data reuse framework, and Section 4 our buffer size/communication volume optimization algorithm. Finally, Section 5 presents our fast design space exploration framework and experimental results.

## 2. RELATED WORK

Design automation and optimization for data reuse have been studied for decades. The data transfer and storage exploration (DTSE) methodology [14, 15] is one of the milestones in this field. A data reuse graph is introduced to express the possible data reuse candidates between array references in the source program [28], where a polyhedral model is used to analyze the data dependence. Then, heuristics based on reuse buffer size and bandwidth reduction can be applied to decide the allocation of the reuse candidates and their memory hierarchy [13, 29]. A large body of previous work has also considered data locality optimization, but focuses exclusively on CPU and data caches optimization [8, 30, 39]. Loop transformations for data locality optimization are only an enabler for effective on-chip data reuse. Numerous previous work for FPGAs and GPUs, such as [9, 14, 15, 19, 24, 31], have considered automatic techniques to promote memory references on-chip. However, previous work had systemic limitations based either on the program representation used (which for instance only approximates the data accessed by a reference), and/or constrained to managing an on-chip buffer that corresponds precisely to a tile. Other work studied the power of the polyhedral transformation framework for FPGA design. For instance, DEFACTO combines a parallelizing compiler technology (SUIF) with early hardware synthesis tools to propose a C-to-FPGA design flow [21, 36], and MMAlpha [25] focused on systolic designs. These works illustrated the benefit of using advanced compiler technologies for memory optimization and parallelization analysis. However, to the best of our knowledge, none of those frameworks consider a space of program transformation as large as ours, and/or have limited loop tiling capabilities. Bayliss et al. [11] used the polyhedral model to compute an address generator exploiting data reuse, however they do not consider any loop transformation and therefore do not restructure the program to better exploit its inherent data locality potential. In contrast, loop transformations for improving data locality is the starting point of our framework.

Tiling in particular is a crucial loop transformation for data locality improvement, and is one key transformation used in our framework. As an illustration, on a matrix-multiply example previous work by Cong. et al using only loop permutation, (limited) loop skewing, and loop fusion/distribution reduces the communication volume from $3.N^3$ to $N^3$, using a buffer of size $2.N$ [19]. Using a simple square tiling with tile size $T$ reduces the communication volume to to roughly $N^3/T^2$, for a buffer of size $T^2$, and even better solutions can be achieved with rectangular tiles, as used in this paper. However in [19], finer-grain data reuse opportunities are explored in a combined problem searching for buffer allocation and loop transformation simultaneously, which can lead to even smaller buffer sizes than achievable by our present work. Loop tiling often requires a complex sequence of complementary loop transformations such as skewing, fusion/distribution, shifting, etc., to be applied [6, 12, 27, 40], and finding such sequence is a challenging problem. In this work, we address it in an automatic fashion by using the Tiling Hyperplane scheduling method, which is geared towards maximizing data locality and program tilability [12].

Recently, the importance of considering platform-dependent cost modeling in optimizing the loop transformation has been emphasized [32, 41]. Loop transformation and data reuse optimization are loosely coupled by introducing fast hierarchical memory size estimators [26, 33] to evaluate the promising transformations. But the search process lacks an analytic model for guidance, which makes it inefficient to search a large transformation space. Previous work tries to establish analytic optimization formulations for the combined problem, such as optimizations of loop tiling parameters and reuse buffer selections are formulated into quadratic programming [9] and geometric programming [31] respectively. Alias et al. uses tiling and prefetching to reduce the memory traffic [7], focusing on the Altera tool-chain. They proposed a formulation for the prefetching problem and the pipelining of communications, but their approach does not consider the balance between communication volume and scratchpad size/energy, nor any design-space exploration, contrary to the present work.

# 3. AUTOMATIC DATA REUSE FRAMEWORK

## 3.1 Overview of the Method

In our framework, we perform a multi-stage process to automatically optimize C programs for effective execution on a FPGA. Our approach uses design-space exploration to determine the best performing program variant. Specifically, we search for best performance through the evaluation of different *rectangular* tile sizes. Our framework is built so that different tile sizes lead to different program candidates, with distinct features in terms of the communication schedule, buffer size, loop to be tiled (e.g. when a tile size of 1 is used for this loop), etc. Each candidate is built as follows.

1. We first transform the input program, using polyhedral loop transformations. The objective is to restructure the program so that data locality is maximized (e.g., the "time" between two accesses to the same memory cell is minimized), and at the same time the number of loops that can be tiled is maximized. This is presented in Section 3.2. Tilable loops are tiled using a tile size given as input.

2. We then promote all memory accesses to on-chip buffers in the transformed program, and automatically generate off-chip / on-chip communication code. Data reuse between consecutive iterations of a loop is automatically exploited. This is presented in Section 3.3. The hardware constraints on the maximal buffer size are automatically satisfied, using a lightweight search algorithm that trades off communication volume for buffer size. This is presented in Section 4.

3. We conclude the code transformation process by performing a set of HLS-specific optimizations, such as coarse-grain and fine-grain/task-level parallelism extraction. This is presented in Section 3.4.

## 3.2 Polyhedral Loop Transformations

Unlike the internal representation that uses abstract syntax trees (AST) found in conventional compilers, polyhedral compiler frameworks use an internal representation of imperfectly nested affine loop computations and their data dependence information as a collection of parametric polyhedra, this enables a powerful and expressive mathematical framework to be applied in performing various data flow analysis and code transformations.

Significant benefits over conventional AST representations of computations include the effective handling of symbolic loop bounds and array index function, the uniform treatment of perfectly nested versus imperfectly nested loops, the ability to view the selection of an arbitrarily complex sequence of loop transformations as a single optimization problem, the automatic generation of tiled code for non-rectangular imperfectly nested loops, etc.

### 3.2.1 Polyhedral Program Representation

The *polyhedral model* is a flexible and expressive representation for loop nests with statically predictable control flow. Loop nests amenable to this algebraic representation are called *static control parts* (SCoP) [22, 23], roughly defined as a set of consecutive statements such that loop bounds and conditionals involved are affine functions of the enclosing loop iterators and variables that are constant during the SCoP execution (whose values are unknown at compile-time). Numerous scientific kernels exhibit those properties; they can be found typically in image processing filters (such as medical imaging algorithms) and dense linear algebra operations.

```
1   for (t = 0; t < T; ++t) {
2     for (i = 1; i < N-1; ++i)
3       for (j = 1; j < N-1; ++j)
4   R:      B[i][j] = 0.2*(A[i][j-1] + A[i][j] + A[i][j+1]
5                          + A[i-1][j] +A[i+1][j]);
6     for (i = 0; i < N; ++i)
7       for (j = 0; j < N; ++j)
8   S:      A[i][j] = B[i][j];
}
```

**Figure 1: Jacobi2D example**

First, a program is analyzed to extract its polyhedral representation, including iteration domain, access pattern and dependence information.

*Iteration Domains.* For all textual statements in the program, for example $R$ in Figure 1, the set of its dynamic instances is captured with a set of affine inequalities. When the statement is enclosed by loop(s), all iterations of the loop(s) are captured in the iteration domain of the statement. Considering the jacobi2D kernel in Figure 1, the iteration domain of $R$ is:

$$\mathcal{D}_R = \{(t,i,j) \in \mathbb{Z}^3 \mid 0 \le t < T \wedge 1 \le i < N-1 \wedge 1 \le j < N-1\}.$$

The iteration domain $\mathcal{D}_R$ contains only integer vectors (or, integer points if only one loop encloses the statement $R$). The *iteration vector* $\vec{x}_R$ is the vector of the surrounding loop iterators; for $R$ it is $(t,i,j)$ and takes values in $\mathcal{D}_R$. Each vector in $\mathcal{D}_R$ corresponds to a specific set of values taken by the surrounding loop iterators (starting from the outermost to the innermost enclosing loop iterator) when $R$ is executed.

*Access functions.* They represent the location of the data accessed by the statement. In SCoPs, memory accesses are performed through array references (a variable being a particular case of an array). We restrict ourselves to subscripts of the form of affine expressions which may depend on surrounding loop counters and global parameters. For instance, the subscript function for the read reference A[i-1][j] of statement $R$ is simply $f_A(t,i,j) = (i-1,j)$.

The sets of statement instances between which there is a producer-consumer relationship are modeled as equalities and inequalities in a *dependence polyhedron*. This is defined at the granularity of the array cell. If two instances $\vec{x}_R$ and $\vec{x}_S$ refer to the same array cell and one of these references is a write, then they are said to be in dependence. Therefore to respect the program semantics, the transformed program must execute $\vec{x}_R$ before $\vec{x}_S$. Given two statements $R$ and $S$, a dependence polyhedron, written $\mathcal{D}_{R,S}$, contains all pairs of dependent instances $\langle \vec{x}_R, \vec{x}_S \rangle$.

Multiple dependence polyhedra may be required to capture all dependent instances, at least one for each pair of array references accessing the same array cell (scalars being a particular case of array). It is possible to have several dependence polyhedra per pair of textual statements, as some may contain multiple array references.

### 3.2.2 *Program Transformation for Locality and Parallelism*

The next step in polyhedral program optimization is to compute a transformation for the program. Such a transformation captures, in a single step, what may typically correspond to a sequence of several tens of textbook loop transformations [23]. It takes the form of a carefully crafted affine multidimensional schedule, together with (optional) iteration domain or array subscript transformations.

In order to expose coarse-grain parallelization as well as data locality optimizations, we first compute a polyhedral transformation which is geared towards maximizing data locality while exposing coarse-grain parallelism when possible. This optimization is implemented via a possibly complex composition of multidimensional tiling, fusion, skewing, interchange, shifting, and peeling. It is known as the Tiling Hyperplanes method [12]. The Tiling Hyperplane method has proved to be very effective in integrating loop tiling into polyhedral transformation sequences [12,27]. Bondhugula et al. proposed an integrated optimization scheme that seeks to maximally fuse a group of statements, while making the outer loops permutable (i.e., tilable) [12] when possible. A schedule is computed such that parallel loops are brought to the outer levels,

if possible. This technique is applied on each SCoP of the program. When coarse-grain parallelism is exposed (such as pipelined tile parallelism), we automatically exploit it to support concurrent execution on the FPGA.

From a data reuse standpoint, the Tiling Hyperplane method schedules iterations that access the same data elements as close to each other as possible, maximizing temporal data locality under the framework constraints. We note that the Tiling Hyperplane method attempts to maximize the number of loops that *can* be tiled, but operates seamlessly on non-tilable (or non-fully tilable) programs, also maximizing locality in those cases. In our framework, loop tiling is applied on the set of loop nests that are made permutable after applying the Tiling Hyperplane method. Finally, Syntactically correct transformed code is generated back from the polyhedral representation, and this code scans the iteration spaces according to the schedule we have computed with the Tiling Hyperplane method. We use the CLooG, a state-of-the-art code generator [10] to perform this task.

## 3.3 Automatic On-Chip Buffer Management

Most ICs, especially embedded systems, use on-chip buffer memories for fast and energy-efficient access to the most frequently used data. For FPGAs, the total data for the application is much larger than on-chip memory capacity. In contrast to general-purpose processors that use hardware-managed caches to hold frequently accessed data, the use of on-chip buffers with explicit copy-in and copy-out of data is a key optimization for embedded systems [18]. By storing frequently accessed data in the on-chip buffer, the bandwidth contention is decreased, and the overall performance increases significantly as the latency of accessing on-chip data is significantly faster than off-chip accesses. In the following we present a fully automated approach for on-chip buffer management that consists of promoting to local memory (e.g., the on-chip buffer) all memory references in the program.

Promoting the entire data accessed by a program to local memory is often infeasible, in particular for FPGA design where the on-chip buffer resource is limited. Therefore, we want to enable the promotion all program references to an on-chip buffer, while still controlling its size. We chose to solve this problem by using the granularity of the loop iteration, for any of the loops in the program. That is, given an arbitrary loop in the program (which may very well be surrounded by other loops), our technique will compute the minimal on-chip buffer size requirement and associated communications to execute one iteration of this loop, while exploiting the reuse between consecutive iterations of said loop. This implicitly offers a lot of freedom for the on-chip buffer size. By considering the innermost loop, its size will be similar to the number of registers required to execute the computation. By considering the outermost loops it will be equivalent to the entire data space of the program. Any loop in-between will trade off communication count for on-chip buffer size (and its associated static energy).

For example, in Figure 1 if we put on-chip the data accessed by one full execution of the $j$ loop in line 3 (that is exactly one iteration of the $i$ loop), we need to store the $i^{th}$ row of $A$ and $B$, as well as the $(i-1)^{th}$ and $(i+1)^{th}$ rows of $A$, leading to a buffer requirement of $4.N$. This buffer must be filled for each iteration of the $i$ loop, that is roughly $T.N$ times (total communication volume is roughly $4.N^2.T$). Putting on-chip the full computation (that is, along the $t$ loop on line 1) leads to a $2.N^2$ buffer requirement, but to be filled only once (total communication volume is reduced to $2.N^2$). So, the trade-off here is between a buffer size $N$ times smaller versus a communication volume increase of $2.T$. Below, we show how to build better solutions exploiting reuse across executions of a loop.

### 3.3.1 Parametric Data Spaces for On-Chip Buffer Support

We now present our formalization to effectively promote memory references for on-chip buffer usage. Our technique operates on each array individually, and promotes optimally (under the framework constraints) all references to this array into a dedicated on-chip buffer for this array. Our approach is based on the concept of *parametric polyhedral sets* to express the set of data elements being used at various specific points of the computation. Those sets correspond exactly to the data to be communicated, reused, or stored. We then use a polyhedral code generator to scan those sets, and properly modify the program by inserting the code that scans communications sets, and change main memory references in the modified source code to on-chip buffer references.

We first define the data space of an array $A$ for a program. The data space is simply the set of all data elements accessed through the various access functions referencing this array, for each value of the surrounding loop iterators where the reference is done. We use the concept of the image of a polyhedron (e.g., the iteration domain) by an affine function (e.g., the access function). The image of a polyhedron $\mathcal{D}$ by an affine function $F$ is defined as the set $\{\vec{y} \mid \forall \vec{x} \in \mathcal{D}, F(\vec{x}) = \vec{y}\}$.

**DEFINITION 1** (DATA SPACE). *Given an array $A$, a collection of statements $\mathcal{S}$, and the associated set of memory references $F_S^A$ with $S \in \mathcal{S}$, the data space of $A$ is the set of unique data elements accessed during the execution of the statements. It is the union of the image of the iteration domain by the various access functions:*

$$DS(A) = \bigcup_{S \in \mathcal{S}} Image(F_S^A, \mathcal{D}_S)$$

We remark that $DS(A)$ is not necessarily a convex set, but can still be manipulated with existing polyhedral libraries. For example, in Figure 1, the data space of $DS_R(B)$ for the first statement ($R$ : line 4) is the 2-dimensional square set going from 1 to $N-2$ in each dimension. But for the second statement ($S$ : line 7), $DS_S(B)$ is the 2D square set going from 0 to $N$. As we make the union, it means $DS(B)$ is the 2D square set going from 0 to $N$ in each dimension.

In order to capture the data accessed at a particular loop level, we must fix the value of the surrounding loop iterators to a certain value in the data space expression, while preserving all inner loop iterations. For the data space computation to be valid for any execution of this loop (nest), we resort to using parametric constants (i.e., whose value is fixed but unknown) in the formulation. All sets and expressions computed will be parametric forms of those constants, and therefore valid for any value these constants can take; they will consequently be valid for any value the surrounding loop iterators can take during the computation.

We first define the parametric domain slice, that will be the enabler for defining the data space of a loop iteration.

**DEFINITION 2** (PARAMETRIC DOMAIN SLICE). *Given a loop nest with a loop $l$ of depth $n$ surrounded by $k-1$ loops, and an integer constant $\alpha$, the parametric domain slice (PDS) of loop $l$ is a subset of $\mathbb{Z}^n$ defined as follows:*

$$P_{l,\alpha} = \{(x_1, \ldots, x_n) \in \mathbb{Z}^n \mid x_1 = p_1, \ldots, x_{k-1} = p_{k-1}, x_k = p_k + \alpha\}$$

*where $p_1, \ldots, p_n$ are parametric constants unrestricted on $\mathbb{Z}$.*

For example, for loop $i$ in line 3 of Figure 1, we have:

$$P_{i,1} = \{(t,i,j) \in \mathbb{Z}^3 \mid t = p_1, i = p_2 + 1\}$$

This is a (parametric) set of 3D integer points with the first two components of each point always having the same (parametric) values.

This set contains an infinite number of points, as the third component takes any value in $\mathbb{Z}$.

We can now adapt the definition of a data space to the subset of data which is accessed by a loop iteration.

**DEFINITION 3** (DATA SPACE OF A LOOP ITERATION). *Given an array $A$, a collection of statements $\mathcal{S}$ surrounded by a loop $l$ and their associated set of memory references $F_S^A$ with $S \in \mathcal{S}'$, and $\vec{P}_{l,0}$ a PDS for loop $l$, the data space of $A$ is the set of unique data elements accessed during one iteration of $l$:*

$$DS(A, \vec{P}_{l,0}) = \bigcup_{S \in \mathcal{S}} Image\left(F_S^A, \left(\mathcal{D}_S \cap P_{l,0}\right)\right)$$

To illustrate the power and generality of this approach, in Figure 2 we show the sets $DS(A, \vec{P}_{j,0})$ (left) and $DS(A, \vec{P}_{j,-1})$ (center), the data space of the immediately preceding iteration, for the first $j$ loop (line 3) in the Jacobi2D example. By computing the difference or intersection between those sets (right), we can capture naturally the data reused between two consecutive iterations, as well as the data that is not alive at the previous iteration.

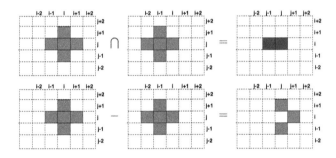

**Figure 2: Computation of the *Reuse* (top) and *PerIterC* (bottom) sets for the j loop of jacobi2D**

Formally, the reused data space between consecutive iterations of a loop is defined as follows. All data which is reused does not need to be communicated at the next iteration.

**DEFINITION 4** (REUSE SPACE). *Given an array $A$, and $\vec{P}_{l,0}$ and $\vec{P}_{l,-1}$ two PDS for loop $l$, the reused data space between two consecutive iterations of $l$ is:*

$$Reuse(A, \vec{P}_{l,0}) = DS(A, \vec{P}_{l,-1}) \cap DS(A, \vec{P}_{l,0})$$

The communication required for each loop iteration is defined as follows. It consists in only the data elements that were not accessed by the previous iterations.

**DEFINITION 5** (PER-ITERATION COMMUNICATION). *Given an array $A$, and $\vec{P}_{l,0}$ a PDS for loop $l$, then assuming the data reused between two consecutive iterations is still in local memory, the data space required to communicate in order to compute a given iteration of $l$ is:*

$$PerIterC(A, \vec{P}_{l,0}) = DS(A, \vec{P}_{l,0}) - Reuse(A, \vec{P}_{l,0})$$

Finally, to ensure that for the first loop iteration, all data is ready in the on-chip buffer, we must communicate the per-iteration data set but also initialize the on-chip buffer with the reuse set at the first loop iteration, as no previous iteration has already loaded the data.

**DEFINITION 6** (INITIALIZATION). *Given an array $A$, the data to be stored in the buffer before the loop starts is:*

$$Init(A, l) = Reuse(A, \vec{P}_{l,c})$$

with $c = lb(l) - p_k$, where $lb(l)$ is the lower bound expression of the loop $l$ and $p_k$ is the parameter associated with the loop $l$.

It is also required to store back to main memory any data element that is produced. This is captured by the copy-out set as defined below.

DEFINITION 7 (PER-ITERATION COPY-OUT). *Given an array $A$ and $\vec{P}_{l,0}$ a PDS for loop $l$, the copy-out set $CopyOut(A, \vec{P}_{l,0})$ storing written data in on-chip buffer back to main memory is the data space $DS^w(A, \vec{P}_{l,0})$ which considers only the access functions $F_S^A$ that correspond to written references.*

We remark that as our framework computes the data reuse only between two consecutive iterations, it does not necessarily capture all the reuse potential in a loop nest. In particular, reuse between two non-consecutive iterations (e.g., A[3i] and A[3i+6]) is not exploited. We believe that is is not a strong limitation in practice, as those cases only rarely occur, especially after having applied the Tiling Hyperplane method to transform the original program.

### 3.3.2 Code Generation

*Local buffer computation.* The polyhedral set defining the buffer requirement for a given loop $l$ is $DS(A, \vec{P}_{l,0})$. We take a simple approach, which is based on computing the rectangular hull of $DS$ (that is, the smallest rectangle that contains the set $DS$). It offers the advantage of generating a simple code with equally simple access functions. On the other hand, space can be wasted in particular when $DS$ is not convex and contains holes, and/or when $DS$ is a skewed parallelogram. In our experiments, buffer sizes of up to $2\times$ the minimal required size have been allocated, due to this over-approximation. Optimal allocation techniques do exist [20], and we plan to investigate their implementation as future work.

We compute the rectangular hull of $DS(A, \vec{P}_{l,0})$ dimension by dimension, using the following formula, for each dimension $i$:

$$dim_i = project(rectangularHull(DS(A, \vec{P}_{l,0})), i)$$
$$bs_i = lexmax(dim_i, 1) - lexmin(dim_i, 1)$$

where $project(DS, i)$ projects the set $DS$ onto the dimension $i$, and $lexmax(dim_i, 1)$ returns the coordinate of the extremal (maximal) point of the one-dimensional set $dim_i$. We remark that this stage, this coordinate and the entire sets are parametric forms of the loop bounds.

*Code generation algorithm.* Because of our generalized formalism above, the communication scheduling and final code generation has become straightforward. Our algorithm for the local memory promotion of an array at a given loop is shown in Figure 3. Function createLocalBufferDecl creates a declaration to a local buffer of same data type as the argument array, and its size is computed as the rectangular hull of the argument set. Function createScanningCodeIn creates an imperative C program that scans all elements of the polyhedral set given as an argument. For each point in this set, a statement A_l[i%bsi].. = A[i].. (or the opposite assignment for createScanningCodeOut) is executed, where $bs_i$ is the buffer size along dimension $i$. All parameters $p_i$ introduced by the PDS used are replaced with the loop iterator variable symbol they were assigned to. convertGlobalToLocalRef replaces all references to the original array with references to the local array, using modulo indexing similar to the copy statement above.

*Correctness of the algorithm.* Our algorithm is robust to any value taken by the loop iterator for which the buffer communication

```
LocalMemoryPromotion:
Input:
  A: array to promote
  l: loop along which A is promoted
Output:
  l: in-place modification of l

1   A_l ← createLocalBufferDecl(A, DS(A,l))
2   pre ← createScanningCodeIn(A_l, Init(A,l))
3   pic ← createScanningCodeIn(A_l, PerIterC(A,l))
4   wout ← createScanningCodeOut(A_l, WriteOut(A,l))
5   convertGlobalToLocalRef(l,A,A_l)
6   insertFirstInLoopBody(l,pic)
7   insertLastInLoopBody(l,wout)
8   prependBlock(l,pre)
9   prependBlock(getEnclosingFunc(l),A_l)
```

**Figure 3: Code generation algorithm for a loop $l$**

is computed, per virtue of the PDS mechanism. As a consequence, simply translating the various sets described above for each value of the surrounding and current loop iterators is sufficient to capture exactly the data accessed by each iteration. We also note that this algorithm is a data layout transformation only: the scheduling of the operations remains unchanged after application of the local memory promotion pass. Finally, to ensure correctness we write back all data elements written during a loop iteration at the end of the iteration. While there are occurrences where a lower amount of write communications may be performed, such as with reduction loops, this ensures that an element being written and then accessed at a much later iteration will hold the correct value.

## 3.4 HLS-Specific Optimizations

Despite very significant advances in HLS, a variety of complementary source-level transformations are often needed to produce the best result. In particular, fine-grain parallelism exposure and explicit overlapping of computation and communications dramatically impacts the performance. We leverage the power of the polyhedral model to precisely capture all sources of parallelism, reorganize the computation to pack sequential tasks together and recognize sets of parallel tasks, and produce a fine-grain task dependence graph that is used for task scheduling by the HLS tool.

### 3.4.1 Communication Prefetching and Overlapping

It is critical to properly overlap communication and computation, in order to minimize the penalty of data movements. A common technique is to prefetch in advance the data that will be required later by the computation. Following our paradigm of managing communications at the loop iteration level, the set of data elements that should be prefetched at the current iteration is defined as follows.

DEFINITION 8 (COMMUNICATION PREFETCH). *Given an array $A$, and $\vec{P}_{l,0}$ and $\vec{P}_{l,1}$ two parametric iteration vectors for loop $l$, the data that needs to be communicated to execute the next iteration is:*

$$Prefetch(A, \vec{P}_{l,0}) = PerIterC(A, \vec{P}_{l,1})$$

When operating on tiled programs, we remark that if the loop along which we bufferize is a tile loop, this set corresponds to the data set being used by the next tile, minus elements which are reused between consecutive tiles. Therefore inter-tile reuse between consecutive tiles is automatically captured in our framework.

This set is scanned at the beginning of the current loop iteration, and the associated code segment is put in a dedicated function (i.e., a task) that can be executed in parallel with the rest of the loop iteration that has also been put in a dedicated function.[1] In terms of storage, one can implement a simple double-buffer for the *PerIterC* and *Prefetch* sets, with a buffer swap at the beginning of each loop iteration.

### 3.4.2 Loop Pipelining and Task Parallelism

One of the most important hardware optimizations for high-performance RTL design leverages the fine-grain parallelism available in the program. *Loop pipelining* pipelines consecutive iterations of the loop, and this amounts to executing loop iterations in parallel if the loop is synchronization-free. In this work we automatically apply post-transformations to expose parallelism at the innermost loop level, if possible. Previous work on SIMD vectorization for affine programs has proposed effective solutions to expose inner-loop-level parallelism [12, 37], and we seamlessly reuse those techniques to enable effective loop pipelining on the FPGA. This is achieved by using additional constraints during and after the tiling hyperplanes computation, to preserve one level of inner parallelism. As a result, we mark all innermost loops with a specific `#pragma AP pipeline II=1`, and let the HLS tool find the best II it can for this loop. And for all innermost parallel loops, we also insert `#pragma AP dependence inter false` pragmas for all variables which are written in the loop iteration, to prevent conservative dependence analysis.

There exists a significant amount of parallelism *inside* loop iterations, in particular when prefetching is implemented. That is, some operations inside a loop iteration can be executed concurrently, and synchronization is (possibly) required at the end of the loop iteration. Such parallelism can be captured effectively in the polyhedral representation by focusing the analysis on the modeling of the possible order of statements within an iteration of a given loop. We implemented this analysis as a post-pass, after polyhedral code generation for the parallelism/locality extraction. Polyhedral transformations may indeed expose more task-level parallelism inside a loop iteration after code generation (precisely, after the separation step [10]) has been been performed. Focusing on a single loop at a time by using the appropriate PDS, we are able to automatically compute a graph of dependent operations within a given iteration of the loop body. This dependence graph is used to restructure the code as a collection of separate functions with distinct arguments for functions/tasks that can be run in parallel.

### 3.4.3 Additional Optimizations

Finally, we have implemented a series of complementary optimizations that have a significant impact on the performance of the final design. Specifically, we implemented a simple common sub-expression elimination, loop bound normalization [8], simplification and hoisting, and a simplification of the circular buffer access functions. Indeed, affine loops generated increment by stride of 1, and modulo expressions can easily be replaced by a simple loop increment and a test against the modulo value at the end of each loop iteration.

## 4. MANAGEMENT OF ON-CHIP BUFFER RESOURCE CONSTRAINTS

The algorithm presented above to compute communications and the associated on-chip buffer size is designed to work seamlessly for any loop in the program. We now show how to leverage the generality of this approach to transform any affine program to use on-chip memory for all computations, while meeting any user-defined resource constraint on the maximal on-chip buffer size. We proceed

in two steps: first we present how to build the solution space, and then we show how to find an optimal solution satisfying both bandwidth minimization and buffer size requirement.

### 4.1 Search Space Construction

The first step is to build the set of possible solutions for each array and each loop in the program. This is shown in Figure 4. In order to build the solution set, we simply apply the process described in the previous section for each arrays and each loop individually. That is, for the cross-product of all arrays and loops, we produce a tuple containing the buffer size requirement (*BS*) if bufferizing this specific array along this specific loop, and the bandwidth requirement (*BW*). *BS* is computed using the formula shown in Section 3.3.2, and *BW* is computed as the product of the cardinality of the *PerIterC* set by the number of executions of the loop, which can be exactly computed at compile-time for SCoPs, as later shown in Section 5.

```
BuildSolutionSet:
Input:
  P: input SCoP
Output:
  solset: solution set for loop selection

  solset ← createEmptySetofTuples
  forall arrays a in P do
    forall loops l in P do
        ldup ← cloneAST(l)
        LocalMemoryPromotion(a,ldup)
        BS ← getBufferVolume(ldup)
        BW ← getCommVolume(ldup)
        insertTuple(solset,{a,l, (BW,BS)})
    end do
  end do
  return solset
```

**Figure 4: Create solution space**

By design of the algorithm, the number of possibilities is very tractable. It is the product of the number of loops in the program by the number of arrays; in practice most of the time for SCoPs this number is below 100. Our implementation is very fast, and computing all solutions is achieved in a matter of seconds for complex tiled 3D stencil programs.

We note that in order to guarantee correctness for the case of imperfectly nested loops, we enforce that, for a given array, all loops at a same nesting level are bufferized. This may lead to conservative solutions, but greatly simplifies the code generation process.

### 4.2 Optimization Problem

We seek a solution that will systematically satisfy the objective that the sum of the buffer sizes required does not exceed the available on-chip resources (e.g., the number of BRAMs). That is, we want to find the loops *l* for all arrays *a* such that:

$$\sum_{a \in Arrays(P)} BS(a,l) < maxBuffSize$$

We note that as soon as the largest data space of a single iteration of the inner loops (that is usually in the order of the number of registers required to execute the iteration, assuming no spilling) is below *maxBuffSize*, our algorithm will find a solution. In practice, the number of BRAMs available on-chip is significantly larger than the number of registers required to execute a single iteration; hence our method will always find a valid solution.

Satisfying the above constraint let us find a solution that will meet hardware resource limitations. In order to find an (optimal) solution, we need to add the optimization objective. In this work we choose to minimize the bandwidth requirement (i.e., the communication vol-

---

9[1]AutoESL is able to exploit task-level parallelism in this case.

ume). We note that this solution relates only to the communication scheduling, for a given fully specified program. We aim here at computing a valid generated code *for a given tiled program whose tile sizes have been already set*. The problem of finding a final solution that will maximize bandwidth usage is addressed in the next section, and is framed as a tile size selection problem, solved using fast design-space exploration techniques. The final constrained bandwidth minimization problem is stated as:

$$minimize \sum_{a \in Arrays(P)} BW(a,l)$$

$$s.t. \sum_{a \in Arrays(P)} BS(a,l) < maxBuffSize$$

Solving this problem is achieved by repeatedly scanning the solution set obtained with `BuildSolutionSet`. For each array and each loop we compute the total bandwidth and buffer size requirement to find the solution with minimal bandwidth that meets the buffer size constraint. The complexity of finding the optimal solution is $n^d$, where $n$ is the number of loops in the program and $d$ the number of arrays. Despite being an exponential solver, in practice it is extremely fast. For instance a 3D image processing algorithm we tested has 12 loops and 4 arrays, leading to computing about 20,000 sums of 4 elements, which is done in a negligible time on modern processors. For too large spaces, one can implement approximate solving heuristics based for instance on dynamic programming. No such case has been encountered in our test suite.

## 5. DESIGN SPACE EXPLORATION

### 5.1 Methods for Fast DSE

Our objective is to enable quality of result (QoR) computation by AutoESL without having to resort to complete synthesis/simulation, in order to speed up the design-space exploration phase. This is particularly important for our method as we employ DSE to search the space of possible tile sizes, for tilable programs.

#### 5.1.1 Capturing the Exact Control Flow

In order to obtain accurate metrics from AutoESL RTL latency estimator, we must provide it with complete information about each loop in the program. The loop trip count (minimal, average and maximal) of a loop must be provided for each and every loop to be mapped to the FPGA. While for general programs it is impossible to accurately compute the loop trip count at compile-time, this is not an issue with SCoPs as addressed in this paper. As the control flow is static and therefore not data dependent, we can compute the number of times each statement in the loop body is executed, thus deducing the trip count of the surrounding loop. This is a critical benefit of manipulating SCoPs: *design-space exploration can be accurately achieved without synthesizing/running or simulating the application*. We use again our concept of PDS to capture the trip count of a statement in the following formula.

DEFINITION 9 (STATEMENT TRIP COUNT FOR A LOOP). *Given a statement S surrounded by a loop l, and $\vec{P}_{l,0}$ a parametric iteration vector, the trip count (noted STC) of l for S is:*

$$\mathcal{D}_{S,l} = \mathcal{D}_S \cap P_{l,0}$$
$$STC(\mathcal{D}_{S,l}, l) = lexmax(\mathcal{D}_{S,l}, k+1) - lexmin(\mathcal{D}_{S,l}, k+1)$$

*where k is the number of loops surrounding l dimension.*

The computation of the minimal and maximal trip count of a loop follows naturally.

DEFINITION 10 (LOOP TRIP COUNT). *Given a loop l and a collection $S_l$ of statements surrounded by l. The minimal and maximal trip count of l are given by:*

$$TC_{min}(l) = \min_{S \in S_l}(STC(\mathcal{D}_S, l)) \qquad TC_{max}(l) = STC((\bigcup_{S \in S_l} \mathcal{D}_S), l)$$

This trip count computation is performed for each loop of the program. We note that as we have described the communication sets in a purely polyhedral fashion, loops introduced to scan the various data sets are necessarily following the static control flow requirements, and can be exactly analyzed at compile-time. When entering the final design space exploration stage, only numerical values can be provided to AutoESL to represent the loop trip count. At this stage, parameters (such as problem size, etc.) are inlined to their numerical value, leading to simple scalar expressions for the loop trip count.

#### 5.1.2 Accurate Memory Latency Estimation

Off-chip SDRAM memory access has a high latency and limited bandwidth. To fully utilize the memory bandwidth, we use two FIFOs as to bufferize (a) the memory requests and (b) the fetched data, and access the off-chip memory in bursts. AutoESL does not natively model the latency consumed by off-chip memory accesses. To model this latency and throughput of the off-chip accesses, we modify the functions scanning the various communication sets. We insert cycle-wasting operations to emulate the time spent doing the corresponding off-chip accesses.

A property of our approach is that communications are executed in bursts, for each array and set to be scanned. So, at the beginning of each chunk of off-chip accesses we insert a `burst_wait()` function call, which corresponds to the burst time overhead (startup latency). We also insert `data_wait()` function calls for each word access. We have implemented these functions to force the design of a $p$-cycle long operation in the critical path of the function, so that AutoESL will count the additional latency introduced by `burst_wait()` and `data_wait()` in the final execution latency report, so as to emulate the time taken by transferring data to/from off-chip memory. In our experiments, we have micro-benchmarking on the Convey HC-1ex, and obtained $p = 131$ cycles for the burst waiting time, and $p = 1.15$ cycles for the per-word access time. Using this mechanism we accurately capture the bandwidth throughput per communication FIFO in our target platform.

#### 5.1.3 Communication/Computation Functions

Finally, in order to effectively exploit the FIFO communication mechanism, and in order to simplify the DSE method, we perform a final AST-based transformation to the generated program. First, we create a *communication prefetch* function by cloning the entire program generated by the previous algorithms and removing all loops/code segments that do not relate to off-chip/on-chip communication. We then replace all communications by non-blocking FIFO send requests. That is, all requests are sent as fast as possible until the request buffer of the FIFO module is full (the number of in-fly requests is limited by the implementation), which makes the prefetch function wait.

Second, we modify the transformed program (that contains the actual computations) such that all communications are blocking FIFO receive requests. That is, until the data is available on the FIFO, the program will wait. We finish by encapsulating the program in a *computation function*.

We conclude the transformation process by calling the communication prefetch and computation functions simultaneously in the main FPGA function, so that communication prefetch and computation are perfectly overlapped. We note that for the fast DSE approach, the cycle wasting functions are inserted in the prefetch function, thus emulating the time taken to transfer the data from off-chip memory to the FIFOs.

## 5.2 Experimental Results

### 5.2.1 Implementation Details

The entire tool-chain presented in this paper has been fully implemented as an open-source software, PolyOpt/HLS.[2] Specifically, we have based our work on the PolyOpt/C polyhedral compiler [34] we have implemented, which is itself based on the LLNL ROSE source-to-source compiler; and on PoCC, the Polyhedral Compiler Collection [4] we have implemented. All polyhedral operations are performed using Sven Verdoolaege's ISL library [38], and we use CLooG [10] for the polyhedral code generation part. Starting from an input sequential C program to be executed on the CPU, our tool-chain automatically extracts regions where the framework can be applied, performs data locality, parallelization and tiling loop transformations, local memory promotion and all the additional HLS-specific optimizations mentioned above. Each SCoP is mapped to the FPGA, using a custom FIFO data management module.

### 5.2.2 Experimental Setup

*Target FPGA platform.* We design the optimized codes for a multi-FPGA platform Convey HC-1ex [2], which provides four Xilinx Virtex-6 FPGAs (xc6vlx760-1-ff1760) and total bandwidth up to 80GB/s. We use the Xilinx ISE toolchain, version 14.2, which has been validated by Convey for the HC-1. For HLS, we use AutoESL, version 2011.4 [3]. The RTL is connected to memory interfaces and control interfaces provided by Convey, which have been designed to operate at 150MHz. Hence the working frequency of our core design is set to 150MHz. Off-chip memory runs at 300HMz.

*Benchmark Description.* We evaluate our framework using two core image processing algorithms for 3D MRI, denoise and segmentation. These algorithms are taken from the CPU implementation of the CDSC medical imaging pipeline [1, 16, 17]. We also evaluate 2 benchmarks from the PolyBench/C test suite, representative of compute-bound and memory-bound numerical kernels. They are described in Table 1. We report the total number of operations as $x \times y$ where $x$ indicates the number of operations per loop iteration, and $y$ the number of iterations. All benchmarks use single-precision floating point arithmetic in the input C code. is well-known that

Table 1: Description of the benchmarks used

| Benchmark | Description | #fp ops |
|---|---|---|
| denoise | 3D Jacobi+Seidel-like 7-point stencils | $61 \times 256^3 \times 15$ |
| segmentation | 3D Jacobi-like 7-point stencils | $67 \times 256^3 \times 150$ |
| DGEMM | matrix-multiplication | $3 \times 2048^3 + 2048^2$ |
| GEMVER | sequence of mv | $11 \times 2048^2$ |

### 5.2.3 Details of DSE Results

The time taken by our framework is decomposed as follow. For each point in the design space (e.g., a different tile size), the end-to-end transformation from the original C program to the AutoESL-friendly input C file (this includes program transformations for locality, on-chip buffer management and optimizations, and HLS-specific optimizations) takes about one minute, for the most complex program. AutoESL transforms the input C program and generates RTL as well as complete latency/usage reports in at most two minutes in

our experiments. So, testing 100 points takes at most five hours, and took usually around two hours in our experiments.

We have set a maximal buffer size limit to 1440 BRAMs, as it is the maximum for the Virtex-6 FPGA on the Convey HC-1. To capture multiple scenarios of bandwidth usage, we evaluated about 100 different rectangular tile sizes, using different power-of-two values in each of the three tile dimensions. Each tile size will have a different buffer requirement, and a different communication volume.

Figure 5 plots the results of the fast DSE framework that we implemented on three representative benchmarks, for a subset of the entire computation. In this figure, we compare side-by-side the off-chip communication volume on the $y$ axis, in number of 32-bit elements communicated, with the total off-chip communication time on the $x$ axis, as reported by AutoESL. DSE results are reported using a single PE per FPGA.

We observe significant variations in the communication volume that can be transferred in the same amount of time. For instance, the time to transfer the same amount of data can vary by more than $3 \times$ for Segmentation. This is because the quality of the RTL generated by AutoESL depends on the source code generated by our framework. Multiple factors influence the performance of the generated code. First, loop bounds used to compute the data space to communicate may be significantly more complex between two tile sizes. This is an artifact of polyhedral code generation, where generated loop bounds may contain tens or more sequences of *min*, *max*, *ceil* and *floor* functions. For some tile sizes not evenly dividing the data space to communicate, more complex code is generated and the QoR is lowered. Second, the benefit of loop pipelining depends on the loop trip count of the innermost loops. For loops with a too-small trip count (lower than the pipeline depth), the benefit of pipelining will be reduced. As a consequence, two tile sizes having a similar communication volume (e.g., $4 \times 8 \times 1$ and $1 \times 4 \times 8$) will see a different QoR. While analytical modeling of those specific factors may be achievable, it is important to note that AutoESL is a *production compiler*. As such, it is fragile and sensitive to the input program shape, as different source codes triggers different internal optimizations, therefore leading to different QoR. Such effect is a well-known artifact of compilers, and has been widely observed and discussed for production compilers [35].

All those factors confirm our claim that using fast DSE addresses important considerations for the final performance. It is very unlikely that all artifacts related to QoR obtained by the HLS tools can be modeled analytically, as it would be equivalent to building an analytical model of an optimizing compiler. In addition, because of the very fast speed of AutoESL, this modeling effort is non-necessary. So, RTL generation is used to capture those effects such as as how good a compiler (our framework or AutoESL) will be at optimizing different program variants.

Figure 6 shows, for the same benchmark and design space, the Pareto-optimal points for total time and buffer size requirement.

We observe a trade-off between the buffer size requirement and the total time, illustrative of tile size exploration results. Indeed, the majority of data reuse is achieved with tile sizes that fit in a few tens of kB; for instance for segmentation a tile size of $4 \times 8 \times 256$ uses only 73 BRAMs, and has achieved a communication volume reduction of $20 \times$ with respect to a non-tiled variant. Using a larger tile size requires a significantly larger buffer size (typically holding a complete 2D slice of the image), but achieves only a small communication improvement ($21 \times$ vs. $20 \times$ above). In addition, as pointed out above, one key challenge in improving the total execution time is taking into account all compiler optimization effects. With our DSE approach, we can select the transformed variant that achieves the best estimated total time, this takes into account all high-level synthesis/RTL generation artifacts.

---

9[2]Available at http://cadlab.cs.ucla.edu/PolyOptHLS.

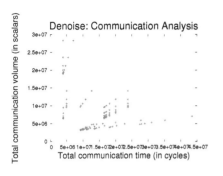
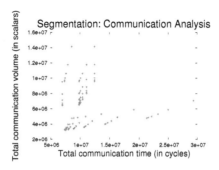
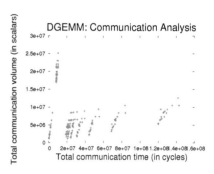

**Figure 5: Communication time vs. Communication volume**

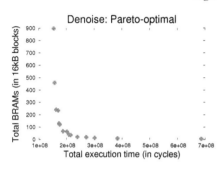
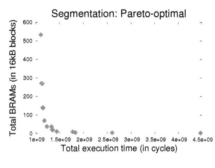
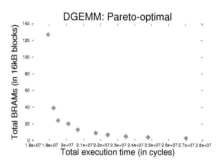

**Figure 6: Total time vs. On-Chip Buffer Size Requirement, Pareto-optimal points**

### 5.2.4 Complete Results

Table 2 summarizes the best version found by our framework, for each tested benchmark. We report #PEs the number of replications of the full computation we have been able to place on a single Virtex-6 FPGA as in the Convey HC-1, showing the level of coarse-grain parallelization we have achieved. BRAM and LUT are totals for the set of PEs placed on the chip.

**Table 2: Characteristics of Best Found Versions**

| Benchmark | tile size | #PEs | #BRAM | #LUT |
|---|---|---|---|---|
| denoise | 4×8×128 | 2 | 132 | 178544 |
| segmentation | 4×8×256 | 8 | 584 | 177288 |
| DGEMM | 8×256×32 | 16 | 320 | 112672 |
| GEMVER | 128×128 | 10 | 500 | 140710 |

Table 3 reports the performance, in GigaFlop per second, of numerous different implementations of the same benchmark. out-of-the-box reports the performance of a basic manual off-chip-only implementation of the benchmark, without our framework. PolyOpt/HLS-E reports the performance achieved with our automated framework. Those are AutoESL results obtained with our fast DSE framework. Hand-tuned reports the performance of a manually hand-tuned version serving as our performance reference, from Cong et al. [17]. It has been designed through time-consuming source code level manual refinements, specifically for the HC-1ex machine. It demonstrated that a 4-FPGA manual design for denoise and segmentation systematically outperforms a CPU-based implementation, both in terms of performance improvement (from 2× to 20×) and energy-delay product (up to 2000×), therefore showing the great potential of implementing such 3D image processing algorithms on FPGAs [17].

We observe that for denoise (only 2 PEs were generated by PolyOpt/HLS) the final performance, despite being significantly better than an off-chip-based solution, remains far from the manual design (which uses 4 PEs). On one hand, the code we generate, and especially the loop structures, are more complex for denoise than, e.g., segmentation. This leads to under-performing execution for our au-

tomatically generated code. On the other hand, the reference manual implementation uses numerous techniques not implemented in our automatic framework, such as in-register data reuse, fine-grain communication pipelining, and algorithmic modifications leading to near-optimal performance for this version.

For segmentation, we outperform the manual design, despite the clear remaining room for improvement our framework still has, as shown by the denoise number. We mention that semi-automated manual design can be performed on top of our framework, to address optimizations we do not support, such as array partitioning.

**Table 3: Side-by-side comparison**

| Benchmark | out-of-the-box | PolyOpt/HLS-E | hand-tuned [17] |
|---|---|---|---|
| denoise | 0.02 GF/s | 4.58 GF/s | 52.0 GF/s |
| segmentation | 0.05 GF/s | 24.91 GF/s | 23.39 GF/s |
| dgemm | 0.04 GF/s | 22.72 GF/s | N/A |
| gemver | 0.10 GF/s | 1.07 GF/s | N/A |

Finally Table 4 compares the latency as reported by AutoESL using our memory latency framework for fast DSE, against the wall-clock time observed on the machine after full synthesis of the generated RTL. We report the performance of a single PE call executing a subset (slice) of the full computation.

**Table 4: AutoESL vs. full synthesis comparison (in cycles)**

| Benchmark | AutoESL only | full synthesis |
|---|---|---|
| denoise-1PE (1/32 slice) | 23732704 | 25254164 (+6%) |
| segmentation-1PE (1/32 slice) | 131984559 | 148878928 (+12%) |
| dgemm-1PE (1/64 slice) | 5022287 | 5055335 (+1%) |

## 6. CONCLUSION

High Level Synthesis (HLS) tools for synthesizing designs specified in a behavioral programming language like C/C++ can dramatically reduce the design time especially for embedded systems. HLS systems have now reached a level of advancement to be able to generate RTL that comes quite close to hand generated designs.

However, the current state-of-the art is still very far from being able to take a simple high-level description of a system in C/C++ and derive an efficient FPGA implementation. Currently, an expert designer must perform a number of manual source-level transformations of the input C/C++ code to create an "HLS-friendly" C/C++ program before an effective hardware design can be synthesized by the HLS tool.

We have provided in this paper a complete and fully implemented compiler support to alleviate the burden of manually transforming an input sequential C program into a version that can be effectively mapped to FPGA using HLS tools. Our approach leverages the polyhedral compilation framework to automatically transform the input program for data reuse improvement, as well as for outer and inner parallelism extraction. We have designed and implemented a novel and powerful end-to-end solution for on-chip buffer optimization, that automatically implements the available data reuse in a loop nest. This approach is able to meet any hardware-based resource constraint on the maximal buffer size. In addition we presented a complete fast design space exploration technique, leveraging the specifics of polyhedral program. As a result, we have performed extensive design space exploration using the Xilinx ISE tool-chain on medical imaging algorithms. Experiments showed very significant performance improvements over purely out-of-the-box off-chip automatic solutions, and our automated framework even beats in one case a hand-tuned reference implementation of a segmentation algorithm.

*Acknowledgment.* This work was supported by the Center for Domain-Specific Computing (CDSC) funded by NSF "Expeditions in Computing" award 0926127, and the Gigascale Systems Research Center (GSRC).

# 7. REFERENCES

[1] Center for domain-specific computing. http://cdsc.ucla.edu.

[2] Convey. http://www.conveycomputer.com.

[3] http://www.xilinx.com/products/design-tools/ise-design-suite/index.htm.

[4] Pocc 1.1. http://pocc.sourceforge.net.

[5] An independent evaluation of the autoesl autopilot high-level synthesis tool. Technical report, Berkeley Design Technology, Inc., 2010.

[6] N. Ahmed, N. Mateev, and K. Pingali. Tiling imperfectly-nested loop nests. In *ACM/IEEE Conf. on Supercomputing (SC'00)*, Dallas, TX, USA, Nov. 2000.

[7] C. Alias, A. Darte, and A. Plesco. Optimizing remote accesses for offloaded kernels: application to high-level synthesis for fpga. *SIGPLAN Not.*, 47(8):285–286, Feb. 2012.

[8] J. Allen and K. Kennedy. *Optimizing Compilers for Modern Architectures.* Morgan Kaufmann Publishers, 2002.

[9] M. M. Baskaran, U. Bondhugula, S. Krishnamoorthy, J. Ramanujam, A. Rountev, and P. Sadayappan. Automatic data movement and computation mapping for multi-level parallel architectures with explicitly managed memories. In *ACM Symposium on Principles and practice of parallel programming*, pages 1–10. ACM, 2008.

[10] C. Bastoul. Code generation in the polyhedral model is easier than you think. In *IEEE Intl. Conf. on Parallel Architectures and Compilation Techniques (PACT'04)*, pages 7–16, Sept. 2004.

[11] S. Bayliss and G. A. Constantinides. Optimizing sdram bandwidth for custom fpga loop accelerators. In *Proceedings of the ACM/SIGDA international symposium on Field Programmable Gate Arrays*, FPGA '12, pages 195–204, New York, NY, USA, 2012. ACM.

[12] U. Bondhugula, A. Hartono, J. Ramanujam, and P. Sadayappan. A practical automatic polyhedral program optimization system. In *ACM SIGPLAN Conference on Programming Language Design and Implementation*, June 2008.

[13] E. Brockmeyer, M. Miranda, and F. Catthoor. Layer assignment techniques for low energy in multi-layered memory organisations. In *Design, Automation and Test in Europe Conference and Exhibition, 2003*, pages 1070–1075, 2003. DATE.

[14] F. Catthoor, K. Danckaert, K. Kulkarni, E. Brockmeyer, P. Kjeldsberg, T. v. Achteren, and T. Omnes. *Data access and storage management for embedded programmable processors.* Kluwer Academic Publishers, Norwell, MA, USA, 2002.

[15] F. Catthoor, E. d. Greef, and S. Suytack. *Custom Memory Management Methodology: Exploration of Memory Organisation for Embedded Multimedia System Design.* Kluwer Academic Publishers, Norwell, MA, USA, 1998.

[16] J. Cong, K. Guruaj, M. Huang, S. Li, B. Xiao, and Y. Zou. Domain-specific processor with 3d integration for medical image processing. In *IEEE Intl. Conf. on Application-Specific Systems, Architectures and Processors*, pages 247 –250, sept. 2011.

[17] J. Cong, M. Huang, and Y. Zou. Accelerating fluid registration algorithm on multi-fpga platforms. In *Proc. of Intl. Conf. on Field Programmable Logic and Applications (FPL'11)*. IEEE, 2011.

[18] J. Cong, B. Liu, S. Neuendorffer, J. Noguera, K. Vissers, and Z. Zhang. High-level synthesis for fpgas: From prototyping to deployment. *Computer-Aided Design of Integrated Circuits and Systems, IEEE Transactions on*, 30(4):473 –491, april 2011.

[19] J. Cong, P. Zhang, and Y. Zou. Optimizing memory hierarchy allocation with loop transformations for high-level synthesis. In *Design Automation Conference (DAC'12)*, June 2012.

[20] A. Darte, R. Schreiber, and G. Villard. Lattice-based memory allocation. *IEEE Trans. Comput.*, 54(10):1242–1257, 2005.

[21] P. Diniz, M. Hall, J. Park, B. So, and H. Ziegler. Bridging the gap between compilation and synthesis in the defacto system. In *LCPC'03*, pages 52–70. 2003.

[22] P. Feautrier. Some efficient solutions to the affine scheduling problem. Part II. Multidimensional time. *Int. J. Parallel Program.*, 21(5):389–420, 1992.

[23] S. Girbal, N. Vasilache, C. Bastoul, A. Cohen, D. Parello, M. Sigler, and O. Temam. Semi-automatic composition of loop transformations for deep parallelism and memory hierarchies. *Intl. J. of Parallel Programming*, 34(3), 2006.

[24] A. Grosslinger. Precise Management of Scratchpad Memories for Localising Array Accesses in Scientific Codes. In *Compiler Construction*, pages 236–250, 2009.

[25] A.-C. Guillou, F. Quilleré, P. Quinton, S. Rajopadhye, and T. Risset. Hardware design methodology with the Alpha language. In *FDL'01*, Lyon, France, Sept. 2001.

[26] Q. Hu, P. G. Kjeldsberg, A. Vandecappelle, M. Palkovic, and F. Catthoor. Incremental hierarchical memory size estimation for steering of loop transformations. *ACM Trans. Des. Autom. Electron. Syst.*, 12, September 2007.

[27] F. Irigoin and R. Triolet. Supernode partitioning. In *ACM SIGPLAN Principles of Programming Languages*, pages 319–329, 1988.

[28] I. Issenin, E. Brockmeyer, M. Miranda, and N. Dutt. Drdu: A data reuse analysis technique for efficient scratch-pad memory management. *ACM Trans. Des. Autom. Electron. Syst.*, 12, April 2007.

[29] M. Kandemir and A. Choudhary. Compiler-directed scratch pad memory hierarchy design and management. In *Design Automation Conference, 2002. Proceedings. 39th*, pages 628–633, 2002.

[30] I. Kodukula, N. Ahmed, and K. Pingali. Data-centric multi-level blocking. In *ACM SIGPLAN'97 Conf. on Programming Language Design and Implementation*, pages 346–357, Las Vegas, June 1997.

[31] Q. Liu, G. A. Constantinides, K. Masselos, and P. Cheung. Combining data reuse with data-level parallelization for fpga-targeted hardware compilation: A geometric programming framework. *Trans. Comp.-Aided Design of Integr. Circuits and Systems*, 28(3):305–315, 2009.

[32] M. Palkovic, F. Catthoor, and H. Corporaal. Trade-offs in loop transformations. *ACM Trans. Des. Autom. Electron. Syst.*, 14:22:1–22:30, April 2009.

[33] P. R. Panda, N. D. Dutt, and A. Nicolau. Local memory exploration and optimization in embedded systems. *IEEE Trans. on CAD of Integrated Circuits and Systems*, 18:3–13, January 1999.

[34] PolyOpt: A complete source-to-source Polyhedral Compiler, http://www.cse.ohio-state.edu/~pouchet/polyopt.

[35] L.-N. Pouchet, C. Bastoul, A. Cohen, and N. Vasilache. Iterative optimization in the polyhedral model: Part I, one-dimensional time. In *IEEE/ACM Intl. Symp. on Code Generation and Optimization (CGO'07)*, pages 144–156, 2007.

[36] B. So, M. W. Hall, and P. C. Diniz. A compiler approach to fast hardware design space exploration in fpga-based systems. In *Programming Language Design and Implementation*, 2002.

[37] K. Trifunovic, D. Nuzman, A. Cohen, A. Zaks, and I. Rosen. Polyhedral-model guided loop-nest auto-vectorization. In *IEEE Intl. Conf. on Parallel Architectures and Compilation Techniques*, pages 327–337, 2009.

[38] S. Verdoolaege. isl: An integer set library for the polyhedral model. In *Mathematical Software - ICMS 2010*, pages 299–302, 2010.

[39] M. Wolf and M. Lam. A data locality optimizing algorithm. In *ACM SIGPLAN'91 Conf. on Programming Language Design and Implementation*, pages 30–44, New York, June 1991.

[40] M. Wolfe. Iteration space tiling for memory hierarchies. In *3rd SIAM Conf. on Parallel Processing for Scientific Computing*, pages 357–361, Dec. 1987.

[41] W. Zuo, Y. Liang, P. Li, K. Rupnow, D. Chen, and J. Cong. Improving High Level Synthesis Optimization Opportunity Through Polyhedral Transformations. In *Proc. of the ACM/SIGDA Intl. Symp. on Field Programmable Gate Arrays (FPGA'13)*, 2013.

# Faithful Single-Precision Floating-Point Tangent for FPGAs

Martin Langhammer
Altera European Technology Centre,
High Wycombe, UK

Bogdan Pasca
Altera European Technology Centre,
High Wycombe, UK

## ABSTRACT

This paper presents an FPGA-specific implementation of the floating-point tangent function. The implementation inputs values in the interval $[-\pi/2, \pi/2]$, targets the IEEE-754 single-precision format and has an accuracy of 1 *ulp*. The proposed work is based on a combination of mathematical identities and properties of the tangent function in floating point. The architecture was designed having the Stratix-IV DSP and memory blocks in mind but should map well on any contemporary FPGA featuring embedded multiplier and memory blocks. It outperforms generic polynomial approximation targeting the same resource spectrum and provides better resources trade-offs than classical CORDIC-based implementations. The presented work is widely available as being part of the Altera DSP Builder Advanced Blockset.

## Categories and Subject Descriptors

B.2.4 [**Arithmetic and Logic Structures**]: High-Speed Arithmetic— *Algorithms*; G.1 [**Numerical Analysis**]: General—*Computer Arithmetic, Error Analysis*

## Keywords

tangent; floating-point; single-precision; FPGA

## 1. INTRODUCTION

Many hardware implementations of trigonometric functions use the CORDIC family of algorithms [16, 11]. Iterative implementations consume low resources and are preferred when implemented in the floating-point unit of embedded processors. Unrolled implementations are often encountered in computational datapaths targeting high throughputs. These are recognized to be very stressful to support in FPGAs due to the multiple, deep arithmetic structures, with each level containing a wide adder. Chip-filling designs using such structures are usually unable to close timing at high fmax [6].

Architectures based on polynomial approximations can be used to implement the sine, cosine and division based on the inverse [14]. These approaches map better to the recent FPGAs containing thousands of multiplier and embedded memory blocks but can be

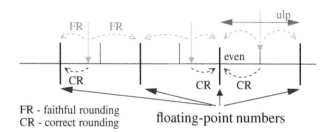

FR - faithful rounding
CR - correct rounding

floating-point numbers

**Figure 1: IEEE-754 correct rounding for round to nearest and the non-standard and faithful rounding**

quite wasteful when implementing the tangent operation by operator assembly [7, 12]

In this work the floating-point tangent function is implemented as a *fused operator*. We present a step-by-step error analysis which allows optimizing the internal operations by computing just-right for obtaining a faithfully rounded implementation. The results presented in Section 5 show the superiority of this approach compared to the best polynomial approximation implementations.

## 2. BACKGROUND

The IEEE-754 standard for floating-point arithmetic (revised in 2008) [2] represents binary floating-point numbers using a three element tuple: sign (1 bit), exponent ($w_E$ bits) and fraction ($w_F$ bits) - (s, e, f) such that: $x = (-1)^s 2^e 1.f$. The widths of the fields defines the supported formats: (1, 8, 23) for single precision and (1, 11, 52) for double precision.

Let $x, y$ and $q$ be floating-point numbers such that $q = \circ(x \text{ op } y)$ where ($\circ$) denotes rounding an infinitely accurate result to the target format. Rounding to nearest is desired as it provides the best accuracy (maximum error of $1/2$ *ulp* where the *ulp* denotes the unit in the last place). For elementary functions round to nearest is very difficult to obtain - problem called the Table Maker's Dilemma [13]. For these functions implementations diverge from the standard and implement the relaxed *faithful rounding* (Figure 1) with a maximum error of 1 *ulp*.

In this work we present a multiplier and memory based architecture of the floating-point tangent function having an accuracy of 1 ulp.

Recent Altera FPGAs such as Stratix-III/-IV [3, 4] contain thousands of such embedded resources. One Stratix-IV half-DSP block (each half can be configured independently) can be configured to implement either 2 $18 \times 18$ multipliers or one $36 \times 36$ multiplier. Embedded memory blocks can also have various configurations, most relevant for this work being the $256 \times 36$ and $512 \times 18$ modes of the M9K block.

## 3. ALGORITHM

We present here the algorithm used to compute a faithfully accurate floating-point tangent in single precision, where the input interval is restricted to $[-\pi/2, +\pi/2]$. This type of operator can be directly used in datapaths where we can bound beforehand the range of the the input variable. In order to obtain an operator for the full floating-point input range a supplementary range-reduction step is required [9, 15] which is currently outside the scope of this work.

Tangent is symmetrical to the origin: $\tan(-x) = -\tan(x)$; this allows restricting the computation to positive arguments $[0, \pi/2)$.

The Taylor expansion for the tangent is

$$\tan(x) = x + \frac{1}{3}x^3 + \frac{2}{15}x^5 + \dots x \in \left(\frac{-\pi}{2}, \frac{\pi}{2}\right) \qquad (1)$$

If $x$ is very small ($< 2^{-w_F/2}$) a good approximation for $tan(x)$ is $x$. This is due to the fact that the higher order terms in Equation 1 have weights lower than the LSB of $x$ and are shifted-out in the final summation. This is a well known property of the floating-point sine and tangent functions. The dynamic range of the input is therefore limited to $[2^{-w_F/2}, +\pi/2]$, allowing the input to the function to be represented in an error-free fixed-point format with $1 + w_F + \lceil w_F/2 \rceil$ bits (24+12=36 bits for single precision).

The following mathematical identity holds true for tangent:

$$\tan(a+b) = \frac{\tan(a) + \tan(b)}{1 - \tan(a)\tan(b)} \qquad (2)$$

this can be expanded to:

$$\tan(a+b+c) = \frac{\frac{\tan(a) + \tan(b)}{1 - \tan(a)\tan(b)} + \tan(c)}{1 - \frac{\tan(a) + \tan(b)}{1 - \tan(a)\tan(b)}\tan(c)} \qquad (3)$$

Building a faithfully accurate floating-point tangent requires the final error to be less than $1ulp$. The final error has two components: $E_{total} = E_{approx} + E_{round}$. The rounding error ($E_{round}$) is a bound on the maximal error done when packing a possibly infinitely accurate result into the target format. Rounding to nearest will yield a maximal error of $1/2ulp$. The approximation error ($E_{approx}$) sums the both the method errors and the errors due to implementation optimizations (datapath trimmings). The objective is to keep the sum of these errors smaller than $1/2ulp$.

The proposed architecture is based on Equation 3, which is implemented as a floating-point multiplication between the numerator (n) and the inverse of the denominator (id): $p = n \times id$. In the following equation, tilde variables are approximations. The approximation error is computed as $E_{approx} = |(\tilde{p} - p)/p|$.

$$p = n \times id;$$
$$\tilde{p} = \tilde{n} \times \tilde{id}$$
$$= n(1+\varepsilon) \times id(1+\varepsilon)$$
$$= n \cdot id + 2 \cdot n \cdot id \cdot \varepsilon + n \cdot id \cdot \varepsilon^2.$$
$$E_{approx} = |(p - \tilde{p})/p|$$
$$= |(2 \cdot n \cdot id \cdot \varepsilon + n \cdot id \cdot \varepsilon^2)/(n \cdot id)|$$
$$= |2\varepsilon + \varepsilon^2| \le 1/2 \cdot 2^{-p} \qquad (4)$$

**Figure 2: The fixed-point decomposition of the input argument** $x$

From inequality 4, where $p = 24$ for single-precision results that the value of $\varepsilon$ should be slightly smaller than $2^{-26}$ which translates into slightly better than $1/4ulp$ error bound for both the numerator and denominator.

The complexity of computing the numerator in Equation 3 to the required accuracy can be reduced, for single-precision, by using the fixed-point decomposition presented in Figure 2. This decomposition favours tabulating the tangent computations for $\tan(a)$ and $\tan(c)$ using embedded memory blocks. In addition, as both $\tan(a)$ and $\tan(b)$ are small, $\tan(a)\tan(b)$ is also very small. Moreover, as $b < 2^{-17}$ it is safe to use $\tan(b) \approx b$. Therefore, we will use the follwing approximation for computing the numerator:

$$n = \tan(c) + \tan(a) + b \qquad (5)$$

We need to compute a bound on the error of this approximation. We do this for two cases. First, $\tan(c) = 0$ and $\tan(a)\tan(b)$ maximal:

```
a =   .          111111111
b =   .                   1111111111111111000
```

In this case the relative error is slightly less than $2^{-25}$, and should be $2^{-26}$. However, in this case the denominator value is 1 and carries no error, so the accuracy is reached. Second, for $\tan(c)$ minimal but greater than zero and $\tan(a)\tan(b)$ maximal, the value for $\tan(a)$ has a lower weight than $\tan(c)$, which pushes the relative error in the summation to $2^{-26}$. Consequently, computing both $\tan(a)$ and $\tan(b)$ with $1 + w_F + 2$ bits of accuracy suffices.

The denominator will be computed using a similar approximation as for the numerator.

$$d = 1 - (\tan(a) + b)\tan(c) \qquad (6)$$

This computation involves a possible cancellation which can amplify an existing error by an amount equal to the cancellation size. This would require computing the subtracted term with additional accuracy. As the cancellation occurs when the input is close to $\pi/2$ we use an additional table for the final $256ulp$ before $\pi/2$. Hence, the largest cancellation can now be produced by the following input:

```
c = 1.10010010;
a =   .          000111001;
b =   .                   010000;
```

The cancellation size is 3 bits, and therefore we require 3 additional bits of accuracy in computing the right term of the subtraction. This requires computing both $\tan(a)$ and $\tan(c)$ with $1 + w_F + 2 + 3$ bits of precision and $0.5ulp$ of accuracy.

## 4. IMPLEMENTATION

The implemented architecture is presented in Figure 3. As $a$ and $c$ are small subsections (9 bits) of the fixed point input, the tangents for all possible bit combinations can be stored in 36-bit wide data tables:

- $\tan(c)$ has a dynamic range between $2^{-8}$ and $2^{11}$. It will be stored in a normalized floating-point format with an exponent on 5 bits and a fraction on $w_F + 5$ bits. The hidden '1' is also stored explicitly in order to save on the decoding logic for 0. The total data width in this table is therefore 34 bits (M9K have a width of 36-bits).

- $\tan(a)$ has a dynamic range of just 9 positions. We store this value directly in fixed-point for a total width of $9 + 23 + 5 = 36 + 1$ which one bit wider than the M9K block in Stratix-IV/-III devices.

The problem has now been reduced to a 36 bit fixed-point multiply and a 36 bit fixed-point divide. There are also some additions required: although they will be a form of floating point, explained below. The subtraction will be a simple fixed-point subtraction.

The input number is first converted to a 36 bit fixed-point number by shifting the difference between the number and the maximum biased input exponent. The fixed point input is then split into three numbers: $c$ - bits (35 downto 27), $a$ - bits(26 downto 18), and $b$, the least significant 18 bits.

The numerator is calculated largely on the left side of Figure 3. The $\tan(a)$ and $b$ numbers are in fixed-point format, and can immediately be added together. The $\tan(a) + b$ sum may grow by one bit when both $a$ and $b$ approach their maximums. The sum must then be aligned to the exponent of $c$, which can range from 0 to 19 (127 to 146 in single precision offset equivalent).

After right shifting the sum $\tan(a) + b$ it can finally be added to the mantissa of $c$. Next, $\tan(c) + \tan(a) + b$ sum is then normalized. The numerator now exists in a floating point format.

The denominator is calculated largely on the right side of the diagram. The $\tan(a) + b$ sum is normalized before the multiplication by the mantissa of $\tan(c)$. The local exponent is used to denormalize the product to a fixed-point number again. The now fixed-point value of $(\tan(a) + b) \cdot \tan(c)$ is subtracted from 1, and is normalized again before the division. The maximum cancellation size is 3 positions which simplifies the normalizer implementation.

As presented in the error analysis section, the final division is implemented as an inverse of the denominator, which is then multiplied by the numerator. The division uses a normalized denominator, and the multiplier input is a normalized numerator. The product therefore requires only a single bit normalization, which is implemented as a 2-1 multiplexer. Finally, a rounding stage, along with the application of special or signalling conditions, is performed.

If the biased input exponent is less than 115, the output and the input are considered the same, as this is the point where $\tan(x) = x$. This is implemented as an input in the final multiplexer in Figure 3. If the input is within the $256ulp$ prior to $\pi/2$ a tabulated value is used, which is also an input in the final multiplexer.

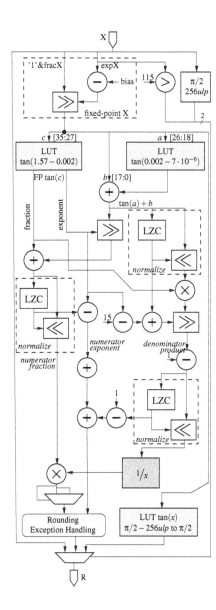

**Figure 3: The architecture for the faithful single-precision floating-point tangent**

# 5. RESULTS

Table 1 presents the synthesis results for our proposed implementation on a Stratix-IV C2 speedgrade FPGA. The *Resources* numbers are given as returned by QuartusII: number of DSP blocks is given in terms of 18-bit multipliers (4 18-bit multipliers compose a 36 x 36 block). The 18 18-bit multipliers also comprise the units needed for implementing the inverse calculation.

We first compared our proposed solution against the $\tan(\pi x)$ implementation available in Altera DSP Builder Advanced [1] block set. This implementation also performs a simple range reduction, so it is expected to be 100-200LUT smaller when the input range is limited to $-\pi/2$ to $\pi/2$. Nevertheless, the proposed fine-tuned implementation has a significantly shorter latency, consumes fewer

**Table 1: Synthesis results for Stratix-IV C2. MUL = 18-bit multipliers**

| Architecture | Lat @ Freq. | Resources |
|---|---|---|
| ours | 30 @ 314MHz | 18MUL, 8M9K, 1172LUT, 1078Reg |
| $\tan(\pi x)$ [1] | 48 @ 360MHz | 28MUL, 7M9K, 2633LUT, 4099Reg |
| $\sin\cos(\pi x)$ [10] | 85ns | 10 MUL, 2*1365 LUTs |
| div [7] | 16 @ 233MHz | 1210LUT, 1308REG |
| div [14] | 11 @ 400MHz | 8MUL, 4M9K, 274LUT, 291Reg |

multipliers, roughly the same number of memory blocks and less than half the logic.

We have also compared this implementation against the sin cos operator presented in [10]. This is a combinatorial design, targeting a VirtexII-Pro and uses a fused sin cos operator. Similar to [1], it inputs an argument of $\pi x$ which slightly penalizes the implementation compared to ours. In the bottom part of Table 1 we give two top divider implementations, each targeting different resources spectrum: the FloPoCo [7] divider uses a digit recurrence method whereas the DSPBuilder Advanced version [14] uses polynomial approximation. The full tangent implementation based on [10] would require an extra division. Additionally, pipelining the implementation is also expected to increase resource usage. All this considered, the proposed architecture manages to outperform this implementation.

# 6. CONCLUSION

We have presented the architecture of a faithfully accurate single-precision tangent. Unlike previous works, the tangent is viewed as a fused operator which, in combination with a careful error analysis, allows significantly reducing implementation cost. The implementation targets recent Stratix-III/-IV devices and resizes the internal datapath in order to: 1/ use the larger multiplier granularity – one 36-bit multiplier is equivalent in cost to two 18-bit ones 2/ make good use of the available block memory size.

Future work includes generalizing these techniques for larger precision. In such a case $\tan(c)$ and $\tan(a)$ will be too large for direct tabulation. Using the HOTBM approach by Detrey and de Dinechin [8] would allow computing these to higher precisions with little cost. The larger multipliers needed in these operators would benefit from the truncated multiplier techniques presented by Banescu et. al. [5].

# 7. REFERENCES

[1] DSP Builder Advanced Blockset.
http://www.altera.com/technology/dsp/advanced-blockset/dsp-advanced-blockset.html.

[2] IEEE Standard for Floating-Point Arithmetic. *IEEE Std 754-2008*, pages 1–58, 29 2008.

[3] *StratixIII Device Handbook*, 2010. http://www.altera.com/literature/hb/stx3/stratix3_handbook.pdf.

[4] *StratixIV Device Handbook*, 2011. http://www.altera.com/literature/hb/stratix-iv/stx4_5v1.pdf.

[5] S. Banescu, F. de Dinechin, B. Pasca, and R. Tudoran. Multipliers for floating-point double precision and beyond on FPGAs. In *International Workshop on Higly-Efficient Accelerators and Reconfigurable Technologies (HEART)*. ACM, jun 2010.

[6] I. Berkeley Design Technology. An Independent Analysis of Altera's FPGA Floating-point DSP Design Flow. 2011.

[7] F. de Dinechin and B. Pasca. Designing custom arithmetic data paths with FloPoCo. *IEEE Design and Test*, 2011.

[8] J. Detrey and F. de Dinechin. Table-based polynomials for fast hardware function evaluation. In S. Vassiliadis,

N. Dimopoulos, and S. Rajopadhye, editors, *16th IEEE International Conference on Application-Specific Systems, Architectures, and Processors (ASAP'05)*, pages 328–333, Samos, Greece, July 2005. IEEE Computer Society.

[9] J. Detrey and F. de Dinechin. Floating-point trigonometric functions for FPGAs. In *International Conference on Field Programmable Logic and Applications*, pages 29–34, Amsterdam, Netherlands, aug 2007. IEEE.

[10] J. Detrey and F. de Dinechin. Floating-point trigonometric functions for FPGAs. In K. Bertels, W. Najjar, A. van Genderen, and S. Vassiliadis, editors, *17th International Conference on Field Programmable Logic and Applications (FPL'07)*, pages 29–34, Amsterdam, Netherlands, Aug. 2007. IEEE.

[11] E. Garcia, R. Cumplido, and M. Arias. Pipelined cordic design on fpga for a digital sine and cosine waves generator. In *Electrical and Electronics Engineering, 2006 3rd International Conference on*, pages 1 –4, sept. 2006.

[12] M. Langhammer and T. VanCourt. FPGA floating point datapath compiler. *Field-Programmable Custom Computing Machines, Annual IEEE Symposium on*, 17:259–262, 2009.

[13] J.-M. Muller, N. Brisebarre, F. de Dinechin, C.-P. Jeannerod, V. Lefèvre, G. Melquiond, N. Revol, D. Stehlé, and S. Torres. *Handbook of Floating-Point Arithmetic*. Birkhauser Boston, 2010.

[14] B. Pasca. Correctly rounded floating-point division for DSP-enabled FPGAs. In *22th International Conference on Field Programmable Logic and Applications (FPL'12)*, Oslo, Norway, Aug. 2012. IEEE.

[15] M. H. Payne and R. N. Hanek. Radian reduction for trigonometric functions. *ACM SIGNUM Newsletter*, 18(1):19–24, Jan. 1983.

[16] Y. Shang. Implementation of ip core of fast sine and cosine operation through FPGA. *Energy Procedia*, 16, Part B(0):1253 – 1258, 2012. 2012 ICFEEM.

# Accelerating ncRNA Homology Search with FPGAs

Nathaniel McVicar[†]        Walter L. Ruzzo[§]        Scott Hauck[‡]

[††]Department of Electrical Engineering and [§]Department of Computer Science and Engineering
and [§]Department of Genome Sciences        University of Washington, Seattle, WA 98195
[§]Fred Hutchinson Cancer Research Center, Seattle, WA 98109

nmcvicar@u.washington.edu        ruzzo@cs.washington.edu        hauck@ee.washington.edu

## ABSTRACT

Over the last decade, the number of known biologically important non-coding RNAs (ncRNAs) has increased by orders of magnitude. The function performed by a specific ncRNA is partially determined by its structure, defined by which nucleotides of the molecule form pairs. These correlations may span large and variable distances in the linear RNA molecule. Because of these characteristics, algorithms that search for ncRNAs belonging to known families are computationally expensive, often taking many CPU weeks to run. To improve the speed of this search, multiple search algorithms arranged into a series of progressively more stringent filters can be used. In this paper, we present an FPGA based implementation of some of these algorithms. This is the first FPGA based approach to attempt to accelerate multiple filters used in ncRNA search. The FPGA is reconfigured for each filter, resulting in a total system speedup of 25x when compared with a single CPU.

## Categories and Subject Descriptors

B.7.1 [**Integrated Circuits**]: Types and Design Styles–
*Algorithms implemented in hardware;* J.3 [**Life and Medical Sciences**]: Biology and genetics

## General Terms

Algorithms, performance

## Keywords

FPGA, ncRNA, reconfigurable computing, Viterbi, CYK

## 1. INTRODUCTION

Proteins are well known as the workhorse molecules for living organisms. The traditional view of ribonucleic acid (RNA) held that its main role was to encode proteins. It was a temporary product transcribed from deoxyribonucleic acid (DNA) and then translated into protein. In contrast with this role are functional non-coding RNA molecules. These ncRNAs fill a variety of biological roles, performing protein-like functions as diverse as catalyzing reactions and regulating gene expression or metabolism [1][2][3]. Recent discoveries include specific links between ncRNA and human diseases, including cancer and Alzheimer's [4].

One key problem in ncRNA bioinformatics is homology search: finding additional instances of a known ncRNA family across multiple genomes. The current software search algorithms can

have very long runtimes, on the order of days, weeks or even longer depending on the problem size. Faster implementations would also allow for searches to be run routinely that are currently impossible due to their complexity, opening up entirely new avenues of research. For these reasons, we have developed a field programmable gate array (FPGA) based implementation to reduce the runtime of the ncRNA search problem.

## 2. BACKGROUND

Like DNA, ncRNA is made up of a chain of nucleotides. From an abstract viewpoint, each of these nucleotides can be represented by a single base selected from an alphabet of A, C, G or U. The string of bases that make up the ncRNA molecule is called the sequence or primary structure. Much like DNA, the bases in ncRNAs can bond, or pair, with one another. The strongest bonds form between adenine (A) and uracil (U), and between guanine (G) and cytosine (C). In addition to these Watson-Crick pairs, ncRNAs also form weaker G-U wobble pairs, as well as other interactions. After being transcribed, some of the bases in the ncRNA molecule will bond with their complements, creating various two-dimensional features. This shape, known as the secondary structure, depends both on the sequence and on which bases ultimately end up paired. The actual location of each nucleotide in three-dimensional space is the tertiary structure.

The Rfam database is an attempt to classify all known ncRNAs into families based on their functions [5]. Much like proteins, these functions strongly depend on the three-dimensional structure of the ncRNA molecule, but, also like the case for proteins, this information is intensely difficult to compute. For RNA, the secondary structure provides a partial proxy and allows the use of much more efficient algorithms when determining if a given ncRNA is a member of a functional family [6]. The use of the secondary structure, instead of the primary structure, is necessary because ncRNA of the same family (in the same or different species) may have very different sequences while sharing the same secondary structure.

Rfam seeks to maximize the accuracy of its ncRNA homology searches by modeling each family [7]. This is a particularly challenging problem for Rfam because traditional sequence alignment techniques are not appropriate. Tools like BLAST, Smith-Waterman and profile HMMs are designed for matching sequences. They make no use of secondary structure information, so it would be very hard for a single model to match two ncRNAs with the same secondary structure but radically different primary sequences without a huge sacrifice in specificity. To get around this limitation, Rfam uses covariance models (CMs) to represent families [6]. Covariance refers to the fact that for the secondary structure to be preserved, paired bases must remain complementary across different members of the family even if the bases themselves change; i.e., paired bases tend to covary.

Figure 1 shows the sequence for an Iron response element (IRE) ncRNA in four different species. The IRE plays an important role in iron metabolism and has over 3,000 instances in Rfam. The shaded sections of the sequence represent two helixes, as illustrated by the secondary structure shown in Figure 2. Note that each species has a different sequence for positions 3, 4 and 5 from the left, but the bases in the 5th, 4th and 3rd positions from the right change accordingly (covary) to preserve Watson-Crick (or G-U wobble) pairs. The gaps in the sequences, represented by dots in Figure 1, mean that these pairs are not at a fixed spacing. The color coding in Figure 2 represents another important concept captured by the CM. Warmer colors represent highly conserved bases, the ones that rarely change between species. Cooler colors represent bases that are more likely to vary. Highly conserved regions of ncRNAs reflect regions that are critical to the molecule's function [8]. For example, the highly conserved loop on the end of the IRE binds with important iron response proteins to help regulate iron metabolism [9]. Notice that the base-paired regions are also highly conserved, but in the more subtle sense that pairing is preserved, rather than specific nucleotides. CMs are especially useful for ncRNA homology search because they are capable of capturing these features, specifically variably spaced conserved sequences and pairs embedded in less well-conserved regions.

```
rainbow smelt    AUUCUUGCCUCAACAGUGAUUGAACGGAAC
red junglefowl   AUUAUC..GGGGACAGUGUUUCCC.AUAAU
human            UUUCCUGCUUCAGCAGUGCUUGGACGGAAC
gray wolf        UCGUUC..GUCCUCAGUGCAGGGC.AACAG
```

**Figure 1. The sequence for an IRE ncRNA in four species**

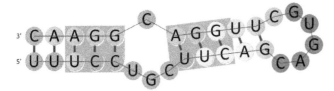

**Figure 2. The secondary structure of the IRE, based on IRE_I summary [5]**

Using CMs, it is possible to perform ncRNA homology searches relatively efficiently, but the computation is still very time-consuming. A typical search for a single family against a large sequence database can take days of CPU time [10]. The work presented in this paper is focused on accelerating the CM search pipeline in the Infernal 1.0 software package [11]. In addition to many other features, Infernal provides a very fast CM-based ncRNA homology search component. The speed of the search is due to three main features: 1) The use of efficient CM algorithms; 2) Highly optimized code; 3) Prefiltering the sequences using hidden Markov models (HMMs). This use of HMM filters is especially important for speedup, since the algorithmic complexity of an efficient HMM algorithm is $O(N^2)$ compared with $O(N^3)$ for a CM.

Infernal 1.0's search pipeline is made up of two filters followed by a final CM search. The first filter is HMM-based, and so it is asymptotically more efficient than a CM. This filter typically eliminates 98% or more of the dataset from consideration. The second filter is CM-based, and uses a slower but more sensitive search algorithm. This filter eliminates a large portion of the remaining input sequences, and the final most sensitive CM search algorithm, known as Inside, is run against what remains to find potential ncRNA family members.

## 3. PREVIOUS WORK

Infernal uses the Viterbi dynamic programming algorithm for scoring sequences against HMMs and CYK for CM scoring [11]. Both of these algorithms have a number of FPGA implementations [12][13][14][15]. However, to our knowledge there have been no previous efforts to accelerate Infernal's entire ncRNA homology search pipeline. Given the massive performance gains from prefiltering, any approach that only attacks a single stage of the Infernal pipeline is severely limited in terms of the speedup it can realize. Infernal without any filters is orders of magnitude slower, and with all pipeline stages enabled each of the three main stages is roughly equal in runtime.

Significant work has been done on using hardware to improve the runtime of the CYK portion of Infernal. The approach used by [16] is more geared to an application-specific integrated circuit (ASIC) than an FPGA, due to the shared memory and very large switches it requires to handle CMs with many states. On a large Virtex-5 FPGA from Xilinx, this work is limited by the available logic and maxes out at around 20 processing elements (PEs). By way of contrast, the approach is designed to scale well to over 300 PEs on an ASIC. Although this is reasonable given that ASICs are the stated focus of the design, the FPGA performance is not optimized.

The Infernal CYK accelerator presented in [17] is much more FPGA centric. This design makes use of an array of processors that require minimal access to data that is not stored in the PE or available from one of its neighbors. This approach requires much less memory bandwidth and yields 32 PEs on a Virtex-5. Ultimately, it ends up being block RAM (BRAM) limited and it is most similar to the CYK acceleration approach presented in this paper. The significant differences are discussed below. Note that [17] does not address HMM filtering, so its speedup is limited to only the CYK stage of the pipeline.

Of the FPGA Viterbi implementations, the most relevant are those that implement HMMER HMMs. HMMER is a software package that makes use of Plan 7 HMMs to perform protein homology search [18]. This protein search, using families found in Pfam, is very similar to ncRNA homology search. However, given their size and structural restrictions, the primary structure alone provides sufficient sensitivity for finding protein family members. Of the efforts to accelerate HMMER on FPGAs, [14] is the most relevant. It presents a very fast FPGA implementation of Plan 7, with the ability to fit over 50 PEs on a Virtex-4. Plan 7 HMMs form the basis for the Plan 9 HMMs used in Infernal 1.0 [8], but Plan 9 is significantly different from Plan 7, and so is the FPGA implementation. The next section covers these differences in detail.

## 4. VITERBI

This section provides an overview of the Viterbi algorithm, as well as details and results for the Viterbi FPGA implementation.

### 4.1 Viterbi Algorithm and Plan 9 HMMs

The Viterbi algorithm is a two-dimensional dynamic programming algorithm [19]. Given an observed sequence and an HMM featuring a set of states with emission and transition probabilities for those states, the algorithm produces the highest scoring path through the states. This is the most likely path to have emitted the particular input sequence. Although the Viterbi algorithm itself is general and can be used with any HMM, the implementations used in HMMER and Infernal are limited to supporting only Plan 7 and Plan 9 HMMs respectively. Although they are very similar, there are some significant differences that affect the CM Plan 9 (CP9) FPGA design. The states of CP9 HMMs are shown in Figure 3.

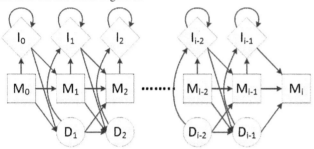

**Figure 3. CM Plan 9 HMM States**

In CP9, each node consists of three states: Insert, Match and Delete. The Match state emits a base that matches the one expected by the model. The Insert state emits an unexpected base, optionally advancing to the next node. Finally, the Delete state advances to the next node without emitting. Note that every node is the same except for the first and last. For the first node, there is no Delete state and $M_0$ is equivalent to a Begin state, which represents the start of the model. For the final node there is no Insert or Delete and $M_i$ represents an End state. The CP9 HMMs are built by Infernal from each family's CM. This process is based on the techniques described in [20] and creates a filter with a much faster runtime than the CM due to the better asymptotic efficiency of the Viterbi algorithm.

The first key difference between Plan 7 and CP9, and therefore between the FPGA Viterbi accelerator presented here and the previous work, is which state transitions are available. In Plan 7, there are no transitions from Insert to Delete or vice versa. Supporting these edges requires slightly more complex PEs in CP9. There are two more significant differences, but these require a discussion of the CP9 Viterbi algorithm first.

The Viterbi algorithm makes use of a two-dimensional dynamic programming table to store the log-probability scores computed for each state. The work for each node involves computing the log-probability of each transition into that node given the current sequence element and the scores of previous nodes. For example, to compute the Insert score for some node requires taking the sum of the Insert emission log-probability for that state, given the current base in the sequence, and the maximum of the scores of the three states that could transition into an Insert. Each of these scores must have the correct transition log-probability added to it before the max is computed. The final equation for an Insert score

is as follows:

$$\text{Insert}(j,i) = \text{emit\_prob}(\text{Insert}_j, \text{Seq}_i) + \max \begin{cases} \text{Insert}(j, i-1) + \text{trans\_prob}(\text{Insert} \rightarrow \text{Insert}_j) \\ \text{Match}(j, i-1) + \text{trans\_prob}(\text{Match} \rightarrow \text{Insert}_j) \\ \text{Delete}(j, i-1) + \text{trans\_prob}(\text{Delete} \rightarrow \text{Insert}_j) \end{cases}$$

During the Viterbi run, the table cell $j,i$ contains a score representing the log-probability of the sequence up to some element $i$ matching the model up to some state $j$, and by the end of the run the entire table will be filled in this manner. The equations for the remaining transitions are very similar to those used in Plan 7 and can be found in the previous work [12]. Notice that the Insert equation above has the additional Delete to Insert transition. The others must be similarly modified.

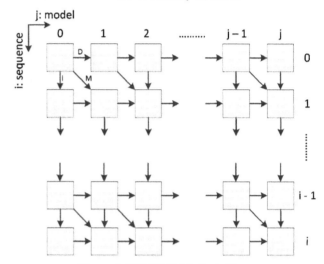

**Figure 4. CP9 DP Table Data Flow**

One dimension of the dynamic programing table is the model, so moving one cell to the right in Figure 4 is equivalent to moving to the next state in the model. The other dimension represents the sequence being scored, so moving down the table represents emitting one base. Each cell in Figure 4 represent an entire node, meaning that they each contain a Match, Insert and Delete state. The Delete state does not emit a base, instead it represents a state in the model that is not found in the sequence. For this reason, Delete is a transition from one node to its right hand neighbor in the table. Similarly, Insert emits a base that does not match any model state, so it moves down the table. The Match state is used when a base fits the model's expectations. In this case it both emits the base and moves on to the next model state, moving right and down one node in the table.

These data dependencies are such that the CP9 HMM has no backwards paths. This means that a computation can be performed along a wavefront starting with node (0, 0) (which depends on no other nodes) followed by computing (1, 0) and (0, 1) in parallel, then (2, 0), (1, 1) and (0, 2) also in parallel and so on. In other words, the lack of backwards data flow means that there is a huge amount of parallelism available in the computation. Note that communication is not all local from one node to the next. Not shown here are the Begin and End state transitions. These provide some (typically very low) probabilities to jump from the Begin state to any position in the model, and similarly from any state to End. Although these transitions are not local like the transitions in Figure 4, they are still entirely feedforward, so no parallelism is lost.

The fact that there are no feedback paths in CP9 HMMs is the second critical difference between CP9 and Plan 7 HMMs. The feedback path in Plan 7 allows for the model to match multiple copies of itself in succession [14]. This feedback requires special consideration for an FPGA implementation, and so the lack of it in CP9 gives us greater design freedom.

Among the changes from Plan 7, the third and most significant is the introduction of another state type. This End Local (EL) state only exists for some nodes along the model, and allows for large portions of the model to be bypassed. Because EL states also have a self-loop, like Inserts, they allow for a number of bases to be emitted while skipping over a potentially large portion of the model. More specifically, when the CP9 HMM is built from the CM, some nodes will contain an EL state and a probability to transition from Match to this state. The only other way to reach the EL state is through a self-loop which emits a base and stays in the same state. The only transition from the EL state is to some subsequent Match state. This transition is unique in CP9 in that it is the only transition other than from Match to End that can jump forward many states. It is also different from other states in that not every Match has an associated EL state. In addition, a single Match can have multiple incoming EL transitions. See Figure 5 for an example of some of these properties. Because of these properties a more flexible design is required to handle EL states.

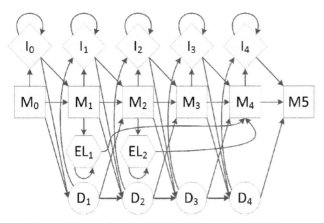

**Figure 5. Example of a CP9 HMM Featuring EL States**

## 4.2 FPGA Implementation

Figure 6 shows a block diagram of the CP9 Viterbi implementation developed in this work. For all of the results presented in this and subsequent sections, our FPGA designs targeted a Pico Computing system featuring an EX-500 backplane equipped with an M-503 module. This module features a Xilinx Virtex-6 LX240T as well as 8GB of DRAM and 27MB of SRAM. The design operates on a streaming paradigm. This is appropriate because a single, relatively small HMM may be run against a very long sequence or set of sequences. The sequence is streamed in from offchip and scores are streamed out on a similar channel. No other external memory or offchip communication is used.

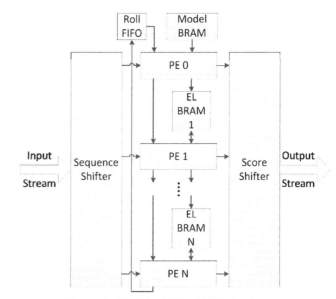

**Figure 6. CP9 Viterbi FPGA Block Diagram**

The CP9 Viterbi FPGA design is based on a linear array of PEs. Once the processor pipeline has filled, this allows all PEs to operate in parallel along the wavefront described in the previous section. Given the dynamic program table in Figure 4, it makes the most sense for a single PE to either move down a column, computing scores for many bases from the sequence for a single state, or across a row, handling all states for a single base. Either of these arrangements allows for neighbors to communicate model and score values. Because CP9 does not have a feedback path, but it does have EL states, it is most feasible for a single PE to handle all states for a given base, for the next PE to handle the next base, and so on down the sequence as shown in Figure 7. Every PE will be computing at all times except for the beginning and end of the sequence. There are some cases that break this parallelism, for example, a very short model with fewer states than there are PEs. However, this situation can be handled by replicating the model multiple times and shifting in the next base after reaching the end of the first copy of the model.

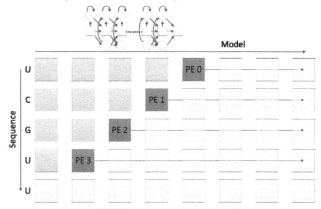

**Figure 7. CP9 Viterbi PE Allocation and Wavefront**

The Sequence Shifter itself is simply a set of shift registers. The first shifts bases in from the input stream and loads them into a second shift register when required. After a PE has completed work on a base, a new base is loaded from the PE's second shift register. The Score Shifter operates on similar principles and also filters output scores to avoid saturating output bandwidth.

The Model BRAM stores the CP9 HMM parameters, which include emission scores for Insert and Match states and transition scores for all possible state transmissions. These scores are stored as the logarithm of an odds ratio measuring the likelihood of a given event, known as log-odds form. This form converts multiplications to addition of precomputed logs. Viterbi also requires maximum operations, which can use the same hardware in log and regular integer format. In addition, the precision of the calculations can be adjusted by changing the number of bits used to store the scores throughout the system. The amount of BRAM required to store the models depends on this width. Every state requires an emission probability for each base for Match and Insert, or 8 emission probabilities per state. There are transmission probabilities between each of the three states in the nodes for a total of 9 different values. In addition, there are transition probabilities for Begin, End and EL for each state, bringing the total up to 20. Letting $w_s$ represent the number of bits per score, this requires $20 \times w_s$ bits per state. Setting the maximum model length to 2k, which can handle all of the current Rfam models, and given that the Virtex-6 series features 36 Kb BRAMs, this means that the total model BRAM requirement is $2k \times 20 \times w_s / 36k = 1.25 \times w_s$. For our current system, a $w_s$ value of around 18 bits is sufficient, requiring about 24 of our FPGA's 416 BRAMs for model tables, due to padding.

The Processing Elements themselves are fairly simple. The first PE receives model information from the BRAM. Since the computation wavefront, shown in Figure 7, is such that each PE is always one node in the HMM behind the previous PE, this model information can be passed from one PE to the next as well. Dark grey cells represent current computation while light grey cells have already been scored. The alternative approach, where each PE handles many sequence bases for the same state, requires that each PE have access to its own portions of the table, potentially reducing efficiency of BRAM use or introducing additional multiplexers.

In addition to the transition and emission probability and sequence data discussed above, the PEs need some way to access and update the DP score table. Because all communication is either between adjacent bases or across many states but within the same base, there is no need to actually store the entire table in memory. Instead, the values that are required at any given time are only those at the computation wavefront. Values that do require longer communications, such as Begin and End scores (with an End score for each base being the ultimate output of the FPGA accelerator) can be stored in the local PE. The only exception to this local communication is the EL state, which we will discuss. Since the input sequence proceeds down the PEs in order, the next base after PE N has to be handled by PE 0. At this point, all score information must be transferred back to PE 0. For models longer than the number of PEs, PE 0 will still be busy computing its current base, so this score information must be stored in the Roll FIFO shown in Figure 6. The total amount of score information required for each base is one score each from the Match, Insert, Delete and EL states, or $4 \times w_s$. There is also an EL BRAM (not shown) for PE 0 located after the FIFO.

The PEs themselves are simple pipelined arithmetic units. They perform the addition and max operations required to calculate the scores for the DP table cells they are processing before moving on to the next cell in the next cycle. It is worth noting that although the current version with a two stage pipeline can run at slightly over 100 MHz, it is challenging to add more pipeline stages. This

is due to the various local dependencies for individual HMM states like EL and End. In addition to computing table values for the current cell, the PE stores the running best scores for the current base for long transitions. These include scores for EL, Begin and End.

EL states are a special case for a number of reasons introduced earlier. To summarize, EL states introduce data dependencies between nonadjacent cells. EL states also have a self-loop with a score penalty that transitions to the next base similar to an Insert state. In order to handle these irregularities, we introduce the EL memory. This memory is necessary because unlike the End state, storage for many EL scores could be required simultaneously. See Figure 5 for an example of how this could happen. In this case, a PE computing $M_4$ requires data from both $EL_1$ and $EL_2$. More complex models require storage for many more ELs. Furthermore, there are some situations with much greater EL fan-in. Although these situations are handled with a simple loop over the EL input states when computing a Match score in the Infernal software, that luxury is not available for an FPGA implementation. Instead, our design handles this problem by combining ELs in a tree-like structure while running along the model. The shape of this combination tree is computed in software and stored with the model information prior to a Viterbi run. This is possible because EL states are typically generated from states that pair in the CM, and physical limitations on the molecule shape prevent overly complex EL patterns. In fact, for many CP9 HMMs a stack would be sufficient for EL storage. The algorithm for EL combination is presented in Figure 8.

```
combineELs(ELMap)
Input: ELMap, containing list of all EL transitions
Output: ELCmd, containing EL memory and register
        commands for each CP9 HMM state

Convert ELMap to ELCmd equivalent (EL memory ops)
foreach link l in ELMap
    if l has only one destination state and
    if next l has only the same destination state
        remove l's EL memory ops from ELCmd
        add equivalent EL register op to ELCmd
foreach command c in ELCmd
    while c has reads from > 2 EL memory locations
        let wl be the origin state of data for reads in c
        sort wl by state
        foreach HMM state s starting at second state in wl
            if s has no EL memory ops (register ops are OK)
                add two reads (based on order in wl) to s
                remove those reads from ELCmd for c
                add write of combined data to ELCmd for s
                add a read of combined data to ELCmd for c
                terminate foreach
            if s = state of c
                insert dummy state after second state in wl
                terminate foreach
```

**Figure 8. EL Combination Algorithm for CP9 HMMs**

The EL combination algorithm above is capable of giving all states a maximum of one EL write and two EL reads, in addition to the use of an EL register inside the PE. In the FPGA, this translates to a pair of mirrored BRAMs for a total of one write port and two read ports. For an example of the algorithm's operation, see Figure 9. A represents the initial state after software EL states are converted into EL memory commands. States 4 and 7 both require three reads, so this is not a legal set of commands for our hardware. In B, after the EL register conversion has taken place, the extra reads on state 4 have been resolved. The register operations automatically combine EL scores and are represented with a dotted line. Finally, in part C, the first two EL reads in state 7 are reduced to a single read by doing an EL combination in state 5. Now no state has more than two reads and one write, resulting in a legal set of EL commands.

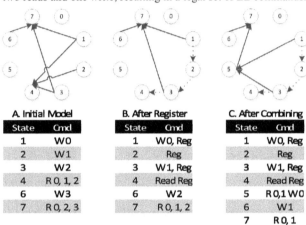

| A. Initial Model | | B. After Register | | C. After Combining | |
|---|---|---|---|---|---|
| State | Cmd | State | Cmd | State | Cmd |
| 1 | W0 | 1 | W0, Reg | 1 | W0, Reg |
| 2 | W1 | 2 | Reg | 2 | Reg |
| 3 | W2 | 3 | W1, Reg | 3 | W1, Reg |
| 4 | R 0, 1, 2 | 4 | Read Reg | 4 | Read Reg |
| 6 | W3 | 6 | W2 | 5 | R 0,1 W0 |
| 7 | R 0, 2, 3 | 7 | R 0, 1, 2 | 6 | W1 |
| | | | | 7 | R 0, 1 |

**Figure 9. EL Combination Algorithm Example**

Currently, two BRAMs per PE is not a limiting factor, as can be seen in the next section, but if it becomes an issue in the future it would be possible to double-pump the BRAM ports and use a single BRAM for each PE. Finally, although it is possible to conceive of a scenario where the dummy states inserted by the combination algorithm could have a substantial impact on runtime, or even make an HMM too long to fit in the Model BRAM, we have not yet encountered any Rfam families that require even a single dummy state.

## 4.3 Viterbi Results

Running at 100 MHz, the CP9 Viterbi implementation is limited by the available logic resources on our Virtex-6, as seen in Table 1. This is the expected result, given that each PE has many adders and max units. The current PEs make use of parallel maxes, a poison bit for overflow and other frequency optimizations that result in larger PEs. Determining the optimal tradeoff between frequency and quantity of PEs on an FPGA remains in the domain of future work.

**Table 1. Post-map Logic Utilization of Viterbi Design**

| PEs | Slices | LUTs | BRAMs |
|---|---|---|---|
| 4 | 14% | 9% | 13% |
| 16 | 27% | 15% | 19% |
| 64 | 67% | 43% | 42% |
| 128 | 97% | 77% | 73% |

The performance of the FPGA-based solution is very good when compared with Infernal. Figure 10 shows the speedup vs. Infernal 1.0 software running on a single Intel Xeon E5520 core and compiled using GCC -O2. Adding PEs to the system results in nearly linear speedup, and this is to be expected given that there is

no significant overhead. Speedup over Infernal 1.0 decreases as model size (shown in parentheses) increases, leveling out at around 230x. This is most likely due to inefficiencies in the software Viterbi implementation for very small models. Note that the median HMM model length in Rfam is under 100 states. This chart compares only the runtime of the Viterbi algorithm itself, not the entire FPGA and software systems.

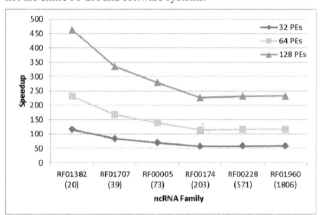

**Figure 10. Speedup of FPGA Viterbi vs. Single CPU Infernal**

## 5. CYK

This section provides an overview of the CYK algorithm, as well as details and results for the CYK FPGA implementation.

## 5.1 CYK Algorithm

To achieve high performance, Infernal's HMM filter stage removes the non-local dependencies in the ncRNA structure and simply looks at features detectable in a linear search. While this ignores important elements of the structure, the filter runs quickly and can eliminate most of the input data. However, the HMM will accept many regions that do not actually include the target ncRNA. Further filtering requires looking at the secondary structure of the ncRNA model for which we are searching, and is performed by the Cocke-Younger-Kasami (CYK) algorithm [21].

CYK is a dynamic programing algorithm, in some ways analogous to a three-dimensional version of Viterbi. Also like Viterbi, CYK is a general algorithm that can be used to parse any probabilistic context-free grammar in Chomsky normal form. CMs fit this description, as they are constructed using only a few rules of the appropriate form [6]. The CM directly represents the pairings and branchings found in the secondary structure of an ncRNA. This is done through Match Pair and Bifurcate nodes respectively. As can be seen in Figure 11, Match Pair nodes represent pairings of potentially distant bases in the ncRNA sequence, something the HMM model cannot support. In Hammerhead_3, the second and second-to-last bases are emitted by the same Match Pair node. Bifurcation nodes represent branches in the ncRNA secondary structure. Handling Bifurcations will require breaking the problem up into two smaller subproblems (one for the left branch and one for the right branch). Unfortunately, since each subproblem can use varying lengths of the target RNA, given that biological evolution can change the length of individual branches, we cannot know ahead of time where the split point occurs in the candidate sequence. This is solved by simply trying every possible split-point and picking the highest scoring match, a fairly time-consuming process. In Figure 11, the Bifurcate node takes place before the sets of Match Pairs that make up Hammerhead_3's two arms. This requires a Bifurcation state, because without one there would be no way to express two separate helices, or sets of paired bases. Instead, the Match state that emitted the U at the base of the arm would emit an A at the other end of the entire molecule, and the arms would be merged into a single arm with bulges in the middle.

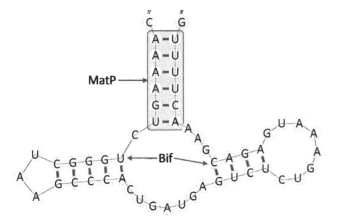

**Figure 11. Secondary Structure of a Hammerhead_3 ncRNA**

The CYK algorithm starts with a sequence of length N and a CM, and scores that sequence against the model with a better match resulting in a higher score. It converts this into a three-dimensional dynamic programming problem by creating layers of triangular DP matrixes, one for each state in the CM as in Figure 12. These matrixes are triangular because position $j, i$ in state S represents the best matching of states $S...S_{End}$ to region $i...j$ of the target sequence. It does not make sense to match to a region whose start is after its end, so entries $j, i$ where $j < i$ are useless. Emissions of single bases are achieved through Match Left and Right states, where Left states move up one cell in the DP matrix by subtracting one from $i$ as shown in Figure 12. Similarly, Right states move right one cell by adding one to $j$. The final dimension, $k$, refers to the state.

As the CYK algorithm proceeds, it works from the last CM state $S_{End}$ back to the starting state $S_{Root}$, and processes from small sequences of length 1 (i.e. squares $i$, $i+1$) towards longer sequences. The probability score for each subsequence is stored in the DP table to be reused without being recomputed. This process handles most parts of the model (including Match Pair) very efficiently, with only local communication. The one exception is the Bifurcation state. In this state, processing a sequence from $i$ to $j$ requires finding the best split point, mid, where $i < mid < j$. Since we don't know where the bifurcation point is in the target sequence, CYK must compute the highest score for all possible mids by maximizing the score($i$, $mid$, branch$_1$) + score($mid$, $j$, branch$_2$) where branch$_1$ and branch$_2$ are the states containing the total scores for the subtrees. The first two cells of this calculation are shown in Figure 12 and the equation can be found in [6]. This computation is very similar to matrix multiplication and requires $O(n^3)$ arithmetic operations for each Bifurcation resulting in a total CYK runtime on the order of $O(kn^2 + bn^3)$ where k is the number of non-bifurcation states, b is the number of bifurcations and n is the sequence length. Because of the expense of this operation, it can dominate the computation time for very large models as seen in Figure 13. In practice, the impact of Bifurcation states is not always as extreme as this chart makes it appear because over half of all Rfam CMs are under 100 nodes long.

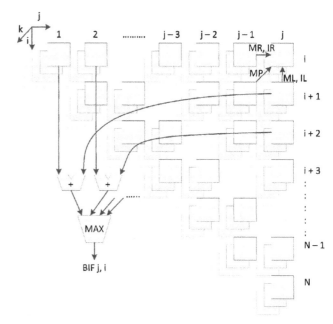

**Figure 12. CM CYK Three-dimensional DP Table**

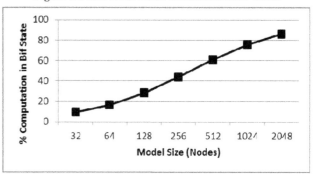

**Figure 13. Computation in Bif State Assuming 0.9% Bifs**

## 5.2 FPGA Implementation

Our implementation of CYK for CMs, diagrammed in Figure 14, is based around a linear array of PEs, similar to the one used for Viterbi. The most significant difference in the design is the use of off-chip memories. Because it has a three-dimensional DP table, CYK requires substantially more storage than Viterbi. By dividing the entire matrix into stripes and letting each PE handle a single column of the DP table as in Figure 16, most of this memory can be made local to the PE in the form of BRAM [17]. This method of striping the model is possible because, much like Viterbi, there are no non-local or backwards data dependencies for non-Bifurcation states. The calculations for a given cell in a non-Bifurcation state only require data from the same cell and its immediate neighbors from layers in the previous node. This means the computation wavefront is similar to Viterbi, and a similar arraignment of PEs inside the stripes is most effective. After completing one state for a given stripe, the PEs can begin work on the next layer. After completing all layers, the PEs begin work on the next stripe until computation is complete. Each PE contains many simple arithmetic units to update all states in the node simultaneously. This requires striping the state data across many local BRAMs.

49

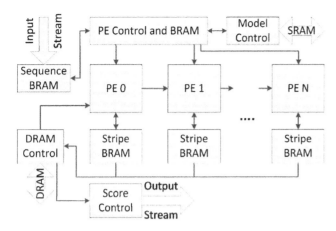

**Figure 14. CM CYK FPGA Implementation Block Diagram**

All of the DP cells for the current stripe can be stored in the local BRAM associated with each PE. Values from cells to the left can be passed from the previous PE. The values computed at the end of a stripe are written out to DRAM, to be reloaded when the same layer is reached during the next stripe. The only other time that DRAM storage is required is for one of the Begin layers prior to a Bifurcation state. Because the Bifurcation computation uses non-local data, it requires substantially more cells from DRAM. Figure 16 shows that PE operation is substantially different for Bifurcations and this requirement explains why. The row data used in the Bifurcation computation discussed in the previous section is streamed in from DRAM and passed from one PE to the next. Column data is loaded from BRAM as with other states. Every PE is equipped with multiple Bifurcation arithmetic units allowing for the use of multiple DRAM rows simultaneously, improving use of memory bandwidth for Bifurcation states. This can be seen in Figure 15.

Although the striping pattern is similar to [17], the novel aspect of this design is the parallel computation of the scores for an entire node. Eliminating the need of a layer in the DP table for each state (the standard implementation described in [22]), yields a substantial performance advantage for non-Bifurcation nodes. The parallel Bifurcation units in the PE confer a similar advantage for Bifurcation states. Increasing performance and memory operations, while keeping BRAM requirements constant, also results in better DRAM bandwidth utilization than [17]. Although this requires a larger PE, FPGA logic is not the limiting resource, as explained below. Our design also precomputes all memory addresses and other information required to access the model and DP table data and stores this information in SRAM, resulting in an extremely simple control structure. The resulting savings help to offset the increased PE logic.

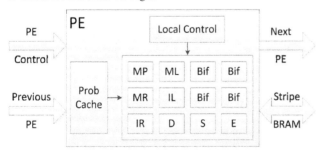

**Figure 15. CM CYK PE Block Diagram**

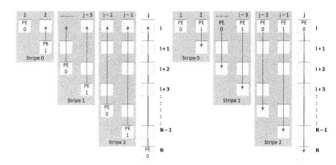

**Figure 16. Striping for Normal (left) and Bif (right) states**

The CM model itself can be much larger than the Viterbi model, and BRAM is the limiting resource for this design, so the model is stored off-chip. BRAM becomes the limiting factor because it would be impossible to achieve high performance if the data required by all stripes was loaded from DRAM. Our M-503 platform offers two 64-bit DDR interfaces running at 400MHz for a total of 12.8 GB/s of DRAM bandwidth. Ignoring the bandwidth required to load the data along the first row, each PE requires as many as four DP table values each cycle for Match Pair, Match Left, Match Right and Delete states. This means that again assuming a score width of $w_s$ the bandwidth required for a single PE is $4 \times$ FPGA speed $\times w_s$. Using $w_s$ of 21 bits [16], slightly more than Viterbi, and a speed of 100 MHz, this gives a requirement of about 1 GB/s of bandwidth for each PE. This result would limit our design to 12 PEs on the M-503.

When using the striped approach with BRAM there is sufficient DRAM bandwidth available and BRAM capacity becomes the limiting factor. Assuming a maximum sequence length of 6144 bases, reasonable given the length of CMs in Rfam, the BRAM requirement for the largest stripe becomes $4 \times 4096 \times w_s$. Again using 21 bits, this yields a storage requirement of 504 Kb. Given the Virtex-6's 36 Kb BRAMs, this would require 14 BRAMs for each PE, allowing 24 PEs per FPGA after accounting for other BRAM usage. This solution is clearly superior, with over twice as many PEs on-chip compared to a design that stores the entire table in DRAM. Another advantage is that as the PE clock speed increases the DRAM bandwidth would be able to support even fewer PEs.

Another way the CYK design differs from Viterbi is in the input sequence handling. For Viterbi, the sequence can be streamed in, sent to the PEs and then discarded. Unfortunately, this is not the case for CYK. Because the use of stripes results in each stripe requiring the same parts of the sequence, the entire sequence must be stored for reuse after being streamed in. The sequence BRAM, shown on the block diagram, serves this purpose.

The last significant CYK module is the Controller. This module contains the Finite State Machine (FSM) responsible for the CYK algorithm operation. The Controller also contains BRAM that stores model-specific instructions. These consist of a number of fields generated by software and written to the FPGA prior to accepting sequence input. Entries in this table include DRAM and SRAM addresses and lengths for each stripe as well as state and other model information for the stripe. The CM itself can be large and is stored in off-chip SRAM. The FSM currently follows a simple schedule of loading the stripe information from the controller BRAM, loading appropriate DRAM values and then executing to completion while writing values back to DRAM.

Future versions of the design could feature a more complex controller that performs some of these operations in parallel.

## 5.3 CYK Results

Running at 100 MHz, the FPGA CYK implementation is limited by BRAMs available on chip, as seen in Table 2. This is the expected result given the discussion of BRAM utilization in the previous section. Future designs may contain additional parallel logic in an attempt to achieve better performance with the same memory utilization.

**Table 2. Post-map Logic Utilization of CYK Design**

| PEs | Slices | LUTs | BRAMs |
|-----|--------|------|-------|
| 6 | 45% | 29% | 35% |
| 12 | 54% | 36% | 56% |
| 24 | 61% | 42% | 96% |

CYK performance shows much more unpredictable variation between different CMs than Viterbi, as seen in Figure 17. This is because the CYK algorithm's runtime depends on a number of factors other than model size, including the prevalence of Bifurcation states. In addition, the speedup from adding PEs is sublinear for some models due to the overhead of switching between stripes and computing scores for cells in the stripe that are not actually part of the DP triangle. This effect is substantially more pronounced in very small models because the average height of a stripe is much less. Overall speedup is still good, with a geometric mean speedup of over 60x for 24 PEs.

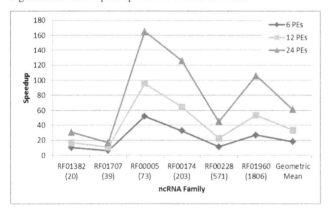

**Figure 17. Speedup of FPGA CYK vs. Single CPU Infernal**

To get an estimate of the performance of Infernal's final search algorithm, Inside, it is necessary to determine the number of Inside PEs that would fit on our FPGA. The large increase in size from a CYK PE to an Inside PE is due to the use of floating point (FP) addition. The CYK and Viterbi implementations avoid FP arithmetic and multiplication by using log-odds scores where those operations become integer additions. However, Inside requires addition of scores, instead of only multiplication, which is expensive in the logarithmic representation. For FPGAs, single precision FP addition requires approximately 20x more area than log multiplication (integer addition), which is still only half as expensive as log addition [23]. Based on these numbers, and our calculations showing that the CYK design becomes FPGA logic limited at around 80 PEs (logic, not BRAM, will limit Inside), a very conservative estimate for Inside would allow for 4 PEs and one sixth the speedup of CYK. This estimate is very likely

excessively pessimistic because the Infernal 1.0 implementation of Inside is also slower than CYK.

## 6. FPGA BASED SYSTEM

Although the performance of the individual FPGA implementations of Viterbi and CYK is important, the ultimate goal of this work is to accelerate Infernal 1.0 in a way that is useful to biologists and others in the field. To measure progress towards this goal, it is valuable to look at the performance of Infernal 1.0 as a whole. Infernal performance using the FPGA runtimes for Viterbi and CYK are shown in Figure 18. Although no novel techniques for integrating the accelerators into an FPGA system are currently modeled, one advantage of a system that uses FPGA implementations to accelerate Viterbi and CYK is the possibility to reconfigure a single FPGA to run both filters if multiple FPGAs are not available. A multi-FPGA system could divide FPGAs between Viterbi and CYK as required given that some ncRNA families spend more time in one algorithm or the other, as seen in Figure 18. This is due to a number of factors, including the filtering fraction achieved by each filter and the asymptotically worse runtime of CYK, which begins to dominate for larger models. The ability to reconfigure the same hardware and allocate resources as required for a wide variety of genomics applications gives the FPGA implementation an advantage over potential ASIC designs like [16]. Finally, many bioinformatics laboratories already have FPGA platforms installed.

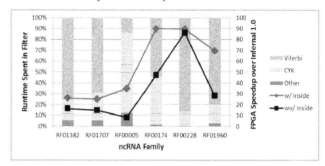

**Figure 18. Estimated Infernal 1.0 FPGA System Speedup**

The speedup here is less than that of the individual accelerators □ particularly without Inside acceleration □ for two major reasons. First, without an accelerated version of the Inside algorithm sequences that make it past both the Viterbi and CM filters must still run in software. Although a very small percentage of the sequence passes both filters, the Inside algorithm is much slower than CYK, so a substantial amount of time is still spent running Inside. This time is less than 10% of the total prior to acceleration, but dominates afterwards. The other reason for the reduction in speedup is that these results include all software tasks performed by the system, not just Inside and the two filters. Although for large enough sequences the time spent in these tasks becomes very small, averaging less than 1% of the total runtime for a 60 million base sequence, they cannot be ignored. It is also worth noting that the ncRNA families selected for this experiment tend to be among the more frequently occurring, so speedup would likely be better for a more typical family because Inside would have fewer possible matches to score. With estimated Inside acceleration, the expected overall system speedup is much better in the worst case. For tRNA (RF00005), a particularly unusual ncRNA, speedup improves from 8x to 35x.

# 7. CONCLUSION

This work presented an FPGA accelerator for the biologically important ncRNA homology search problem. The accelerator features FPGA implementations of the two filtering algorithms used by the Infernal 1.0 software package. The FPGA version of the first of these algorithms, Viterbi, gets a speedup of over 200x. The second, CYK, achieves a speedup of 60x over the software version. When combined into an Infernal-like system, we anticipate that these accelerators alone can run 25x faster than pure software. This speedup is limited by the fact that our current system has no accelerator for the Inside algorithm used as the final stage in Infernal's search pipeline. Given the results of our other accelerators, we anticipate that an Infernal 1.0 system featuring an FPGA implementation of the Inside algorithm could achieve a total system speedup of over 48x. To our knowledge, this is the first system to accelerate multiple stages of an ncRNA homology search pipeline, which we achieved using FPGA reconfiguration.

# 8. ACKNOWLEDGMENTS

This work was supported in part by Pico Computing.

This material is based upon work supported by the National Science Foundation Graduate Research Fellowship under Grant No. DGE-0718124.

# 9. REFERENCES

[1] J. P. Bachellerie, J. Cavaillé, and A. Hüttenhofer, "The expanding snoRNA world," *Biochimie*, vol. 84, no. 8, pp. 775–790, 2002.

[2] D. P. Bartel, "MicroRNAs: genomics, biogenesis, mechanism, and function," *Cell*, vol. 116, no. 2, pp. 281–297, 2004.

[3] J. S. Mattick, "The genetic signatures of noncoding RNAs," *PLoS genetics*, vol. 5, no. 4, p. e1000459, 2009.

[4] M. Esteller, "Non-coding RNAs in human disease," *Nature Reviews Genetics*, vol. 12, no. 12, pp. 861–874, 2011.

[5] S. Griffiths-Jones, S. Moxon, M. Marshall, A. Khanna, S. R. Eddy, and A. Bateman, "Rfam: annotating non-coding RNAs in complete genomes," *Nucleic Acids Research*, vol. 33, no. suppl 1, pp. D121–D124, 2005.

[6] S. R. Eddy and R. Durbin, "RNA sequence analysis using covariance models," *Nucleic Acids Research*, vol. 22, no. 11, pp. 2079–2088, 1994.

[7] S. R. Eddy, "Computational genomics of noncoding RNA genes," *Cell*, vol. 109, no. 2, pp. 137–140, 2002.

[8] E. P. Nawrocki and S. R. Adviser-Eddy, "Structural RNA homology search and alignment using covariance models," 2009.

[9] K. J. Addess, J. P. Basilion, R. D. Klausner, T. A. Rouault, and A. Pardi, "Structure and dynamics of the iron responsive element RNA: implications for binding of the RNA by iron regulatory binding proteins1," *Journal of Molecular Biology*, vol. 274, no. 1, pp. 72–83, 1997.

[10] Z. Weinberg and W. L. Ruzzo, "Faster genome annotation of non-coding RNA families without loss of accuracy," *Proceedings of the Eighth Annual International Conference on Research in Computational Molecular Biology*, pp. 243–251, 2004.

[11] E. P. Nawrocki, D. L. Kolbe, and S. R. Eddy, "Infernal 1.0: inference of RNA alignments," *Bioinformatics*, vol. 25, no. 10, pp. 1335–1337, 2009.

[12] T. Oliver, L. Y. Yeow, and B. Schmidt, "Integrating FPGA acceleration into HMMer," *Parallel Computing*, vol. 34, no. 11, pp. 681–691, 2008.

[13] N. Abbas, S. Derrien, S. Rajopadhye, P. Quinton, and others, "Accelerating HMMER on FPGA using Parallel Prefixes and Reductions," 2010.

[14] T. Takagi and T. Maruyama, "Accelerating HMMER search using FPGA," *Field Programmable Logic and Applications, 2009. FPL 2009. International Conference on*, pp. 332–337, 2009.

[15] C. Ciressan, E. Sanchez, M. Rajman, and J. C. Chappelier, "An FPGA-based coprocessor for the parsing of context-free grammars," *Field-Programmable Custom Computing Machines, 2000 IEEE Symposium on*, pp. 236–245, 2000.

[16] J. Moscola, R. K. Cytron, and Y. H. Cho, "Hardware-accelerated RNA secondary-structure alignment," *ACM Transactions on Reconfigurable Technology and Systems (TRETS)*, vol. 3, no. 3, pp. 1–44, 2010.

[17] F. Xia, Y. Dou, D. Zhou, and X. Li, "Fine-grained parallel RNA secondary structure prediction using SCFGs on FPGA," *Parallel Computing*, vol. 36, no. 9, pp. 516–530, 2010.

[18] S. R. Eddy, "Profile hidden Markov models.," *Bioinformatics*, vol. 14, no. 9, p. 755, 1998.

[19] G. D. Forney Jr, "The Viterbi algorithm," *Proceedings of the IEEE*, vol. 61, no. 3, pp. 268–278, 1973.

[20] Z. Weinberg and W. L. Ruzzo, "Sequence-based heuristics for faster annotation of non-coding RNA families," *Bioinformatics*, vol. 22, no. 1, pp. 35–39, 2006.

[21] D. H. Younger, "Recognition and parsing of context-free languages in time n^3," *Information and control*, vol. 10, no. 2, pp. 189–208, 1967.

[22] S. Eddy, "A memory-efficient dynamic programming algorithm for optimal alignment of a sequence to an RNA secondary structure," *BMC Bioinformatics*, vol. 3, no. 1, p. 18, 2002.

[23] M. Haselman, M. Beauchamp, A. Wood, S. Hauck, K. Underwood, and K. S. Hemmert, "A comparison of floating point and logarithmic number systems for FPGAs," *Field-Programmable Custom Computing Machines, 2005. FCCM 2005. 13th Annual IEEE Symposium on*, pp. 181–190, 2005.

# Accelerating Subsequence Similarity Search Based on Dynamic Time Warping Distance with FPGA

Zilong Wang[1], Sitao Huang[1], Lanjun Wang[2], Hao Li[2], Yu Wang[1], Huazhong Yang[1]

[1]E.E. Dept., TNLIST, Tsinghua University; [2]IBM Research China
{wang-zl11, hst10}@mails.tsinghua.edu.cn, {wangljbj, haolibj}@cn.ibm.com,
{yu-wang, yanghz}@mail.tsinghua.edu.cn

## ABSTRACT

Subsequence search, especially subsequence similarity search, is one of the most important subroutines in time series data mining algorithms, and there is increasing evidence that Dynamic Time Warping (DTW) is the best distance metric. However, in spite of the great effort in software speedup techniques, including early abandoning strategies, lower bound, indexing, computation-reuse, DTW still cost too much time for many applications, e.g. 80% of the total time. Since DTW is a 2-Dimension sequential dynamic search with quite high data dependency, it is hard to use parallel hardware to accelerate it. In this work, we propose a novel framework for FPGA based subsequence similarity search and a novel PE-ring structure for DTW calculation. This framework utilizes the data reusability of continuous DTW calculations to reduce the bandwidth and exploit the coarse-grain parallelism; meanwhile guarantees the accuracy with a two-phase precision reduction. The PE-ring supports on-line updating patterns of arbitrary lengths, and utilizes the hard-wired synchronization of FPGA to realize the fine-grained parallelism. It also achieves flexible parallelism degree to do performance-cost trade-off. The experimental results show that we can achieve several orders of magnitude speedup in accelerating subsequence similarity search compared with the best software and current GPU/FPGA implementations in different datasets.

## Categories and Subject Descriptors

H.2.8 [**Database Management**]: Database application – *Data mining*

B.7.1 [**Integrated Circuits**]: Types and Design Styles – *Algorithms implemented in hardware, Gate arrays*

## General Terms

Algorithms, Design, Performance

## Keywords

DTW, FPGA, subsequence similarity search, time series

## 1. INTRODUCTION

There is an increasing interest in subsequence similarity search of time series in many domains, such as database and knowledge discovery. For example, in a bridge health monitoring database system, finding the bridge vibration which has some specific patterns may help maintenance personnel predict the bridge cracking problem. In subsequence similarity search, a key subroutine is to measure the distance between the subsequences and the pattern. In spite of dozens of similarity distance metrics which have been proposed in the last decades, there is increasing evidence that the classic **Dynamic Time Warping (DTW) is the best distance metric** [4].

Due to its unique ability to recognize a warping pattern, DTW has been widely used in many domains, like robotics, astronomy, speech recognition, gesture recognition, biometrics or medicine [1][2][3]. However, the application of DTW is greatly limited by its computational complexity. To solve this problem, dozens of techniques and thousands of papers have been proposed to speed up DTW. One of the most effective methods is lower bound, which tries to prune off most of the subsequences based on the lower bound of DTW distance estimated in a cheap way[4][5][8]. Another one is computation-reuse [12], which tries to reuse the temporary data between the neighboring DTW calculations to reduce calculation. The other techniques includes early abandoning strategies [10], data indexing [7][9], embedding. All these software based techniques focus on reducing the calling times of DTW, instead of accelerating DTW itself, while the DTW calculation still takes too much time, **accounting for about 80% of the total time** [17]. Therefore, even with so many techniques and several orders of magnitude speedup, the whole subsequence similarity search is still the bottleneck of many applications [2] [3].

A recent work [10] combines all possible existing speedup techniques and achieved a very fast speed, which makes us believe that we have almost exploited all potential from software and we must turn to hardware if we want to get a further speedup. However, since DTW is a 2-dimension dynamic search, the high data dependency makes it not easy to be accelerated by parallel hardware. This may explain that in spite of the continuous interest in software speedup techniques, there are very few efforts exploiting the effectiveness of parallel hardware. Most of the existing hardware efforts are implemented in coarse-grained parallelism, i.e. they try to allocate DTW calculation of different subsequences into different processing elements, such as computer-cluster [14], multi-cores [13], or GPU [17]. Limited by the huge transfer load of subsequences, these methods cannot get further speedup, and they still do not accelerate DTW itself. The first and only implementation using FPGA [12] to accelerate DTW itself is generated by a C-To-VHDL tool. The lack of insight into the FPGA limits their achievement, and their work can only be applied in small-scale problems. Actually, there is still fine-grained parallelism potential in DTW, and we find that this parallelism can be only exploited by FPGA, instead of GPU or multi-cores. However, Unlike GPU or multi-cores, FPGA is considered to be not suitable for if-not-break algorithms because of the fixed pipeline structure, which means most of the software speedup techniques may not be able to be utilized by FPGA. To address these problems and to explore how FPGA can go further than GPU or other parallel hardware in subsequence similarity search, we propose the subsequence similarity search based on DTW distance on FPGAs. The major contributions of our work are as follows:

1) We propose a stream oriented framework for subsequence similarity search. Based on the assumption that we can do normalization on subsequence of a little longer length, we realize coarse-grained parallelism by reusing data of different DTW calculations. This framework uses a two-phase precision reduction technique to guarantee accuracy while reducing resource cost.

2) We propose a PE-ring structure for DTW calculation. Benefited from the hard-wired synchronization only provided by FPGA, the PE-ring can exploit all the fine-grained parallelism of DTW. The flexible ring structure allows on-line updating patterns of arbitrary length without re-compilation or re-configuration. Besides, flexible parallelism degree is achieved to do performance-cost trade-off.

3) Our work achieves significant speedup. The experimental results show that we achieve several orders of magnitude speedup in accelerating subsequence similarity search, compared with the best software and current GPU/FPGA implementations in different datasets.

## 2. BACKGROUND AND RELATED WORK

### 2.1 Subsequence Similarity Search

Subsequence similarity search aims to find a subsequence which is similar to a certain pattern from a time series, using the following definition:

A *time series* $S$ is a sequence of tuples: $S = s_1, s_2 ..., s_N$, where $N$ is the length of the whole sequence.

A *tuple* $s_i$ consists of sample time $t_i$ and sample value $v_i$: $s_i = [t_i, v_i]$;

A *subsequence* $S_{ik}$, which starts from $i$ and ends at $k$, is a continuous subset of $S$: $S_{ik} = s_i, s_{i+1}..., s_k$ where $1 \leq i < k \leq N$;

A *pattern* $P$ is a certain subsequence to be found: $P = p_1, p_2..p_M$, where $M$ is the length of the pattern.

Note that for a sequence of length $N$, there will be $N$-$M$ subsequences of length $M$, which are usually picked out by a sliding window. A distance metric is used to define how similar the two subsequences are. The DTW distance's definition can be found in Section 2.2. There are two kinds of subsequence similarity search:

***Best-match search***: Given sequence $S$ of length $N$ and pattern $P$ of length $M$, find the subsequence $S_{ik}$ whose distance from $P$ is the minimum among all the subsequences, that is to say: $Distance(S_{ik}, P) < Distance (S_{ab}, P)$ for any $1 \leq a \leq n$ and b=1 $\leq$ b $\leq$ n.

***Local-best-match search***: Given sequence $S$ of length $N$ and pattern $P$ of length $M$, find all the subsequences $S_{ik}$ whose distance from P is the minimal among their neighboring subsequences whose distance from the pattern $P$ is under the threshold.

We focus on the second one in our paper.

### 2.2 Dynamic Time Warping

DTW is a measure of the distance between two subsequences. Suppose we have two time series: $P = p_1, p_2, p_3..p_M$ and $S = s_1, s_2,$

$s_3..s_M$, where $P$ is the pattern and $S$ is the subsequence picked out by the sliding window. The DTW distance between $P$ and $S$ is defined as follows:

$$DTW(S, P) = D(M, M);$$

$$D(i, j) = dist(s_i, p_j) + min \begin{cases} D(i-1, j) \\ D(i, j-1) \\ D(i-1, j-1) \end{cases} \qquad (1)$$

$$D(0,0) = 0; D(i, 0) = D(0, j) = \infty, 1 \leq i \leq M, 1 \leq j \leq M;$$

where $M$ is the length of pattern, *dist()* is the distance between two tuples. Either absolute difference or squared difference is fine.

The calculation process of DTW can be illustrated in the following intuitive way: to align two sequences of length $M$ using DTW, an $M$-by-$M$ warping matrix is generated, with the $(i, j)$ cell being the distance between $s_i$ and $p_j$, i.e., $dist(s_i, p_j)$. The DTW algorithm aims to search for an optimal path from the left-bottom cell to the right-top cell, as shown in Figure 1. The accumulated value of the cells in this path should be the minimum of all paths. The accumulated value is defined as the DTW distance, and the path implies the mapping relationship between the tuples of these two sequences. In addition, researchers often constrain the path that it cannot deviate more than $R*M$ cells from the anti-diagonal, as the green line in Figure 1, which is called the Sakoe-Chiba band constraint [4]. $R$ can be seen as the allowed warping degree of the pattern, ranging from 0 to 1.

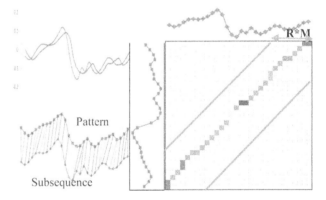

**Figure 1:** *(left-top)* **two similar time series;** *(right)* **search for the optimal path in the warping matrix;** *(left-bottom)* **the final mapping between two time series.**

Obviously, DTW is actually a 2-Diminson dynamic path search, whose time complexity is O($M*M$). For a sequence of length $N$, there will be $N$-$M$ subsequences of length $M$, so the time complexity is up to O($N*M*M$) for the whole sequence search. If Sakoe-Chiba path constraint is used, it is reduced to O($N*M*M*R$), which is still too large. However, DTW is considered as the best distance metric [4], since it allows the subsequence to have some stretching, shrinking, warping, or even length difference compared with the pattern. Many research efforts would like to use DTW, but find it very time-consuming [5,14,15,16]. Therefore, DTW is the right measure to accelerate.

### 2.3 Related Work

Accelerating DTW attracts thousands of research work in these decades, and almost all of them are software-based techniques.

Y. Sakurai et al. propose a computation-reuse algorithm called SPRING [11]. However, the data-reuse requires the sequence not to be normalized, which limits its applications. S. H. Lim et al. use indexing techniques to speed up the search, which need to specify the length of pattern beforehand [9]. E. Keogh et al. build a multiple index for various length patterns [7], which may be quite complex if the patterns have a wide range of length. Besides, no one can index on an infinitely-long streaming data. A. Fu, E. Keogh et al. try to estimate the lower bound of DTW distance in a cheap way, called LB_Keogh. If the lower bound has exceeded the threshold, the DTW distance also exceeds the threshold, so the subsequence can be pruned off. Although the lower bound technique is widely used and effective, the conflict of tightness and complexity limits the further speedup. The same research group claims to be able to search data even larger than all the other work in a recent paper [10], which can be seen as one of the best software implementations. It utilizes almost all the software techniques to do speedup.

All the former software techniques can be seen as pre-processing techniques, as they mainly focus on how to reduce the calling times of DTW calculation, instead of accelerating DTW itself. However, because it is too complex, DTW still costs a large part of the total time in many applications, which limits the further speedup of software techniques.

S. Srikanthan et al. exploit the possibility of CPU clusters to speed up DTW. They send subsequences starting from different positions of the time series to different processors, and each processor executes DTW calculation in the naive way [13]. N. Takhashi et al. choose multi-cores [14]. They separate different patterns into different cores, and each subsequence will be sent to different cores to be compared with different patterns in the naive way. As a subsequence consists of several hundreds or thousands of tuples, the data transfer becomes the bottleneck of the whole system in both implementations. M. Grimaldi et al. propose a GPU implementation [6] similar to [13].

All the former works using parallel hardware are implemented in coarse-grained parallelism, as they focus on how to separate different DTW calculations into different processing units. However, the cost of coarse-grained parallelism is very high. A sequence of length $N$ includes ($N$-$M$) subsequences of length $M$, If we would like to achieve a parallelism up to $W$, the data transfer bandwidth will be $W*M$ tuples/cycle, which will soon become the bottleneck as the $W$ or $M$ increases, so it is hard to get speedup from coarse-grained parallelism.

Y. Zhang et al. propose another GPU implementation [17]. Multi threads are used to generate the warping matrix in parallel, but they used another thread to do path search serially. This implementation exploits partial fine-grained parallelism of DTW itself. Because it separates the matrix generation phase and the path search phase into two kernels, it needs to store and transfer the whole warping matrix for each DTW calculation, which is also a heavy burden of the whole system. D. Sart et al. claim themselves to be "the first to present hardware acceleration techniques for similarity search in streams under the DTW measure" [12], and to the best of our knowledge, this is also the only work using FPGA to accelerate DTW. Their GPU implementation is similar to [13]. Their FPGA implementation consists of two modules: *Normalizer* and *Warper* (DTW calculation). Though their system is generated by a C-to-VHDL tool called ROCCC, based on their performance, we think the tool has smartly exploited the fine-grained parallelism of the DTW. However, the lack of insight into the FPGA makes their work suffers from lacking flexibility and scalability: it must be re-compiled if updated to a new pattern of different length, the data

precision is only 8 bits, and it cannot support patterns longer than 1024. Their work focuses on the naive subsequence similarity search, and do not exploit any pre-processing techniques, which also limits them to get further speedup.

# 3. ALGORITHM

Both software solution and our hardware solution share the similar algorithm framework, consisting of three modules: normalization, lower bound, and DTW calculation, as shown in Figure 2. In normalization step, we make two assumptions to enable the data-reusability for DTW calculation and guarantee the accuracy while using lower precision representation in FPGAs. We try to construct a hybrid lower bound structure based on the existing lower bounds techniques to do performance-resource trade-off in different applications. After lower bound's pruning, the rest subsequences are usually located in continuous interval, so we modify the SPRING algorithm to calculate the DTW distances of multiple continuous subsequences in single search.

**Figure 2: The algorithm framework**

## 3.1 Normalization

In some applications, the subsequences must be normalized to get a meaningful result, which is emphasized in some existing works [10][12]. This is mainly caused by the time-varying offset (or amplitude) of the sequence, which has a quite bad impact on the accurate distance calculation.

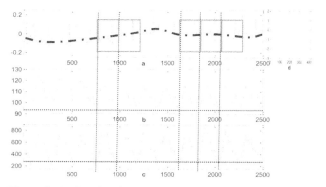

**Figure 3: (a) the blue line is the electrocardiogram (ECG), and the dotted line is the approximate offset; (b) the DTW distance without normalization, only five heartbeats can be recognized; (c) the DTW distance with normalization on subsequence of length $M$ (red) and $M$+$M$(blue), all the heartbeats have been recognized in both cases; (d)the pattern we want to find.**

As shown in Figure 3 (a), the offset of the heartbeat wave starts below zero, then goes up and finally descends. If we directly do DTW calculation without normalization, we can get a result like Figure 3 (b). Some correct subsequences are missed or some false subsequences are recognized, no matter how we set the threshold. If we do normalization just once on the whole sequence, we will find that the sequence has not changed, because the mean of the whole sequence is still about zero. The right way, just like what they do in [10][12], is to do normalization in every subsequence, for example, $S'_{i,i+M} = normalize(S_{i,i+M})$ and $S'_{i+1,i+M+1} = normalize(S_{i+1,i+M+1})$. In fact, it implies an assumption that the offset (or the amplitude) can be approximately seen as time-invariant in a short length of $M$, where $M$ is the length of pattern, so bad impact of the offset can be removed by normalization. If the offset can't be seen as time-invariant, we cannot get meaningful result even with normalization. This motivates us that it is the time-varying offset leading to the accuracy degradation, instead of the nonstandard offset itself. In fact, if several subsequences share the same nonstandard offset, the most similar one to the pattern will still be the most similar one to the pattern after normalization. Since our objective is to find the subsequence which is most similar to the pattern in a local interval, we can normalize these several subsequences once if they share the same offset. Although these subsequences' offset may still be nonstandard after such normalization, it makes no change to us to find the most similar one to the pattern. Here we make a little stronger assumption, which will be used in Section 3.3.

**Assumption 1**: the offset or the amplitude can be approximately seen as time-invariant in a little longer length of $M+C$, where $M$ is the length of pattern, and $C$ is a constant no larger than $M$.

With this assumption, we can pick out $M+C$ tuples once and do normalization on these tuples. Note that $M+C$ tuples include $C+1$ subsequences of length $M$, so we actually normalize $C+1$ subsequences once. The experimental results show that this assumption is effective in most real world time series. As shown in Figure 3 (c), the red curve is the DTW distance after normalization in every subsequence, which means normalized by every $M$ tuples, while the blue curve is the DTW distance after normalization in every $M+M$ tuples, where we set $C$ to be $M$. There is little difference between each other, but the correct subsequences similar to the pattern have been recognized in both cases. Anyway, the purpose is to find the similar subsequence in a local interval under the threshold, not to calculate the exact distance between the subsequence and pattern.

To reduce computation and process the streaming data, we do subsequence normalization based on the following equations:

$$\mu = \frac{1}{m}\left(\sum_{i=1}^{k} s_i - \sum_{i=1}^{k-m} s_i\right) \tag{2}$$

$$\sigma^2 = \frac{1}{m}\left(\sum_{i=1}^{k} s_i^2 - \sum_{i=1}^{k-m} s_i^2\right) - \mu^2 \tag{3}$$

$$s_i = \frac{s_i - \mu}{\sigma} \tag{4}$$

With formula (2) and (3), the mean and standard deviation of the subsequence in the sliding window can be updated only with the new-come tuple and the last tuple in the window.

Because floating point operation or wide fixed point operation cost much resource in FPGAs and most applications don't need such high precision, it's necessary to explore how many bits is enough to represent a number without sacrificing accuracy. Here we make another assumption.

**Assumption 2**: the subsequence can be represented with a shorten width fixed point number after normalization, that is to say, low precision number.

Note the fact that the dynamic range of the data is usually very small after offset removed and amplitude compressed, this assumption is rather trivial in most applications. We select "short" type (16 bit fixed point number) as the default data format, but it can be replaced by any wider fixed point number if needed. The experiment also shows that this assumption only leads to a little difference in distance, without sacrificing the matching accuracy.

Unlike lower bound technique or DTW calculation of the mathematical completeness, normalization is usually considered as an empirical pre-processing technique. There is no theoretical evidence that which normalization and how to do normalization is the best choice. For example, z-normalization as formula (4) is used based on the assumption that the sequence follows the normal distribution, while we can also simply set the maximum to be "1" as another kind of normalization. Whether we do normalization on the whole sequence, or on every subsequence, or on several continuous subsequences as assumption 1 is dependent on whether the accuracy can be improved. The time-varying offset (or amplitude) can also be removed by many other techniques, such as Kalman-filter, which is widely used in sensors for motion detection. However, we do normalization not only for improving accuracy, but also for the data representation in hardware, as shown in section 4.1.2.

## 3.2 Lower Bound

A classic way to speed up subsequence similarity search based on an expensive distance metric such as DTW is to use a cheap-to-compute distance to estimate the lower bound of the real distance[4][7]. If the lower bound has exceeded the threshold, the DTW distance will exceed the threshold, too. There are many lower bound techniques, and their tightness and complexity are all different. T. Rakthanmanon et al. propose a cascade lower bound, [10] consisting of LB_Kim [8], LB_Keogh [4][9] and reversed-LB_Keogh. The complexity of these three lower bounds is increasing as well as the tightness. If a former lower bound's result is not large enough to prune off a subsequence, the latter lower bound will be executed. As such if-not-break algorithm is not suitable for FPGA, we propose a hybrid structure consisting of LB_partial DTW (LB_pDTW), LB_Keogh and reversed-LB_Keogh. Actually, this can been seen as a combination of lower bound technique and early abandoning technique.

LB_pDTW is defined as the DTW distance between the partial subsequence and the partial pattern, for example, the DTW distance between the first X tuples of the subsequence and the first X tuples of the pattern. It can be seen as a strengthened version of LB_Kim. LB_Keogh constructs an upper envelope and a lower envelope, and accumulate the distance falling out of the envelope as the lower bound. Reversed-LB_Keogh uses the same algorithm as LB_Keogh, only reversing the position of the pattern $P$ and the subsequence $S$. The definition is as follows:

$$U_i = max \ \{p_{i-R}, p_{i-R+1} ... p_{i+R-1}, p_{i+R}\};$$

$$L_i = min \ \{\ p_{i-R}, p_{i-R+1} ... p_{i+R-1}, p_{i+R}\ \}; \tag{5}$$

$$D_i = \begin{cases} s_i - U_i & if \ s_i > U_i \\ L_i - s_i & if \ L_i > s_i \\ 0 & else \end{cases} \tag{6}$$

$$LB(P_{1,Y}, S_{1,Y}) = \sum D_i \tag{7}$$

where $1 \leq i \leq Y$, and $R$ is the parameter indicating the allowed warping degree, defined as the green line in Figure 1.

In our hybrid lower bound, LB_pDTW processes the first $X$ tuples of every subsequence, while LB_Keogh and reversed-LB_Keogh process the following $Y$ tuples. Note that $Y$ is usually set to be $M-X$, where $M$ is the length of the pattern. The final lower bound is defined as **LB_pDTW + max{LB_Keogh, reversed-LB_Keogh}**. LB_pDTW is a rather tight lower bound, but its time complexity is up to $O(X*X)$. LB_Keogh has the highest performance-cost-ratio, which costs only about $O(Y)$ time complexity to prune a lot of subsequences. The effectiveness of LB_Keogh highly depends on the parameter $R$, which is usually set to a small value, such as 5%~10%. If we set $R$ to a little larger value, for example, 20%, the performance will significantly degrade, and if $R$ is set to 100%, which is used in the classic DTW, this method will be absolutely useless. So a hybrid structure of LB_pDTW and LB_Keogh/ reversed LB_Kegoh can do performance cost trade-off with the ratio of X/Y.

With lower bound technique, we can prune off many subsequences whose hybrid lower bound distance has exceeded the threshold. As shown in Figure 3, if we set the threshold to be 40, only a small portion of the subsequences still need the DTW calculation, as the red star line shown in Figure 4.

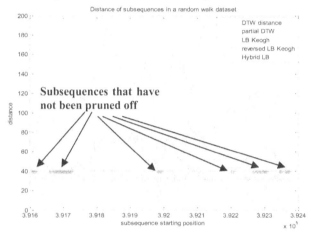

**Figure 4: DTW distance and different lower bound distance in a random walk dataset, where $M$= 128, $X$=10, $Y$=118, $R$=5%.**

## 3.3 DTW

Since candidate subsequences, which still need DTW calculation, is usually continuous, we can use a computation-reuse DTW algorithm, like SPRING [11], to calculate the DTW distance of multiple subsequences in a single search. In classic DTW algorithm, one $M$-by-$M$ warping matrix is generated for every subsequence. Note that there are $N$-$M$ subsequences of length $M$ in the whole sequence of length $N$, so totally $N$-$M$ matrixes are generated. In the neighboring two subsequences, for example, $S_{i,k}$ and $S_{i+1,k+1}$, only one tuple is different, which means that only one column is different in the two warping matrixes. Based on this data reusability, the SPRING algorithm modifies the boundary condition of the classic DTW, generates a single $M$-by-$N$ matrix and finds the matching subsequences only in one search. N paths grow from all cells in the bottom line of the M-by-N matrix at the same time, instead of only from the left-bottom cell, with extra labels recording the starting positions of the paths. The less similar paths will be replaced by the more similar paths when the paths grow. The SPRING algorithm is defined as follows:

$$DTW(S_{s,e}, P) = D(e,M)$$

$$D(i,j) = dist(s_i, p_j) + min \begin{cases} D(i\text{-}1, j) \\ D(i\text{-}1, j\text{-}1) \\ D(i, j\text{-}1) \end{cases} \quad (8)$$

$$Sp(i,j) = \begin{cases} Sp(i\text{-}1, j) & if\ D(i\text{-}1, j)\ \ is\ the\ minimum \\ Sp(i\text{-}1, j\text{-}1) & if\ D(i\text{-}1, j\text{-}1)\ is\ the\ minimum \\ Sp(i, j\text{-}1) & if\ D(i, j\text{-}1)\ \ is\ the\ minimum \end{cases} \quad (9)$$

$$D(i, 0) = 0; D(0, j) = \infty;$$

$$Sp(i, 0)=i;\ Sp(0, j)=0; where\ 1 \leq i \leq N, 1 \leq j \leq M;$$

Obviously, SPRING reduces the time complexity from O((M-N)*M*M) to O(M*N), which is a quite high speedup. However, some researchers reject this algorithm because if we do normalization on every subsequence, all the tuples are different even in the neighboring subsequences, thus the data reusability does not exist. However, as the assumption 1 in section 3.1, we can do normalization on $C+1$continuous subsequences, because the offset can be seen as time-invariant in a small interval. Then we can apply SPRING to $C+1$subsequences, e.g. the red-star-line shown in Figure 4, to achieve a coarse-grained parallelism up to $C+1$, as they are normalized with the same coefficients.

We slightly modify the SPRING algorithm to allow constrains R: In formula (8), the former $D(u,v)$ can be selected only if $u - R \leq SP(u, v) + v \leq u + R$, which means the current cell is in the constraint line. In boundary condition, $D(i,0)$ can be set to $0$ only if the current subsequence is *valid*, which means it has not been pruned off. Or $D(i,0)$ is set to infinite, too.

## 4. IMPLEMENTATION

### 4.1 System Architecture

The following figure is our hardware framework:

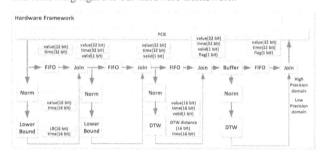

**Figure 5: Hardware framework of the whole system**

Compared with the algorithm framework in Figure 2, our hardware framework has two main differences: one is that we separate DTW and lower bound into two individual loops without direct connection; another one is that we place duplicate loops for both lower bound and DTW. In our system, $C$ subsequences are seen as a group, where $C$ is the constant in Assumption 1, and we set $C$ to be $M$, where $M$ is the length of the pattern.

Our system works as follows:

Firstly, the CPU sends the basic configuration information to the FPGA, for example, the normalized pattern, the threshold.

Secondly, the streaming time series will be transferred through PCIE to FPGAs. Each of the normalizer has a sliding window of length $M+M$, which is the total length of $M+1$continuous subsequences. The *normalizer* in the first loop picks out the first $M$ continuous subsequences and normalizes them, while the second loop picks out the next $M$ continuous subsequences. Then the two windows both slide in a step of $2*M$ tuples to prepare for the next calculation, just like a Ping-Pong buffer. The normalized subsequences will be represented by a shorter width number, before they are sent to *Hybrid Lower Bound* modules. Then the lower bound result will be joined with the original sequence, based on the sample time tag. In the *Join* module, if the lower bound distance has exceeded the threshold, the starting tuple of this subsequence will be asserted *invalid* with a label, which means it has been pruned off.

Thirdly, if a tuple with *valid* tag high is founded in the first *M* tuples of the sliding window of the third loop, which means this subsequence still needs DTW calculation, the normalizer will pick out all the *2\*M* continuous tuples in the window and do normalization. Then the *DTW* module will calculate the DTW distance for the subsequences which are asserted *valid*. All the first *M* tuples of the original sequence will be asserted "invalid" after they flow into the *DTW* module, indicating they do not need DTW calculation again. The DTW result will be joined with the original sequence, too. If the DTW distance is smaller than the threshold, the *Join* module will assert another tag *flag* high, indicating that this subsequence is what we want. If the DTW module is busy, the normalizer stops normalization until the DTW module is idle again, but still slides and updates the mean& standard, which means the original sequence flows without stop.

Fourthly, the whole sequence will be stored in a buffer and very few tuples are still asserted *valid*. The fourth loop works just as the third loop, but the first *M* tuples in the sliding window will be output to the last FIFO only if they are all asserted "invalid".

Finally, the sequence will be sent back to CPU tagged with label *flag* indicating which subsequences are the similar ones.

### 4.1.1 Four loops to guarantee streaming
The main reason for the duplicate loops of lower bound and DTW is that we try to guarantee the streaming processing. As we describe before, the first loop picks out *M+M* tuples and executes normalization and lower bound calculation on them. Only *M* subsequences starting from the first *M* tuples have been processed. If we place a duplicate loop, the second *M* subsequences starting from the second *M* tuples will be processed by the second loop. In this way, all the tuples can just flow through the both loops for once without stop. The third loop also tries to guarantee the streaming processing of the original sequence. However, as the DTW module is not implemented in full-pipeline and needs many cycles to finish the processing, so the last loop must work in a stop-wait way. An extra buffer is used, and the stream may stop before the fourth loop. Since most subsequences have been pruned off by the lower bound, the burden of these two loops is not heavy and usually can process the sequence in streaming. This can be seen as another kind of coarse-grained parallelism.

The main reason for separating the DTW and lower bound into two loops, instead of directly connecting each other in one loop, is that not all the subsequences need to calculate DTW distance as they may have been pruned off.

### 4.1.2 Two-phase precision reduction
The researchers using FPGA often encounter the precision problem. As floating point arithmetic or wide fixed point arithmetic does not scale well in FPGAs, precision reduction is often used to save resource cost. We try to maintain more precision in precision reduction. In our system, we separate the precision reduction into two phases. The first phase is executed by CPU, if the data are represented by floating number or very wide fixed point number, the CPU converts them into 32 bits fixed point number (shifted left x bits to maintain x bits fraction); and then send them into the *high precision domain*, which is used for data transfer, as shown in Figure 5. The second precision reduction phase is executed after normalization. With Assumption 2, the dynamic range of the values has been significantly reduced after normalization, so fixed point number of the same width can maintain more accuracy. For example, after z-normalization as formula (4), most of the tuples range from -1 to 1, and nearly no tuple's absolute value is larger than 2, no matter what the range of

the original time series is. So we can represent the subsequence with 2 bit for integer, 14 bits for fraction, and 1 bit for sign. Then the subsequence will be sent into the *low precision domain*, which is the data processing domain. Finally, all the results will be converted into a label, before they are joined with the original high-precision sequence. In the next time the subsequences need to be processed, they are normalized and precision-reduced again to make sure that the precision error will not be accumulated.

### 4.1.3 Support for multi FPGAs
A common solution to the scalability problem is to do performance-resource trade-off, i.e. support the large scale problem at the cost of performance degradation. This is a good feature, and is also what our system has. But what we can do if we don't want to slow down the performance even in the largest scale problem? The answer is to use more FPGAs (or other more devices like GPU). With this motivation, we design a loose coupling data path in our system. In fact, the data transfer between different loops only includes the original time series, tagged with two bits labels. The loose coupling makes it easy to use multi FPGA to get a further speedup. This is not a trivial or useless idea. It is very common that people would like to search for a very long pattern, for example, DNA chains. We can simply map the four loops into four boards. In fact, we can place more than one loops as same as the third loop to reduce the burden of the last loop and thus improve the throughput of the whole system.

## 4.2 Normalizer

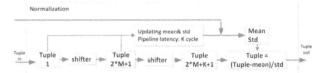

**Figure 6: Architecture of the normalizer**

As shown in Figure 6, all the tuples of the sequence will flow into the normalizer one by one. A RAM-based shifter is used to delay the sequence for *2\*M* cycles, and we use the input tuple and output tuple of the shifter to update the normalization coefficients (mean & standard deviation) in every cycle, based on Equation (2,3). As the updating of coefficients needs another *K* cycles, we use another shifter to delay the sequence for *K* cycles. Then at the $(2*M+K)^{th}$ cycle, if we assert the *enable* signal high for one cycle, the coefficients of the first *2\*M* tuples will be stored in the register *Mean Std*, and the normalizer will start to output the normalized *2\*M* tuples. In the same way, if we assert "enable" high at the $(4*M+K)^{th}$ cycle, the normalizer will output the following normalized 2\*M tuples.

## 4.3 Hybrid Lower Bound
Our hybrid lower bound consists of LB_pDTW, LB_Keogh and reversed-LB_Keogh, as shown in Figure 7.

Firstly, the subsequences will flow into the LB_pDTW module. In this module, we place a processing elements (PE) matrix, as shown in Figure 8, corresponding to the partial warping matrix generated by the first *X* tuples of every subsequence and the pattern, to calculate the partial DTW distance. Each PE only calculates the accumulated distance in one cell, based on Equation (1), for example, the PE (1,1) only calculate the distance between the first tuple of every subsequence and the first tuple of the pattern. In this full-pipeline way, this module can process one subsequence per cycle. We also use a max/min filter to generate the envelopes of LB_Keogh, as Equation (5).

Secondly, the following $Y$ tuples of every subsequence are sent to the LB_Keogh module, while the envelope of these $Y$ tuples will be sent to the reversed LB_Keogh module. The main structure of LB_Keogh/reversed LB_Keogh module consists of a multiplexer array and an adder tree: the multiplexer array is used to select the distance of the corresponding tuples as Equation (6), and the adder tree is used to accumulate the distance as Equation (7). Note that if $X+Y>M$, the redundant element will be masked; if $X+Y<M$, we actually use a partial LB_Keogh to replace the LB_Keogh.

Finally, we use *LB_pDTW +max{LB_Keogh, reversed LB_Keogh}* as the final lower bound.

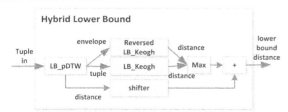

**Figure 7: Architecture of the hybrid lower bound**

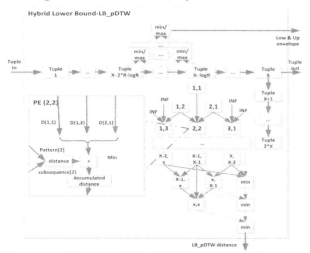

**Figure 8: Architecture of LB_pDTW. To make the figure clear, the connecting line between tuple delayed registers for tuple and the PE-matrix are not exhibited in the figure.**

## 4.4 PE-ring for DTW

Note that the SPRING algorithm only extends the warping matrix to *2M-by-M*, aiming to get multiple results with one search, but it makes no difference to the path search or data dependency. Based on Equation (1), it is easy to find that only the cells on the diagonals of the warping matrix, as the green cells in Figure 10, have no data dependency and can be calculated in parallel, with parallelism up to *M*. A trivial way to exploit this parallelism is to place a PE-array on the diagonals of the matrix. This way is used in [12], though it is generated by a C-to-VHDL tool. The PE-array structure exploits the full parallelism, but suffers from lacking flexibility and scalability. The parallelism degree (PD) changes in the starting phase, e.g. PD=1 at the first cycle and PD =2 at the second cycle, so the PEs in the array need to be frequently switched. The max parallelism degree must be equal to the pattern length and cannot be tuned, so we cannot do performance-cost trade-off and it cannot support long pattern limited by the logic resource. If a new pattern of different length is wanted, the parameter of the PE array's length must be modified, and the compilation of several hours may be unacceptable in real-time systems.

We propose a simple but effective PE-ring structure, as shown in Figure 9. All the PEs are connected one by one, and the temporal results are only transferred between the neighboring PEs. A multiplexer is used to send the pattern and the boundary condition into the ring in the starting phase, and then it is switched to the FIFO. The FIFO is used to buffer the temporal result of the last PE when all the PEs are busy. When the first PE is idle again, the FIFO sends out the temporal results to the first PE, acting as a delayed PE. A tuple router is used to route every tuple of the subsequence to the next idle PE one by one. A result router is used to route the final results of all PEs to the output port.

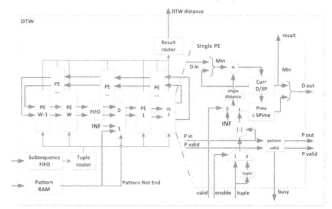

**Figure 9: PE-ring structures for DTW**

A single PE is only used to calculate one column of the warping matrix, as shown in Figure 10. With SPRING algorithm, the PE needs to record an extra label *SP*, indicating the starting position of the path, as the number in bracket in Figure 10. To finish the calculation of one column, every PE only needs the left and down boundary condition, as Equation (8,9), as well as the pattern. The left boundary condition can be obtained from the input port *D in* from the former PE, and the down boundary condition can be obtained from the delayed registers *Prev D/SP* of the previous result. The pattern only needs to be sent into the ring at the starting phase for once, and then all the tuples of the pattern flow around the ring without stop. In this way, all the PEs in the ring can surely obtain all the tuples of the pattern from the former PE.

We illustrate the process intuitively in Figure 10, where we have a ring of 7 PEs to search a pattern of length 7 in a sequence of length 14. At the 1st cycle, the first tuple of the subsequence, $s_1=8$, is sent into PE *1* from the router, along with the first tuple of pattern, $p_1=0$, from the *Pattern RAM* and the left boundary, INF. Then PE *1* records the starting position, $sp=1$, and starts to do calculation of cell *(1,1)* in the matrix. At the 2nd cycle, the second tuple, $s_2=1$, is sent into PE *2* from the router, along with the first tuple of pattern, $p_1=0$, from PE *1*, and the left boundary, $D(1,1)=8$, from PE 1. At the same time, PE *1* calculates cell *(1,2)* based on the second tuple of pattern, $p_2=5$ from the *Pattern RAM* and the left boundary, INF from the multiplexer. In this way, all the PEs in the ring start one by one at different time. At the 8th cycle, the PE 1 has finished all the calculation of the first column, and is idle again. Then PE 1 start to calculate cell *(8,1)* based on the 8th tuple of the subsequence, $s_8=0$, from the router. At the same time, the *Pattern Not End* signal is asserted low to switch the multiplexer from the pattern RAM to the FIFO, as the whole pattern has flowed into the ring. So the temporary results of PE *7* are used as new boundary condition to be sent into PE *1*, and PE 1 acts exactly as a virtual PE *8*. In this way, all the PEs finish the calculation, just like a ring rolling over the matrix. Note that here we just want to give out an intuitive working process of our PE-ring and ignore the latency of the real FIFO.

| PE | | PE1 | PE2 | PE3 | PE4 | PE5 | PE6 | PE7 | PE1 | PE2 | PE3 | PE4 | PE5 | PE6 | PE7 |
|---|---|---|---|---|---|---|---|---|---|---|---|---|---|---|---|
| P7=0 | INF | 26(1) | 19(1) | 23(2) | 16(2) | 12(2) | 14(2) | 12(2) | 6(2) | 14(2) | 17(8) | 11(8) | 12(8) | 14(8) | 12(8) |
| P6=5 | INF | 18(1) | 19(1) | 19(2) | 7(2) | 5(2) | 9(2) | 9(2) | 11(2) | 10(8) | 8(8) | 5(8) | 7(8) | 9(8) | 11(8) |
| P5=9 | INF | 15(1) | 22(1) | 18(2) | 3(2) | 5(2) | 5(2) | 9(2) | 7(2) | 7(8) | 4(8) | 7(8) | 9(8) | 11(8) | 17(8) |
| P4=10 | INF | 14(1) | 21(1) | 13(2) | 3(2) | 5(2) | 5(2) | 8(2) | 7(2) | 8(8) | 4(8) | 7(8) | 9(8) | 11(8) | 17(11) |
| P3=9 | INF | 12(1) | 13(2) | 7(2) | 2(2) | 4(2) | 4(2) | 7(2) | 14(8) | 4(8) | 9(8) | 6(8) | 8(8) | 10(11) | 11(14) |
| P2=5 | INF | 11(1) | 5(2) | 2(2) | 6(2) | 8(2) | 11(5) | 7(7) | 5(8) | 3(8) | 7(8) | 8(11) | 9(13) | 5(14) |
| P1=0 | INF | 8(1) | 1(2) | 4(3) | 9(4) | 7(5) | 9(6) | 6(7) | 0(8) | 8(9) | 9(10) | 6(11) | 7(12) | 7(13) | 3(14) |
| value | | 8 | | 4 | 9 | 7 | 9 | 6 | 0 | 8 | 9 | 6 | 7 | 7 | 3 |
| time | | 1 | 2 | 3 | 4 | 5 | 6 | 7 | 8 | 9 | 10 | 11 | 12 | 13 | 14 |

**Figure 10: Illustration of SPRING algorithm. The arrows imply the data dependency of DTW, and we can calculate the green cells in parallel; the red subsequence $S_{2,8}$ is the final result, as its final accumulated distance 6 is the minimum. The number in the cell is the accumulated distance, while the number in the bracket is the corresponding starting position.**

### 4.4.1 Why only FPGA can exploit the parallelism

In our design, each column of the matrix is calculated serially in different PEs, and the parallelism is obtained by multiple running PEs. One of the most important things supports us to do this is that we can exactly control the behavior of PEs in a cycle-accurate way. As PEs start one cycle by one cycle, they operate exactly on the diagonals cells of the matrix all the time. For example, at the $13^{th}$ cycle, PE 6 is calculating the cell(13,1), PE 5 is calculating the cell(12,2)...PE 7 is calculating the cell(7,7). In the next cycle, PE 6 needs the temporal result D out from PE 5 to continue its calculation, and PE 5 needs the temporal result D out from PE 4...Benefited from the hard-wired synchronization of FPGA, the former PE can just send the result to the output port, and the temporal result can be received by the latter PE in the next cycle. However, if GPU is used in this algorithm, different threads must be placed on the diagonals of the matrix to exploit the fine-grained parallelism, but the temporal result must be stored into the shared memory and be read out to the latter PE. The latency of memory and the extra protocol to prevent the memory coherence problem slow down the next thread to continue its calculation. The only solution for GPU is to transfer all the temporal results of the whole column to the next thread through the shared memory, but this means the next thread must wait until the whole calculation of the former thread is finished, which becomes actually serial processing. Besides, the huge memory access becomes another new burden.

### 4.4.2 Support for patterns of arbitrary lengths

In the previous FPGA implementation [12], the fabric of the PE array is fixed and the number of PEs in the array must be equal to the length of the pattern. If a new pattern of different length is wanted, we must modify the parameter of the PE number, re-compile the design and re-configure the FPGAs, which may cost several hours and be unacceptable in an on-line system. However, in our PE-ring, there are no constraints about the PE number or the pattern length. If the PE number is larger than the pattern length, the redundant PE will be idle without changing the structure. If the PE number is smaller the pattern length, the temporal result can be stored into the FIFO and wait until the next PE is idle, which slows down the performance but will not lead to function errors. In a single PE, the structure is also independent of the pattern length, as the PE only needs to know whether a tuple of pattern is *valid*, which can be easily realized by tagging the tuple with a label. So when a pattern of different length is wanted, we only need to write the new pattern into the *Pattern RAM*.

Limited by the on chip logic resource, the previous PE-array cannot support very long pattern, while our PE-ring supports almost infinite long patterns if the external memory used as FIFO is large enough.

### 4.4.3 Support for flexible parallelism degree

The ring topology hides the specificity of each isomorphic PE. PE 1 will become virtual PE $W+1$, and PE 2 will become virtual PE $W+2$, if there are $W$ PEs in the ring. Any PE in the ring can be removed without causing functional errors of the whole system, and the saved resource can be allocated to other modules, at the cost of linear performance degradation of the PE-ring. If there is abundant resource, a new PE can be simply inserted into the ring to improve the performance of the ring. The flexible performance-resource trade-off can be used to tune the bottleneck of the whole system.

### 4.4.4 Performance analysis of PE-ring

If we place $W$ PEs in the ring, and we need to find a pattern of length $M$ in a sequence of length $N$, then we can approximately estimate the worst throughput of our system, assuming that there is no lower bound technique pruning any subsequences.

As we pick out $M$ subsequences of length $2*M$ tuples from the whole sequence to generate a $2*M$-by-$M$ matrix, it will need $M$ cycles for one PE to finish the calculation of one column. If $W>M$, all the tuples can be sent to the PE-ring without stopping, as every PE only need $M$ cycles to process one column of the matrix. Considering that only $M$ subsequences are processed once, the throughput is $M/(2*M)$ tuple/cycle, and **1 tuple/cycle** for the whole two loops. If $W<M$, we can only send $W$ tuples before all the PEs are busy, and the next tuple must be sent at the $M^{th}$ cycle, when the first PE is idle again. This means the input rate is $W/M$ tuples/cycle. So we averagely need $2*M/(W/M)$ cycles to send all the $2*M$ tuples into the PE-ring. Extra $M$ cycles are needed to wait for the calculation of the last column of the warping matrix, because we are not sure whether the first PE is idle now and we use the worst case to do estimation. Then we need totally $2*M/(W/M)+M$ cycles to get the result of the $M$ subsequences, achieving a throughput up to $M/(2*M/(W/M)+M) = W/(2*M+W)$. As we have two DTW modules, the total throughput will be $2*W/(2*M+W)$ **tuples/cycle.** In our system, there are two rings, each consisting of 512 PEs. Our system runs at 150MHz, and we use 64 bits to store one tuple. So without the lower bound's pruning effect, the worst throughput is $1228.80/(2*M+512)$ GB/s if $M>512$, and 1.2 GB/s if $M<512$.

## 5. EXPERIMENTAL RESULT

### 5.1 Experiment Setup

Our system is implemented on TERASIC Company's Altera DE 4 Board with a Stratix IV GX EP4SGX530 FPGAs[15]. The board has an X8 PCI Express interface and is housed in an ASUS workstation PC with a 2.8GHz Intel i7-930 CPU, 16GB 1333MHz DDR3, and running Windows 7. The software program is also executed on this PC.

The resource cost of our system is shown as follows, with parameter $X=8$, $Y=512$ in lower bound, $W=512$ in DTW, and data precision is 16 bits. The following experiments are all conducted under this setting.

| Combinational ALUTs | 362,568/424,960 | (85%) |
|---|---|---|
| Dedicated logic registers | 230,160/424,960 | (54%) |
| Memory bits | 1,902,512/21,233,664 | (9%) |

The "TimeQuest Timing Analysis" in Quartus II 11.0 reports the frequency max is 167.8MHz, and we run it on 150MHz quite well.

## 5.2 Comparison with Software

T. Rakthanmanon et al. exploit almost all the possible software speedup techniques and got a high performance [10]. Their fast speed helps them to win the SIGKDD 2012 best paper award. So we choose their method as the best software implementation to be compared with. We download their open source program, and run it with different datasets. Unlike the parallel hardware solution in section 5.3, their software constrains the path with the parameter R, as in section 2.2. Although some other researchers insist that there should be no (or larger) constrain to improve the fault tolerance, they claim that the constraint should be as small as about 5% to prevent pathological warping. In our opinion, the constraint R is an application-dependent parameter. Though we test their program in cases that R is set to be a large one in some dataset, we only show the result as a comparison of computation power in extreme cases, not standing for that the larger constraint can improve the high level accuracy in these applications.

### 5.2.1 Dataset 1: random walk

Random walks are often used to model many applications. To avoid the difference of the random number generator and the seeds used, we use the existing sequence attached with their code [10] and search for the same pattern, which are both attached with their code. This dataset has 1 million points, and the pattern (query) length is 128. We try to modify the parameter R, which means we try to find patterns of different warping degrees, and show the result in logarithmic coordinates in Figure 11. Benefited from the great power of PE-ring structure in DTW calculation, our performance does not depend on the parameter R in the case that pattern length is shorter than 512, while their performance significantly decreases as R increases. We achieve two orders of magnitude (1.924s/0.008s=240) speedup in the case that R=5%, and four orders of magnitude (223.7s/0.008s =27962) speedup in the case that R=100%, which is the classic unconstrained DTW.

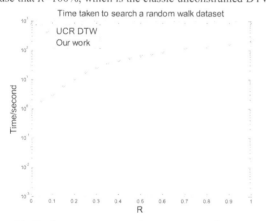

**Figure 11: Performance comparisons on a random walk data set, pattern length =128 (logarithmic coordinates).**

### 5.2.2 Dataset 2: medical data

This is a traditional domain in which subsequence similarity search is greatly needed, for example, temperature monitoring, electrocardiogram, motion monitoring, gesture recognition, etc. We download a dataset of electrocardiogram (ECG) from the web site of [10]. This dataset has about 8G points, and we need to find a pattern of length 421, as shown in Figure 3(d), with R = 5%. We get a 19.28x faster performance compared with their work.

**Table 1: Time taken to search one year of ECG data**

|  | UCR_DTW[10] | Our work | Speedup |
|---|---|---|---|
| ECG | 18.0 minutes | 56 seconds | 19.28 |

### 5.2.3 Dataset 3: speech recognition

Speech recognition is another domain where needs DTW as a kernel subroutine. We download the CMU_ARCTIC speech synthesis databases from [16], and construct a speech of 1 minute by splicing together the first 21 utterances of all the 1132 utterances. Then we get a time series of about 1 million points, and we randomly cut out patterns from this speech. Some of the software cases are too time-consuming that we don't finish the test in more than one day, so we do not list them. Note that in traditional speech recognition, DTW distance is usually defined upon some features, instead of time series, e.g. MFCC, which are extracted from the frames of the speech. As we only want to evaluate the subsequence similarity search, we directly search the pattern on the speech time series, without any feature extraction or other operations. We achieve two orders of magnitude (0.827s/0.008s =103) speedup in the case that the pattern length =128, R=5%, and three orders of magnitude (634s/0.6s =1057) speedup in the case that pattern length = 16384, R=5%. Larger speedup can be achieved in the cases that R is larger than 5%, for example, in the case that pattern length = 16384, R=20%, the speedup is up to 63432(31716s/0.5s).

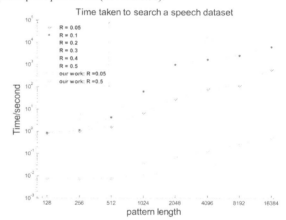

**Figure 12: Performance comparisons on a Speech Recognition dataset (logarithmic coordinates). Only the up bound (R=0.5) and low bound(R=0.05) of our work is shown to make the figure clear.**

In [10], they do best-match-search while we do local-best-match search in our design. When their work encounters a similar subsequence at an early position, the threshold will be significantly reduced to the distance between the current subsequence and the pattern, and then lower bound technique can prune off more subsequences in the following search. Therefore, the search speed is highly dependent on where the first similar subsequence is, and this explains their fast search speed in ECG data set, which consists of repeated heartbeats pattern. As we mentioned before, lower bound aims to prune off subsequences in a cheap way, so the larger constraint makes lower bound less-effective and leads to more calling times of DTW. Besides, the DTW complexity increases with square of pattern length, while the lower bound complexity increases linearly with the pattern length. They both explain the higher speed-up in the cases that the pattern length is larger or the constraint R is larger.

## 5.3 Comparison with Hardware

D. Sart et al. [12] claim themselves to be the first using FPGAs to accelerate DTW based subsequence similarity search, though their FPGA design is generated by a C-To-VHDL tool. In their experiment, a data set records a fluctuating voltage occurring when the insect's stylet penetrates the plant, called the Electrical Penetration Graph (EPG) signal. This data set has 1,499,000 points, and the pattern length is 360. They need 80.39s with GPU, and 2.24 seconds with FPGAs, for the whole search, while we only need 0.011 second, achieving two orders of magnitude speedup to their FPGA implementation, and three orders of magnitude speedup to their GPU implementation.

**Table 2: Time taken to search EPG data set**

| EPG data set | D. Sart [12] | Our work | speedup |
|---|---|---|---|
| GPU | 80.39s | | 7398 |
| FPGA | 2.24s | 0.011s | 203 |

The main reason for the huge speedup is that GPU can't exploit the fine-grained parallelism of DTW, as stated in Section 4.4; although their FPGAs implementation exploits the fine-grained parallelism, the lack of computation-reuse feature makes them lose the speedup from the coarse-grained parallelism, which is also up to *C+1 by SPRING*. Both of their GPU and FPGA designs do not use lower bound pruning technique, which also slows down their performance. Their FPGA implementation cannot support pattern longer than 1024, while we can support nearly unlimited long pattern, benefited from our flexible and scalable PE-ring. Besides, the parallelism degree of their work cannot be tuned, as discussed in section 4.4.2.

Y. Zhang et al. [4] propose another GPU implementation, which parallelize the generation of the warping matrix but still process the path search serially. We cannot access to their dataset. Besides, in their implementation, DTW based subsequence similarity search is embedded in feature extraction of the speech recognition application. So we do not have a direct comparison, but we try to evaluate our work in an indirect approach: they claimed their work is 2 times faster than the GPU implementation of [12], so our work should be about 3,699 times faster than theirs. The reason for the speedup is similar. Although the parallel generation of the distance matrix makes it a little faster than the former GPU implementation, the serial path search limits the further speedup.

## 6. CONCLUSION

In this paper, we propose a novel stream-oriented framework for subsequence similarity search, and a novel PE-ring structure for DTW calculation. The framework guarantees accuracy with two-phase precision-reduction while reducing resource cost. It uses lower bound technique to prune off most of the subsequence, and utilizes the computation reusability to exploit the coarse-grained parallelism of subsequences similarity search. The PE-ring exploits the full fine-grained parallelism of DTW while supports on-line updating pattern of arbitrary lengths. Besides, flexible parallelism degree is achieved to do performance-cost trade-off. We also analyze why only FPGA can exploit such parallelism. The experimental results show that we can achieve several orders of magnitude speedup in accelerating subsequence similarity search compared with the best software and current GPU/FPGA implementations.

## 7. ACKNOWLEDGMENTS

This work was supported by IBM Research China University Relationship Program, National Science and Technology Major Project (2011ZX03003-003-01), National Natural Science Foundation of China (No.61271269, 61028006), and Tsinghua University Initiative Scientific Research Program.

## 8. REFERENCES

[1] Adams, N., Marquez, D., and Wakefield, G. 2005. Iterative deepening for melody alignment and retrieval. *ISMIR*.

[2] Alon, J., Athitsos, V., Yuan, Q., and Sclaroff, S. 2009. A unified framework for gesture recognition and spatiotemporal gesture segmentation. *IEEE PAMI* 31, 9, 1685-1699.

[3] Chadwick, N., McMeekin, D., and Tan, T. 2011. Classifying eye and head movement artifacts in EEG Signals. *DEST*, 285-291.

[4] Ding, H., Trajcevski, G., Scheuermann, P., Wang, X., and Keogh, E. J. 2008. Querying and mining of time series data: experimental comparison of representations and distance measures. *PVLDB* 1, 2, 1542-52.

[5] Fu, A., Keogh, E. J., Lau, L., Ratanamahatana, C., and Wong, R. 2008. Scaling and time warping in time series querying. *VLDB J.* 17, 4, 899-921

[6] Grimaldi, M., Albanese, D., Jurman, G., and Furlanello, C. 2009. Mining Very Large Databases of Time-Series: Speeding up Dynamic Time Warping using GPGPU. *NIPS Workshop*

[7] Keogh, E. J., Wei, L., Xi, X., Vlachos, M., Lee, S. H., and Protopapas, P. 2009. Supporting exact indexing of arbitrarily rotated shapes and periodic time series under Euclidean and warping distance measures. *VLDB J.* 18, 3, 611-630.

[8] Kim, S., Park, S., and Chu, W. 2001. An index-based approach for similarity search supporting time warping in large sequence databases. *ICDE*, 607-61.

[9] Lim, S. H., Park, H., and Kim, S. W. 2007. Using multiple indexes for efficient subsequence matching in time-series databases. *Inf. Sci.* 177, 24, 5691-5706.

[10] Rakthanmanon, T., Campana, B. J. L., Mueen, A., Batista, G. E. A. P. A., Westover, M. B., Zhu, Q., Zakaria, J. and Keogh, E. J. 2012. Searching and mining trillions of time series subsequences under dynamic time warping. *KDD*, 262-270.

[11] Sakurai, Y., Faloutsos, C., and Yamamuro, M. 2007. Stream Monitoring under the Time Warping Distance. *ICDE*, 1046-1055

[12] Sart, D., Mueen, A., Najjar, W., Niennattrakul, V., and Keogh, E. J. 2010. Accelerating Dynamic Time Warping Subsequence Search with GPUs and FPGAs. *ICDM*, 1001-1006

[13] Srikanthan, S., Kumar, A., and Gupta, R. 2011. Implementing the dynamic time warping algorithm in multithreaded environments for real time and unsupervised pattern discovery. *IEEE ICCCT*, 394-398.

[14] Takhashi, N., Yoshihisa, T., Sakurai, Y., and Kanazawa, M. 2009. A Parallelized Data Stream Processing System using Dynamic Time Warping Distance. *CISIS* 1100-1105

[15] www.terasic.com.tw

[16] www.festvox.org/cmu_arctic/

[17] Zhang, Y., Adl, K., and Glass, J. 2012. Fast spoken query detection using lower-bound Dynamic Time Warping on Graphical Processing Units. *ICASSP*, 5173 – 5176.

# Video-Rate Stereo Matching Using Markov Random Field TRW-S Inference on a Hybrid CPU+FPGA Computing Platform

Jungwook Choi
Department of Electrical and Computer Engineering
University of Illinois at Urbana-Champaign
201 N. Goodwin Avenue, Urbana, IL 61801-2302
jchoi67@illinois.edu

Rob A. Rutenbar
Department of Computer Science
University of Illinois at Urbana-Champaign
201 N. Goodwin Avenue, Urbana, IL 61801-2302
rutenbar@illinois.edu

## ABSTRACT

We demonstrate a video-rate stereo matching system implemented on a hybrid CPU+FPGA platform (Convey HC-1). Emerging applications such as 3D gesture recognition and automotive navigation demand fast and high quality stereo vision. We describe a custom hardware-accelerated Markov Random Field inference system for this task. Starting from a core architecture for streaming tree-reweighted message passing (TRW-S) inference, we describe the end-to-end system engineering needed to move from this single frame message update to full stereo video. We partition the stereo matching procedure across the CPU and the FPGAs, and apply both function-level pipelining and frame-level parallelism to achieve the required speed. Experimental results show that our system achieves a speed of 12 frames per second for challenging video stereo matching tasks. We note that this appears to be the first implementation of TRW-S inference at video rates, and that our system is also significantly faster than several recent GPU implementations of similar stereo inference methods based on belief propagation (BP).

## Categories and Subject Descriptors

B.7.1 [Integrated Circuits]: Types and Design Styles—Algorithms implemented in hardware; I.3.1 [Computer Graphics]: Hardware Architecture—Parallel Processing

## General Terms

Performance, Design, Experimentation.

## Keywords

Video-rate stereo matching, Markov random field energy minimization methods, tree-reweighted message passing, Convey hybrid-core computing platform

## 1. INTRODUCTION

Stereo matching extracts 3D information from two or more images with different viewpoints. This fundamental problem has been studied for many years in computer vision and appears in a wide variety of applications. For example, the desire for video-rate stereo matching comes from applications as diverse as gesture recognition [2] and automotive navigation [3]. Because our

broader interests focus on hardware acceleration of statistical *inference* methods in *machine learning* (ML) problems, we choose solution methods that treat this problem as an inference task on video frames treated as *probabilistic graphical models* [4]. Thus, we formulate the stereo matching problem as energy minimization over a parameterized undirected graph called a *Markov Random Field* (MRF), which can be solved using statistical inference algorithms such as Graph Cuts [5] and Belief Propagation (BP) [6].

There is an extensive literature on MRF inference-based attacks on the stereo matching problem [7,8,9,10]. Algorithmically, there are broad tradeoffs available between result quality and speed, and heuristics for speeding up these methods (both domain-specific and domain-independent) are the subject of broad interest (e.g., [11,12]).

Nevertheless, software implementations of popular global inference methods are just too slow for high-quality video tasks. This is one significant motivation for hardware (which has a quite long history for this application, e.g., [13]). Custom hardware implementations of message passing algorithms that implement variants of BP have recently appeared ([14,15,16]) as have some GPU implementations ([16,17,18]). We have chosen to implement a particularly challenging BP method known as *sequential tree-reweighted* inference (TRW-S, [19,20]). Broadly speaking, BP methods are attractive because they are very parallel and easy to implement. However, they often fail to converge to a useful answer. TRW-S is a recent theoretical advance that avoids many of these convergence problems – but does so with an explicitly sequential computational process. Thus, we showed in [1] how the core message-passing update of TRW-S could be effectively parallelized for single-frame stereo tasks. In this paper, we describe the missing steps in [1] – hardware/software partitioning, data preprocessing, IO issues, macro-level pipelining and parallelism, mapping to multiple FPGAs – needed to build a working stereo video system.

The organization of the rest of the paper is as follows. In section 2, we briefly introduce background about our stereo matching technique, MRF inference as energy minimization, and our target hybrid-core computing platform. Then, implementation issues for a video-rate stereo matching system are discussed in section 3. The overall architecture of our stereo matching system and the details about its components are described in section 4, followed by the experimental results and the conclusion in section 5 and 6, respectively.

## 2. BACKGROUND

In this section, we will explain how MRF inference maps to an energy minimization method for the stereo matching problem. In particular, we describe the preprocessing part of this method, which is necessary for the standalone stereo matching system: the MRF parameter computation. Also we introduce the Convey HC-1 hybrid-core computing device used for our target platform.

## 2.1 Stereo Matching as MRF Energy Minimization

Stereo matching can be formulated as a *maximum a posteriori* (MAP) discrete-label inference problem, where we seek the most probable disparity labels, whose values are related to the depth, for all the pixels given the left and right images. This MAP problem can be formulated in terms of the parameters defined on an undirected grid graph (i.e., a grid MRF), where nodes ($\mathcal{V}$) of the graph correspond to the pixels and edges ($\mathcal{E}$) are assigned between all four pairs of neighboring vertical/horizontal nodes. Here, a node represents a random variable that encodes the probability of each label being selected as the best one for each pixel, and an edge explains the probabilistic relationship between two neighboring pixels [7,8]. It is numerically convenient to transform from probabilities to $-log$(Probability), which we refer to as *energy*; the probability maximization problem then becomes an energy minimization problem as follows:

$$\min_{l} E(\boldsymbol{l}) = \min_{l} \left\{ \sum_{s \in \mathcal{V}} d_s(l_s) + \sum_{(s,t) \in \mathcal{E}} V_{st}(l_s, l_t) \right\}, \quad (1)$$

where $d_s(l_s)$ and $V_{st}(l_s, l_t)$ are parameters which penalize certain choices of labels $\boldsymbol{l}$, and are called the *data cost* and the *smoothness cost*, respectively. $d_s(l_s)$ is related to the likelihood of a disparity label $l_s$ being assigned to the node $s$ and $V_{st}(l_s, l_t)$ models the prior preference of two neighboring nodes, defined on edge $(s,t)$, to have similar labels. For example, a label $l_s$ is less likely to be selected if the value of $d_s(l_s)$ is large, and labels $l_s$ and $l_t$ tend to agree if the value of $V_{st}(l_s, l_t)$ is large. The goal of (1) is to find the set of labels $\boldsymbol{l}$ such that minimizes the overall summation over $d_s(l_s)$ and $V_{st}(l_s, l_t)$ terms (i.e., energy) among all possible per-pixel label choices.

The energy minimization problem (1) can be solved efficiently using message passing algorithms, and one of the most popular algorithms in hardware implementation is *belief propagation* (BP) [7,8]. In BP, a node tells its neighbor about its "belief" of which label is the most probable by passing "messages". Thus, a message is a vector of size $|l_s|$, whose values correspond to the probability of the label not being chosen (recall that these values mean the "cost"). For inference of the best label assignment, BP repeats updating the messages until they converge. The best label for each node can be chosen based on the messages from its neighbors. Since message passing is neighbor pixel local and highly parallelizable, BP is widely used in custom hardware and GPU implementations [14,15,16,17,18].

However, simple loopy BP on stereo matching problems does not produce the best disparity labeling results in practice ([10]) and can occasionally diverge. Thus, we chose instead *sequential tree reweighted message passing* (TRW-S), which shows superior quality thanks to an attractive convergence property for its sequential order of update [19,20]. To overcome this intrinsic sequential characteristic of TRW-S, we introduced a novel streaming TRW-S hardware architecture which parallelizes the update order to perform message update of multiple nodes in a diagonal row in the stereo image [1]. This streaming architecture achieves high throughput and maintains the convergence property at the same time. Thus, we start with our novel message passing from [1] as the core MRF inference engine.

## 2.2 MRF Parameter Computation

The message passing architecture of [1] assumes that the MRF for each frame is properly initialized with a set of complex data and smoothness costs. So, as prologue to MRF inference, we must first compute these MRF parameters defined in (1).

For stereo matching, the data cost models the (dis)similarity between a pixel in one image, and each of several horizontally displaced pixels in the other image. The depth (disparity) information we seek is recovered from this horizontal separation between where a left-image pixel is to be found in the right image. For data cost, we employ the sampling insensitive matching model of [21]. When comparing dissimilarity of one pixel $s$ in the left image $I_L$ and a pixel $s' = (s - l_s)$ displaced by distance $l_s$ in the right image $I_R$, we first compute interpolated pixel intensity values for neighbor pixels as follows:

$$I_L^- = \frac{1}{2}\big(I_L(s), I_L(s-1)\big), \quad (2.a)$$

$$I_L^+ = \frac{1}{2}\big(I_L(s), I_L(s+1)\big), \quad (2.b)$$

$$I_R^- = \frac{1}{2}\big(I_R(s'), I_R(s'-1)\big), \quad (2.c)$$

$$I_R^+ = \frac{1}{2}\big(I_R(s'), I_R(s'+1)\big). \quad (2.d)$$

These interpolated intensity values are used to compute the intensity difference of two pixels $s$ and $s'$ as follows:

$$di_L(s,s') = \max\big\{0, I_L(s) - I_{R\_max}, I_{R\_min} - I_L(s)\big\}, \quad (3.a)$$

$$di_R(s,s') = \max\big\{0, I_R(s') - I_{L\_max}, I_{L\_min} - I_R(s')\big\}, \quad (3.b)$$

where $I_{min}$ and $I_{max}$ are $\min\{I^-, I^+, I\}$ and $\max\{I^-, I^+, I\}$, respectively. Then, the dissimilarity vector for the node $s$ (which contains one element for each possible disparity label) is computed as:

$$d_s(l_s) = \min\{0, di_L(s, s - l_s), di_R(s, s - l_s)\}. \quad (4)$$

Note that $d_s(l_s)$ is a vector of costs measured from pixel $s$ in the left image to the horizontally displaced pixel $s' = s - l_s$ in the right image. It is shown in [22] that this matching cost is well suited to MRF inference since it corrects blurring effects.

The smoothness cost models the fact that neighbor pixels are more likely to have the same (or similar) depth, because most pixels are not boundary edges in the resulting disparity map. We use truncated smoothness functions with image boundary information considered as follows:

$$V_{st}(l_s, l_t) = w_{st} \cdot \min\{|l_s - l_t|^k, V_{max}\}, \quad (5)$$

where $k$ is 1 or 2, $V_{max}$ is the maximum smoothness cost, and $w_{st}$ is a per-edge weight. The smoothness cost is limited by $V_{max}$ in order to allow disagreement in labels between two nodes across the object boundary in the image. In addition, the per-edge weight is not set only for the case where the gradient of image intensity is larger than a threshold, which implies the existence of the boundaries. Note that $w_{st}$ exists for every edge. Thus there are weights in four directions from one node. [8] shows that including

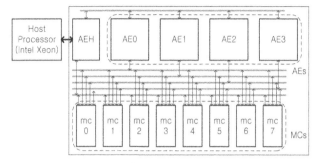

**Figure 1. Overall architecture of Convey HC-1 ([23]).**

lower-level visual cues such as object boundary information in the smoothness cost improves stereo matching. Thus, we use truncated functions with the gradient cues as our smoothness cost.

## 2.3 Hybrid Multicore+FPGA Platform

Our implementation targets a Convey HC-1 hybrid-core computing system containing an Intel Xeon dual core processor and four Xilinx Virtex-5 (V5LX330) FPGAs [23]. Figure 1 shows the overall architecture [23]. The FPGA-fabric consists of three major parts: the application engine hub (AEH) which interfaces the Xeon to the FPGAs; the memory controllers (MCs); and the FPGAs themselves, which Convey refers to as *application engines* (AEs). Each FPGA is connected to eight MCs, which control 16 DRAM DIMMs to provide 20Gbyte/sec (or 1Kbit/cycle) of memory bandwidth per FPGA.

The platform also provides a single, cache-coherent virtual memory system across both the host processor and the FPGA fabric [24]. Any data written by any host processor core can be used in any FPGA through the front side bus (FSB), and vice versa. This flexibility offers a broad space of hardware-software partitioning tradeoffs to the designer; we shall explore this next.

## 3. PARTITIONING & MAPPING ISSUES

In this section, we discuss issues of partitioning the stereo matching computations onto the platform, and mapping options that exploit both parallelism and pipelining that allow us to move from single frame [1] to full video-rate computation.

### 3.1 Hardware/Software Partitioning

Given the hybrid-core platform, it is important to determine which computations will be accelerated by the FPGA hardware. The overall procedure of running video stereo matching is as follows:

```
Initialize
For (idx=0; idx<numFrame; idx=idx+1)
Begin
    Get left and right frame images            (5.a)
    Compute MRF parameters                     (5.b)
    Run MRF energy minimization algorithm      (5.c)
    Obtain the best labeling result            (5.d)
    Produce disparity map frame                (5.e)
End
```

It is straightforward to determine the partitioning for (5.a), (5.c), (5.d) and (5.e). It is shown in [1] that (5.c) can be done at high speed using a custom hardware implementation of TRW-S. Also, (5.a) and (5.d,e) can be done by the host processor to exploit widely used image processing libraries [25,26].

However, (5.b) can be done either by the host processor or in FPGAs. But there are two advantages in putting (5.b) in FPGA.

First, we can parallelize the computation of MRF parameters, since the computations of the matching cost and the cues for one disparity label of a node are *independent* of the computations of all *other* labels. Thus, it is advantageous to utilize the parallel hardware resources in the FPGAs.

Second, we can reduce the size of data transferring from the host processor to the custom hardware. The input data for [1] are the parameters of a graph, which consist of a vector of size equal to the number of disparity labels for each node. For example, if the input images are of width $W$ and height $H$ pixels, and the number of labels is $nD$, then the number of parameters transferred is $W*H*nD$. In contrast, if (5.b) is done in hardware, we need to transfer only the pixel intensity of two images, which is $W*H*2$(left and right images)*3(for red, green and blue intensity). Since the bit-width of a parameter (= 64bits) is much larger than the 8bit color intensity, and the number of disparity levels $nD$ is usually greater than 6, the size of the data that the host processor needs to transfer is much reduced if (5.b) is done in hardware. According to our experiments, total time for the execution of (5.b) and the data transfer is reduced to about 3% if it is partitioned onto FPGA.

### 3.2 Frame Level Parallelism

In section 3.1, we discussed pixel and label-wise parallelism for computation of MRF parameters. We can further speed-up the stereo matching by utilizing the multiple FPGAs available on the platform. For example, we can process two frames of stereo input in parallel by implementing two inference engines on two different FPGAs. Note that each FPGA has its own memory bandwidth of 20GB/sec. Thus, we can simply put the MRF parameters for two image frames in a different location of the shared memory and then run the two inference engines independently. Thus, a multiple-FPGA stereo matching system is attractive since 1) the frame level parallelism is obvious and easily accessible in this video application, and 2) larger memory bandwidth can be utilized by employing multiple FPGAs, which is the prime bottleneck of performance in [1].

### 3.3 Pipelining the Stereo Matching

The stereo matching procedure can be decomposed into three groups of tasks: input data preparation (5.a); inference (5.b,c); and the output data processing (5.d,e). The next obvious question is how to *overlap* the execution time of these groups. Since the inference is done in hardware, the host processor is available while the FPGA is busy in doing inference. Thus, we can apply basic software pipelining ([27]) so that the FPGA performs inference for the current frame while the host processor is preparing the input for the next frame, as well as processing the labeling results of the previous frame.

It is not difficult to see that we can combine this functional pipelining and the frame level parallelism to achieve the most speed-up. However, there is a balancing issue: the more frames that are processed by the inference engines in parallel, the longer time it takes to manage the input and output data of the inference. If the time for input and output data management is shorter than the time for parallel inference, the total stereo matching time can be reduced because the time for data preparation can be overlapped with the inference. But if the number of frames processed in parallel is too large, then the time for data management becomes dominant in the entire execution, and the benefit of exploiting multiple FPGAs vanishes. Therefore, it is important to make the two balanced.

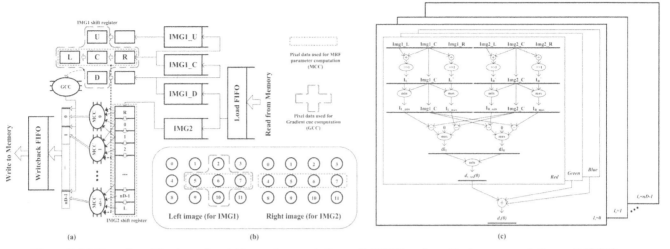

**Figure 2. (a)** Overall architecture of matching cost computation unit (MCC) and gradient cue computation unit (GCC). **(b)** Example of image data. Nodes (circles with numbers) inside the red dotted line and blue dotted line are used as input for MCC and GCC, respectively. **(c)** Detailed architecture of MCC.

## 4. VIDEO-RATE SYSTEM DESIGN

In this section, we describe the detailed architectures of our custom FPGA accelerators as well as the parallel and the function level pipelined processing of image frames in our stereo system.

### 4.1 Streaming TRW-S Inference Hardware

Our streaming TRW-S hardware (STRM_TRWS) is an FPGA implementation of the message update MRF inference algorithm from [1]. STRM_TRWS employs a novel diagonal ordering of MRF nodes to update messages in a deep pipeline and utilizes FIFO interfaces to access memory in a streaming manner for high throughput. Input data consists of the data cost and the gradient cues, which are packed along with the bits for the messages and the most likely label. The messages and the best label for each node are updated during the inference. The STRM_TRWS performs a core role in our stereo matching system; we refer the reader to [1] for details.

### 4.2 Matching Cost and Gradient Cue Units

The matching cost and the gradient cues are computed independently using a *Matching Cost Computation* unit (MCC) and a *Gradient Cue Computation* unit (GCC). To exploit the maximum parallelism, the MCC is designed to be label-wise and color-wise parallel, and the GCC is designed to be color-wise and direction-wise parallel. Thus, the MCC reads three (left, center, right) pixel data from the left image and $(nD+2)$ pixel data from the right image for the $nD$ label data cost. The GCC reads five pixels of intensity data to compute gradient of intensity in four directions (right, down, left, and up) from the center node.

FIFOs and shift registers are utilized to feed the required pixel data from the left (IMG1) and the right images (IMG2). Figure 2(a) shows the overall architecture of the MCC and the GCC. The (red, green, blue) pixel data for both left and right images are loaded from shared memory and fetched into the IMG1 and IMG2 FIFOs. There are three FIFOs for IMG1: IMG1_U, IMG1_C, and IMG_D. These IMG1 FIFOs are managed to temporarily store the pixel data for the up, center, and down rows of the left image, which are fetched from the memory in row-major order. For example, if all the pixels in the left image of Figure 2(b) are loaded, IMG1_U, IMG1_C, and IMG_D will contain data for pixels {0,1,2,3}, {4,5,6,7}, and {8,9,10,11},

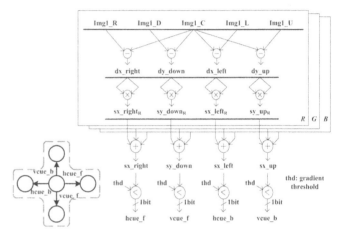

**Figure 3. Detailed architecture of GCC.**

respectively. Also, the IMG2 FIFO temporarily stores the pixel data from the right image. The IMG1 and IMG2 FIFO depths are sized as the width of the image to align the pixel data by the rows of the image.

The pixel data stored in the IMG1 and IMG2 FIFOs are used to fill the shift registers. The depth of the IMG1 shift register is 3, since the MCC and the GCC require only the center pixel from IMG1 along with its right and left neighbors. On the other hand, the depth of IMG2 shift register is $nD+2$, since the MCC requires three (left, center, right) pixel data for each $nD$ label. For example, if $nD=2$ and the pixel 6 in Figure 2(b) is the center pixel, the MCC_0 and the MCC_1 read {5,6,7} and {4,5,6} for IMG2 to compute $d_6(0)$ and $d_6(1)$, respectively.

Figure 2(c) shows the detailed hardware architecture of the MCC. As discussed before, the matching cost of each color for all the labels are computed in parallel, and then merged at the last stage to generate a vector of data cost with the size of $nD$. The computations are equivalent to (2,3,4) in section 2.2, which are pipelined to maximize the throughput as well as to reduce the critical path.

Figure 3 shows the detailed architecture of the GCC. The color intensity values are subtracted (*dx_right, dy_down, dx_left, and dy_up*) and squared (*sx_right, sy_down, sx_left, and sy_up*) to

**Table 1. List of Stereo Matching Functions.**

| Function name | Partition | Description |
|---|---|---|
| RD_IMGS | SW | Get left and right frame images |
| COM_COST | HW | Compute MRF parameters |
| STRM_TRWS | HW | Run STRM_TRWS |
| GET_LABEL | SW | Obtain the best labeling result |
| WR_DISP | SW | Produce disparity map |

find the gradient. The computations for the four directions for the three colors are done in parallel, and then merged at the last stages. Note that the actual value of the smoothness cost as well as the per-edge weight are not computed. This is because the smoothness cost is a function of the labels and the per-edge weight, and the weight is an on-off function so that it has non-unity value only if the gradient value is less than the threshold. Thus, we can simply store only the one bit signals to indicate whether the per-edge weight needs to be applied or not. In this way, we can again reduce the size of the input data.

The computed matching costs for a node are packed with the four bit gradient cue flags, and then put in the write back FIFOs to dump into the memory. These MRF parameters are used in the inference engine to compute the most probable labels.

## 4.3 Processing Multiple Frames in Parallel

Our MCC, GCC and STRM_TRWS are implemented in FPGA, they can be invoked by the host processor like other software functions to perform stereo matching. The full list of these custom software and hardware functions that comprise our video stereo system is shown in Table 1. Here, we use a simple naming convention for these functions based on where they are executed: SW (software) and HW (hardware) functions. Thus, RD_IMGS, GET_LABEL, and WR_DISP belong to SW functions since they are mapped to be executed in the host processor, and COM_COST and STRM_TRWS belong to HW functions for their implementation on FPGAs.

As described in section 2.3, there are four FPGAs available on the Convey HC-1. Since COM_COST and STRM_TRWS occupy one FPGA each, we can launch multiple COM_COST or STRM_TRWS functions in parallel to process more than one frame at the same time. The following pseudo code is an example of processing two frames in parallel using two FPGAs for COM_COST and STRM_TRWS each:

```
Initialize
For (idx=0; idx<numFrame; idx+=2)
    Even_frame   RD_IMGS [idx];
    Odd_frame    RD_IMGS [idx+1];
    COM_COST    (Even_frame@AE0, Odd_frame@AE1);
    STRM_TRWS (Even_frame@AE2, Odd_frame@AE3);
    GET_DISP (Even_frame from AE2);
    GET_DISP (Odd _frame from AE3);
    WR_DISP  (Even_frame);
    WR_DISP  (Odd_frame);
End
```

In this example, two image frames (even and odd) are read by the host processor and passed to two FPGAs (called AE1 and AE3) for COM_COST of two frames in parallel. MRF parameters computed by COM_COST are used by another two other FPGAs (AE2 and AE4) to perform inference (STRM_TRWS) for two frames in parallel. Then, disparity map results are retrieved (GET_DISP) and output (WR_DISP) by the host processor sequentially. Note that data transfer between the host processor and the FPGAs is managed by the cache coherent shared-memory, and can be expedited by using a dedicated data mover [28]. Also,

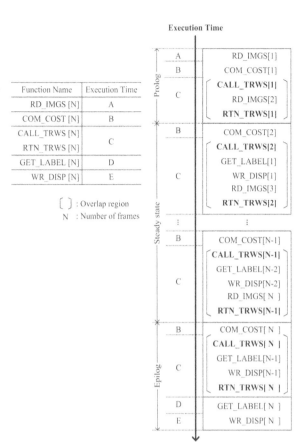

**Figure 4 Pipelining of stereo matching functions.**

we can observe that the number of calls for RD_IMGS, GET_DISP, and WR_DISP increase in proportion to the number of frames processed in parallel, as per the discussion in section 3.3.

## 4.4 Pipelining Stereo Matching Functions

On the Convey HC-1, FPGA functions appear as callable procedures, which can be invoked by software on the host, and pass parameters back and forth. Because the platform supports *non-blocking* calls for these custom FPGA functions ([28]), we can further increase the speed of stereo matching by overlapping the execution time for the software functions and these hardware functions. Figure 4 shows an example of applying the non-blocking call for STRM_TRWS. Note that STRM_TRWS is now divided into two sub-functions: CALL_TRWS (the "call") and RTN_TRWS (the "return"). Thus, the computation time of the host function calls between CALL_TRWS and RTN_TRWS (overlap region in Figure 4) are hidden by the execution time of the FPGAs. We can estimate the ideal execution time $T$ for $N$ frame stereo matching by the execution time of each function ($A \sim E$) defined in Figure 4 as follows:

$$T = A + N \times (B + C) + (D + E). \qquad (6)$$

Thus, the computation time of the host processor ($= A+D+E$) can be neglected if ($B+C$) is greater than ($A+D+E$) and $N$ is large enough. This is the case when the time for data management on the host processor and the time for inference on FPGAS are well balanced, as discussed in section 3.3.

**Table 2. Execution time (in msec) of stereo matching functions.**

| Tsukuba Stereo Matching Benchmark (384x288,16 labels) ([29]) | | |
|---|---|---|
| # Inference Iterations | 5 | 40 |
| RD_IMGS | 22.3 | 22.4 |
| COM_COST (SW / HW) | **146.9 / 4.5** | **147.0 / 4.5** |
| STRM_TRWS (SW / HW) | **500.0 / 18.9** | **3720.0 / 127.1** |
| GET_LABEL | 1.9 | 1.9 |
| WR_DISP | 10.9 | 10.6 |
| Minimum energy | 394,434 | 370,359 |
| Min. energy of VLSI impl. [16] | 396,953 in 137.4 msec | |

**Table 3. Comparison of execution time (in msec) for Tsukuba benchmark between GPU implementations [16,17,18] and streaming TRW-S system.**

| | GPU platform | Number of iterations | Exec. Time |
|---|---|---|---|
| Real-time BP [17] | NVIDIA GeForce 7900 GTX | (4 coarse to fine scales) = (5, 5, 10, 2) | 79.7 |
| Tile-based BP [16] | NVIDIA GeForce 8800 GTS | (B, $T_I$, $T_O$) = (16, 20, 5) | 97.3 |
| Fast BP [18] | NVIDIA GeForce GTX 260 | (3 coarse to fine scales) = (9, 6, 2) | 61.4 |
| Our streaming TRW-S system | N/A | 5 | **23.4** |

# 5. EXPERIMENTAL RESULTS

In this section, we present the experimental results for our stereo matching system to evaluate our overall hardware/software partitioning, and various pixel, frame, and video parallelism optimizations. Our implementation runs entirely on the Convey HC-1 platform; the host processors and all FPGA functions are run at 2.13GHz and 150MHz, respectively.

## 5.1 Single-Frame Performance by Function

We begin with a detailed analysis of performance at the level of single stereo frames. We do this for two reasons. First, many of our optimizations are at frame level, and so they are most easily explained here. Second, much of the literature and common benchmarks are actually on single frames; it is interesting that many of these efforts assert real-time performance while neither actually demonstrating video-rate benchmarks (e.g. [14,15,16,18]) nor providing detailed analysis (e.g. [17]). As we hope to show here, the path from frame to video is rather less than trivial.

So to begin, we first run the well-known Tsukuba stereo matching benchmark from the Middlebury suite ([29]) on our full stereo video matching system, and we evaluate its performance by function for a single frame image.

Table 2 shows the execution time of the stereo matching functions, with different number of iterations for the inference. As the MRF inference minimizes the energy over the iterations, the number of iterations can be either adaptively increased to achieve a desired minimum energy, or pre-determined for some fixed latency of the entire inference engine. In the latter case, the

minimum energy is a metric to evaluate the quality of solutions, as is used in [10]. In this work, therefore, we demonstrate performance for our hardware in terms of the execution time (determined by a fixed number of iterations) and the minimum energy we obtain.

Since RD_IMGS, GET_LABEL, and WR_DISP functions are partitioned as SW functions, they are processed in the host side. For COM_COST and STRM_TRWS functions, *both* SW and HW execution time are measured for comparison. As shown in Table 2, the hardware implementation of COM_COST and STRM_TRWS run 32.6 and 26.5 times faster than the same functions run in the host processor, respectively. Thus, we can conclude that it is beneficial to accelerate both COM_COST and STRM_TRWS functions in the FPGA side.

To take advantage of functional pipelining, it is important to balance the execution time for SW and HW functions. As shown in Table 2, execution time for SW functions is insensitive to the number of inference iterations, and is about 57.9msec. However, with more inference iterations in the hardware, we can achieve a lower minimum energy. Note that the minimum energy decreases from 394,434 to 370,359 as the number of iterations increases from 5 to 40. As will be discussed later, this minimum energy achieved by 40 iterations is much lower compared to the minimum energy obtained by a competing VLSI implementation [16] of the MRF inference within a similar time frame. Since it takes 130msec for inference with 40 inference iterations, and this is smaller than the SW execution time, we can hide the SW execution time by pipelining the SW and HW functions.

Next, let us turn to some comparison of similar efforts to accelerate inference-based solutions to the stereo matching problem, again at the level of individual stereo frames. One recent group of efforts has focused on GPUs to accelerate these tasks, again using variants of Belief Propagation – though not, we will note, the TRW-S variant with its attractive convergence guarantees.

There are several notable efforts to use GPUs to accelerate belief propagation algorithms for stereo matching [16,17,18]. (These include both older and newer GPU architectures.) Real-time BP ([17]) and Fast BP ([18]) exploit the idea of applying BP in a hierarchical manner (from coarse to fine scales) to speed up convergence of BP [11]. In Tile-based BP ([16]), the entire graph is divided into small tiles; BP is performed on each tile but only messages on the boundary are kept to reduce memory access. Since all of these implementations are based on BP, there is no convergence property which leads closer to the optimum solution or the lower minimum energy, unlike TRW-S.

Table 3 shows execution time for each implementation for stereo matching of the standard Tsukuba single-frame benchmark with its own GPU platform and iteration settings. Here, GPU execution time includes *only* the time for inference, whereas execution time of our system includes *both* data cost computation and inference processed in FPGA. As we can see, the execution time of our system is faster than the execution time of these other GPU implementations, although our hardware is running at a much slower clock frequency (150MHz). We believe that aggressively custom design with a tightly coupled streaming memory interface is what leads to such significant speed-ups.

Next, let us consider some recent efforts in fully custom hardware for this task. VLSI implementation of tile-based BP ([16]) can run up to 64-label stereo matching of a 320x240 image in 137.4msec for a high quality result. For the Tsukuba benchmark, it obtains the lowest minimum energy of 396,953 with the same setting. Note that the lowest minimum energy corresponds to a high quality stereo result for the MRF. In

| | | |
|---|---|---|
| Left | Right | Disparity map |

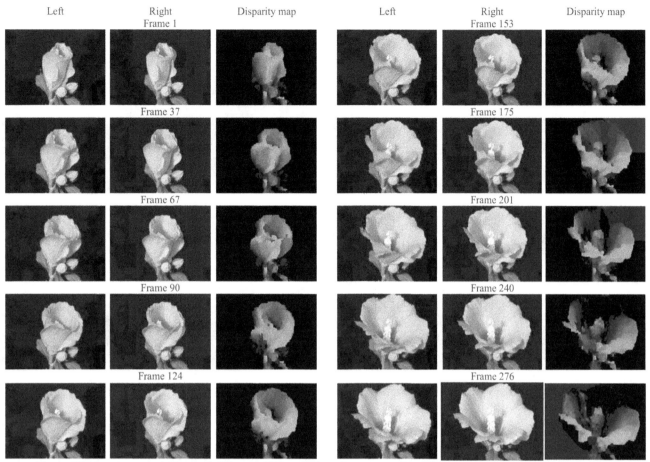

**Figure 5 Video stereo matching task (Flower, [28]) and disparity map results. (Lighter grey means closer to camera.)**

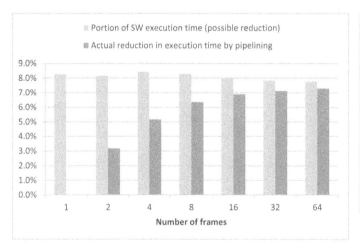

**Figure 6 Possible reduction versus actual reduction in overall execution time due to function-level pipelining**

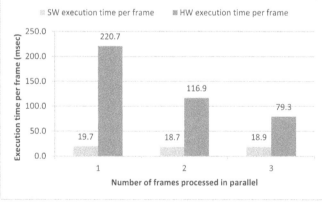

**Figure 7 Per-frame execution time of SW and HW functions.**

comparison, for single frame performance, our system can achieve about 6 times faster speed in inference with a slightly lower minimum energy (when the number of iterations is 5), or about the same speed but with much lower minimum energy (when the number of iterations is 40), as shown in Table 2. More detail discussion about this related work can be found in [1].

## 5.2 Video Performance

Next, we show results from full video experiments. Benchmarks like the single-frame Middlebury set ([29]) are less common here. We use a set of real-world stereo examples from [30] for our experiments.

We perform stereo matching of a stereo video task (Flower) from [30] on our system with the non-blocking function calls to analyze the effect of function level pipelining. This stereo video

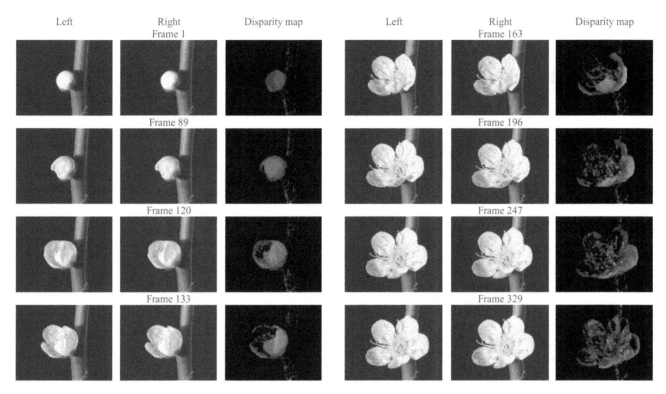

| Left | Right | Disparity map | | Left | Right | Disparity map |
| --- | --- | --- | --- | --- | --- | --- |

Frame 1 ... Frame 163
Frame 89 ... Frame 196
Frame 120 ... Frame 247
Frame 133 ... Frame 329

**Figure 8 Video stereo matching task (Ume, [30]) and disparity map results. (Lighter grey means closer to camera.)**

**Table 4. Analysis of total execution time (in sec) for Flower video stereo matching (276 frames).**

| Num. FPGAs | 1 | 2 | 3 |
| --- | --- | --- | --- |
| Total Exec Time ($T_t$) | 61.3 | 33.3 | **23.4** |
| Estm. Time with Pipelining ($T_p$) | 60.9 | 32.3 | 21.9 |
| Estm. Time w/o Pipelining ($T_{np}$) | 66.4 | 37.4 | 27.1 |

task consists of 276 frames of 360x262 stereo flower images as input. The 16-label (disparity levels) stereo matching is performed for 80 iterations to obtain the disparity map results in Figure 5, since it requires considerable effort to propagate the depth information on the body of flower to its empty background. This task is more challenging than Tsukuba, for which TRW-S produces reasonable outcome within only 5~40 iterations.

Next, we analyze the effect of the function-level pipelining used in our implementation. Figure 6 shows possible reduction versus actual reduction in overall execution time due to the function-level pipelining. The possible reduction comes from the portion of the SW execution time relative to the total execution time. The actual reduction is calculated as the difference of execution time with and without applying the function level pipelining. In case of one-frame stereo matching, the actual reduction is zero since there is no possible overlap between SW and HW execution time. However, the actual reduction becomes closer to the portion of the SW execution time as the number of frames increases. In the case of 64-frame stereo matching, the difference between the possible reduction and the actual reduction is only 0.5%. Thus, we can conclude that the pipelining of the functions improves the speed of the stereo matching by hiding most of the SW execution time. (Since the portion of the SW execution time is around 8% of the entire execution time, there is ample time for the host processor.)

We further examine our stereo matching system for parallel processing of multiple frames. Among the four FPGAs available on the Convey HC-1, we assign one for the MCC and GCC, and the other FPGAs for STRM_TRWS. The number of FPGAs used for STRM_TRWS is equal to the number of frames processed in parallel. We compare the execution time of the SW and HW functions, normalized by the number of frames processed concurrently. As shown in Figure 7, the HW execution time per frame decreases inversely proportional to the number of FPGAs. Thus, we can conclude that the computations for multiple frames are well parallelized. In contrast, the SW execution time per frame does not change as more hardware is utilized, as expected from section 4.3. Since the SW per frame execution time is smaller than the HW execution time, we can exploit functional pipelining to fully overlap SW execution time with HW execution time.

We now analyze the total execution time for Flower video stereo matching. The execution time is measured for different number of frames processed in parallel, and function level pipelining is applied for all the cases. To provide an idea of how well our optimization techniques work for entire frames, we also present estimated execution time with and without applying function level pipelining for each parallel processing of frames. Table 4 shows the total execution time of stereo matching of 276 stereo flower images ($T_t$) along with the estimated execution time of either applying the pipelining ($T_p$) or not ($T_{np}$) using different number of FPGAs. $T_p$ is computed by (6), and $T_{np}$ is the execution time of one parallel processing of frames multiplied by the number of parallel processing calls (e.g. multiply 92 if the number of FPGAs is 3). Thus, $T_p$ and $T_{np}$ are the lower and the upper bound of the total execution time. Since $T_t$ is more close to $T_p$ than $T_{np}$, we can see that our stereo matching system takes advantage of pipelining. In case of using three FPGAs for STRM_TRWS, the speed of the stereo matching is 11.8 frames per second.

Using the analysis, we chose to run 3 frames in parallel. So, next, we evaluate our 3-frame-parallel video stereo matching system using a different video stereo task (Ume, [30]). The Ume task consists of 342 frames of 320x240 stereo images, and it also takes 80 iterations per frame for 16-label stereo matching. Figure 8 shows disparity map results by frame. Our stereo system finishes this challenging stereo matching task in 27.4sec, which is equivalent to a speed of 12.5 frames per second.

# 6. CONCLUSION

We have designed and benchmarked a video-rate stereo matching system implemented on a hybrid CPU+FPGA platform (Convey HC-1). We model the stereo task as statistical inference on a Markov Random Field model, and show how to implement TRW-S style inference at video rates. We described the hardware/software partitioning, and various sources of parallelism in this application. We note that this appears to be the first implementation of TRW-S inference at video rates, and that our system is also significantly faster than recently published GPU implementations of similar stereo inference methods based on belief propagation (BP).

# 7. ACKNOWLEDGMENTS

The authors acknowledge the support of the C2S2 Focus Center, one of six research centers funded under the Focus Center Research Program (FCRP), a Semiconductor Research Corporation entity. We also thank our colleague, Abner Guzmán-Rivera, of the department of Computer Science at the University of Illinois, for his insight in probabilistic graphical models. Special thanks also to Glen Edwards of Convey Computer for thoughtful help in working with the Convey HC-1 platform, and Takashi Aizawa for generous permission to use his stereo video clips for evaluation of our hardware.

# 8. REFERENCES

[1] Choi , J. and Rutenbar, R. A. 2012. Hardware implementation of MRF MAP inference on an FPGA platform. In *Proc. IEEE 22nd Int. Conf. Field Programmable Logic and Applications.* 209-216.

[2] Ko, D. –I. and Agarwal, G. 2011. Gesture recognition--first step toward 3D UIs? *EETimes.* http://www.eetimes.com/design/embedded/4231057/Gesture-recognition-first-step-toward-3D-UIs-

[3] Gong, H., Sim, J., Likhachev, M. and Shi, J. 2011. Multi-hypothesis motion planning for visual object tracking. In *Proc. IEEE Int. Conf. Computer Vision.* 619-626.

[4] Koller, D. and Friedman, N. 2009. *Probabilistic graphical model.* MIT press.

[5] Boykov, Y. and Veksler, O. and Zabih, R. 2001. Fast approximate energy minimization via graph cuts. *IEEE Trans. Pattern Analysis and Machine Intelligence (PAMI).*11:1222-1239.

[6] Pearl, J. 1988. *Probabilistic reasoning in intelligent systems: networks of plausible inference.* Morgan Kaufmann

[7] Tappen, M. F. and Freeman, W. T. 2003. Comparison of graph cuts with belief propagation for stereo, using identical MRF parameters. In *Proc. IEEE 9th Int. Conf. Computer Vision.* 900-907.

[8] Sun, J., Zheng, N. N., and Shum, H. Y. 2003. Stereo matching using belief propagation. *IEEE Trans. PAMI.* 7:787-800.

[9] Li, Y. and Huttenlocher, D.P. 2008. Learning for stereo vision using the structured support vector machine. In *Proc. IEEE Int. Conf. Computer Vision and Pattern Recognition (CVPR).* 1-8.

[10] Szeliski, R., et al. 2008. A comparative study of energy minimization methods for Markov random fields with smoothness based priors. *IEEE Trans. PAMI.* 6:1068-1080.

[11] Felzenszwalb, P. F. and Huttenlocher, D. P. 2004. Efficient belief propagation for early vision. In *Proc. IEEE Int. Conf. CVPR.* 1261-1268.

[12] Gonzalez, J., Low, Y. and Guestrin, C. 2009. Residual splash for optimally parallelizing belief propagation. In *Proc. 12th Int. Conf. Artificial Intelligence and Statistics.*

[13] Kanade, T., Kano, H., Kimura, S., Yoshida, A. and Oda, K. 1995. Development of a video-rate stereo machine. *In Proc. IEEE/RSJ Int. Conf. Intelligent Robots and Systems.* 95-100.

[14] Park, S., Chen, C., and Jeong, H. 2007. VLSI architecture for MRF based stereo matching. In *Proc. 7th Int. Conf. Embedded Computer Systems: Architectures, Modeling, and Simulation.* 55-64.

[15] Park, J., Lee, S., and Yoo, H.J. 2010. A 30fps stereo matching processor based on belief propagation with disparity-parallel PE array architecture. In *Proc. IEEE Int. Symp. Circuits and Systems.* 453-456.

[16] Liang, C. –K., Cheng, C. C., Lai, Y. C., Chen, L. G., and Chen, H. H. 2011. Hardware-efficient belief propagation. *IEEE Trans. Circuits and Systems for Video Technology.* 5:525-537

[17] Yang , Q., Wang, L., Yang, R., Wang, S., Liao, M., and Nister, D. 2006. Real-time global stereo matching using hierarchical belief propagation. *The British Machine Vision Conference.* 989-998.

[18] Xiang, X., Zhang, M., Li, G., He, Y., and Pan, Z. 2012. Real-time stereo matching based on fast belief propagation. *Machine Vision and Applications,* 1-9.

[19] Wainwright, M., Jaakkola, T. S., and Willsky, A. S. 2005. Map estimation via agreement on trees: message-passing and linear programming. *IEEE Trans. Information Theory.* 11:3697-3717.

[20] Kolmogorov, V. 2006. Convergent tree-reweighted message passing for energy minimization. *IEEE Trans. PAMI.* 10:568-1583.

[21] Birchfield, S. and Tomasi, C. 1998. A pixel dissimilarity measure that is insensitive to image sampling. *IEEE Trans. PAMI.* 4:401-406.

[22] Hirschmuller H. and Scharstein, D. 2009 Evaluation of stereo matching costs on images with radiometric differences. *IEEE Trans. on PAMI.* 9:1582-1599.

[23] Convey computer. 2012. Convey Reference Manual. http://www.conveycomputer.com.

[24] Bakos, J.D. 2010. High-performance heterogeneous computing with the convey hc-1. *Computing in Science & Engineering. 12(6):80-87.*

[25] zlib: a massively spiffy yet delicately unobtrusive compression library. http://www.zlib.net.

[26] libpng. http://www.libpng.org.

[27] Lam, M. 1988. Software pipelining: an effective scheduling technique for VLIW machines. In *Proc. ACM SIGPLAN Conf. Programming Language design and Implementation.* 7:318-328.

[28] Convey computer. 2012. Convey Programmers Guide. http://www.conveycomputer.com.

[29] D. Scharstein and R. Szeliski. 2002. A taxonomy and evaluation of dense two-frame stereo correspondence algorithms. International Journal of Computer Vision, 47(1/2/3):7-42.

[30] Stereo movie sample. http://www.stereomaker.net/sample/index.html.

# Fully-Functional FPGA Prototype with Fine-Grain Programmable Body Biasing

Masakazu Hioki, Toshihiro Sekigawa,
Tadashi Nakagawa and Hanpei Koike
National Institute of Advanced Industrial Science
and Technology (AIST)
Tsukuba, Japan
{m.hioki, t.sekigawa, nakagawa.tadashi,
h.koike}@aist.go.jp

Yohei Matsumoto
Tokyo University of Marine Science and Technology
Tokyo, Japan
matumoto@kaiyodai.ac.jp

Takashi Kawanami
Kanazawa Institute of Technology
Kanazawa, Japan
t-kawanami@neptune.kanazawa-it.ac.jp

Toshiyuki Tsutsumi
Meiji University
Kawasaki, Japan
tsutsumi@cs.meiji.ac.jp

## ABSTRACT

A fully-functional FPGA prototype chip in which the programmable body bias voltage can be individually applied to elemental circuits such as MUXes, LUT and DFF is fabricated using low-power 90-nm bulk CMOS technology and the area overhead, dynamic current, static current and operational speed are evaluated in silicon. In measurements, 10 ISCAS benchmark circuits are implemented by employing newly developed CAD tools which consist of VT mapper as well as placer and router. Mask layout shows that well-separated margins, programmable body bias circuits, and additional configuration memories occupy 54% of the FPGA tile area. Measurement results show that the fabricated FPGA reduces the static current by 91.4% in average. In addition, evaluations by implementing ring oscillator with various body bias voltage pairs demonstrate the static current reduction from 23.1 μA to 1.0 μA by assigning low threshold voltage and high threshold voltage to MOSFETs on a critical path and the rest of the MOSFETs, respectively while maintaining the same oscillation frequency of 6.6 MHz as the frequency when all MOSFETs are assigned low threshold voltage. Moreover the fine-grain programmable body bias technique accelerates the oscillation frequency of ring oscillator implemented on FPGA by aggressively applying forward body bias voltage, while assignment of HVT to MOSFETs on the non-critical path by applying the reverse body biasing effectively suppresses exponential increase of static current caused by the forward body biasing.

## Categories and Subject Descriptors

B.7.1 [INTEGRATED CIRCUITS]: Types and Design Styles - VLSI (very large scale integration)

## General Terms

Measurement, Design, Verification.

## Keywords

Programmable Body Biasing, Threshold Voltage, Static Current Reduction.

## 1. INTRODUCTION

Field-programmable gate arrays (FPGAs) can implement various functions by storing circuit construction information in configuration memories. This flexibility enables FPGAs to be adapted for various applications such as prototyping, automotive, consumer products, industrial equipment, military equipment, aerospace applications, video/picture processing, and telecommunications. Because FPGAs are ensured wide implementation and extremely high productivities due to these applications, FPGAs can be fabricated by advanced semiconductor process technologies. Production costs can be reduced and device performance can be improved by rapidly shrinking the silicon die area.

On the other hand, FPGAs suffer from various problems caused by the higher MOSFET densities in advanced process technology. One such problem is an increase in power, especially static power. Static power mainly originates from subthreshold and gate leakage currents. The gate leakage current can be exponentially reduced by using a high-k material as the gate insulator and increasing the gate insulator thickness. The subthreshold leakage current generally tends to increase when the MOSFET performance is improved by applying device scaling theory. The subthreshold leakage current depends on parameters such as the threshold voltage. Fig. 1 compares the Id–Vg characteristics of MOSFETs with different threshold voltages. Ioff denotes the subthreshold leakage current. Reducing the MOSFET threshold voltage will increase the currents Ion and Ioff; conversely, a higher threshold voltage will reduce Ion and Ioff. Thus, a trade-off relationship exists between the static power and the operating speed, which can be controlled by the threshold voltage.

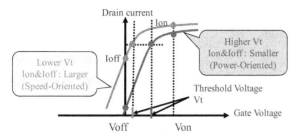

Figure 1: Comparison of Id-Vg characteristics of two MOSFETs with different threshold voltages.

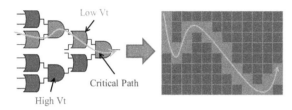

Figure 2: Critical-path-aware lower threshold voltage assignment in FPGA.

We have proposed low-power FPGA architecture with fine-grain programmable body biasing, called Flex Power FPGA, in which the above-mentioned relationship is applied cleverly. The FPGA can reduce the subthreshold leakage current by electrically controlling threshold voltage of MOSFETs. Assignment of lower threshold voltages to MOSFETs on critical paths and higher threshold voltages to the rest of the MOSFETs (see Fig. 2) reduces the static power in FPGAs without reducing the operating speed.

The concept of Flex Power FPGA is proposed for the first time in [8] and it is shown that the FPGA provides static power reduction of 1/30 using predicted 70nm bulk CMOS process technology. Simulation result of [9] shows that the FPGA can realize the increase of operation frequency from 66MHz to 121MHz with 30% reduction of energy-delay product in a best case. In [10], when a simple critical path and a simple model of the FPGA only are assumed for evaluations, static power reduces less than 1/5 of original level, while increase an area overhead of less than 40%. If an area increase of 50% is allowed, then the reduction in static power consumption to 1/10 or less is obtained. [11] shows that optimal set of body bias voltage for the FPGA is explored.

In the past, various preliminary evaluations Flex Power FPGA with are based on computer simulations and calculations. In contrast, this study demonstrates the effectiveness of static current reduction and evaluates area overhead of the Flex Power FPGA in silicon designed in low-power 90-nm CMOS technology.

The remainder of this paper is organized as follows: In Section 2, we introduce previous technologies for reducing the static current in FPGAs. Section 3 describes the architecture of Flex Power FPGA with fine-grain programmable body biasing used in this research. Section 4 presents a CAD flow that includes newly developed VT mapper as well as placement and routing tools. In Section 5, the Flex Power FPGA prototype chip is evaluated in terms of area overhead, dynamic current, static current and operating speed by implementing 10 ISCAS benchmark circuits

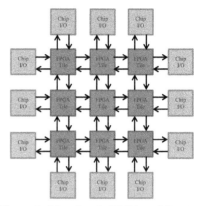

Figure 3: Island-style FPGA architecture

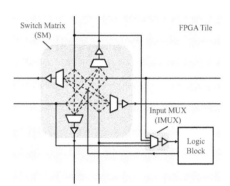

Figure 4: Tile architecture.

and ring oscillator with various body bias voltage pairs. Finally, the conclusions are given in Section 6.

## 2. RELATED WORK

Various techniques to reduce static current in FPGAs are proposed. In [1], leakage current of LUT is reduced by increasing threshold voltage of SRAM transistors in LUT. [2] evaluates the effectiveness of various low-leakage techniques such as redundant SRAM cell design, dual threshold voltage design, body biasing and gate biasing for programmable multiplexers and switch block design. [3] aims at leakage current reduction in logic slices which occupies 45% of total leakage current in their Xilnx style FPGA architecture by switching off the power supply in each unused region using sleep transistors. Threshold voltage of the configuration SRAM is increased to obtain a 98% reduction in leakage energy of SRAM while increasing configuration time by 20%. Programmable low-power routing switch in [4] has three operational modes such as high-speed mode, low-power mode and sleep mode by arranging two transistors between power supply and virtual power supply. Leakage in low-power mode is reduced by 36-40% vs. high-speed mode. Sleep mode offers leakage reduction of 61%. The low leakage interconnects via fine-grained power-gating reduce total power by 38.18% for the FPGA in 100nm technology as shown in [5]. In [6], heterogeneous routing architecture in which minimum channel length devices and longer channel length devices are mixed, resulting in the reduction of standby power dissipation of FPGA routing fabric by 33% without any area penalty and at the cost of less than 5% performance degradation. [7] shows the standby power reduction by 99% using higher Vt low-leakage memory cells and power-

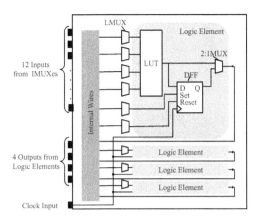

**Figure 5: Logic block architecture.**

**Table 1: Summary of FPGA architecture**

| Architecture specification | | | # of elemental circuit / tile | |
|---|---|---|---|---|
| # of tiles | 121 (11x11) | | 16:1 SMUX | 8 |
| Wire length | 4 | | 32:1 IMUX | 12 |
| Routing architecture | disjoint, uni-direction, single driver | | 16:1 LMUX | 24 |
| | | | 4-inputs LUT | 4 |
| | | | DFF with set/reset | 4 |
| Routing channel width (number of wires) | 16 | | 2:1MUX | 4 |
| # of BLEs per a CLB | 4 | | PO MUX | 1 |
| # of CLB inputs (including clk) | 13 | | Total | 57 |
| # of CLB outputs | 4 | | | |
| # of BLE inputs (including clk) | 7 | | | |
| # of Vt control domains | 57 | | | |

gating technique in a Xilinx Startan-3 style FPGA architecture. [13] explorers the size of power control region and fraction of high-speed region and low-power region for power management technique using body biasing in their Altera style FPGA architecture. The authors of [13] present the static power reduction ratio in case that the body bias control region is the LAB granularity and the ALM granularity, respectively. In both granularities, static power reduces by nearly 60% in maximum case. While their approach is a real product design under the current fabrication restriction, our study investigates the related technology in the extreme circumstance which might be available in the future.

# 3. FPGA ARCHITECTURE

In this section, the architecture of Flex Power FPGA with fine-grain programmable body biasing is explained in more detail.

Flex Power FPGA is the typical island-style and tileable FPGA as shown in figure 3. Wire segments are arranged around FPGA tiles to provide connection between FPGA tiles. Unidirectional and single-driver routing architecture [12] is employed as programmable interconnects. The wire segment length is 4 tile spans and the vertical and horizontal channel width is 16, respectively.

Figure 4 illustrates the FPGA tile architecture. Switch matrix (SM) interconnects between wire segments or between outputs from the logic blocks and wire segments. A switch matrix that has a disjoint topology contains eight 16:1 switch multiplexers (SMUXes). Input multiplexers (IMUXes) select signals from wire segments and input signals to a logic block. In this architecture, the number of IMUXes is 12 and the number of inputs in IMUX is 32 (32:1 IMUX). The population is set to 100%.

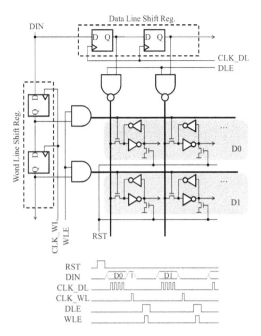

**Figure 6: Configuration memories.**

A logic block with 13 inputs and 4 outputs clusters the 4 logic elements as show in Figure 5. The number of inputs in each logic element is 7 (i.e.: 4 logic signals, set and reset signals for a D Flip Flop (DFF) and a clock signal). The logic signals, set and reset signals selected by IMUXes are connected to logic elements via the local multiplexers (LMUXes). There are twenty four 16:1 LMUX in a logic block. 12 inputs of a LMUX are connected to each IMUX output and the remaining 4 inputs of a LMUX receive local feedback signals from each logic element output. A logic element has a 4-input look-up table (LUT), a DFF, and a 2:1 MUX. Output signals from 4 logic elements are exported to SMUXes in SM directly. Table 1 summarizes the FPGA architecture.

Configuration memories are constructed by an inverter latch as shown in Figure 6. Word-lines and data-lines are connected to word-line shift registers and data-line shift registers, respectively. Configuration is performed row-by-row in a configuration memory array. First, all configuration memories are initialized by activating RST. Next, a part of the bit stream data inputted from DIN is filled in data line shift registers. Subsequently, a high or low state is stored in a configuration memory by activating WLE after setting DLE to high state to transfer configuration data from data line shift registers to data line. To fill of bit stream data and to activate word-line are repeated until the configuration procedure is completed.

Special feature in this FPGA architecture is to be able to apply body bias voltage to each elemental circuit individually and programmably. Body bias voltage in 57 elemental circuits per an FPGA tile, namely, 8 SMUXes, 12 IMUXes, 24 LMUXes, 4 LUTs, a DFF, a 2-1MUX and a PAD Output MUX (PO MUX) explained later, are individually controlled by programmable body bias circuits, enabling precise adjustment of the subthreshold leakage current.

Generally, some additional elements are needed to control body bias of MOSFETs as shown in Figure 7. As an essential process technique, transistor's wells have to be separated by triple well

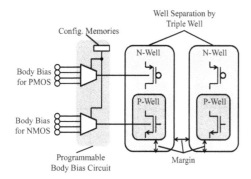

Figure 7: Additional elements for programmable body biasing of MOSFETs.

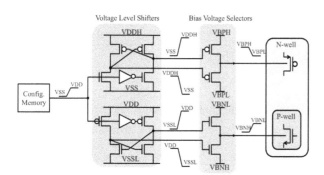

Figure 8: Detailed schematic of programmable body bias circuit.

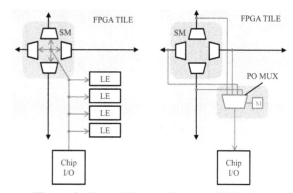

Figure 9: Simple I/O circuits in the FPGA tile.

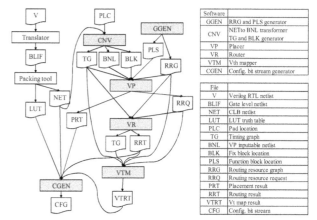

Figure 10: CAD flow.

process to apply body bias voltage to each MOSFET's body individually. In addition, separation margins are needed to prevent huge current flow between power line and well bias line or between ground line and well bias line via transistor's wells and active areas. Moreover, as a circuit technique, body bias control circuits, especially programmable body bias circuits in this FPGA architecture, have to be prepared.

The programmable body bias circuit in this study consists of a configuration memory, voltage level shifters, and bias voltage selectors as shown in Figure 8. A voltage level shifter shifts the voltage swing of VDD/VSS from an output of the configuration memory to the voltage swing of VDDH/VSS and VDD/VSSL for PMOS and NMOS bias voltage selectors, respectively. Body bias selectors select a body bias voltage of VBPH or VBPL for the PMOS body and VBNH or VBNL for the NMOS body.

In the circuit design of programmable body bias circuits, high-voltage MOSFETs are employed because power supply voltages higher than VDD or lower than VSS are applied to MOSFETs connected to VDDH or VSSL. Moreover, body bias voltages VBPH and VBPL for PMOS or VBNH and VBNL for NMOS are set between VDDH and VDD or between VSS and VSSL, respectively. In this condition, short circuit between power lines and well bias lines via well regions and diffusion regions of MOSFETs has to be prevented by applying VDDH to n-type wells and VSSL p-type wells. Therefore, programmable body bias circuits need to be isolated electrically in the same way as elemental circuits of FPGA, e.g. MUXes and buffers, by triple well process.

Additional function in the FPGA tile is to be able to communicate signals between FPGA tile and Chip I/O directly as shown in

Figure 9. Though I/O tiles which are the dedicated tiles for the communication to chip I/Os are prepared in the typical FPGA architecture, dedicated I/O tiles don't exist in this FPGA architecture. Instead, simple I/O circuits are implemented in the FPGA tile for the connection to a chip I/O. A wire from a chip I/O is connected to 4 logic elements in a logic block and SM in a FPGA tile directly. In the SM, one input port of each SMUX receives a signal from a chip I/O. In each logic element, one input port of 4 inputs can select a signal either from chip I/O or from wire segments. Output signals from 4 logic elements are inputted to Pad Output MUX (PO MUX) via SMUXes in SM. PO MUX transfers 1 of 8 signals which are outputted from 8 SMUXes to a chip I/O.

## 4. CAD FLOW

Fig. 5 introduces CAD flow for the Flex Power FPGA. It is very difficult to apply the finished VPR tool flow [14] to our FPGA architecture. Particularly, it is necessary to modify a complicated resource graph generation part of VPR to output a resource graph corresponding to our FPGA architecture using VPR. Therefore each program such as GGEN, CNV, VP, VR, CGEN, and VTM is newly developed. GGEN generates routing resource graph that reflects our FPGA architecture. In addition, logic synthesis and packing need to be performed beforehand for a target circuit. CNV translates and generates some files required for placement and routing. Placement and routing are subsequently performed by VP and VR, respectively. VTM maps body biasing information based on placement and routing results for each elemental circuit in FPGA. Finally, CGEN generates a

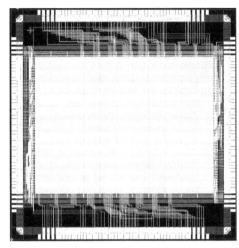

**Figure 11: Whole chip layout.**

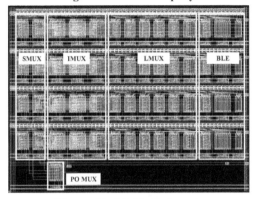

**Figure 12: FPGA tile layout.**

configuration bit-stream file. FPGA tile I/Os are assigned to package pins flexibly by describing the correspondence of FPGA tile number to package pin number in a setting file.

# 5. CHIP EVALUATION

The goal is to evaluate how many static current of the FPGA can be reduced in silicon chip implemented various benchmark circuits when the body bias control grain size is made as small as possible. Another aim of this research is to quantitatively show the additional area overhead for applying body bias voltage in finest granularity by designing mask layout. Though the concerting point is the increase of area overhead by allowing control of body bias voltage in finest granularity, we don't make aggressive efforts to reduce the area overhead in this research. From a standpoint of academic research as shown by above, relatively small FPGA chip is designed, while relatively small benchmark circuits are selected for the FPGA chip in subsection 5.2.

A fully-functional Flex Power FPGA with the 11×11 is fabricated by 1P9M 90-nm low-power bulk CMOS process technology. The main elemental circuits of FPGA such as buffers and MUXes are constructed by built-in low threshold voltage (LVT) MOSFETs, while configuration memories and word-line shift registers and data-line shift registers are constructed by built-in high threshold voltage (HVT) MOSFETs. Voltage level shift circuits and body bias select circuits are designed by a high-voltage 3.3 V MOSFETs to employ higher voltage than VDD or lower voltage than VSS. Configuration memories are not applied to the body

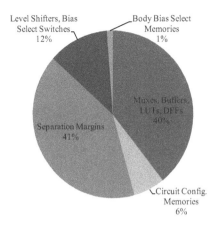

**Figure 13: Tile area breakdown.**

bias voltage. There are about 1.34 million transistors, including chip I/Os. The number of FPGA I/Os is 121. Supply voltages are set as follows. Power supply for FPGA core circuits, configuration memories and related control circuits are set to +1.2 V. Ground voltage of VSS is 0 V. VDDH/VSSL for voltage level shifters is set to +2.25 V/–1.05 V. VBPH/VBPL for PMOS body and VBNH/VBNL for NMOS body in the body bias selector are set to +2.25 V/+1.2 V and –1.05 V/0 V, respectively for ISCAS benchmark circuit evaluations. In ring oscillator evaluations, various body bias voltage pairs for VBPH/VBPL and VBNH/VBNL are employed. The total number of body biasing domains is 6,897. All layout macros except chip I/O macro such as elemental circuits, configuration memories, programmable body bias circuits, FPGA tiles and whole chip macro are designed manually. Because of implementing simple I/O circuits in a FPGA tile, all you have to do is designing only one kind of FPGA tile and placing them simply to construct FPGA macro with 11×11 tile array, resulting in shortening global mask layout design and verification periods.

## 5.1 Area

Figure 11 show the whole chip layout of the fabricated FPGA. The FPGA tile size is 290 μm × 217 μm so that the 11×11 FPGA tile array size is 3.2 mm × 2.4 mm. Word-line shift registers and data-line shift registers are arranged in the left side and the upper side of the11x11 FPGA tile array respectively. In the FPGA tile layout as shown in Figure 12, 2 SMUXes, 3 IMUXes, 6 LMUXes, a LUT, a DFF and a 2:1 MUX are arranged in a straight line. Configuration memories and programmable body bias circuits are placed on upper side and lower side of them, respectively, resulting in the construction of the FPGA tile sub-macro. The FPGA tile macro design almost completes by arranging 4 sub-macros and wiring between them appropriately. PO MUX is placed at the lowest part of FPGA tile.

In our FPGA tile architecture with simple I/O circuits, it is worried that each wire length between an FPGA tile and a chip I/O is different in FPGA tile position because FPGA tiles are arranged as two-dimensional array, while chip I/Os are located around FPGA tile array, causing delay variation between FPGA tiles and chip I/Os. Though it is expected that the connections between FPGA tiles and pads by isometric wires mitigate delay variations, this method is not applied to the fabricated FPGA in this research because of the wiring design complexity.

Figure 13 shows the FPGA tile area breakdown. Elemental circuits such as MUXes, LUTs, DFFs, buffers, and configuration

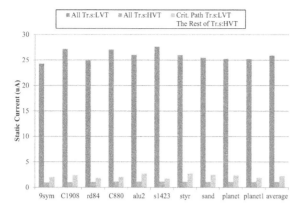

**Figure 14: Evaluation results of measured static current in 10 ISCAS benchmark circuits.**

memories that make up an FPGA tile occupy 46% of the tile area. The remaining 54 % of the FPGA tile area is occupied by well separation margins, voltage level shifters, body bias selection circuits, and configuration memories for programmable body bias circuits. In particular, the well-separation margins occupy 41 % of the tile area. The finest partition of the body biasing domain of 57 in the FPGA tile doubles the area. Further progress in device and process technologies such as deep trench isolation or SOI devices has possibility to reduce the well-separation space dramatically.

## 5.2 Evaluations of static current reduction

In this subsection, an effectiveness of the fabricated FPGA on static current reduction is evaluated by implementing ISCAS 10 benchmark circuits. Benchmark circuits are selected by following manners in this evaluation. First, some benchmark circuits are distilled from many kinds of ISCAS benchmark circuits from the viewpoint of the number of LUTs and the number of I/Os. After that, placement and routing tests are carried out to confirm whether above-distilled benchmark circuits can be implemented or not. Finally, 5 combinational circuits and 5 sequential circuits are picked up from the benchmark circuits in which placement and routing have successfully completed.

Table 2 shows the FPGA tile utilization in selected 10 benchmark circuits. 9sym, C1908, rd84, C880 and alu2 are the combinational circuits, and s1423, styr, sand, planet and planet1 are the sequential circuits. Utilization of used tile exceeds 96 % in average. Fraction of the used tile, in which both logic blocks (LB) and switch matrix (SM) are used, and in which only SM is used, is 47.5 % and 48.8 %, respectively. Moreover, Table 3 shows the utilization of elemental circuits of the FPGA. LUT utilization is 45.9 % and utilization of SMUX is closely 60 %.

Packing can be carried out effectively because the utilization of LB and SM used tiles is almost same value as LUT utilization. On the other hand, higher utilization results of 48.8 % in SM only used tile and of 59.6 % in SMUX show that plural FPGA tiles which have connectability each other are not able to be placed closely, as a result, the cases increase that the FPGA tiles are placed to the distance farther than wire segment length of 4. In short, routing resources of fabricated FPGA are insufficient in case that selected 10 benchmark circuits are implemented in this research.

Figure 14 shows evaluation results of measured static current in implemented 10 ISCAS benchmark circuits and static current in

**Table 2: FPGA tile utilization.**

| Benchmark Circuit | Used Tile | | | Unused Tile (%) |
| --- | --- | --- | --- | --- |
| | (1) LB and SM Used Tile (%) | (2) SM Only Used Tile (%) | (1)+(2) Total (%) | |
| 9sym | 32.2 | 46.3 | 78.5 | 21.5 |
| C1908 | 45.5 | 54.5 | 100.0 | 0.0 |
| rd84 | 34.7 | 56.2 | 90.9 | 9.1 |
| C880 | 52.9 | 47.1 | 100.0 | 0.0 |
| alu2 | 43.0 | 56.2 | 99.2 | 0.8 |
| s1423 | 48.8 | 49.6 | 98.3 | 1.7 |
| styr | 51.2 | 47.9 | 99.2 | 0.8 |
| sand | 52.9 | 47.1 | 100.0 | 0.0 |
| planet | 57.0 | 42.1 | 99.2 | 0.8 |
| planet1 | 57.0 | 40.5 | 97.5 | 2.5 |
| average | 47.5 | 48.8 | 96.3 | 3.7 |

**Table 3: Elemental circuit utilization.**

| Benchmark Circuit | IMUX (%) | SMUX (%) | LMUX (%) | LUT (%) | DFF (%) | 2:1MUX (%) | PO MUX (%) | Total (%) |
| --- | --- | --- | --- | --- | --- | --- | --- | --- |
| 9sym | 19.8 | 35.8 | 16.8 | 31.6 | 0.0 | 31.6 | 0.8 | 20.7 |
| C1908 | 24.4 | 66.5 | 17.5 | 36.8 | 0.0 | 36.8 | 20.7 | 27.4 |
| rd84 | 21.8 | 44.6 | 19.6 | 34.1 | 0.0 | 34.1 | 3.3 | 23.9 |
| C880 | 28.5 | 63.4 | 21.7 | 48.3 | 0.0 | 48.3 | 21.5 | 31.2 |
| alu2 | 28.0 | 64.7 | 24.0 | 42.8 | 0.0 | 42.8 | 5.0 | 31.2 |
| s1423 | 25.8 | 59.8 | 25.8 | 49.4 | 15.3 | 49.4 | 4.1 | 32.8 |
| styr | 32.9 | 64.6 | 28.0 | 51.0 | 1.0 | 51.0 | 8.3 | 35.2 |
| sand | 33.6 | 69.6 | 28.9 | 52.5 | 1.0 | 52.5 | 7.4 | 36.6 |
| planet | 35.7 | 62.9 | 31.3 | 56.4 | 1.2 | 56.4 | 15.7 | 37.8 |
| planet1 | 36.0 | 64.0 | 31.3 | 56.4 | 1.2 | 56.4 | 15.7 | 38.0 |
| average | 28.7 | 59.6 | 24.5 | 45.9 | 2.0 | 45.9 | 10.2 | 31.5 |

**Table 4: Summary of static current evaluation results.**

| Benchmark Circuit | (1) All Tr.s:LVT (μA) | (2) All Tr.s:HVT (μA) | (3) Crit. Path Tr.s:LVT The Rest of Tr.s:HVT (μA) | (1)/(2) | (1)/(3) | (3)/(1)-1 Static Current Reduction (%) |
| --- | --- | --- | --- | --- | --- | --- |
| 9sym | 24.25 | 0.93 | 2.03 | 26.04 | 11.92 | -91.6 |
| C1908 | 27.19 | 1.03 | 2.41 | 26.40 | 11.27 | -91.1 |
| rd84 | 24.93 | 1.05 | 1.85 | 23.80 | 13.49 | -92.6 |
| C880 | 27.06 | 1.13 | 2.06 | 23.86 | 13.13 | -92.4 |
| alu2 | 26.02 | 1.11 | 2.68 | 23.54 | 9.71 | -89.7 |
| s1423 | 27.62 | 1.14 | 1.75 | 24.26 | 15.78 | -93.7 |
| styr | 25.99 | 1.10 | 2.72 | 23.55 | 9.56 | -89.5 |
| sand | 25.43 | 1.07 | 2.48 | 23.83 | 10.26 | -90.3 |
| planet | 25.25 | 1.07 | 2.32 | 23.68 | 10.87 | -90.8 |
| planet1 | 25.18 | 1.06 | 1.89 | 23.70 | 13.29 | -92.5 |
| average | 25.89 | 1.07 | 2.22 | 24.23 | 11.66 | -91.4 |

**Table 5: Fraction of elemental circuits assigned LVT.**

| Benchmark Circuit | IMUX (%) | SMUX (%) | LMUX (%) | LUT (%) | DFF (%) | 2:1MUX (%) | PO MUX (%) | Total (%) |
| --- | --- | --- | --- | --- | --- | --- | --- | --- |
| 9sym | 3.3 | 8.1 | 3.2 | 13.0 | 0.0 | 14.5 | 0.8 | 5.1 |
| C1908 | 3.3 | 10.1 | 3.0 | 14.5 | 0.0 | 19.2 | 4.1 | 5.8 |
| rd84 | 2.0 | 5.6 | 2.3 | 9.5 | 0.0 | 11.2 | 2.5 | 3.7 |
| C880 | 1.9 | 5.0 | 2.4 | 10.5 | 0.0 | 18.6 | 3.3 | 4.2 |
| alu2 | 4.1 | 14.0 | 3.5 | 14.3 | 0.0 | 18.0 | 2.5 | 6.6 |
| s1423 | 1.5 | 3.2 | 1.6 | 7.0 | 0.8 | 12.2 | 0.0 | 2.8 |
| styr | 3.9 | 13.9 | 3.2 | 14.5 | 1.0 | 17.1 | 1.7 | 6.4 |
| sand | 3.0 | 13.4 | 2.8 | 13.0 | 1.0 | 17.4 | 3.3 | 6.0 |
| planet | 3.2 | 11.9 | 2.4 | 11.4 | 1.2 | 15.5 | 1.7 | 5.4 |
| planet1 | 1.8 | 7.5 | 1.7 | 8.9 | 1.2 | 13.4 | 0.0 | 3.8 |
| average | 2.8 | 9.3 | 2.6 | 11.7 | 0.5 | 15.7 | 2.0 | 5.0 |

the 3 body bias conditions and their static current ratios are summarizes in Table 4.

Here, the terms, described in the Figure14 and Table 4, and related body bias conditions are explained. "ALL Tr.s:LVT" means that all MOSFETs of elemental circuits in the FPGA are low-threshold voltage (LVT) condition. In this condition, body bias voltages are not applied to transistor's body. "ALL Tr.s:HVT" stands that all MOSFETs of elemental circuits are high-threshold voltage (HVT) condition by applying body bias voltages of +2.25 V for pmos body and –1.05 V for nmos body, respectively. "Crit. Path Tr.s:LVT, The Rest Tr.s:HVT" shows that threshold voltage of MOSFETs in elemental circuits on critical paths is set to LVT and the rest of MOSFETs are remaining HVT.

Static current becomes about 1/24 in average of 10 benchmark circuits by setting threshold voltage of all MOSFETs to HVT by applying body bias voltage to all MOSFETs bodies compared with the case that the threshold voltage of all MOSFETs is LVT. On the other hand, by assigning LVT to MOSFETs on critical paths, static current becomes 1/15.8 in maximum case by implementing a benchmark circuit of s1423 and 1/11.7 in average of 10 benchmark circuits. In short, fabricated Flex Power FPGA can reduce static current by 91.4 %.

When transistors on critical paths are assigned LVT while the rest of transistors are set to HVT, it is expected that the critical path delay is the same value as the case all MOSFETs are LVT condition. However, dynamic operations in case that 10 benchmark circuits are implemented can't be evaluated because we don't have information about input vectors and reasonable expectations of these benchmark circuits.

Table 5 shows the fraction of elemental circuits assigned LVT in each benchmark circuit. The fraction of LVT elements in SMUX, LUT and 2:1MUX becomes relatively higher than the other elemental circuits in which the fraction of LVT elements is lower than 3 %. The fraction of LVT in all elemental circuits is only 5 % in average of 10 benchmark circuits.

## 5.3 Implemented Ring Oscillator Evaluations

In this subsection, oscillation frequency, dynamic current and static current are evaluated by implementing a ring oscillator on the fabricated FPGA.

Figure 15 shows measured oscillation frequency, dynamic current and static current of implemented 22-stage ring oscillator (RO) with 21 inverters and 1 buffer when several body bias pairs are applied. Similar method has been employed in the previous work of [11]. When non body bias voltage are applied to MOSFETs on both a signal path and non-signal paths (0 V/0 V in figure), the oscillation frequency, dynamic current and the static current is 6.6 MHz, 291.4 μA and 23.1 μA respectively. By assigning HVT to all MOSFETs (–1.05 V/–1.05 V), the static current decreases to 1.0 μA, while the oscillation frequency becomes slower to 4.8 MHz while reducing dynamic current to 195.9 μA in proportion to the degradation of oscillation frequency . On the other hands, in case that LVT and HVT is assigned to the MOSFETs on signal path and the rest of the MOSFETs, respectively by applying body bias pair of (0 V/–1.05 V), the static current decreases to 1.5 μA while maintaining the same oscillation frequency of 6.6 MHz as the frequency in case that all MOSFETs are assigned LVT (0 V/0 V). Further static current reduction of 0.5 μA can be realized when the body bias voltage of –1.3 V is applied to MOSFETs on the non-signal path.

Moreover, by forward body biasing for all MOSFETs (+0.35 V/+0.35 V), oscillation frequency becomes fast from 6.6 MHz to 7.7 MHz, namely by 17 % compared with no body bias condition (0 V/0 V), while static current increases exponentially from 23.1 μA to 227.9 μA. Here, by applying body biasing of -1.3 V to MOSFETs on the non-signal paths (+0.35 V/–1.3 V), static current decreases to 4.1 μA drastically while maintaining oscillation frequency of 7.7 MHz in forward body bias condition (+0.35 V/+0.35 V). Total current consumption in this case (+0.35 V/–1.3 V) increases only by 8 % compared with the non-body bias condition of (0 V/0 V).

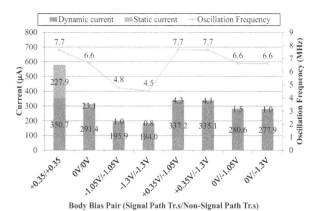

**Figure 15: Evaluation results of implemented ring oscillator.**

## 6. CONCLUSIONS

A fully-functional Flex Power FPGA with fine-grain programmable body biasing is fabricated using low-power 90-nm bulk CMOS technology. By individually controlling the body bias voltage of all the elemental circuits in the FPGA tile, fabricated FPGA drastically reduces the static current by 92.6% in the maximum case and by 91.4% on average, while the FPGA tile area is increased by well-separation margins and programmable body bias circuits. In particular, well-separation margins occupy 41% of the tile area. Moreover, by implementing ring oscillator in which LVT and HVT is assigned to MOSFETs on signal path and the rest of the MOSFETs respectively, the static current decreases from 23.1 μA to 1.0 μA while maintaining the same oscillation frequency of 6.6 MHz as the frequency when all MOSFETs are assigned LVT. Evaluation results show that fabricated Flex Power FPGA achieves drastic static current reduction without degrading operation speed. Moreover the fine-grain programmable body bias technique accelerates the oscillation frequency of ring oscillator implemented on FPGA by aggressively applying forward body bias voltage, while Assignment of HVT to MOSFETs on the non-critical path by applying the reverse body biasing effectively suppresses exponential increase of static current caused by the forward body biasing. The oscillation frequency becomes fast from 6.6 MHz to 7.7 MHz by applying body bias voltage pair of (+0.35 V/–1.3 V) compared to the FPGA with non-body bias condition (0 V/0 V). The increase of total current is only 8%.

## 7. ACKNOWLEDGMENTS

This work is supported by the Japan Science and Technology Agency (JST/CREST).

## 8. REFERENCES

[1] F. Li, Y. Lin, L. He, and J. Cong, "Low-power FPGA using predefined dual-Vdd/dual-Vt fabrics," in ISFPGA, pp.42-50, 2004.

[2] A. Rahman, and V. Polavarapuv, "Evaluation of low-leakage design techniques for field programmable gate arrays," in ISFPGA, pp.23-30, 2004.

[3] A. Gayasen, Y. Tsai, N. Vijaykrishnan, M. Kandemir, M. J. Irwin, and T. Tuan, "Reducing leakage energy in FPGAs using region-constrained placement," in ISFPGA, pp.51-58, 2004.

[4] J. H. Anderson, and F. N. Najim, "Low-power programmable routing circuitry for FPGAs," in ICCAD, pp.602-609, 2004.

[5] Y. Lin, F. Li, and L. He, "Routing track duplication with fine-grained power-gating for FPGA interconnect power reduction," in ASP-DAC, pp.645-650, 2005.

[6] A. Rahman, S. Das, T. Tuan and A. Rahut, "Heterogeneous Routing Architecture for Low-Power FPGA Fabric," in CICC, pp. 183-186, 2005.

[7] T. Tuan, S. Kao, A. Rahman, S. Das, and S. Trimberger, "A 90nm lowpower FPGA for battery-powered applications," in ISFPGA, pp.3-11, 2006.

[8] T. Kawanami, M. Hioki, H. Nagase, T. Tsutsumi, T. Nakagawa, T. Sekigawa, and H. Koike, "Preliminary evaluation of Flex Power FPGA: A power reconfigurable architecture with fine granularity," IEICE Trans. Information and Systems, E87-D(8):2004–2010, August 2004.

[9] M. Hioki, T. Kawanami, T. Tsutsumi, T. Nakagawa, T. Sekigawa, and H. Koike, "Can a cool chip be hot? yes, Flex Power FPGA can," in COOL Chips VII, pp.49–57, 2004.

[10] M. Hioki, T. Kawanami, T. Tsutsumi, T. Nakagawa, T. Sekigawa, and H. Koike, "Evaluation of Granularity on Threshold Voltage Control in Flex Power FPGA," in ICFPT, pp.17-23, 2006.

[11] T. Kawanami, M. Hioki, Y. Matsumoto, T. Tsutsumi, T. Nakagawa, T. Sekigawa, and H. Koike, "Optimal Set of Body Bias Voltages for an FPGA with Field-Programmable Vth Components," in ICFPT, pp.329-332, 2006.

[12] G. Lemieux, E. Lee, M. Tom, and A. Yu, "Directional and Single-Driver Wires in FPGA Interconnect," in ICFPT, pp.41-48, 2004.

[13] D. Lewis, E. Ahmed, D. Cashman, T. Vanderhoek, C. Lane, A. Lee, and P. Pan, "Architectural Enhancements in Stratix-III™ and Stratix-IV™," in Proc. FPGA, pp. 33–42, 2009.

[14] J. Luu, I. Kuon, P. Jamieson, T. Campbell, A. Ye, W. Fang, and J. Rose, "VPR 5.0: FPGA cad and architecture exploration tools with single-driver routing, heterogeneity and process scaling," in Proc. FPGA, pp. 133–142, 2009.

# GROK-LAB: Generating Real On-chip Knowledge for Intra-cluster Delays Using Timing Extraction

Benjamin Gojman
Department of Computer and
Information Systems
University of Pennsylvania
3330 Walnut Street
Philadelphia, PA 19104
bgojman@seas.upenn.edu

Sirisha Nalmela
Juniper Networks
10 Technology Park Drive
Westford, MA 01886
snalmela@juniper.net

Nikil Mehta
Department of Computer
Science California Institute of
Technology MC 305-16
1200 E. California Blvd.
Pasadena, CA 91125
nikil@caltech.edu

Nicholas Howarth
nhowarth@seas.upenn.edu

André DeHon
andre@acm.org

Department of Electrical and Systems Engineering
University of Pennsylvania
200 S. 33rd St. Philadelphia, PA 19104

## ABSTRACT

Timing Extraction identifies the delay of fine-grained components within an FPGA. From these computed delays, the delay of any path can be calculated. Moreover, a comparison of the fine-grained delays allows a detailed understanding of the amount and type of process variation that exists in the FPGA. To obtain these delays, Timing Extraction measures, using only resources already available in the FPGA, the delay of a small subset of the total paths in the FPGA. We apply Timing Extraction to the Logic Array Block (LAB) on an Altera Cyclone III FPGA to obtain a view of the delay down to near individual LUT granularity, characterizing components with delays on the order of a few hundred picoseconds with a resolution of $\pm 3.2$ ps. This information reveals that the 65 nm process used has, on average, random variation of $\sigma/\mu = 4.0\%$ with components having an average maximum spread of 83 ps. Timing Extraction also shows that as $V_{DD}$ decreases from 1.2 V to 0.9 V in a Cyclone IV 60 nm FPGA, paths slow down and variation increases from $\sigma/\mu = 4.3\%$ to $\sigma/\mu = 5.8\%$, a clear indication that lowering $V_{DD}$ magnifies the impact of random variation.

## Categories and Subject Descriptors

B.7.2 [**Integrated Circuits**]: Design Aids—*placement and routing*; B.8.1 [**Performance and Reliability**]: Reliability, Testing, and Fault-Tolerance; C.4 [**Performance of Systems**]: Measurement techniques

## General Terms

Algorithms, Measurement, Reliability

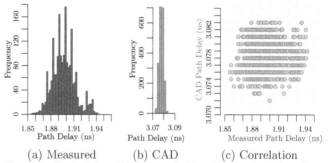

(a) Measured    (b) CAD    (c) Correlation

Figure 1: Path delay of 1000 nearly identical paths of length 7 LUTs, comparing measured delays to delays reported by the CAD tools for a Cyclone III 65 nm FPGA

## Keywords

Component-Specific Mapping; Variation Measurment; Variation Characterization; In-System Measurement

## 1. INTRODUCTION

Circuit variation is quickly becoming one of the biggest problems to overcome if the benefit from Moore's Law scaling is to continue. It is no longer possible to maintain an abstraction of identical devices without incurring huge yield losses, performance penalties, and high energy costs. Current techniques such as margining and speed grade binning are used to deal with this problem. However, they will become prohibitively conservative, only offering a limited solution that will not scale as variation increases.

Fig. 1 concretely demonstrates the price we pay for these techniques. We carefully measured 1,000 paths consisting of seven buffers in one logic array block (LAB) of an Altera Cyclone III 65 nm FPGA. Fig. 1a shows a histogram of the results of these measurements. Similarly, Fig. 1b shows the distribution of delays as computed by the CAD tools for these paths. Observe that the mean of the measured distribution is significantly lower than that reported by the CAD tools. This illustrates the magnitude of conservative margining, showing that the fabricated paths are only 60%

the delay predicted by the CAD tools. Moreover, the measured distribution has a much larger spread — 96 ps vs. 11 ps. Fig. 1c demonstrates there is no correlation between the delays measured and those reported by the CAD tools.

FPGAs have the unique advantage over ASICs that they can use more fine-grained and aggressive techniques that carefully choose which resources to use after fabrication in order to mitigate adverse variation effects. In [10] we show that a component-specific mapping solution reduces energy needs by 50% and will be a necessity to extend beneficial scaling as variation increases. This approach requires measurement of the underlying resource delays for the CAD tools to generate a custom mapping perfectly adapted to the variation in the FPGA. In this paper we present Timing Extraction, a methodology that allows the kind of fine-grained measurement of fabricated component delays necessary for [10] in an efficient and inexpensive manner, utilizing only resources already available on conventional FPGAs. To practically validate Timing Extraction, we apply it to clusters (LABs) in the Altera Cyclone III and Cyclone IV FPGAs and confirm that the measurements and calculations reflect underlying process variation.

The key challenge in Timing Extraction is that it is not possible to directly measure the characteristics of every LUT or wire in an FPGA. Nonetheless, we show that it is possible to obtain fine-grain delays using an indirect approach to measure, compute and characterize the variation of small groups of components. Work in [18] demonstrated the feasibility of measuring path delays without the need of any dedicated test circuitry, by surrounding the path with two registers that are already part of the reconfigurable fabric. Timing Extraction takes advantage of this measurement technique but goes further by demonstrating how to use the measurements to resolve the delays of individual resources.

The measured path is composed of multiple components, the individual delays of which we would we would like to know. By configuring and measuring a small set of overlapping paths, we can setup a linear system of equations that, when solved, gives the individual delay of each component in the paths [5]. A simple example will give better intuition as to what the technique actually accomplishes. Consider that we measure three paths. Path 1 composed of component $A$ and $B$. Path 2, $B$ and $C$. Finally, Path 3, $C$ and $A$. Suppose the delays of the paths are 5ps, 4ps and 3ps respectively. That leads to the system of equations below:

$$A + B = 5ps \qquad \text{Path 1}$$
$$B + C = 4ps \qquad \text{Path 2}$$
$$C + A = 3ps \qquad \text{Path 3}$$

Even though we did not measure the delays directly, with little work we can solve for the delay of $A$, $B$, and $C$ to be 2ps, 3ps and 1ps respectively.

Timing Extraction does exactly this but at a level that allows us to characterize a full FPGA. Formulating the naive problem, where every wire and transistor in the FPGA is represented by a separate variable in the system of equations, invariably leads to an underdetermined system without a unique solution (Sec. 3.2). However, Timing Extraction judiciously groups components into discrete units of knowledge (DUKs) which, combined with a careful selection of measured paths, guarantee a solution to the delay of each DUK in the system (Sec. 3.3). With that information, we can predict the delay of any path that could be used when mapping logic to the FPGA.

We begin with a brief review of the required background (Sec. 2). Sec. 3 develops the ideas of Timing Extraction by using the Cyclone III as a case study. Results from our measurements are presented in Sec. 4. While we present concrete details on how to measure the Cyclone III, the general technique can be extended to any modern FPGA; in Sec. 5 we briefly sketch how to port the ideas and why they are generally applicable. An outline of future work is explored in Sec. 6, before concluding (Sec. 7).

Novel contributions of this work include:

- First identification and demonstration of techniques for determining the delay of individual LUTs and the unique interconnect delay between pairs of LUTs using only on-chip FPGA resources.
    - Identification of smallest delay-measurable groups of components
    - Identification of smallest set of measurements necessary to extract complete fine-grain delay information within a cluster (LAB)
    - Algorithm for calculating component delays from path measurements
- Technique for predicting delay of any path in a cluster (LAB) using component LUT delay measurements.
- First set of measurements to fully characterize the delay components within a cluster (LAB) in a commercial FPGA.
- Quantification of process variation at a near LUT-level granularity.
- Quantification of increased random variation with voltage scaling.
- Characterization of significant contribution from random variation in process variation.

## 2. BACKGROUND

### 2.1 Process Variation

Process variation refers to differences between device parameters due to manufacturing. These differences ultimately affect the delay and energy requirements of the device. Correlated variation has historically comprised the majority of process variation, where the amount a device varies is correlated to some parameter, such as location on the wafer. Consequently, most techniques aim to reduce correlated variation. Binning, for example, mitigates die-to-die variation, while biasing reduces correlated regional variation. In essence, correlated variation provides a model which can be used to reduce process variation. However, as feature sizes continue to shrink, more and smaller transistors fit on one chip, greatly increasing the contribution of random variation to process variation. Unfortunately, unlike correlated, random variation is not easily modeled and mitigated.

Fig. 2 shows how the three main contributors to random variation – oxide thickness, line edge roughness, and random dopant fluctuations – lead to a significant increase in variation experienced by $V_{th}$, the transistor's threshold voltage, as technology scales.

The value of $V_{th}$ has a direct and profound effect on the performance and energy requirements of a transistor. Eqs. 1 and 2 represent the current through a transistor during the saturation and subthreshold operating points [6, 11]. Although physical parameters such as transistor geometry, $W$, $L$, and dopant concentration, $\eta$, have a strong stochastic

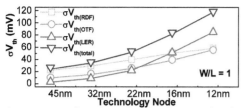

Figure 2: $\sigma_{V_{th}}$ as a function of technology nodes, based on predictive technology models. Considering the individual effects of random dopant fluctuations (RDF), line edge roughness (LER) and oxide thickness (OTF) from [19]

variation component, it is the exponential dependence on $V_{th}$ that brings about the harmful effects of random variation on the current through a transistor.

$$I_{ds,sat} = W v_{sat} C_{ox} \left( V_{gs} - V_{th} - \frac{V_{d,sat}}{2} \right) \quad (1)$$

$$I_{ds,sub} = \frac{W}{L} \eta C_{ox} (n-1) \cdot v_T^2 \cdot e^{\frac{V_{gs}-V_{th}}{n \cdot v_T}} \left( 1 - e^{\frac{-V_{ds}}{v_T}} \right) \quad (2)$$

In turn, the propagation delay $\tau_{pd}$ and leakage energy of the circuit are a function of current (Eqs. 3, 4).

$$\tau_{pd} = C_l \cdot \frac{V_{ds}}{I_{ds}} \quad (3) \qquad E_{leak} = I_{ds,sub} \cdot V_{ds} \cdot \tau_{cycle} \quad (4)$$

As such, random physical variation expresses itself in differences in the energy efficiency and delay of a transistor.

Statistical static timing analysis (SSTA) [14] attempts to model the expected random variation and with it the expected behavior of the FPGA. With this model, the CAD tools can generate a mapping that, statistically speaking, will reduce the effects of random variation. Unfortunately, this solution inherently fails to accommodate every FPGA. Instead of employing this one-size-fits-all solution, Timing Extraction measures and extracts detailed delay information from the FPGA after fabrication. This can then be provided to the CAD flow which generates a component-specific mapping tailoring the design to the particular FPGA.

The delay of a component in the FPGA is not only affected by process variation but can also fluctuate due to environmental and temperature changes [7] as well as aging effects [15]. To ensure that measured delays consistently represent process variation, Timing Extraction requires that measurements be taken in a highly controlled manner. Sec. 4.1 details the controls employed for our application on the Cyclone FPGA. The consistency of the results presented in Sec. 4.3 concretely demonstrates that Timing Extraction does measure process variation.

## 2.2 Altera Cyclone LAB Architecture

Timing Extraction is a general methodology that provides fine-grain delay measurement of small groups of components within an FPGA. Although it is applicable to any FPGA, to ground the presentation in this paper, we focus our application to the logic array blocks (LAB) of the Altera Cyclone III and Cyclone IV FPGAs.

The LAB in these FPGAs is composed of 16 Logic Elements (LE) each having a 4-LUT and optional register output, a set of 38 routing channels for external inputs, and 16 local routing channels for LE-to-LE communication with 50% depopulation (Fig. 4). The scope of this paper limits delay measurements to the 16 LEs and the 16 local routing channels in the LAB.

To better understand the results presented later in Sec. 4, it is worth noting that the architecture of the LUTs is such that nominally, the first two inputs, $A$ and $B$, have similar delays and by design are slower than input $C$ which in turn is tailored to be slower than input $D$. Moreover, inputs $A$ and $B$ form a complete input set, where every LE can connect to every other LE in the LAB by using either input $A$ or $B$, and similarly inputs $C$ and $D$ form a complete input set.

## 2.3 Path-Delay Measurements

We use a launch-capture technique to measure the delay of a path in an FPGA. In this approach, a combinatorial circuit, known as the circuit under test (CUT), is configured between a launch register and a capture register. Starting at an initial frequency and increasing to a maximum frequency, signals are sent from the launch register to the capture register. When a signal fails to reach the capture register within half of a clock cycle, we know that the delay of the path is greater than twice the frequency at which that signal was clocked. This technique has been successfully used to capture the delay of paths on FPGAs for many applications [8, 12, 13, 18].

A limitation of this measurement technique, however, is that it cannot measure a path that is faster than twice the highest frequency supported by the FPGA's on-chip PLLs. Twice the frequency comes from the fact that the launch and capture registers are clocked on opposite clock edges. Therefore, any work that exclusively uses this measurement technique will be limited to reporting delays of long paths. To ground this, consider that the maximum frequency for the Cyclone III PLLs used in this work is 402.5 MHz. This means that the fastest path we can measure is $\frac{1}{2 \cdot 402.5} = 1.24$ ns. Fig. 1a shows that, on average, a path of length 7 LUTs is measured to take 1.90 ns, meaning that, roughly on average, the delay through one LUT is 271 ps. Combining this fact with our maximum frequency leads to the conclusion that the smallest path we can measure is 5 LUTs long. This ignores the expected variation spread. Therefore, to err on the side of caution, we do not measure anything with less than 6 LUTs in a path. Nevertheless, as we will later show, this work reports on delays on the order of one LUT by taking delay measurements of long paths and breaking them into smaller parts. [18] and [17] take only a single measure within each LAB or CLB and make no attempt to characterize within-LAB variation. The most closely related technique used in [3] and [20] takes the difference between two ring oscillators to extract sub-cluster delays. However, this approach fails to account for the unique interconnect delay between pairs of LUTs, nor is it able to account for register delays.

Due to the nature of CMOS and FPGA circuit design that uses NMOS pass transistors, there is a marked delay difference in a rising transition, as compared to a falling transition. In order to separate the falling and rising delays, our CUT is composed of buffers in series. In this way, all elements in a path transition in the same direction, allowing us to separate the rising transition through the path from falling transitions (Fig. 14). Fig. 3 shows a diagram of the path-delay measurement circuit used. A signal with a 50% duty cycle is provided to the launch register. The signal propagates through the CUT and the capture register records its output. Errors are detected by the two error detection circuits, one monitoring rising failures, the other, falling failures.

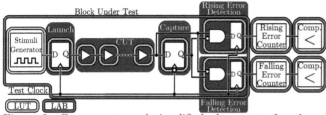

Figure 3: Components and simplified placement of path-delay measurement circuit

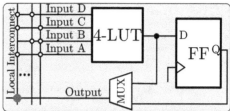

Figure 4: Block diagram of a Cyclone FPGA LE (4-LUT and register), including local interconnect

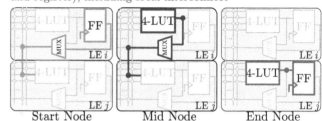

Start Node          Mid Node          End Node

Figure 5: Highlighted, an example of the components that form each of the three types of LC Nodes in a Cyclone LAB

Because of operating variation such as clock jitter, it is not sufficient to observe one failure to declare the delay of a path. Instead, the path is tested at one frequency many times, and two counters, for rising and falling transitions, keep track of how many failures occurred at that frequency, for that transition. If at frequency $f$, the number of failures reaches a percent of the total number of transitions, the delay of that circuit is reported as $\frac{1}{f}$. The transition from no failures to 100% failures is gradual. If we assume that the variation that caused this gradual failure rate is mostly stochastic and has a symmetric probability distribution, then the 50% failure rate provides the most accurate estimate of delay given a small number of samples. We do not use this frequency for regular operation, since at this frequency signals fail timing 50% of the time. Knowing the variance in cycle time, we can then select a suitable operating frequency that keeps timing errors down to an acceptable level.

## 3. TIMING EXTRACTION

The general idea behind Timing Extraction is easy to understand. It is not possible to measure the delay of every component in an FPGA directly since individual transistors or wires cannot be isolated from their surrounding components. Nevertheless, by measuring the delay of different paths through an FPGA, it is possible to decompose the delays of these paths into their constituents. Essentially, each path consists of a linear sum of the delay of its parts; therefore, we can cast this problem as a linear system of equations where each equation represents a path and equals the measured delay of the path. With enough equations, we can solve for all the unknowns and directly acquire the delays of every component used in these paths. In order for the system of equations to have a unique solution, it is imperative to carefully select what the variables in the equations represent. In this section, we use the Altera Cyclone LAB architecture to ground the development of the general Timing Extraction methodology. We begin by considering what is individually calculable, followed by an analysis of what paths must be measured. This leads to the realization that our initial assessment of what is individually calculable is flawed, which ultimately arrives at the notion of discrete units of knowledge (DUKs), allowing for a complete solution.

### 3.1 Logical Components

It is not possible to measure the delay of a single wire or transistor in the FPGA, even indirectly. To explain, consider the simple representation of the Cyclone LUT in Fig. 4. Suppose we want to know the delay of only the highlighted crosspoint in isolation. This is not possible since any path that uses that crosspoint must use the labeled Local Interconnect, Output and MUX. However, since any path that uses this crosspoint will naturally use the other components,

there is no practical reason to measure its delay independent of these components. This gives the notion of a Logical Component or LC Node, and the first attempt at defining what the variables in our system of equations represent.

As explained in Sec. 2.3, measured paths start at a register, go through zero or more buffers, and end at a register. A path in a LAB will begin at a register, go through some number of LUTs and end at a second register. Fig. 5 shows how we decompose this path into three types of LC Nodes. The path begins at an LC Node whose first component is a register, known as a *Start Node*, goes through zero or more LC Nodes with no registers, *Mid Nodes*, and ends at an *End Node*, an LC Node whose last component is a register.

Fig. 6a represents a path using groups of Start, Mid and End Nodes. Thus, we let LC Nodes correspond to variables in our system of equations and represent each measured path delay by a linear sum of the delays of these LC Nodes.

To solve for the delay of all LC Nodes, we must measure at least a number of paths equal to the number of LC Nodes in a LAB. A Start Node and Mid Node start at one LE and end at a second LE. Considering there are 16 LEs in a LAB and two input sets (Sec. 2.2), this gives a total of $16 \times 15 \times 2 = 480$ Start and 480 Mid Nodes per LAB. Since End Nodes only use one LE, there are only 16 End Nodes per LAB. In total, there are $480 + 480 + 16 = 976$ LC Nodes in a LAB, which is the minimum number of paths we must measure to solve for their delay.

### 3.2 Matrix Representation

Once we measure a correct set of 976 paths and solve for the delay of all LC Nodes, it will be possible to reconstruct the delay of any of the approximately $10^{18}$ paths within a LAB. Therefore, the problem is deciding which 976 paths to measure. To better discuss this solution, we formulate our system of equations as a matrix. A path is represented by a row, while a column describes an LC Node. An entry $L_{ij}$ in the matrix is 1 if LC Node $j$ forms part of path $i$, 0 otherwise. Since there are 976 LC Nodes, and we need at least 976 paths, our matrix will be at least as large as $976 \times 976$. Once the delays of the paths are measured, we use this matrix and the path delays to solve for all LC Nodes.

Linear algebra tells us that if the rank of the original matrix is equal to the number of LC Nodes, then we can solve

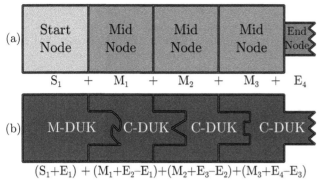

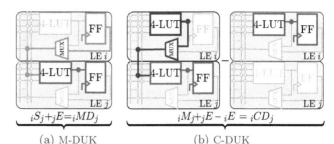

$$_iS_j + _jE = _iMD_j \qquad\qquad _iM_j + _jE - _iE = _iCD_j$$

(a) M-DUK  (b) C-DUK

Figure 7: Highlighted, an example of the LC Nodes that form the two types of DUKs in a Cyclone LAB

$$(S_1+E_1) + (M_1+E_2-E_1)+(M_2+E_3-E_2)+(M_3+E_4-E_3)$$

Figure 6: Equivalence between LC Node basis and DUK basis. To build intuition, the shapes give a geometric interpretation to the delay of each LC Node or DUK. The Equations below each figure show it mathematically

for the delay of each LC Node. Otherwise, if it is less than the number of LC Nodes, the system is underdetermined and, in general, contains an infinite number of solutions. Unfortunately, even if we measure the delay of all $10^{18}$ paths, the rank of the matrix is 960, 16 less than the total number of LC Nodes in a LAB. Sec. 5 provides some intuition as to why this is the case for any FPGA in which we let LC Nodes represent the variables in the system of equations.

Even though the matrix is rank deficient, it must have a non-empty vector space which comprises its basis. In turn, this means that there must be a set of linearly independent paths, which, when taken together and measured, allow us to compute the delay of any other measurable path in the circuit. Since the LAB has a matrix with rank 960, we only need to measure a linearly independent set of 960 paths to compute the delay of any path in the LAB. Essentially, instead of using a basis where every path in the matrix is represented by a linear combination of LC Nodes, we use a basis where every path is represented by a linear combination of the 960 paths measured.

Although this approach provides the delay of any path, it does not achieve the desired results for two reasons. First, it is difficult to incorporate these results into conventional routing algorithms when a component-specific route is sought, since routing algorithms [9] tend to expand routes incrementally and we only have complete path delay information. Second, the basis does not provide a fine-grained understanding of the variation. The next section addresses these shortcomings by defining a particularly convenient basis that spans the matrix yet provides the fine-grain, incremental variation information desired.

## 3.3 DUK Basis

Timing Extraction's objective is to provide fine-grain delay information that can then be used to characterize the variation in the FPGA as well as perform a component-specific mapping to the FPGA. We know it is not possible to solve for the delay of every LC Node; however, our solution should allow us to formulate path delays as a linear sum of a small number of components. By definition, an LC Node is the smallest delay we care to measure; however, since we cannot solve for LC Nodes, we consider the next best thing, a basis where the variables represent a small linear combination of LC Nodes. We refer to this small linear combination of LC Nodes as a *Discrete Unit of Knowledge*, or *DUK*. First we introduce the vectors that compose the

DUK basis, then we show the equivalence between an LC-based and a DUK-based model, finally we demonstrate that unlike LC Nodes, we can compute the delay of DUKs.

Instead of having three types of variables which are combined to represent a path, this basis contains two types of DUKs. The delay of a Start Node plus an End Node forms the first DUK (Eq. 5). On its own, this DUK forms a complete measurable path, starting at a register and ending at a second register. Moreover, all paths stem from this DUK, therefore, we refer to it as a Mother DUK, or *M-DUK*. The second DUK is known as a Child DUK, or *C-DUK*. As its name suggests, it follows the Mother DUK and incrementally grows a path. A C-DUK consists of the delay of a Mid Node plus the difference of two End Nodes (Eq. 6).

$$\text{M-DUK} = S_i + E_j \qquad (5)$$
$$\text{C-DUK} = M_i + E_j - E_k \qquad (6)$$

Assuming we have their delays, together, these two types of DUK allow us to compose any measurable path in exactly the same way that LC Nodes did. In general, a measurable path will be represented by an M-DUK and zero or more C-DUKs. For a path to be measurable, it must start and end at a register, M-DUKs naturally represent such paths. The function of a C-DUK is to replace the End Node and extend the path by adding a Mid Node and a new End Node. Consider, for example, the path shown in Fig. 6a consisting of a Start Node, 3 Mid Nodes and an End Node. We can easily represent this path in the DUK basis using one M-DUK and 3 C-DUKs, as shown in Fig. 6b. Fig. 6b represents each DUK as a jigsaw piece to give a geometric meaning to the notion that two DUKs must complement each other in order to correctly represent a path. Here, instead of each DUK having a different delay, each DUK has a unique shape. The concave left side of a C-DUK represents the carved out delay of the subtracted End Node, while the convex right side of a DUK shows the addition of an End Node.

In general, given a path represented by LC Nodes, we can easily re-express it using the DUK basis by replacing the Start Node with an M-DUK containing the same Start Node, and every Mid Node by a C-DUK composed in part by the Mid Node and subtracting the same End Node that is added to the DUK before it. The last C-DUK must also contain the End Node of the path in question.

## 3.4 DUKs in Cyclone LAB

Fig. 7 shows how DUKs map to LE $i$ and $j$ in a Cyclone LAB. Similar to the Start Node, the M-DUK spans two LEs. Since there are 16 LEs in a LAB, and two input sets (Sec. 2.2), there are $16 \times 15 \times 2 = 480$ M-DUKs. An equal number of C-DUKs exist, since a C-DUK also spans two LEs. Using the 960 DUKs in a LAB, it is possible to represent any path in the LAB originally represented by a set of LC Nodes. Under Fig. 7 appear two LC Node equations leading to the corresponding DUKs. A subscript prefix on both the LC Nodes and the DUKs indicate the source LE and a subscript suffix signals the sink LE. We can establish a one-to-one correspondence between Start Nodes and M-DUKs (Fig. 7a) by observing that the prefix and suffix on the Start Node matches the prefix and suffix of the M-DUK. Essentially, it indicates that if the Start Node begins in LE $i$ and ends in LE $j$, the M-DUK will as well. A similar bijection exists between Mid Nodes and C-DUKs (Fig. 7b). The equations in Fig. 7 also indicate which End Nodes must be added or subtracted to correctly form the DUK.

These equations and this notation allows us to trivially transform a path based on LC Nodes into one using DUKs. We replace the Start Node with the M-DUK that has the same source and sink LE. Similarly we replace every Mid Node with the matching C-DUK. The delay contributed by the End Node will already form part of the last DUK. An example will help solidify this transformation.

Consider the path with four LC Nodes

$$_iS_j + {}_jM_k + {}_kM_l + {}_lE$$

Applying the transformation algorithm described above leads to the path

$$_iMD_j + {}_jCD_k + {}_kCD_l$$

Expand each DUK to its LC Node representation leads to

$$\underbrace{_iS_j + {}_jE}_{_iMD_j} + \underbrace{_jM_k + {}_kE - {}_jE}_{_jCD_k} + \underbrace{_kM_l + {}_lE - {}_kE}_{_kCD_l}$$

Which, after simplifying the terms, equals the original LC Node-based path.

It is not a coincidence that the number of DUKs, 960, matches the rank of the matrix formed by paths × LC Nodes. The algorithm above shows how a linear combination of DUKs can be used to represent an arbitrary measurable path. This is the definition of a basis for the matrix. Therefore, these DUKs form a basis for the path-LC Node matrix. As such, by obtaining the delay of the 960 DUKs, we can compute the delay of any of the $10^{18}$ paths in the LAB.

This basis is superior to the one suggested at the end of Sec. 3.2, where 960 linearly independent paths are selected to form the basis, for several reasons. First, DUKs can be composed incrementally, allowing routing algorithms to easily incorporate this delay information into their path search. Second, DUKs provide a uniformity that the other basis lacks. There is no guarantee that all paths in the other basis will be of the same length or use similar LUT inputs. Therefore, it is not easy to compare delays between and within LABs. DUKs, on the other hand, have two consistent forms, M-DUKs and C-DUKs. We can directly compare one C-DUK using LUT input A to another C-DUK using LUT input A, and know that if one is faster, it is due to process variation and not because of differences in what they represent. Finally, DUKs provide very fine-grain delay information, almost on the order of one LE, while the other basis only has delays of paths.

## 3.5 Obtaining DUK Delays

It should come as no surprise that it is impossible to measure C-DUKs directly, since one term subtracts the delay of an End Node. It is relatively simple, however, to figure out which paths combine to give a C-DUK's delay. Consider C-DUK $_iM_j + {}_jE - {}_iE$ from Fig. 7b. To get this delay we simply measure a path starting with a set of Nodes represented by path prefix $A$ and ending in Nodes $_iM_j + {}_jE$ and subtract from it a path starting with the Nodes in $A$ and ending in Node $_iE$. This leads to the path equation:

$$(A + {}_iM_j + {}_jE) - (A + {}_iE) = {}_iM_j + {}_jE - {}_iE$$

In a sense, this mathematically demonstrates the purpose of a C-DUK, removing the last End Node in a path and replacing it with a new Mid Node and End Node.

Since every M-DUK represents the delay of a Start Node plus an End Node and a path must begin at a Start Node and end at an End Node, our path measurement technique (Sec. 2.3) should allow us to directly measure the delay of every M-DUK. Unfortunately, as established in Sec. 2.3, the shortest path we can confidently measure is of length 6, while an M-DUK forms a much smaller path of length 1 LUT and 2 registers (Fig. 7a). Therefore, we take an indirect approach to measuring the delay of an M-DUK by measuring three paths and taking a linear combination of these paths.

To compute the delay of M-DUK $_iS_j + {}_jE$, we measure one path that begins by a set of nodes represented by $A$ and ends with $_lM_j + {}_jE$. Then measure a second path which begins with $_iS_j + {}_jM_k$ and ends with a set of nodes represented by $B$. Finally we measure a path which is similar to the second path at the beginning and similar to the first path at the end: $A + {}_lM_j + {}_jM_k + B$. Adding the first two paths and subtracting the third leads to the delay of the M-DUK as shown in the following path equation:

$$(A + {}_lM_j + {}_jE) + ({}_iS_j + {}_jM_k + B) - (A + {}_lM_j + {}_jM_k + B) = {}_iS_j + {}_jE$$

There exist a few requirements on which nodes may form part of $A$ and $B$. Since the third path uses both $A$ and $B$, we must make sure that each of the 16 LUTs in the LAB is used only once between the Nodes in $A$, $B$, and the two Mid Nodes $_lM_j + {}_jM_k$. Also, $A$ and $B$ should not use the LUT $i$ or $j$. These requirements are easy to satisfy and allow for long paths that we can measure using the limited frequency resources in the Cyclone III and Cyclone IV FPGAs.

All told, we measure two paths for every C-DUK and three for each M-DUK, at worst, this means we must measure $2 \times 480 + 3 \times 480 = 2,400$ paths per LAB. Although this is slightly larger than the minimum of 960 given by performing Gaussian Elimination on the path × LC Node matrix, it is still a small number compared to the total possible paths, and it meets the Timing Extraction goals: Fine-grain measurements suitable for direct variation characterization and component-specific routing.

## 4. EXPERIMENTAL RESULTS

We applied Timing Extraction both to 18 Arrow BeMicro boards which have a Cyclone III FPGA EP3C16F256C8N [2] and one Terasic DE0-Nano with a Cyclone IV FPGA EP4CE22F17C6N [16], modified to allow control over the FPGA's internal $V_{dd}$. In this section we present the main results from our measurement experiments on both boards.

## 4.1 Methodology

The delay of a path in an FPGA is subject to many sources of variation beyond process variation. These include effects such as CAD tool decisions, local supply voltage IR-drop, crosstalk and temperature fluctuations. To annul the effects of these variation sources we perform our measurements in a very structured and systematic way. We divide the FPGA into a control region, where logic required to control the measurement tests is placed on 66 LABs, and a measurement region containing the LABs that will be measured. This keeps the control logic away from the paths under test so that noise effects in the control circuitry will have minimal impact on the measured circuitry. Leveraging the constraints provided by QUIP [1], the placement and routing of all but the LABs being measured is fixed and consistent for all our measurements. This assures us that signal path lengths and compositions are identical across test and do not directly contribute to the differences in measured delays. QUIP is also used to dictate the placement and routing of the path being measured within a LAB. Moreover, to reduce the overall activity in the FPGA, we do not measure LABs in parallel, but rather measure LABs one at a time. This guarantees that local heating and switching-activity-dependent IR drop do not impact the delay measurements. What's more, all measurements are taken in a temperature controlled room, and we perform our measurement several times to reach a stable internal temperature before recording the final path delay. All these precautions lead to path delays measured in a consistent and precise manner with repeatable results, suggesting the measurements reveal the underlying process variation and allowing us to compare results between LABs and FPGAs without worry that other variation effects cloud our results.

We use the path measurement technique (Sec. 2.3) on 18 Cyclone III FPGAs, to measure the 2,400 paths per LAB necessary to compute all DUK delays. Each measurement set taking on average 20 minutes per LAB. Due to limitations in the Cyclone III PLLs, for our measurements, we increment the frequency at linear intervals of 1.6 ps and at each frequency, perform $2^{15}$ path measurements, taking as the delay of the path the frequency that yields a 50% failure rate for that path. Unless otherwise specified, throughout this section we present results related to C-DUKs in LAB (27,22) of a Cyclone III. Where appropriate, we indicate more general results.

## 4.2 Extracted Characterization

Fig. 8 shows the resulting distribution of the paths measured to compute C-DUKs in a LAB. We highlight four separate distributions to isolate two sources of known systematic difference, the path length (7 and 8 LUTs) and the LUT inputs used (A&B or C&D). From these paths, we compute DUK delays, Fig. 9 shows these distributions for C-DUKs in a LAB. In this case, the different colors indicate the LUT input used by the DUK. Fig. 10 shows the individual delays for each C-DUK over LUT inputs $A$ and $B$. Note that there is no single delay associated with a LUT; each source-sink pair has a unique delay, demonstrating the importance of accounting for LUT to LUT routing. Within a LAB, on average, over all 18 FPGAs we see a standard deviation of $\sigma/\mu = 3\%$ for M-DUKs and $\sigma/\mu = 5\%$ for C-DUKs.

Fig. 11a and 11b compare the C-DUK delay distribution of two LABs in one FPGA, and of one LAB in two FPGAs, respectively. The results indicate that the variation is composed of a spatially correlated component, a within-die correlated component, and a random component. If the variation was only correlated, the data points on these graphs would lie on the $\Delta 0ps$ diagonal line. Similarly, if it was all random variation, the data points would resemble Fig. 1c. The correlated components are less apparent, but random variation is clear when reviewing Fig. 12 which compares the

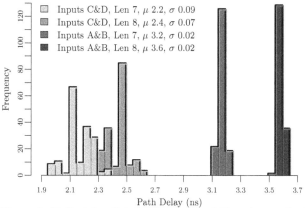

Figure 8: Path delay distribution for the 960 paths required to solve all C-DUKs, differentiating known systematic variation, Cyclone III LAB (27,22)

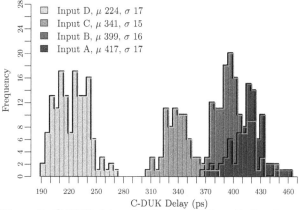

Figure 9: C-DUK delay distribution, differentiating known systematic variation, Cyclone III LAB (27,22)

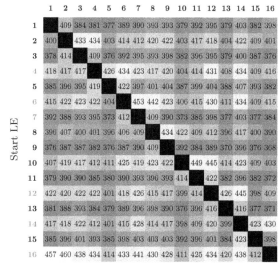

Figure 10: C-DUK delays in picoseconds over LUT inputs $A$ and $B$. Rows index start LE of C-DUK, columns index end LE. LUT input $A$ shown by highlighted row header, $B$ otherwise. Cyclone III LAB (27,22)

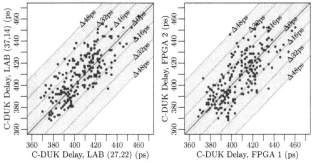

(a) LAB vs LAB, same FPGA  (b) FPGA vs FPGA, same LAB

Figure 11: Correlation between C-DUKs in two LABs in one FPGA (a) and between two FPGAs for the same LAB (27,22) (b). Diagonal lines indicate difference between results in terms of $d_\Delta = 1.6$ ps. Thicker lines indicate $10d_\Delta$. Red lines at $\pm 2d_\Delta$ region. Cyclone III

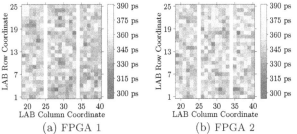

(a) FPGA 1  (b) FPGA 2

Figure 12: Delay heatmap for the C-DUK that goes from LE 10 to LE 8, over a region of $21 \times 25$ LABs for two different FPGAs. White columns represent location of embedded blocks. Cyclone III

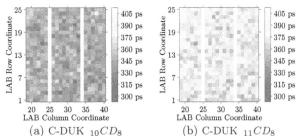

(a) C-DUK $_{10}CD_8$  (b) C-DUK $_{11}CD_8$

Figure 13: Delay heatmap for the C-DUK that goes from LE 10 to LE 8 (a) and C-DUK from LE 11 to LE 8 (b), over a region of $21 \times 25$ LABs for the same FPGA. White columns represent location of embedded blocks. Figs. 12a and 13a show same C-DUK using different heat scales. Cyclone III

delay of the same C-DUK over a region of $21 \times 25$ LABs between two FPGAs. Fig. 13, which compares two C-DUKs in one FPGA over the same region, does show correlated variation, where one C-DUK is clearly slower than the other; however, there still exists a strong random component.

We also see strong evidence of a mixture of variation types when considering the DUK delays for rising transitions as compared to falling transitions (Fig. 14). As previously pointed out, the nature of CMOS and the use of NMOS pass transistors in the FPGA lead us to expect a difference in the delay of rising and falling transitions. On average, falling transitions are 9% faster. However, the spread in Fig. 14a shows a strong random component, due to the fact that

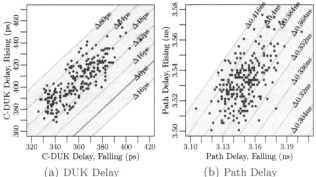

(a) DUK Delay  (b) Path Delay

Figure 14: Correlation between Rising and Falling delays for C-DUKs (a) and paths (b). Diagonal lines indicate difference between results. Cyclone III LAB (27,22)

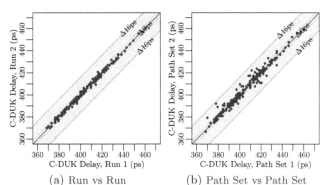

(a) Run vs Run  (b) Path Set vs Path Set

Figure 15: Correlation between C-DUKs when measuring the same paths twice (a) and measuring different path sets yielding the same DUKs (b). Diagonal lines indicate difference between results in terms of $d_\Delta = 1.6$ ps. Thicker lines indicate $10d_\Delta$. Red lines at $\pm 2d_\Delta$ region. Cyclone III LAB(27,22)

PMOS and NMOS transistors do not have perfectly correlated relative parameters and can vary independent of each other.

## 4.3 Measurement Validation

The measurement of the delay of a path can be subject to many sources of noise; therefore, we would like to build confidence that we are not measuring that noise but rather the actual delay of paths and DUKs in a consistent manner. As explained in Sec. 4.1, we control as many aspects as possible when performing our measurements. To measure if these controls achieve consistency, we perform the measurements twice by measuring paths, computing all DUK delays and repeating. Fig. 15a shows the resulting C-DUK delay when we measure paths twice. We see high correlation with nearly all DUKs differing by less than $\pm 3.2$ ps (region between red diagonal lines) between the first and second measurement.

A second form of validation comes from the fact that we can measure distinct sets of paths that allow us to compute the delay of the same set of DUKs. Recall from Sec. 3.5 that we need two paths to compute the delay of C-DUKs and three for M-DUKs. These paths have a fixed set of LC Nodes that determine which DUK will be computed from their delays, and a prefix of LC Nodes that do not form part of the final DUK. We can select a different set of LC Nodes to use for the prefix without affecting which DUKs we compute. Fig. 15b shows the resulting C-DUKs when we compute them using two different sets of paths. Considering that the path measurement

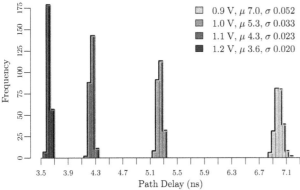

Figure 16: Path delay distribution for Length 8 Paths over LUT inputs $A$ and $B$ required to solve C-DUKs, differentiating varying $V_{dd}$, Cyclone IV LAB (28,22)

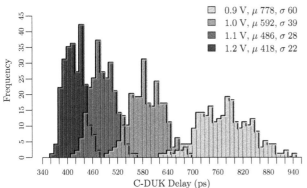

Figure 17: C-DUK delay distribution for LUT inputs $A$ and $B$, differentiating varying $V_{dd}$, Cyclone IV LAB (28,22)

inherently introduces a difference of $\pm 3.2$ ps, Fig. 15b shows that it matters little which set of paths are measured as long as we can compute the complete set of DUKs from these paths. Together these figures show that we can trust our technique to correctly and consistently compute the delay of DUKs.

## 4.4 Effects of Varying $V_{DD}$

Lowering $V_{DD}$ is a common and important way to save power and energy. In this section we examine the effect that reducing $V_{DD}$ has on variation. In particular we ask whether scaling $V_{DD}$ has a purely systematic effect on the variation distributions or is there a random component as well. To do this we modify a DE0-Nano board containing a Cyclone IV FPGA so that we can control the internal $V_{DD}$. Nominally, the board provides a 1.2 V $V_{DD}$. For our tests, we scale at 100 mV increments. At $V_{DD} = 0.8$ V, a large percent of our measurements fail and at 0.7 V the board fails to power up.

We know that a lower $V_{DD}$ increases the propagation delay of a circuit, as well as the standard deviation of the path delay distribution [4]. We clearly see this effect in Fig. 16, the delay distribution for the paths of length 8 used to compute C-DUKs. As we lower $V_{DD}$ the distribution shifts right and becomes wider. This effect is even more pronounced when we look at the C-DUK delay distributions in Fig. 17.

To see how the distribution changes when we go from 1.2 V to 0.9 V we plot correlation graphs (Fig. 18). We would expect a graph similar to Fig. 15a if lowering $V_{DD}$ only had a systematic effect on the distribution. However, we observe a significant random component, indicating that lowering $V_{DD}$ magnifies the impact of random variation.

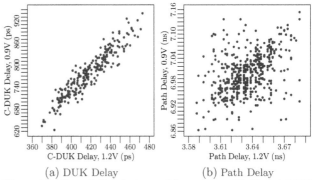

(a) DUK Delay      (b) Path Delay

Figure 18: Correlation between Measuring with $V_{dd}$ at 1.2V and 0.9V for C-DUKs (a) and paths of length 8 (b) for LUT input $A$ and $B$. Cyclone IV LAB (28,22)

## 5. GENERALIZING TIMING EXTRACTION

Although Sec. 3 introduces Timing Extraction by applying it to a Cyclone III LAB, the approach generalizes to any FPGA that has registers and configurable PLLs. We can distill the essence of Timing Extraction into five concepts.

1. We can measure the delay of a group of components in the FPGA using only resources already in the FPGA.

2. LC Nodes represent the smallest group of components for which we need to compute a delay, since, if we use any component in an LC Node, we must use all other components in the LC Node.

3. When using the measurement technique from Sec. 2.3, it is not possible to solve for the delay of every LC Node when a measured path begins at a Start Node, goes through zero or more Mid Nodes, and terminates at an End Node.

4. When representing all measurable paths as a matrix, there exists a basis that will allow us to compute the delay of any path in the FPGA using only the delay of vectors in that basis.

5. We can formulate a basis where every vector is a DUK composed of a small linear combination of LC Nodes.

The first, second, and fourth points are immediate; however, it is not obvious why the third and fifth hold true. Although a full explanation, formalization, and proof is beyond the scope of this paper, we can build some intuition to address the third point. Consider a simplified circuit that, when represented in LC Nodes, has all paths being composed by just a Start Node and an End Node. Moreover, there exists a physical path in the circuit formed by combining any Start Node with any End Node. We can represent this situation as a fully connected bipartite graph with Start Nodes forming one set and End Nodes the second. For simplicity, assume that the delay of every path is measured to be 500 ps. It is easy to show that at least two solutions to the delay of the nodes exist. One solution assigns a delay of 200 ps to all Start Nodes and a delay of 300 ps to all End Nodes. The second solution does the opposite, assigning 300 ps to Start Nodes and 200 ps to End Nodes. A similar circuit with fewer paths suffers from the same problem. Therefore, this circuit, and any subset, leads to an underdetermined system. The argument becomes somewhat more complicated when considering the more general problem which also includes Mid Nodes; however, the intuition remains the same.

Showing the fifth point to be true remains part of our future work. We have already introduced two types of DUKs, yet it is likely that more will be necessary to decompose an arbitrary path into DUKs. The exact form and number is not yet clear;

however, we expect that the regularity of FPGAs will help limit the total number of DUK types. By defining enough DUK types to be able to decompose an arbitrary measurable path into DUKs, we will be able to form a DUK basis. Finally, by defining new DUKs also as a small linear combination of LC Nodes, we can keep all DUKs small enough to provide fine-grain, meaningful delay information.

## 6. FUTURE WORK

The previous section suggests that Timing Extraction is more generally applicable. This paper applies Timing Extraction exclusively to the LABs. To get the full, intended benefits of this technique, it is essential to also apply Timing Extraction to inter-cluster routing and LUT logic. Moreover, the results section hints at the existence of different types of variation: systematic, spatially correlated, random, and shows that Timing Extraction is able to provide the raw information necessary to understand variation in the FPGA. To fully harness the power of Timing Extraction, however, a mathematical analysis of the information it provides should be performed to quantify how much and what kind of variation exists within the FPGA.

Finally, we perform our measurements in a highly controlled setting (Sec. 4.1), this leads to clean and consistent results, yet, it is not clear which controls are necessary for good results. Careful experimentation will reveal how the results change when we change or relax the strong restrictions on our measurement technique, allowing us to simplify and accelerate path measurements.

## 7. CONCLUSIONS

We presented Timing Extraction, a method used to extract the fine-grained delay information necessary to understand variation within the FPGA and to generate component-specific mappings. We acquire this information using only resources already present in the FPGA. Essentially, we apply a launch and capture technique to measure a subset of all paths in the FPGA, and extract small Discrete Units of Knowledge (DUKs) from these measurements. We can then compose DUKs to compute the delay of any path in the FPGA and use them to understand the amount and type of variation present.

We applied this technique to the Logic Array Blocks in both the Altera Cyclone III and Cyclone IV FPGAs. The results indicate that, on average, we see $\sigma/\mu = 4\%$ variation in the 65 nm process used for the Cyclone III. Moreover, there is clear indication that random variation forms a significant part of the total variation. We expect that as we measure smaller technology nodes, both the total variation and the contribution from random variation will increase. By using Timing Extraction we will be able to characterize and reduce the adverse effects from this increase.

### Acknowledgments

This research was funded in part by National Science Foundation grant CCF-0904577. Any opinions, findings, and conclusions or recommendations expressed in this material are those of the authors and do not necessarily reflect the views of the National Science Foundation. The authors gratefully acknowledge donations of software and hardware from Altera Corporation that facilitated this work.

## 8. REFERENCES

[1] Altera. Quartus II University Interface Program. http://www.altera.com/education/univ/research/quip/unv-quip.html.

[2] Arrow. BeMicro FPGA Evaluation Kit. http://www.arrownac.com/offers/altera-corporation/bemicro/.

[3] W. B. Culbertson, R. Amerson, R. Carter, P. Kuekes, and G. Snider. Defect tolerance on the TERAMAC custom computer. In *FCCM*, pages 116–123, April 1997.

[4] M. Eisele, J. Berthold, D. Schmitt-Landsiedel, and R. Mahnkopf. The impact of intra-die device parameter variations on path delays and on the design for yield of low voltage digital circuits. *IEEE Trans. VLSI Syst.*, 5(4):360–368, Dec. 1997.

[5] B. Gojman, N. Mehta, R. Rubin, and A. DeHon. Component-specific mapping for low-power operation in the presence of variation and aging. In *Low-Power Variation-Tolerant Design in Nanometer Silicon*, chapter 12, pages 381–432. Springer, 2011.

[6] S. Hanson, B. Zhai, K. Bernstein, D. Blaauw, A. Bryant, L. Chang, K. K. Das, W. Haensch, E. J. Nowak, and D. M. Sylvester. Ultralow-voltage, minimum-energy CMOS. *IBM J. Res. and Dev.*, 50(4–5):469–490, July/September 2006.

[7] X. Li, J. Tong, and J. Mao. Temperature-dependent device behavior in advanced CMOS technologies. In *ISSSE*, volume 2, pages 1–4, Sept. 2010.

[8] M. Majzoobi, E. Dyer, A. Elnably, and F. Koushanfar. Rapid FPGA delay characterization using clock synthesis and sparse sampling. In *Proc. Intl. Test Conf.*, 2010.

[9] L. McMurchie and C. Ebeling. PathFinder: A negotiation-based performance-driven router for FPGAs. In *FPGA*, pages 111–117, 1995.

[10] N. Mehta, R. Rubin, and A. DeHon. Limit study of energy & delay benefits of component-specific routing. In *FPGA*, pages 97–106, 2012.

[11] J. M. Rabaey, A. Chandrakasan, and B. Nikolic. *Digital Integrated Circuits*. Prentice Hall, 2nd edition, 1999.

[12] P. Sedcole, J. S. Wong, and P. Y. K. Cheung. Modelling and compensating for clock skew variability in FPGAs. *ICFPT*, pages 217–224, 2008.

[13] J. R. Smith and X. Tian. High-resolution delay testing of interconnect paths in Field-Programmable Gate Arrays. *IEEE Trans. Instrum. Meas.*, 58(1):187–195, 2009.

[14] A. Srivastava, D. Sylvester, and D. Blaauw. *Statistical Analysis and Optimization for VLSI: Timing and Power*. Integrated Circuits and Systems. Springer, 2005.

[15] E. A. Stott, J. S. J. Wong, P. Pete Sedcole, and P. Y. K. Cheung. Degradation in FPGAs: measurement and modelling. In *FPGA*, page 229, 2010.

[16] Terasic. DE0-Nano Development and Education Board. http://www.terasic.com.tw/cgi-bin/page/archive.pl?\Language=English&CategoryNo=139&No=593.

[17] T. Tuan, A. Lesea, C. Kingsley, and S. Trimberger. Analysis of within-die process variation in 65nm FPGAs. In *ISQED*, pages 1–5, March 2011.

[18] J. S. Wong, P. Sedcole, and P. Y. K. Cheung. Self-measurement of combinatorial circuit delays in FPGAs. *ACM Tr. Reconfig. Tech. and Sys.*, 2(2):1–22, June 2009.

[19] Y. Ye, S. Gummalla, C.-C. Wang, C. Chakrabarti, and Y. Cao. Random variability modeling and its impact on scaled CMOS circuits. *J. Comput. Electron.*, 9(3-4):108–113, Dec. 2010.

[20] H. Yu, Q. Xu, and P. H. Leong. Fine-grained characterization of process variation in FPGAs. In *ICFPT*, pages 138–145, 2010.

# Side-Channel Attacks on the Bitstream Encryption Mechanism of Altera Stratix II

## Facilitating Black-Box Analysis using Software Reverse-Engineering

Amir Moradi
Horst Görtz Institute
for IT-Security
Ruhr University Bochum
Germany
amir.moradi@rub.de

David Oswald
Horst Görtz Institute
for IT-Security
Ruhr University Bochum
Germany
david.oswald@rub.de

Christof Paar
Horst Görtz Institute
for IT-Security
Ruhr University Bochum
Germany
christof.paar@rub.de

Pawel Swierczynski
Horst Görtz Institute
for IT-Security
Ruhr University Bochum
Germany
pawel.swierczynski@rub.de

## ABSTRACT

In order to protect FPGA designs against IP theft and related issues such as product cloning, all major FPGA manufacturers offer a mechanism to encrypt the bitstream used to configure the FPGA. From a mathematical point of view, the employed encryption algorithms, e.g., AES or 3DES, are highly secure. However, recently it has been shown that the bitstream encryption feature of several FPGA product lines is susceptible to side-channel attacks that monitor the power consumption of the cryptographic module. In this paper, we present the first successful attack on the bitstream encryption of the Altera Stratix II FPGA. To this end, we reverse-engineered the details of the proprietary and unpublished Stratix II bitstream encryption scheme from the Quartus II software. Using this knowledge, we demonstrate that the full 128-bit AES key of a Stratix II can be recovered by means of side-channel analysis with 30,000 measurements, which can be acquired in less than three hours. The complete bitstream of a Stratix II that is (seemingly) protected by the bitstream encryption feature can hence fall into the hands of a competitor or criminal — possibly implying system-wide damage if confidential information such as proprietary encryption schemes or keys programmed into the FPGA are extracted. In addition to lost IP, reprogramming the attacked FPGA with modified code, for instance, to secretly plant a hardware trojan, is a particularly dangerous scenario for many security-critical applications.

## Categories and Subject Descriptors

K.6.5 [**Security and Protection**]: [Unauthorized access]; D.4.6 [**Security and Protection**]: [Cryptographic controls]

## General Terms

Security, Experimentation

## Keywords

Side-channel attack, bitstream encryption, Altera, Stratix II, AES, hardware security, reverse-engineering

## 1. INTRODUCTION

Ubiquitous computing has become reality and has began to shape almost all aspects of our life, ranging from social interaction to the way we do business. Virtually all ubiquitous devices are based on embedded digital technology. As part of this development, the security of embedded systems has become an increasingly important issue. For instance, digital systems can often be cloned relatively easily or Intellectual Property (IP) can be extracted. Also, ill-intended malfunctions of the device or the circumvention of business models based on the electronic content — which is regularly happening in the pay-TV sector — are also possible. Another flavor of malicious manipulation of digital systems was described in a 2005 report by the US Defense Science Board, where the clandestine introduction of hardware trojans was underlined as a serious threat [1]. In order to prevent these and other forms of abuse, it is often highly desirable to introduce security mechanisms into embedded systems which prevent reverse-engineering and manipulation of designs.

In the field of digital design, FPGAs close the gap between powerful but inflexible Application Specific Integrated Circuits (ASICs) and highly flexible but performance-limited microcontroller ($\mu$C) solutions. FPGAs combine some advantages of software (fast development, low non-recurring engineering costs) with those of hardware (performance, relative power efficiency). These advantages have made FPGAs an important fixture in embedded system design, especially for applications that require heavy processing, e.g., for routing, signal processing, or encryption.

Most of today's FPGAs are (re)configured with bitstreams, which is the equivalent of software program code for FPGAs. The bitstream determines the complete functionality of the device. In most cases, FPGAs produced by the dominant vendors use volatile memory, e.g., SRAM to store the bitstream. This implies that the FPGA must be reconfigured after each power-up. The bitstream is stored in an external Non-Volatile Memory (NVM), e.g., EEPROM or Flash, and is transferred to the FPGA on each power-up.

One of the disadvantages of FPGAs, especially with respect to custom hardware such as ASICs, is that an attacker who has access to the external NVM can easily read out the bitstream and clone the system, or extract the IP of the design. The solution that industry has given for this issue is a security feature called *bitstream encryption*. This scheme is based on symmetric cryptography in order to provide confidentiality of the bitstream data. After generating the bitstream, the designer encrypts it with a secure symmetric cipher such as the Advanced Encryption Standard (AES), using a secret key $k_{design}$. The encrypted bitstream can now be safely stored in the external NVM. The FPGA possesses an internal decryption engine and uses the previously stored secret key $k_{FPGA}$ to decrypt the bitstream before configuring the internal circuitry. The configuration is successful if and only if the secret keys used for the encryption and decryption of the bitstream are identical, i.e., $k_{design} = k_{FPGA}$. Now, wire-tapping the data bus or dumping the content of the external NVM containing the encrypted bitstream does not yield useful information for cloning or reverse-engineering the device, given the adversary does not know the secret key.

The cryptographic scheme used by Xilinx FPGAs starting from the old and discontinued Virtex-II family to the recent 7 series is Triple-DES (3DES) or AES in Cipher Block Chaining (CBC) mode [12, 21]. Recent findings reported in [14] and [15] show the vulnerability of these schemes to state-of-the-art Side-Channel Analysis (SCA). Indeed, it has been shown that a side-channel adversary can recover the secret key stored in the target FPGA and use it for decrypting the bitstream. More recently, similar findings have been reported for bitstream security feature of a family of flash-based Actel FPGAs of Microsemi [20].

Side-channel attacks exploit physical information leakage of an implementation in order to extract the cryptographic key. In the particular case of power analysis, the current consumption of the cryptographic device is used as a side channel for key extraction. The underlying principle is a divide-and-conquer approach, i.e., small parts of the key, e.g., 8 bit, are guessed, and the according hypotheses are verified. This process is repeated until the whole key has been revealed [9, 11].

In this work, we analyze the bitstream protection mechanism of Altera's Stratix II FPGA families called *design security*. A detailed description of this real-world attack illustrating the steps required to perform a black-box analysis of a mostly undocumented target, i.e., the design security feature of the targeted FPGA family, is given. Similar to the attacks on the bitstream encryption of Xilinx and Actel FPGAs, our attack on the targeted Altera FPGA makes use of the physical leakage of the embedded decryption module. However, a detailed specification of the design security scheme is not publicly available. By reverse-engineering the Quartus II software application, we recovered all details and proprietary algorithms used for the design security scheme. Our results show the vulnerability of the bitstream encryption feature of Altera's Stratix II FPGAs to power analysis attacks, leading to a complete break of the security feature and the anti-counterfeiting mechanism.

The remainder of this paper is organized as follows. In Section 2, we describe the steps needed to reverse-engineer the Quartus II application in order to reveal the details of the design security scheme. Also, basic security problems of the according scheme are illustrated. The details of our side-channel attacks are presented in Section 3 and Section 4. Finally, in Section 5, we conclude, summing up our research results.

## 2. REVERSE-ENGINEERING – DESIGN SECURITY SCHEME

For a side-channel analysis, all details of the bitstream encryption scheme are required. However, this information cannot be found in the public documents published by Altera. In this section, we thus illustrate the method we followed to reveal the essential information, including the proprietary algorithms used for the key derivation and the encryption scheme.

### 2.1 Preliminaries

The main design software for Altera FPGAs is called "Quartus II". To generate a bitstream for an FPGA, the Hardware Description Language (HDL) sources are first translated into a so called .SOF file. In turn, this file can then be converted into several file types that are used to actually configure the FPGA, cf. Table 1.

For the purposes of reverse-engineering the bitstream format, we selected the .RBF type, i.e., a raw binary output file. This format has the advantage that it can be used with our custom programmer, cf. Section 3.1.

| File extension | Type |
| --- | --- |
| .HexOut | Hexdecimal Output |
| .POF | Programmer Object File |
| **.RBF** | **Raw Binary File** |
| .TTF | Tabular Text File |
| .RPD | Raw Programming Data |
| .JIC | JTAG Indirect Configuration |

**Table 1: Bitstream file formats generated by Quartus II**

For transferring the bitstream to the FPGA, Altera provides several different configuration schemes [4, p.131-132]. Table 2 gives an overview on the different available schemes. For our purposes, we used the Passive Serial (PS) configuration scheme, because it supports bitstream encryption and moreover, because the configuration clock signal is controlled by the configuration device.

Regarding the actual realization of the bitstream encryption, relatively little information is known. In the public documents [5] it is stated that Stratix II uses the AES with

| Mode | Bitstream Enc. |
|---|---|
| Fast Passive Parallel (FPP) | Yes |
| Active Serial (AS) | Yes |
| **Passive Serial (PS)** | **Yes** |
| Passive Parallel Asynch. (PPA) | No |
| JTAG | No |

**Table 2: Configuration modes for the Stratix II**

128-bit key. Furthermore, a key derivation scheme is outlined that generates the actual encryption key given two user-supplied 128-bit keys. Apart from that, no information on the file format, mode of operation used for the encryption, etc. was initially available to us. Thus, in the following, we analyze the functional blocks of Quartus II and completely describe the mechanisms used for bitstream encryption on the Stratix II.

## 2.2 RBF File Format

In order to understand the file structure of an .RBF file, we generated both the encrypted and the unencrypted .RBF files for an example design and compared the results. We found that the file can be divided into a header and a body section. Comparing the encrypted and the unencrypted .RBF files, we figured out that only a few bytes vary in the header. In contrast, the bodies containing the – possibly encrypted – actual bitstream are completely different. The unencrypted file's body contains mainly zero, while the encrypted file consists of seemingly random bytes.

We encrypted the same input (.SOF file) twice, using the same key both times. It turned out that the resulting encrypted bitstreams are completely different, with differences in some header bytes and the complete body. Thus, the encryption process appears to be randomized in some way. Experimentally, we found that this randomization is based on the current PC clock only. Using a small batch script, we fixed the PC clock to a particular value and again generated two encrypted .RBF files. The resulting files were completely identical, confirming the conjecture that the PC clock is used as an Initialization Vector (IV) for the bitstream encryption.

To gain further insight into the internals of the file format, we used the reverse-engineering tool Hex-Rays IDA Pro [2]. Amongst others, this program allows analyzing the assembly code of an executable program (i.e., in our case the Quartus II bitstream tool) and run a debugger (i.e., display register values etc. ) while the target program is running. Using IDA Pro, we obtained the file structure depicted in Figure 1 (for the specific FPGA fabric EP2S15F484C5N).

Both the unencrypted and encrypted .RBF files start with a fixed 33-byte "pre-header". The following 40 bytes include the IV used for the encryption. For the unencrypted file, the IV is always set to 0xFF...FF, while for the encrypted file the first (left) 32-bit half is randomized (using the PC clock). The right 32-bit half is set to a fixed value. However, the IV is not directly stored in plain; rather, the single bits of the IV are distributed over several bytes of the header. Using IDA Pro, we determined the byte (and bit) positions in the header at which a particular IV bit is stored.

Table 3 shows the resulting IV bit positions. The notation $Y_{bitX}$ refers to bit X (big endian, $X \in [0,7]$) of the byte at position Y in the .RBF file. Note that the byte positions

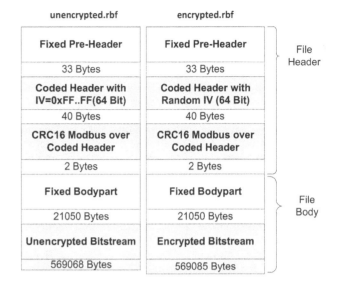

**Figure 1: Structure of an unencrypted and an encrypted .RBF file**

are counted starting from the beginning of the .RBF file, i.e., including the fixed 33-byte pre-header.

| IV bit | 63 | 62 | 61 | 60 | 59 | 58 | 57 | 56 |
|---|---|---|---|---|---|---|---|---|
| Position | $49_{bit3}$ | $48_{bit3}$ | $47_{bit3}$ | $46_{bit3}$ | $45_{bit3}$ | $44_{bit3}$ | $43_{bit3}$ | $42_{bit3}$ |
| **IV bit** | 55 | 54 | 53 | 52 | 51 | 50 | 49 | 48 |
| Position | $57_{bit3}$ | $56_{bit3}$ | $55_{bit3}$ | $54_{bit3}$ | $53_{bit3}$ | $52_{bit3}$ | $51_{bit3}$ | $50_{bit3}$ |
| **IV bit** | 47 | 46 | 45 | 44 | 43 | 42 | 41 | 40 |
| Position | $65_{bit3}$ | $64_{bit3}$ | $63_{bit3}$ | $62_{bit3}$ | $61_{bit3}$ | $60_{bit3}$ | $59_{bit3}$ | $58_{bit3}$ |
| **IV bit** | 39 | 38 | 37 | 36 | 35 | 34 | 33 | 32 |
| Position | $33_{bit4}$ | $72_{bit3}$ | $71_{bit3}$ | $70_{bit3}$ | $69_{bit3}$ | $68_{bit3}$ | $67_{bit3}$ | $66_{bit3}$ |
| **IV bit** | 31 | 30 | 29 | 28 | 27 | 26 | 25 | 24 |
| Position | $41_{bit4}$ | $40_{bit4}$ | $39_{bit4}$ | $38_{bit4}$ | $37_{bit4}$ | $36_{bit4}$ | $35_{bit4}$ | $34_{bit4}$ |
| **IV bit** | 23 | 22 | 21 | 20 | 19 | 18 | 17 | 16 |
| Position | $49_{bit4}$ | $48_{bit4}$ | $47_{bit4}$ | $46_{bit4}$ | $45_{bit4}$ | $44_{bit4}$ | $43_{bit4}$ | $42_{bit4}$ |
| **IV bit** | 15 | 14 | 13 | 12 | 11 | 10 | 9 | 8 |
| Position | $57_{bit4}$ | $56_{bit4}$ | $55_{bit4}$ | $54_{bit4}$ | $53_{bit4}$ | $52_{bit4}$ | $51_{bit4}$ | $50_{bit4}$ |
| **IV bit** | 7 | 6 | 5 | 4 | 3 | 2 | 1 | 0 |
| Position | $65_{bit4}$ | $64_{bit4}$ | $63_{bit4}$ | $62_{bit4}$ | $61_{bit4}$ | $60_{bit4}$ | $59_{bit4}$ | $58_{bit4}$ |

**Table 3: Mapping between the IV bits and the header bytes**

Only the third and fourth bit of a byte is used to store the IV bits. The other bits of the header are constant and independent of the IV. We assume that these bits store configuration options, e.g., whether the bitstream is encrypted. The header is followed by a two-byte Modbus CRC-16 [3] computed over the preceding 40 header bytes for integrity check purposes.

The body starts with a 21050-byte block that is equal for both encrypted and unencrypted files. This block is followed by the actual bitstream (in encrypted or unencrypted form). The unencrypted bitstream has a length of 569068 bytes. For the encrypted bitstream, 17 additional bytes are added. This is due to the fact that for the encrypted format several padding bytes are added. For the purposes of our work, the details of this padding are irrelevant, as the additional block does not carry data belonging to the actual bitstream.

## 2.3 AES Key Derivation

In the publicly available documents it is stated that the

128-bit AES key used for the bitstream encryption is not directly programmed into the Stratix II. Rather, two 128-bit keys denoted as KEY1 and KEY2 are sent to the FPGA during the key programming. These keys are then passed through a key derivation function that generates the actual "real key" used to decrypt the bitstream. The idea behind this approach is that if an adversary obtains the real key (e.g., by means of a side-channel attack), he should still be unable to use the same (encrypted) bitstream to program another Stratix II (e.g., to create a perfect clone of a product). Since the real key (of the second Stratix II) can only be set given KEY1 and KEY2, an adversary would have to invert the key derivation function, which is supposed to be hard. We further comment on the security of this approach in the case of the Stratix II in Section 2.3.2.

Initially, the details of the key derivation were hidden in the Quartus II software, i.e., the software appears as a complete black-box. As depicted in Figure 2, Quartus II produces a key file (in our case Keyfile.ekp) that stores the specified KEY1 and KEY2. This key file is later passed to the FPGA, e.g., via the Joint Test Action Group (JTAG) port using a suitable programmer.

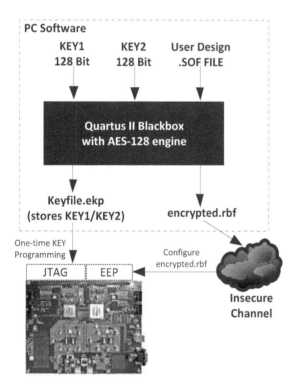

**Figure 2: Quartus II black-box generating encrypted Stratix II bitstreams**

However, the key derivation function obviously has to also be implemented in Quartus II because the real key is needed to finally encrypt the bitstream. Hence, we again reverse-engineered the corresponding scheme from the executable program. Most of the cryptographic functions are implemented in the DLL file pgm_pgio_nv_aes.dll. Apparently, the developers of Quartus II did not remove the debugging information from the binary executable; hence the original function names are still present in the DLL.

Figure 3 shows the corresponding function calls for the

key derivation and the bitstream encryption. First, we focus on the key derivation, i.e., the upper part of Figure 3. Note that due to the available debugging information, all function names are exactly those chosen by the Altera developers.

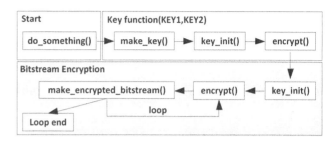

**Figure 3: Quartus II call sequence during the bitstream encryption**

First, the do_something() function checks the used key length. Then, the make_key() function copies the bytes of KEY1 to a particular memory location. The key_init() function then implements the key schedule algorithm of the AES, generating 160 bytes of round keys in total. encrypt() then encrypts KEY2 with KEY1. Hence, the – previously unknown – key derivation function is given as

$$\text{Real Key} := \text{AES128}_{\text{KEY1}}(\text{KEY2}),$$

where KEY1 and KEY2 are those specified in the Quartus II application.

### 2.3.1 Worked Example

In order to further illustrate the details of the key derivation function, in the following we give the inputs and outputs for the chosen KEY1 and KEY2 we used for our analysis.

**KEY1 (Quartus input, little endian)**
0x0F 0E 0D 0C 0B 0A 09 08 07 06 05 04 03 02 01 00

**KEY2 (Quartus input, little endian)**
0x32 00 31 C9 FD 4F 69 8C 51 9D 68 C6 86 A2 43 7C

**Real Key = AES128$_{\text{KEY1}}$(KEY2) (big endian)**
0x2B 7E 15 16 28 AE D2 A6 AB F7 15 88 09 CF 4F 3C

### 2.3.2 Security of the Key Derivation Function

At first glance, the approach of deriving the real key within the device appears to be a reasonable countermeasure to prevent cloning of products even if the real key has been discovered. Yet, it should be taken into account that an adversary knowing the real key is still able to decrypt the bitstream and re-encrypt it with a different key for which he has chosen KEY1 and KEY2. Nevertheless, a product cloned in such a way could be still identified, because the re-encrypted bitstream will differ from the original one.

However, the way the AES is used for the key derivation in the case of the Stratix II does not add to the protection against product cloning in any way: a secure key derivation scheme requires the utilized function to be one-way, i.e., very hard to invert. For the Stratix II scheme, this is not the case. An adversary can pick *any* KEY1 and then decrypt the – previously recovered – real key using this KEY1. The resulting KEY2 together with KEY1 then forms one of $2^{128}$ pairs that lead to the same (desired) real key when programmed into a blank Stratix II. The device will thus still accept the original (encrypted) bitstream, and the clone cannot be identified as such because KEY1 and KEY2 are never stored in the FPGA by design.

## 2.4 AES Encryption Mode

Having revealed the key derivation scheme, we focus on the details of the actual AES encryption, i.e., analyze the lower part of Figure 3. First, the `key_init` function is executed in order to generate the round keys for the (previously derived) real key. Then, `encrypt()` is invoked repeatedly in a loop. Using the debugger functionality of IDA Pro, we exemplary observed the following sequence of inputs to `encrypt()`:

```
0xB4 52 19 50 76 08 93 F1 B4 52 19 50 76 08 93 F1
0xB5 52 19 50 76 08 93 F1 B5 52 19 50 76 08 93 F1
0xB6 52 19 50 76 08 93 F1 B6 52 19 50 76 08 93 F1
...
```

Note that the first and the second eight bytes of each AES input are equal. Moreover, this 64-bit value is incremented for each encryption, yielding (in this case) the sequence B4, B5, B6 for the first byte. Apparently, the AES is not used to directly encrypt the bitstream. Rather, it seems that the so-called Counter (CTR) mode [17] is applied. Figure 4 shows the corresponding block diagram.

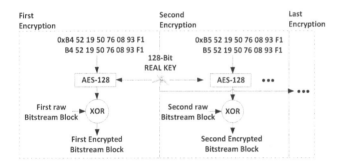

**Figure 4: AES in CTR mode**

In CTR mode, an IV is encrypted using the specified key (in our case the real key). The output (i.e., ciphertext) of the AES is then XORed with the 16-byte data block to perform the encryption (of the bitstream blocks for the case of Stratix II). For each block, the IV is incremented to generate a new ciphertext to be XORed with the corresponding data block. The XOR operation is implemented in the function `make_encrypted_bitstream()`.

As mentioned in Section 2.2, the IV is generated based on the PC clock. Indeed, we found that the first four bytes of the IV correspond to the number of seconds elapsed since January 1, 1970. More concretely, the (little endian) value `0xB4 52 19 50` represents the date `2012.08.01 18:00:52`. The remaining four bytes are constant. The overall structure of the IV is thus:

$$0x\ \underbrace{\textbf{B4 52 19 50}}_{\text{Timestamp}}\ \underbrace{\text{76 08 93 F1}}_{\text{Fixed bytes}}\ \underbrace{\textbf{B4 52 19 50}}_{\text{Timestamp}}\ \underbrace{\text{76 08 93 F1}}_{\text{Fixed bytes}}.$$

Having figured out the details of the AES key derivation and encryption, we implemented the aforementioned func-

tions to decrypt a given encrypted bitstream. Given the correct real key and IV, we successfully decrypted the bitstream of an encrypted .RBF file. Figure 5 summarizes the details of the bitstream encryption process of Stratix II.

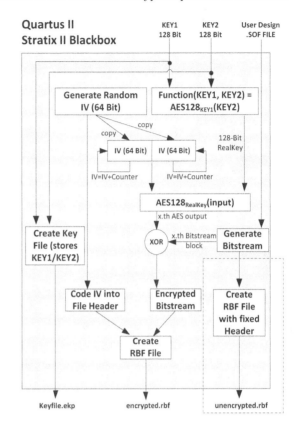

**Figure 5: Overview of the bitstream encryption process for the Stratix II FPGAs**

## 3. SIDE-CHANNEL PROFILING

With the knowledge of the bitstream encryption process presented in Section 2, we are able to analyze the Stratix II from a side-channel point of view. To this end, in this section we first describe the measurement setup and scenario. Then, as a prerequisite to the according key extraction attack (Section 4), we apply SCA to find out the point in time at which the AES operations are executed. In the following, we refer to the used Stratix II FPGA as Device Under Test (DUT). Also, we call – following the conventions in the side-channel literature – the current consumption curves during the configuration process *(power) traces*.

### 3.1 Measurement Setup

Our DUT, a Stratix II FPGA (EP2S15F484C5N), is soldered onto a SASEBO-B board [6] specifically designed for SCA purposes. The SASEBO-B board provides a JTAG port that allows one-time programing KEY1 and KEY2 into the DUT. For our experiments we set the real key to `0x2B 7E 15 16 28 AE D2 A6 AB F7 15 88 09 CF 4F 3C`, cf. Section 2.3.1.

We directly configure the DUT using the passive serial mode. For this purpose, we built an adapter that is conformant to [4, p.599]. We developed a custom programmer based on an ATmega256 μC. Thus, we have precise control over the configuration process and are additionally able to set a trigger signal for starting the measurement process. This helps to record well-aligned power traces. Finally, our μC also provides the configuration clock signal to avoid (unwanted) internal clock effects that could e.g., lead to clock jitter and therefore to misaligned traces.

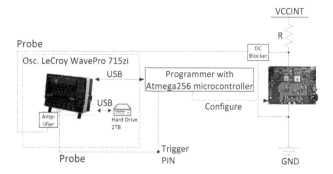

**Figure 6: Measurement setup for SCA**

According to [4, p.148], the DUT has three different supply voltage lines: $V_{CCINT}$ (internal logic, 1.15V-1.255V), $V_{CCIO}$ (input and output buffers, 3.00V-3.60V) and $V_{CCPD}$ (pre-drivers, configuration, and JTAG buffers, 3.135V-3.465V).

For our analysis, we recorded the power consumption during the configuration of the DUT by inserting a small shunt resistor into the $V_{CCINT}$ path and measuring the (amplified, AC-coupled) voltage drop using a LeCroy WavePro 715Zi Digital Storage Oscilloscope (DSO) as depicted in Figure 6. We acquired 840,000 traces with 225,000 data points each at a sampling rate of 500 MS/s. The respective (encrypted) bitstreams were generated on the PC built into the DSO and then sent to the DUT via the μC. The measurement process was triggered using a dedicated μC pin providing a rising edge shortly before the first bitstream block is sent.

During the decryption process of the encrypted bitstream, the AES is used in CTR mode. Hence, it might be possible that the DUT performs the first AES encryption when the header is being sent because from that time onwards, the DUT knows the IV (first AES input). Therefore, we decided to perform a new power-up of the FPGA for each power trace that we measured. The corresponding steps are described in more detail in Algorithm 1.

### 3.2 Difference between Unencrypted and Encrypted Bitstream

Using our measurement script, we recorded 10,000 power traces for the time range that includes the transmission of 48 fixed, encrypted bitstream bytes. The FPGA decryptor hence each time has the same input. In addition to that, we performed the same measurements while sending 48 bytes of unencrypted bitstream. Finally, we computed the average power consumption over the set of our measured power traces, once for the unencrypted and once for the encrypted bitstream. Figure 7 illustrates the corresponding mean traces.

As it is clearly visible in Figure 7, there is a significant difference in the average power consumption between the processing of the unencrypted bitstream and the encrypted bitstream. While the FPGA processes an encrypted bitstream,

---

**Algorithm 1** Measurement steps

**for** i=1 to numberOfTraces **do**
  [μC] Perform DUT reset
  [μC] Transfer fixed 33-byte pre-header to DUT
  [PC] myIV[0..7] ← rand
  [PC] myHeader[] ← Get header from .RBF file
  [PC] Code myIV[] into myHeader[] (Table 3)
  [PC] Compute CRC-16 over coded header
  [PC] Send coded header with CRC-16 (42 bytes) to μC
  [μC] Transfer coded header (42 bytes) to DUT
  [μC] Transfer fixed body part (21050 bytes) to DUT
  [PC] Bitstream[0..47] ← rand
  [PC] Send Bitstream[] (48 bytes) to μC
  [μC] Set trigger. Transfer bitstream (48 bytes) to DUT
  [DSO] Record power trace of the DUT
  [PC] Store trace i
  [PC] Store myIV[]
**end for**

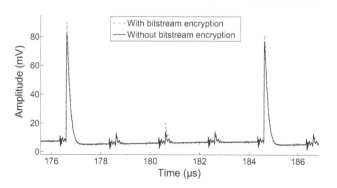

**Figure 7: Average power consumption (10k traces) while sending an unencrypted (solid) and an encrypted (dashed) bitstream. Zoom on one byte.**

it consumes more energy compared to the processing of an unencrypted bitstream. A difference is already visible at the point where the first bitstream block is being transferred to the DUT. Thus, we assume that the AES encryption engine processes the first AES input (IV) while the programmer transfers the first encrypted bitstream block to the DUT. We further conjecture that while the programmer sends the second encrypted bitstream block, the DUT computes the XOR of the first AES output with the encrypted bitstream and configures the corresponding FPGA blocks.

### 3.3 Locating the AES Encryption

To verify our assumption on the correct time instance of the first AES encryption, we recorded another set of measurements and measured 840,000 power traces, this time exactly as described in Algorithm 1. Then, for our profiling, we used the known key to compute all intermediate AES values for each IV challenge/trace.

For a Correlation Power Analysis (CPA), [8], we used this set of power traces to compute the correlation curves of about 220 different prediction models, e.g., each S-box bit of the first AES round, several Hamming Distance (HD) models with different predicted register sizes, and several Hamming Weight (HW) models for the intermediate AES states. As a result, the majority of our power models revealed a data dependency between the predicted power models and the measured power traces. Hence, the FPGA evidently leaks sensitive information. Figure 8 shows nine of the correlation curves for the states after each AES round.

The first correlation curve (black) that exhibits a peak up to an approximate value of 0.05 between 30 and 65 microseconds is for the HW model of the 128-bit state after the first round of the first AES encryption. The second correlation curve (red) is almost the same prediction model as before, but this time for the second round, etc. . Each round of the first AES encryption leaks and therefore, the correct time instance of the first AES encryption is located between 30 and 160 $\mu s$.

In Figure 8, one can also spot the processing of the second AES encryption (starts at 180 $\mu s$). Due to the fact that only two bytes of the IV are incremented each time, for the second AES encryption, the first output state (128 bits) is similar to that of the first AES encryption. Therefore, the prediction of the first state of the first AES encryption automatically fits to the second encryption as well. Thus, the same leakage (black curve in Figure 8) appears for both the first and second AES encryption. Even the states after round 2 of both encryptions are slightly similar, and the leakage peak (red curve) appears for both encryption runs. Since the states (starting from round 3) are completely different for both encryptions, the predicted state of round $\geq 3$ does not leak for the second encryption anymore.

## 4. SIDE-CHANNEL KEY EXTRACTION

As shown in Section 3, the DUT exhibits a clear relationship between the power consumption and the internal states during the AES operation. In this section, we show how this side-channel leakage can be utilized to extract the full 128-bit AES key from a Stratix II with approximately three hours of measurements and a few hours of offline computation.

### 4.1 Digital Pre-Processing

As commonly encountered in SCA, the effect of the AES encryption on the overall power consumption is rather small (cf. Section 3). Hence, digital pre-processing of the traces to isolate the signal of interest (and thus reduce the Signal-to-Noise Ratio (SNR)) is often suggested in the literature in order to reduce the number of required measurements [7]. In

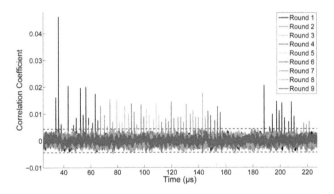

**Figure 8: Correlation coefficient for one full AddRoundKey 128-bit state (one curve for each round). Utilized models: $1^{st}$ curve $\leftrightarrow$ HW of round 1, $2^{nd}$ curve $\leftrightarrow$ HW of round 2, etc.**

the case of the Stratix II, we experimentally determined a set of pre-processing steps before performing the actual key extraction.

First, the trace is band-pass filtered with a passband from 500 kHz to 100 MHz. Then, the signal is subdivided into windows of 750 sample points (i.e., 1.5 $\mu s$ at the sampling rate of 500 MHz), with an overlap of 50 percent between adjacent windows. Each window is zero-padded to a length of 7000 points. Then, the Discrete Fourier Transform (DFT) of each window is computed, and the absolute value of the resulting complex coefficients is used as the input to the CPA. Note that we found the frequency with the maximum leakage to be around 2 MHz, hence, we left out all frequencies above 8 MHz to reduce the number of data points as well as the computational complexity of the CPA. Hence, each window (0 ... 8 MHz) has a length of 112 points.

This approach was first proposed in [10] under the name of Differential Frequency Analysis (DFA). Since then, several practical side-channel attacks successfully applied this method to improve the signal quality, cf. for instance [18, 19].

### 4.2 Hypothetical Architecture

For a side-channel attack to succeed, an adequate model for the dependency between the internal architecture and the measured power consumption is needed. Common models include the HW, which states that the consumed power depends on the number of set bits in a register, and the HD, which predicts the power consumption to be proportional to the number of switching bits in a register.

In the case of the Stratix II, the internal realization of the AES was initially unknown. Hence, we experimentally tested many (common) different models, as mentioned in Section 3.3. As a result, it turned out that the leakage present in the traces is best modeled by the HD *within* the AES state after the ShiftRows step [16]. More precisely, it appears that each column of the AES state is processed in one step, and that the result is shifted into a register, overwriting the previous column (that in turn is shifted one step to the right). The corresponding hypothetical architecture is depicted in Figure 9.

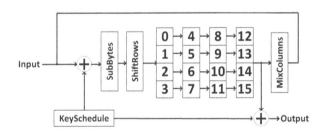

**Figure 9: Hypothetical architecture of the AES implementation.**

For the key extraction in Section 4.3, we thus use for instance the HD byte $0 \to 4$ (after ShiftRows in the first AES round) to recover the first key byte, byte $1 \to 5$ to recover the second key byte, and so on. As common in SCA, each key byte can be recovered separately from the remaining bytes, i.e., in principle $16 \times 2^8$ instead of $2^{128}$ key guesses for an exhaustive search have to be tested.

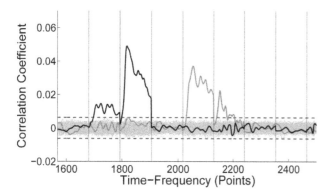

Figure 10: Correlation coefficient for the first S-box after 400k traces using DFT pre-processing. Correct key candidate 0x2B: black curve.

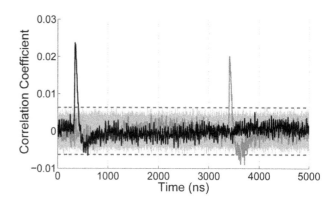

Figure 11: Correlation coefficient for the first S-box after 400k traces without DFT pre-processing. Correct key candidate 0x2B: black curve.

Note that, however, the initial state (i.e., the column overwritten with byte 0 ... 3) is unknown. Hence, we consider each row of the first two columns together and recover the key bytes 0 and 4, 1 and 5, 2 and 6, and 3 and 7 together, corresponding to $2^{16}$ key candidates each. After that, the remaining eight key bytes 8 ... 15 yield $8 \times 2^8$ candidates in total because the previous (overwritten) column values are known. The total number of key candidates is thus $8 \times 2^8 + 4 \times 2^{16} = 264,192$ for which the CPA can be conducted within a few hours using standard hardware.

## 4.3 Results

Using the described power model, we computed the correlation coefficient for the respective (byte-wise) HD of the AES states. Figure 10 shows the result for the first S-box, i.e., the HD between byte 0 and 4. Evidently, the correct key candidate 0x2B (black curve) exhibits a maximum correlation of approximately 0.05 after 400,000 traces, clearly exceeding the "noise level" of $4/\sqrt{\#traces} = 0.006$ [13].

All other (but one) key candidates stay below the noise level. However, a second key candidate 0xAB (red curve) also results in a significant peak at a different point in time. This is due to the fact that, as explained in Section 2, the first 64-bit half of the plaintext (i.e., the IV) equals the second half. Hence, a second key candidate (from the second 64-bit half) also exhibits a significant correlation. Indeed, the second peak (red one) belongs to the correct key candidate 0xAB for the corresponding key byte 8 in the second 64-bit half. As expected, due to the serial nature of the hypothetical architecture, the correlation occurs at a later point in time.

We conducted the CPA for all 16 AES S-boxes and obtained a minimal correlation coefficient (determining the required number of traces) of $\rho_{min} = 0.031$ for the fourth S-box. Hence, according to the estimation given in [13], the minimal number of traces to extract the full AES key is approximately $2^8/\rho_{min}^2 = 29,136$.

Figure 11 depicts the according correlation coefficient for the first S-box when leaving out the DFT pre-processing step. In general, the results are similar to those of Figure 10, however, the observed correlation is halved compared to the CPA with the DFT pre-processing. Overall, we obtained a $\rho_{min} = 0.021$, i.e., 63,492 traces would be needed when leaving out the DFT pre-processing.

Using our current measurement setup, 10,000 traces can

be recorded in approximately 55 min. Note that the speed of the data acquisition is currently limited by the $\mu$C; thus, this time could be reduced with further engineering efforts. Nevertheless, the amount of traces required to perform a full-key recovery can be collected in less than three hours.

## 5. IMPLICATIONS – FUTURE WORKS

After reverse-engineering the relevant functions of the Quartus II program, all details of the bitstream encryption, including the proprietary algorithms of the design security scheme have been revealed. Using this knowledge, a side-channel adversary can mount a successful key recovery attack on the dedicated decryption hardware. As a consequence of our attacks, cloning of products employing Altera Stratix II FPGAs for which the bitstream encryption feature is enabled becomes straightforward. Moreover, an attacker can not only extract and reverse-engineer the bitstream, but might also modify it or create a completely new one that would be accepted by the device. This fact is especially sensitive in military applications, but could also have a major impact in other cases, e.g., surveillance and trojan hardware scenarios. Furthermore, an unencrypted bitstream allows an adversary to read out secret keys from security modules or to recover classified security primitives.

Since the Stratix II family belongs to an older generations of Altera FPGAs, the fact that SCA countermeasures have been ignored during the development appears likely. However, recent families like Stratix V or Arria II probably feature an only slightly different scheme for bitstream encryption. At least, these FPGAs are supposed to provide 256-bit security compared to the 128-bit security of Stratix II. Therefore, analyzing the security of the more recent Altera FPGAs from an SCA point of view is interesting for future work.

# 6. REFERENCES

[1] Defense Science Board.
http://www.acq.osd.mil/dsb/.

[2] Hex-Rays SA. http://www.hex-rays.com.

[3] On-line CRC calculation and free library. http://www.lammertbies.nl/comm/info/crc-calculation.html.

[4] Stratix II Device Handbook, Volume 1. Technical report, Altera, 2007. http://www.altera.com/literature/hb/stx2/stratix2_handbook.pdf.

[5] AN 341: Using the Design Security Feature in Stratix II and Stratix II GX Devices. Technical report, Altera, 2009.
http://www.altera.com/literature/an/an341.pdf.

[6] AIST. *Side-channel Attack Standard Evaluation Board SASEBO-B Specification*, 2008.
http://www.risec.aist.go.jp/project/sasebo/download/SASEBO-B\_Spec\_Ver1.0\_English.pdf.

[7] A. Barenghi, G. Pelosi, and Y. Teglia. Improving First Order Differential Power Attacks through Digital Signal Processing. In *Security of Information and Networks - SIN 2010*, pages 124–133. ACM, 2010.

[8] E. Brier, C. Clavier, and F. Olivier. Correlation Power Analysis with a Leakage Model. In *CHES 2004*, volume 3156 of *LNCS*, pages 16–29. Springer, 2004.

[9] T. Eisenbarth, T. Kasper, A. Moradi, C. Paar, M. Salmasizadeh, and M. T. M. Shalmani. On the Power of Power Analysis in the Real World: A Complete Break of the KeeLoq Code Hopping Scheme. In *CRYPTO 2008*, volume 5157 of *LNCS*, pages 203–220. Springer.

[10] C. Gebotys, C. Tiu, and X. Chen. A countermeasure for EM attack of a wireless PDA. In *ITCC 2005*, volume 1, pages 544–549. IEEE Computer Society, 2005.

[11] P. Kocher, J. Jaffe, and B. Jun. Differential Power Analysis. In *CRYPTO 99*, volume 1666 of *LNCS*, pages 388–397. Springer, 1999.

[12] R. Krueger. Application Note XAPP766: Using High Security Features in Virtex-II Series FPGAs. Technical report, Xilinx, 2004.
http://www.xilinx.com/support/documentation/application_notes/xapp766.pdf.

[13] S. Mangard, E. Oswald, and T. Popp. *Power Analysis Attacks: Revealing the Secrets of Smart Cards*. Springer, 2007.

[14] A. Moradi, A. Barenghi, T. Kasper, and C. Paar. On the vulnerability of FPGA bitstream encryption against power analysis attacks: extracting keys from xilinx Virtex-II FPGAs. In *CCS 2011*, pages 111–124. ACM, 2011.

[15] A. Moradi, M. Kasper, and C. Paar. Black-Box Side-Channel Attacks Highlight the Importance of Countermeasures - An Analysis of the Xilinx Virtex-4 and Virtex-5 Bitstream Encryption Mechanism. In *CT-RSA 2012*, volume 7178 of *LNCS*, pages 1–18. Springer, 2012.

[16] NIST. FIPS 197 Advanced Encryption Standard (AES). http://csrc.nist.gov/publications/fips/fips197/fips-197.pdf.

[17] NIST. *Recommendation for Block 2001 Edition Cipher Modes of Operation*, 2001. http://csrc.nist.gov/publications/nistpubs/800-38a/sp800-38a.pdf.

[18] D. Oswald and C. Paar. Breaking Mifare DESFire MF3ICD40: Power Analysis and Templates in the Real World. In *CHES 2011*, volume 6917 of *LNCS*, pages 207–222. Springer, 2011.

[19] T. Plos, M. Hutter, and M. Feldhofer. Evaluation of Side-Channel Preprocessing Techniques on Cryptographic-Enabled HF and UHF RFID-Tag Prototypes. In *RFIDSec 2008*, pages 114–127, 2008.

[20] S. Skorobogatov and C. Woods. In the blink of an eye: There goes your AES key. Cryptology ePrint Archive, Report 2012/296, 2012. http://eprint.iacr.org/.

[21] C. W. Tseng. Lock Your Designs with the Virtex-4 Security Solution. XCell Journal, Xilinx, Spring 2005.

# Sensing Nanosecond-scale Voltage Attacks and Natural Transients in FPGAs

Kenneth M. Zick[1]
kzick@isi.edu

Meeta Srivastav[2]
meeta@vt.edu

Wei Zhang[3]
wz6pc@virginia.edu

Matthew French[1]
mfrench@isi.edu

[1]University of Southern California Information Sciences Institute (USC ISI), Arlington, VA, USA
[2]Virginia Tech, Blacksburg, VA, USA
[3]University of Virginia, Charlottesville, VA, USA

## ABSTRACT

Voltage noise not only detracts from reliability and performance, but has been used to attack system security. Most systems are completely unaware of fluctuations occurring on nanosecond time scales. This paper quantifies the threat to FPGA-based systems and presents a solution approach. Novel measurements of transients on 28nm FPGAs show that extreme activity in the fabric can cause enormous undershoot and overshoot, more than $10\times$ larger than what is allowed by the specification. An existing voltage sensor is evaluated and shown to be insufficient. Lastly, a sensor design using reconfigurable logic is presented; its time-to-digital converter enables sample rates $500\times$ faster than the 28nm Xilinx ADC. This enables quick characterization of transients that would normally go undetected, thereby providing potentially useful data for system optimization and helping to defend against supply voltage attacks.

## Categories and Subject Descriptors

B.8.1 [**Performance and Reliability**]: Reliability, Testing, and Fault-Tolerance

## General Terms

Measurement, Reliability, Security

## Keywords

Voltage sensing, voltage transient, droop, Ldi/dt, glitch attack, denial of service, time-to-digital converter, FPGA

## 1. INTRODUCTION

State of the art electronic systems need their supply voltages to be within increasingly tight ranges in order to operate correctly. During operation, changes in system activity inevitably cause supply voltages to fluctuate with inductive noise. If strong enough, these *voltage transients* can put the system at risk of both soft and hard errors. Undershoot can cause timing errors and potentially even data retention errors, while overshoot can cause many wear out mechanisms to accelerate super-linearly.

Many state of the art ICs can sense the voltage at various location on the die, and at speeds high enough to detect transient effects shorter than 10ns [1][2]. However, FPGAs are almost entirely lacking in this regard. Some platforms provide a single sensor that can estimate the voltage at a package pin, but these operate far too slowly to catch glitches. The VLSI design of FPGAs is proprietary and simulation models are unavailable, so users cannot model and simulate high-speed voltage transients in their systems. The increasing reliance on power gating complicates the dynamics further [3]. In short, FPGA system designers and users are largely in the dark about their system's voltage noise. Pinpointing the location and timing of droops with on-line sensing could potentially enable improved designs.

On top of naturally occurring noise, there are threats of malicious attacks involving voltage transients. In a voltage glitch attack, an attacker with physical access injects glitches into the power grid to force a system into an invalid state that leaks information [4][5]. Even without physical access, there is a concern as to whether an unauthorized bitstream (or partial bitstream) could actually damage an IC with a supply-related attack, leading to a permanent denial of service.

An existing security standard dictates that supply voltages be continuously monitored in highly secure systems (FIPS PUB 140-2) [6], but much more attention needs to be paid—in FPGA-based systems and many other systems—to monitoring at the rate of nanosecond-scale transients. Xilinx has acknowledged the vulnerability, stating "If detection of very fast changes in temperature or voltages is required, an off-chip solution might be required." [7] Unfortunately, observability from off-chip is obscured by decoupling capacitors and potentially man-in-the-middle attacks. Furthermore, better capabilities are needed for detecting and reacting to attacks *quickly*, in order to minimize potential information leakage.

The problem of sensing voltage transients in FPGA-based systems is thus an important one. This short paper helps to address the problem and points the way to expanded research in this area. The contributions include:

- A novel demonstration of extreme voltage undershoot and overshoot caused by fabric activity on a 28nm FPGA

- A demonstration of why voltage sensing in FPGAs needs to be faster and closer to the circuitry than the existing method

- An implementation of a digital sensor in reconfigurable logic able to quickly characterize nanosecond-scale transients that normally go undetected

- Recommendations for increased protection against transients

## 2. RELATED WORK

Sensing of nanosecond-scale voltage transients is being studied in contexts such as design optimization, test, and debug of microprocessors and ASICs [1][2][8]. Detection of voltage glitches in ASICs for security purposes has begun receiving attention [9]. Little research has addressed FPGAs. Some sensors require analog or custom circuitry not available on FPGAs, while others are entirely digital [10]. Xilinx FPGAs do include a built-in means of sensing the internal supply voltage, but the sample rate is limited to 200K samples/s (Virtex-6) [11] and 1MSPS (7 Series) [12]. Several researchers have explored ring oscillator-based voltage sensing in FPGAs [13][14]. This type of frequency counting allows only clock cycle granularity, requiring that oscillators be run for many cycles to achieve good resolution. Thus it is better suited for sensing static effects or slow transients. By combining multiple oscillators, it may be feasible to achieve rates such as 8MSPS [15], but a sample period of 125ns is still far too slow for detecting and reacting to nanosecond-scale effects.

## 3. SENSING NANOSECOND-SCALE VOLTAGE TRANSIENTS

We propose high-speed voltage transient sensing using the digital reconfigurable logic available on FPGAs. The concept is to pair a delay line which is sensitive to the core voltage with a circuit that can measure small fluctuations in delay—a time-to-digital converter (TDC). A similar strategy is discussed for microprocessors in [10]. Our delay line includes not only LUTs but also latches that are left open to act as buffers; the extra gate delay enhances voltage sensitivity. A block diagram and timing diagram are shown in Fig. 1.

We use a carry chain-based TDC, in which an input signal zooms through the chain, racing against a clock. This style has been used successfully on FPGAs and can enable a resolution of approximately 10ps [16]. The bit position of the transition between 1s and 0s in the output word acts as the sample's bin number, providing an indication of the timing of the original event. The TDC concept is illustrated in Fig. 2. By measuring the delay line output every 2ns, the TDC allows detection of cycle to cycle changes in delay. Level-sensitive latches are used here instead of the conventional flip-flops, allowing a reset and a sample to occur in the same clock phase. The length of the delay line and number of TDC bins can be designed such that the desired dynamic sensor range is achieved.

The key to characterizing transients is to look for abrupt shifts in values across successive samples. The sensor data can be stored in memory for software-based processing, or alternatively, logic can be included for generating alarms based on thresholds or detected shifts. The sensor is of course also sensitive to low-frequency changes in voltage and temperature, but not on the nanosecond time scales of interest. If calibration is required, the clock to the delay line can be phase shifted. When targeting the Xilinx 7 Series, the sensor operates at 500MSPS.

## 4. EXPERIMENTAL RESULTS

We performed experiments addressing a series of questions regarding voltage transients: what amplitudes and time scales are involved, what can be generated using reconfigurable logic, what are the limitations of low sample rate sensing, and what is made possible with the proposed approach to sensing.

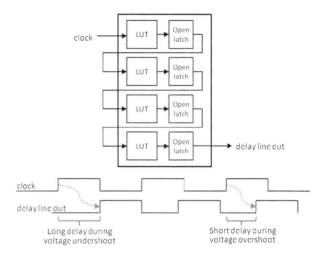

**Figure 1. Voltage sensitive delay line and timing diagram**

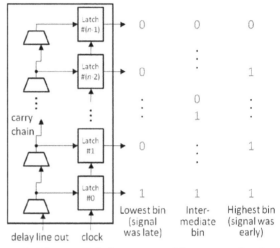

**Figure 2. Time-to-digital converter. Three scenarios shown.**

### 4.1 Generating voltage transients from within

In order to test the power grid and methods of sensing, a technique for generating voltage transients is needed. One existing on-die method requires large analog transistors [1][9] not applicable to FPGAs. A second recent method involves simultaneous switching of many LUT SRAM bits [17]; however, logic blocks are spread sparsely throughout a fabric, and in our testing were not effective at generating the largest transients. We propose a novel method of generating transients: simultaneous switching of dense interconnect resources. Unused wires and programmable interconnect points (PIPs) represent an enormous amount of capacitance that can be charged and discharged. After placement and routing of a design, a signal can be connected to a large number of unused PIPs, for instance with assistance from the Torc tools [18]. Interconnect has been used in the past for unconventional purposes [19], but to our knowledge never for inducing transients. This approach not only enables the generation of transients, it provides insight into an interesting related question: can changes in on-chip activity cause out-of-spec voltage excursions? The answer is yes, and to a surprising extent. We simultaneously switched about half of the PIPs (5M out of 10M) on a Xilinx Kintex-7 FPGA residing on a KC705 board, and measured the response on a package supply

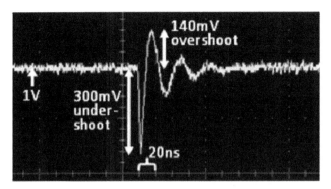

**Figure 3. Example of a very large, very quick excursion in the Kintex-7 core supply voltage measured with an oscilloscope. The origin of the noise was activity in the FPGA fabric.**

pin with an oscilloscope. The events caused a 31% undershoot at the pins, more than ten times the allowed 3% fluctuation. Detection of soft errors was outside the scope of this work, but clearly a 31% undershoot can cause timing errors in aggressive designs. The minimum voltage observed was 688mV, below the specified minimum data retention voltage. Just as surprising was the amount of overshoot, reaching 14% above nominal. A trace is provided in Fig. 3. In general, we found that the amount of voltage swing was nearly linear with the number of PIPs switched.

## 4.2 Limitations of existing sensor

The frequency response of a power distribution system is a complex function of capacitance, inductance, and resistance on the die, package and board [20]. We determined empirically that the Kintex-7/KC705 power grid, as measured at a package pin, would respond to a change in on-chip activity with a large first droop for several ns and smaller ripples lasting roughly 40ns. Even in the most extreme case (Fig. 3) the ripples quickly dissipated after tens of ns. The ADC embedded in Xilinx 7 Series FPGAs is limited to a sample period of 1000ns, so clearly transient effects can be missed. We confirmed this by measuring the Kintex-7 core voltage using the ADC. The ADCCLK was set to 25MHz and averaging was turned off. When two dramatic transients were injected, the ADC detected nothing and reported nominal values for the minimum and maximum voltages. We varied the event timing and confirmed that the ADC would occasionally detect some evidence of fluctuations, but the reported magnitude was highly diminished (e.g. a dip of 30mV instead of 300mV). The sampling capacitor in the ADC cannot track nanosecond-scale dynamics.

## 4.3 Results of proposed sensing approach

The proposed sensing approach from Section 3 was evaluated with a specific implementation tested on two KC705 boards. The delay line was made long enough (>1ns) so the sensor with its 10ps resolution can detect changes in delay smaller than 1%. The TDC was implemented with 64 stages (63 bins), and was calibrated to a nominal value in the low 40s so as to handle the undershoots that tend to be twice as large as the overshoots. A sensor was instantiated in a peripheral with BRAM to store sensor data. A timer circuit was connected to unused resources in the fabric to cause switching events of various sizes. Experiments were controlled with a MicroBlaze program. A

high-level diagram of the experimental system is shown in Fig. 4. The overhead of the sensor itself is small as shown in Table 1. Additional overhead is associated with optional features such as BRAM storage and an AXI interface. Note that determining the voltage range and resolution of the sensor in absolute terms was not attempted; independently measuring the local supply voltages throughout the FPGA fabric is inherently difficult, and not all transients are observable outside the chip. The main goal was to determine whether the sensing approach could detect ns-scale relative shifts indicative of anomalous transients.

With the system operating normally and the MicroBlaze program in a loop, the sensor reported values across a range of just 11 bins. Some fluctuations are expected due to nominal supply noise, clock jitter, measurement error, etc. We then switched 1% of the fabric PIPs simultaneously. The sensor reported a series of values spanning 15 bins, indicating that an abnormal swing was detected. Next, 3% of the PIPs were switched. The sensor reported a span of 22 bins, indicating an obvious anomaly (Table 2). Note that when probing a supply pin on the board with an oscilloscope in this scenario, the fluctuations were damped and nearly indistinguishable from typical noise, confirming the need for sensors embedded near the circuitry of interest. The sequence of samples from the proposed sensor is plotted in Fig. 5. The sensor is able to detect the initial droop, the overshoot, and the characteristic ripples.

**Figure 4. High-level diagram of FPGA-based system**

**Table 1. Overhead of sensor**

| Resource (Xilinx 7 Series) | Utilization |
|---|---|
| Slices for delay line | 1 |
| Slices for TDC | 16 |
| Control register bits | 32 |
| Clocks | 500MHz, 100MHz |

**Table 2. Range of sensor values**

| Size of simultaneous switching events | Range of sensor values |
|---|---|
| 0 (only nominal system activity) | 11 bins |
| 1% of K7 (100,000 PIPs) | 15 bins |
| 3% of K7 (300,000 PIPs) | 22 bins |

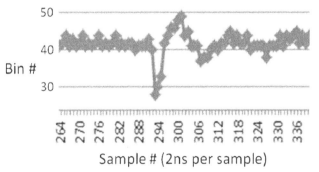

**Figure 5. Sequence of data from the proposed sensor showing clear voltage ripples after a switching event near sample 291**

# 5. DISCUSSION AND FUTURE WORK

The ability to sense momentary voltage anomalies in FPGAs suggests several possibilities. One of the most promising is enhanced protection against cryptographic voltage glitch attacks, whether originating off-chip or on-chip. High-speed sensors would be implemented in a trusted portion of the fabric, or eventually as a hard IP block by the vendor. Upon detection of an anomaly, a system could attempt to zero out its secret information or shutdown. Low latency detection solutions like the one presented here are needed, such that the time the cryptographic module spends in an invalid state is minimized. More research is needed into validating that FPGA-based sensing solutions themselves are resistant to attack.

Another possibility is protection against differential power analysis (DPA). System designers striving for DPA-resistance (e.g. using a special logic style that hides power fluctuations) may be able to deploy multiple voltage sensors optimized for sensitivity to validate their implementation. The effects of tampering with board or package decoupling capacitors (relevant for some DPA attacks [21]) could potentially be inferred. For instance, at appropriate times, a system could inject a distinctive noise event and monitor the transient response of the power grid, looking for abnormalities.

The threat of remote permanent denial of service attacks involving voltage transients needs further study. With microprocessors, GPUs, DRAM and the like, users are separated from the hardware by layers of abstraction, and the power grids are designed to handle worst case conditions, providing some inherent protection. This work highlights that reconfigurable logic is different—it provides fine-grained control of the hardware, and by implication, unprecedented control over physical effects. The power grids and sensors of the chips tested here were overwhelmed by extreme events. Work is needed regarding maximum voltage overshoot and the reliability impact; even natural overshoot can decrease the lifetime of an IC by 5× [22]. In the future, the inherent power of reconfigurable logic will sometimes need to be paired with restrictions in access, automated inspection of bitstreams, and/or additional hardware safeguards.

# 6. CONCLUSION

This work has found that voltage transients can be larger and quicker than expected and can go undetected in FPGA-based systems. Better characterization of transients is needed for optimizing system designs, for guarding against wear out attacks, and for protecting private information. The presented sensing approach can achieve sample rates in the hundreds of millions/s, help detect anomalies quickly, and provide insight into and protection against this dynamic phenomenon.

# 7. ACKNOWLEDGMENT

Our thanks to Aaron Wood and Neil Steiner for providing tools and feedback. This material is based upon work supported by the Defense Advanced Research Projects Agency (DARPA) under Contract No. HR001-11-C-0041. Any opinions, findings and conclusions or recommendations expressed in this material are those of the author(s) and do not necessarily reflect the views of the Defense Advanced Research Projects Agency (DARPA).

# 8. REFERENCES

[1] R. Petersen, P. Pant, P. Lopez, A. Barton, J. Ignowski and D. Josephson, "Voltage transient detection and induction for debug and test," *Proc. Int'l Test Conf.*, pp. 1–10, 2009.

[2] C. Lefurgy et al., "Active management of timing guardband to save energy in POWER7," *Proc. Int'l Symp. Microarchitecture (MICRO)*, pp. 1–11, 2011.

[3] A. Bsoul and S. Wilton, "A configurable architecture to limit wakeup current in dynamically-controlled power-gated FPGAs," *Proc. Int'l Symp. Field Programmable Gate Arrays*, pp. 245–254, 2012.

[4] J.-M. Schmidt and C. Herbst, "A practical fault attack on square and multiply," *Proc. Fault Diagnosis and Tolerance in Cryptography*, pp. 53–58, 2008.

[5] A. Pellegrini, V. Bertacco and T. Austin, "Fault-based attack of RSA authentication," *Design, Aut. & Test in Europe*, pp. 855–860, 2010.

[6] FIPS PUB 140-2, "Security Requirements for Cryptographic Modules," National Inst. Standards and Technology, May 25, 2001.

[7] Xilinx, Inc., "Developing tamper resistant designs with Xilinx Virtex-6 and 7 Series FPGAs," XAPP1084 (v1.2), August 10, 2012.

[8] T. Fischer, J. Desai, B. Doyle, S. Naffziger and B. Patella, "A 90-nm variable frequency clock system for a power-managed Itanium Architecture processor," *IEEE Journal of Solid-State Circuits*, vol. 41, no. 1, pp. 229–237, Jan. 2006.

[9] A.G. Yanci, S. Pickles and T. Arslan, "Characterization of a voltage glitch attack detector for secure devices," *Symp. Bio-inspired Learning and Intelligent Systems for Security*, 2009.

[10] K.A. Bowman, *et al.*, "All-digital circuit-level dynamic variation monitor for silicon debug and adaptive clock control," *IEEE Trans. Circuits and Systems I*, vol. 58, no. 9, pp. 2017–2025, 2011.

[11] Xilinx, Inc., "Virtex-6 FPGA System Monitor User Guide," UG370 (v1.1), June 2010.

[12] Xilinx, Inc., "7 Series FPGAs and Zynq-7000 All Prog. SoC XADC dual 12-bit 1MSPS ADC User Guide," UG480(v1.2), Oct. 2012.

[13] E. Boemo and S. López-Buedo, "Thermal monitoring on FPGAs using ring-oscillators," *Int'l Workshop on Field-Programmable Logic and Applications*, pp. 69–78, 1997.

[14] K.M. Zick and J.P. Hayes, "Low-cost sensing with ring oscillator arrays for healthier reconfigurable systems," *ACM Trans. Reconfigurable Technology and Systems*, vol. 5, no. 1, pp. 1–26, 2012.

[15] A. Le Masle and W. Luk, "Detecting power attacks on reconfigurable hardware," *Field Programmable Logic and Applications*, pp. 14–19, 2012.

[16] H. Menninga, "Implementation, characterization, and optimization of an FPGA-based time-to-digital converter," M.Sc. thesis, Delft Univ. of Technology, May 2011.

[17] D. Ziener, F. Baueregger and J. Teich, "Using the power side channel of FPGAs for communication," *IEEE Field-Prog. Custom Computing Machines*, pp. 237–244, 2010.

[18] N. Steiner, A. Wood, H. Shojaei, J. Couch. P. Athanas and M. French, "Torc: towards an open-source tool flow," *Proc. Int'l Symp. Field Programmable Gate Arrays*, pp. 41–44, 2011. http://torc.isi.edu.

[19] A. Tavaragiri, J. Couch and P. Athanas, "Exploration of FPGA interconnect for the design of unconventional antennas," *Proc. Int'l Symp. Field Programmable Gate Arrays*, pp. 219–226, 2011.

[20] D. Brooks, R.P. Dick and L. Shang, "Power, thermal, and reliability modeling in nanometer-scale microprocessors," *IEEE Micro*, vol. 27, no. 3, pp. 49–62, 2007.

[21] A. Moradi, M. Kasper and C. Paar, "Black-box side-channel attacks highlight the importance of countermeasures," *Proc. Conf. Topics in Cryptology*, pp. 1–18, 2012.

[22] Z. Liu, B. McGaughy and J. Ma, "Design tools for reliability analysis," *Design Automation Conference*, pp. 182–187, 2006.

# Word-length Optimization Beyond Straight Line Code

David Boland and George A. Constantinides
Department of Electrical and Electronic Engineering
Imperial College London
London, UK
{david.boland03, g.constantinides}@imperial.ac.uk

## ABSTRACT

The silicon area benefits that result from word-length optimization have been widely reported by the FPGA community. However, to date, most approaches are restricted to straight line code, or code that can be converted into straight line code using techniques such as loop-unrolling. In this paper, we take the first steps towards creating analytical techniques to optimize the precision used throughout custom FPGA accelerators for algorithms that contain loops with data dependent exit conditions. To achieve this, we build on ideas emanating from the software verification community to prove program termination. Our idea is to apply word-length optimization techniques to find the minimum precision required to guarantee that a loop with data dependent exit conditions will terminate.

Without techniques to analyze algorithms containing these types of loops, a hardware designer may elect to implement every arithmetic operator throughout a custom FPGA-based accelerator using IEEE-754 standard single or double precision arithmetic. With this approach, the FPGA accelerator would have comparable accuracy to a software implementation. However, we show that using our new technique to create custom fixed and floating point designs, we can obtain silicon area savings of up to 50% over IEEE standard single precision arithmetic, or 80% over IEEE standard double precision arithmetic, at the same time as providing guarantees that the created hardware designs will work in practice.

## Categories and Subject Descriptors

G.1.0 [**NUMERICAL ANALYSIS**]: Miscellaneous

## General Terms

Algorithms, Design, Verification.

## Keywords

Precision Analysis, Loop Termination, Word-length Optimization.

## 1. INTRODUCTION

In recent years we have seen an explosion in the use of embedded devices throughout everyday life. These devices demand high performance with minimal power use. FPGAs are often proposed as an alternative to create designs that exhibit much greater energy efficiency than a software counterpart. To obtain this efficiency, it is imperative that the available silicon area is used effectively; this means not performing any unnecessary computation. This ideology should not only apply at an algorithmic level, but also at a much finer arithmetic level. Word-length optimization is a key technique to ensure that every individual bit within an arithmetic operation is computing useful information.

The underlying concept behind word-length optimization is that error is inherent in most numerical algorithms because it is either impossible or infeasible to represent numbers exactly. This means that almost every algorithm operating on real numbers must be tolerant of errors to some extent. Ideally one should choose the minimum precision throughout a design according to this tolerance because this will use the minimum silicon area. This in turn will reduce the power requirements, or allow room for additional parallelism.

A large variety of techniques have been proposed which attempt to realize these performance benefits, as we will discuss in Section 2. To date, these are based upon analyzing the finite precision errors that arise from every individual arithmetic operation and computing bounds on the range or relative error of the output. This information is used to determine the minimum precision required to meet an error specification. Unfortunately this process breaks down in the case of loops with data dependent exit conditions. This is because it is impossible to analyze every arithmetic operation *a priori* since it is unknown how many operations will actually occur.

In this paper, we assume that the loop termination condition embodies the algorithm designer's objective, such as convergence to a desired result. Consequently, we propose that the precision used throughout a custom FPGA design should be the minimum required to ensure that the loop will still terminate. This would guarantee that the hardware would work as desired.

In order to provide such guarantees, we build on concepts to prove program termination described by the software verification community. Firstly, we introduce techniques to model finite precision errors (both fixed and floating point) within a termination argument. We then demonstrate how it is possible to use analysis techniques from the field of word-length optimization to check the validity of this argument for various word-length specifications. We can then select the minimum precision that ensures the loop will terminate. A summary of the main contributions of this work is as follows:

- A method to incorporate finite precision models typically used in numerical analysis into a termination argument.

- A discussion of how to use precision analysis techniques to validate such a termination argument. These techniques are

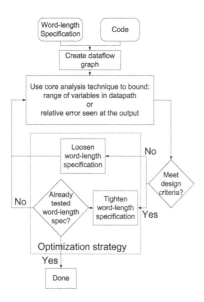

**Figure 1: Overview of word-length optimization.**

applicable where the loop body consists of the basic algebraic operations or smooth elementary functions. This takes it beyond the scope of existing termination proving tools.

- The integration of our analysis technique within a basic word-length optimization framework to illustrate the power of our tool in saving silicon area when creating custom FPGA designs.

We first introduce the reader to the field of word-length optimization in order to highlight how the analysis technique we describe could have a major impact on this body of work. We then walk through the basics of program termination, discuss the state of the art tools to prove termination and their limitations when seen from an FPGA-based computing point of view. After this, through the use of a few simple examples, we introduce our solution to utilize analysis techniques from the field of word-length optimization to prove program termination in the presence of finite precision errors. Finally, we demonstrate how our method can be used to tune the precision throughout an algorithm using four case studies.

## 2. WORD-LENGTH OPTIMIZATION

Figure 1 presents a high-level view of word-length optimization. The typical process first involves constructing a dataflow graph for the desired code and analyzing the error seen at the output of this graph for a given word-length specification. It then iteratively refines this word-length specification to create the smallest, lowest power, or fastest datapath that satisfies the desired design criterion. To date, the focus of word-length optimization frameworks has either been on the high-level optimization strategy to perform the word-length refinement, or the core analysis technique to compute bounds on the range or relative error of the output variables of a datapath over a user-provided input range. In this section, we discuss the main contributions in each of these areas.

Computing bounds on the range of variables in a datapath enables a user to choose the position of the MSB in a fixed point representation, or the number of bits required for the exponent in a floating point representation. Bounds on the relative error seen at the output of a datapath are important when computing metrics such as the signal to quantization noise ratio, or more generally to

ensure the hardware datapath achieves the desired quality of output. Consequently, several core analysis techniques have been described to compute these bounds. As well as Monte-Carlo simulation, these include analytical techniques such as interval arithmetic, linear-time invariant system analysis, affine arithmetic, algebraic analysis and satisfiability modulo theory [10]. While simulation can potentially detect counter examples demonstrating that a word-length specification violates the design criteria, it runs the risk of not allocating sufficient bits because it is impractical to exhaustively simulate over a range of input data. In contrast, the analytical methods can provide guarantees that any word-length specification is appropriate. Unfortunately they will typically over-allocate bits because they are unable to calculate the optimal bounds. The existing tools trade quality of bounds for execution time and scalability of the procedure, as discussed in detail in [2]. Furthermore, various contributions have proposed slightly higher level strategies to help improve the quality of bounds and execution time of the core analysis techniques. For example, allowing expert hints to help improve the analysis [15] or applying some form of combination of these techniques to make the most of their contrasting strengths [17, 21, 22, 24].

The high-level optimization strategies which utilize these core analysis techniques seek to quickly find the best word-length specification that meets the design criterion. This is a complex problem because it has been shown that a variable word-length specification can obtain superior performance-error trade-offs than a uniform word-length specification [8]. Since an exhaustive search is generally impractical, various approaches have been proposed to quickly search for an optimal design. These include integer linear programming [9], simulated annealing [21] and various custom heuristics [8, 20, 29]. Alternatively, techniques have been suggested to reduce the search space by grouping signals to take into account resource sharing [4, 5], or guide the search by applying area and error models for adders and multipliers or other operators [6, 21]. Finally, research has also investigated whether to implement operators using fixed point, floating point or a some combination of the two approaches [19].

However, the fundamental limitation of these analytical word-length optimization techniques is that they need to know exactly how the data flows through the hardware. This means this body of work can only be applied to algorithms where the input code can be converted into static single assignment (SSA) form. Algorithms with conditional statements can be expanded into SSA by exploring each path separately. For example, for the code of Figure 2, the result of $a/b$ lies in the interval $[0.1; 10]$, and the result of $a \times b$ lies in the interval $[1000; 10000]$; consequently, the variable *output* lies somewhere in their union *i.e.* in the interval $[0.1; 10000]$. Similarly, any graph with feedback can be unrolled into SSA form provided the number of iterations is known *a priori*. From the perspective of computing the range or worst-case error of the variable *output* from the code shown in Figure 3, the hardware architectures of Figures 3(b) and 3(c) are equivalent. Using the latter architecture, the framework of Figure 1 is still appropriate.

```
Function absolute_dif(a, b)
//a, b are known to lie in the interval [10; 100];
if  a > b then
    output = a/b;
else
    output = a × b;
end if
```

**Figure 2: Expanding a conditional statement.**

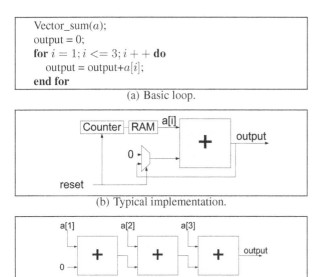

(a) Basic loop.

```
Vector_sum(a);
output = 0;
for i = 1; i <= 3; i + + do
    output = output+a[i];
end for
```

(b) Typical implementation.

(c) Unrolled loop.

Figure 3: Unrolling a for loop.

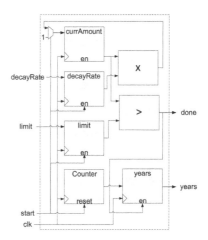

Figure 5: Hardware accelerator for halflife example.

Table 1: Execution of half-life algorithm with currAmount using 5 bits lying between $\frac{1}{32}$ and 1.

| Loop Iteration | Years | currAmount (before rounding) | currAmount (after rounding) |
|---|---|---|---|
| 0 | 0 | 1 | 1 |
| 1 | 1 | 0.9375 | $30/32$ |
| 2 | 2 | 0.87890625 | $28/32$ |
| 3 | 3 | 0.87890625 | $26/32$ |
| 4 | 4 | 0.76171875 | $24/32$ |
| 5 | 5 | 0.703125 | $23/32$ |
| ⋮ | ⋮ | ⋮ | ⋮ |
| 19 | 19 | 0.263671875 | $9/32$ |
| 20 | 20 | 0.234375 | $8/32$ |
| 21 | 21 | 0.234375 | $8/32$ |

However, it is not possible to construct a finite cycle free graph for a loop with data-dependent exit conditions. While it is possible to analyze a single loop iteration, one cannot compute the bound on relative error seen at the final output because any errors will be amplified by feedback [3]. This means that none of the existing analytical word-length optimization tools can be used on these loops, while any simulation based word-length optimization tool will still potentially suffer from under-allocating bits and potentially create unsafe hardware.

To illustrate the difficulty of allocating bits within such a loop, consider the simple example of designing a dedicated hardware accelerator to compute the time for a radioactive substance to decay to a tolerable level. It is specified that the inputs for the rate of decay and tolerable limit are 4-bit values lying between $\frac{1}{16}$ and $\frac{15}{16}$, and the output number of years should be an 8-bit integer. Figure 4 shows the algorithm and a potential hardware implementation for this specification is given in Figure 5. The only unknown is the width of the internal variable $currAmount$. None of the existing word-length optimization tools are capable of choosing the precision of this variable. Suppose we were to arbitrarily choose this precision to be 5 bits lying between $\frac{1}{32}$ and 1. In this case, if the decayRate was $\frac{15}{16}$ and the limit was $\frac{1}{16}$, the algorithm would execute as in Table 1 and would never terminate!

```
Function Halflife(fixed4bit(decayRate), fixed4bit(limit))
int8 years = 0;
fixed?bit currAmount = 1;
while currAmount > limit do
    years = years+1;
    currAmount = currAmount × decayRate;
end while
return(years);
```

Figure 4: Basic function to compute time for radioactive substance to decay to a tolerable level.

Since loop termination is a necessary condition for correctness, this paper proposes to choose the precision such that the loop is guaranteed to terminate. For this case study, because the input has

a very limited range, it is possible to exhaustively simulate until the minimum precision that will guarantee termination is computed. However, for wide input ranges, the execution time prevents such an approach. Instead, we discuss how ideas to prove loop termination can be utilized to allocate bits within such loops.

Tools to automatically generate termination proofs have drawn interest from several communities ever since their use was first demonstrated to find software bugs in real systems code [12]. Since then, many potential further uses of these tools have been identified [13]. In this paper, we seek to extend the use of these tools by making them applicable for optimizing the precision throughout a custom hardware accelerator for numerical algorithms. The next section provides an introduction to the relevant concepts that we have adopted from this community for the unfamiliar reader before discussing the state-of-the-art in termination tools. In Section 4, we then discuss our suggested method that builds on these ideas and enables us to choose the number of bits required in an algorithm with data dependent loop exit conditions.

## 3. PROVING TERMINATION

The main concept we have adopted from termination provers is that of ranking functions. After introducing some notation, we will discuss this technique through the use of some simple examples.

## 3.1 Notation

For a loop containing $n$ variables, we label the loop variables $x_1$ to $x_n$ before the loop update, and $x'_1$ to $x'_n$ after the loop update. We focus on analyzing loops that follow the structure described by Figure 6. These are singly nested loops which contain bounded input variables, linear and conjunctive loop exit conditions and transition statements that consist of the basic algebraic operations $(+, -, \times, /)$ or smooth elementary functions.

```
// Loop input variables with defined input ranges
x₁ = 100 × rand();
x₂ = 5 - 10 × rand();
while ((x₁ > 0)&&(x₂ < 1000))do //Loop exit conditions
    //Loop transition statements
    x₁ = x₁ + 1
    x₂ = x₂ × x₁
end while
```

**Figure 6: Overview of loop structure.**

## 3.2 Ranking functions

Proving program termination using a ranking function is based on the following steps:

1. Construct a ranking function $f(x_1, ..., x_n)$ that maps every potential state within the loop to a positive real number.

2. Prove that for all potential values of the variables $x_1, ..., x_n$ within the loop body, when the ranking function is applied to the loop variables before and after the loop transition statements, it always decreases by more than some fixed amount $\epsilon > 0$, i.e. $f(x'_1, ..., x'_n) < f(x_1, ..., x_n) - \epsilon$.

The reason this proves program termination, is because if the ranking function always decreases by at least the fixed amount $\epsilon$, eventually there will be a loop transition such that $f(x'_1, ..., x'_n) \leq 0$. This corresponds to the loop terminating.

To illustrate this process, we discuss the termination argument for the three examples in Figure 7:

1. (a) Choose a ranking function that maps every state in the loop to a positive real number: $f(i) = i$ is one such function.

    (b) Apply ranking function to loop variables before and after the loop transition statements: $f(i) = i$, $f(i') = i - 1$.

    (c) Prove that $f(i') < f(i)$: $0 < 1 \rightarrow i - 1 < i$.

2. (a) Choose a ranking function that maps every state in the loop to a positive real number: $f(i) = 100 - i$ maps every potential state to the set of integers between 0 and maxInt.

    (b) Apply ranking function to loop variables before and after the loop transition statements: $f(i) = 100 - i$, $f(i') = 100 - (i + 1)$.

    (c) Prove that $f(i') < f(i)$: $0 < 1 \rightarrow 100 - (i + 1) < 100 - i$.

3. (a) Choose a ranking function that maps every state in the loop to a positive real number: $f(i, j, k) = maxInt + 100 - i - j$ maps every potential state to the set of integers between 0 and $2 \times$ maxInt+100.

```
int i;                          int i;
while i > 0 do                  while i < 100 do
    i = i-1;                        i = i+1;
end while                       end while
```
(a) Case study 1.              (b) Case study 2.

```
int i,j,k;
while (i < 100)&&(j < k) do
    temp = i;
    i = j;
    j = temp+1;
    k = k-1;
end while
```
(c) Case study 3.

**Figure 7: Termination case studies.**

    (b) Apply ranking function to loop variables before and after the loop transition statements: $f(i, j, k) = maxInt + 100 - i - j$, $f(i', j', k') = maxInt + 100 - j - (i + 1)$.

    (c) Prove that $f(i', j', k') < f(i, j, k)$: $0 < 1 \rightarrow maxInt + 100 - i - j < maxInt + 100 - j - (i + 1)$.

While it is trivial to demonstrate termination in these benchmarks, for more complex problems, constructing a suitable ranking function and proving that the ranking function argument holds are both difficult tasks. As a result it is desirable to create automated analysis techniques. Any such process must take care when dealing with finite precision number systems.

A trivial example of why it is important to consider finite precision error can be seen in Figure 8, which once again examines the case study in Figure 7(a), but assumes a floating point representation is chosen for $i$. We have shown that this program will terminate under infinite precision. Similarly, the program will terminate for any fixed point number system containing a unit digit. However, the code will not necessarily terminate for a floating point number system, because the decrement can be counteracted by round-off error. To demonstrate this, suppose we had a custom number system of a 4 bit exponent with no bias and a 5 bit mantissa, and our initial value of $i$ was 256. In this loop, we would first perform the computation $1.00000 \times 2^8 - 1.00000 \times 2^0$. The result of this expression is $1.1111111 \times 2^7$ which is unrepresentable in the number system, so a round-to-nearest operation is typically performed, returning $1.00000 \times 2^8$. This means that after the first iteration of the loop, the value of $i$ would be the same as on entering the loop and as a result, the loop would never terminate.

```
float(4,5) i; // This notation implies i is a custom floating
point number with a 4 bit exponent and 5 bit mantissa.
while i > 0 do
    i = i - 1.0;
end while
```

**Figure 8: Potentially non-terminating loop.**

## 3.3 Termination provers

The importance of termination provers within the software verification community has led to many tools that can be used to prove termination. Amongst the techniques using ranking functions, a seminal contribution was the work of Podelski et al. [26] which is guaranteed to compute linear ranking functions for a loop body that consists of linear arithmetic operations. This contribution formed the basis of more powerful tools, such as the TERMINATOR project, that perform more widespread program analysis to detect bugs in systems code [12, 27]. These tools automatically breaks down loops into the simplest possible structure, before using the method by Podelski to prove program termination of these individual loops.

However, from the perspective of numerical algorithms, there are two major limitations of reliance on the method by Podelski: a focus on linear arithmetic, and the absence of support for finite precision arithmetics such as floating point. Being able to model finite precision errors is imperative if we are to apply these tools to optimize the word-length of custom hardware designs, while nonlinear arithmetic operations, such as general multiplication, are common in most software programs.

There already exist several techniques that search for non-linear ranking functions for non-nested loops with non-linear loop transition statements [7, 14, 23]. However, these methods have exponential computational complexity in the number of program variables. To tackle this problem, we make use of scalable precision analysis techniques [1, 2] to check if a ranking function proves termination. Furthermore, we only apply this check for ranking functions that are either specified by a user or of a specific form. While this restriction limits the form of ranking functions that can be discovered, we believe this sacrifice is important for these techniques to be of use on real numerical algorithms. This is especially important since software is generally written in some form of finite precision arithmetic, and modelling finite precision arithmetic errors introduces many extra program variables.

Kittel [16] and Seneschal [11] are two tools that have attempted to incorporate fixed precision arithmetic using term re-write systems and SAT respectively. The analysis is performed at a bit-vector level, and this has the advantage that both techniques are able to consider bit-wise operations such as logical AND, OR and NOT. However, modelling variables at a bit-vector level is not scalable; for example, the number of constraints to represent multiplication using SAT grow quadratically with the word-length [28]. Furthermore, floating point operators are far more complicated than fixed point operators and the majority of algorithms in the field of scientific computing are written in floating point. Instead our approach uses standard safe over approximations from the numerical analysis community to model finite precision arithmetic at the word-level.

The only existing technique that would be applicable to floating point algorithms is bounded model checking. This unrolls the loop for a number of iterations and attempts to find an example of a recurring path within a while loop which demonstrates nontermination. For example, in Table 1, bounded model checking could detect the recurring value for $currAmount$, if it unrolled 21 iterations. However, while there have been substantial developments in speeding up bounded model checking using tools such as SAT, because this technique only explores a limited number unrolled iterations, it cannot prove termination in the general case.

In this paper, we seek to make these tools become more widely applicable in both software and hardware accelerator verification by introducing scalable techniques to deal with finite precision number systems numbers and improve the speed to which these tools handle all the basic arithmetic operations. In addition, we introduce how these techniques can be used to improve custom hardware designs.

## 4. BEYOND SSA

An overview of our approach is given in Figure 9. Firstly, our tool parses a program to extract the relevant information: the input

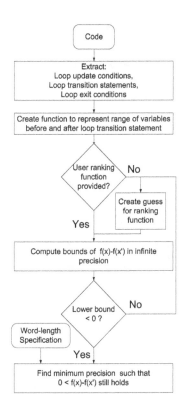

**Figure 9: Overview of our approach.**

variable ranges, loop exit conditions and loop transition statements. Using this information, we construct a representation of the ranges of the loop variables before and after an iteration of the loop body, taking into account finite precision errors. We then apply a chosen ranking function, this is either specified through a user hint, or our tool searches for a suitable ranking function. Provided the ranking function is valid, we proceed to find the minimum precision such that even in the worst-case, the chosen ranking functions will guarantee that the loop still terminates.

In this section, we outline first how we construct the model for the variables within the loop body. We then briefly discuss our technique to search for ranking functions using this model.

### 4.1 Representing the range of a variable

In this work, for floating point error, we have elected to use the multiplicative model of error used throughout numerical analysis literature. This represents the closest radix-2 floating-point approximation $\hat{x}$ to any real value $x$ as in equation (1) [18], where $\eta$ represents the number of mantissa bits used and $\delta$ represents the small unknown roundoff error. It is similarly possible to show that the radix-2 floating-point result of any scalar operation $(\odot)$ is bounded as in (2), provided the exponent is sufficiently large to span the range of the result, allowing us to create a polynomial to represent the potential range of a variable. In the example of Figure 8, the range of $i'$ (after the loop update) could be represented as (3). For fixed point, we use a different model of error (4).

$$\hat{x} = x(1 + \delta) \quad (|\delta| \le 2^{-\eta}). \tag{1}$$

$$\widehat{x \odot y} = (x \odot y)(1 + \delta). \tag{2}$$

$$i' = (i - 1.0)(1 + \delta) \quad (|\delta| \le 2^{-5}). \tag{3}$$

$$\hat{x} = x + \delta \quad (|\delta| \le 2^{-\eta}). \tag{4}$$

## 4.2 Generating ranking functions

To prove termination, we must find a ranking function $f(x_1, ..., x_n)$ such that when it is applied to the loop variables before and after a loop transition, the ranking function will always decrease by more than some fixed amount (5). To represent the range of every loop variable before a loop update, we construct polynomials based upon information prior to entering the loop and on the loop conditions themselves. For the example in Figure 8, if the maximum value is specified to be 256, since the loop exit condition specifies $i > 0$, we could represent the range using equation (6). Similarly, we construct polynomials representing the ranges after the loop transition using the method described in the previous subsection. For the example in Figure 8, this would result in equation (7).

$$f(x_1', ..., x_n') < f(x_1, ..., x_n) - \epsilon \qquad (5)$$

$$i \in 128 + 128i_1, \text{where } |i_1| \leq 1 \qquad (6)$$

$$i' \in (127 + 128i_1)(1 + \delta), \text{where } |i_1| \leq 1, |\delta| \leq 2^{-5} \qquad (7)$$

The next stage involves applying a ranking function to these polynomials to obtain $f(x')$ and $f(x)$. As we have described in Section 3.3, for algorithms that contain non-linear arithmetic operations, currently there are no scalable techniques that can automatically choose the ranking functions that can prove program termination. Indeed, our approach is only capable of checking if a ranking proves termination. Consequently, if no user-defined ranking function is supplied, our approach attempts to find a ranking function of the form described by (8) by exhaustively testing all the combinations of $c_i$ until it finds a ranking function to prove termination in infinite precision.

$$f(x_1, ..., x_n) = c_0 + \sum_{i=1}^{n} c_i x_i \qquad (8)$$

where $c_0 \in \{-maxVal, 0, maxVal\}$, $c_1, ...c_n \in \{-1, 0, 1\}$

To prove termination with these functions, we perform a basic algebraic manipulation to equation (5) to create equation (9). This allows us to construct a single polynomial to which we can apply algebraic techniques to prove polynomial positivity [25] to determine whether the ranking function argument can prove termination. We apply the procedure described in [1, 2] because it satisfies these criteria whilst computing tight bounds in a scalable manner. These papers also highlighted that their procedure can make use of an iterative refinement to accommodate divisions in the input code and apply polynomial approximations to extend this technique for any elementary functions in the input code. This means we could apply our termination analysis to loops where transition statements are any of the basic algebraic operation or smooth elementary functions. Furthermore, this technique can check a termination proof is valid for any user specified ranking function provided that it can be expressed using a polynomial.

$$0 < f(x_1, ..., x_n) - f(x_1', ..., x_n') - \epsilon \qquad (9)$$

If our approach is able to automatically find a ranking function and prove that it terminates using the above search technique, we can repeat this test with different choices of precision to find the minimum precision required to guarantee termination using this ranking function. If the search technique fails to find a ranking function that proves termination, it will require the user to provide a ranking function. Our program can then test if the provided rank-

ing function will lead to termination and if successful, proceed to search for the minimum precision required to guarantee termination using this ranking function. In the example of Figure 8 where $i$ lies in the range $[0; 256]$, if we use the ranking function $f(i) = i$, we would have to satisfy (10) to prove termination. As a result, it is trivial to see that the termination proof will depend on the input range and the chosen precision $\delta$, as one would expect. We can compute that $|\delta| \leq 2^{-9}$ for this function to be positive.

$$0 < 128 + 128i_1 - (127 + 128i_1)(1 + \delta) - \epsilon \qquad (10)$$

## 5. RESULTS

We demonstrate how our termination procedure can be used within a word-length optimization framework to improve a custom FPGA design using four case studies. We first discuss how to choose the fixed-point precision to guarantee termination for our half-life problem in Figure 4, and for a method to compute the greatest common divisor of two numbers. We then discuss two more complex numerical algorithms that require floating-point precision due to the high dynamic range of the variables. All these case studies contain loops with data dependent exit conditions where the loop transition statements contain multiplications and divisions. We also consider finite precision effects. Altogether, this takes it far beyond the scope of the tools described in Sections 2 and 3.3.

## 5.1 Case study: Half-life

The first stage of the process involves extracting the relevant loop information. Taking into account the user-specified input ranges, this is shown in Figure 10.

```
1: decayRate ∈ [1/16; 15/16];
2: limit ∈ [1/16; 15/16];
3: years ∈ [1; 64];
4: currAmount ∈ [1/16; 1];
5: // Transition Statements
6: years' = years + 1
7: currAmount' = currAmount × decayRate
8: Terminates if:
   0 < f(years, currAmount)−f(years′,currAmount′)−ε
```

**Figure 10: Halflife algorithm broken down into transition test.**

The next stage of the process involves choosing the ranking function; the search method described in Section 4.2 will find the ranking function $f(years, currAmount) = currAmount$. First, we test that this is a valid ranking function. For this to be the case, $f(years, currAmount) > 0$. This is trivially the case since we have specified $currAmount$ to lie in the range $[1/16; 1]$. As a result, after applying the model of fixed point error described by equation (4), our procedure will then attempt to bound the function (11), for different values of precision $\delta$. Figure 11 shows the computed lower bound for this function.

$$currAmount - (currAmount \times decayRate + \delta) \qquad (11)$$

This lower bound crosses 0 when 8 bits are used. This means that when 8 bits are used for the variable $currAmount$, it is guaranteed to terminate. For this simple example, we can test that this result is correct by hand. The worst case is when $limit$ is $1/16$ and $decayRate$ is $15/16$. Suppose in this case, $currAmount$ could eventually decrease to the value $1/16$. The result for $1/16 \times 15/16 =$

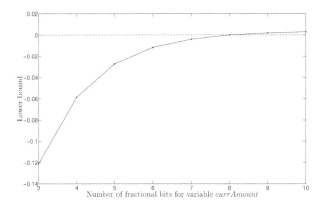

**Figure 11: Computed lower bound of** $f(currAmount) - f(currAmount')$ **using the approach described in [1, 2]. For a given precision, if the lower bound is above zero it is guaranteed to terminate.**

$15/256$ in binary is 0.00001111. With 7 bits, this would round up to 0.000100, which is $1/16$, so this would never terminate. However, with 8 bits, it could exactly represent 0.00001111, so it would terminate.

**Impact on FPGA Implementation:** In order to quantify how much hardware could be saved by making use of this analysis, we have hand-coded a custom FPGA-based accelerator for this algorithm using VHDL according to the architecture of Figure 5. Table 2 shows the post-place and route resource use for different choices of precision for this hardware implementation, targeted to a Virtex 7. We can see that even on this trivial example, it is desirable to choose the minimum precision required to guarantee termination because this design achieves a higher clock frequency and uses fewer resources in terms of slices and DSPs. Furthermore, the reduced silicon area use will result in lower power consumption.

**Table 2: Resource use and max frequency of custom hardware implementations of halflife example.**

| # bits for $currAmount$ | Slices | DSPs | Frequency (MHz) |
|---|---|---|---|
| 8 | 14 | 1 | 275 |
| 12 | 15 | 1 | 275 |
| 16 | 16 | 1 | 275 |
| 20 | 17 | 2 | 210 |

We note that with the exception of exhaustive simulation, none of the existing word-length optimization tools described in Section 2 could be used to determine the precision for $currAmount$. Similarly, none of the termination provers described in Section 3.3 could prove that the smallest design that is guaranteed to terminate. For example, due to the multiplication, Kittel [16] and Seneschal [11] both reach time-outs when attempting to compute a result. Furthermore, exhaustive simulation is only applicable because the inputs to this example only consist of four fractional bits. If the inputs required were described by many more bits, exhaustive simulation would quickly become infeasible. In contrast, because our analysis involves bounding a polynomial (11) and the input range would not affect the size of this polynomial, our approach would compute the minimum precision required to guarantee termination for an example with a wider input range within the same execution time.

In the following case studies, we will study increasingly complex examples where only our approach could compute the minimum precision required to guarantee termination within a tractable amount of time.

## 5.2  Case study: Euclidean Division

Our second case study is Euclid's method to compute the greatest common divisor of two numbers. This algorithm is given in Figure 12. Once again, we shall step through the various steps of our framework. After extracting the relevant loop information, we obtain the information in Figure 13.

```
1: // Algorithm to compute the GCD of two numbers a and b,
2: // where a lies in the interval [0.1; 1000], b lies in the inter-
      val [0.1; 100] and a > b.
3: Function GCD(a, b)
4:   while b > 0.1 do
5:     c = b;
6:     b = a − ⌊a/b⌋b
7:     a = c;
8:   end while
9:   return(a)
```

**Figure 12: Euclid's method to compute the greatest common divisor of two variables.**

```
1: a ∈ [0.1; 1000];
2: b ∈ [0.1; 100];
3: c ∈ [0.1; 1000];
4: // Transition Statements
5: c′ = b
6: b′ = a − ⌊a/b⌋ × b
7: a′ = b
8: Terminates if:
     0 < f(b) − f(b′) − ε
```

**Figure 13: Euclid's method broken down into transition test.**

Once again, the search can be used to select the ranking function, in this case it will find the function $f(a, b, c) = b$. This can trivially be shown to be a valid ranking function because $b$ lies in the range $[0.1; 100]$. In order to apply the polynomial techniques to bound the function, we first must approximate the floor function. To do this, we note that the floor function has a limited range as shown in (12), so we bound this worst case range using (13). We can then once again apply the model of fixed point error described in equation (4), and attempt to compute the lower bound of the function (14), for different values of precision $\delta_i$. This is shown in Figure 14.

$$a/b - 1 \leq \lfloor a/b \rfloor \leq a/b \tag{12}$$

$$a/b - 1 \leq a/b - 0.5 + y \leq a/b, \text{where } |y| \leq 0.5 \tag{13}$$

$$0 < b - (a - ((a/b + \delta_1) - 0.5 + y) \times b + \delta_2) \tag{14}$$

$$\text{where } |y| \leq 0.5 \text{ and } |\delta_i| \leq 2^{-\eta}$$

**Impact on FPGA Implementation:** Figure 15 illustrates a custom FPGA-based accelerator for this algorithm, which we have hand-coded VHDL. For this implementation, using our approach we can see that the lower bound crosses 0 in Figure 14 when 5 fractional bits are used. This implies that to guarantee termination a total of 15 bits (10 integer bits are needed represent the range between 0 and 1000) are required for the variable $b$ as well as all the intermediate variables that are used to compute $b$. The post-place

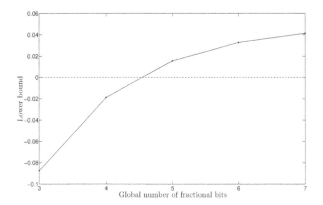

Figure 14: Computed lower bound of $f(b) - f(b')$.

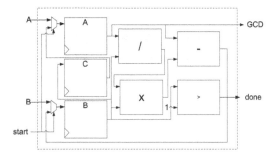

Figure 15: Hardware accelerator for Euclid's method to find the greatest common divisor.

and route resource use for different choices of precision for this example are shown in Table 3. Whereas the last example consisted of only a multiplier, counter, comparator and some registers, this example also contains a subtracter and a divider. As a result, it becomes of even greater importance to choose the minimum precision. Using a single additional fractional bit requires an increase in slices of 30%; using 5 additional fractional bits requires 90% more slices and 2 times the number of DSPs. This is mainly because the divider, created using Xilinx Coregen, consumes substantially more resources with increasing number of bits. This highlights the importance of ensuring the analytical techniques described in this work are available when performing word-length optimization.

Table 3: Resource use and max frequency of custom hardware implementations of Euclid's method to compute the greatest common divisor of two variables.

| # fractional bits | Slices | DSPs | Frequency (MHz) |
|---|---|---|---|
| 5 | 141 | 1 | 230 |
| 6 | 183 | 1 | 225 |
| 7 | 203 | 1 | 220 |
| 8 | 262 | 1 | 190 |
| 9 | 289 | 1 | 195 |
| 10 | 274 | 2 | 180 |

## 5.3 Case study: Newton's Method

Our third case study analyzes how our approach could used when trying to create a dedicated hardware accelerator to compute the square root of any number lying in the interval $[0; 100]$ using Newton's Method, as described in Figure 16.

For this case study, after extracting the loop information, we add a hint that incorporates the fact that the loop will never be entered when $0.9999999 < i < 1.0000001$. This hint tells the tool to

```
1: // Algorithm to find square root of any input number i to a
   tolerance η,
2: // where i lies in the interval [0; 100] and η = 1 × 10⁻⁷
3: Function Newton_SQRT(i)
4:   i₀ = 1, i₁ = i; k = 0
5:   while |iₖ₊₁ − iₖ| > η do
6:     iₖ₊₁ = ½ (iₖ + i/iₖ)
7:     k = k + 1;
8:   end while
9:   return(i)
```

Figure 16: Newton method to compute the square root of a number.

explore regions either side of this range separately. This results in the two tests given in Figure 17, where in the second test we also take into account the condition $|i_{k+1} - i_k| > \eta$ to limit the lower bound. Once it is in this form, our tool applies the floating point model of error described in Section 4.1, to represent the ranges of all the intermediate variables ($i\_sq, num, den$ and $i'$). Finally, our search procedure finds the ranking functions $f(i) = i$ for the first test, and $f(i) = maxFloat - i$ for the second test. We use this information to make a custom FPGA accelerator.

```
1: // First test              1: // Second test
2: i ∈ [1.0000001; 100];      2: i ∈ [0.0000001; 0.9999999];
3: η = 1 × 10⁻⁷;              3: η = 1 × 10⁻⁷;
4: // Transition Statements    4: // Transition Statements
5: i_sq = i × i               5: i_sq = i × i
6: num = i_sq + i             6: num = i_sq + i
7: den = 2 × i                7: den = 2 × i
8: i' = num/den               8: i' = num/den
9: Terminates if:             9: Terminates if:
     f(i') < f(i) − ε              f(i') < f(i) − ε
```

Figure 17: Newton method broken down into transition tests.

**Impact on FPGA Implementation:** A parallel FPGA implementation of this square root circuit is shown in Figure 18. In this example, using the same process, we can calculate that at least 27 bits (or a precision of $7.5 \times 10^{-9}$) are required to guarantee the termination. Table 4 demonstrates the resource use of this circuit using the minimum precision necessary as found by our technique, as well as using IEEE-754 standard single or double precision. We see that our technique can create a circuit that uses over 50% less silicon area than IEEE-754 standard double precision. This could in turn be used to increase the level of parallelism to create a faster square root circuit; a simple technique to achieve this would be to unroll the loop until all the area of the FPGA is consumed.

Table 4: Resource use and max frequency of custom hardware implementations to find square roots using Newton's Method.

| Method | Precision (# bits) | Slices | Frequency (MHz) |
|---|---|---|---|
| Our Approach | 27 | 1,236 | 490 |
| IEEE Single Precision | 24 | 999 | 500 |
| IEEE Double Precision | 53 | 2,667 | 330 |

While one may be tempted to use IEEE-754 single precision throughout a custom hardware implementation as this requires even less silicon area, because we are unable to prove termination in the

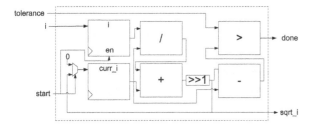

**Figure 18: Hardware accelerator for Newton's method to compute the square root.**

case of round-off errors, such a design may not be safe to use. Furthermore, in a software setting, this highlights how our technique could also be used to locate potential termination bugs; indeed, when running the code of Figure 16 in single precision in Matlab with an input of $i = 1.01$, the loop fails to terminate after 1 minute of execution time. In contrast, the execution time to check if termination is guaranteed for a given precision, was less than 20 seconds using our approach, and it generates a safe implementation that is guaranteed to work.

## 5.4 Case study: Adaptive Euler's Method

The final case study is Euler's Method, which is a numerical method to approximate the solution to a differential equation, described in Figure 19. This example differs from the previous examples in that it has two loops and the latter is a repeat loop. However, the repeat loop can be re-written into a while loop, and provided we treat each loop separately, the same process can be applied to prove termination of the algorithm.

```
/* Algorithm to solve differential equation of the form y = c + dy,
where the initial value y_in lies in the interval [1000; 1100]. The
remaining input variables are bounded as follows:
a ∈ [0; 1] and b ∈ [0; 1], c ∈ [90; 100], d ∈ [0.4; 0.5],
η_1 ∈ [0.1; 1] and η_2 ∈ [10^-6; 1]*/
```

1: Function Euler($a, b, c, d, y_{in}, \eta_1, \eta_2$)
2:   $y_{curr} = y_{in}$
3: **while** $a < b$ **do**
4:     $h = 0.5$
5:     **do**
6:       $y_0 = y_{curr} + h \times (c + d \times y_{curr})$
7:       $mid = y_{curr} + \frac{1}{2}h \times (c + d \times y_{curr})$
8:       $f = c + \frac{1}{2}h + d \times mid$
9:       $y_1 = y_{curr} + \frac{1}{2}h \times ((c + d \times y_{curr}) + f)$
10:      $\tau = y_1 - y_0$
11:      $h = \frac{1}{2}h$
12:     **while** $(\tau > \eta_1)\&\&(h > \eta_2)$
13:     $y_{curr} = y_0;$
14:     $a = a + 2 \times h;$
15: **end while**
16: return($a$)

**Figure 19: Euler's Method for Solving Differential Equations.**

Once again, the search procedure will select the ranking functions, for the inner loop this will be $f(\tau) = \tau$ and for the outer loop $f(a) = 1000 - a$.

**Impact on FPGA Implementation:** After applying our bounding procedure, we can compute that a 9 bit precision is required to guarantee termination of the inner loop and 17 bits for the outer

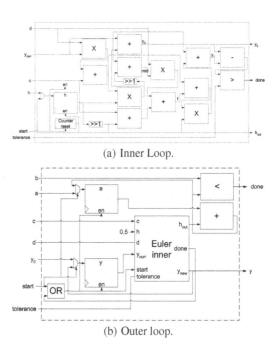

(a) Inner Loop.

(b) Outer loop.

**Figure 20: Hardware accelerator for Euler's method for Solving Differential Equations.**

loop. We note that we could use these different precisions within the inner and outer loops in a custom hardware design. If we were to implement the hardware using 9 bits for every operator in the inner loop and 17 bits for the outer loop, we would create the hardware described in Table 5. In this case, it would save 50% or 80% of the silicon area of an IEEE-754 standard single or double precision arithmetic implementation respectively.

**Table 5: Resource use and max frequency of custom hardware implementations of Euler's Method for Solving Differential Equations.**

| Method | Precision (# bits) | Slices | Frequency (MHz) |
|---|---|---|---|
| Our Approach | 9,17 | 418 | 550 |
| IEEE Single Precision | 24 | 926 | 490 |
| IEEE Double Precision | 53 | 2230 | 480 |

## 6. CONCLUSION

This paper has discussed a novel technique that can be used to determine the minimum precision throughout a loop with data dependent exit conditions. We have shown that we can use it to design safe hardware that is guaranteed to terminate, and this can result in silicon area savings of up to 80% over a naïve approach of using IEEE-754 standard double precision arithmetic. No existing analytical technique could be used to provide such guarantees. Furthermore, the third case study also demonstrated the potential of our work to locate the presence of bugs in software programs. In the future, we wish to refine the techniques described in this paper to make it applicable to more sophisticated algorithms as well as to analyze the relationship between precision and convergence.

## 7. ACKNOWLEDGMENTS

The authors would like to acknowledge the support of the EPSRC (Grant EP/I020357/1 and EP/I012036/1) and the EU FP7 project REFLECT.

# 8. REFERENCES

[1] D. Boland and G. Constantinides. Bounding variable values and round-off effects using Handelman representations. *IEEE Trans. on Computer-Aided Design of Integrated Circuits and Systems*, 30(11):1691–1704, 2011.

[2] D. Boland and G. A. Constantinides. A scalable approach for automated precision analysis. In *Proc. Int. Symp. on Field Programmable Gate Arrays*, pages 185–194, 2012.

[3] G. Caffarena, C. Carreras, J. A. López, and A. Fernández. SQNR estimation of fixed-point DSP algorithms. *EURASIP J. Adv. Signal Process*, 2010:21:1–21:12, 2010.

[4] M.-A. Cantin, Y. Savaria, and P. Lavoie. A comparison of automatic word length optimization procedures. In *Proc. Int. Symp. on Circuits and Systems*, volume 2, pages II–612 – II–615 vol.2, 2002.

[5] M.-A. Cantin, Y. Savaria, D. Prodanos, and P. Lavoie. An automatic word length determination method. In *Proc. Int. Symp. on Circuits and Systems*, pages 53 –56 vol. 5, 2001.

[6] M. L. Chang and S. Hauck. Automated least-significant bit datapath optimization for FPGAs. *Proc. IEEE Symp. on Field-Programmable Custom Computing Machines*, pages 59–67, 2004.

[7] Y. Chen, B. Xia, L. Yang, N. Zhan, and C. Zhou. Discovering non-linear ranking functions by solving semi-algebraic systems. In *Proc. Int. Conf. on Theoretical Aspects of Computing*, pages 34–49, 2007.

[8] G. Constantinides, P. Cheung, and W. Luk. The multiple wordlength paradigm. In *Proc. Int. Symp. on Field-Programmable Custom Computing Machines*, pages 51 –60, 2001.

[9] G. Constantinides, P. Cheung, and W. Luk. Optimum wordlength allocation. *Proc. Int. Symp. Field-Programmable Custom Computing Machines*, pages 219–228, 2002.

[10] G. Constantinides, A. Kinsman, and N. Nicolici. Numerical data representations for FPGA-based scientific computing. *IEEE Design Test of Computers*, 28(4):8–17, 2011.

[11] B. Cook, D. Kroening, P. Rümmer, and C. M. Wintersteiger. Ranking function synthesis for bit-vector relations. In *Proc. Int. Conf. on Tools and Algorithms for the Construction and Analysis of Systems*, pages 236–250, 2010.

[12] B. Cook, A. Podelski, and A. Rybalchenko. Termination proofs for systems code. In *Proc. Conf. on Programming language design and implementation*, pages 415–426, 2006.

[13] B. Cook, A. Podelski, and A. Rybalchenko. Proving program termination. *Commun. ACM*, 54(5):88–98, May 2011.

[14] P. Cousot. Proving program invariance and termination by parametric abstraction, Lagrangian relaxation and semidefinite programming. In *Proc. Int. Conf. on Verification, Model Checking, and Abstract Interpretation*, pages 1–24, 2005.

[15] F. de Dinechin, C. Lauter, and G. Melquiond. Certifying the floating-point implementation of an elementary function using gappa. *IEEE Trans. Computers.*, 60(2):242–253, 2011.

[16] S. Falke, D. Kapur, and C. Sinz. Termination analysis of imperative programs using bitvector arithmetic. In *Proc. Int. Conf. on Verified Software: Theories, Tools, Experiments*, pages 261–277, 2012.

[17] A. A. Gaffar, W. Luk, P. Y. K. Cheung, N. Shirazi, and J. Hwang. Automating customisation of floating-point designs. In *Proc. Int. Conf. on Field-Programmable Logic and Applications*, pages 523–533, London, UK, 2002.

[18] N. J. Higham. *Accuracy and Stability of Numerical Algorithms*. Soc for Industrial & Applied Math, Philadelphia, PA, USA, second edition, 2002.

[19] A. B. Kinsman and N. Nicolici. Robust design methods for hardware accelerators for iterative algorithms in scientific computing. In *Proc. Design Automation Conference*, pages 254–257, 2010.

[20] K.-I. Kum and W. Sung. Combined word-length optimization and high-level synthesis of digital signal processing systems. *IEEE Trans. on Computer-Aided Design of Integrated Circuits and Systems*, 20(8):921–930, Aug 2001.

[21] D.-U. Lee, A. Gaffar, R. Cheung, O. Mencer, W. Luk, and G. Constantinides. Accuracy-guaranteed bit-width optimization. *IEEE Trans. on Computer-Aided Design of Integrated Circuits and Systems*, 25(10):1990–2000, Oct. 2006.

[22] D.-U. Lee, A. A. Gaffar, O. Mencer, and W. Luk. Minibit: bit-width optimization via affine arithmetic. In *Proc. Design Automation Conference*, pages 837–840, New York, NY, USA, 2005. ACM.

[23] Y. Li. Automatic discovery of non-linear ranking functions of loop programs. In *Proc. Int. Conf. on Computer Science and Information Technology*, pages 402 –406, 2009.

[24] W. Osborne, R. Cheung, J. Coutinho, W. Luk, and O. Mencer. Automatic accuracy-guaranteed bit-width optimization for fixed and floating-point systems. In *Int. Conf. on Field Programmable Logic and Applications*, pages 617–620, Aug. 2007.

[25] P. A. Parrilo. Semidefinite programming relaxations for semialgebraic problems. *Mathematical Programming Ser. B*, 96(2-3):293–320, 2003.

[26] A. Podelski and A. Rybalchenko. A complete method for the synthesis of linear ranking functions. In *Proc. int. conf. on Verification, Model Checking, and Abstract Interpretation*, pages 239–251, 2004.

[27] A. Podelski and A. Rybalchenko. ARMC: the logical choice for software model checking with abstraction refinement. In *Proc. Int. Conf. on Practical Aspects of Declarative Languages*, pages 245–259, 2007.

[28] A. Sülfow, U. Kühne, R. Wille, D. Große, and R. Drechsler. Evaluation of sat like proof techniques for formal verification of word level circuits. In *Proc. Workshop on RTL and High Level Testing.*, pages 31Ű–36, 2007.

[29] W. Sung and K.-I. Kum. Simulation-based word-length optimization method for fixed-point digital signal processing systems. *IEEE Trans. on Signal Processing*, 43(12):3087–3090, 1995.

# Placement of Repair Circuits for In-Field FPGA Repair

Michael Wirthlin, Josh Jensen,
Alex Wilson, and Will Howes
Dept. of Electrical and Computer Engineering
Brigham Young University
Provo, UT 84606, USA

Shi-Jie Wen and Rick Wong
Cisco Systems
San Jose, CA 95134, USA

## ABSTRACT

With the growing density and shrinking feature size of modern semiconductors, it is increasingly difficult to manufacture defect free semiconductors that maintain acceptable levels of reliability for long periods of time. These systems are increasingly susceptible to wear-out by failing to meet their operational specifications for an extended period of time. The reconfigurability of FPGAs can be used to repair post-manufacturing faults by configuring the FPGA to avoid a damaged resource. This paper presents a method for repairing FPGA devices with wear-out faults by precomputing a set of repair circuits that, collectively, can repair a fault found in *any* logic block of the FPGA. This approach relies on logic placement to create "repair" circuits that avoid specific logic blocks. Three "repair" placement algorithms will be presented that generate a complete set of repair designs during the conventional placement process. The number of repairs needed to create a complete repair set depends heavily on the utilization of the FPGA resources. The three algorithms are tested against several benchmarks and with multiple area constraints for each benchmark. The best repair placement approach described in the paper generates a full set of repair circuits at a computation cost of $16\times$ that of a conventional placer and with circuits of comparable quality.

## Categories and Subject Descriptors

B.8.1 [**Performance and Reliability**]: Reliability, Testing, and Fault-Tolerance; B.7.2 [**Design Aids**]: Placement and Routing

## Keywords

FPGA; Fault-Tolerance; Repair; Placement; Simulated Annealing

## 1. INTRODUCTION

It is increasingly difficult to design and manufacture semiconductor systems that maintain acceptable levels of reliability while simultaneously taking advantage of the lower power, higher operating speeds, and greater density offered by modern sub-micron fabrication technologies [1]. There is also greater variation in transistor parameters as the technology node decreases causing a greater circuit failure rate. In addition, the effects of wear-out due to electromigration are more pronounced at smaller geometries [2]. To obtain the full benefits of future technologies, future semiconductor systems must tolerate a greater number and variety of permanent faults. The lifetime of these systems could be significantly increased if they are designed to support some form of repair to address manufacturing faults or wear-out faults that occur after manufacturing.

Because of the fine-grain reconfigurability of FPGAs, it is possible to address such wear-out faults by modifying the placement and routing of a design. This modified placement and routing, called a repair configuration, performs the same function as the original circuit but avoids the resource or resources that are permanently faulty. There are many previous efforts that investigate ways of repairing an FPGA by reconfiguring the circuit [3, 4, 5, 6]. These papers exploit the fact that there are many unused resources in a mapped FPGA design and repair circuits can take advantage of these unused resources to avoid faulty resources.

In this paper, we present a technique for generating a set of circuits that repair permanent faults within an FPGA. In particular, this paper identifies a complete set of repair circuits *before* the fault occurs. Unlike most approaches in which the repair circuit is created after the fault occurs, this approach invests a large amount of computation during the technology mapping process to generate a repair circuit for all possible permanent faults. A large set of pre-computed repair circuits, called a "repair set" is created before the system is deployed and made available for use after a permanent fault is found. When a fault occurs and its location identified, one of the pregenerated repair circuits is configured onto the FPGA to "repair" the permanent fault.

The long term objective of this work is to generate a repair set for all FPGA faults including faults within the programmable logic, fixed functions (DSP, BRAM, etc.), and routing resources. This paper will focus on generating repair circuits for faults within logic and fixed function blocks. A parallel effort is investigating the ability to generate repair circuits for routing resources – the results of routing repair will be presented in a future publication. The primary mechanism for repairing logic and fixed function blocks is through circuit placement. Multiple circuit placements are performed to produce a placement that will avoid each allocated resource of a design mapped to a particular device.

This work is based on an in-house placement infrastructure that targets the commercially available Xilinx Virtex 4 family of FPGAs. This placer successfully performs FPGA placement that meets all of the design rules for the Virtex 4 family. Several repair placement algorithms were developed from this baseline placer to generate repair placement configurations. This paper will present three repair placement approaches and contrast the execution time and quality of result.

## 2. OVERVIEW OF APPROACH

In-field repair of FPGA circuits is possible by generating a large set of circuit configurations *before* the circuit is deployed. An initial circuit configuration is generated that performs the operation of the circuit when there are no permanent faults on the FPGA device. The system is configured with this initial configuration and the FPGA uses this initial configuration until a fault is found. In addition to the initial configuration, a set of repair circuit configurations is generated. These repair configurations are used to replace the initial circuit configuration when a permanent fault is found (see Figure 1).

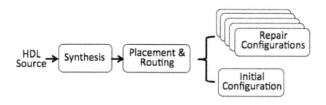

Figure 1: Initial and Repair Configurations.

During normal operation, the system will employ a mechanism for periodically detecting permanent faults within the initial configuration (see Figure 2). Although not the focus of this work, there is a large body of previous work in fault detection and isolation for FPGAs [7]. If a permanent fault is detected, the system identifies the location of the fault and selects a repair configuration that repairs the permanent fault. The set of repair configurations could be cached locally within the system or be made available on an external server and accessed remotely if the system does not have sufficient memory resources. Because the repair configuration has already been created, a repair can be performed relatively quickly and without additional computation.

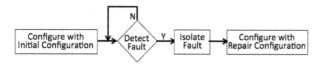

Figure 2: Operational Repair.

This particular repair strategy is best suited for an FPGA design that is deployed in a large number of products and which have network access to a central server as suggested by Figure 3. The central server maintains a set of repair configurations for the design and responds to failure messages from the product in the field. When the server receives a failure message, it identifies the corresponding repair configuration within the repair database and sends the repair configuration to the product in the field. The failed product in the field is then repaired using the appropriate repair configuration. With time, multiple products in the field may fail and the server will provide a different repair circuit for different products since the failure of each product is unique.

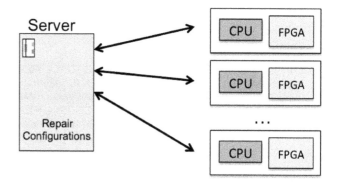

Figure 3: Repair Server Repairing FPGA-Based Products In-Field.

## 2.1 Repair Placement Objectives

The primary goal of the placement approach described in this paper is to determine a valid FPGA placement on a fully functional device and a unique "repair placement" for *every* possible permanent fault in the device. A repair placement is a unique placement of a circuit design that avoids one or more specific FPGA resources. If any of these resources fail, its corresponding repair circuit can be configured onto the device and allow the circuit to continue operating on the faulty FPGA. If a repair configuration is created for *every* possible resource failure, the circuit can be configured to operate on an FPGA in the presence any single resource failure. Tolerating any single permanent fault significantly increases lifetime of the device and addresses the growing problem of device wear-out[1].

The primary disadvantage of this approach is the large amount of computation that must be performed to create repair configurations for the circuit. Creating a custom placement and routing of a circuit for every possible resource failure will obviously take far more time than traditional placement and routing for a fully functional device. However, performing all this placement and routing computation before the circuit is first configured has a number of advantages. First, all the repair information is available when a fault occurs and no additional resource mapping computation is needed to create a repair circuit. This simplifies the process of performing a repair. Second, it is possible to guarantee a repair circuit for each failure. Because the repair configurations are available before failure, there is no concern that a repair circuit cannot be determined. Third, it

---

[1]Repair circuits may also be able to repair more than one permanent fault. Section 6.2 describes the ability of one repair placement approach to repair double faults.

is more efficient to identify all of the repair configurations at the same time during global placement and routing than it is to create repair circuits one at a time as needed. Since all of the design and device information is resident, many of the data structures can be reused and information shared during the process. This savings in time is similar to the time savings performed using incremental placement and routing approaches [4].

The repair placement described in this work will generate an initial placement of a design. Specifically, this initial placement specifies the placement of each primitive of a given design. Each FPGA site, $s_i$, used in this initial placement must have a corresponding repair placement. A corresponding repair placement is a unique placement of the same design such that the given FPGA site, $s_i$, is not used in the design.

The repair placer must generate a complete set of repair placements under several constraints. First, the repair placer should minimize the impact of the of the repair process on the circuit quality. Modifying the placement of a circuit for a repair may impact the timing of the circuit. It is important to minimize this impact and generate placement configurations that have similar timing characteristics of the original circuit configuration.

Second, it is important to minimize the overall size of the repair database. The repair database may be part of an embedded system and may consume a large amount of memory. To make this approach feasible, the size of this repair database needs to be carefully controlled. As described earlier, a repair placement may repair a large number of faults. To reduce the number of repair patches in the repair database, the repair placement should attempt to cover as many faults as possible with each repair configuration.

Third, it is important to minimize the time required to generate the repair placement set. Performing repair placement will certainly increase the run-time of the placement routing process. In some cases, repair placement will be significantly longer than the conventional placement. While this approach for repair must accept longer run-times, the run-times must be carefully controlled and managed.

## 2.2 Related Work

There has been great interest in taking advantage of unused logic and routing resources of FPGAs to tolerate faults. Most FPGA designs, even those that are heavily utilized, contain unused resources (routing and logic). The goal of these techniques is to exploit these unused resources with repair configurations that use these unused resources to avoid a faulty resource.

Incremental approaches have been introduced that allow the ability to perform partial rerouting for repairing with much less effort by saving the routing history [4]. This work also supports the ability to address "Intra-cluster" faults by using unused resources within a cluster. In [8], the authors describe a method for embedding test structures and repair information *within* a bitstream. Decisions are made at configuration load time to determine which configuration information, including alternative repair structures, to use. The authors in [9] describes a yield enhancement scheme that allocates spare interconnect resources to tolerate functional faults. Several efforts exploit repair by pre-allocating rows or columns of logic resources and "shifting" the design to avoid these resources in the event of a fault [10].

## 3. BASELINE PLACEMENT ALGORITHM

A conventional placement algorithm was developed to perform logic placement for Xilinx Virtex 4 designs. Although the focus of this paper is not on the development and improvement of conventional placement algorithms, a conventional placer is necessary to provide a baseline of comparison between the repair placement approaches described later in this paper.

The baseline placer (and all subsequent placers) was written in Java and built upon the RapidSmith toolkit [11, 12]. Like the open source tool Torc [13], RapidSmith facilitates the manipulation (including placement) of FPGA resources using the text-based XDL language. Although the use of the Java programming language for this project will result in slower run-times for placement when compared to natively compiled approaches, the ability to exploit the existing XDL libraries and device databases significantly improved the software development productivity of the project.

The baseline placer operates on XDL files that are created from vendor tools as shown in Figure 4. Vendor tools are used to synthesize the design, perform technology mapping, and convert the internal design representation into the XDL text file. At this point, our baseline placer reads the XDL, performs placement, and saves the placement into the XDL file. The file is converted back into the binary format and vendor tools are used to perform routing and generate a valid FPGA bitstream.

**Figure 4: Design Flow for Baseline Placement.**

The baseline placer was based on the well-known VPR FPGA placement approach [14]. An initial, legal placement is created by randomly choosing sites for FPGA resources. After creating a legal initial placement, simulated annealing is used to explore placement perturbations (moves) in an attempt to improve the design placement [15]. Placement moves are randomly selected and accepted using a carefully controlled annealing schedule.

The cost of a given placement is determined by estimating the wirelength of the routing within the design. This estimate is made by measuring the $x$ and $y$ dimensions of the bounding box that contains all terminals of each net as follows,

$$Cost = \sum_{i \in AllNets} q(i) \cdot (bb_{x_i} + bb_{y_i}), \qquad (1)$$

where $q(i)$ is a fanout-based correction factor, $bb_{x_i}$ is the $x$ dimension of the bounding box and $bb_{y_i}$ is the $y$ dimension of the bounding box. The coarse-grain Virtex 4 Tile coordinate system is used to measure distance between net terminals (i.e., SLICE instances within a tile have no distance between them). At the present time, this baseline placer is not timing driven. A timing driven placer is being created and will be integrated with our ongoing repair routing effort.

To support placement of designs on the commercially available Virtex 4 architecture, a number of issues had to be addressed. First, the Virtex 4 architecture is not homogeneous and there are several different primitive types whose placement locations are not interchangeable (i.e., SLICEL, SLICEM, BRAM, DSP, etc.). Second, there are a number of architecture dependent placement restrictions that complicate the selection of valid placement locations. For example, SLICEL primitives can be placed at either a SLICEM or SLICEL location while SLICEM primitives can only be placed at a SLICEM location. Third, many design instances have relational placement constraints with other instances when certain architecture-specific features are used. For example, all instances using the same carry chain must be placed in the same column and be placed vertically adjacent in the appropriate carry chain order.

To address these issues, this placer identifies and organizes all netlist instances into relationally placed groups (RPGs) and performs placement on multi-site RPGs rather than individual netlist instances. The placement of groups is more challenging as the placement process must consider the shape of each groups and find a placement in which no groups overlap (this is especially challenging with very tight placement constraints). All benchmark designs were successfully placed and validated using the vendor design rule checker.

## 3.1 Benchmark Designs

Five benchmarks will be used to evaluate the various placement algorithms described in this paper (see Table 1). These benchmarks are all real-world designs that have been used for other research projects. The five benchmarks were chosen to provide a wide range of design styles and sizes. All of the designs have been mapped to various devices within the Xilinx Virtex-4 family of FPGAs. The sizes of the benchmark designs are summarized in Table 1 in terms of the number of slices (i.e., the sum of SLICEL and SLICEM primitives), the number of BRAM and DSP elements, and the number of relationally placed groups (RPGs).

| Benchmark | Device | SLICE (utilization) | BRAM, DSP | RPGs |
|---|---|---|---|---|
| top | fx12 | 31 (.56%) | 0, 0 | 1 |
| system_test0 | fx12 | 316 (5.8%) | 2, 0 | 23 |
| mult18 | sx55 | 653 (2.7%) | 0, 0 | 17 |
| crazy | fx12 | 3373 (62%) | 32, 24 | 0 |
| multxor | lx160 | 10585 (16%) | 0, 0 | 473 |

**Table 1: Benchmark Circuits.**

## 3.2 Baseline Results

The execution time and overall cost of circuits placed with our baseline placer are shown in Table 2. The cost represents the quality of result of the placement by measuring the total wirelength using a bounding box span (see Equation 1). To provide a reference, the execution time and cost for vendor placement is also provided. To facilitate comparison, the same cost function was used for both the vendor placement and our baseline placement. On average, our placer executes 6.7 times slower and generates circuits that have a 19% higher clock period than the vendor tools.

The authors recognize that the baseline placement approach described here is inferior to a commercial placement approach in both execution time and quality of results. We

| Design | Baseline RapidSmith | | | Xilinx | | |
|---|---|---|---|---|---|---|
| | Time | Cost | ns | Time | Cost | ns |
| top | .71 | 200 | 3.3 | 7 | 127 | 2.9 |
| test0 | 4.4 | 5834 | 7.6 | 16 | 6115 | 6.7 |
| mult18 | 35.7 | 9160 | 2.5 | 15 | 10866 | 2.3 |
| crazy | 51.5 | 73731 | 4.4 | 35 | 54280 | 3.4 |
| multxor | 3937 | 348792 | 3.9 | 110 | 321098 | 3.0 |

**Table 2: Placement Time (s) and Quality of Result for Baseline and and Vendor Placement Tools**

recognize that there are many ways that we could improve the quality and run time of our approach. However, the focus of this work is not to replicate commercial quality placement but to demonstrate the feasibility of a placement approach that considers repair.

## 4. AREA CONSTRAINTS

As seen in Table 1, most of the benchmark designs use a relatively small amount of the device's FPGA resources. It is relatively easy to repair designs with low FPGA utilization because these designs leave a large number of unused FPGA resources. With a large set of unused resources, it is relatively easy to create a repair design that replaces a used resource from the original design with an unused resource.

Any design that uses less than 50% of an FPGA's resources can repair any permanent fault with a *single* repair circuit. Figure 5 demonstrates this point. This figure demonstrates two different placements of the `multxor` benchmark design. The placement on the left is the original placement and would be used when there is no fault in the device. The placement on the right is the "repair" placement and would be used if there is a permanent fault in the device that affects any of the resources used in the original placement of the design. Since no resources used in the left placement are used in the right placement[2], the device can be configured with the right placement repair *any* failure within device that affects the left placement. Only one alternative placement, the right placement, is needed for a repair configuration.

Generating repair circuits is more difficult for designs that consume more than 50% of the circuit resources. When more than 50% of the device is utilized, more than one repair circuit is needed. For example, if a design uses 67% of the FPGA resources, only 33% of the idle resources are available for a repair. In this case, at least two repair circuits are needed (see Figure 6). One repair configuration could repair half of the design's original resources and the other repair configuration could repair the other half of the original resources.

The number of repair configurations needed to repair any circuit fault grows as the utilization of the device increases. Note that if the device is 100% utilized, there are no idle resources for a repair and no repairs can be made. The minimum number of repair configurations required to cover all utilized resources is the number of resources allocated by the design, $A$, divided by the number of idle resources in the device, $I$, as shown in Equation 2. The number of idle

[2]There are some "fixed" I/O resources in the middle of the device that are common for both placements. These resources cannot be repaired and are not considered in this discussion.

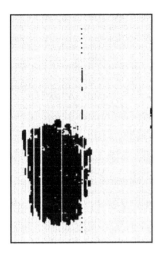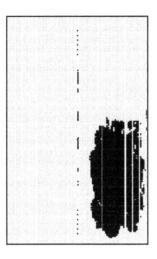

Figure 5: Two Placements for the `multxor` Design. The Left Placement is the Original Placement and the Right Placement is the Repair Placement.

Original          Repair 1          Repair 2

Figure 6: Repair Circuits for 67% Utilized Design.

resources is the total number of resources available on the device, $R$, minus the number of resources allocated by the design (i.e., $I = R - A$),

$$N_{min} = \left\lceil \frac{A}{I} \right\rceil = \left\lceil \frac{A}{R-A} \right\rceil = \left\lceil \frac{1}{R/A-1} \right\rceil = \left\lceil \frac{u}{1-u} \right\rceil . \quad (2)$$

This expression can also be represented in terms of the utilization of the device, $u = A/R$.

For example, if a device contains 10,000 elements (i.e., $R = 10,000$) and a design mapped to the device uses 8,500 of these elements (i.e., $A = 8,500$), then there are 1,500 idle resources in the device (i.e., $I = 1,500$) and the device has a utilization factor of .85. This design will need a minimum of six repair configurations to repair every resource on the device:

$$N_{min} = \left\lceil \frac{1}{10,000/8,500 - 1} \right\rceil = \left\lceil \frac{1}{1.18 - 1} \right\rceil = \lceil 5.667 \rceil = 6$$

Equation 2 represents the minimum number of configurations and in practice more repair configurations will be needed.

A set of artificial placement constraints have been created for the benchmark designs to emulate higher resource utilization. These artificial placement constraints will define a rectangular region within the FPGA that achieves a predetermined utilization. Table 1 describes five different area constraints for each of the benchmarks. These constrains force a utilization of 50% (A), 75% (B), 90% (C), 95% (D),

and 99% (E). There is no 50% constraint for the `crazy` design since this design consumes more than 50% of the logic resources and there are no 95% or 99% constraints for the `top` design since this design is too small. Using equation 2, these constraints will require at least 1, 4, 10, 20, and 100 repair configurations respectively.

For example, the rectangular constraint to provide a 90% utilization for the `mult18` design is 25,29. This means that all of the slices in the `mult18` design must be placed within a square region that is 25 slices wide and 29 slices high. The total area of this bounding box constraint is 725 slices. The utilization of this constrained region for the `mult18` design is $653/725 = 90.1\%$.

| | Constraint | | | | |
|---|---|---|---|---|---|
| | A | B | C | D | E |
| Design | 50% | 75% | 90% | 95% | 99% |
| top | 4,16 | 3,16 | 2,16 | N/A | N/A |
| test0 | 24,26 | 16,26 | 14,25 | 9,37 | 11,29 |
| mult18 | 35,38 | 25,35 | 25,29 | 6,43 | 20,33 |
| crazy | N/A | 47,126 | 47,126 | 47,126 | 47,118 |
| multxor | 140,152 | 99,142 | 105,112 | 116,96 | 115,93 |

Table 3: Bounding Box Area Constraints For Five Different Utilization Levels.

In practice, more repair designs will be needed to provide a complete database of repairs than the amount indicated in Equation 2. Minimizing the number of repair circuits may lead to some repair circuits with a poor quality of result. For example, Repair #1 in Figure 6 is not a particularly good placement result – this particular placement is split into two parts with a significant distance between the two parts.

## 5. NAIVE REPAIR PLACEMENT

The first approach for repair placement is relatively simplistic and thus called the "Naive" approach. This approach, summarized in Algorithm 1, begins by performing a single, initial placement using the conventional placement algorithm described in Section 3. This initial placement is used on the device when there are no device failures. This initial placement defines a set, $S$, of placement sites that are used in the initial placement (see line 3).

---
**Algorithm 1** Naive Repair Placement
---
1: $D \leftarrow$ set of all possible placement sites
2: Perform initial placement
3: $S \leftarrow$ set of occupied sites in initial placement
4: **while** $S \neq \emptyset$ **do**
5:     choose $s \in S$, remove $s$ from $S$
6:     Remove site $s$ from device database
7:     Perform repair placement (site $s$ not available)
8:     $R \leftarrow$ set of occupied sites in repair placement
9:     $G \leftarrow (D - R) \cap S$ (sites repaired)
10:     $S \leftarrow S - G$
11:     Add site $s$ into device database
12: **end while**
---

The algorithm proceeds by performing multiple, independent placements on the design with the goal of "repairing" one or more sites used in the original design. A "repair" placement is an alternative placement of the circuit primitives such that some logic or fixed function sites used in the original placement are not used. To insure that the placement repairs at least one site, one of the physical placement sites, $s$, used in the original placement is removed from the device database (line 5). This prevents the placer from selecting $s$ when choosing random placement moves. Since the site $s$ will never be selected during placement, it will not be used in the repair placement and the repair placement can be used when site $s$ fails. Due to the random nature of the simulated annealing placer, the repair placer will likely repair other sites that were used in the original placement (i.e., some of the sites used in the original placement are not used in the repair placement). Those sites repaired during a repair placement are removed from set of sites needing a repair (line 10). The algorithm will iterate until there are no more sites needing a repair (line 4).

The Naive repair placer was performed on all five benchmarks and each area constraint. The results of this placement approach are summarized in Table 4. This table indicates how many repair placement circuits were created to repair all sites used in the initial placement. For example, 114 different placement configurations were required to repair all 3429 instances for the `crazy` benchmark using the 75% (B) area constraint. For this design, each placement circuit repaired on average 30 placement sites.

| | Constraint | | | | | |
|---|---|---|---|---|---|---|
| Design | 0 | A | B | C | D | E |
| top | 1 | 4 | 6 | 31 | N/A | N/A |
| test0 | 10 | 40 | 71 | 112 | 149 | 243 |
| mult18 | 2 | 51 | 142 | 294 | 340 | 467 |
| crazy | N/A | 76 | 114 | 224 | 413 | 929 |
| multxor | 47 | 150 | 441 | * | * | * |
| Time | 25x | 56x | 132x | 152x | 243x | 468x |

Table 4: Number of Repair Circuits using Naive Repair Placement.

As expected, the number of repair circuits required to repair all sites increases as the area constraint tightens. The number of repair circuits generated by this approach, however, is far higher than the minimum number of repairs suggested by Equation 2. For example, the minimum number of repair circuits for `crazy` using the 75% benchmark (B) is 5 while 114 were created using this approach. Not all of the results have been computed for the `multxor` benchmark. Naive Repair Placement for this benchmark takes a very long time. For example, it took over 17 days to generate the 441 repair placements for constraint B. It is anticipated that the C, D, and E constraints would require several months to complete.

The final row of Table 4 reports the average increase in execution time of the Naive Repair Placer over the conventional placer. As expected, the execution time increases with each tighter area constraint. For these benchmarks, the execution time is growing non-linearly and this approach will take a tremendous amount of time to repair large circuits with a high utilization. The cost of the repair circuits using Equation 1 was measured and compared with the cost of the corresponding initial configurations. The average cost of the repair configurations was found to be 2% higher than

the cost of the initial configurations. Since a complete placement is performed during each iteration, it is expected that the cost of the naive repair configurations will be very similar to the cost of the initial configuration.

Completing the Naive Repair Placer takes a very long time because relatively few repairs are performed during each placement iteration. The number of unique repairs performed during each iteration of the `multxor` benchmark for the 75% **B** constraint is shown in Figure 7. As seen in this figure, the first few iterations of the algorithm perform a large number of repairs (over 900 in the first iteration). However, due to the random nature of site selection, the number of repairs performed quickly decreases. Even though each iteration is guaranteed to repair a single site, fewer than 100 repairs repairs are actually performed after about 30 iterations of the algorithm and only a handful of repairs are made in the final iterations of the algorithm.

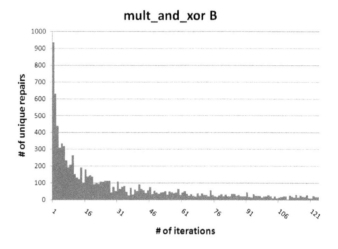

Figure 7: Repairs Per Iteration for `multxor` under Constraint B.

## 6. COST REPAIR PLACEMENT

A second repair placement approach was developed to address the long execution time of the Naive Repair approach. This second approach, called Cost Repair, operates similarly to the Naive Repair – the algorithms begins with an initial placement and performs multiple independent placements to provide repairs for the sites used in the initial placement. The objective of the Cost Repair approach is to perform more repairs during each placement iteration to reduce the number of repair placements required to repair all sites.

A modified cost function is used to meet this objective. Specifically, this modified cost function is used to encourage the placer to perform more repairs during each iteration of the placer. This is done by charging a site-specific cost for each primitive site used in the design (see Equation 3). Placement sites that are unused in the original placement or that have been repaired have no cost – they can be used by the repair placer without incurring additional costs. Sites that have not been repaired (i.e., elements of set $S$ on line 3) are given an initial cost. Because the use of these sites will incur additional cost, the placer will attempt to avoid sites that need to be repaired and favor those sites that do

**Algorithm 2** Cost Repair Placement

1: $D \leftarrow$ set of all possible placement sites
2: Perform initial placement
3: $S \leftarrow$ set of occupied sites in initial placement
4: **while** $S \neq \emptyset$ **do**
5:     choose $s \in S$, remove $s$ from $S$
6:     Remove site $s$ from device database
7:     Perform repair placement (site $s$ not available)
8:     $R \leftarrow$ set of occupied sites in repair placement
9:     $G \leftarrow (D - R) \cap S$ (sites repaired)
10:    $S \leftarrow S - G$
11:    Increase cost of each site in $S$
12:    Add site $s$ into device database
13: **end while**

not need to be repaired (i.e., sites that were not used in the original placement). The placer will not avoid all sites needing repair, however, since avoiding all of these sites will significantly increase the wirelength bounding box.

$$Cost = \sum_{i \in AllNets} q(i) \cdot (bb_x + bb_y) + \sum_{j \in Sites} c_j \qquad (3)$$

Initially, the cost of using sites that need to be repaired is low. As seen in the Naive approach, the random nature of placement will repair a large number of sites during the early iterations. To encourage repair in later iterations of placement, the cost of sites needing repair is increased after each iteration (line 11). The cost of using a site needing repair grows exponentially: $C_{i+1} = C_i \cdot (1 + \mu)$, where $u$ is a experimentally determined parameter.

In addition to a modified cost function, the Cost Repair approach will insure the placer makes greater forward progress by removing more than one site from the device database during each iteration. Specifically, either 5% of the idle sites will be removed or 5% of the used resources are removed as shown in Equation 4. This calculation is rounded up to insure that at least one resource is removed during each iteration.

$$n_t = \min \begin{cases} \lceil .05 \times I \rceil, \\ \lceil .05 \times A \rceil. \end{cases} \qquad (4)$$

## 6.1 Cost Repair Results

The Cost Repair placement approach was applied to all of the benchmarks under each of the placement constraints. The number of placements needed to repair all sites in the original design is summarized in Table 5. These results indicate that the Cost Repair is able to provide a complete repair set with far fewer repair circuits than the Naive approach (see Table 4). For example, the number of repair placements needed for **crazy** using benchmark B drops from 114 using the Naive approach down to 15 using the Cost Repair approach. A similar reductions in the number of repair circuits is seen for the other benchmarks and constraints.

The primary reason that the placement time has been decreased is the ability of the Cost Repair approach to repair a large number of sites during each iteration of the algorithm. Figure 8 plots the number of repairs performed during each iteration of the **multxor** benchmark under the B constraint.

| Design | Constraint | | | | | |
|---|---|---|---|---|---|---|
| | 0 | A | B | C | D | E |
| top | 1 | 2 | 4 | 16 | N/A | N/A |
| test0 | 12 | 7 | 11 | 10 | 17 | 85 |
| mult18 | 4 | 5 | 11 | 11 | 18 | 111 |
| crazy | 15 | 14 | 15 | 16 | 21 | 32 |
| multxor | 8 | 9 | 10 | 12 | 21 | 108 |
| Time | 8.7x | 8.2x | 12.9x | 14.8x | 22.1x | 28.5x |

**Table 5: Number of Repair Circuits using Cost Repair Placement.**

Most of the work is done during the first seven iterations of the algorithm where an average of 1400 repairs are performed during each iteration.

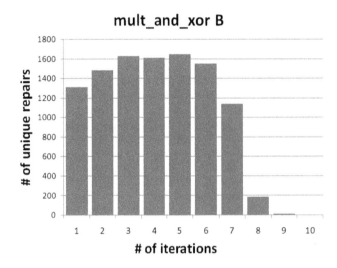

**Figure 8: Cost Repair: Repairs Per Iteration.**

The bottom row of Table 5 indicates the increase in time required for Cost Repair placement when compared with the original, non-repair placement. As expected, the cost increases as the area constraints tighten. On average and across all benchmarks and constraints, the Cost Repair placer executed 13.9× longer than the original, non repair placement. On average, the overall placement cost of the Cost Repair was 105% of the cost of the original placements.

## 6.2 Repairing Multiple Faults

Although the algorithms described in this paper were not designed to repair more than one fault, it is likely that a given repair circuit will repair more than one fault. The repair circuits for the **crazy** benchmark were analyzed to see how many double faults can be repaired. With 3373 slices in this design, there are 3373×3372=11,373,756 possible two-slice pairs. Each pair of circuit resources used in the original design is checked against each of the repair configurations. If there is a repair configuration that does not use both of the faulty sites, the repair configuration is able to repair the given double fault. If either of the sites are used in the repair configuration, the repair configuration cannot repair the double fault. The results of this analysis are shown for all five area constraints in Table 6. For loose area constraints, the repair configurations can repair most double faults. However, as the area constraint tightens, fewer and fewer double faults can be repaired.

| A | B | C | D | E |
|---|---|---|---|---|
| 64.2% | 43.0% | 13.8% | 5.5% | 3.6% |

**Table 6: Percentage of Two-Site Faults That Can Be Repaired on the crazy Benchmark.**

# 7. SHADOW PLACEMENT

While successfully able to create valid repair sets, the Naive and Cost Repair approaches for repair placement do not reuse any placement information from one placement iteration to the next. Another style of repair placement, called Shadow Placement, was developed to exploit the advantages of incremental placement. Unlike the previous two approaches, Shadow Placement will generate a complete repair set within a single placement iteration.

Like traditional placement, a unique FPGA resource is allocated for each circuit primitive in the netlist. This resource is used during the initial configuration and is named the "main" resource. In addition, a replacement resource, named the "shadow" resource, is also allocated for each circuit primitive in the netlist. This shadow resource is reserved for a potential repair if the original resource becomes faulty. Shadow placement operates by placing each circuit primitive at two locations – once for its "main" site (when there are no faults in the device) and once for its "shadow" site (when the main site is at fault).

The "main" resource for each primitive in the netlist must be unique and distinct from the resources used by all other primitives in the netlist. The resource allocated for "shadow" sites, however, can be shared with the "shadow" sites of other circuit primitives. Since this repair strategy will only guarantee the repair of any *single* resource failures, there is no need to allocate a dedicated repair resource for each circuit primitive. In fact, shadow resources are shared as much as possible to reduce the overhead of the repair circuit. These shadow resources are distributed throughout the device as dictated by the placer to insure that adequate redundant resources are available while still minimizing the placement cost.

Figure 9 demonstrates the placement of the main and shadow primitives. In this simplified example, there are four netlist primitives: L1, L2, L3, and L4. Dedicated "main" resources are allocated for each of these primitives and are annotated as bold in the figure. Only one primitive is allocated for each primary resource (site (0,1) for L1, site (1,1) for L2, site (2,1) for L3, and site (0,0) for L4). Shadow resources are also allocated for primitive but these resources can be shared. The shadow resources are indicated in the figure with braces (i.e., L1, L2, L3, and L4). In this example, three shadow primitives (L1, L2, and L4) are allocated at the site (1,0) and L3 is allocated to site (2,0).

When the device is functioning normally and without fault, the four primitives are placed at their "main" sites ( (0,0), (0,1), (1,1), and (2,1)) and the sites (1,0) and (2,0) are idle. If a permanent fault occurs at site (1,1) where primitive L2 is located, a new circuit placement is used in which primitive L2 is moved to its shadow site (1,0) (see Figure 10).

This example is not necessarily an efficient placement of the shadow resources. In this example, two shadow resources

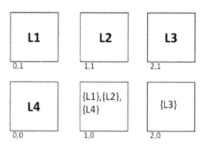

**Figure 9: Placement of "Main" and "Shadow" Resources.**

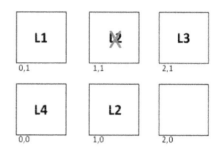

**Figure 10: Repair of a Resource using Shadow Site.**

are allocated for four primary resources for a 50% overhead. Ideally, shadow placement will share more shadow resources and significantly reduce the overhead to support repair.

## 7.1 Shadow Placement Algorithm

The Shadow Placement approach is based on the conventional simulated annealing placer described in Section 3. Unlike the previous repair placement approaches, the Shadow repair placer will determine a repair within a *single* placement iteration. The first difference occurs during the generation of the initial placement. The algorithm begins by placing all of the shadow resources for the design. In particular, the algorithm chooses a small set of placement site within the device in which *all* shadow resources reside. The size of this set is based on the size of the largest placement group. Placing all shadow resources at the same site is done to maximize the remaining sites for main placement. If too many shadow sites are allocated during the initial placement, it may not be possible to find sufficient sites for the main resources and the placement cannot proceed. After placing all shadow resources, the main resources are randomly placed within the remaining sites.

The second major difference is the cost function. The cost function is based on the cost function of Equation 1 but modified to take into account the location of the shadow resources. The wirelength of the routing is estimated by measuring the $x$ and $y$ dimensions of the bounding box that contains *both* the main and shadow terminals of each net (Figure 11 demonstrates this difference). If only the main placement sites are considered, this bounding box has a size of 6 ($x=3$, $y=3$). Since the shadow sites for L1 and L3 lie outside of this bounding box, the bounding box for Shadow placement is expanded. In this case, the bounding box size

122

for this net is 8 (x=4,y=4). To minimize the cost function, the resources allocated for shadow sites must be placed relatively close to its corresponding site and ideally will not increase the bounding box of a net.

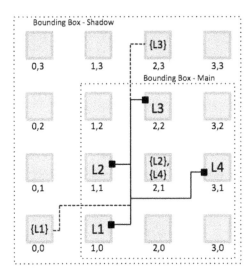

**Figure 11: Shadow Repair Cost Function Bounding Box.**

The third difference between the conventional placer and the Shadow Placer is the way in which potential placement moves are created. Like the conventional annealing placer, a random resource is chosen as a candidate for movement. Since each resource has a corresponding main and shadow resource, the main or shadow version of the resource is randomly selected. Next, a random target site is selected as a potential destination for the selected resource. If the selected target site is free, the move is considered for acceptance. If the target site is not free, the shadow placer will attempt to swap the resource with the resource(s) located at the target site. If the target site contains shadow resources, *all* of the target shadow resources are swapped with the randomly selected resource.

## 7.2 Results

An important figure of merit for the Shadow Placer is the number of shadow sites allocated during placement. Table 7 summarizes the number of shadow sites allocated for each benchmark and constraint pair. As the constraint tightens, fewer idle resources are available and fewer shadow sites are allocated. Although the Shadow Placement executes in a single placement iteration, each iteration must place twice as many resources (i.e., a "main" and a "shadow" for each resource). The average increase in time of the Shadow placer over the conventional placer is summarized in the final row of Table 7. On average, the Shadow placer takes 2.9× longer than the conventional placer and unlike the previous approaches, the amount of time required to complete a shadow placement does not increase with a tighter area constraint.

The primary disadvantage of the Shadow Placer, however, is the lower quality of some repairs. Unlike the other repair placement techniques, the shadow placer must reserve

| | Constraint | | | | | |
|---|---|---|---|---|---|---|
| | None | A | B | C | D | E |
| top | 29 | 23 | 16 | N/A | N/A | N/A |
| test0 | 218 | 122 | 69 | 31 | 19 | N/A |
| mult18 | 482 | 167 | 110 | 52 | 26 | N/A |
| crazy | 884 | 878 | 646 | 357 | 175 | 55 |
| multxor | 4094 | 1773 | 826 | 431 | 282 | 101 |
| Time | 2.12x | 3.43x | 3.01x | 3.1x | 2.48x | 3.03x |

**Table 7: Number of Shadow Sites and Execution Time of Shadow Placement.**

a large number of extra resources for placement of shadow sites. These shadow sites are spread out throughout the area constraint and increase the size of the net bounding boxes. In some cases, shadow sites are placed very far from their corresponding main sites and significantly increase the placement cost. On average, the cost of all circuit repairs using this approach is 41% higher than the original non-repair placement.

The cost of each repair is not the same with shadow placement – some repairs lower the cost while others increase the cost. Figure 12 provides a distribution of the cost deviation from the initial placement of the multxor benchmark. As seen in this distribution, many repairs do not change the cost or even reduce the cost of the placement. However, for this tight constraint (E), the cost increases for a large number of repairs. There are a large number of repairs that significantly increase the placement cost. In summary, the Shadow repair approach has a significant advantage in terms of execution time as the placer only performs one placement iteration. The primary disadvantage of this approach, however, is the relatively low quality of some circuit repairs.

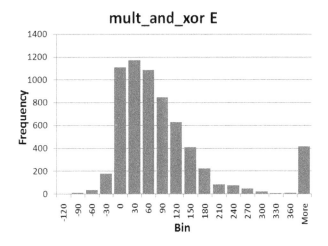

**Figure 12: Distribution of Wirelength Cost Deviation for Shadow Repairs.**

## 8. CONCLUSION

This paper presents three placement algorithms to support in-field repair. These algorithms pre-allocate repair resources for all circuit primitives in the device for use in the presence of a permanent fault. Three different algorithms were presented that vary in approach, execution time, and quality of repair result. The results of each approach are summarized in Table 8. The Naive repair approach is computationally expensive and is not feasible for large, highly utilized designs. The Shadow repair approach is less computationally intensive but generates repair circuits that are inferior to traditional placement approaches. The Cost repair approaches creates circuits that are comparable in quality to traditional placement but require about $16\times$ more execution time than a conventional placer. This work demonstrates that it is possible to perform repair placement that anticipates all possible repairs within a reasonable amount of time.

| Technique | Run Time | Cost |
|---|---|---|
| Naive Repair | $210\times$ | 1.02 |
| Cost Repair | $13.9\times$ | 1.05 |
| Shadow Repair | $2.9\times$ | 1.41 |

**Table 8: Execution Time and Placement Cost of Repair Placement Algorithms When Compared to Non-Repair Placement.**

This work is part of a larger effort of in-field repair that will pre-compute repair configurations before a circuit is deployed. By precomputing repair configurations, it is relatively easy to apply a repair in the field. Future work will integrate timing-driven placer and an incremental repair router that will provide a similar repair function for routing resources. This repair router will reserve redundant routing resources for each net within the design and provide repairs for permanent faults within the routing network. With the ability to repair logic and routing faults, repair configurations can be used to address the growing challenge of permanent faults and circuit wear out.

## 9. ACKNOWLEDGMENTS

This work was supported by a grant from Cisco Corporation.

## 10. REFERENCES

[1] ITRS. *International Technology Roadmap For Semiconductors*, 2011. http://www.itrs.net/Links/2011ITRS/Home2011.htm.

[2] Gregory Ross Wilkinson. Digital circuit wear-out due to electromigration in semiconductor metal lines. Master's thesis, California Polytechnic State University, November 2009.

[3] John Lach, William H. Mangione-Smith, and Miodrag Potkonjak. Efficiently supporting fault-tolerance in fpgas. In *Proceedings of the 1998 ACM/SIGDA sixth international symposium on Field programmable gate arrays*, FPGA '98, pages 105–115, New York, NY, USA, 1998. ACM.

[4] Vijay Lakamraju and Russel Tessier. Tolerating operational faults in cluster-based FPGAs. In *Proceedings of the 2000 ACM/SIGDA eighth international symposium on Field programmable gate arrays*, FPGA '00, pages 187–194, New York, NY, USA, 2000. ACM.

[5] J. Emmert, C. Stroud, B. Skaggs, and M. Abramovici. Dynamic fault tolerance in FPGAs via partial reconfiguration. In *Field-Programmable Custom Computing Machines, 2000 IEEE Symposium on*, pages 165 –174, 2000.

[6] Shu-Yi Yu and E.J. McCluskey. Permanent fault repair for FPGAs with limited redundant area. In *Defect and Fault Tolerance in VLSI Systems, 2001. Proceedings. 2001 IEEE International Symposium on*, pages 125 –133, 2001.

[7] S. Dutt, V. Verma, and V. Suthar. Built-in-self-test of FPGAs with provable diagnosabilities and high diagnostic coverage with application to online testing. *Computer-Aided Design of Integrated Circuits and Systems, IEEE Transactions on*, 27(2):309 –326, 2008.

[8] Raphael Rubin and André Dehon. Choose-your-own-adventure routing: Lightweight load-time defect avoidance. *ACM Trans. Reconfigurable Technol. Syst.*, 4(4):33:1–33:24, December 2011.

[9] George A. Constantinides Nicola Campregher, Peter Y. K. Cheung and Milan Vasilko. Reconfiguration and fine-grained redundancy for fault tolerance in fpgas. In *In Proceedings of the International Conference on Field-Programmable Logic and Applications*, 2006.

[10] John Lach, William H. Mangione-Smith, and Miodrag Potkonjak. Efficiently supporting fault-tolerance in FPGAs. In *Proceedings of the 1998 ACM/SIGDA sixth international symposium on field programmable gate arrays*, pages 105–115, 1998.

[11] C. Lavin, M. Padilla, J. Lamprecht, P. Lundrigan, B. Nelson, and B. Hutchings. Rapid prototyping tools for FPGA designs:RapidSmith. In *Proceedings of the 2010 International Conference on Field-Programmable Technology (FPT)*, pages 353–358, 2010.

[12] C. Lavin, M. Padilla, J. Lamprecht, P. Lundrigan, B. Nelson, and B. Hutchings. Do-it-yourself CAD tools for Xilinx FPGAs. In *Proceedings of the 2011 International Conference on Field-Programmable Technology (FPT)*, 2010.

[13] Neil Steiner, Aaron Wood, Hamid Shojaei, Jacob Couch, Peter Athanas, and Matthew French. Torc: towards an open-source tool flow. In *Proceedings of the 19th ACM/SIGDA international symposium on Field programmable gate arrays*, FPGA '11, pages 41–44, New York, NY, USA, 2011. ACM.

[14] Vaughn Betz and Jonathan Rose. VPR: a new packing, placement and routing tool for FPGA research. In Wayne Luk, Peter Cheung, and Manfred Glesner, editors, *Field-Programmable Logic and Applications*, volume 1304 of *Lecture Notes in Computer Science*, pages 213–222. Springer Berlin / Heidelberg, 1997.

[15] Jimmy Lam and Jean-Marc Delosme. Performance of a new annealing schedule. In *Proceedings of the 25th ACM/IEEE Design Automation Conference*, DAC '88, pages 306–311, Los Alamitos, CA, USA, 1988. IEEE Computer Society Press.

# Heracles: A Tool for Fast RTL-Based Design Space Exploration of Multicore Processors

Michel A. Kinsy     Srinivas Devadas
Department of Electrical Engineering and
Computer Science
Massachusetts Institute of Technology
mkinsy, devadas@mit.edu

Michael Pellauer
Intel Corporation
VSSAD Group
michael.i.pellauer@intel.com

## ABSTRACT

This paper presents *Heracles*, an open-source, functional, parameterized, synthesizable multicore system toolkit. Such a multi/many-core design platform is a powerful and versatile research and teaching tool for architectural exploration and hardware-software co-design. The *Heracles* toolkit comprises the soft hardware (HDL) modules, application compiler, and graphical user interface. It is designed with a high degree of modularity to support fast exploration of future multicore processors of different topologies, routing schemes, processing elements (cores), and memory system organizations. It is a component-based framework with parameterized interfaces and strong emphasis on module reusability. The compiler toolchain is used to map C or C++ based applications onto the processing units. The GUI allows the user to quickly configure and launch a system instance for easy factorial development and evaluation. Hardware modules are implemented in synthesizable Verilog and are FPGA platform independent. The *Heracles* tool is freely available under the open-source MIT license at: http://projects.csail.mit.edu/heracles.

## Categories and Subject Descriptors

C.1.2 [**Computer Systems Organization**]: Processor Architecture - Single-instruction-stream, multiple-data-stream processors (SIMD); B.5.1 [**Hardware**]: Register-Transfer-Level Implementation- Design.

## General Terms

Tool, Design, Experimentation, Performance

## Keywords

Multicore Architecture Design, RTL-Based Design, FPGA, Shared Memory, Distributed Shared Memory, Network-on-Chip, RISC, MIPS, Hardware Migration, Hardware multi-threading, Virtual Channel, Wormhole Router, NoC Routing Algorithm.

## 1. INTRODUCTION

The ability to integrate various computation components such as processing cores, memories, custom hardware units, and complex network-on-chip (NoC) communication protocols onto a single chip has significantly enlarged the design space in multi/many-core systems. The design of these systems requires tuning of a large number of parameters in order to find the most suitable hardware configuration, in terms of performance, area, and energy consumption, for a target application domain. This increasing complexity makes the need for efficient and accurate design tools more acute.

There are two main approaches currently used in the design space exploration of multi/many-core systems. One approach consists of building software routines for the different system components and simulating them to analyze system behavior. Software simulation has many advantages: i) large programming tool support; ii) internal states of all system modules can be easily accessed and altered; iii) compilation/re-compilation is fast; and iv) less constraining in terms of number of components (e.g., number of cores) to simulate. Some of the most stable and widely used software simulators are Simics [14]–a commercially available full-system simulator–GEMS [21], Hornet [12], and Graphite [15]. However, software simulation of many-core architectures with cycle- and bit-level accuracy is time-prohibitive, and many of these systems have to trade off evaluation accuracy for execution speed. Although such a tradeoff is fair and even desirable in the early phase of the design exploration, making final micro-architecture decisions based on these software models over truncated applications or application traces leads to inaccurate or misleading system characterization.

The second approach used, often preceded by software simulation, is register-transfer level (RTL) simulation or emulation. This level of accuracy considerably reduces system behavior mis-characterization and helps avoid late discovery of system performance problems. The primary disadvantage of RTL simulation/emulation is that as the design size increases so does the simulation time. However, this problem can be circumvented by adopting synthesizable RTL and using hardware-assisted accelerators–field programmable gate arrays (FPGAs)–to speed up system execution. Although FPGA resources constrain the size of design one can implement, recent advances in FPGA-based design methodologies have shown that such constraints can be overcome. HAsim [18], for example, has shown using its time multiplexing technique how one can model a shared-memory multicore system including detailed core pipelines, cache hierarchy, and on-chip network, on a single FPGA. RAMP Gold [20] is able to simulate a 64-core shared-memory target machine capable of booting real operating systems running on a single Xilinx Virtex-5 FPGA board. Fleming et al [7] propose a mechanism by which complex designs can be efficiently and automatically partitioned among multiple FPGAs.

RTL design exploration for multi/many-core systems nonetheless remain unattractive to most researchers because it is still a time-consuming endeavor to build such large designs from the ground up and ensure correctness at all levels. Furthermore, researchers are generally interested in one key system area, such as processing core and/or memory organization, network interface, interconnect network, or operating system and/or application mapping. Therefore, we believe that if there is a platform-independent design framework, more specifically, a general hardware toolkit, which allows designers to compose their systems and modify them at will and with very little effort or knowledge of other parts of the system, the speed versus accuracy dilemma in design space exploration of many-core systems can be further mitigated.

To that end we present *Heracles*, a functional, modular, synthesizable, parameterized multicore system toolkit. It is a powerful and versatile research and teaching tool for architectural exploration and hardware-software co-design. Without loss in timing accuracy and logic, complete systems can be constructed, simulated and/or synthesized onto FPGA, with minimal effort. The initial framework is presented in [10]. *Heracles* is designed with a high degree of modularity to support fast exploration of future multicore processors–different topologies, routing schemes, processing elements or cores, and memory system organizations by using a library of components, and reusing user-defined hardware blocks between different system configurations or projects. It has a compiler toolchain for mapping applications written in C or C++ onto the core units. The graphical user interface (GUI) allows the user to quickly configure and launch a system instance for easily-factored development and evaluation. Hardware modules are implemented in synthesizable Verilog and are FPGA platform independent.

## 2. RELATED WORK

In [6] Del Valle *et al* present an FPGA-based emulation framework for multiprocessor system-on-chip (MPSoC) architectures. LEON3, a synthesizable VHDL model of a 32-bit processor compliant with the SPARC V8 architecture, has been used in implementing multiprocessor systems on FPGAs. Andersson *et al* [1], for example, use the LEON4FT microprocessor to build their Next Generation Multipurpose Microprocessor (NGMP) architecture, which is prototyped on the Xilinx XC5VFX130T FPGA board. However, the LEON architecture is fairly complex, and it is difficult to instantiate more than two or three on a medium-sized FPGA. Clack *et al* [4] investigate the use of FPGAs as a prototyping platform for developing multicore system applications. They use the Xilinx MicroBlaze processor for the core, and a bus protocol for the inter-core communication. Some designs focus primarily on the Network-on-chip (NoC). Lusala *et al* [13], for example, propose a scalable implementation of NoC on FPGA using a torus topology. Genko *et al* [8] also present an FPGA-based flexible emulation environment for exploring different NoC features. A VHDL-based cycle-accurate

RTL model for evaluating power and performance of NoC architectures is presented in Banerjee *et al* [2]. Other designs make use of multiple FPGAs. H-Scale [19], by Saint-Jean *et al*, is a multi-FPGA based homogeneous SoC, with RISC processors and an asynchronous NoC. The S-Scale version supports a multi-threaded sequential programming model with dedicated communication primitives handled at runtime by a simple operating system.

## 3. HERACLES HARDWARE SYSTEM

*Heracles* presents designers with a global and complete view of the inner workings of the multi/many-core system at cycle-level granularity from instruction fetches at the processing core in each node to the flit arbitration at the routers. It enables designers to explore different implementation parameters: core micro-architecture, levels of caches, cache sizes, routing algorithm, router micro-architecture, distributed or shared memory, or network interface, and to quickly evaluate their impact on the overall system performance. It is implemented with user-enabled performance counters and probes.

### 3.1 System overview

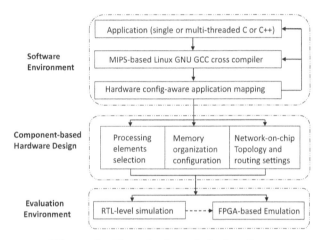

**Figure 1: *Heracles*-based design flow.**

Figure 1 illustrates the general *Heracles*-based design flow. Full applications–written in single or multithreaded C or C++–can be directly compiled onto a given system instance using the *Heracles* MIPS-based GCC cross compiler. The detailed compilation process and application examples are presented in Section 5. For a multi/many-core system, we take a component-based approach by providing clear interfaces to all modules for easy composition and substitutions. The system has multiple default settings to allow users to quickly get a system running and only focus on their area of interest. System and application binary can be executed in an RTL simulated environment and/or on an FPGA. Figure 2 shows two different views of a typical network node structure in *Heracles*.

### 3.2 Processing Units

In the current version of the *Heracles* design framework, users can instantiate four different types of processor cores, or any combination thereof, depending on the programming model adopted and architectural evaluation goals.

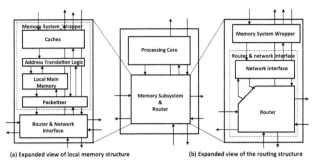

(a) Expanded view of local memory structure    (b) Expanded view of the routing structure

**Figure 2: Network node structure.**

### 3.2.1  Injector Core

The injector core (iCore) is the simplest processing unit. It emits and/or collects from the network user-defined data streams and traffic patterns. Although it does not do any useful computation, this type of core is useful when the user is only focusing on the network on-chip behavior. It is useful in generating network traffic and allowing the evaluation of network congestion. Often, applications running on real cores fail to produce enough data traffic to saturate the network.

### 3.2.2  Single Hardware-Threaded MIPS Core

This is an integer 7-stage 32-bit MIPS–Microprocessor without Interlocked Pipeline Stages–Core (sCore). This RISC architecture is widely used in commercial products and for teaching purposes [17]. Most users are very familiar with this architecture and its operation, and will be able to easily modify it when necessary. Our implementation is generally standard with some modifications for FPGAs. For example, the adoption of a 7-stage pipeline, due to block RAM access time on the FPGA. The architecture is fully bypassed, with no branch prediction table or branch delay slot, running MIPS-III instruction set architecture (ISA) without floating point. Instruction and data caches are implemented using block RAMs, and instruction fetch and data memory access take two cycles. Stall and bypass signals are modified to support the extended pipeline. Instructions are issued and executed in-order, and the data memory accesses are also in-order.

### 3.2.3  Two-way Hardware-Threaded MIPS Core

A fully functional fine-grain hardware multithreaded MIPS core (dCore). There are two hardware threads in the core. The execution datapath for each thread is similar to the single-threaded core above. Each of the two threads has its own context which includes a program counter (PC), a set of 32 data registers, and one 32-bit state register. The core can dispatch instructions from any one of hardware contexts and supports precise interrupts (doorbell type) with limited state saving. A single hardware thread is active on any given cycle, and pipeline stages must be drained between context switches to avoid state corruption. The user has the ability to control the context switching conditions, e.g., minimum number of cycles to allocate to each hardware thread at a time, instruction or data cache misses.

### 3.2.4  Two-way Hardware-Threaded MIPS Core with Migration

The fourth type of core is also a two-way hardware-threaded processor but enhanced to support hardware-level thread migration and evictions (mCore). It is the user's responsibility to guarantee deadlock-freedom under this core configuration. One approach is to allocate local memory to contexts so on migration they are removed from the network. Another approach which requires no additional hardware modification to the core, is using Cho et al [3] deadlock-free thread migration scheme.

### 3.2.5  FPGA Synthesis Data

All the cores have the same interface, they are self-contained and oblivious to the rest of the system, and therefore easily interchangeable. The cores are synthesized using Xilinx ISE Design Suite 11.5, with Virtex-6 LX550T package ff1760 speed -2, as the targeted FPGA board. The number of slice registers and slice lookup tables (LUTs) on the board are 687360 and 343680 respectively. Table 1 shows the register and LUT utilization of the different cores. The two-way hardware-threaded core with migration consumes the most resources and is less than 0.5%. Table 1 also shows the clocking speed of the cores. The injector core, which does no useful computation, runs the fastest at $500.92MHz$ whereas the two-way hardware-threaded core runs the slowest at $118.66MHz$.

**Table 1: FPGA resource utilization per core type.**

| Core type | iCore | sCore | dCore | mCore |
|---|---|---|---|---|
| Registers | 227 | 1660 | 2875 | 3484 |
| LUTs | 243 | 3661 | 5481 | 6293 |
| Speed (MHz) | 500.92 | 172.02 | 118.66 | 127.4 |

## 3.3  Memory System Organization

The memory system in *Heracles* is parameterized, and can be set up in various ways, independent of the rest of the system. The key components are main memory, caching system, and network interface.

### 3.3.1  Main Memory Configuration

The main memory is constructed to allow different memory space configurations. For Centralized Shared Memory (CSM) implementation, all processors share a single large main memory block; the local memory size (shown in Figure 2) is simply set to zero at all nodes except one. In Distributed Shared Memory (DSM), where each processing element has a local memory, the local memory is parameterized and has two very important attributes: the size can be changed on a per core-basis, providing support for both uniform and non-uniform distributed memory, and it can service a variable number of caches in a round-robin fashion. Figure 3 illustrates these physical memory partitions. The fact that the local memory is parameterized to handle requests from a variable number of caches allows the traffic coming into a node from other cores through the network to be presented to local memory as just another cache communication. This illusion is created through the network packetizer. Local memory can also be viewed as a memory controller. Figure 4 illustrates the local structure of the memory sub-system. The *LOCAL_ADDR_BITS* parameter is used to set the size of the local memory. The *Address Translation Logic* performs the virtual-to-physical address lookup using the high-order bits, and directs cache traffic to local memory or network.

For cache coherence, a directory is attached to each local memory and the MESI protocol is implemented as the

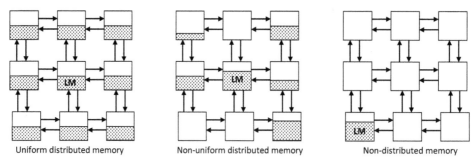

Figure 3: Possible physical memory configurations.

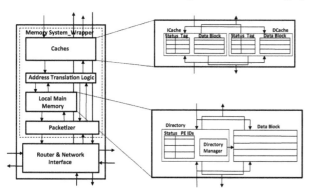

Figure 4: Local memory sub-system structure.

default coherence mechanism. Remote access (RA) is also supported. In RA mode, the network packetizer directly sends network traffic to the caches. Memory structures are implemented in FPGA using block RAMs. There are 632 block RAMs on the Virtex-6 LX550T. A local memory of $0.26MB$ uses 64 block RAMs or 10%. Table 2 shows the FPGA resource used to provide the two cache coherence mechanisms. The RA scheme uses less hardware resources than the cache-coherence-free structure, since no cache-line buffering is needed. The directory-based coherence is far more complex resulting in more resource utilization. The *SHARERS* parameter is used to set the number of sharers per data block. It also dictates the overall size of the local memory directory size. When a directory entry cannot handle all sharers, other sharers are evicted.

**Table 2: FPGA resource utilization per coherence mechanism.**

| Coherence | None | RA | Directory |
|---|---|---|---|
| Registers | 2917 | 2424 | 11482 |
| LUTs | 5285 | 4826 | 17460 |
| Speed (MHz) | 238.04 | 217.34 | 171.75 |

### 3.3.2 Caching System

The user can instantiate direct-mapped Level 1 or Levels 1 and 2 caches with the option of making Level 2 an inclusive cache. The *INDEX_BITS* parameter defines the number of blocks or cache-lines in the cache where the *OFFSET_BITS* parameter defines block size. By default, cache and memory structures are implemented in FPGA using block RAMs, but user can instruct *Heracles* to use LUTs for caches or some combination of LUTs and block RAMs. A single $2KB$ cache uses 4 FPGA block RAMs, 462 slice registers, 1106 slice LUTs, and runs at $228.8MHz$. If cache size is increased to $8KB$ by changing the *INDEX_BITS* parameter

from 6 to 8, resource utilization and speed remain identical. Meanwhile if cache size is increased to $8KB$ by changing the *OFFSET_BITS* parameter from 3 to 5, resource utilization increases dramatically: 15 FPGA block RAMs, 1232 slice registers, 3397 slice LUTs, and speed is $226.8MHz$. FPGA-based cache design favors large number of blocks of small size versus small number of blocks of large size [1].

### 3.3.3 Network Interface

The *Address Resolution Logic* works with the *Packetizer* module, shown in Figure 2, to get the caches and the local memory to interact with the rest of the system. All cache traffic goes through the *Address Resolution Logic*, which determines if a request can be served at the local memory, or if the request needs to be sent over the network. The *Packetizer* is responsible for converting data traffic, such as a load, coming from the local memory and the cache system into packets or flits that can be routed inside the Network-on-chip (NoC), and for reconstructing packets or flits into data traffic at the opposite side when exiting the NoC.

### 3.3.4 Hardware multithreading and caching

In this section, we examine the effect of hardware multithreading (HMT) on system performance. We run the 197.parser application from the SPEC CINT2000 benchmarks on a single node with the dCore as the processing unit using two different inputs–one per thread–with five different execution interleaving policies:

- setup 1: threads take turns to execute every 32 cycles; on a context switch, the pipeline is drained before the execution of another thread begins.
- setup 2: thread switching happens every 1024 cycles.
- setup 3: thread context swapping is initiated on an instruction or a data miss at the Level 1 cache.
- setup 4: thread interleaving occurs only when there is a data miss at the Level 1 cache.
- setup 5: thread switching happens when there is a data miss at the Level 2 cache.

Figure 5 shows the total completion time of the two threads (in terms of number of cycles). It is worth noting that even with fast fine-grain hardware context switching, multithreading is most beneficial for large miss penalty events like Level 2 cache misses or remote data accesses.

## 3.4 Network-on-Chip (NoC)

To provide scalability, *Heracles* uses a network-on-chip (NoC) architecture for its data communication infrastructure. A NoC architecture is defined by its topology (the

---

[1] Cache-line size also has traffic implications at the network level

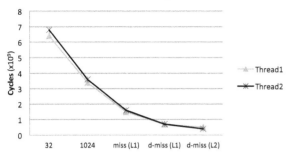

**Execution Cycles**

Figure 5: Effects of hardware multithreading and caching.

physical organization of nodes in the network), its flow control mechanism (which establishes the data formatting, the switching protocol and the buffer allocation), and its routing algorithm (which determines the path selected by a packet to reach its destination under a given application).

### 3.4.1 Flow control

Routing in *Heracles* can be done using either bufferless or buffered routers. Bufferless routing is generally used to reduce area and power overhead associated with buffered routing. Contention for physical link access is resolved by either dropping and retransmitting or temporarily misrouting or *deflecting* of flits. With flit dropping an acknowledgment mechanism is needed to enable retransmission of lost flits. With flit deflection, a priority-based arbitration, e.g., *age-based*, is needed to avoid livelock. In *Heracles*, to mitigate some of the problems associated with the lossy bufferless routing, namely retransmission and slow arbitration logic, we supplement the arbiter with a routing table that can be statically and off-line configured on a per-application basis.

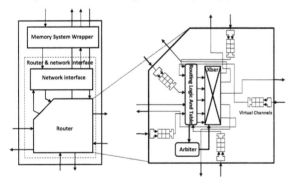

Figure 6: Virtual channel based router architecture.

The system default virtual-channel router conforms in its architecture and operation to conventional virtual-channel routers [5]. It has some input buffers to store flits while they are waiting to be routed to the next hop in the network. The router is modular enough to allow user to substitute different arbitration schemes. The routing operation takes four steps or phases, namely routing (RC), virtual-channel allocation (VA), switch allocation (SA), and switch traversal (ST), where each phase corresponds to a pipeline stage in our router. Figure 6 depicts the general structure of the buffered router. In this router the number of virtual channels per port and their sizes are controlled through *VC_PER_PORT* and *VC_DEPTH* parameters. Table 3 shows the register and LUT utilization of the bufferless router and different buffer

configurations of the buffered router. It also shows the effect of virtual channels on router clocking speed. The key takeaway is that a larger number of VCs at the router increases both the router resource utilization and the critical path.

Table 3: FPGA resource utilization per router configuration.

| Number of VCs | Bufferless | 2 VCs | 4 VCs | 8 VCs |
|---|---|---|---|---|
| Registers | 175 | 4081 | 7260 | 13374 |
| LUTs | 328 | 7251 | 12733 | 23585 |
| Speed (MHz) | 817.18 | 111.83 | 94.8 | 80.02 |

### 3.4.2 Routing algorithm

Algorithms used to compute routes in network-on-chip (NoC) architectures, generally fall under two categories: *oblivious* and *dynamic* [16]. The default routers in *Heracles* primarily support *oblivious* routing algorithms using either fixed logic or routing tables. Fixed logic is provided for dimension-order routing (DOR) algorithms, which are widely used and have many desirable properties. On the other hand, table-based routing provides greater programmability and flexibility, since routes can be pre-computed and stored in the routing tables before execution. Both buffered and bufferless routers can make usage of the routing tables. *Heracles* provides support for both static and dynamic virtual channel allocation.

### 3.4.3 Network Topology Configuration

The parameterization of the number of input ports and output ports on the router and the table-based routing capability give *Heracles* a great amount of flexibility and the ability to metamorphose into different network topologies; for example, *k*-ary *n*-cube, 2D-mesh, 3D-mesh, hypercube, ring, or tree. A new topology is constructed by changing the *IN_PORTS*, *OUT_PORTS*, and *SWITCH_TO_SWITCH* parameters and reconnecting the routers. Table 4 shows the clocking speed of a bufferless router, a buffered router with strict round-robin arbitration (Arbiter1), a buffered router with weak round-robin arbitration (Arbiter2), and a buffered router with 7 ports for a 3D-mesh network. The bufferless router runs the fastest at $817.2MHz$, Arbiter1 and Arbiter2 run at the same speed ($\sim 112$), although the arbitration scheme in Arbiter2 is more complex. The 7-port router runs the slowest due to more complex arbitration logic.

Table 4: Clocking speed of different router types.

| Router type | Bufferless | Arbiter1 | Arbiter2 | 7-Port |
|---|---|---|---|---|
| Speed (MHz) | 817.18 | 111.83 | 112.15 | 101.5 |

Figure 7 shows a 3×3 2D-mesh with all identical routers. Figure 8 depicts an unbalanced *fat-tree* topology. For a *fat-tree* [11] topology, routers at different levels of the tree have different sizes, in terms of crossbar and arbitration logic. The root node contains the largest router, and controls the clock frequency of the system.

## 4. HERACLES PROGRAMMING MODELS

A programming model is inherently tied to the underlying hardware architecture. The *Heracles* design tool has no directly deployable operating system, but it supports both sequential and parallel programming models through various

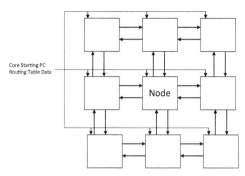

Figure 7: 2D mesh topology.

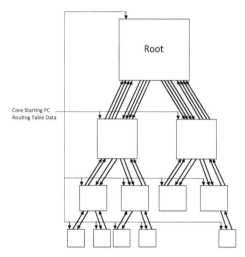

Figure 8: Unbalanced fat-tree topology.

application programming interface (API) protocols. There are three memory spaces associated with each program: instruction memory, data memory, and stack memory. Dynamic memory allocation is not supported in the current version of the tool.

## 4.1 Sequential programming model

In the sequential programming model, a program has a single entry point (starting program counter–PC) and single execution thread. Under this model, a program may exhibit any of the follow behavior or a combination thereof:

- the local memory of executing core has instruction binary;
- PC pointer to another core's local memory where the instruction binary resides;
- the stack frame pointer– SP points to the local memory of executing core;
- SP points to another core's local memory for the storage of the stack frame;
- program data is stored at the local memory;
- program data is mapped to another core local memory.

Figure 9 gives illustrating examples of the memory space management when dealing with sequential programs. These techniques provide the programming flexibility needed to support the different physical memory configurations. They also allow users:

- to run the same program on multiple cores (program inputs can be different); in this setup the program binary is loaded to one core and the program counter at other cores points to the core with the binary;

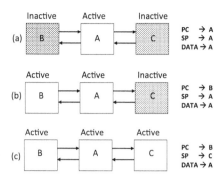

Figure 9: Examples of memory space management for sequential programs.

- to execute one program across multiple cores by migrating the program from one core to another.

## 4.2 Parallel programming model

The *Heracles* design platform supports both hardware multi-threading and software multi-threading. The keywords *HHThread1* and *HHThread2* are provided to specify the part of the program to execute on each hardware thread. Multiple programs can also be executed on the same core using the same approach. An example is shown below:

```
...
int HHThread1 (int *array, int item, int size) {
    sort(array, size);
    int output = search(array, item, size);
    return output;
}

int HHThread2 (int input,int src,int aux,int dest){
    int output = Hanoi(input, src, aux, dest);
    return output;
}
...
```

Below is the associated binary outline:

```
@e2       // <HHThread1>
27bdffd8  // 00000388 addiu sp,sp,-40
...
0c00004c  // 000003c0 jal 130 <search>
...


@fa       // <HHThread2>
27bdffd8  // 000003e8 addiu sp,sp,-40
...
0c0000ab  // 00000418 jal 2ac <Hanoi>
...


@110      // <HHThread1_Dispatcher>
27bdffa8  // 00000440 addiu sp,sp,-88
...
0c0000e2  // 000004bc jal 388 <hThread1>
...


@15e      // <HHThread2_Dispatcher>
27bdffa8  // 00000440 addiu sp,sp,-88
...
0c0000fa  // 000004d8 jal 3e8 <HHThread2>
...
```

*Heracles* uses OpenMP style pragmas to allow users to directly compile multi-threaded programs onto cores. Users specify programs or parts of a program that can be executed in parallel and on which cores. Keywords *HLock* and *HBarrier* are provided for synchronization and shared variables are encoded with the keyword *HGlobal*. An example is shown below:

```
...
#pragma Heracles core 0 {
  // Synchronizers
  HLock lock1, lock2;
  HBarrier bar1, bar2;

  // Variables
  HGlobal int arg1, arg2, arg3;
  HGlobal int Arr[16][16];
  HGlobal int Arr0[16][16] = { { 1, 12, 7, 0,...
  HGlobal int Arr1[16][16] = { { 2, 45, 63, 89,...

  // Workers
  #pragma Heracles core 1 {
    start_check(50);
    check_lock(&lock1, 1000);
    matrix_add(Arr, Arr0, Arr1, arg1);
    clear_barrier(&bar1);
  }

  #pragma Heracles core 2 {
    start_check(50);
    check_lock(&lock1, 1000);
    matrix_add(Arr, Arr0, Arr1, arg2);
    clear_barrier(&bar2);
  }
}
...
```

Below is the intermediate C representation:

```
...
int core_0_lock1, core_0_lock2;
int core_0_bar1, core_0_bar2;
int core_0_arg1, core_0_arg2, core_0_arg3;
int core_0_Arr[16][16];
int core_0_Arr0[16][16] = { { 1, 12, 7, 0,...
int core_0_Arr1[16][16] = { { 2, 45, 63, 89,...

void  core_0_work (void)
{
  // Synchronizers
  // Variables
  // Workers
  // Main function
  main();
}
void  core_1_work (void)
{
  start_check(50);
  check_lock(&core_0_lock1, 1000);
  matrix_add(core_0_Arr, core_0_Arr0, core_0_Arr1,
  core_0_arg1);
  clear_barrier(&core_0_bar1);
}
...
```

Below is the associated binary outline:

```
@12b      // <Dispatcher>
27bdffe8  // 000004ac addiu sp,sp,-24
...
0c000113  // 000004bc jal 44c <core_0_work>
...
```

## 5. PROGRAMMING TOOLCHAIN

### 5.1 Program compilation flow

The *Heracles* environment has an open-source compiler toolchain to assist in developing software for different system configurations. The toolchain is built around the GCC MIPS cross-compiler using GNU C version 3.2.1. Figure 10 depicts the software flow for compiling a C program into the compatible MIPS instruction code that can be executed on the system. The compilation process consists of a series of six steps.

- First, the user invokes *mips-gcc* to translate the C code into assembly language (e.g., *./mips-gcc -S fibonacci.c*).
- In step 2, the assembly code is then run through the isa-checker (e.g., *./checker fibonacci.s*). The checker's role is to: (1) remove all memory space primitives, (2) replace all pseudo-instructions, and (3) check for floating point instructions. Its output is a *.asm* file.
- For this release, there is no direct high-level operating system support. Therefore, in the third compilation stage, a small kernel-like assembly code is added to the application assembly code for memory space management and workload distribution (e.g., *./linker fibonacci.asm*). Users can modify the *linker.cpp* file provided in the toolchain to reconfigure the memory space and workload.
- In step 4, the user compiles the assembly file into an object file using the cross-compiler. This is accomplished by executing *mips-as* on the *.asm* file (e.g., *./mips-as fibonacci.asm*).
- In step 5, the object file is disassembled using the *mips-objdump* command (e.g., *./mips-objdump fibonacci.o*). Its output is a *.dump* file.
- Finally, the constructor script is called to transform the dump file into a Verilog memory, *.vmh*, file format (e.g., *./dump2vmh fibonacci.dump*).

If the program is specified using *Heracles* multi-threading format (*.hc* or *.hcc*), c-cplus-generator (e.g., *./c-cplus-generator fibonacci.hc*) is called to first get the C or C++ program file before executing the steps listed above. The software toolchain is still evolving. All these steps are also automated through the GUI.

### 5.2 Heracles graphical user interface

The graphical user interface (GUI) is called *Heracles Designer*. It helps to quickly configure and launch system configurations. Figure 11 shows a screen shot of the GUI. On the core tab, the user can select: (1) the type of core to generate, (2) the network topology of the system instance to generate, (3) the number of cores to generate, (4) traffic type, injection rate, and simulation cycles in the case of an injector core, or (5) different pre-configured settings.

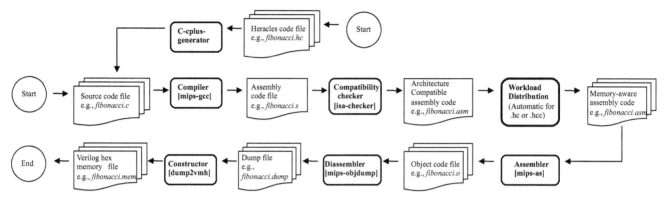

Figure 10: Software toolchain flow.

Figure 11: *Heracles* designer graphical user interface.

*Generate* and *Run* buttons on this tab are used to automatically generate the Verilog files and to launch the synthesis process or specified simulation environment. The second tab–memory system tab–allows the user to set: (1) maim memory configuration (e.g., Uniformed Distributed), (2) total main memory size, (3) instruction and data cache sizes, (4) Level 2 cache, and (5) FPGA favored resource (LUT or block RAM) for cache structures. The on-chip network tab covers all the major aspects of the system interconnect: (1) routing algorithm, (2) number of virtual channels (VCs) per port, (3) VC depth, (4) core and switch bandwidths, (5) routing tables programming, by selecting source/destination pair or flow ID, router ID, output port, and VC (allowing user-defined routing paths), and (6) number of flits per packet for injector-based traffic. The programming tab is updated when the user changes the number of cores in the system; the user can: (1) load a binary file onto a core, (2) load a binary onto a core and set the starting address for another core to point to that binary, (3) select where to place the data section or stack pointer of a core (it can be local, on the same core as the binary or on another core), and (4) select which cores to start.

# 6. EXPERIMENTAL RESULTS

## 6.1 Full 2D-mesh systems

The synthesis results of five multicore systems of size: 2×2, 3×3, 4×4, 5×5, and 6×6 arranged in 2D-mesh topology are summarized below. Table 5 gives the key architectural characteristics of the multicore system. All five systems run at $105.5MHz$, which is the clock frequency of the router, regardless of the size of the mesh.

Figure 12 summarizes the FPGA resource utilization by the different systems in terms of registers, lookup tables, and block RAMs. In the 2×2 and 3×3 configurations, the local memory is set to $260KB$ per core. The 3×3 configuration uses 99% of block RAM resources at $260KB$ of local memory per core. For the 4×4 configuration the local memory is reduced to $64KB$ per core, and the local memory in the 5×5 configuration is set to $32KB$. The 6×6 configuration, with $16KB$ of local memory per core, fails during the mapping and routing synthesis steps, due to the lack of LUTs.

## 6.2 Evaluation results

We examine the performance of two SPEC CINT2000 benchmarks, namely, 197.parser and 256.bzip2 on *Heracles*. We modify and parallelize these benchmarks to fit into our evaluation framework. For the 197.parser benchmark, we identify three functional units: file reading and parameters setting as one unit, actual parsing as a second unit, and er-

Table 5: 2D-mesh system architecture details.

| Core | |
|---|---|
| ISA | 32-Bit MIPS |
| Hardware threads | 1 |
| Pipeline Stages | 7 |
| Bypassing | Full |
| Branch policy | Always non-Taken |
| Outstanding memory requests | 1 |
| Level 1 Instruction/Data Caches | |
| Associativity | Direct |
| Size | variable |
| Outstanding Misses | 1 |
| On-Chip Network | |
| Topology | 2D-Mesh |
| Routing Policy | DOR and Table-based |
| Virtual Channels | 2 |
| Buffers per channel | 8 |

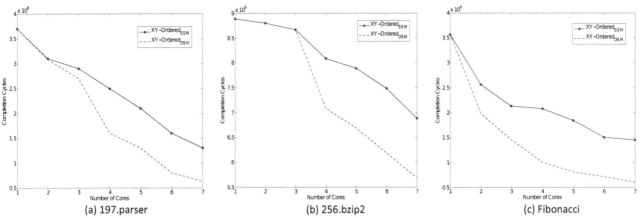

(a) 197.parser      (b) 256.bzip2      (c) Fibonacci

Figure 13: Effect of memory organization on performance for the different applications.

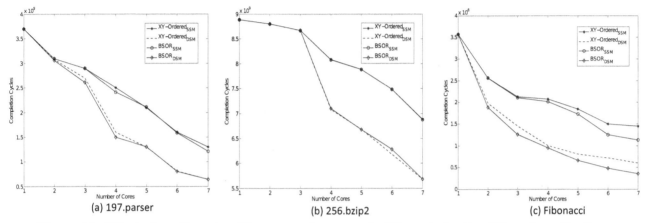

(a) 197.parser      (b) 256.bzip2      (c) Fibonacci

Figure 14: Effect of routing algorithm on performance in 2D-mesh for the different applications.

## Resource Utilization

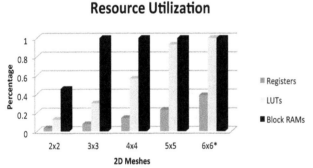

Figure 12: Percentage of FPGA resource utilization per mesh size.

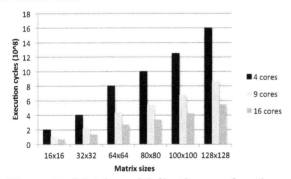

Figure 15: Matrix multiplication acceleration.

ror reporting as the third unit. When there are more than three cores, all additional cores are used in the parsing unit. Similarly, 256.bzip2 is divided into three functional units: file reading and cyclic redundancy check, compression, and output file writing. The compression unit exhibits a high degree of data-parallelism, therefore we apply all additional cores to this unit for core count greater than three. We also present a brief analysis of a simple Fibonacci number calculation program. Figures 13 (a), (b), and (c) show 197.parser, 256.bzip2, and Fibonacci benchmarks under single shared-memory (SSM) and distributed shared-memory (DSM), using *XY-Ordered* routing. Increasing the number of cores improves performance for both benchmarks; it also exposes the memory bottleneck encountered in the single shared-memory scheme. Figures 14 (a), (b), and (c) highlight the impact of the routing algorithm on the overall system performance, by comparing completion cycles of *XY-Ordered* routing and BSOR [9]. BSOR, which stands for Bandwidth-Sensitive Oblivious Routing, is a table-based routing algorithm that minimizes the maximum channel load (MCL) (or maximum traffic) across all network links in an effort to maximize application throughput. The routing algorithm has little or no effect on the performance of 197.parser and 256.bzip2 benchmarks, because of the traffic patterns in these applications. For the Fibonacci application, Figure 14 (c), BSOR routing does improve performance, particularly with 5 or more cores. To show the multithreading and scalability properties of the system, Figure 15 presents the execution times for matrix multiplication given matrices of different size. The *Heracles* multicore programming format is used to automate of the workload distribution onto cores.

# 7. CONCLUSION

In this work, we present the new *Heracles* design toolkit which is comprised of soft hardware (HDL) modules, an application compiler toolchain, and a graphical user interface. It is a component-based framework that gives researchers the ability to create complete, realistic, synthesizable, multi/many-core architectures for fast, high-accuracy design space exploration. In this environment, user can explore design tradeoffs at the processing unit level, the memory organization and access level, and the network on-chip level. The *Heracles* tool is open-source and can be downloaded at http://projects.csail.mit.edu/heracles. In the current release, RTL hardware modules can be simulated on all operating systems, the MIPS GCC cross-compiler runs in a Linux environment, and the graphical user interface has a Windows installer.

# 8. ACKNOWLEDGMENTS

We thank the students from the MIT 6.S918 IAP 2012 class who worked with early versions of the tool and made many excellent suggestions for improvement. We thank Joel Emer, Li-Shiuan Peh, and Omer Khan for interesting discussions throughout the course of this work.

# 9. REFERENCES

[1] J. Andersson, J. Gaisler, and R. Weigand. Next generation multipurpose microprocessor. 2010.

[2] N. Banerjee, P. Vellanki, and K. Chatha. A power and performance model for network-on-chip architectures. In *Design, Automation and Test in Europe Conference and Exhibition, 2004. Proceedings*, volume 2, pages 1250 – 1255 Vol.2, feb. 2004.

[3] M. H. Cho, K. S. Shim, M. Lis, O. Khan, and S. Devadas. Deadlock-free fine-grained thread migration. In *Networks on Chip (NoCS), 2011 Fifth IEEE/ACM International Symposium on*, pages 33 –40, may 2011.

[4] C. R. Clack, R. Nathuji, and H.-H. S. Lee. Using an fpga as a prototyping platform for multi-core processor applications. In *WARFP-2005: Workshop on Architecture Research using FPGA Platforms*, Cambridge, MA, USA, feb. 2005.

[5] W. J. Dally and B. Towles. *Principles and Practices of Interconnection Networks*. Morgan Kaufmann, 2003.

[6] P. Del valle, D. Atienza, I. Magan, J. Flores, E. Perez, J. Mendias, L. Benini, and G. Micheli. A complete multi-processor system-on-chip fpga-based emulation framework. In *Very Large Scale Integration, 2006 IFIP International Conference on*, pages 140–145, oct. 2006.

[7] K. E. Fleming, M. Adler, M. Pellauer, A. Parashar, A. Mithal, and J. Emer. Leveraging latency-insensitivity to ease multiple fpga design. In *Proceedings of the ACM/SIGDA international symposium on Field Programmable Gate Arrays*, FPGA '12, pages 175–184, New York, NY, USA, 2012.

[8] N. Genko, D. Atienza, G. De Micheli, J. Mendias, R. Hermida, and F. Catthoor. A complete network-on-chip emulation framework. In *Design, Automation and Test in Europe, 2005. Proceedings*, pages 246–251 Vol. 1, march 2005.

[9] M. Kinsy, M. H. Cho, T. Wen, E. Suh, M. van Dijk, and S. Devadas. Application-Aware Deadlock-Free Oblivious Routing. In *Proceedings of the Int'l Symposium on Computer Architecture*, June 2009.

[10] M. Kinsy, M. Pellauer, and S. Devadas. Heracles: Fully synthesizable parameterized mips-based multicore system. In *Field Programmable Logic and Applications (FPL), 2011 International Conference on*, pages 356 –362, sept. 2011.

[11] C. E. Leiserson. Fat-trees: universal networks for hardware-efficient supercomputing. *IEEE Trans. Comput.*, 34(10):892–901, 1985.

[12] M. Lis, P. Ren, M. H. Cho, K. S. Shim, C. Fletcher, O. Khan, and S. Devadas. Scalable, accurate multicore simulation in the 1000-core era. In *Performance Analysis of Systems and Software (ISPASS), 2011 IEEE International Symposium on*, pages 175–185, april 2011.

[13] A. Lusala, P. Manet, B. Rousseau, and J.-D. Legat. Noc implementation in fpga using torus topology. In *Field Programmable Logic and Applications, 2007. FPL 2007. International Conference on*, pages 778–781, aug. 2007.

[14] P. S. Magnusson, M. Christensson, J. Eskilson, D. Forsgren, G. Hållberg, J. Högberg, F. Larsson, A. Moestedt, and B. Werner. Simics: A full system simulation platform. *Computer*, 35(2):50–58, feb 2002.

[15] J. Miller, H. Kasture, G. Kurian, C. Gruenwald, N. Beckmann, C. Celio, J. Eastep, and A. Agarwal. Graphite: A distributed parallel simulator for multicores. In *High Performance Computer Architecture (HPCA), 2010 IEEE 16th International Symposium on*, pages 1–12, jan. 2010.

[16] L. M. Ni and P. K. McKinley. A survey of wormhole routing techniques in direct networks. *Computer*, 26(2):62–76, 1993.

[17] D. Patterson and J. Hennessy. *Computer Organization and Design: The Hardware/software Interface*. Morgan Kaufmann, 2005.

[18] M. Pellauer, M. Adler, M. Kinsy, A. Parashar, and J. Emer. Hasim: Fpga-based high-detail multicore simulation using time-division multiplexing. In *High Performance Computer Architecture (HPCA), 2011 IEEE 17th International Symposium on*, pages 406–417, feb. 2011.

[19] N. Saint-Jean, G. Sassatelli, P. Benoit, L. Torres, and M. Robert. Hs-scale: a hardware-software scalable mp-soc architecture for embedded systems. In *VLSI, 2007. ISVLSI '07. IEEE Computer Society Annual Symposium on*, pages 21–28, march 2007.

[20] Z. Tan, A. Waterman, R. Avizienis, Y. Lee, H. Cook, D. Patterson, and K. Asanovict' and. Ramp gold: An fpga-based architecture simulator for multiprocessors. In *Design Automation Conference (DAC), 2010 47th ACM/IEEE*, pages 463–468, june 2010.

[21] W. Yu. Gems a high performance em simulation tool. In *Electrical Design of Advanced Packaging Systems Symposium, 2009. (EDAPS 2009). IEEE*, pages 1–4, dec. 2009.

# Are FPGAs Suffering from the Innovator's Dilemna?

*Organized by:*

Vaughn Betz
University of Toronto
Dept. of Electrical and Computer Engineering
10 King's College Road, Toronto, ON, Canada
vaughn@eecg.utoronto.ca

Jason Cong
UCLA
Dept. of Computer Science
4731J, Boelter Hall, Los Angeles, CA
cong@cs.ucla.edu

## ABSTRACT

FPGAs constitute a highly profitable industry, with approximately $5 billion of sales per year. High barriers to entry keep most companies away, and enable high profit margins for the incumbents. The industry has grown greatly over the years, but still constitutes a small portion of the overall semiconductor market. This raises the question to be addressed by this panel: is the FPGA community innovating as much as it should, or is a bias to maintain high profit margins and protect the cash flow of the current FPGA market holding us back from exploring new ideas and products that could greatly expand the appeal of and market for FPGA-related technology? This would be a classic case of the innovator's dilemma defined by Clayton Christensen: it is difficult for a company to engage in creative destruction of a cash cow product.

Our distinguished panel of experts will discuss whether we are seeing major innovation in architectures, design flows and applications, or only incremental improvements. We will also discuss if any new (possibly low margin) application domain is left out by the FPGA industry, what radical ideas should be explored, and whether large incumbents, new startups, academia or some combination are best able to attack these new areas.

## Categories and Subject Descriptors

B.7.1 [**Integrated Circuits**]: VLSI, Gate Arrays

## General Terms: Economics

## Keywords: Field Programmable Gate Arrays

# Location, Location, Location—The Role of Spatial Locality in Asymptotic Energy Minimization

André DeHon
Department of Electrical and Systems Engineering
University of Pennsylvania
200 S. 33rd St., Philadelphia, PA 19104
andre@acm.org

## ABSTRACT

Locality exploitation is essential to asymptotic energy minimization for gate array netlist evaluation. Naive implementations that ignore locality, including flat crossbars and simple processors based on monolithic memories, can require $O(N^2)$ energy for an $N$ node graph. Specifically, it is important to exploit locality (1) to reduce the size of the description of the graph, (2) to reduce data movement, and (3) to reduce instruction movement. FPGAs exploit all three. FPGAs with a Rent Exponent $p < 0.5$ running designs with $p < 0.5$ achieve asymptotically optimal $\Theta(N)$ energy. FPGA designs with $p > 0.5$ and implementations with metal layers that grow as $O(N^{p-0.5})$ require only $O(N^{p+0.5})$ energy; this bound can be achieved with $O(1)$ metal layers with a novel multicontext design that has heterogeneous context depth. In contrast, a $p > 0.5$ FPGA design on an implementation technology with $O(1)$ metal layers requires $O(N^{2p})$ energy.

## Categories and Subject Descriptors

B.7.1 [**Integrated Circuits**]: Type and Design Styles—*VLSI*; C.2.1 [**Computer Communication Newtorks**]: Network Architecture and Design; C.1.3 [**Processor Architectures**]: Other Architecture Styles—*Adapative Architextures*

## General Terms

Theory, Design

## Keywords

VLSI Theory, Energy, Energy Complexity, Low Power, FPGA, Rent's Rule, Locality, Multicontext

## 1. INTRODUCTION

Energy is now the dominant concern for many applications and systems. This shows up directly as hours of operation for battery powered devices and indirectly as power density

limits for air-cooled laptops and servers. Consequently, considerable research over the last decade has focused on energy reduction at all levels in FPGA design (CAD, microarchitecture, circuit, technology). Microarchitecture studies (*e.g.* [23, 21]) ask detailed questions about parameters in a basic FPGA design such as how long interconnect segments should be, how switchboxes should be populated, how many input a LUT should have, or how many LUTs should be in a cluster. Here we address a broader architecture question: is the basic architectural organization of configured gates and wires energy efficient? or would it be more energy efficient to sequentially evaluate gates as instructions on a processor? is there an inherent energy advantage or disadvantage to multicontext FPGAs?

Since this is a broad question, we stick with an asymptotic energy analysis, ignoring constants. The asymptotic picture is necessarily crude, but it has the advantage of being independent of technologies and a host of implementation assumptions that can obfuscate or, if chosen poorly, invalidate a comparison. The comparison we make is in the spirit of VLSI complexity theory, but focuses on architecturally determined energy complexity rather than application-driven Area-Time complexity (See Secs. 2.3 and 10 for details).

We start by defining a gate-array evaluation model that defines the computation required to evaluate all the gates in a netlist and a VLSI model for the area and energy in the physical substrate (Sec. 3). We consider strawman implementations on spatial crossbars and sequential processors with monolithic memories (Sec. 4) as a baseline.

From this starting point, we derive the need to exploit locality in the problem and use Rent's Rule [19] to characterize the locality in a design. We successively see that there is an asymptotic energy advantage to exploiting locality in:
- *descriptions*—referring to gates with fewer bits when they are "closer" to a consumer rather than using a fixed number of bits to refer to all gates–Sec. 5
- *data movement*—laying out data elements to minimize the distance we need to bring the inputs to a gate together for evaluation; this leads us to give each gate a location and move data to it rather than storing all gate values in a common memory–Sec. 6
- *instruction movement*—placing instructions adjacent to the resources they control, particularly interconnect, rather than centrally or with the gates–Sec. 7

Combining these localities gives us the typical FPGA organization. Despite the fact that FPGA organization may be physically larger than a processor with a dense memory or an ASIC, it is asymptotically optimal ($\Theta(N)$ energy to evaluate $N$ gates) when locality is high (Rent's Rule $p < 0.5$).

Lack of locality is a common challenge for spatial designs and is a key driver in the $AT^2$ VLSI complexity bounds. For these less local designs ($p > 0.5$), when limited to a constant number of metal layers, traditional FPGA designs require $O(N^{2p})$ energy. We introduce architectures that constructively achieve energy as low as $O(N^{p+0.5})$, including a sequential design and a novel multicontext design. The multicontext design differs from prior proposal for multicontext FPGAs (*e.g.*, [6, 27]) in that it uses a different context depth at different levels in its hierarchical interconnect—a depth driven both by the Rent's Rule demand for interconnect and the availability of wire tracks when limited to a constant number of metal layers (Sec. 7.3). Furthermore, if our technology allows us to add wire layers fast enough, we show that FPGA-like designs can achieve the $O(N^{p+0.5})$ energy bound as well (Sec. 8).

## 2. BACKGROUND

### 2.1 Energy Matters

We have now hit the point where power density limits (*e.g.* 100W/cm$^2$ for force-air cooling, 1–10W/cm$^2$ for ambient cooling), not transistor integration density, is the key limitation for computations [12]. That is, we cannot afford to turn on all the transistors that we can integrate onto an integrated circuit [15], a phenomenon now termed "Dark Silicon" [29, 10]. This power density limit has driven the end of microprocessor clock scaling [12], and it may drive the end of useful VLSI feature size scaling [11]. *As energy reduction from scaling diminishes, architectural solutions that reduce energy grow in importance.* Even when power does not limit what designers can do, energy consumption is a primary concern for battery life and operating costs.

### 2.2 Energy Efficiency Hints

A wealth of papers at this conference and the International Symposium on Field-Programmable Custom Computing Machines regularly show FPGA designs that require substantially less energy than processor designs. In one of the early, direct comparisons Budiu maps computational benchmarks to spatial designs and shows order of magnitude lower energy than sequential processor designs [4]. Stitt showed that kernels could be moved from a processor to an attached FPGA co-processor to reduce energy [25]. More recently, Venkatesh shows that custom spatial implementation of basic blocks saves considerable energy compared to sequential implementation on general-purpose processors [29]. Dally shows that the dominant energy in low power embedded processor is in instruction and data memories and this can be reduced by using an array of processors with shallower memories [5]. Trimberger's original paper on multicontext FPGAs [27] noted the high power requirement of instruction memory reads as a potential drawback.

All of this work suggests that spatial designs save energy compared to sequential designs since they avoid the need to read data and instructions from memories. However, we also know that computations on FPGAs can be less compact than processors and, consequently, must pay energy to send bits over longer physical distances than processor. The examples above suggest that the savings in memory energy is more substantial than the cost in interconnect energy. It

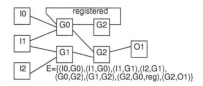

**Figure 2: Example Gate Array Netlist**

is therefore desirable to understand if there are fundamental effects that drive the previous observations. While there are many effects at play that are beyond the scope of this paper (See Sec. 11), our results begin to show that there are asymptotic effects that favor spatial implementations as well as showing conditions under which hybrid designs may be better than either spatial or sequential designs.

### 2.3 VLSI Theory

There is a well-developed theory of VLSI complexity (*e.g.*, [26, 24, 20]). Notably, by modeling the finite width of wires and focusing on graph cut sizes in algorithms, it has been possible to obtain non-trivial bounds on the area of a VLSI design with a particular level of parallelism [2]. For designs with high communication requirements, and hence cut widths, such as sorting and FFT, this led to $AT^2$ bounds. This says that to run these problems twice as fast, it will require 4 times the area. This area expansion comes not from the need to place more processing elements, but from the need to layout more wiring. Our results in this paper take careful account of wiring and layout to identify constructive organizations and achievable energy bounds.

The energy complexity of VLSI has received less attention than area and time, and most of the VLSI complexity results ignore the area and delay impacts of memory. We believe this is the first work to establish energy complexity results for memories. Section 10 characterizes work on VLSI energy complexity and relates it to the result we develop here.

## 3. MODELS

### 3.1 Gate Array Evaluation Model

To model a typical FPGA circuit, we use a gate array netlist model. Informally, this is a graph where every node has bounded fanin $k$ and evaluates once per evaluation cycles (*e.g.* Fig. 2). $k$ can be taken as the number of inputs to the LUTs in the FPGA. We take $k$ to be a small constant and make no attempt to differentiate among different choices for $k$. We characterize a graph by the number of nodes $N = |V|$. Since $k$ is bounded, the number of edges in the graph $|E| \le kN = O(N)$.

Note that one model simplification here is that every edge is assumed to switch once per evaluation. This is essentially making a worst-case assumption about switching. Said another way, we assume homogeneous activity on all edges in the graph. That is, the asymptotic results are unchanged if we say every edge switches 10% of the time. Consequently, we will not specifically reason about variable activity on the netlist graph. Prior work has addressed heterogeneous net activity (See Sec. 10), and treatment of heterogeneous net activity for this model is an important direction to extend our results (Sec. 11).

Since we assume $k$ is a constant, every node is of size $O(1)$ and will require $O(1)$ energy per cycle simply to perform the

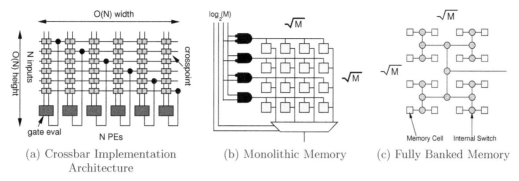

(a) Crossbar Implementation
Architecture

(b) Monolithic Memory

(c) Fully Banked Memory

Figure 1: Crossbar and Memory Organizations

gate evaluation. Since we assume every gate evaluates and potentially switches its output on every cycle, we must, at least, pay energy for the $N$ gates for each evaluation of the netlist. *This means $\Omega(N)$ is a lower bound on the energy that will be required to evaluate the netlist.*

## 3.2 VLSI Area and Energy Model

We focus on the energy of operations. However, since the energy for a physical wire will depend on the length of the wire, it is also important that we carefully account for area and lengths in the implementation. All gates used in the implementations have $O(1)$ inputs, and hence $O(1)$ area and width. Each wire has $O(1)$ width, and we initially assume $O(1)$ wire layers, so that it takes $O(w)$ width to layout $w$ wires leaving a region of the chip. Energy per fanin, gate switch, or unit length of wire is $O(1)$. Consequently, energy of a physical net is proportional to its total wire length.

## 3.3 Asynchronous Evaluation

In a combinational circuit implementation, glitches might make the activity on a node greater than 1.0 [18]. That is, the inputs to a gate might change at different times causing the output to switch multiple times per circuit evaluation. As a partial justification of the homogeneous switching model, we note that an asynchronous implementation of the gate that performs a handshake with the inputs can guarantee $O(1)$ switching without changing the asymptotic size of the implementation or number of switching events. If CAD and tuning (*e.g.* [18]) can adequately control glitching, the asynchronous assumption is not necessary to achieve the bounds derived for the fully spatial designs (including traditional FPGAs) (Sec. 7.2 and 8). However, as we will see starting in Sec. 4.2.3, the asynchronous handshaking is necessary to achieving the tightest bounds derived in this paper for the sequential and multicontext designs.

## 4. SIMPLE STARTING POINTS

We start by analyzing the simplest, most direct architectures for implementing the gate array evaluation model (Sec. 3.1). We see that these are much more expensive than the $\Omega(N)$ lower bound.

## 4.1 Full Crossbar

For a full crossbar implementation of the gate array evaluation model, we arrange the gates in a line of size $N$ at the outputs of the crossbar (See Fig. 1(a)). Since each gate has at most $k$ inputs, there are at most $kN$ outputs from the crossbar feeding into the gates. Except for the circuit

outputs, each gate output is fed back into the crossbar. As a result, the crossbar has $N$ inputs by $kN$ outputs, for a total area that is $O(N^2)$. Significantly, every output drives a wire of length $O(N)$ and every input is of length $O(N)$. A memory cell at each crossbar crosspoint can hold its configuration without changing the asymptotic size of the crossbar. The energy of evaluation for each gate is $O(N)$ to drive its output, plus $O(1)$ for the gate evaluation, plus $O(N)$ for its $k$ inputs to be driven for a total energy of $O(N)$. Evaluating $N$ gates means a total of $O(N^2)$ energy—a factor of $N$ larger than the lower bound of $\Omega(N)$.

## 4.2 Memory

The crossbar is known to be area expensive because we dedicate a physical connection for every edge in the graph and a physical gate for every vertex. We should be able to store the state in the graph and the description of the edges more compactly in memories. In particular, the vertex outputs require at most $O(N)$ memory locations. If we give each of the $N$ vertices a $\log_2(N)$ bit address, we can describe the connectivity in the graph with $O(N\log(N))$ bits of memory. In order to develop models for architectures that exploit memories, in this section, we characterize the asymptotic energy requirements of memories.

### 4.2.1 Monolithic

The simplest case is a monolithic memory bank where we store $M$ bits in one large array. We arrange the $M$ bits into a $\sqrt{M} \times \sqrt{M}$ array and use $\log_2(M)$ bits to specify the bit in the array (Fig. 1(b)). This address is broken in half with $\log_2(M)/2$ bits specifying the row address and $\log_2(M)/2$ bits specifying the column address. This organization allows each memory bit to take up $O(1)$ area in the middle of the array. Each memory bit also contributes $O(1)$ capacitance, and hence energy, to the row select and column read lines. Reading out of the core of the memory takes $O(\sqrt{M})$ energy to drive the single activated row select line and $O(\sqrt{M})$ to drive each column read line. Since there are $O(\sqrt{M})$ column read lines, this is a total of $O(M)$ energy. Selecting the row line demands driving $O(\log(M))$ lines of length $O(\sqrt{M})$ for $O(\log(M)\sqrt{M})$ and $O(\log(M)\sqrt{M})$ energy in gates, asymptotically less energy than the $O(M)$ energy in the core. Performing the final bit selection from the $O(\sqrt{M})$ column results takes $O(\sqrt{M})$ energy for a mux tree reduction and less than $O(\log(M)\sqrt{M})$ to connect the column address lines to the muxes; both of these are also asymptotically less than the $O(M)$ energy in the core. Con-

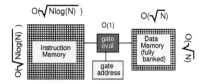

**Figure 3: Processor with Memory Organization**

sequently, a memory read takes $O(M)$ energy to obtain each randomly accessed bit.

### 4.2.2 Sequential Access

Accessing a single bit is potentially wasteful since we pay energy to bring $\sqrt{M}$ bits out of the array core, but only use one. If we can arrange to read the memory sequentially, we can amortize the energy reading from the array core across all the $\sqrt{M}$ bits read. In particular, instead of using a multiplexer to select the column, we read the column bits into a shift register. We then shift the bits serially out of the shift register. For this case, we perform one read from the core that still takes $O(M)$ energy. For each of the $\sqrt{M}$ bits read, we shift the shift register for a cost of $O(\sqrt{M})$. After $\sqrt{M}$ shifts, we have spent $\sqrt{M} \times O(\sqrt{M}) = O(M)$ energy on the shifts and $O(M)$ energy on the read from the core or a total of $O(M)$ energy. Each bit thus costs us $O(\sqrt{M})$ energy.

Sequential access is an important component of "spatial locality" as the term is used for processor caches. Otherwise, the processor cache use of "spatial locality" is, at best, loosely related to the physical spatial locality developed in the rest of this paper (Secs. 5–7).

### 4.2.3 Fully Banked

Random access into the monolithic memory (Sec. 4.2.1) suffers because we must activate the entire memory. We can reduce the energy by breaking the memory into separate banks and only activating the bank that stores the data being addressed. For example, simply breaking the memory into two banks, means we activate a memory core of half the size and hence half the energy. We do have to pay some energy controlling bank selection, but that is on the order of the address selection $O(\log(M)\sqrt{M})$, which is small compared to compared to the energy of the cores $O(M)$. To get an asymptotic benefit, we recursively subdivide the memory banks, building a tree-based memory access.

Constructively, we layout the fully banked memory as an H-tree (Fig. 1(c)). The leaves of the H-tree are the memory cells of size $O(1)$. Each internal tree node in the H-tree is of size $O(1)$ and serves to route addresses down to the leaves and route results out of the H-tree. The entire H-tree is of size $O(M)$, since the number of internal nodes is also $O(M)$ and the wiring only spreads the leaves and internal nodes by $O(1)$. We cannot afford to clock the memory access tree as that would take $O(M)$ energy per cycle. If we clocked operation at each level of the tree, that would mean $O(M \log(M))$ energy, which is greater than the monolithic memory. Instead, we use asynchronous handshaking at each tree node and are careful to only send address bits down the necessary branch of the tree. Addresses are fed in serially from the top. The first address bit is used by the root node and sets the tree node to send down the left or right branch as appropriate. The remaining address bits follow through the root, each setting the internal node one level

down the tree. When the path reaches a leaf node, the value from the leaf is sent back up the tree. As a result, we send $\log(M)$ bits down through the top node, $\log(M) - 1$ through the next, $\log(M) - 2$ through the next, and eventually one bit to the final internal node above the leaf. Each of these $\log(M)$ active internal nodes then sees one bit coming back out. This means $O(\log^2(M))$ energy spent by the switching gates within the tree. However, we must also account for the energy on the wires. The wires at the top of the tree are of length $\sqrt{M}$. Roughly, the wires at the next level are $\sqrt{M}$ as well. At the following level, the wires have length $\sqrt{M}/2$.

$$
\begin{aligned}
E_{wire} &= \sqrt{M} \sum_{i=0}^{\log_2(M)} \left( i \times \frac{1}{2^{\lceil (\log_2(M)-i)/2 \rceil}} \right) \\
&\leq \log_2(M)\sqrt{M} \sum_{i=0}^{\log_2(M)} \left( \frac{1}{2^{\lceil i/2 \rceil}} \right) \\
&\leq \log_2(M)\sqrt{M} \sum_{i=0}^{\log_2(M)/2} \left( \frac{2}{2^i} \right) \quad (1)
\end{aligned}
$$

The sum is a geometric series that converges to $O(1)$,[1] so we have:

$$
E_{wire} \leq O(\log_2(M)\sqrt{M}) \quad (2)
$$

Wire energy asymptotically dominates gate energy, so the total energy for a bit read from this fully banked memory is $O(\log(M)\sqrt{M})$, which is asymptotically smaller than the bit read energy for a monolithic memory. Writes behave similarly and take the same asymptotic energy.

## 4.3 Processor with Memory

A simple, sequential case might store the graph description in one memory (instruction memory) and the data value of each gate in another (data memory) as shown in Fig. 3. The sequential processor would process the graph in topological order. For each node, it would:

1. read the gate description from the instruction memory $= 2^k$ bits $= O(1)$ bits since we take $k$ to be a constant
2. read the address of each of the $k$ inputs from the instruction memory; since there are $O(N)$ sources, this is $k\log(N)$ or $O(\log(N))$ bits
3. read the $k$ input bits from the data memory
4. perform the gate evaluation
5. store the result into the current gate address in the data memory
6. increment the gate address

Each vertex requires $O(\log(N))$ bits to specify its inputs, so the total instruction memory holds $O(N \log(N))$ bits. The instruction memory is accessed sequentially, so it can use the more efficient sequential access pattern into memory (Sec. 4.2.2). The data memory only holds $O(N)$ bits, but these must be accessed randomly, so we use a fully banked memory (Sec. 4.2.3). The instruction memory reads (operations 1 and 2) take $O(\log(N)\sqrt{N \log(N)})$ energy. The data memory reads (operation 3) and write (operation 5) take $O(\log(N)\sqrt{N})$. The gate evaluation (operation 4) takes $O(1)$ energy, and the gate address increment (operation 6) takes $O(\log(N))$. Instruction memory dominates, such that

---

[1]Throughout, we make use of the relationship: $a\left(1 + r + r^2 + \ldots\right) \leq \frac{a}{1-r}$ when $r < 1$.

each memory read takes $O(\log^{1.5}(N)\sqrt{N})$. Processing the entire graph with $N$ nodes takes $O((N\log(N))^{1.5})$.

If we had used a monolithic memory instead of the fully banked memory for the data memory, the data memory would have dominated with energy $O(N)$, for a total energy of $O(N^2)$—comparable to the crossbar.

# 5. DESCRIPTION LOCALITY

The analysis in the previous section assumes each input to a vertex may come from any other vertex. However, in typical circuits, we expect a certain amount of locality. Most inputs will come from a subset of the vertices that can be made close to the gate. In circuit design, including the design of FPGA architectures [7, 8, 16], it is typical to characterize this locality using Rent's Rule [19] which says the number of wires that exit a region containing $N$ gates is proportional to a fractional power of the gates in the region:

$$IO = cN^p \qquad (3)$$

This can be directly mapped to Leighton's $\alpha$-bifurcator definition [2]. Both characterizations recursively bisect designs minimizing the cut size between regions and use the cut sizes out of each subregion to characterize the locality. In both cases, they suggest a geometric relationship on the cut sizes at successive tree levels in the recursive bisection.

For designs with locality where $p < 1$, not all edges are cut by the top bisection. In particular, only $cN^p$ edges are cut. These edges cut by the top bisection will need all $\log_2(N)$ bits to describe their source. However, the other edges are contained in smaller subtrees and can use fewer bits. This can be used to show that the total number of bits needed to specify routing is $O(N)$ [8]. The number of bits required to specify an edge is proportional to the logarithm of the capacity of the smallest subtree that contains the edge. We can count the number of bits required by charging each edge for each subtree it must exit. That is, when a graph edge needs to cross out of the top of a tree at level $i$, we need one bit to specify which way the edge connects at that tree level. Thus we need:

$$N_{bits} = \sum_{i=0}^{\log_2(N)} \left( \frac{N}{2^i} \times c \left(2^i\right)^p \right) \qquad (4)$$

The first term $\frac{N}{2^i}$ is the number of subtrees at height $i$ from the leaf, while the second term is Rent's Rule (Eq. 3) applied to the size of the subtree $(2^i)$. Pulling out $c$ and $N$ and combining the $2^i$ terms we get:

$$N_{bits} = cN \sum_{i=0}^{\log_2(N)} \left( \left(2^i\right)^{(p-1)} \right) \qquad (5)$$

For $p = 1$, the term being summed is one, so $N_{bits}$ becomes $O(N\log(N))$ as we saw in the previous section when we did not assume any locality. However, when $p < 1$, the exponent $p - 1$ is less than one, making the term being summed a fraction that decreases geometrically with $i$. As a result, the sum converges to $O(1)$, and we have $N_{bits}=O(N)$.

**Impact on Processor Case** If we exploit this locality when $p < 1$, the instruction memory in the processor (Sec. 4.3) only needs to be of size $O(N)$. This reduces the area for the processor to $O(N)$. Furthermore, the total bits read from the instruction memory will be $O(N)$ instead of $O(N\log(N))$. The total instruction memory energy reduces

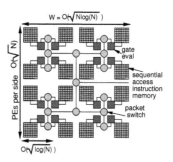

**Figure 4: Sequential Communication Exploiting Data Locality**

from $O((N\log(N))^{1.5})$ to $O(N^{1.5})$. The data memory energy of $O(\sqrt{N}\log(N))$ per gate means a total energy across all $N$ gates of $O(N^{1.5}\log(N))$ which now dominates instruction energy and determines the asymptotic energy of operation. *Exploiting description locality saves us a factor of* $\sqrt{\log(N)}$.

# 6. DATA LOCALITY

After exploiting description locality, the dominant energy arises from accessing the data memory. Here, since we bring the data to a single location to evaluate the gate, we must pay $O(\sqrt{N}\log(N))$ energy for every data fetch from the banked memory. That is, we are **not** exploiting any locality in movement of the data.

Alternately, we can perform the gate evaluation at different places and arrange the data for minimal movement. Again, we consider performing the recursive bisection of the graph to minimize cut sizes for Rent's Rule. Each node lives at the leaf of a tree. We layout the tree as an H-Tree (Fig. 4). For this case, we additionally limit the fanout associated with a node to $k$ (See Sec. 6.1). At the leaf associated with a node we include:

1. asynchronous logic to recognize when all $k$ inputs have arrived = $O(1)$
2. storage space for the $k$ inputs to each gate = $O(1)$
3. the description of the behavior of the gate = $O(1)$
4. memory to store the address of the $k$ successors to the gate = $O(\log(N))$

Since each leaf node needs $O(\log(N))$ memory, the entire structure requires area $O(N\log(N))$. If we did not limit the fanout to a constant, we could not guarantee the node memories could be this small.

All links in the H-tree are $O(1)$ wide so that the H-tree has the same asymptotic area as the leaves. The internal nodes in the tree serve as a bit-serial, packet-switched network. This is similar to the fully banked memory, except that routing bits are needed both to route up the tree to the point of cross-over and back down. Since the path up the tree is the same length as the path back down, adding bits to route up the tree does not asymptotically change the number of bits needed to address a destination.

Each leaf node behaves as follows:

1. wait for all inputs to arrive
2. evaluate gate
3. send result bit to all $\leq k$ successor vertices; this also depends on the fanout limit.

Evaluation energy at the leaf nodes remains $O(1)$ per node or $O(N)$ total. We can sequentially access the successor gate address memory. We must read $O(\log(N))$ bits at energy $O(\sqrt{\log(N)})$ per read, for a total of $O(\log^{1.5}(N))$ energy per node or $O(N \log^{1.5}(N))$ energy to perform these reads from all nodes.[2] This leaves the energy required to route the data to the successors over the H-tree network. Here, we must account for the number of edges that must be routed to each height in the tree, the bits that specify the destination, and the lengths of the wires at each level in the tree.

- There are $\frac{N}{2^i}$ subtrees at height $i$ from the leaf.
- By Rent's Rule, we know we have $c\left(2^i\right)^p$ edges that must cross out of each of those subtrees.
- The number of bits in an address will be less than $\log(N)$; for simplicity, we make no further attempt to account for the fact that many stages see fewer bits.
- The length of the top wire in the tree is $O(\sqrt{N \log(N)})$.
- Wire lengths halve every other stage as noted for the fully banked memory.

Putting this together, we get:

$$
\begin{aligned}
E_{comm} &\leq \sum_{i=0}^{\log_2(N)} \left( \frac{N}{2^i} \times c\left(2^i\right)^p \times \log(N) \right. \\
&\qquad\qquad \left. \times O\left(2^{\lceil i/2 \rceil} \sqrt{\log(N)}\right) \right) \\
&\leq O(N \log^{1.5}(N)) \sum_{i=0}^{\lceil \log_2(N)/2 \rceil} \left( \left(2^i\right)^{(2p-1)} \right)
\end{aligned}
$$

For $p = 0.5$, the term in the sum is one, making the total:

$$
E_{comm}(p = 0.5) \leq O(N \log^{2.5}(N)) \qquad (6)
$$

For $p > 0.5$, the sum is largest at the maximum value of $i = \lceil \log_2(N)/2 \rceil$ where it evaluates to $O(N^{p-0.5})$. The other terms recede geometrically from the maximum value, so the entire sum comes to $O(N^{p-0.5})$. As a result, we have:

$$
E_{comm}(p > 0.5) \leq O(N^{p+0.5} \log^{1.5}(N)) \qquad (7)
$$

At $p = 1$, this is $O(\sqrt{\log(N)})$ larger than the memory case in Sec. 5 due to the area increase to hold $O(N \log(N))$ bits for the description; however, for any $p < 1$, the benefit from locality of data movement is greater, and this is scheme has asymptotically lower energy. *Picking spatial locations for computations and moving the data minimally to these locations saves a factor of $O(N^{(1-p)}/\sqrt{\log(N)})$.* For $p < 0.5$, the sum is largest at the minimum value of $i = 0$ where it evaluates to one. Again, the other terms form a receding geometric sum as $i$ increases, so the summation comes to $O(1)$. For $p < 0.5$, we have:

$$
E_{comm}(p < 0.5) \leq O(N \log^{1.5}(N)) \qquad (8)
$$

In all cases this data communication energy equals or dominates gate evaluation and memory read energy.

## 6.1 Fanout Limit

Imposing a fanout bound does not limit the netlists we can support nor change the asymptotic results. We can transform any netlist with bounded fanin and unbounded

---

[2] Strictly speaking, by exploiting the description locality, we read a total of $O(N)$ successor address bits rather than $O(N \log(N))$ when $p < 1$, so, the total energy is $O(N\sqrt{\log(N)})$ for $p < 1$, but this doesn't change the total asymptotic result that follows since the data movement term dominates the asymptotic energy use.

fanout into one with bounded fanout without asymptotically changing the number of nodes in the network or its depth [14]. Roughly, an $N$ node graph with a fanin bound of $k$ and unbounded fanout can be transformed into a graph with a bounded fanout of $k$ that has no more than $2N$ nodes. Consequently, the asymptotic results here hold even if we think about starting with a netlist with unbounded fanout.

## 7. INSTRUCTION LOCALITY

While data communication locality reduces the cost of communication, we spend more energy providing the address for routing the data than we do for actually sending the data. Furthermore, we are forced to give up the full area compactness of description locality. Instead of storing the location address bits at the leaves, we can save additional energy by storing the routing bits in the tree local to the switches that they control.

### 7.1 Sequential

Starting with the sequential case from the previous section, storing the configuration in the tree means we time-multiplex the switches rather than packet switching with route addresses stored at the leaves. Each internal switch at level $i$ now has a memory of size $O\left(\left(2^i\right)^p\right)$ to tell it the sequence of configurations it must perform in order to route the data (See Fig. 5(a)). The switches remain asynchronous. Each switch reads $O(1)$ bits form the memory to tell it the next route operation to perform, waits for input to arrive on the specified source, handshakes with the source, switches the input data to the specified output, and handshakes with the destination LUT or switch. The Rent's Rule subtree IO model already captures fanout effects. That is, some switches may switch data out two sides, and this effect is already accounted for in the Rent IO of the subtrees to which they connect. Consequently, it is not necessary to assume bounded fanout as in Sec. 6 for the designs in this section and the next (Sec. 8). Each LUT at the leaf waits for all inputs to arrive, computes the result, and sends the result.

To achieve the $O(\sqrt{M})$ energy for reading from each of the switch memory banks, we must layout the switch memories as a square. This means that the width of the switch at tree level $i$ becomes $O(\sqrt{(2^i)^p})$. For $i = \log_2(N)$, there is one switch width at the root of the tree. Every two tree levels, we double the number of switch widths we must accommodate across the width. Consequently, the width of the tree of capacity $N$ becomes:

$$
\begin{aligned}
W &= \sum_{i=0}^{\log_2(N)/2} \left( \frac{\sqrt{N}}{2^i} \times O\left(\sqrt{(2^{2i})^p}\right) \right) \\
&= \sqrt{N} \sum_{i=0}^{\log_2(N)/2} \left( O\left(\left(2^i\right)^{p-1}\right) \right) \qquad (9)
\end{aligned}
$$

For $p < 1$, this is a receding geometric sum, so we have $W = O(\sqrt{N})$. This tells us that the entire design requires only $A = W^2 = O(N)$ area. It further tells us that the wire lengths for each subtree of capacity $N$ are only $O(\sqrt{N})$, asymptotically the same as if we did not have memories embedded in the tree.

The energy of operation is now composed of:
- Energy per gate evaluation = $O(1)$ per gate.
- Energy for each communication link including the energy reading from the switch instruction memory. At

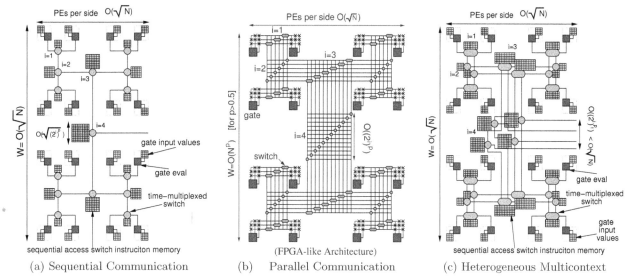

| (a) Sequential Communication | (b) Parallel Communication | (c) Heterogeneous Multicontext |

**Figure 5: Instruction Locality Architectures**

level $i$ of the tree, we drive a wire of length $O(\sqrt{2^i})$ and spend memory read energy $O(\sqrt{(2^i)^p})$. Since $p < 1$, the energy reading from the memory is less than the energy driving the wire, so the energy per link at level $i$ is $O(\sqrt{2^i})$.

We perform a similar sum to the previous section to account for the number of switches of a given height, the wirelengths driven by each switch height, and the number of edges that must be switched through that switch height.

$$E_{comm} \leq \sum_{i=0}^{\log_2(N)} \left( \frac{N}{2^i} \times c\left(2^i\right)^p \times O\left(2^{\lceil i/2 \rceil}\right) \right)$$

$$\leq O(N) \sum_{i=0}^{\log_2(N)} \left( O\left( \left(2^i\right)^{p-0.5} \right) \right) \quad (10)$$

For $p = 0.5$, the term in the sum is $O(1)$, so the communication energy, and hence total energy, is $O(N \log(N))$. For $p < 0.5$, $p - 0.5 < 0$, so the sum converges to $O(1)$ and the communication and total energy is $O(N)$; since this matches the lower bound of $\Omega(N)$, we can conclude the $p < 0.5$ case requires $\Theta(N)$ energy. For $p > 0.5$, the term in the sum is maximum at $i = \log_2(N)$ and takes on the value $O(N^{p-0.5})$. As $i$ decreases, the terms are geometrically smaller, so the sum converges to $O(N^{p-0.5})$, making communication and total energy $O(N^{p+0.5})$. *Keeping the instructions local to the switches they are configuring saves a factor of $O(\log^{1.5}(N))$ and achieves asymptotically optimal energy for $p < 0.5$.*

## 7.2 Parallel (FPGA)

Alternately, we can dedicate spatial wiring for each edge in the graph. This gives us an architecture analogous to an FPGA. To simplify analysis and build on the designs and calculations we have already performed, we consider a butterfly fat-tree-based spatial interconnect [13, 28]. Instead of having a single wire from each subtree, and hence a single switch linking subtrees, we have a number of switches proportional to the Rent's Rule proscribed IO for each subtree (See Fig. 5(b)). Switches are passively configured with $O(1)$ local configuration bits; as with an FPGA these are continuously applied rather than being read from memory.

As such, switches simply pass values combinationally; there is no need for any sequenced behavior. Gates at the leaves perform as in the sequential case, waiting for all inputs to arrive, computing the output, handshaking with the inputs and handshaking with the outputs.

Again, we start by assessing the width of the entire tree. The width of each of the switch groups combining subtrees at height $i$ is now $O\left((2^i)^p\right)$ instead of $O(\sqrt{(2^i)^p})$, but the number of switch groups across the width remains the same. We get a width:

$$W = \sum_{i=0}^{\log_2(N)/2} \left( \frac{\sqrt{N}}{2^i} O\left(2^{2pi}\right) \right) = \sqrt{N} \sum_{i=0}^{\log_2(N)/2} \left( \left(2^i\right)^{2p-1} \right)$$

For $p < 0.5$, the sum converges to $O(1)$, for $p = 0.5$, it converges to $O(\log(N))$, and for $1.0 > p > 0.5$, it becomes $O(N^{p-0.5})$. This makes the width $O(\sqrt{N})$, $O(\log(N)\sqrt{N})$, and $O(N^p)$, respectively, and area $O(N)$, $O(N \log(N))$, and $O(N^{2p})$.

With these lengths, we can calculate communication energy. *The $p < 0.5$ case is the same as the previous sum (Eq. 10), so also achieves $O(N)$ communication energy and $\Theta(N)$ total energy.* The $p > 0.5$ case becomes:

$$E_{comm}(p > 0.5) \leq \sum_{i=0}^{\log_2(N)} \left( \frac{N}{2^i} \times c\left(2^i\right)^p \times O\left(\left(2^i\right)^p\right) \right)$$

$$\leq O(N) \sum_{i=0}^{\log_2(N)} \left( O\left( \left(2^i\right)^{2p-1} \right) \right)$$

The sum converges to $O(N^{2p-1})$ bringing communication and total energy to $O(N^{2p})$. For $p = 0.5$, we get:

$$E_{comm} \leq \sum_{i=0}^{\log_2(N)} \left( \frac{N}{2^i} \times c\left(2^i\right)^{0.5} \times O\left( \left(2^{\lceil i/2 \rceil}\right) \log(2^i) \right) \right)$$

$$\leq O(N) \sum_{i=0}^{\log_2(N)} \left( O\left(i\right) \right)$$

The sum converges to $O\left(\log^2(N)\right)$, and hence communication and total energy converge to $O(N \log^2(N))$. *For*

$p \geq 0.5$, *the energy requirements are asymptotically larger than the sequential case in the previous section due to the larger area and hence longer wires.*

If CAD mapping can avoid glitching, or limit it to a constant effect, this fully parallel design could be synchronous without damaging the asymptotic result; only the registers at the leaves need to be clocked, and they only need to be clocked once per evaluation cycle. This can be done with no more than $O(N + W \times \sqrt{N}) = O(N + N^{p+0.5})$ energy, which is no larger than the communication energy.

## 7.3 Multicontext

The fully spatial, fully parallel, FPGA-like case requires asymptotically more energy than the sequential locality case (Sec. 7.1) when the spatial case requires asymptotically more area and hence asymptotically longer wires. Note that the $p < 0.5$ case that did not require asymptotically longer wires did not require asymptotically more energy. This suggests that we might be able to achieve the same asymptotically low energy as the sequential case without giving up all communication parallelism. However, we must be careful not to include too much communication hardware.

Specifically, the previous case suggests that as long as the number of wires at a tree root grows as $O\left(\left(2^i\right)^{p_t}\right)$ with $p_t < 0.5$, we can keep the side length of the tree to $O(\sqrt{2^i})$. Consequently, we build a tree with $p_t < 0.5$ and provide the same asynchronous context memories for the upper level switches as we did in the sequential case (Sec. 7.1) as shown in Fig. 5(c). However, we size these memories based on their required wire sharing. The memory for a switch at the root of a tree at level $i$ must be have $O\left(\max\left(1, \frac{(2^i)^p}{(2^i)^{p_t}}\right)\right)$. For the interesting cases where $p > p_t$, this is: $O((2^i)^{p-p_t})$. *This means that the switches have heterogeneous context depth, increasing toward the root of the tree where edge growth exceeds available 2D wiring.* Switching behavior is the same as the sequential case except that some tree switches have multiple physical parent connections like the spatial case.

The designs fits in $O(N)$ area with width $O(\sqrt{N})$ and the same asymptotic energy as the sequential case. To properly demonstrate this result we need to:

1. validate memory area is asymptotically small enough: At height $i$, the wire width for the channel is $O\left(\left(2^i\right)^{p_t}\right)$ and the height of the channel is $O(\sqrt{2^i})$. This gives area $O\left(\left(2^i\right)^{p_t+0.5}\right)$. Each of the $O\left(\left(2^i\right)^{p_t}\right)$ memories is of size $O\left(\left(2^i\right)^{p-p_t}\right)$ for a total area of $O\left(\left(2^i\right)^p\right)$, which is less than $O\left(\left(2^i\right)^{p_t+0.5}\right)$ as long as $p < p_t+0.5$. We can guarantee this holds by selecting $p_t \geq p - 0.5$, which we can do and keep $p_t < 0.5$ for any $p < 1$.

2. make sure we can place and route to the memories without changing the asymptotic area or side lengths: The previous calculation assumed that we could pack switches anywhere in the channel. This is possible if we can route the signals from the lower channel to the point of the switch. Since the number of wires from the lower channel are within a constant factor of the number of wires in a channel, if we space out the root wires to allow the lower channel wires to route alongside them to the point where the switch is placed, it only makes the channel a constant amount wider,

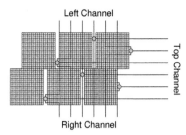

**Figure 6: Routing to Multicontext Memories**

thus leaving the asymptotic channel width unchanged (See Fig. 6).

3. account for the read energy from memories: The read energy for a switch at level $i$, $O(\sqrt{(2^i)^{p-p_t}})$, is never greater than the $O(\sqrt{2^i})$ energy of the associated wire.

4. account for the communication energy: This is the same as the sequential case since the wire lengths are asymptotically the same length.

*When limited to $O(1)$ metal layers for planar VLSI, this heterogeneous, multicontext FPGA saves $O(N^{p-0.5})$ compared to a fully spatial FPGA that allocates a wire for every edge, achieving the same asymptotic energy as the sequential case.*

## 8. MULTILEVEL METALIZATION

The fully spatial, FPGA-like case with $p \geq 0.5$ consumed more energy than the sequential case because the wires grew asymptotically longer. This is driven by growing channel widths when limited to a constant number of wire layers. *If we can instead use a suitably growing number of wire layers, we can avoid this cost and achieve the same asymptotic energy as the sequential instruction locality case (Sec. 7.1).* In particular, if the wire layers grow as $O((2^i)^{p-p_{2D}})$, where $p_{2D} < 0.5$, we can keep the 2D channel widths down to $O((2^i)^{p_{2D}})$. We must account for both the 2D and z-axis wire lengths in routing, but if we pick $p_{2D} \geq p/2$, the z-axis wire length of $O((2^i)^{p-p_{2D}})$ is never greater than the planar wire length of $O((2^i)^{p_{2D}})$. For $p < 1$, we can pick a $p_{2D} < 0.5$ that satisfies that constraint, so the total wire energy remains asymptotically the same as the sequential and multicontext case. We must guarantee that we can perfectly use the additional wire layers. DeHon and Rubin showed that this was possible using a Mesh-of-Trees interconnect structure [9]. As with the $O(1)$ metal layer FPGA, if we can contain glitching effects, the asynchronous assumption is not necessary to achieve this bound. The total clock energy would only be $O(N)$ per evaluation cycle.

## 9. LESSONS

Table 1 summarizes the asymptotic bounds developed in this paper. It shows a rich landscape where energy reduces both with the exploitation of more locality in the architecture (roughly top to bottom) and with the gate array netlist locality (Rent $p$, left to right). The locality exploitation in FPGAs does give them an asymptotic energy advantage compared to processors. The sequence of optimizations shows that exploiting locality to reduce the distances that edge data travel is a larger benefit than being able to share a single physical compute operator. *Locality exploitation is more important than physical operator sharing.*

Table 1: Asymptotic Energy Required for $N$-node Gate Array Evaluation

| Organization | Locality | Sec. | Asynch. Handshake | Rent Exponent $p$ | | | |
|---|---|---|---|---|---|---|---|
| | | | | 1 | 1>p>0.5 | 0.5 | <0.5 |
| Crossbar | none | 4.1 | No | $O(N^2)$ | | | |
| P Monolithic Mem. | none | 4.3 | No | $O(N^2)$ | | | |
| P Fully Banked | description | 4.3, 5 | Yes | $O\left((N\log(N))^{1.5}\right)$ | $O\left(N^{1.5}\log(N)\right)$ | | |
| Sequential Comm. | data | 6 | Yes | $O\left(N^{p+0.5}\times\log^{1.5}(N)\right)$ | | $O(N\log^{2.5}(N))$ | $O(N\log^{1.5}(N))$ |
| Sequential Comm. | instruction | 7.1 | Yes | $O\left(N^{1.5}\log^{0.5}(N)\right)$ | $O(N^{p+0.5})$ | $O(N\log(N))$ | $\theta(N)$ |
| Parallel (FPGA) | instruction | 7.2 | No | $O\left(N^{2p}\right)$ | | $O(N\log^2(N))$ | $\theta(N)$ |
| Hetero Multicontext | instruction | 7.3 | Yes | $O\left(N^{1.5}\log^{0.5}(N)\right)$ | $O(N^{p+0.5})$ | $O(N\log(N))$ | $\theta(N)$ |
| Multilevel (FPGA) | instruction | 8 | No | $O\left(N^{1.5}\log^{0.5}(N)\right)$ | $O(N^{p+0.5})$ | $O(N\log(N))$ | $\theta(N)$ |

Multicontext designs can have lower energy than FPGAs when the number of metal layers is limited, but the multicontext designs must be organized differently from previous proposal for multicontext FPGAs. *Sharing of interconnect is important for $p \geq 0.5$ (when limited to $O(1)$ metal layers).* We must be careful not to overbuild wiring to the point that it makes wire lengths grow faster than $O(\sqrt{N})$. For constant numbers of metal layers, this means it is beneficial to share interconnection links to keep the layout size down.

*Parallelism is (asymptotically) energy neutral at the architectural level.* At fixed voltages, more parallel solutions demand no more asymptotic energy than sequential ones as long as wire lengths do not grow faster than $O(\sqrt{N})$. If we do have fixed performance goals and allow voltage scaling, the parallel solutions may actually be lower energy, since they can use the parallelism to achieve the performance goal with lower operating voltage.

*Programmability is (asymptotically) energy neutral.* The presence of configuration bits does not impact the asymptotic analysis for the FPGA-like cases (Secs. 7.2 and 8). The constants become smaller, but the asymptotes do not.

## 10. RELATED WORK

Most of the theoretical work on energy complexity deals with activity factors for particular types of computations (*e.g.*, [1, 17]). This is complementary to the current work that addresses general bounds where circuit classes are only differentiated by their locality.

Another class of work specifically deals with energy-time tradeoffs that arise form VLSI circuits (*e.g.*, [22, 3]). These explore the impact of tuning voltage and sizing ($ET^2$), which we did not address in this paper. These tradeoffs are important, but not valid over large enough of a range to be fully asymptotic. These works almost entirely address tradeoffs in specific circuits and do not address architectural tradeoffs for general classes of computations. As such, this tuning is also largely complementary to the work described here.

## 11. OPEN QUESTIONS

The results obtained so far show that there are fundamental reasons that FPGA-like architectures can offer energy advantages. However, there are other phenomena that must be characterized to capture the complete story.

*How large are the associated constants and when do the asymptotes matter?* We have deliberately focused on asymptotic bounds only. Certainly an asynchronous switch is larger than single SRAM cell and the multicontext design is larger than the sequential instruction locality design. It will be useful to establish how large $N$ must be for various asymptotes to matter (*e.g.* when the fully banked design is lower energy than the monolithic memory, when the sequential instruction locality is lower energy than the processor using fully banked memory). Constants will also be necessary to differentiate the energy in the cases that achieve the same asymptotic energy.

Processors have the option to describe a large computation, but only exercise a small portion of it, or to only exercise portions of the computational graph infrequently. Similarly, gates and wires that do not toggle on a cycle need not consume energy if controlled properly. We deliberately assumed homogeneous *activity* to keep the analysis simple and the results general. As the prior theoretical work show (Sec. 10), specific designs have structurally different activities that can be exploited to identify even lower energy bounds. It will be useful to explore a richer model that accounts for non-homogeneous activities and understand how this impacts the energy picture.

GPGPUs, vector processors, and even scalar microprocessor exploit the fact that instructions can often be productively shared across collections of bits (*e.g.* multi-bit words) and across operations (*e.g.* SIMD, SPMD) or reused (*e.g.*, subroutines, looping), such that the operation description is small compared to the bit operations performed. For this work, we assumed that every gate needed a unique instruction. To complete the picture, it will be useful to characterize the impact of this *instruction sharing and reuse* on the asymptotic energy bounds.

This paper has focused on constructive upper bounds. Except for the $p < 0.5$ case where the constructive upper bound matches the trivial *lower bound*, we have not established non-trivial lower bounds on the energy requirements.

## 12. CONCLUSIONS

Asymptotically, communication locality exploitation matters. Architectures that are organized to minimize the movement of data and instructions can operate with asymptotically lower energy than alternatives that do not, including sequential processors that move data from a central memory to a single, shared computational block. This gives FPGA-like designs an inherent energy advantage compared to processors. The same energy advantage can be achieved with designs that share interconnect, but operators and data must be spatially distributed similar to FPGAs. Since communication locality is essential, FPGA-like designs must contain processor to processor wiring distances to $O(\sqrt{N})$ (where $N$ is the capacity of the smallest subtree that includes both processors) to achieve the tightest bounds; designs that allow switching or wiring to grow asymptotically faster will not be able to achieve the lowest energy bounds demonstrated. For designs with moderate locality ($0.5 \leq p < 1.0$), wiring requirements grow too fast to achieve the $O(\sqrt{N})$ distance when limited to a constant number of metal layers. It is necessary to either use multilevel metalization with wiring levels growing sufficiently fast or multicontext designs that contain physical interconnect links below $p_t = 0.5$ in order to achieve the lowest energy bounds identified.

## 13. ACKNOWLEDGMENTS

This work was inspired in part by insights gained from Cory Waxman's time-multiplexed FPGA energy modelling effort. This research was funded in part by National Science Foundation grant CCF-0904577. Any opinions, findings, and conclusions or recommendations expressed in this material are those of the authors and do not necessarily reflect the views of the National Science Foundation.

## 14. REFERENCES

[1] A. A. Ashok, Chandra, and P. Raghavan. Energy consumption in VLSI circuits. In *Proceedings of the ACM symposium on Theory of computing*, pages 205–216, 1988. 10

[2] S. Bhatt and F. T. Leighton. A framework for solving VLSI graph layout problems. *Journal of Computer System Sciences*, 28:300–343, 1984. 2.3, 5

[3] B. D. Bingham and M. R. Greenstreet. Modeling energy-time trade-offs in VLSI computation. *IEEE Trans. Comput.*, 61(4):530–547, April 2012. 10

[4] M. Budiu, G. Venkataramani, T. Chelcea, and S. C. Goldstein. Spatial computation. In *Proc. ASPLOS*, pages 14–26, 2004. 2.2

[5] W. J. Dally, J. Balfour, D. Black-Shaffer, J. Chen, R. C. Harting, V. Parikh, J. Park, and D. Sheffield. Efficient embedded computing. *IEEE Computer*, 41(7):27–32, July 2008. 2.2

[6] A. DeHon. DPGA utilization and application. In *FPGA*, pages 115–121, February 1996. 1

[7] A. DeHon. Balancing Interconnect and Computation in a Reconfigurable Computing Array (or, why you don't really want 100% LUT utilization). In *FPGA*, pages 69–78, February 1999. 5

[8] A. DeHon. Rent's Rule Based Switching Requirements. In *Proc. SLIP*, pages 197–204. ACM, March 2001. 5, 5

[9] A. DeHon and R. Rubin. Design of FPGA Interconnect for Multilevel Metalization. *IEEE Trans. VLSI Syst.*, 12(10):1038–1050, October 2004. 8

[10] H. Esmaeilzadeh, E. Blem, R. S. Amant, K. Sankaralingam, and D. Burger. Dark silicon and the end of multicore scaling. In *ISCA*, pages 365–376, 2011. 2.1

[11] D. J. Frank. Power constrained CMOS scaling limits. *IBM J. Res. and Dev.*, 46(2/3):235–244, March 2002. 2.1

[12] S. H. Fuller and L. I. Millett, editors. *The Future of Computing Performance: Game Over or Next Level?* The National Academies Press, 2011. 2.1

[13] R. I. Greenberg and C. E. Leiserson. *Randomness in Computation*, volume 5 of *Advances in Computing Research*, chapter Randomized Routing on Fat-Trees. JAI Press, 1988. Earlier version MIT/LCS/TM-307. 7.2

[14] H. J. Hoover, M. M. Klawe, and N. J. Pippenger. Bounding fan-out in logical networks. *Journal of the ACM*, 31(1):13–18, January 1984. 6.1

[15] M. Horowitz, E. Alon, D. Patil, S. Naffziger, R. Kumar, and K. Bernstein. Scaling, power, and the future of CMOS. In *IEDM*, pages 7–15, December 2005. 2.1

[16] M. Hutton. Interconnect predition for programmable logic devices. In *Proc. SLIP*, pages 125–131, 2001. 5

[17] G. Kissin. Upper and lower bounds on switching energy in VLSI. *JACM*, 38(1):222–254, January 1991. 10

[18] J. Lamoureux, G. G. F. Lemieux, and S. J. E. Wilton. GlitchLess: Dynamic Power Minimization in FPGAs Through Edge Alignment and Glitch Filtering. *IEEE Trans. VLSI Syst.*, 16(11):1521–1534, November 2008. 3.3

[19] B. S. Landman and R. L. Russo. On pin versus block relationship for partitions of logic circuits. *IEEE Transactions on Computers*, 20:1469–1479, 1971. 1, 5

[20] F. T. Leighton. New lower bound techniques for VLSI. In *Proc. Symp. FOCS*, pages 1–12. IEEE, 1981. 2.3

[21] Y. Lin and J. Cong. Power modeling and characteristics of field programmable gate arrays. *IEEE Trans. Computer-Aided Design*, 24(11):1712–1724, November 2005. 1

[22] R. Melhem and R. Graybill, editors. *Power-Aware Computing*, chapter ET$^2$: A Metric For Time and Energy Efficiency of Computation. Kluwer Academic Publishers, 2001. 10

[23] K. Poon, S. Wilton, and A. Yan. A detailed power model for field-programmable gate arrays. *ACM Tr. Des. Auto. of Elec. Sys.*, 10:279–302, 2005. 1

[24] J. E. Savage. Planar circuit complexity and the performance of VLSI algorithms. In *VLSI Systems and Computations*, pages 61–68, 1981. 2.3

[25] G. Stitt, B. Grattan, J. Villarreal, and F. Vahid. Using on-chip configurable logic to reduce embedded system software energy. In *FCCM*, pages 143–151, 2002. 2.2

[26] C. Thompson. Area-time complexity for VLSI. In *Proc. ACM STOC*, pages 81–88, May 1979. 2.3

[27] S. Trimberger, D. Carberry, A. Johnson, and J. Wong. A time-multiplexed FPGA. In *FCCM*, pages 22–28, April 1997. 1, 2.2

[28] W. Tsu, K. Macy, A. Joshi, R. Huang, N. Walker, T. Tung, O. Rowhani, V. George, J. Wawrzynek, and A. DeHon. HSRA: High-Speed, Hierarchical Synchronous Reconfigurable Array. In *FPGA*, pages 125–134, February 1999. 7.2

[29] G. Venkatesh, J. Sampson, N. Goulding, S. Garcia, V. Bryksin, J. Lugo-Martinez, S. Swanson, and M. B. Taylor. Conservation cores: reducing the energy of mature computations. In *Proc. ASPLOS*, pages 205–218, 2010. 2.1, 2.2

# Architectural Enhancements in Stratix V™

David Lewis*, David Cashman*, Mark Chan, Jeffery Chromczak*, Gary Lai,
Andy Lee, Tim Vanderhoek*, Haiming Yu
Altera Corporation, 101 Innovation Drive, San Jose, CA, 95134
(*) Altera Corporation, 150 Bloor St W., Suite 400, Toronto, Ont., Canada M5S 2X9
{dlewis,dcashman,mchan,jchrmomcz,glai,alee,tvanderh,hyu}@altera.com

## Abstract

This paper describes architectural enhancements in the Altera Stratix-V™ FPGA architecture, built on a 28nm TSMC process, together with the data supporting those choices. Among the key features are time borrowing flip-flops, a doubling of the number of flip-flops per LUT compared to previous Stratix architectures, a simplified embedded 20kb dual-port RAM block, and error correction that can correct up to 8 adjacent errors. Arithmetic performance is significantly improved using a fast adder with two levels of multi-bit skip. We also describe how the routing architecture and layout is optimized for the 28nm process to take advantage of a wider range of wire thicknesses offered on the different layers, and improvements in performance and routability are obtained without dramatic changes to the repeated floorplan of the logic plus routing fabric.

## Categories and Subject Descriptors

B.7.1 [Integrated Circuits]

## General Terms

Design

## Keywords

FPGA, logic module, routing

## 1. INTRODUCTION

This paper describes core logic architecture enhancements in the Stratix-V™ FPGA architecture. This device is manufactured in a 28nm CMOS process, in the revision of the Stratix family architecture, which has logic capacity of up to 950K equivalent 4 LUTs. While Moore's law continues to offer native density increases of approximately 2X per generation, this also introduces new challenges for FPGA architecture. The metal RC delay per physical distance increases with process shrink, making it necessary for users to pipeline designs. This both increases the demand for registers, and also the importance of providing high speed long distance routing. Similarly, decreasing SRAM cell size and the increasing number of bits on an FPGA causes an increase in soft errors that needs to be addressed. As designs

grow, taking advantage of the increased logic capacity, memory demand also changes, requiring ongoing optimization of embedded memory architecture every generation. Finally, process technology offers only modest gains for FPGA circuits, requiring that architecture continue to find ways to meaningfully improve performance.

The remainder of the paper is organized as follows. First we give a brief overview of Stratix-style architectures and experimental methodology employed in developing new architectures. Next, in Section 3, we will describe the enhancements made to the logic architecture to improve density and performance of flip-flops. Section 4 describes improvements to LUT-based memory and the overall memory architecture. Some enhancements to the routing fabric are given in Section 5, while Section 6 describes a new architectural structure for faster addition. Section 7 provides conclusions.

## 2. STRATIX™ ARCHITECTURE AND EXPERIMENTAL INFRASTRUCTURE

For background information to help understand the remainder of the paper, we provide a short summary of Stratix-style architectures.

Stratix and Cyclone based architectures use logic elements (LEs) of different types arranged into logic array blocks (LABs). Each LAB contains some number of LEs, which in the case of Stratix II and later are adaptive logic modules (ALMs). The term LAB in this paper also refers to the programmable routing fabric associated with each group of LEs, so throughout this paper, a Stratix LAB means 10 ALMs and all inter-LAB and intra-LAB routing.

Figure 1 shows that LABs and other embedded blocks such as memories and DSP blocks are arranged in a row-column fashion conceptually between the horizontal and vertical routing wires. Each block in the array can communicate with the inter-LAB routing on three of the four sides of the block such that each output can drive onto either of the adjacent vertical routing channels or one horizontal routing channel, and the inputs can receive signals from any of these three channels [2]. Figure 2 illustrates that routing wires are driven by multiplexers called driver input muxes (DIMs), and select inputs from other routing wires to implement stitching and corner turning, as well as the outputs of the LAB. Inputs to the LAB are provided by LAB input muxes (LIMs) which select from the inter-LAB routing wires and drive the LAB lines. Inputs to the LEs are driven by LE input muxes (LEIMs) which select from the LAB lines and outputs from the LEs in that LAB (local lines.)

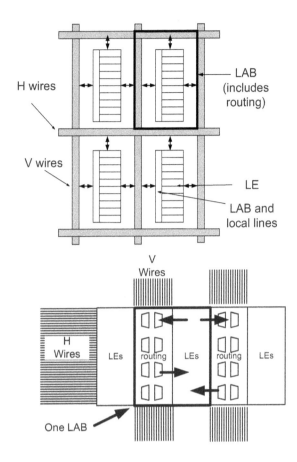

**Figure 1: LAB inputs and outputs connect to 3 routing channels; logical view on top, physically oriented view on bottom. A LAB consists of both logic and routing.**

An adaptive logic module (ALM) contains a 6 LUT that can be fractured into two 5 LUTs [2]. In the case of two 5-LUTs in a single ALM, there must be no more than 8 unique inputs, so that a pair of 5 LUTs must share at least two inputs. In arithmetic modes, the 6-LUT can be used as four 4-LUTs, with two pairs of 4-LUT providing inputs to a two-bit adder. Each pair of 4-LUTs has common inputs. Each LAB contains a number of LEs together with LAB lines that can route signals to the input pins of the various LEs, and local lines that route signals from the output of the LEs to the inputs of LEs in the same LAB. Control signal conditioning selects and conditions wide fanout signals such as clears and clock enables. Figure 2 shows a simplified overview of a LAB, using a 4-LUT LE for simplicity. Note that global signals such as clocks and clears are distributed on separate high speed networks, and brought into the LAB via separate routing muxes or conventional routing, and distributed to the LEs in that LAB.

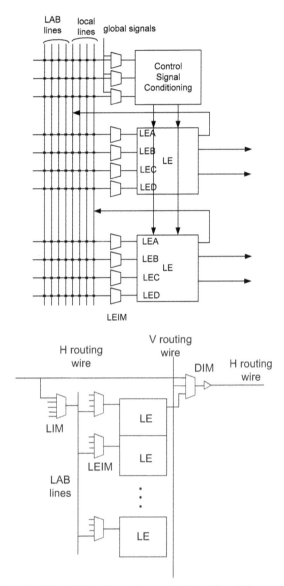

**Figure 2: LEs with local routing on LAB and local lines. Connectivity of LEs and LEIM to DIM and LIM.**

## 2.1 Architecture Evaluation CAD Flow

All CAD experiments in this paper were performed using the FPGA Modeling Toolkit (FMT) which is an extended version of the VPR placement and routing software [1] developed at Altera. A set of customer designs is mapped to the Stratix ALM, memories, and DSP blocks, and placement, routing, and timing analysis is performed. The Altera Quartus II logic synthesis software provides the input, a LUT-level netlist, used in FMT experiments. The FMT is used for the clustering, placement, and routing. The area of the fabric is calculated and an overall area/performance tradeoff is determined.

The experiments described in this paper were performed over a range of time from 2006 onwards using customer designs as well as Altera-generated designs. The circuit set typically comprises 80 to 100 circuits with sizes ranging from 10,000 LUTs to 300,000 equivalent 4-LUTs, with average size of 45,000 LUTs increasing to 110,000 4-LUTs over time. About half of these circuits use DSP blocks.

This paper will present various results that depend on the circuit area of blocks in these architectures. The details of these exact areas are confidential and cannot be disclosed, however the paper does present quantitative results for a number of metrics relevant to the decisions that were made.

## 3. FLIP FLOP ARCHITECTURE

For the Stratix-V architecture, we explored two related aspects of flip-flops in the architecture. Increasing performance requirements has led to deeper pipelining, which increases both the number of flip-flops in designs, as well as the importance of their speed on overall system performance as they contribute a larger fraction of critical path delay in shallower logic.

### 3.1 Flip-Flop Count

To accommodate the increasing demand for flip-flops, we explored increasing the number of flip-flops from 2 to 4 per ALM. Since designs that are dominated by flip-flops are still less common, we avoid increasing the cost of these additional flip-flops with a low cost modification. In particular, since routing pins are relatively expensive, we share the data inputs for the flip-flops with the existing LE inputs as shown in Figure 3. A data mux for each flip-flop allows the flip-flop to select an input that is shared with either one pin on its half-ALM, or an input on the other half-ALM. The former is useful for synchronous loads, such as counters, where a data input is common with a LUT, and the latter for using the flip-flop independently of that half-ALM when the other one is free. This input sharing makes it more difficult to simultaneously use both the LUTs to their fullest extent as well as all four flip-flops, but is a good area/density tradeoff since it avoids adding expensive routing. There are still a total of 8 inputs available to feed one or two LUTs, plus up to four flip-flops. This approach increases LAB cost by only a few percent, but can decrease the LAB count significantly, as shown in the following experiment, which measured the density advantage of the 4 flip-flop/ALM compared to 2 flip-flop /ALM. The design set is packed, placed and routed as usual, and the number of LABs measured for each of the two cases. Figure 4 shows, on the Y-axis, the ratio of LAB count for a 4- flip-flop ALM to a 2- flip-flop ALM for each design in the set. The X-axis gives the ratio of number Flip-flops to LUTS (FF:LUT) for each design. The results show the increasing benefit of more flip-flop intensive designs. Designs with fewer flip-flops than LUTs have small benefit, but flip-flop intensive designs can achieve significant density improvement. Across the entire design set, a 7% reduction in LAB count is achieved. We expect the advantage of the extra flip-flops to increase over time, as more pipelining causes a higher FF:LUT ratio, and future designs will likely be more pipelined as described in the introduction. In designs with FF:LUT ratio larger than 1, an average of 10% LAB count reduction is seen, with reductions up to 28% LAB count at the maximum win. In denser packing modes, performance can be traded for even better LAB count reduction, possibly enabling use of a smaller part.

### 3.2 Time-Borrowing Flip-Flops

A second optimization of the flip-flops in Stratix V contributes to system performance. Performance improvement in FPGAs has been explored using configurable clock skews [14,16,17]. Time borrowing or skew absorbing flip-flops (TBFF) are commonly used in processors to absorb clock skew and jitter [5] [6] and have been used in high performance processors [7] [8]. Pulse latches can also be used to perform small amounts of time borrowing between consecutive sequential paths. The use of latches in FPGAs to support time borrowing has also been explored in [15, 18] with positive results in performance improvement. In contrast to selectively using pulse latches, we provided ubiquitous pulse latches in the Stratix V logic fabric.

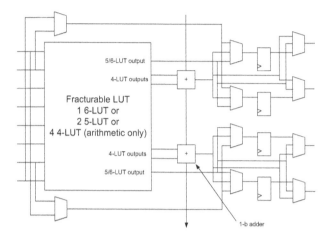

**Figure 3: Stratix V ALM with 4 flip-flops**

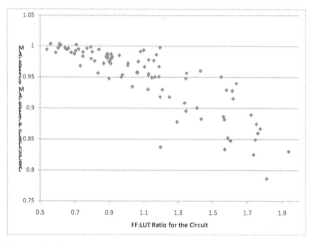

**Figure 4: Scatter plot of LAB count ratio of 4 flip-flop vs 2 flip-flop architecture, vs FF:LUT. Each dot represents one circuit.**

TBFF may be understood either from a physical implementation as a level sensitive latch and pulse generator, or a logical model of it as a conventional edge-triggered flip-flop (ETFF) with adjustable clock skew. Figure 5 shows an schematic of a pulse latch with a configurable pulse width $T_{pw}$. A delay chain with a programmable setting is used to generate a pulse that connects to the enable of a level sensitive latch. n_clk_d is a delayed version of the clock, which is ANDed with the clock to generate the clock pulse cp which enables a level-sensitive latch.

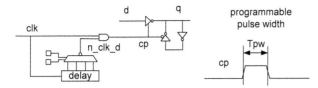

**Figure 5: TBFF implemented as latch with configurable pulse generator.**

Figure 6 (a) and (b) show the timing of a pulse latch for data arrival times before and during the transparent window respectively. cp represents the pulse generated as shown in Figure 5, and it will be assumed that cp rises at t=0. The data arrives at t=a, and the output value launches at t=A. The behavior of the pulse latch is defined by the pulse width $T_{pw}$, the setup time of the latch with respect to falling edge, $T_{sul}$, the clock to out time $T_{cq}$, and the data to out time $T_{dq}$. The data must arrive at least the setup time, $T_{sul}$, before the falling edge of the pulse, as expressed by the constraint:

$$a < T_{pw} - T_{sul}$$

If the data arrival time is in advance of the clock pulse, the output, q, is launched at some time $T_{cq}$ after the clock pulse asserts. If the data arrives while the clock pulse is asserted, then the q launches some constant time $T_{dq}$ later. Simply stated, for a clock pulse starting at t = 0

$$A = \max(T_{cq}, a + T_{dq})$$

The behaviour of a pulse latch can be summarized as:

```
if (a < Tpw – Tsul) then
        if (a > Tcq – Tdq) then
                A = a + Tdq
        else
                A = Tcq
        end
else /* failed setup */
        A = ∞
end
```

This is shown graphically in Fig 6(c), including the region from $T_{cq} - T_{dq}$ to $T_{pw} - T_{sul}$ where the output launch time A increases linearly with the input arrival time a. This has a width of $T_{pw} - T_{sul} + T_{dq} - T_{cq}$ which represents the amount of time that can be borrowed using the pulse latch. Although conventional latch analysis can be used to exactly model latch-based timing, it is possible to present a simpler user model by modeling the TBFF as an edge-triggered flip-flop (ETFF) with a clock skew. The pulse latch can be modeled as an ETFF with a delay line that can be selected arbitrarily in the range shown in Figure 6(d). An ETFF has timing parameters $T_{suf}$ and $T_{co}$ reflecting its setup and hold time ($T_{suf}$ to distinguish from the latch setup time $T_{sul}$.) The modeling of the ETFF in relationship to the pulse latch may be seen by examining the timing with respect to notional clock clk' in Figure 4. To model the ETFF, first observe the case when a is early ($a < T_{cq} - T_{dq}$), so A is at $T_{cq}$ and no time borrowing is required. This corresponds to the ETFF with $T_{pd} = 0$ and $T_{co} = T_{cq}$. When $a > T_{cq} - T_{dq}$, we will borrow time by selecting a notional clock delay $T_{pd}$. $T_{pd}$ is determined by the constraint that $A = a + T_{dq}$, due to latch transparency during this time, and also $A = T_{pd} + T_{co} = T_{pd} + T_{cq}$ to model the ETFF behavior. Therefore $a + T_{dq} = T_{pd} + T_{cq}$, so $T_{pd} = a + T_{dq} - T_{cq}$.

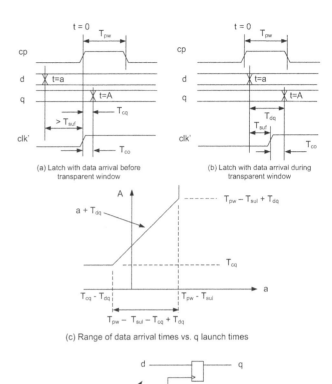

(a) Latch with data arrival before transparent window

(b) Latch with data arrival during transparent window

(c) Range of data arrival times vs. q launch times

(d) Equivalence of pulse latch to ETFF with infinitely precise clock skew

**Figure 6: Timing of TBFF can be modeled as infinitely variable and precise clock delay and ETFF.**

The setup time of the notional ETFF must correspond to having the same total time through the ETFF as the pulse latch, constraining $T_{suf} + T_{co} = T_{dq}$, and since $T_{co} = T_{cq}$, the notional $T_{suf}$ of the ETFF is modeled as $T_{suf} = T_{dq} - T_{cq}$. When the latch is borrowing time, the nominal clk' is positioned $T_{pd} = a + T_{dq} - T_{cq}$, and the output data launches $T_{cq}$ after clk'.

A consequence of the TBFF is increased hold time. The data input must be valid until the falling edge of the pulse, so is $T_{pw}$ plus the hold time of the level sensitive latch, with respect to clk, not clk'.

Figure 7 shows an example of time borrowing with a loop with two unequal combinational delays of 2450ps and 2550ps. With a edge triggered flip-flop and fixed $T_{su} + T_{co}$ of 200ps, the cycle time is limited to the larger of the combinational delays plus the 200ps, or 2750ps. In the example, retaining the total $T_{dq} = 200$ps, but by allowing 50ps to be shifted between the two sequential stages, a cycle time of 2700ps is achieved.

Time borrowing, achieved by using pulse latches, has several advantages compared to configurable clock skewing. As mentioned above, a pulse latch is intrinsically faster than a full ETFF. Second, it is not limited by a finite number of discrete clock delays which restrict the clocks to specific relative delays. Both of these advantages can be captured by modeling the pulse latch as an ETFF plus configurable clock skew. Third, delay chains for clock skewed ETFF contribute to clock cycle uncertainty and must be included in cycle time, while delay chain uncertainty in pulse latches only contributes to hold time. Other advantages also exist, but need more detailed timing analysis than the skewed clock model. Time borrowing can absorb clock uncertainty in the form of both skew and jitter while configurable clock delays cannot. A downside of TBFF compared to clock skews with ETFF is the increased hold time that can negatively affect the ability to borrow time.

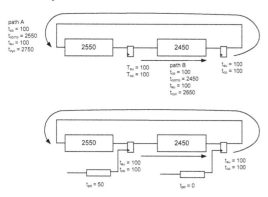

**Figure 7: Using clock skewing with TBFF can balance sequential stages and improve fmax. Top: ETFF has 2750 cycle time; bottom: 50ps is borrowed to reduce cycle time to 2700.**

To evaluate the set of possible pulse widths we performed two experiments. These experiments were performed using Quartus because it has support for hold time timing analysis and avoidance, while FMT does not. Modest modifications to Quartus used the minimum propagation delay to determine the maximum possible hold time, and used this to set the maximum possible $T_{pw}$. Quartus then performed notional clock skewing on each FF to optimize performance, and re-analyzed the timing. Initially, we swept the range of time that can be borrowed. In this experiment we modeled a delay chain with taps every 100ps, and varied the total number of taps. We observed a knee of performance improvement around approximately 200ps, as shown in Figure 8(a). Figure 8(a) also includes the performance increase ignoring hold time requirements. This shows a higher performance, so hold time requirements do reduce the performance improvement achieved using TBFF.

Each tap requires a multiplexer input and hence hardware cost, so it is desirable to use as few taps as possible. A second experiment performed a more detailed investigation of the discrete sets of values to use in the delay chain settings, the results of which are shown in Figure 8(b). Each vertical bar represents a particular combination of possible delay settings that can be selected. Each case also include a minimum pulse width that does not allow any time borrowing. The figure shows performance improvement obtained for each of the sets of possible delay chain settings. Each vertical bar represents the fmax improvement achieved with a particular set of possible configurable delay chain settings for setting $T_{pw}$. Performance is limited due to the need to meet hold time constraints on short routing paths. A single small delay chain setting on the order of 200ps provides the majority of the benefit, with decreasing performance at larger delay chain settings due to hold time.

A TBFF has an additional performance advantage compared to ETFF beyond that provided by time borrowing, since the total $T_{dq}$ is also reduced due the the reduction of logic stages from the data input to the output compared to ETFF. As shown in the simplified circuit in Figure 5, there is potentially only a single inverter delay comprising $T_{dq}$. The use of TBFF provides a performance improvement even without using time borrowing.

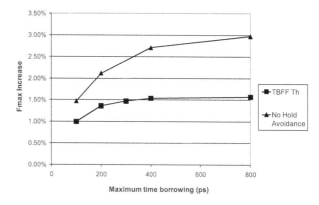

(a) Varying delay with one tap per 100ps, with and without hold time avoidance

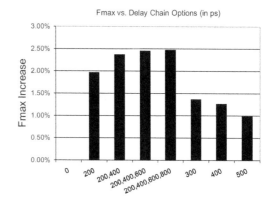

(b) Discrete set of delay chain settings

**Figure 8: Performance improvement obtained with various delay chain taps**

# 4. MEMORY ARCHITECTURE

The embedded memory in the Stratix family architectures up to Stratix III used three distinct embedded memory block sizes, while Stratix III and Stratix IV replaced the smallest of these, the 512b block, with LUT RAM (which programmably converts LUTs into RAM) and two embedded blocks of 9Kb and 144Kb. For Stratix V we revisited the RAM size and functionality with a goal of addressing soft errors and optimizing core density.

## 4.1 Soft Error Correction

With increasing memory density and decreasing memory cell size, soft errors become more important to circuit reliability. The Stratix V product family includes parts containing up to 52Mb of embedded memory. Consequently, we explored the addition of hardened error correction circuits (ECC) in the memory block. Each memory block in Stratix V includes dedicated circuits to perform error code generation and checking. Previous Stratix architectures have included dual-ported memory blocks allowing independent clocks on both ports. The memories support configurable widths, up to a maximum of 36b. ECC is most efficient on wider words, since the width of the code grows proportionally to log(N). However to correct even a single bit error requires that the number of error correcting bits M for an N bit data word satisfy M > log (N + M) [9, 10]. This means that a 32b data word requires at least M=6, so at least a 38b native width in the RAM.

A second issue is the frequency of *multi*-bit errors. Shrinking RAM cell size means an increasing probability that an error can affect more than a single bit, but these errors will be adjacent bits in a word. The impact of an ionizing particle produces a linear charge that spans some distance, and as cell sizes decrease, this distance can span more adjacent memory bits Conventional single-error correcting codes only need 38 bits, however double-error correcting codes require at least 12 extra bits for a 32 data bit word, leading to an excessive overhead [9,10,11]. Since we are primarily concerned with adjacent bit errors, it is possible to consider double adjacent error correcting codes that can be constructed with 39 bits. By itself, this is still inadequate for a small percentage of multi-bit errors. A complementary technique used to address this is spatial interleaving [12] using column muxing, shown in Figure 9. That is, for an N bit wide memory, the physical memory core is constructed as some multiple of N bits, say 4. Each memory read therefore accesses 4*N bits, and N 4:1 muxes are used to select a desired word. The bits are interleaved such that each mux selects from 4 physically adjacent bits. This means that consecutive words select from adjacent bits, but any given logical word reads bits that are 4 bit cells apart in a given row. This is not only most efficient from an implementation standpoint, but enables correction of errors that affect multiple physically adjacent bits. An error that affects up to 4 adjacent bits in a row will only affect a single bit in the accessed word. As long as each word can correct a single bit error, the memory core is immune from a 4 bit adjacent error.

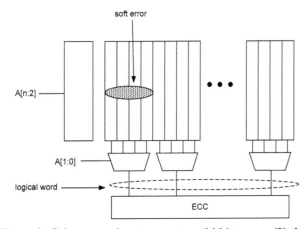

**Figure 9: Column muxing to correct multi-bit errors 4X the width native capability of an ECC code. Example 4b adjacent error only affects one bit in each of 4 consecutive logical words**

Since the minimum 39b word width to support double adjacent error correction (DAEC) is relatively uncommon, and does not have any useful division into smaller word sizes, the decision was made to increase word width to 40b, which supports sizes of 512*40, 1024*20, 2048*10, 4096*5, 8192*2, and 16384*1. This also provides enough width to enable the correction of errors up to 2 adjacent bits using inexpensive hardware. Our solution is

similar to the SEC-DED-DAEC code of [13]. We wrote a program to define a boolean satisfiability problem to generate a code, and use a low cost code that can correct adjacent errors of up to two bits and detect any error of up to three adjacent bits. Combined with 4-way column muxing, the embedded memory can correct any error that affects any subset of bits including up to 8 adjacent bits and detect any error that affects up to 12 adjacent bits. The hardened logic for ECC provides outputs from the block indicating the presence of correctable and uncorrectable errors. The maximum number of adjacent bits that can be upset in 28nm are well below this, so an error that cannot be corrected has a probability that is essentially 0.

## 4.2 Block RAM Size

We revisited the memory block size with a view to optimizing cost for designs using a significantly larger amount of memory in the new generation device. Increasing design size trends are expected to increase the size of the most area efficient embedded memory block. As a result of introducing the ECC described above, it would be necessary to increase the size of the 9Kb block to 10Kb. Recall that prior generations employed a medium-size block (of 9Kb) and a large RAM block of size 144Kb. We compared FPGAs with a mix of 10Kb and 144Kb memory blocks to architectures that consisted of a mixture of 20Kb blocks and 40Kb blocks. In the case of the 20Kb block we also explored whether a single embedded block could provide comparable area efficiency to a mix of two types.

To make these comparisons, the experiment models a family of FPGAs with a fixed LAB:medium-sized memory block ratio across all family members. We find the smallest device that each user design can fit into, and measure its area. The experiment measures the geometric mean of the die area required as we vary the LAB:medium-sized memory ratio.

Figure 10 shows the results, showing the LAB:medium-sized memory block ratio on the X axis, and total core area required across a design set on the Y axis. The 20Kb block and no large memory block can match the efficiency of the 10Kb block with 144Kb memory. The single 40Kb architecture is less area efficient. Due to the reduced design effort of a single type of RAM, as well as the greater placement flexibility of a single type of memory block, we chose to provide only a 20Kb embedded memory block.

## 4.3 LUT RAM Architecture

Reusing the memory cells in the LUT as a user RAM has been provided since relatively early generations of FPGAs [20]. The Stratix III generation introduced LUT RAM into the Stratix family, offering the ability to configure each ALM as a 64b 1R1W dual port SRAM, providing a total of 640b per LAB. Because the ALM provides 8 inputs for a 64b LUT, and only 6 inputs are required for a read address, there are 2 extra inputs available to provide other signals such as write data, write address, and byte enable. This allows all of the ALMs in a LAB to be used for LUT RAM, without wasting any ALMs merely to provide inputs.

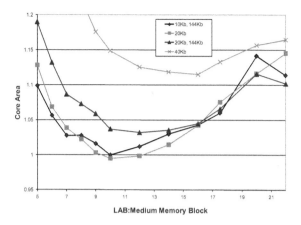

**Figure 10: Core area vs LAB:medium memory block ratio for various medium and large memory block sizes**

In the initial version of LUT RAM, the focus was entirely on low cost, and consequently as much functionality as reasonably possible was left in soft logic. In particular, the Stratix III device included 2 flip-flops per ALM, or 20 per LAB, which was just sufficient for the write data registers. All other logic, in particular input address and output registers (if present in the user circuit), were implemented in the regular ALM flip-flops in other LABs.

This approach forced Stratix III to use relatively loose timing for the write cycle. The write was performed on the negative edge of the clock, allowing the write address ½ clock cycle to propagate from the source LAB to the LUT RAM. Although this is reasonably generous for nearby connections, the addition of routing delay, especially for wide RAMs with large address fanout, clock skew, clock duty cycle distortion, and the internal delays in the write address can create a performance limit in high speed designs. Therefore it was decided to add hardened write address registers in the write control logic. A total of 6 flip-flops are added to the control region in the LAB to implement the write address and improve LUT RAM timing as shown in Figures 11 and 12. Fig 11 shows the previous Stratix style write, where routing was required between the write address flip-flops and the LAB containing the LUT RAM. Consequently the write is performed on the falling edge. In Stratix V and later, the write address is contained in dedicated flip-flops so the write can start shortly after the positive clock edge. Figure 12 shows simplified logic for this design.

The addition of two extra flip-flops per ALM was also used to improve LUT RAM usability. With the availability of 4 flip-flops per ALM (as described in Section 3.1), both read data and write data can be registered in the ALM flip-flops. The read address registers continue to be soft and implemented in other flip-flops, since this is purely a single LUT combinational logic path.

# 5. ROUTING ENHANCEMENTS

Every FPGA generation experiences the benefits of Moore's law, with approximate doubling of density, and its concurrent demand for increased routing. Altera FPGAs are implemented with a highly modular structure that is area efficient, but also requires constructing the various multiplexers in quantities that have suitable integral ratios with respect to the logic. Figure 13 shows an overview of a one ALM high slice of a full LAB, including the various routing muxes as well as logic. The LE input muxes

(LEIM) are pitch matched to the ALM, as are the inter LAB routing muxes (the DIMs) and LAB input muxes (the LIMs.) Routing, including all DIM, LIM, and LEIM consistently occupies about 50% of total LAB area, while LEs occupy the other 50%, across all Stratix and Cyclone devices. Inter-LAB routing, in the form of the DIMs, is about 20% of LAB area while LIMs occupy 10% and LEIMs the remaining 20%. Thus, the amount of LAB area that is used to implement inter-LAB routing is relatively small. When referenced to total die area, LAB soft logic and routing typically comprise 30-35% of die area (with the remainder taken up by I/O, memory and DSP blocks), so all programmable routing is less than 17% of die area, and inter-LAB routing in the form of DIMs is less than 8% of die area.

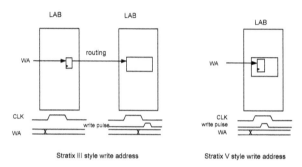

**Figure 11: Stratix III vs. Stratix V LUT RAM Timing**

Although relatively small, the modularity results in a desire to accommodate a moderate increase in routing demand with adjustments to wire length, rather than the coarser quantization of increasing columns of routing multiplexers. Consequently rather than completely re-architect the routing, we explored minor variations that could keep pace with the increase in routing demand as well as obtain performance improvement.

Simultaneously, the increased resistance of metal with process shrinkage causes a need to mitigate its effects. In addition to using architectural changes to the fabric, modern processes offer an increasing variety of metal thicknesses which can be used to mitigate resistance effects [19]. However, thicker metal is also necessarily wider, and consumes more space. Architectural techniques to efficiently and selectively exploit middle thickness metal produces better performance for given LAB area, as described below.

The basic technique used in Stratix V is another variation on the heterogeneous routing architectures described in [1]. As has been used in many FPGA architectures, a subset of faster resources can be used preferentially for more timing-critical paths by a timing-aware router. This technique is used in two ways in Stratix V. While Stratix II, III, and IV included length 4 wires in both horizontal and vertical directions (H4 and V4 wires). With Stratix V, more heterogeneity is introduced in both directions, but using different techniques. This is motivated by the physical layout of the LAB, which resembles that shown in the figures, being considerably taller than it is wide. Consequently V wires of a given logical length are physically longer than an H wire of the same logical length. Our experiments explored a few varieties of homogeneity in the H wires, all of which had small performance and routability impacts. Ultimately we decided to split the H wires into two lengths, 3 and 6 LABs respectively (H3 and H6 wires.) This reduces delay on short connections, since the H3 wires are not only less capacitive, but less affected by metal resistance. Using a mix of H3 and H6 wires provides slightly more total channel width and routability for a fixed number of DIMs compared to H4 wires. For example, using 100 DIMs, we could create either 400 H4 wires, or using 50 DIM each for H3 and H6, 150 H3 wires and 300 H6 wires for a total channel width of 450. The balance between H3 and H6 wires and other wire lengths is chosen to optimize routability and improve performance, and the use of H3/H6 provides approximately 1% performance improvement.

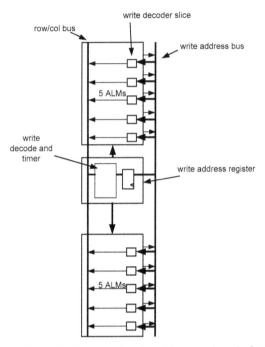

**Figure 12: Hardened write address register in Stratix V**

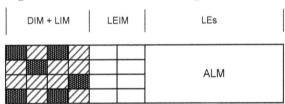

**Figure 13: Modular layout of routing muxes and logic**

As mentioned earlier, because the LAB is taller than it is wide, resistance effects are more pronounced on the vertical wires. We moved 50% of the V wires to a mid-thickness layer with much lower resistance and about half the delay. Nevertheless, the use of a timing driven router ensures that when a V wire is used on a critical path, 80% of the time it is on a fast V wire. Based on FMT performance evaluation on our benchmark set, this single architecture change improved average performance by 8% compared to using thin metal only.

The Stratix family programmable routing fabric also includes long wires optimized for high-fanout global nets and fast long-distance communication. To keep resistance low these wires use the thickest metal layers available. Their thickness typically stays constant from one generation to the next instead of scaling with the fabrication process. As a result, the most performance tuned physical length of these wires does not scale as aggressively as

wires on lower metal layers. Thus, the *logical* length of global routing wires needs to be increased as LAB size is reduced, but a longer wire results in needing a higher channel width, and less routability since average required connection length does not increase as fast. We chose to increase the long wire length to 24 LABs (H24) in the horizontal direction and 14 in the vertical direction (V14). Compared to the H20 and V12 used in Stratix IV these lengths reduce delay for long-distance connections by 5% while maintaining metal efficiency and performance on mid-length connections.

Thick metal requires large wire pitch so fewer long wires are available per channel. Wide input muxes are used to give a sufficient fraction of local interconnect access to the long wires, but these muxes can have large delay. In past architectures multi-level muxes were used to reduce diffusion loading at each mux stage. In Stratix V fast sneak paths are added for stitching connections, as shown in Figure 14. This reduces long-distance delay by 15% while adding minimal delay to the initial connection from short to long wires. The combination of a moderate increase in logical length of the wire and introduction of fast stitching maintains fast corner to corner routing connections with minimal impact on demand for thick metal.

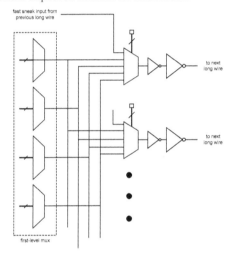

**Figure 14: Fast Stitching in long wires**

## 6. ADDER ENHANCEMENTS

As FPGAs increase in density and are used more as a computational fabric in systems, the importance of fast arithmetic increases. Although DSP blocks efficiently implement multiplication, addition is primarily done in the soft logic fabric. Figure 3 shows that the LUTs can provide 4 outputs (from 4 4-LUTs, not shown) as inputs for the two adders.

Early generations of FPGAs used ripple carry circuits [20]. Stratix I contained a carry select adder that had a delay of 3 muxes per 10 bits, but the cost of this is relatively high. The carry select requires duplicating the carry chain and adding an output select mux, which is relatively expensive and was found not to be worth the cost. The adder circuitry evolved incrementally in subsequent architectures. Stratix II and later architectures included an ALM based architecture with 2 bits of addition per ALM using a full adder with one bit ripple carry, shown in Figure 15, and eliminated the carry select. The cin to cout path of the mux is speed critical and is optimized for high speed across the LE high wire that cascades between adjacent LEs.

For Stratix IV, a first level of speed improvement was applied. A 2-bit carry skip was generated within each ALM. Figure 16 shows a simplified circuit diagram, not including the intermediate carry. Each adder bit produces a propagate and

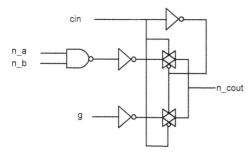

**Figure 15: Single bit ripple carry in Stratix II, III**

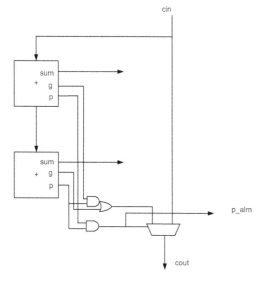

**Figure 16: Two-bit carry skip introduced in Stratix IV. The ALM provides two bits of arithmetic. p_alm is not used in Stratix IV but is used in Stratix V for second level skip.**

generate bit, which are combined into a two-bit level generate and skip with a few gates. The multiplexer allows cin to directly propagate to cout with a single stage of logic when the carry will propagate. Although this adds several more logic gates, because the 2b carry propagate and generate is not on the critical path, these can be very small. The same multiplexing structure as previous was employed for a 2b carry chain. The critical path is now a single mux per two bits, and only this needs to use large transistors. The area savings of eliminating one large mux per ALM was more than sufficient to provide the area for the carry lookahead logic that generates the skip signal. As a result we achieved a modest area savings per LE while halving the delay per bit.The critical path on long carry chains is now a single mux per 20 bits. The critical path of a wide adder begins with a 10 bit two-bit carry skip (5 stages), followed by a carry skip per 20 bits, and a final 10 bit two-bit skip (5 more stages) through the last half LAB. Figure 18 shows a SPICE simulation of an early timing prediction of carry chain delay. This also includes a version that performed carry select, but was not found to be any faster than the basic carry skip. As a result, the speed of long carry chains is estimated to be improved by a factor of 5 with a modest increase in LAB area.

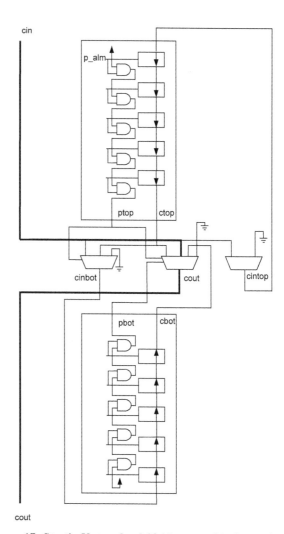

**Figure 17: Stratix V two level 20 bit carry skip has a single mux delay per 20 bits, and one mux delay per two bits within a ALM.**

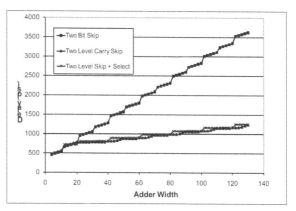

**Figure 18: SPICE simulation of carry skip adder**

# 7. CONCLUSIONS

The Stratix V architecture introduces logic fabric, routing, and memory architecture changes to improve performance and density for modern, million logic element designs. Doubling the number of flip-flops in a low cost manner offers improved density for flip-flop intensive designs, while the use of pulse latches and a small configurable pulse width generator enables time borrowing and improved performance. The memory architecture is improved by hardening more logic for the LUT RAM, exploiting the extra flip-flops, as well as by introducing a simpler unified embedded memory architecture comprising a single type of block. An error correction scheme makes this memory immune to soft errors of up to 8 adjacent bits as well as detecting any errors within 12 adjacent bits. The routing architecture exploits heterogeneity in wire length and metal layers for better performance, while providing a moderate increase in routing density. Finally, the adder now includes two levels of multi-bit skip to reduce carry delay in long chains to a single multiplexer per 20 bits.

# 8. REFERENCES

[1]    V. Betz, J. Rose, and A. Marquardt, "Architecture and CAD for Deep-Submicron FPGAs", Kluwer Academic Publishers, 1999

[2]    D. Lewis et al, "The Stratix-II™ Routing and Logic Architecture", *Proc FPGA 2005*, pp. 14-20

[3]    D. Lewis et al, "The Stratix™ Routing and Logic Architecture", *Proc FPGA 2003*, pp. 12-20

[4]    D. Lewis et al, "Architectural Enhancements in Stratix-III™ and Stratix-IV™", *Proc FPGA 2009*, pp. 33-42

[5]    N. Nedovic et al, "A Clock Skew Absorbing Flip-Flop", *Proc ISSCC 2003*, pp. 342-343

[6]    V. G. Oklobdzija, "Clocking and clocked storage elements in a multi-gigahertz environment", *IBM J. Res. Dev*, Sept 2003, pp. 567-583

[7]    B. Stackhouse et al., "A 65nm 2-Billion Transistor Quad-Core Itanium® Processor", *IEEE JSSC*, Jan 2009 pp. 18-31

[8]    D. Wendel et al, "Power7®, a Highly Parallel, Scalable Multi-Core High End Server Processor", *IEEE JSSC*, Jan 2011, pp. 145-161

[9]    M. Y. Hsiao, "A Class of Optimal minimum Odd-weight-column SEC-DED Codes", *IBM J. Res. Dev.*, Jul 1970, pp. 395-401

[10]   C. L. Chen and M. Y. Hsiao, "Error-correcting codes for semiconductor memory applications: A state-of-the-art review", *IBM J. Res. Dev.*, Mar 1984, pp. 124-134

[11]   R. Naseer and J. Draper, "DEC ECC Design to Improve Memory Reliability in Sub-100nm Technologies", *IEEE Intl. Conf. on Electronics, Circuits, and Systems*, 2008, pp. 586-589

[12]   R. Goodman and M. Sayano, "The Reliability of Semiconductor RAM Memories with On-Chip Error-Correction Coding", *IEEE Trans. Information Theory*, May 1991, pp. 884-896

[13]   A. Dutta and N. Touba, "Multiple Bit Upset Tolerant Memory Using a Selective Cycle Avoidance Based SEC-DED-DAEC Code", *IEEE VLSI Test Symp.*, 2007, pp. 349-354

[14]   D. Singh and S. Brown, "Constrained Clock Shifting for Field Programmable Gate Arrays", *IEEE Intl. Symp. FPGAs 2002*, Monterey, CA, Feb 2002, pp. 121-126.

[15]   B. Teng and J. Anderson, "Latch-Based Performance Optimization for FPGAs", *Proc FPL 2011*, pp. 53-64

[16]   C.-Y. Yeh and M. Marek-Sadowska, "Skew-Programmable Clock Design for FPGA and Skew-Aware placement", *Proc. FPGA 2005*, pp. 33-40

[17]   X. Dong and G. Lemieux, "PRG: Period and Glitch Reduction Via Clock Skew Scheduling, Delay Padding, and GlitchLess", *Proc. FPT 2009*, pp. 88-95

[18]   B. Teng and J.H. Anderson, "Latch-based Performance Optimization for FPGAs," accepted to appear *IEEE Trans. VLSI*

[19]   S.Y. Wu *et al.*, "A 32nm CMOS Low Power SoC Platform Technology for Foundry Applications with Functional High Density SRAM", *Proc IEDM 2007*, pp. 263-266

[20]   H-C. Hsieh, et al, "Third-generation architecture boosts speed and density of field-programmable gate arrays," *Custom Integrated Circuits Conference*, 1990, pp. 31.2.1-31.2.7

# Minimum Energy Operation for Clustered Island-Style FPGAs

Peter Grossmann[1]
Department of Electrical
and Computer Engineering
Northeastern University
Boston, MA

grossmann@ll.mit.edu

Miriam Leeser
Department of Electrical
and Computer Engineering
Northeastern University
Boston, MA

mel@coe.neu.edu

Marvin Onabajo
Department of Electrical
and Computer Engineering
Northeastern University
Boston, MA

monabajo@ece.neu.edu

## ABSTRACT

Despite the advantages offered by field-programmable gate arrays (FPGAs) for low-power systems requiring flexible computing resources, applications with the lowest power budgets still favor microprocessors and application-specific integrated circuits (ASICs). In order for such systems to exploit FPGAs, an FPGA achieving minimum energy operation is needed. Minimum energy points have been found for ASICs and microprocessors to occur at operating voltages that are typically below the transistor threshold voltage. This paper presents two clustered island-style test chips capable of operating with a single supply voltage as low as 260 mV. This supply voltage represents the lowest voltage at which an FPGA has been successfully programmed. Test chip measurements show that the minimum energy point of both circuits is at or below this minimum operating voltage. Operation at 260 mV leads to a 40X power-delay product reduction vs. 1.5V operation. The results demonstrate a clear path forward for fabricating low voltage FPGAs that are fully compatible with existing tool flows.

## Categories and Subject Descriptors

B.7.1 [**Hardware**]: Design Types and Style – *advanced technologies, gate arrays, VLSI.*

## Keywords

Subthreshold, FPGA

## 1. INTRODUCTION

Field Programmable Gate Arrays (FPGAs) offer system designers a flexible, energy-efficient platform for computing that requires moderate costs in terms of designer time and hardware expense, as well as reconfigurability to adapt to diverse applications or changing environments after fabrication of integrated systems. While not as high performance or energy-efficient as application-specific integrated circuits (ASICs), nor as efficient and fast to design for as microprocessors, the advantages of cost and reconfigurability over ASICs and performance over microprocessors make FPGAs the best choice for an increasing number of applications. Presently, the lowest-power systems, such as wireless sensor networks and implantable medical devices, prefer custom ASICs [12] or ultra-low power microcontrollers. While ultra-low power designers have begun to adopt the Actel Igloo FPGA [4], there are few published results using it. To gain traction in such systems, FPGA manufacturers need to shift from designing for low power to designing for minimum energy consumption. This shift has already begun in the ASIC community, where circuit designers have exploited the relaxed system performance requirements by pursuing minimum energy operation of circuits. Research in ASICs has shown that while the minimum energy point of a circuit is dependent upon the details of the circuit itself and its activity factor, the minimum energy point obtained for a given circuit is generally near or below the threshold voltage of the transistors [1]. While subthreshold transistor operation yields minimum energy operation, there are tradeoffs: the exponential relationship between current and voltage below threshold results in drastic increases in circuit delay and vulnerability to process, voltage, and temperature variations. The increased variability of subthreshold circuits restricts which circuit topologies can be used; tall series stacks and ratioed circuits in particular must be avoided [17].

This paper presents the implementation and measurement results of an FPGA test chip fabricated in 0.18 μm SOI that is capable of operating at subthreshold supply voltages. All the leaf cells required to build FPGAs (SRAM bit cells and digital logic gates) have been well-studied for subthreshold operation, and alternatives are available for implementing each. Previous subthreshold SRAM studies have had design objectives not relevant for FPGAs. A previous subthreshold FPGA operating logic and routing resources as low as 200 mV used a second supply voltage to program SRAM-based configuration bits at 400 mV [16]. A comparison of the architectures used in [16] and in this work is given in [6]. It will be shown that latches can replace SRAM in subthreshold FPGAs to mitigate sensitivity to process variation with simplified circuit design, enabling programming at lower voltages. The contributions of this work are:

- Demonstration that replacement of SRAM with latches enables low voltage FPGA programming without write assist circuitry.

- Measurement results for an FPGA test chip showing low voltage operation with a single, subthreshold supply.

---

[1]Attends Northeastern through the MIT Lincoln Laboratory Lincoln Scholars Program. The Lincoln Laboratory portion of this work was sponsored by the Department of the Air Force under Air Force Contract #FA8721-05-C-0002. Opinions, interpretations, conclusions, and recommendations are those of the author and are not necessarily endorsed by the United States Government.

- Measurement results showing that FPGA activity factors can be made high enough to bring the minimum energy point below threshold

- Definition of a path forward for minimum energy analysis of FPGAs prior to tapeout.

Section 2 introduces the test chip architecture. Section 3 presents an evaluation of two-input multiplexer implementation options. Section 4 discusses the replacement of SRAM with interruptible latches and presents simulation results showing the benefits of this circuit for low voltage operation. Section 5 shows measurement results for test chip minimum operating voltage and minimum energy analysis. Section 6 proposes an approach for revising this chip with the support of a standard academic (VPR-based) CAD tool flow for programming, and performing minimum energy analysis prior to fabrication with commercial CAD tools. A summary follows.

## 2. FPGA TEST CHIP ARCHITECTURE
The test chip architecture is based upon the clustered, island-style class of FPGA architectures [5]. The array element in these architectures is called a tile and is comprised of a configurable logic block (CLB), a switch block (SB), and upper and lower connection blocks (CBs) that interface the CLBs to the SBs. Figure 1 shows a block diagram of the tile.

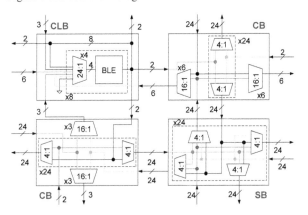

**Figure 1. Test Chip Tile Block Diagram.**

The CLBs in this work are eighteen-input, eight output circuits containing eight four-input basic logic elements (BLEs). Figure 2 shows a block diagram for a BLE like the one used in this work. A four-input lookup table (LUT) is built by connecting configuration bit outputs, usually implemented with SRAM, to a 16:1 multiplexer. The four BLE inputs are connected to the select bits of the multiplexer. A flip-flop is connected along with the LUT output to an output multiplexer that drives the BLE output. Eight BLEs per CLB has been shown to be a good number per CLB for low power design [11]. The eighteen inputs can be routed to any input of each of the eight LUTs using a nearly full crossbar [19] built with 24:1 multiplexers. This 24:1 muxes represent a significant amount of hardware overhead but the resulting input flexibility simplifies synthesis, placement, and routing to the FPGA.

The CBs and SBs are arrays of multiplexers, buffered at the inputs and outputs by inverters. It was shown in [9] that single-driver, unidirectional routing resources such as these are more efficient than bidirectional routing resources, reducing capacitance on each

routing track while offering comparable routability per wire. The switch block is a subset switch box providing 48 total routing tracks in both vertical and horizontal directions. For unidirectional routing tracks, this requires 24 copies of a circuit containing four 4:1 multiplexers. Each 4:1 mux selects which of the four incoming sides is driven on the output and generates the output for one of the four sides.

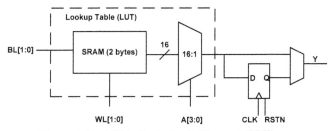

**Figure 2. Test Chip Basic Logic Element (BLE).**

The connection blocks contain arrays of multiplexers generating two types of signals: inputs to adjacent CLBs and inputs to adjacent SBs. Each CB interfaces to the CLB and SB in its own tile and to one CLB and one SB in adjacent tiles. To generate each CLB input, the CB selects from one of sixteen SB outputs. Eight of these come from within the tile and eight come from an adjacent tile. The switch block routing tracks are divided evenly amongst the 16:1 multiplexers driving the CLB inputs. In the lower CB, each routing track goes to one 16:1 mux; in the upper CB, each goes to two. The CLB inputs are divided unevenly between the CBs in order to prevent multiplexer inputs from being left unused. To generate each SB input, 4:1 multiplexers are provided so that each CLB output can be routed to any SB routing track. This flexibility comes at the expense of requiring buffering on the CLB outputs to cope with the high fanout of these nets.

The tile in Figure 1 is replicated sixteen times on the test chip to form a 4x4 array. CLB and CB I/O are connected to test chip pads, which eliminates the need to design I/O blocks (IOBs) and facilitates verification of the tile functionality.

## 3. MULTIPLEXER EVALUATION
Figure 3 shows the multiplexer alternatives that were considered for the test chips. Four conventional topologies were evaluated: ganged tri-state, logic function, buffered transmission gate, and buffered pass transistor. The ganged tri-state, transmission gate, and pass transistor circuits were also evaluated in dynamic threshold (DTMOS) configurations, i.e. with transistor gates connected to bodies.

Table 1 compares the average current, average delay, and area of the multiplexer options in Figure 3. Both conventional and DTMOS pass transistor multiplexer results are omitted due to the poor robustness of these circuits as discussed below. Results are normalized to the ganged tri-state mux, which appears to be the best all-around performer of the options considered. Although the transmission gate multiplexers are faster, the delay improvement is outweighed by the power penalty. The results also show that for a 2.6X area penalty and 1.3X delay penalty, a 2.2X power reduction can be obtained with DTMOS ganged tri-state muxes. This makes it unclear whether the standard or DTMOS configuration would provide better overall results. For this reason, both a conventional and a DTMOS chip were fabricated.

To investigate the relative robustness of these circuits, Spectre simulations with foundry-supplied IBM 0.18 μm SOI process device models were performed with each topology in Figure 3. The figure of merit for robustness was the ratio of standard deviation to the mean (σ/μ) of the multiplexer propagation delay; a lower σ/μ is used as an indication of a more robust circuit. For all multiplexers, transistors were sized with PMOS W/L = 1 μm/0.18 μm and NMOS W/L = 0.5 μm/0.18 μm. To introduce process variations to the large number of voltage and multiplexer combinations without excessive simulation runtime, each test case was simulated over 100 Monte Carlo iterations. Note that each circuit was both driven and loaded by multistage inverter networks that were also subject to variation. This adds an element of realism to the simulations by requiring that the devices under test function correctly even in the presence of potentially very weak drivers. Correct operation of the multiplexer at a given voltage was defined as the existence of valid 10-90% rise and fall times for all 100 iterations.

Figure 4 shows the σ/μ of the various multiplexers as a function of supply voltage for PMOS-controlled output rising edges, while Figure 5 shows the σ/μ for NMOS-controlled output edges. The separate graphs show that output rising edges are generally more vulnerable to variation. All multiplexers met the pass criterion above 0.1V except for the DTMOS pass transistor mux. It is therefore omitted from Figure 4 and Figure 5. The standard pass transistor mux is much less robust than the rest for output falling edges. Significant increases in σ/μ versus the nominal $V_{DD}$ for this process (1.5V) begin at around 0.5V for all multiplexer types. At subthreshold (below 0.4V in this process), the DTMOS circuits exhibit significantly lower PMOS-controlled σ/μ compared to the other types. Since the PMOS-controlled edges are less robust, they will dictate the robustness of the overall circuit. This suggests that the DTMOS multiplexers have a meaningful advantage over their conventional counterparts.

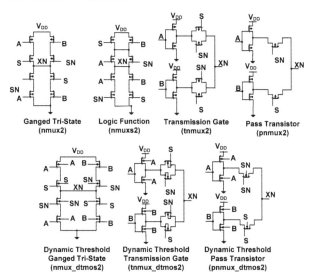

**Figure 3. Multiplexer configuration alternatives.**

**Table 1. Power/Performance Area Evaluation for Multiplexer Alternatives (values are normalized to nmux2 in Figure 3)**

|  | nmux2 | nmuxs2 | nmux_dtmos2 | tnmux2 | tnmux_dtmos2 |
|---|---|---|---|---|---|
| **Avg. Current** | 1.00 | 0.98 | 0.45 | 2.32 | 0.75 |
| **Avg. Static Current** | 1.00 | 1.07 | 0.32 | 2.31 | 0.66 |
| **A/B-Y Delay** | 1.00 | 0.95 | 1.40 | 0.86 | 1.18 |
| **S-Y Delay** | 1.00 | 1.20 | 1.28 | 0.66 | 1.09 |
| **Area** | 1.00 | 1.00 | 2.60 | 0.99 | 2.59 |

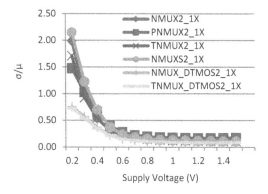

**Figure 4. Simulated standard deviation to mean ratio of the FPGA multiplexer propagation delay vs. supply voltage for output rising edges**

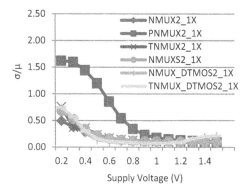

**Figure 5. Simulated standard deviation to mean ratio of the FPGA multiplexer propagation delay vs. supply voltage for output falling edges.**

## 4. REPLACEMENT OF SRAM WITH LATCHES

A storage element is required for FPGA configuration bits. Since the storage element is not actively used once the FPGA is programmed, minimization of static power consumption and area are most important for choosing a storage element. In commercial FPGA design, the common case for storage is SRAM that minimizes static power by using high-Vt transistors [14]. The SOI process used in this work does not have high-Vt transistors, leaving voltage scaling as the primary means of minimizing static power. A compact, robust storage element capable of very low voltage operation is thus required.

While it is known that the conventional 6T SRAM bit cell, shown in Figgure 6 (a), is not appropriate for large memory arrays at subthreshold supply voltages, its suitability for use as configuration storage in FPGAs, where write speed is not critical and bit lines can be made short and local, is less clear. However, the contention between the access transistors and the cross-coupled inverter outputs remains an issue for the 6T SRAM cell in subthreshold. Previous SRAM bit cells targeting low voltage operation have addressed contention primarily through write assist techniques—either boosting the word line voltage, compressing the supplies of the cross coupled inverters, or both. An example that also addresses contention through circuit topology 6T bit cell shown in Figure 6 (b). In addition to compressing supplies, this circuit uses a full transmission gate for the write driver, thereby improving its drive strength [18].

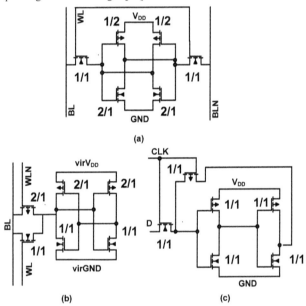

**Figure 6. (a) Conventional 6T SRAM; (b) 6T subthreshold SRAM bit cell [2]; (c) 6T interruptible latch.**

In this work, an interruptible latch is used instead of SRAM to store FPGA configuration bits. The latch eliminates contention entirely and, along with it, the need for write assist circuitry and associated extra supply voltages. Latches have been used previously in FPGAs [19], but have not been considered for FPGAs operating at subthreshold. Figure 6 (c) shows the schematic of the proposed latch. Transistor count is maintained at six by using an NMOS pass transistor for write access and a PMOS pass transistor for feedback to a pair of inverters whose outputs are not cross-coupled. The two primary conditions leading to variation robustness are that no node in the circuit is driven by two transistors simultaneously, and that no node is ever undriven.Simulations were conducted using the IBM 0.18 µm SOI process foundry SPICE models to compare the speed and robustness of the latch to the conventional 6T SRAM in Figure 6 (a), and the 6T subthreshold SRAM in Figure 6 (b). A minimum sized device for this experiment was defined as W = 500 nm (the width required to fit diffusion contacts), and L = 260 nm to

provide up-front additional robustness against process variation. The W/L ratios shown in Figure 6 are scalar factors applied to these minima. The conventional 6T bit cell is sized with its traditional sizing ratio. The subthreshold 6T cell is sized with twice minimum PMOS devices for consistency with its use in [18]. The latch is sized with minimum width transistors.

A Spectre post-layout simulation exercises the propagation delay from the word line to the output as a function of both supply voltage (varied from 0.1-0.5 V) and word line pulse width (varied from 10 ns to 1 µs). Word line pulse width was shown as the preferred criterion for SRAM bit cell write stability at subthreshold in [20]. For the 6T subthreshold SRAM bit cell, the supply was reduced by $0.25V_{DD}$ and the ground rail were raised by $0.25V_{DD}$ whenever the word line was high. To introduce process variations, each test case was simulated over 100 Monte Carlo iterations. The settings controlling process variation were the default settings provided for the foundry models. Each circuit was both driven and loaded by a network of multistage inverters that were also subjected to variations. This adds an element of realism to the simulations by requiring that the devices under test function correctly even in the presence of potentially very weak drivers. At each voltage, the minimum pulse width at which the write was successful for all 100 iterations was determined. "Success" was defined by obtaining a valid propagation delay result for both rising and falling output transitions.

Figure 7 shows each circuit's minimum pulse width as a function of supply voltage. The 6T subthreshold SRAM has the smallest minimum pulse width, benefiting from supply compression, while the latch has the largest. Figure 8 shows a plot of the standard deviation to mean ratio of propagation delay for each cell. Results are divided between PMOS pullup transitions and NMOS pulldown transitions due to the large discrepancy in values between them. For the two SRAM cells, pulldown transition variation dominates at 0.2-0.3V. In this voltage range, pullup transition variation for all three are comparable, but the latch has the best pulldown transition variation. The elimination of node contention of the 6T latch thus offers a tradeoff vs. SRAM—in exchange for slower write operations, comparable or superior robustness can be obtained along with the elimination of write assist circuitry.

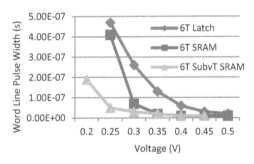

**Figure 7. Minimum word line pulse width vs. supply voltage for the 6T conventional SRAM, 6T subthreshold SRAM, and 6T latch.**

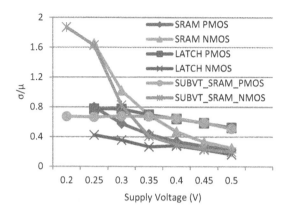

**Figure 8. Standard deviation to mean ratio of propagation delay in the 6T SRAM bit cell, subthreshold 6T SRAM bit cell and 6T latch.**

# 5. TEST CHIP MEASUREMENT RESULTS

The test chips with conventional and DTMOS multiplexers were both fabricated on the same wafer run in the IBM 0.18 μm SOI process. A die photograph of the test chip with conventional multiplexers is shown in Figure 9. The chips are pin compatible and used identical 4.1 × 4.4 mm pad frames. The conventional array core measured roughly 1.8 × 2.3 mm, while the DTMOS array core measured roughly 2.9 × 3.3 mm. The total transistor count was circa 360,000.

Test chips were wafer probed on an Agilent SoC 93000 test system. For the chip with conventional multiplexers, an average minimum operating voltage of 300 mV was obtained across eleven dice, with three operating at 260 mV. For the test chip with DTMOS multiplexers, of four chips tested three operated at 260 mV and the fourth at 270 mV.

Performance testing was conducted by programming the test chip to function as an array of sixteen four-bit counters. The activity factor for this programming across all transistors in the design, including programming circuitry, was 0.11. While for many ASICs this might be nominal, for FPGAs this represents a high activity factor. A sample chip consumed 34.6 μW at 260 mV and 322 kHz when programmed with the counter array, versus 76.5 mW at 16.7 MHz and 1.5V. Minimum voltage operation thus led to a 43X reduction in power-delay product (PDP) compared against nominal voltage operation. For the same test, a sample DTMOS chip consumed 23.7 μW at 260 mV and 202 kHz; the corresponding PDP is 1.1X that of the sample with conventional multiplexers.

Figure 10 shows the power-performance tradeoff within the subthreshold region for a chip with conventional multiplexers. At 0.4V, below the NMOS threshold voltage and slightly above the PMOS threshold voltage, the maximum frequency increases to 1.6 MHz. The DTMOS configuration does not permit nominal voltage operation and for this reason the second test chip was not characterized this way.

Minimum energy analyses of the four DTMOS chips and four sample chips with conventional multiplexers are shown in Figure 11. The PDP of each chip is plotted as a function of voltage. All plots begin at the lowest voltage at which the chips function correctly. The PDP of the DTMOS chips is slightly higher at a

given voltage than that of the chips with conventional multiplexers. In both cases the PDP steadily decreases as the supply voltage decreases, indicating a minimum energy point well below threshold. Since the activity factor for the programming used in Figure 11 is on the high side, the minimum energy point obtained is on the low side of the range of minimum energy points the test chip can produce. This result suggests that there is an incentive to use FPGA programming with high activity factor when minimum energy operation is critical.

**Figure 9. Die photograph of the subthreshold FPGA test chip.**

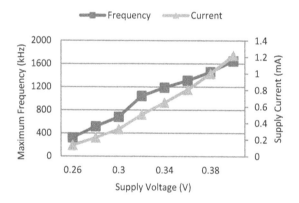

**Figure 10. Maximum operating frequency and supply current at maximum frequency vs. voltage for subthreshold region operation of the FPGA.**

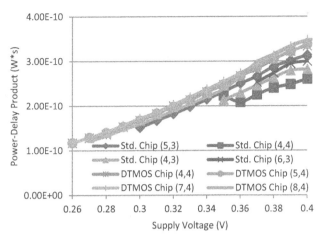

Figure 11. Power-delay product vs. supply voltage for four FPGA test chip dice.

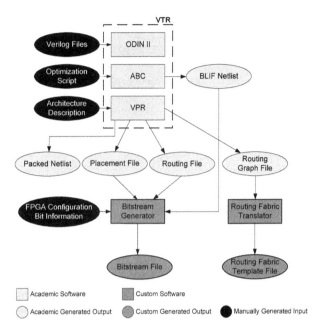

Figure 12. VTR CAD flow augmented with components required for FPGA test chip revision.

# 6. CAD FOR PRE-FABRICATION MINIMUM ENERGY ANALYSIS OF FPGAs

The test chips shown in previous sections demonstrate complete FPGA functionality at 260 mV—programming, logical operation, and routing. Additional work will extend these results in a number of ways, including improving minimum operating voltage increasing the number of tiles in the array, and providing CAD tool support for the FPGA. Of these, the CAD support will be the most beneficial for a revised minimum energy FPGA. In addition to providing infrastructure to support FPGA end users, CAD tools enable efficient estimation of energy consumption of the FPGA prior to fabrication. They can also be used to verify that circuit design techniques for reduction of the minimum operating voltage translate into net energy savings at the chip level.

For academic study of minimum energy FPGAs, the Verilog-To-Routing (VTR) flow consisting of ODIN II for logic synthesis [7], ABC for logic optimization [3], and VPR 6.0 for place-and-route [15], is the preferred option; each tool in this flow is well-established and the tool flow supports a range of architecture alternatives. The test chip architecture presented in Section 2 is ready for use with ODIN II and ABC, but not with VPR due to the design of the routing fabric and the lack of IOBs. Revising the CBs and SB for compatibility with VPR will greatly improve the routability of the test chip architecture in addition to enabling use of the VTR flow. To verify that these revisions are correct, tools beyond the scope of VTR are required. Figure 12 shows a flow diagram depicting the role of VTR in an FPGA CAD flow supporting revision of the test chip architecture. Two additional required components are addressed in this work: a bitstream generator to enable simulation of FPGA programming prior to fabrication and a routing fabric translator to guide revision of the CB and SB. The GILES software [8] performed these tasks for older VPR architecture files, but is not compatible with VPR 6.0.

The remainder of this section presents prototype software used to revise the routing fabric described in Section 2 to make it compatible with VPR 6.0, and a bitstream generator compatible with the revised FPGA. Following the discussion of the software implementation, a CAD approach composed using commercial ASIC EDA tools is presented to perform minimum energy analysis with the support of VTR, the routing fabric translator, and the bitstream generator.

## 6.1 Routing Fabric Translation

To revise the routing fabric for the test chip architecture presented in Section 2, this work proposes to translate the contents of a VPR routing graph file into an easy-to-read text file that can be quickly and reliably, albeit manually, converted into schematics for simulation with industry standard simulation tools. This file will be referred to as a routing template file.

The routing graph translator proposed in this work generates the routing template file with the following steps: First, translate the routing graph into a comprehensive list of every routing multiplexer in the FPGA, with inputs and outputs defined by the nodes in the routing graph. Second, prune the multiplexer list to contain only those multiplexers located within the tiles at X,Y coordinates (0,2), (X,2), (2,0), (2,Y), and (2,2), where X is the number of columns in the FPGA minus two and Y is the number of rows in the FPGA minus two. The pruning step populates the template with a single tile for the interior of the FPGA and a single tile for the I/O blocks on each side of the FPGA. Avoidance of (X,Y) coordinates where either coordinate is one ensures that boundary conditions are avoided when populating the template. Third, apply a set of rules for naming the multiplexer inputs and outputs such that the names directly imply how the tiles are connected to each other. Fourth, write the multiplexers with renamed I/O to a text file.

## 6.2 Bitstream Generation

For bitstream generation, this work proposes to generate bitstreams by aggregating required information for programming from VPR output files and manually created files. The following values are required for bitstream generation:

- Each bit in each LUT occupied by the user circuit
- I/O-related configuration bits in IOBs occupied by the user circuit
- Each select bit in each multiplexer in the routing fabric (SB and CB)
- Each select bit in each multiplexer in the CLB input crossbar
- The select bits that choose whether or not the BLE output is registered with the D flip-flop

In addition, the bitstream generator must order the programming bits so that they are loaded into the correct locations in the FPGA. For the test chips presented in Sections 2-5, programming bits are organized into eight-bit words. Each eight-bit word within a tile is assigned a seven-bit address. One-hot encoded row and column values select which tile is being programmed. Each programming bit in the FPGA must thus be mapped to a particular tile row number, column number, address, and bit position.

The bitstream generator targets chips similar to those presented in previous sections. It obtains bit mappings defined by input text files. The bit values of occupied LUTs, routing fabric multiplexer select bits, input crossbar select bits, and flip-flop configuration bits are obtained from information generated by VPR and the routing fabric translator. IOB-specific configuration is restricted in this work to selection of whether I/Os act as inputs or outputs and whether I/Os are registered within the IOBs. This information is provided by an input text file.

## 6.3 Software Implementation

Figure 13 shows a flow diagram for a prototype software bundle that couples architecture template generation and bitstream generation called vpr2bitstream. The bundle is organized into three major components: a VTR output processor, a routing graph translator, and a bitstream generator. The VTR output processor reads the BLIF netlist, packed netlist, placement file, and routing file and produces two output files: a logic data file summarizing information required for programming logic resources, and a mux select file summarizing information required for programming routing resources. The routing graph translator reads the VPR routing graph file and produces three files used by the bitstream generator. The mux map file defines the mapping of routing multiplexer select bits to address numbers and bit positions within a tile. The mux list file defines a list of multiplexers available in the FPGA that map directly to VPR routing graph nodes, used in the routing file to define how signals are routed. This file also defines which routing nodes are equivalent to the multiplexer inputs. The mux list map file addresses connections between IOBs and non-IOBs. The matching of these connections in the VPR routing file to multiplexers in the mux list file must be treated as a special case. In addition to files used by the bitstream generator, the routing graph translator produces the routing template file. The bitstream generator takes output files from VPR and the routing graph translator hand-generated map files defining the programming word address mappings for the I/O blocks, CLB LUTs, flip-flop muxes, and input crossbars, along with a pin definition file defining the programming of the IOBs, and produces a formatted bitstream file defining the programming word values for each word in each tile in the array.

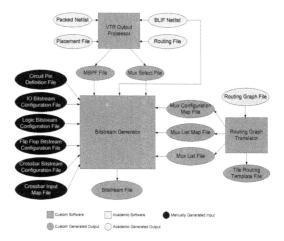

**Figure 13. Flow diagram for routing graph translation with bitstream generation.**

## 6.4 Minimum Energy Estimation CAD Flow

Figure 14 shows a flow diagram of the proposed CAD flow for minimum energy estimation of FPGAs. Implementation of the complete flow is in progress. The user's result is shown with the white bubble; it is a plot of power-delay product versus supply voltage. The plot is specific to a particular place-and-route solution for a particular user circuit being programmed onto the FPGA, and being stimulated with a particular set of input vectors. It is also specific to a particular set of process parameters for the process technology in which the FPGA is designed. A complete minimum energy analysis of an FPGA should exercise this flow across multiple benchmark circuits, multiple input vector patterns for each benchmark, and multiple process corners. The use of the flow is summarized in Figure 14 and described below for a single benchmark circuit and single process corner.

The routing template file (not shown) is used as the basis for generating a set of schematics in Cadence Virtuoso Composer that in turn are used to generate a gate level Verilog netlist of the FPGA. The gate level netlist must be supported by a cell library containing timing and energy information for each leaf cell in the FPGA (multiplexers, flip-flops, inverters, latches, and other logic gates used to implement programming circuitry and IOBs). The cell library is generated using Silvaco's Accucell cell characterization software. Separate cell libraries must be generated for each operating voltage for which energy analysis is to be performed. The timing information obtained from each cell library must be incorporated into the VPR architecture file so that VPR can estimate the minimum clock period of the circuit at that voltage during place-and-route. Incorporation of timing information into the architecture file may make the place-and-route solution voltage-specific. It will be determined during future work what impact this has on the minimum energy point and what VPR options are best for minimum energy analysis. The minimum clock period estimate given by VPR will be used to calculate the power-delay product.

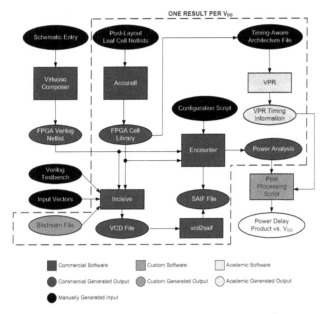

ONE RESULT PER V_DD

Commercial Software
Custom Software
Academic Software
Commercial Generated Output
Custom Generated Output
Academic Generated Output
Manually Generated Input

**Figure 14. CAD flow for FPGA minimum energy analysis**

The bitstream file generated from the voltage-specific place-and-route solution and a set of input vectors are used to simulate the FPGA with Incisive, a commercial Verilog simulator. Waveform information is saved to a value change dump (VCD) file and converted to an industry standard switching activity interchange format (SAIF) file with the Synopsys vcd2saif utility. The netlist, cell library, and SAIF file can be analyzed using Cadence Encounter, a commercially available RTL-to-GDSII software tool for ASIC design that includes commands to perform power analysis. The VPR timing information can then be combined with Encounter power information to compute a power-delay product that is equivalent to the average energy consumption per clock cycle for the FPGA under the programming and activity defined by the bitstream and input vectors. By characterizing the cell library at voltages ranging from below to above threshold and recalculating the power-delay product at each voltage, the minimum energy point of the FPGA can be estimated. This approach to energy analysis is comparable conceptually to the VPR 5.0-based approach used in [13], but the gate-level Verilog representation of the FPGA is a much more explicit representation of the hardware than VPR's internal data structures. As of this writing, schematic generation has been completed for a 6x6 array of tiles plus IOBs. The bitstream generator creates bitstream files for the 6x6 array for use in simulation. The schematics have been verified with small benchmark circuits using Incisive with random input vectors and a Verilog testbench. Development of the rest of the flow is in progress.

## 7. CONCLUSION

This paper presents a pair of related FPGA test chips capable of operating at subthreshold supply voltages. Simulation results of multiplexers, SRAM, and latches have motivated the use of static CMOS multiplexers for routing resources and interruptible latches for configuration bit storage in order to get both good energy efficiency and robustness against process variations without excessive area penalties. One test chip replaced conventional static CMOS multiplexers with DTMOS multiplexers to explore an area vs. energy efficiency tradeoff. The chips were fabricated

in IBM 0.18 µm SOI. Measurement results showed minimum operating voltage of 260 mV for both test chips. This represents the lowest supply voltage at which an FPGA has been successfully programmed. The power-delay product savings at 260mV was ~40X for both chips vs. 1.5V operation for the chip with conventional multiplexers. For a sample test pattern, the energy efficiency of the FPGAs continued to improve as voltages were reduced, revealing a minimum energy point well below threshold.

The presented test chips provide guidance for circuit-level implementation of low voltage FPGAs. To further study minimum energy operation of FPGAs, a software technique was introduced for translating VPR routing graph files into hardware representations of FPGA routing resources. A bitstream generator was also presented for this translated routing fabric coupled with logic blocks comprised of clusters of 4-LUTs. These two software components and the VTR CAD tool suite provide adequate CAD support to enable gate level Verilog simulation of an entire FPGA. Augmenting this tool flow with commercial software for integrated circuit design, simulation, and power estimation will enable future work to perform pre-fabrication estimation of the minimum energy point of FPGAs on a per-user circuit basis.

## 8. ACKNOWLEDGEMENTS

The authors wish to thank Antonio Soares and WeiLin Hu from MIT Lincoln Laboratory for assistance with Agilent 93000 setup.

## 9. REFERENCES

[1] Blaauw, D. and Zhai, B. 2006. Energy efficient design for subthreshold supply voltage operation. *Circuits and Systems, 2006. ISCAS 2006. Proceedings. 2006 IEEE International Symposium on* (2006), 29–32.

[2] Bo Zhai et al. 2008. A Variation-Tolerant Sub-200 mV 6-T Subthreshold SRAM. *Solid-State Circuits, IEEE Journal of*. 43, 10 (2008), 2338–2348.

[3] Brayton, R. and Mishchenko, A. 2010. ABC: an academic industrial-strength verification tool. *Proceedings of the 22nd international conference on Computer Aided Verification* (Berlin, Heidelberg, 2010), 24–40.

[4] Consul-Pacareu, S. et al. 2011. High performance DT-CNN camera device design on ACTEL IGLOO low power FPGA. *Circuit Theory and Design (ECCTD), 2011 20th European Conference on* (Aug. 2011), 37 –40.

[5] Fang, W.M. and Rose, J. 2008. Modeling routing demand for early-stage FPGA architecture development. *Proceedings of the 16th international ACM/SIGDA symposium on Field programmable gate arrays - FPGA '08* (Monterey, California, USA, 2008), 139.

[6] Grossmann, P. et al. Minimum energy analysis and experimental verification of a latch-based subthreshold FPGA. Accepted for publication in *IEEE Trans. on Circuits and Systems II: Express Briefs*.

[7] Jamieson, P. et al. 2010. Odin II-an open-source verilog HDL synthesis tool for CAD research. *Field-Programmable Custom Computing Machines (FCCM), 2010 18th IEEE Annual International Symposium on* (2010), 149–156.

[8] Kuon, I. et al. 2005. Design, layout and verification of an FPGA using automated tools. *Proceedings of the 2005 ACM/SIGDA 13th international symposium on Field-*

*programmable gate arrays* (New York, NY, USA, 2005), 215–226.

[9]   Lemieux, G. et al. 2004. Directional and single-driver wires in FPGA interconnect. *Field-Programmable Technology, 2004. Proceedings. 2004 IEEE International Conference on* (2004), 41–48.

[10]  Lesea, A. et al. 2005. The rosetta experiment: atmospheric soft error rate testing in differing technology FPGAs. *IEEE Transactions on Device and Materials Reliability.* 5, 3 (Sep. 2005), 317 – 328.

[11]  Li, F. et al. 2003. Architecture evaluation for power-efficient FPGAs. *Proceedings of the 2003 ACM/SIGDA eleventh international symposium on Field programmable gate arrays* (Monterey, California, USA, 2003), 175–184.

[12]  Liu, X. et al. 2012. An Ultra-Low Power ECG Acquisition and Monitoring ASIC System for WBAN Applications. *Emerging and Selected Topics in Circuits and Systems, IEEE Journal on.* 2, 1 (Mar. 2012), 60 –70.

[13]  Mehta, N. et al. 2012. Limit study of energy & delay benefits of component-specific routing. *Proceedings of the ACM/SIGDA international symposium on Field Programmable Gate Arrays* (New York, NY, USA, 2012), 97–106.

[14]  Power Consumption at 40 and 45nm: *http://www.xilinx.com/support/documentation/white_papers/wp298.pdf.*

[15]  Rose, J. et al. 2012. The VTR project: architecture and CAD for FPGAs from verilog to routing. *Proceedings of the ACM/SIGDA international symposium on Field Programmable Gate Arrays* (New York, NY, USA, 2012), 77–86.

[16]  Ryan, J.F. and Calhoun, B.H. 2010. A sub-threshold FPGA with low-swing dual-VDD interconnect in 90nm CMOS. *Custom Integrated Circuits Conference (CICC), 2010 IEEE* (2010), 1–4.

[17]  Wang, A. 2006. *Sub-threshold design for ultra low-power systems.* Springer.

[18]  Wang, J. et al. 2008. Analyzing static and dynamic write margin for nanometer SRAMs. *Low Power Electronics and Design (ISLPED), 2008 ACM/IEEE International Symposium on* (Aug. 2008), 129 –134.

[19]  Ye, A.G. 2010. Using the Minimum Set of Input Combinations to Minimize the Area of Local Routing Networks in Logic Clusters Containing Logically Equivalent I/Os in FPGAs. *Very Large Scale Integration (VLSI) Systems, IEEE Transactions on.* 18, 1 (2010), 95–107.

# Improving Bitstream Compression by Modifying FPGA Architecture

Seyyed Ahmad Razavi, Morteza Saheb Zamani
Department of Computer Engineering and Information Technology
Amirkabir University of Technology, Tehran, Iran
{a.razavi,szamani}@aut.ac.ir

## ABSTRACT

The size of configuration bitstreams of field-programmable gate arrays (FPGA) is increasing rapidly. Compression techniques are used to decrease the size of bitstreams. In this paper, an appropriate bitstream format and variable symbol lengths are proposed to utilize the routing patterns for enhancing the compression efficiency. An order of inputs of multiplexers in switch modules is also proposed to improve the symbol statistics and hence, the compression efficiency. A framework to generate the bitstream and hardware description of FPGAs is developed as well. Experimental results over 20 MCNC benchmarks show that by applying the proposed approaches, the compression rate is improved by 46% on average compared to the methods with fixed symbol lengths without any area and performance degradation.

## Categories and Subject Descriptors

B.7.1 [**Integrated Circuits**]: Types and Design Styles—Gate Arrays

## General Terms

Performance, Design.

## Keywords

Bitstream, compression, entropy.

## 1. INTRODUCTION

Field-programmable gate arrays (FPGA) are widely used due to their reconfigurability, short time to market and ease of use. FPGAs are continuously growing to support various modern applications. As a result, the size of configuration bitstreams is increasing rapidly. Nowadays, there are some FPGA families with bitstreams longer than 400 Mega bits. A bitstream is usually saved in an expensive non-volatile memory chip on an FPGA board. Longer bitstream means larger and more expensive memory chips, and also long time to load the bitstream from the on-board memory which is undesirable in some applications.

To reduce the size of bitstream, they are compressed. Most compression techniques firstly convert the segments of bitstream into symbols, and then compress the produced stream of symbols. Several bitstream compression techniques have been presented. However the effects of routing resource structure on the bitstream compressibility have not been studied. Authors of [1] modified the placement and routing tool to reduce the number of frames

used by the design. Hence, the size of the bitstream decreased. A method was proposed in [2] to reduce the configuration bits of the lookup tables by removing redundancies. In [3], various compression methods such as Huffman, arithmetic coding and LZW are applied to the Xilinx Virtex II bitstream, with the assumption of fixed symbol length of either 6 or 9 bits. In [4], the authors introduced a decoding-aware compression method that is a combination of bitmask-based compression techniques and run-length encoding. They used a fixed symbol length of 8 bits. Authors of [5] divide the bitstream of an FPGA into some regions, i.e. logic, routing resources, and IO blocks, with different statistics and compress those regions separately.

In this paper, we present two modifications in structure of the bitstream and routing resources to enhance the efficiency of the subsequent compression methods. These modifications do not necessitate any changes in either the place and route tool or the interconnect architecture. Hence, our method does not affect the performance of the design and the area of FPGA. Our contributions are as follows:

1-A proper order for the configuration bits and an appropriate bit length for the symbols are found in a way that the routing patterns can be utilized appropriately for a compression method.

2-The inputs of multiplexers (MUXs) in switch modules are reordered to increase the number of identical symbols in the symbol stream. It is noteworthy that more compression can be obtained for streams with a large number of identical symbols. Our input reordering method makes it possible to represent the frequently-used similar routing patterns by similar symbols. Such an approach can produce identical symbols for a large part of the stream.

To verify the efficiency of our approach, we developed a framework based on VPR 5 CAD tool [6]. This framework is used to (a) generate the gate level netlist of the basic tiles of the target FPGA that is described by VPR 5 and (b) to produce bitstreams for the circuits that are placed and routed by VPR. To make the evaluation of our method independent of the compression techniques, we used the concept of Shannon entropy [7]. Shannon entropy presents a lower bound on the effectiveness of entropy-based compression methods such as Huffman and arithmetic coding. The rest of the paper is organized as follows: Section 2 provides a background for FPGA architectures and their programmer circuit, and explains the concept of entropy. The proposed approach is described in Section 3. The framework and experimental results are presented in Section 4. Finally, we conclude the paper in Section 5.

## 2. BACKGROUND

### 2.1 FPGA architecture

Island-style FPGAs have a regular structure containing a two-dimensional array of CLBs within a large set of routing resources. Therefore, the chip can be viewed as a set of basic tiles. Figure 1.a illustrates one of the basic tiles of the FPGA that consists of a CLB and its routing resources. The CLB contains a number of basic logic elements (BLE) which are programmed to implement logic functions. The routing resources, which include a connection block and a switch module, are unidirectional and consist of wire segments, MUXs and configuration SRAM cells. The wire segments lie in horizontal (CHANX) or vertical (CHANY) channels. Half of the wire segments in each channel are increasing (decreasing) that is their directions are from low (high) to high (low) coordinates in the FPGA. There are a large number of MUXs in the FPGA that are mainly used for routing, and a dominant part of the configuration SRAM cells are dedicated to them. MUXs can have fully encoded, fully decoded or hybrid structures. In this paper, we focus on the fully encoded MUX structures. Nevertheless, our approach can be extended to FPGAs with fully decoded or hybrid MUX structures.

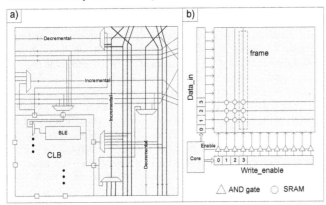

**Figure 1. a) One of the basic tiles of the FPGA b) The FPGA programmer**

SRAM cells are used to configure the FPGA programmable modules. During the configuration, the SRAM cells are loaded with the bits of the bitstream using data and write lines. An on-chip programmer circuit is used to feed the FPGA with the bitstream. The structure of a typical programmer is shown in Figure 1.b. As illustrated in this figure, the programmer consists of two shift registers (i.e. *Data_in* and *Write_enable*) and a core. *Data_in* and the *Write_enable* registers are connected to the data and write lines of the SRAM cells. During the configuration, the core pushes the bitstream into the *Data_in* shift register, and then loads them into the SRAM cells by activating the appropriate *Write_enable* and *Enable* line. After loading the data of one frame into SRAM cells, the Enable line is deactivated to prepare the circuit for loading another frame of the configuration bits. This procedure continues until all of the configuration SRAM cells are loaded with the bitstream.

## 2.2 Shannon entropy

Shannon entropy [7] is a criterion for measuring the amount of information. If the entropy of data is low, the amount of information stored in the data is small and it can be compressed better. Entropy presents a lower bound for the efficiency of entropy-based compression methods as well. Huffman and arithmetic coding are two popular entropy-based compression methods. Entropy is defined by $H = -\sum_{i=1}^{n}[p(i)\times\log_2(p(i))]$ where $p(i)$ is the probability that symbol $i$ occurs in the data, and $n$ is the number of unique symbols. The value of $H$ shows the average number of bits needed to represent a symbol. Entropy-based compressors reduce the size of data because they encode symbols

with higher frequencies by shorter codes. If the data has some more frequent symbols, the entropy would be lower, hence, more compression rate. For example, if each letter represents a symbol, the entropy of the string "aaaab" will be lower than the entropy of "aaabb" because of more occurrence of symbol "a" in the former string. The method of representing the data (i.e., bitstream format and symbol length) has a significant effect on the symbol statistics and entropy. For example, let the bitstream be "00010001". If each bit is used as a symbol (symbol length=1), then the entropy and the number of symbols will be is 0.81 and 8, respectively. Therefore, the total size of the transferred data, that is the multiplication of entropy and symbol count, is 6.48. However, if each pair of consequent bits is considered as a symbol (symbol length=2), the symbols will be '00','01' and '01' and the entropy, the number of symbols and the total size will be 1, 4 and 4, respectively.

## 3. THE PROPOSED APPROACH

As described in the previous section, the bitstream format, the symbol length, and the frequency of symbols have a significant effect on the entropy. Therefore, in this paper, we attempt to modify the bitstream format, set an appropriate symbol length and increase the occurrence of frequent symbols to reduce the entropy. To do this, we modified the bitstream and the routing resource structure in two ways:

1-The configuration of each MUX is represented by individual symbols. To do this, the bitstream format (i.e. the order of configuration bits in the bitstream) is changed in a way that the configuration bits of each MUX can be placed together. Furthermore, we did not use a fixed symbol length. The symbol lengths are set to the number of configuration bits of each MUX. To modify the bitstream format, the *Write-enable* and *Data_in* lines of SRAM cells are rearranged.

2-The structure of switch module MUXs are modified to have better symbol statistics in the stream, which leads to an increase in the occurrences of more frequent symbols and a decrease in the occurrences of others. Our approach is based on the fact that some routing patterns occur more frequent than others. To have better symbol statistics, the frequent routing patterns are represented with identical symbols by arranging the input of the switch module MUXs. As a result, the occurrences of those identical symbols will increase and the other ones will decrease. Therefore, the generated bitstream will be more compressible.

## 3.1 The bitstream format and symbol lengths

A simple method to represent the routing patterns that could be used for compression is to have them in individual symbols. To this end, the configuration bits of each MUX should be kept together. Therefore, the interconnections of SRAM cells are modified in a way that the configuration SRAM cells of each MUX have a common *Write-enable* line and chronological *Data_in* lines. If the SRAM cells of a MUX have different *Write_enable* lines, then according to the structure of the programmer in Figure 1.b, their configuration bits will place in different frames. Moreover, if they have a common *Write_enable* line but they are not arranged contiguously, their configuration bits are placed within a frame but they may be separated. In both of these cases, the configuration bits of a MUX could not be represented by one symbol because they do not take place sequentially in the bitstream. The only way that an individual symbol can be used to configure a MUX is to rearrange its configuration SRAM cells to have a common *Write_anable* line and contiguous sequential *Data_in* lines. This does not affect the

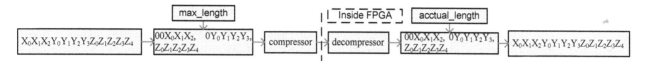

**Figure 2. The block diagram of the proposed bitstream compression and decompression method**

capacitance load on write_enable line significantly because SRAM cells are exchanged and the number of SRAM cells of each frame is almost the same before and after the rearrangement.

As described before, the symbol length has a significant effect on the compression rate. By choosing an appropriate symbol length, the configuration of each MUX could be represented by a symbol so the symbol statistics and the compression rate can improve. In our approach, the configuration bits of each MUX constitute a single symbol. Due to the different sizes of MUXs in the FPGA, a unique symbol length cannot be used for all MUXs. An example is shown in Table 1. Assume that a segment of the bitstream is "$x_0x_1x_2y_0y_1y_2y_3z_0z_1z_2z_3z_4$" where $m_i$ ($m \in \{x, y, z\}$) is the $i_{th}$ configuration bit of the MUX M. If the symbol length is set to a fixed value of 3 or 4 bits, the symbols cannot represent the configuration patterns of the MUXs. On the contrary, if the symbol length is variable, and equal to the number of configuration bits, the symbols will represent the patterns of the related MUXs. However, different symbol lengths imply that the length of all symbols must be saved in masks to make the bitstream decompression possible. Nonetheless, due to the tileability of FPGAs, the overhead of saving the symbol lengths is fairly low because a single mask could be used for multiple tiles. Our FPGA consists of 25 basic tiles for which the symbol lengths must be defined. All tiles are generated by replicating the basic tiles.

**Table 1. The symbols of a bitstream using different symbol lengths**

| bitstream | $x_0x_1x_2y_0y_1y_2y_3z_0z_1z_2z_3z_4$ |
|---|---|
| 3-bit symbol | $x_0x_1x_2, y_0y_1y_2, y_3z_0z_1, z_2z_3z_4$ |
| 4-bit symbol | $x_0x_1x_2y_0, y_1y_2y_3z_0, z_1z_2z_3z_4$ |
| Variable length symbol | $x_0x_1x_2, y_0y_1y_2y_3, z_0z_1z_2z_3z_4$ <br> Related mask: 3, 4, 5 |

To prepare the variable length symbols for compression, they are represented by their maximum length. For example, as illustrated in Figure 2, let the length of symbols for the configuration of switch module MUXs be 3, 4 and 5 bits. First, the symbols are represented with 5 bits by appending extra zeros as the most significant bits. Afterward, the compressor encodes these fixed length symbols. Inside the FPGA, after decoding the compressed bitstream using the decompressor, the real sizes of symbols are restored using the appropriate symbol length masks and the extra zeros are eliminated. In the case that the compression method needs to transfer the symbol probabilities, as in Huffman and arithmetic coding, if the symbol length is long, then the size of symbol probabilities will be large (e.g. $2^{16}$ for a symbol length of 16). Therefore, it is better to use multiple shorter symbols instead of a long symbol. To this end, we divided the large symbols into smaller symbols. For example if a symbol length is 16 bits, it is divided into four 4-bit symbols. Although appending the extra zeros increases the number of bits before compression, it reduces the size of the compressed bitstream due to the improved symbols statistics.

## 4. The order of inputs for switch modules' MUXs

In FPGAs with bidirectional wire segments, some routing patterns in the design are more frequent than the others [8]. We

obtained similar results for the FPGAs with unidirectional wire segments in our experiments. Assigning identical symbols to frequent patterns increases the number of identical symbols and makes the final bitstream more compressible. We categorized the routing patterns into straight (CHANX_to_CHANX and CHANY_to_CHANY segments), orthogonal (CHANX_to_CHANY and vice versa) and starting (output port of CLB into the switch module MUXs). Each routing pattern has a wire segment or the output port of a CLB as its source, and a wire segment as its destination. The target FPGA in our experiments has ten 4-input LUTs in each CLB, and each wire segment spans one CLB. The switch module architecture is Wilton and the flexibility of switch modules (Fs) is 3. All wire segments are unidirectional and they are either increasing or decreasing. To choose the best order for the MUX inputs, as in [8], we counted the routing patterns of routed MCNC benchmarks.

The statistical information of one of MCNC benchmarks (seq.net) is brought in Table 2. As can be seen in the table, straight patterns occur much more frequent than the other patterns for the attempted benchmark. Each MUX can produce only one straight pattern, so the inputs of all the MUXs are ordered in a way that a unique symbol (e.g. "0000") represents all straight patterns. Next to the straight patterns, the orthogonal patterns are more frequently used than the rest of patterns. Therefore, identical symbols are used for representing such patterns to improve the compression rate further. In FPGAs with segment lengths of one, two orthogonal patterns can be produced for each MUX. Thus, two symbols (e.g. "0001" and "0010") are sufficient to represent all orthogonal patterns. The 10 different outputs of each CLB lead to different starting patterns for the MUX that connected to that CLB. Different symbols must be assigned to each of these starting patterns. As a result, each distinctive starting pattern occurs about 10 times less than 1436 which implies a less occurrence frequency than that of straight and orthogonal patterns. It is noticeable that based on our experiments, other MCNC benchmarks have similar statistical information; therefore, the appropriate input orders for them are the same as those for seq.net benchmark.

**Table 2. The number of switch module routing patterns of seq**

| | Mux in X direction | | | | Mux in Y direction | | | | |
|---|---|---|---|---|---|---|---|---|---|
| Destination direction | increasing | | decreasing | | increasing | | decreasing | | Sum |
| Source direction | Inc. | Dec. | Inc. | Dec. | Inc. | Dec. | Inc. | Dec. | |
| Straight | 2066 | -- | -- | 1327 | 1652 | -- | -- | 1951 | 6996 |
| Orthogonal | 504 | 281 | 543 | 466 | 609 | 534 | 308 | 424 | 3669 |
| Starting | 352 | | 400 | | 340 | | 344 | | 1436 |

Some of switch module MUXs do not have required connections for particular routing pattern (e.g. straight pattern in fringe tiles). For these MUXs, symbols with smaller values are assigned to patterns with the higher probabilities of occurrence (e.g. "0000" and "0001" are assigned to the orthogonal patterns in MUXs that do not have straight pattern).

This approach is explained by a simple example. Consider a switch module architecture as illustrated in Figure 3.a. The "0101", "1010", "0010", and "0000" symbols form horizontal and vertical straight patterns. Assume that each of these patterns appears in the design by an average of α times. Therefore, each symbol occurs in the bitstream for at least α times. If the order of MUX inputs is set to what is shown in Figure 3.b, then the horizontal and vertical straight patterns can be represented by "0000". As a result, there will be only one symbol for straight patterns which occurs in the symbol stream 4*α times and will lead to a better symbol statistics and an improved compression rate. It is clear that the symbols associated with patterns in MUXs cannot be changed after fabrication since they depend on the orders of the MUX inputs that are hard wired. There are potential overheads by restricting the design of layout to the specific MUX input order and frame structure such as increase in the wire length of *write_enable* and *data_in* lines. However, by considering them in designing the layout of the tiles, they could be negligible.

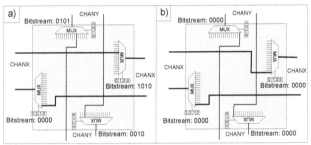

**Figure 3. A switch module a) without and b) with ordered MUX inputs and bitstream for straight patterns**

## 5. EMPERIMENTAL RESULTS

We developed a framework which generates the gate level netlist of basic tiles, the whole FPGA and circuit bitstreams based on architecture file used by VPR 5. The framework supports various unidirectional architectures (i.e. different FPGA sizes, CLB sizes, channel width sizes, switch module topologies, segment lengths, $F_c$ and $F_s$). As the default architecture described by VPR is not tileable, in this paper the tool was modified slightly to generate tileable architectures. The modified tool is used to place and route designs with the minimum channel width. Subsequently, the HDL code of the basic tiles, the hardware description of the FPGA in Verilog, and the bitstream is generated using the developed framework.

After generating the bitstream, the entropy of the bitstream is calculated. Although specifying the don't care bits, which are related to the unused resources, in a suitable way improves the compression rate, they are excluded for a fair evaluation. The architecture attempted in the experiments was the same as the one used in Section 3.2. Shannon entropy presents the lower bound on the effectiveness of entropy-based compression methods. Therefore, this compression rate, called *theoretical compression rate*, can be calculated by dividing the entropy of the bitstream by the symbol length. Figure 4 shows the theoretical compression rate for 20 MCNC benchmarks. In our experiments (the proposed approaches), the maximum length of symbols is chosen to be 4 and the shorter symbols are converted to 4-bit symbols, as described in Section 3.1.

The first proposed approach (App.1), that is the use of variable symbol length, improves the average theoretical compression rate by 35%, 30%, 34%, and 30% compared to the fixed symbol length of 3, 4, 5, and 6 bits, respectively. By applying the second proposed approach, which is the reordering of MUX inputs, on top of the first proposed approach (App.1+App.2), the theoretical compression rate is improved by 24% and 46% on average, compared to the first proposed approach and the best fixed symbol length, respectively. For all the benchmarks, the proposed

approaches led to better results than the approaches which use fixed symbol length. The proposed approaches, does not affect the placement and routing of the design, so the critical path of circuit and the area of FPGA is untouched. It should be pointed out that the base architecture, which the ordered inputs architecture was compared, was produced by VPR 5. This architecture is not the worst case and the order of its MUX inputs can improve the entropy rate compared to the worst case.

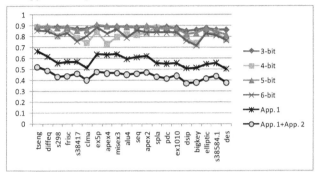

**Figure 4. The theoretical compression rate of switch module bitstream in various approaches**

## 6. CONCLUSION AND FUTURE WORKS

In this paper, we modified the bitstream format and chose the appropriate symbol lengths to have the configuration of MUXs in separate symbols. Then, we arranged the inputs of MUXs in the switch modules to improve the symbol statistics. By applying both approaches, the theoretical compression rate is improved by 46% over 20 MCNC benchmarks compared to the approaches which use fixed symbol length. In this work, we focused on the MUXs of switch modules. Research on other MUXs in other parts of the FPGA, such as connection blocks and CLBs is underway.

## 7. Acknowledgment

We would like to thank Mr. Mohammad Hossein Shekarian for his useful discussions.

## 8. REFERENCES

[1] P. Stepien and M. Vasilko, "On Feasibility of FPGA Bitstream Compression During Placement and Routing," FPL 2006.

[2] A. Abdelhadi and G. Lemieux, "Configuration Bitstream Reduction for SRAM-based FPGAs by Enumerating LUT Input Permutations," ReConFig 2011.

[3] Z. Li and S. Hauck, "Configuration Compression for Virtex FPGAs," FCCM 2001.

[4] X. Qin, et al, "Decoding-Aware Compression of FPGA Bitstreams," IEEE Trans. on VLSI, March 2011.

[5] M. Martina, et al, "A New Approach to Compress the Configuration Information of Programmable Devices," DATE 2006.

[6] J. Luu, et al, "VPR 5.0: FPGA CAD and Architecture Exploration Tools with Single-Driver Routing, Heterogeneity and Process Scaling," FPGA 2009.

[7] C. E. Shannon, "Prediction and Entropy of Printed English," Bell Syst. Tech. J. 30, 50–64, 1951.

[8] G. Wang, et al, "Statistical Analysis and Design of HARP FPGAs," IEEE Trans. on CAD, Oct. 2006.

# Elastic CGRAs

Yuanjie Huang[¶§]
huangyuanjie@ict.ac.cn

Paolo Ienne[†]
paolo.ienne@epfl.ch

Olivier Temam[‡]
olivier.temam@inria.fr

Yunji Chen[¶]
cyj@ict.ac.cn

Chengyong Wu[¶]
cwu@ict.ac.cn

[¶]CARCH, ICT, CAS, China    [†]EPFL, Switzerland    [‡]INRIA, Saclay, France    [§]GUCAS, China

## ABSTRACT

Vital technology trends such as voltage scaling and homogeneous multicore scaling have reached their limits and architects turn to alternate computing paradigms, such as heterogeneous and domain-specialized solutions. *Coarse-Grain Reconfigurable Arrays (CGRAs)* promise the performance of massively spatial computing while offering interesting tradeoffs of flexibility versus energy efficiency. Yet, configuring and scheduling execution for CGRAs generally runs into the classic difficulties that have hampered *Very-Long Instruction Word (VLIW)* architectures: efficient schedules are difficult to generate, especially for applications with complex control flow and data structures, and they are inherently static—thus, inadapted to variable-latency components (such as the read ports of caches). Over the years, VLIWs have been relegated to important but specific application domains where such issues are more under the control of the designers; similarly, statically-scheduled CGRAs may prove inadequate for future general-purpose computing systems. In this paper, we introduce *Elastic CGRAs*, the *superscalar processors* of computing fabrics: no complex schedule needs to be computed at configuration time, and the operations execute dynamically in the CGRA when data are ready, thus exploiting the data parallelism that an application offers. We designed, down to a manufacturable layout, a simple CGRA where we demonstrated and optimized our elastic control circuitry. We also built a complete compilation toolchain that transforms arbitrary C code in a configuration for the array. The area overhead (26%), critical path overhead (8%) and energy overhead (53%) of Elastic CGRAs over non-elastic CGRAs are significantly lower than the overhead of superscalar processors over VLIWs, while providing the same benefits. At such moderate costs, elasticity may prove to be one of the key enablers to make the adoption of CGRAs widespread.

## Categories and Subject Descriptors

C.1.3 [**Computer Systems Organization**]: Processor Architectures — Other Architecture Styles; B.6.3 [**Logic Design**]: Design Aids — Automatic synthesis

## General Terms

Design, Performance

## Keywords

CPGA, elastic circuit, dataflow, reconfigurable computing

## 1. INTRODUCTION

*Coarse-Grained Reconfigurable Arrays (CGRAs)* are an appealing paradigm to implement accelerators in these days and times when both voltage scaling and homogeneous multicore scaling approach their ultimate limits [30, 16]: On one hand, as it is the case for *Field Programmable Gate Arrays (FPGAs)*, CGRAs are good candidates to create massively spatial application-specific accelerators. On the other hand, and in contrast to FPGAs, they are word-oriented and hence naturally more efficient in area, timing, and energy when used for complete applications originally designed for pure software implementation. Yet, despite such appeal and despite more than a decade of focused research, they have not yet made it into widespread commercial use.

CGRAs aggressively exploit spatial parallelism, much as *Very Long Instruction Word (VLIW)* processors [18] exploit *Instruction Level Parallelism (ILP)*, with CGRAs being vastly more complex, and thus potentially powerful, than VLIWs due to the affordable number of operators, routing, and configuration control [36]. Yet, one of the biggest impediments to the diffusion of VLIWs has always been the compiler technology required to efficiently schedule programs with complex control and memory behavior. Thus, superscalar processors, which also aim at leveraging ILP, albeit using a purely automated hardware approach (on-the-fly resolution of register dependences, memory dependences and extraction of ILP), have become the de facto standard for general-purpose computing (epitomized by Intel x86 architecture), and they are now making in-roads in energy-conscious embedded systems as well, e.g., ARM Cortex A9 [2], Intel Atom Z2460 [19]. The difficulty of compiling efficient VLIW code has ultimately relegated VLIWs to some important but niche applications such as digital signal-processing – far away from general-purpose computing.

Existing CGRA designs, such as ADRES [26], MATRIX [27], Tartan [28], MorphoSys [34], or HSRA [40], similarly

171

rely on complex compiler technology to schedule operations. In fact, considerable research efforts have already gone in adapting for CGRAs the *classic* VLIW compilation techniques [31, 41]. To improve the chances of CGRAs to become a viable architecture for reconfigurable accelerators, we introduce an *Elastic CGRA*, where scheduling occurs entirely in hardware and control signals follow computation in a dataflow manner, adapting to the actual execution of the application: Our scheme requires practically no compiler scheduling effort, much like the hardware issuing of operations in superscalar processors removes the burden of VLIW code scheduling. And, while superscalar processors come with a significant hardware overhead which has incited decades of research on VLIW processors, we show that the hardware overhead of Elastic CGRAs, with respect to a statically scheduled CGRA, is comparatively low, even though they bring the same benefits as superscalar processors.

As the name suggests, our idea is based on *elastic circuits* [11], which are data paths where the exact scheduling of operations is not fixed in advance but is dynamically determined at runtime by the availability of operands, much like in asynchronous circuits. Yet, despite a strong conceptual similarity with asynchronous circuits, elastic circuits are perfectly synchronous circuits which can be designed with any modern EDA flow. Starting from a *Control and Data Flow Graph (CDFG)*, we show that it is relatively straightforward to generate two strongly interconnected circuits, one processing the data and the other controlling the flow of operation. These two circuits seamlessly map onto the units of an Elastic CGRA. As a result, creating a configuration for an Elastic CGRA requires less assumptions on the exact device implementation, such as the latency of the individual components or the unit topology. This property also provides some form of "binary compatibility" of the code mapping onto the CGRA across different Elastic CGRA microarchitectures, much like superscalar processors achieve compatibility across successive generations of microarchitectures whereas VLIWs do not.

In this paper, we design a tile of a possible Elastic CGRAs, which we synthesize and place and route with standard cells in a common 65nm technology. In order to demonstrate the programmability of Elastic CGRAs, we implement a GCC-based tool chain which performs a simple conversion of programs into elastic circuits. We retarget VPR [6], typically used for placement and routing on FPGAs, to place and route the combined data and control networks onto an Elastic CGRA. We automatically generate the RTL description of the elastic circuits of five benchmarks, which are then mapped and executed on the Elastic CGRA. We also implement a more classic statically-scheduled version of our CGRA to assess the cost of "elasticity" in terms of area, critical path, and energy consumption. We conclude that the area overhead is 26%, the critical path delay overhead is 8% and the energy overhead is 53%. Overall, the energy and area overhead of Elastic CGRAs over non-elastic CGRAs is significantly lower than the overhead of superscalar processors over VLIWs, while providing the same dynamic schedule and portability benefits.

In Section 2, we present the method for converting a program into elastic circuits. In Section 3, we explain how to generalize the elastic circuit concepts into an Elastic CGRA. In Section 4, we present the different elements of the tool chain. We present the experimental methodology in Sec-

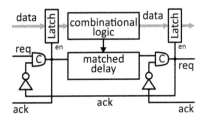

**Figure 1:** *Asynchronous handshaking control circuit.*

tion 5, the performance evaluations in Section 6, and the related work in Section 7.

## 2. FROM SOURCE CODE TO ELASTIC CONTROL CIRCUITS

We first present the concept of elastic control, then we describe the conversion process from source code to elastic circuits (for both ASICs and Elastic CGRA), we outline the interface of such circuits with the memory hierarchy, we explain why such circuits are deadlock-free, and we conclude with a code conversion example.

### 2.1 Elastic Control

The principle of elastic control is to replace statically scheduled control with dynamic dataflow-like control in a circuit. The benefit of dataflow-like control is the avoidance of a statically precomputed schedule: data propagates down the circuit with the respective control token. As a result, complex scheduling cases occurring when the latency of certain operators varies—e.g., complex operators or memory accesses, or where multiple operators must all complete before moving to the next operation—are seamlessly handled with token propagation, as we will later see. This notion of dataflow-like control is not new but, until recently, it was mostly accomplished using asynchronous circuits or through ad-hoc solutions. Budiu et al. [7] had already noted the great potential of dataflow-like asynchronous control for easily converting programs into circuits. However, there is no mature industrial tool chain for designing asynchronous circuits yet, even if promising tool chains are emerging [14]. The key contribution of elastic control [11] is to propose dataflow asynchronous-like control in perfectly synchronous circuits, at a very low energy and area cost. We first briefly recap a few notions about asynchronous control and then we present the main principles of elastic control.

**Asynchronous control.** In an asynchronous pipeline, the control parts of two consecutive pipeline stages are connected through an asynchronous circuit, see Figure 1. The main component of this circuit is the Muller C gate [29] (see gate $C$ in Figure 1) which implements a behavior similar to an SR latch. In an asynchronous circuit controlling a pipeline, the output of that gate is 1 only if the previous pipeline stage is valid (i.e., it has a data to pass) and the next pipeline stage is not stalled (i.e., it can accept the data). This output signal controls the pipeline latch between two pipeline stages in the data path of the circuit (see Figure 1).

The circuit in Figure 1 has the typical issue of needing a delay closely matched to that of the functional unit—something that is unfeasible and simply requires taking large margins.

**Elastic control.** Elastic control aims at emulating a similar behavior, with similar signals handshaking, except that it is based on clocked circuits, and thus it is fully compatible with existing EDA toolchains. Cortadella et al. [11] proposed the SELF protocol and a structure named Elastic Buffer to connect pipeline stages. In our design, Elastic Buffers are modified to use flip-flops for implementation convenience, see Figure 2. Elastic control circuits are always tied to a data path component, forming a *data-control pair*. For instance, the Elastic Buffer in the control path (bottom) is always tied to a pipeline register in the data path (top). This circuit uses the same *valid* and *stall* signals as the corresponding asynchronous circuit. The completion detection signal is replaced by a standard stall signal at a clock-cycle resolution. A data path implemented using elastic control circuits, including loops, has been proved to be deadlock and race free with proper initialization [22].

## 2.2 Conversion Process

Three elastic operators have been previously introduced [20, 11] for implementing elastic control circuits: *Elastic Buffer* (EB), *Eager Fork* (EF), which corresponds to the control token forking to two or more targets, and the reciprocal circuit *Join* (JO), which merges multiple control paths into one. In order to implement program control flow statements such as `if` or `switch`, we also need *Branch* (BR) and the reciprocal *Merge* (MG) [35] elastic control circuits, where Branch corresponds to an operator with multiple potential control flow paths, and only a single token is issued into one of the paths.

In the remainder of this section, we describe these operators in detail, and we illustrate the conversion process with the *Finite Impulse Response* (FIR) filter code shown in Figure 8. The first step consists in converting the program into a control flow graph of its basic blocks, as shown in Figure 9.

### 2.2.1 Across Basic Blocks

By definition, a basic block is a control flow graph node with a single *control flow* entry point and a single *control flow* exit point. Note that "single control flow entry point" or "single control flow exit point" should not be confused with "single control flow predecessor" or "single control flow successor": a basic block can have multiple predecessors all entering the basic block at the same program statement—i.e., entry point—and similarly, a single exit point can potentially fork out to multiple successors. Consider, for instance, BB3 in the control flow graph of Figure 9: It has a single entry point (statement i < NP), but two predecessors, BB2 and BB4. Also, BB3 has a single exit point, but it can branch out to two successors: BB4 and the exit of the function.

**Merge.** If a basic block has several predecessors, the control circuit of the corresponding entry point is an elastic *Merge* circuit, shown in Figure 6. For instance, the control flow token can reach BB3 from two possible predecessors, BB2 and BB4: the entry basic block, and the body of the loop (see Figure 9). However, at any given time, only one of the two successors can have the control flow token.

**Branch.** Similarly, if a basic block has several successors, the control circuit of the corresponding exit point is an elastic Branch circuit, shown in Figure 5. Across basic blocks, the control flow token necessarily flows out to only one of several successors. For instance, one can notice that the exit

```
int i,t0;
int x1=0;
for (i=0;i<N;i++)
{
  t0=x[i];
  y[i]=t0*C0+x1*C1;
  x1=t0;
}
```

**Figure 8:** *FIR code.*

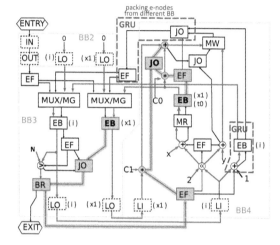

**Figure 9:** *Control flow graph of FIR.*

**Figure 10:** *FIR circuit. LI and LO stand for live-in and live-out respectively, and are only wire annotations. MR and MW are memory read and write ports.*

point of BB2 in Figure 9 can branch out to two successors: either BB4 or exit.

### 2.2.2 Within Basic Blocks

In this section, we explain how the elastic operators Eager Fork and Join, previously introduced by Cortadella et al. [11], can be used for basic block conversion. The control flow subgraph corresponding to a basic block is always a directed acyclic graph of the basic block statements, by definition of a basic block.

**Variables.** The first step consists in converting scalar accesses. There are three types of scalar accesses within a basic block: live-ins, live-outs, and temporary values. Both live-ins and live-outs must exist beyond the basic block data flow graph, and thus, they are implemented using Elastic Buffers. Temporary values require no physical storage. For instance, variables `x1` and `i` in Figure 9 correspond to both live-ins and live-outs in BB3 and BB4, and, thus, they are each implemented with an Elastic Buffer, as shown in Figure 10; `t0` corresponds to a basic block temporary value and has no corresponding register in Figure 10.

**Eager Fork.** When the same value flows from one statement to two or more statements in parallel, the control flow token splits into multiple tokens which, similarly to the corresponding data, flow in parallel. This can only happen *within* a basic block but never across basic blocks, since basic blocks are executed sequentially. This control flow token multiplication is implemented with the Eager Fork elastic

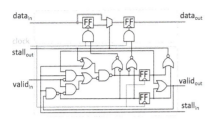

**Figure 2:** *Elastic Buffer (EB).*

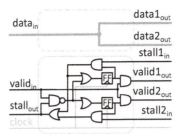

**Figure 3:** *Eager Fork (EF).*

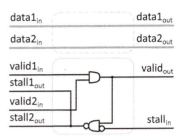

**Figure 4:** *Join (JO).*

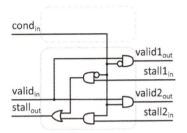

**Figure 5:** *Branch (BR).*

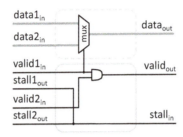

**Figure 6:** *Merge (MG).*

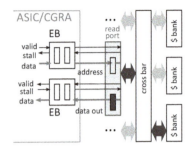

**Figure 7:** *Virtual memory port.*

control circuit (see Figure 3). This fork is called "eager" because the control flow token can be sent to each branch as soon as the branch can accept it. Consider for instance the entry point of the body of the innermost loop in Figure 8: the statements x1*C1, i<<2, i++ can all be executed in parallel and, as a result, the entry point is implemented with an Eager Fork, instead of an Elastic Buffer, as one can see with the EF at the bottom of BB4 in Figure 10.

**Join.** When two or more parallel statements are followed by a sequential flow of execution, or reach the end of the basic block, the multiple control tokens join back to become a single token as soon as they are all available. Again, this can only occur within a basic block. This is implemented with an elastic Join, see Figure 4. Consider for instance the JO at the top of BB4 in Figure 10.

**Dependent statements.** Conversely, dependent statements are implemented with serially connected elastic control circuits. Consider for instance the data flow dependence due to the + operation between t0*C0 and x1*C1: these two statements are respectively implemented with control handshake from an EB through an operator then connected to an elastic Join—i.e., the two control tokens join back to become a single token, as shown by the shaded boxes connected by highlighted lines in Figure 10.

## 2.3 Memory Interface

In order to seamlessly integrate memory accesses within the translation process—and thus easily convert load and store instructions, we introduce the notion of *elastic virtual memory ports*. Each read/write memory access is replaced with a read/write elastic virtual memory port. This memory port supports the same control interface as an Elastic Buffer—i.e., the same two-signal handshake channel. The write port has two data flow inputs (data and address), and the read port has one data flow input (address) and one output (data), as shown in Figure 7. For instance, in a read port, the outgoing *valid* signal becomes true when the data has been fetched from memory and is ready. The

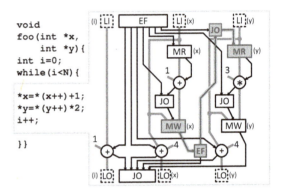

```
void
foo(int *x,
    int *y){
int i=0;
while(i<N){

*x=*(x++)+1;
*y=*(y++)*2;
i++;

}}
```

**Figure 11:** *Memory dependences: the four different accesses to x and y are implemented using 2 read ports (MR) and 2 write ports (MW); the highlighted elastic circuit corresponds to the dependence between the x write and the y read.*

outgoing *stall* signal becomes false when the read port can accept a new memory request—i.e., a new address.

**Memory Dependences.** Distinct references are mapped to different memory ports, so two ports could potentially access the same address. The memory dependence is implemented by creating a lockstep between the corresponding elastic virtual memory ports. Consider the example of Figure 11. Read and write references to pointer x and y are mapped to four memory ports, two for read and two for write. Now, for instance, due to pointer aliasing, the y read can depend upon the x write. So we create a lockstep between the two ports using the highlighted JO and EF: one x write must occur before the next y read takes place. In superscalar processors, such dependences are detected by the *Load/Store Queue* (LSQ). Although nothing would prevent us from implementing an LSQ too, for the sake of simplicity and without loss of generality, we imple-

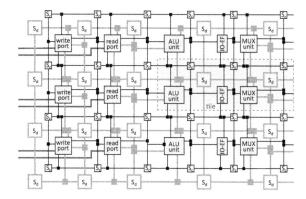

**Figure 12:** *Elastic CGRA.*

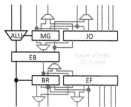

**Figure 13:** *Naive elastic ALU unit.*

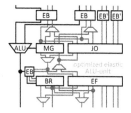

**Figure 14:** *Optimized elastic ALU unit*

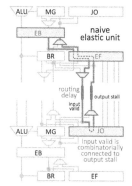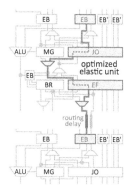

**Figure 15:** *Critical paths of naive and optimized units.*

ment a cheaper, albeit semi-manual solution, for now. If the compiler cannot automatically find which memory references are dependent—e.g., in case of pointer aliasing—the user has to annotate the code. These dependence annotations will be converted into the lockstep circuit of Figure 11.

## 2.4 Putting It All Together

Each control and data flow part of the program is converted as explained above, and all data flow and control flow components are then connected. One of the strengths of an asynchronous-like circuit is the ability to convert each operator in isolation, yet obtain an efficient global circuit. For instance, assuming single-cycle memory accesses, the loop body of the program in Figure 8 can execute in 4 cycles—i.e., one cycle per operation (read t0, two parallel multiplications, one addition, store into y[i] in parallel with register write into x1).

## 3. CGRA

In this section, we adapt the notion of elastic control to reconfigurable circuits, and CGRA in particular. We build an elastic-controlled reconfigurable network and units on which any data and control flow cases can be mapped.

## 3.1 Tile

A tile, shown in the dashed box in Figure 12, is actually a bundle of one ALU-unit, one MUX-unit, and an elastic synchronizer-unit composed of a Join and an Eager Fork. This structure was derived from empirical evaluation of typical control and data flow patterns in programs. The intuition for adding a stand-alone MUX is that operators within basic blocks often receive their inputs either from inside the basic block (e.g., a loop) or outside the basic block (i.e., an initial value), hence the need for a MUX. As we will see below, the ALU also contains a generic set of elastic operators. In addition to these operators, we add a separate JO/EF pair in order to avoid wasting a whole ALU unit for purely Eager-Join-and-then-Fork synchronization, which occur frequently. We describe the different components of the ALU unit below.

**Elastic control bundle.** The elastic control circuit of the ALU is shown in Figure 13. In order to implement any elastic control case, we found that the simplest solution is to bundle all possible elastic operators together (MG, BR, JO, EF, and one EB). Usually only one or two of these operators are used in each unit, but since they are 1-bit operators, their

cost is very low, and such waste is a negligible overhead, as we will see in Section 6. The MG and JO units have similar roles as they perform an action based on all possible incoming tokens, while BR and EF have the dual role on outgoing tokens—hence the symmetric structure of the tile. The EB holds the register at the output of the ALU. The JO and EF have been empirically dimensioned to handle 8 handshakes, and we draw 4 handshakes in Figure 13, 14 and 15 only to be visually clear.

**ALU.** The ALU can perform the following operations: addition, subtraction, multiply, comparison, arithmetic, and logical shifts; all these operations can be signed or unsigned. There are 6-input multiplexers connecting the ALU to the routing network. Moreover, because of address computations, left-shift by 2 are frequently needed, so we add two multiplexers, one at the output of each of these two large multiplexers, in order to select the normal or shifted input. In addition to arithmetic and logic computations, the ALU itself can also behave as a multiplexer (leveraging an unused slot of the ALU multiplexer) for dynamic control flow purposes (*if* statements). The control bit of that multiplexer is coming from the Merge operator in the elastic control part of the unit.

**Read/Write ports.** All read/write ports are placed on one side of the grid, where they are connected to the memory subsystem. This placement was preferred over read/write ports spread around the periphery in order to avoid long connections between closely related memory references in the data flow graph. We implemented these ports on only one side of the array in order to later connect it more easily to cache.

## 3.2 Optimized Tile

The elastic implementation shown in Figure 13 suffers from a problem that limits its clock rate: the input valid signal can be combinatorially connected to the output stall signal through the JO elements at the entrance of a unit, and consequently the inward and outward routing networks for these two control signals are merged into one long timing path. Though it is possible to split the critical path with an extra EB, it is costly solution with the current CGRA structure because one full unit must be used.

In order to overcome that timing limitation, we developed an optimized version where the input valid signal and the output stall signal are separated by registers; this is accomplished by moving the EB to the entrance of the unit; as a result, the EB must be duplicated for each handshake pair. The resulting unit organization is shown in Figure 14. Its critical path is illustrated in Figure 15. Since an ALU unit has only two data inputs, we eliminated data registers in all but two input EBs in order to save area. Another specialized EB with a 1-bit data register is placed before the BR in order to split the long path that goes through the ALU, BR and JOIN and ends up at the input EB.

This optimization trades a small increase of area and energy for a significantly higher clock rate, as later shown in Section 6.

## 3.3 Grid

The Elastic CGRA grid is shown in Figure 12. The high-level structure of the grid is strongly inspired from that of FPGAs. The routing network is composed of switches (or switch boxes, also called *S-boxes*) connecting horizontal and vertical lines, and the units themselves are connected to the network through connect boxes (*C-boxes*) shown as solid black and grey squares. Our Elastic CGRA routing network has some differences from an FPGA routing network, though: Firstly, it is composed of two networks, not one—the elastic control network shown in thin black lines ($S_c$ stands for control switch) and the data network shown in thick grey lines ($S_d$ is a data switch). Moreover, the data network consists of 32-bit channel bundles, whereas FPGAs usually have 1-bit channels; 32-bit data channel bundles share configuration bits. Finally, the valid and stall signals of elastic control share a single 1-bit channel. All channels are unidirectional as in modern FPGAs [23]. For the switches, we have used the popular pattern proposed by Wilton [43]. Based on the benchmarks later presented in Section 5, we empirically found (after exploration with VPR) that six (32-bit) data channels and sixteen (1-bit) control channels are sufficient. Note that, because VPR (used for placement and routing) imposes that all units in a column to be identical, we arrange the three blocks of the unit (ALU, elastic control, and MUX) in a row, see Figure 12.

The elastic control and data configuration is implemented using several multiplexers shown in Figure 12. Note that the configuration of JO and EF requires to indicate how many tokens they should respectively wait upon or issue. No such configuration is needed for MGs and BRs.

## 4. TOOL CHAIN

The overall structure of the tool chain is described in Figure 16. The tool chain first generates a circuit intermediate representation from the source code, then converts it into an elastic circuit. This elastic circuit can either be mapped into Verilog and used to create an ASIC, or mapped onto a CGRA and then placed and routed. We briefly describe the different tool chain components below.

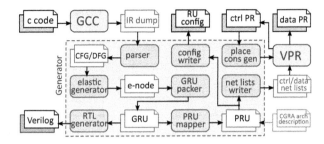

**Figure 16:** *Work flow and structure of the tool chain.*

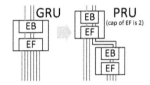

**Figure 17:** *GRU mapping to PRU.*

The front-end of the infrastructure is the GCC compiler (version 4.6.1). In order to generate our intermediate representation, we piggyback on the GCC 32-bit MIPS back-end. We generate the intermediate representation just before the hardware register allocation pass, because a CGRA can potentially implement a far greater number of registers than a core, and the code should not be hampered by the side-effects of a limited number of registers (especially by spill code).

## 4.1 Elastic Circuit

The elastic circuit generator is implemented outside GCC, communicating through the generated intermediate representation instead of being plugged into GCC, only to limit the overhead of keeping pace with the rapid evolution of GCC, and still to benefit from the most recent high-level optimizations.

The elastic generator builds the data flow graph of each basic block, and the control flow graph between basic blocks. Then it generates the elastic components using the elastic operators (stored as templates) described in Section 2. Several of these templates have a configurable number of inputs or outputs (Join, Eager Fork, Merge, and Branch). The output is a directed graph of *e-nodes*, where one e-node corresponds to an elastic operator. For instance, in Figure 10, each solid box or circle stands for an e-node corresponding to a physical elastic operator, while dotted boxes are virtual e-nodes which keep track of various information. For example, the two e-nodes labeled LO in BB2 indicate that the initial value of i and x0 are set in BB2 and that they are live-outs. Thin black edges are control handshakes (arrow showing the valid signal direction), while bold gray edges are 32-bit data channels.

## 4.2 CGRA Generator

The CGRA generator is significantly more complex. It first maps every elastic node onto a *Generic Reconfigurable Unit* (GRU). A GRU is a virtual unit, i.e., an ALU, an Elastic Buffer and the set of elastic control primitives. However, at that stage, the Merge, Join, and Eager Fork primitives are assumed to have an infinite number of inputs and outputs respectively. Moreover, the number of GRU units is

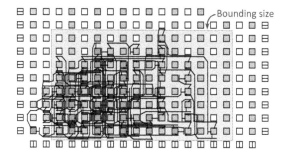

**Figure 18:** *VPR routing result of Susan_s' data nets.*

| Benchmark | Domain | Description | Hot function |
|---|---|---|---|
| *blowfish_e* (Cbench) | security | Symmetric block cipher with a variable length key. | BF_encrypt |
| *fir* (UTDSP) | signal processing | 256-tap Finite Impulse Response filter. | fir |
| *fft* (EEMBC) | telecom | Fast-Fourier-Transformation. | fxpfft |
| *latnrm* (UTDSP) | signal processing | 32nd-order Normalized Lattice filter. | latnrm |
| *susan_s* (Cbench) | auto-motive | An image recognition algorithm, it can smooth the image. | susan_ smoothing |

**Table 1:** *Benchmarks description.*

also considered infinite. The GRU abstract unit representation allows to perform several optimizations independently of the number of units and the capacity of each unit. For instance, an e-node storing a constant does not consume one unit because it is stored in the constant register contained in each unit, see Section 3.1. A GRU is obtained from one or several e-nodes. For instance, if an EB stores the result of an adder, both are packed into the same GRU. Or, if an EF follows a JO, both are also packed into a single GRU. These two examples are marked in Figure 10 with dashed boxes. Finally, GRUs are transformed into *Physical Reconfigurable Units* (PRU) which correspond to the target CGRA unit architecture. For instance, if one GRU contains an Eager Fork with more outputs than a PRU, it is split accordingly and mapped onto several PRUs, see Figure 17. A netlist of the PRUs is then generated for the placement and routing phases.

### 4.3 Place and Route

We use VPR [6] for the placement and routing phases, VPR being the most popular open-source tool for that task. Normally, VPR is designed to place LUTs and route 1-bit channels. Replacing LUTs with PRUs is trivially done. On the other hand, we have two networks to route: the 32-bit data network, and the 1-bit elastic control network (which contains the valid/stall signals). There is no notion of dual networks in VPR and we therefore perform a 2-phase routing: First, we let VPR place the PRUs and route the 1-bit control channels. After that phase, we obtain a placement of all PRUs, because all PRUs must have control connections. Then, we impose this placement and we perform a second routing for data channels, presenting them as 1-bit channels to VPR. In Figure 18, we show the placement of PRUs for *susan_s* and the routing of its data network.

## 5. METHODOLOGY

### 5.1 Synthesis

CGRA tiles are synthesized with Synopsys Design Compiler Ultra 2009 onto a TSMC 65nm library, and layout was done using Synopsys IC Compiler 2009. We employed 9 metal layers, with 1 to 7 for routing, and 8 and 9 dedicated to power distribution. The energy measurements are obtained using Synopsys PrimeTime PX 2009 with post-layout activities captured by by Synopsys VCS 2010. All data presented in Section 6 are collected in the Normal Case COMmercial (NCCOM) condition.

### 5.2 Non-Elastic CGRA

To quantitatively assess the overhead of elastic control, we derived a non-elastic CGRA from the elastic one by substituting elastic control with a distributed statically-scheduled controller as in B. Mei et. al's paper[26]. The elastic control of each unit, shown in Figure 14, is replaced with a distributed local storage containing the contexts of each unit, where one context corresponds to the configuration bits of the ALU, input MUXes and output register write control. In addition, the unit contains the simple context address generation logic allowing to iterate through, or jump to, contexts. As each non-elastic CGRA unit corresponds to an ALU-unit or a MUX-unit in elastic CGRA, we extract contexts for them from the activity of corresponding units in the simulation of the same benchmark on elastic CGRA. Note that, unlike elastic controlled CGRAs, such statically scheduled control can only be used to map codes with regular control flow, e.g., loops, so we focus the comparison on the main (most time-consuming) loop of each benchmark The data routing network remains unchanged.

### 5.3 Benchmarks

We use five benchmarks from the embedded benchmark suites UTDSP [33], MiBench [17] and EEMBC [15] to evaluate our proposal. The five benchmarks are chosen from three different domains: automotive, security, and telecom. For each of these benchmarks, we use gprof to identify the hot function, and convert this function into a circuit.

We simulated these benchmarks using the data sets provided in their benchmark suite. Data sets of *susan_s* were slightly trimmed to achieve acceptable post-layout simulation time. The memory subsystem is emulated in the test bench using a memory array preloaded with a memory image, obtained after running each benchmark on a MIPS CPU. The memory subsystem is assumed to be perfect (no cache misses) and all requests return in one cycle because detailed memory behavior is out of scope of this study.

## 6. PERFORMANCE EVALUATION

In this section, we compare the area, critical path delay and energy of elastic vs non-elastic CGRAs. The non-elastic CGRA is the *baseline*, the naive elastic control of Section 3.1 is called *naive*, and the optimized elastic control of Section 3.2 is called *optimized*.

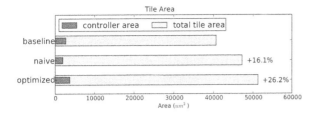

**Figure 19:** *Tile area of non-elastic , naive elastic and optimized elastic implementations.*

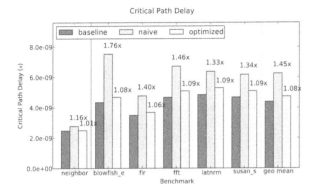

**Figure 20:** *Critical Path Delay of non-elastic CGRA, naive and optimized elastic CGRAs.*

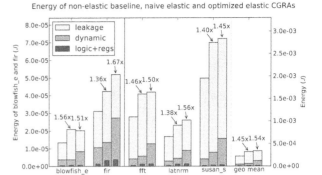

**Figure 21:** *Total energy and breakdown.*

## 6.1 Area

In Figure 19, we compare the area of the non-elastic CGRA (baseline), the optimized tile version of Section 3.2, and the naive tile version of Section 3.1. The naive version has an area overhead of 16.1% over the baseline, and most of this overhead is due to the 1-bit elastic control routing network. The optimized version has an overhead of 26.2% due to the addition of registers, see Section 3.2. In all cases (non-elastic or elastic), the controller logic itself accounts for a small fraction of the overall tile area.

## 6.2 Critical Path Delay

We report the critical path delay in Figure 20. On average, the naive implementation is 1.45× slower than the baseline, while the optimized one is only 1.08× slower. For neighbor-to-neighbor communications, the optimized elastic unit can achieve the same clock rate as the non-elastic unit, as shown in bar *neighbor*. The control handshake wires increases the total wire density which, in turn, degrades the wire quality and results in slightly longer wires, hence the slight slowdown of the optimized elastic CGRA.

## 6.3 Energy

The energy for executing each benchmark on each CGRA is shown in Figure 21, with the number on the top showing the energy ratio with respect to the non-elastic CGRA. On average, the naive and optimized elastic CGRAs respectively require 43.2% and 53.8% more energy than the non-elastic CGRA. We also provide a breakdown into leakage and dynamic energy. Leakage is higher for elastic CGRAs due to the higher area, and dynamic energy is higher due to the elastic control routing network; the dynamic energy of the optimized version is even higher due to the higher register switching activity. We further highlight the fraction of dy-

namic energy due to the logic and registers (the rest being the clock tree and routing network), and we show that the dynamic energy due to the clock tree and routing network dominates.

## 7. RELATED WORK

Schedules generated for CGRA have been universally static, as discussed by De Sutter et al. in their recent survey [36]. This naturally limits the chances to convert efficiently arbitrary programs and adds constraints to the source code: ADRES [26], like others, assumes no control flow in loop bodies to generate VLIW-like static schedules. There exists a considerable body of work on adapting classic VLIW compilation techniques to the mapping and scheduling problems of CGRA (for instance, Park et al. developed variations of modulo scheduling targeted to reconfigurable accelerators [31]). Elastic CGRA is quite different because its elastic nature considerably simplifies program conversion with essentially no constraints. There is a large body of works on compiling programs onto dataflow architectures, e.g. Arvind et .al's TDDA [3], or more recently, Wavescalar [37] and Ambric [39]. While our design follows similar dataflow principles, our focus is on the detailed circuit implementation of such dataflow constructions based on elastic circuits, it relies on a more simple FPGA-like static routing network, and an almost direct translation from C code. Recently, Budiu et. al. [7] have proposed to implement dataflow circuits using asynchronous elements, but such approaches are limited by some classic issues of asynchronous designs; our Elastic CGRA benefits from being fully synchronous. We are also significantly different from Achronix's pipoPIPE [1], which is an asynchronous platform which promises to improve over current FPGAs but remains a fine-grain bit-level device, at a completely different granularity. Park et al. [32], on the other hand, have used data tokens in a CGRA, but their control is only partially distributed: their CGRA is still driven by instructions, stored in a central structure, the goal of the tokens is limited to driving the fetching of instructions into the functional units.

Program translation into arbitrary circuits (both targeting ASICs and FPGAs) is the focus of *High-Level Synthesis (HLS)*, widely researched since the nineties. One of the classic phases of HLS is scheduling, and some ideas in this area are similar to what is or could be done in CGRAs. Academic tools, such as ROCC [42], and commercial tools, such as CatapultC [25], are emerging and can convert programs, with certain limitations, into circuits, mostly targeting FPGAs. To our knowledge, most or all of these tools generate architectures limited to static schedules and cannot accommodate efficiently variable latency components, such as the ports of typical general-purpose memory hierarchies. In fact, from early notable examples of translation of high-level programming constructs into circuits [8] until more recent experiences [24, 38], generated controllers have almost universally taken the form of horizontally microcoded sequencers, single monolithic FSMs, or networks of smaller FSMs [12]. Here too, as in CGRAs, the focus is mostly on VLIW-like loop modifications to allow efficient pipelining of fixed-latency components [41]. The importance of variable-latency components became apparent in the late nineties with work by Benini et al. on *Telescopic Units*, variable-latency units obtained automatically from standard fixed-latency designs [4, 5] but little was done for the generation of efficient controllers. More recently, the design of controllers for such variable-latency units has been revisited in more details, showing the possibility of complex networks of FSMs accounting for all the dependencies in the dataflow specification [13]. To escape the complexity and scalability difficulties of these solutions, *latency insensitive protocols*, *synchronous interlocked pipelines*, and other forms of *elastic circuits* have emerged in the last few years as an elegant, natural, and effective method to control large circuits composed of variable-latency units [9, 21, 11]. Although conceptually similar, these techniques have subtle differences among them [10]; without loss of generality, we have elected SELF [11] as our base methodology to bring elasticity to CGRAs.

# 8. CONCLUSIONS AND FUTURE WORK

We have introduced an Elastic CGRA, a word-based configurable circuit which requires no scheduling thanks to a dataflow-like control. We have implemented a toolchain based on GCC and VPR which can automatically map C code to this Elastic CGRA. The area overhead of elastic control is only 26.2%; the critical path delay overhead is even lower at 8.2%, and moreover it shall be more than compensated by the ability to tolerate variable memory latencies which is beyond the capability of statically scheduled CGRAs, much like superscalar processors have a significant variable latency tolerance advantage over VLIWs. The energy overhead of elastic control is 53.8%, due to additional control routing and registers. However, Elastic CGRAs provide the same benefits as superscalar processors over VLIWs (dynamic scheduling, portability across CGRA designs) with a much lower energy penalty.

Some of our next steps include creating a cost-effective CGRA-to-cache interface in order to plug into and be compatible with existing heterogeneous multi-cores, and introducing local memories for faster and energy-efficient access to data, as common in state-of-the-art FPGAs.

# 9. ACKNOWLEDGMENTS

We thank the anonymous reviewers for suggestions which helped improving this paper. This research is supported by the National Natural Science Foundation of China under project No.61003064 and No.61222204.

# 10. REFERENCES

[1] Achronix. *Introduction to Achronix FPGA*, 2008.

[2] ARM Ltd. The ARM Cortex-a9 processors. White Paper, 2009.

[3] Arvind and R. S. Nikhil. Executing a program on the MIT tagged-token dataflow architecture. *IEEE Transactions on Computers*, 39(3):300–318, Mar. 1990.

[4] L. Benini, E. Macii, and M. Poncino. Efficient Controller Design for Telescopic Units. In *Proceedings of the Second Annual {IEEE} International Conference on Innovative Systems in Silicon*, pages 290–299, Oct. 1997.

[5] L. Benini, E. Macii, M. Poncino, and G. De Micheli. Telescopic Units: A new paradigm for performance optimization of VLSI designs. *{IEEE} Transactions on Computer-Aided Design of Integrated Circuits and Systems*, CAD-17(3):220–232, Mar. 1998.

[6] V. Betz and J. Rose. VPR: A new packing, placement and routing tool for FPGA research. In *Field-Programmable Logic and Applications*, pages 213–222. Springer, 1997.

[7] M. Budiu, G. Venkataramani, T. Chelcea, and S. C. Goldstein. Spatial computation. In *International Conference on Architectural Support for Programming Languages and Operating Systems*, page 14, Boston, Massachussets, Dec. 2004.

[8] R. Camposano. From behavior to structure: High-Level Synthesis. *IEEE Design and Test of Computers*, 7(5):8–19, Oct. 1990.

[9] L. P. Carloni, K. L. McMillan, and A. L. Sangiovanni-Vincentelli. Theory of Latency-Insensitive Design. *IEEE Transactions on Computer-Aided Design of Integrated Circuits and Systems*, CAD-20(9):1059–1076, Sept. 2001.

[10] M. R. Casu and L. Macchiarulo. Adaptive Latency Insensitive Protocols and Elastic Circuits with Early Evaluation: A Comparative Analysis. *Electronic Notes in Theoretical Computer Science*, 245:35–50, Aug. 2009.

[11] J. Cortadella, M. Kishinevsky, and B. Grundmann. Synthesis of Synchronous Elastic Architectures. In *Proceedings of the 43rd Design Automation Conference*, pages 657–662, San Francisco, Calif., July 2006.

[12] G. De Micheli. *Synthesis and Optimization of Digital Circuits*. McGraw-Hill, New York, 1994.

[13] A. A. Del Barrio, S. Ogrenci Memik, M. C. Molina, J. M. Mendias, and R. Hermida. A Distributed Controller for Managing Speculative Functional Units in High Level Synthesis. *IEEE Transactions on Computer-Aided Design of Integrated Circuits and Systems*, CAD-30(3):350–363, Mar. 2011.

[14] D. Edwards and A. Bardsley. Balsa: An asynchronous hardware synthesis language. *The Computer Journal*, 45(1):12–18, 2002.

[15] Embedded Microprocessor Benchmark Consortium. *EEMBC benchmark suite*, 2009.

[16] H. Esmaeilzadeh, E. Blem, R. S. Amant, K. Sankaralingam, and D. Burger. Dark Silicon and the End of Multicore Scaling. In *Proceedings of the 38th International Symposium on Computer Architecture (ISCA)*, June 2011.

[17] M. Guthaus, J. Ringenberg, D. Ernst, T. Austin, T. Mudge, and R. Brown. Mibench: a free, commercially representative embedded benchmark suite. In *2001 IEEE International Workshop on Workload Characterization*, pages 3–14. IEEE, 2001.

[18] J. L. Hennessy and D. A. Patterson. *Computer Architecture: A Quantitative Approach*. Morgan Kaufmann, San Mateo, Calif., fifth edition, 2012.

[19] Intel Cooperation. Intel Atom processor z2460. Product Brief, 2012.

[20] H. Jacobson, P. Kudva, P. Bose, and P. Cook. Synchronous interlocked pipelines. In *Proceedings of the 8th International Symposium on Asynchronus Circuits and Systems*, pages 292–293. IEEE, 2002.

[21] H. M. Jacobson, P. N. Kudva, P. Bose, P. W. Cook, S. E. Schuster, E. G. Mercer, and C. J. Myers. Synchronous Interlocked Pipelines. In *Proceedings of the 8th International Symposium on Advanced Research in Asynchronous Circuits and Systems*, pages 3–12, Manchester, Apr. 2002.

[22] E. Kilada and S. Das. Synchronous Elasticization: Considerations For Correct Implementation and MiniMIPS Case Study. In *Proceedings of the Conference on Design, Automation and Test in Europe*, pages 7–12, 2010.

[23] G. Lemieux, E. Lee, M. Tom, and A. Yu. Directional and Single-Driver Wires in FPGA Interconnect. In *International Conference on Field-Programmable Technology*, pages 41–48. IEEE, 2004.

[24] S. Mahlke, R. Ravindran, M. Schlansker, R. Schreiber, and T. Sherwood. Bitwidth Cognizant Architecture Synthesis of Custom Hardware Accelerators. *IEEE Transactions on Computer-Aided Design of Integrated Circuits and Systems*, CAD-20(11):1355–1371, Nov. 2001.

[25] S. McCloud. Catapult c synthesis-based design flow: Speeding implementation and increasing flexibility. *White Paper, Mentor Graphics*, 2004.

[26] B. Mei, S. Vernalde, D. Verkest, H. De Man, and R. Lauwereins. ADRES: An Architecture with Tightly Coupled VLIW Processor and Coarse-Grained Reconfigurable Matrix. In P. Y. K. Cheung and G. Constantinides, editors, *Field Programmable Logic and Application*, volume 2778, pages 61–70. Springer Berlin / Heidelberg, 2003.

[27] E. Mirsky and A. DeHon. MATRIX: a reconfigurable computing architecture with configurable instruction distribution and deployable resources. In *Proceedings on IEEE Symposium on FPGAs for Custom Computing Machines, 1996*, pages 157–166, Apr. 1996.

[28] M. Mishra, T. J. Callahan, T. Chelcea, G. Venkataramani, M. Budiu, and S. C. Goldstein. Tartan: evaluating spatial computation for whole program execution. In *Proceedings of the 12th International Conference on Architectural Support for Programming Languages and Operating Systems, 2006*, 2006.

[29] D. E. Muller and W. S. Bartky. A Theory of Asynchronous Circuits. In *International Symposium on Theory of Switching*, pages 204–243. Harvard University Press, 1959.

[30] M. Muller. Dark Silicon and the Internet. In *EE Times "Designing with ARM" virtual conference*, 2010.

[31] H. Park, K. Fan, S. A. Mahlke, T. Oh, H. Kim, and H.-s. Kim. Edge-centric modulo scheduling for coarse-grained reconfigurable architectures. In *Proceedings of the 17th International Conference on Parallel Architecture and Compilation Techniques*, pages 166–76, Toronto, Oct. 2008.

[32] H. Park, Y. Park, and S. Mahlke. Reducing Control Power in CGRAs with Token Flow. In *Preceedings of Workshop on Optimizations for DSP and Embedded Systems*, 2009.

[33] S. H.-e. Peng. *UTDSP: A VLIW Programmable DSP Processor*. PhD thesis, University of Toronto, 1999.

[34] H. Singh, F. Kurdahi, N. Bagherzadeh, and E. Chaves Filho. MorphoSys: an integrated reconfigurable system for data-parallel and computation-intensive applications. *IEEE Transactions on Computers*, 49(5):465–481, May 2002.

[35] J. Sparsø and S. Furber. *Principles of Asynchronous Circuit Design: a Systems Perspective*. Kluwer, 2001.

[36] B. D. Sutter, P. Raghavan, and A. Lambrechts. Coarse-Grained Reconfigurable Array Architectures. *Elements*, (1), 2010.

[37] S. Swanson, K. Michelson, A. Schwerin, and M. Oskin. WaveScalar. In *Proceedings of the 36th annual IEEE/ACM International Symposium on Microarchitecture*, MICRO 36, pages 291–302, Washington, DC, USA, 2003. IEEE Computer Society.

[38] R. Taylor and D. Stewart. Coprocessor Generation from Executable Code. In P. Ienne and R. Leupers, editors, *Customizable Embedded Processors—Design Technologies and Applications*, Systems on Silicon Series, chapter 9, pages 209–232. Morgan Kaufmann, San Mateo, Calif., 2006.

[39] P. Top and M. Gokhale. Application experiments: Mppa and fpga. In *Preceedings of the 17th IEEE Symposium on Field Programmable Custom Computing Machines*, pages 291–294, Apr. 2009.

[40] W. Tsu, K. Macy, A. Joshi, R. Huang, N. Walker, T. Tung, O. Rowhani, V. George, J. Wawrzynek, and A. DeHon. Hsra: high-speed, hierarchical synchronous reconfigurable array. In *Proceedings of the 1999 ACM/SIGDA seventh international symposium on Field programmable gate arrays*, FPGA '99, pages 125–134, New York, NY, USA, 1999. ACM.

[41] K. Turkington, G. A. Constantinides, K. Masselos, and P. Y. K. Cheung. Outer loop pipelining for application specific datapaths in FPGAs. *IEEE Transactions on Very Large Scale Integration (VLSI) Systems*, VLSI-16(10):1268–80, Oct. 2008.

[42] J. Villarreal, A. Park, W. A. Najjar, and R. Halstead. Designing Modular Hardware Accelerators in C with ROCCC 2.0. In *International Symposium on Field-Programmable Custom Computing Machines*, number May, pages 127–134. IEEE, 2010.

[43] S. Wilton. *Architectures and Algorithms for Field-Programmable Gate Arrays with Embedded Memory*. Phd. thesis, University of Toronto, 1997.

# Embedding-Based Placement of Processing Element Networks on FPGAs for Physical Model Simulation

Bailey Miller
Dept. of Computer Science
and Engineering
University of California, Riverside
bmiller@cs.ucr.edu

Frank Vahid
Dept. of Computer Science
and Engineering
University of California, Riverside
Also with CECS, UC Irvine
vahid@cs.ucr.edu

Tony Givargis
Center for Embedded Computer
Systems (CECS)
University of California, Irvine
givargis@uci.edu

## ABSTRACT

Physical models utilize mathematical equations to model physical systems like airway mechanics, neuron networks, or chemical reactions. Previous work has shown that physical models can execute fast on FPGAs (field-programmable gate arrays). We introduce an approach for implementing physical models on FPGAs that applies graph theoretic techniques to make use of a physical model's natural structure—tree, ring, chain, etc.— resulting in model execution speedups. A first phase of the approach maps physical model equations to a structured virtual PE (processing element) graph using graph theoretic folding techniques. A second phase maps the structured virtual PE graph to physical PE regions on an FPGA using graph embedding theory. We also present a simulated annealing approach with custom cost and neighbor functions that can map any physical model onto an FPGA with low wire costs. Average circuit speedup improvements over previous works for various physical models are 65% using the graph embedding and 35% using the simulated annealing approach. Each approach's more efficient use of FPGA resources also enables larger models to be implemented on an FPGA device.

## Categories and Subject Descriptors

B.5.2 [**Design Aids**]: Automatic synthesis
C.3 [**SPECIAL-PURPOSE AND APPLICATION-BASED SYSTEMS**]: Real-time and embedded systems

## Keywords

Real-time emulation, field-programmable gate array (FPGA), ordinary differential equations, physical models, cyber-physical systems, differential equation synthesis, high-level synthesis, system-level synthesis, processing elements, PE networks, graph embedding, placement, simulated annealing, emulation

## 1. INTRODUCTION

Fast physical model simulations are required in various domains, including biomedical engineering, physics, chemistry, and much more. A physical model represents some observable physical phenomena, usually as a set of normal, partial differential, or ordinary differential equations. The set of equations can be solved using time-stepping equation solvers.

In the cyber-physical system domain, previous work uses physical models to interact with and test devices such as ventilators [16], pacemakers [13], and unmanned aerial vehicles [9]. Using physical model simulations for testing can be preferable over the actual physical environment when such an environment is difficult, expensive, or dangerous to create or use. Physical models may also be more accurate than physical analogs, e.g., a balloon may capture some of the behavior of a lung, but may not be able to accurately model various lung diseases.

Our previous research has been able to speed up physical model simulation up to three orders of magnitude versus multicore desktop processors, by partitioning physical model computation across hundreds of processing elements (PEs) on an FPGA [12], each PE optimized to execute time-stepping equation solvers [11].

Many physical models share the same natural structure as the corresponding physical system. For example, a Weibel lung model [27] utilizes a binary tree structure because the lung physiology itself is a tree in which the trachea is the root and where gas exchange occurs at the leaves. Similarly, atrial cell models utilize a three-dimensional mesh structure to simulate the propagation of electrical signals across tissues of cardiac cells [29]. Equations of the physical system are grouped naturally, e.g., the volume and pressure of a lung branch have data dependencies and thus should ideally be placed within the same PE to minimize communication costs. Generally, the natural structure of a physical model provides an optimal grouping of equations that minimizes communication costs.

A key contribution of this work is utilizing the natural structure of simulated physical model during placement of a PE network onto an FPGA. By using graph embedding techniques that have been

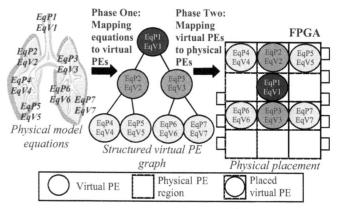

**Figure 1: Two-phase approach of mapping physical model equations onto a structured graph of virtual PEs, and mapping virtual PEs onto a FPGA utilizing graph embedding techniques.**

extensively researched in graph theory literature, the structure of the physical model can be embedded onto a two-dimensional grid of PE elements on an FPGA. By performing graph embeddings, the resulting circuit incurs less communication cost and enables higher circuit frequencies, translating to faster execution of physical models. A secondary contribution is the definition of a simulated annealing approach that provides cost and neighbor functions for minimizing distances between PEs placed on a grid of physical regions on a FPGA, used for unknown model structures and also for evaluating the first contribution.

Figure 1 details a two-phase approach for embedding a physical model onto an FPGA. The first phase maps the physical model equations to a structured virtual PE graph. A structured virtual PE graph has virtual PE nodes that contain groups of equations, have connections to other virtual PE nodes, and is structured in the form of the physical model. Physical placement can then be performed by defining physical PE regions where virtual PEs may be mapped, and then either applying the appropriate graph embedding algorithm or using a general simulated annealing approach to perform the mapping. In the right side of Figure 1, a graph embedding algorithm maps a binary tree to a two-dimensional grid by placing the root in a physical PE region in middle of the grid, and expanding the child subtrees out in different directions.

The rest of the paper is structured as follows. Section 2 describes past work on accelerating physical models, as well as other applications of graph embedding theory. Section 3 describes some example physical models with specific structures. Section 4 describes the process of partitioning equations to virtual PEs. Section 5 describes the mapping of virtual PEs to physical PE regions, either by using a graph embedding or simulated annealing approach. Section 6 discusses experiments showing circuit frequency speedups when using different placement strategies.

## 2. RELATED WORK

Our past research efforts on fast execution of physical models on FPGAs [11][12] have achieved orders of magnitude of acceleration over executing on desktop processors and several times speedups over graphical processing units, with improvements even when considering time/dollar-cost. Speedup was achieved by parallelization of differential equations across hundreds of PEs, for complete applications and not just kernels. FPGAs excel at executing physical models because the massively-parallel local-neighbor communication of physical models represents an excellent match for FPGA fabrics, avoiding common memory or external input/output bottleneck problems. An automated flow was presented that translates a specification of the physical model into an equation dependency graph, partitions equations into PEs via simulated annealing, schedules computations and custom point-to-point communications, and finally generates HDL for commercial tool synthesis. PEs may be either generic computation units with an ALU and programmable instructions, or a custom datapath targeted at a specific equation.

Recent work has shown additional speedups by creating heterogeneous networks of general, programmable PEs, and PEs with custom datapaths for solving specific equations [12]. de Pimentel also utilized an FPGA to accelerate a heart model on an FPGA [19], and interfaced the simulation with a pacemaker via analog-digital converters. Tagkopoulos built a custom FPGA for the simulation of gene regulatory networks [22].

While the above past efforts used heuristics to map equations to PEs and have relied on commercial tools to place PEs, we propose that a mapping of equations to PEs that maintains physical model natural structure and performs placement based on the structure can yield faster circuits and faster execution of physical models.

The problem of mapping algorithms with communication structures that differ from the interconnection scheme of the host architecture was first considered in the 1980s. Bokhari summarized the issue and offered a heuristic for mapping algorithm tasks to adjacent processors in a "finite element machine" array processor [5]. Later, Berman and Snyder offered a general solution for embedding common structures such as cubes, meshes, linear arrays, and trees [3]. Much of that research has been used in distributed and high-performance computing domains for mapping tasks to processors to minimize communication costs [4]. VLSI design has also utilized graph embedding techniques, including minimizing communication between a binary-tree structured processor network implemented on an optimally sized square [23].

The general problem of placing logic into a programmable FPGA fabric has previously been considered as a graph embedding problem, as opposed to the typical approach of iterative heuristics and recursive partitioning. Banerjee proposed converting netlists into hypergraphs and embedding the hypergraphs onto the two-dimensional grid of FPGA resources using a recursive space-filling curve [2]. This approach can yield up to 2x faster runtimes for placement, but yields little improvement to the critical path delays needed for faster physical model simulations. Gopalakrishnan proposed a new approach called CAPRI to create an initial placement of a design based on the embedding of a netlist into the target FPGA platform [10]. CAPRI models the routing delays of the target FPGA platform in a metric space and uses matrix projections to minimize distortion between graph abstractions of the netlist and platform. These previous works have focused on mapping to low-level FPGA resources like CLBs, whereas our work focuses on the best placement of a network of hundreds of individual PEs in abstracted FPGA physical regions.

## 3. PHYSICAL MODEL STRUCTURES

Physical models often have a natural structure associated with a corresponding layout in the physical world. Consider a human lung, which begins at the trachea and splits into nearly identical left and right lobes. Each lung contains more than twenty additional splits as the airway passage diameters decrease and

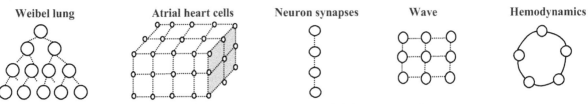

| Weibel lung | Atrial heart cells | Neuron synapses | Wave | Hemodynamics |

**Figure 2: Various physical models and graphs of their representative structures.**

eventually are able to support blood-gas exchange alveoli. The lung has thus often been modeled as a binary tree of twenty or more generations such that gas flow at the trachea can be used to compute the pressure and volume of internal branches [27]. Similarly, cell models that simulate electrical activity across heart atrium walls utilize a three-dimensional mesh structure to allow neighboring cells to propagate signals. Figure 2 shows some examples of physical models and their corresponding structures, which are described below.

*Weibel lung*: The classical binary tree shaped lung model, in which an inlet flow at the root of the tree is used to compute volume and pressure at lower branches [27]. Each node of the tree computes the volume $V$ and flow $F$ of the corresponding branch:

$$\frac{dV_i}{dt} = F_{parent} \cdot C_1 + V_i \cdot C_2 + F_i$$

$$\frac{dF_i}{dt} = V_i \cdot C_3 - F_i \cdot C_4 - V_{R\_child} \cdot C_5 - V_{L\_child} \cdot C_6$$

*Atrial heart cells:* A 3-dimensional mesh of cells, where each cell propagates signals to its neighbors [29]. $v_i$ is the membrane potential of cell $i$ and is computed by the following equation.

$$\frac{dv_i}{dt} = (c_1 + (v_{x1} + v_{x2} + v_{y1} + v_{y2} + v_{z1} + v_{z2} - c_3 \cdot v_i) \cdot c_2) \cdot c_3$$

*Neuron synapses:* A 1-dimensional array of cells that simulates the firing of neuron synapses. $s$ is the synaptic variable, $v$ is the membrane potential, and $w$ is a channel gating variable [21].

$$\frac{dv_i}{dt} = c_1 \cdot v_i + w_i - c_2 \cdot (v_i - c_3) \cdot (s_{i-1} + s_{i+1})$$

$$\frac{dw_i}{dt} = c_1 \cdot w_i - v_i$$

$$\frac{ds_i}{dt} = c_1 \cdot (1 - s_i) \cdot (v_i - c_2) - c_3 \cdot s_i$$

*Wave:* A wave model has a two-dimensional mesh network structure and is often used to model the propagation of sound, acoustics, etc [17]. The amplitude of the signal at node $i$ is given by:

$$\frac{du_i}{dt} = c_1 \cdot (u_{x1} + u_{x2} + u_{y1} + u_{y2}) + c_2 \cdot u_i$$

*Hemodynamics:* A model that simulates the circulation of the human body, and includes submodels for the left/right heart ventricle and pulmonary/systemic tissues [25]. The hemodynamic model is arranged in a circular structure. Since there are many different types of equations to model this system, we omit the detailed descriptions here.

Large physical models such as those described above can be partitioned to hundreds of PEs in a network to achieve very fast simulation speeds. By maintaining the structure associated with the physical model during physical placement of PEs onto an FPGA, the routing overhead between PEs can be minimized. The natural structure of a physical model typically uses an optimally minimal number and length of wires, because only local communication between cells, lung branches, etc. is required.

Previous work in physical model simulation attempted to recover the physical model structure via heuristic annealing algorithms, after having converted the specification of the physical model's equations to an equation dependency graph [11]. However, finding the globally optimal solution for physical models containing thousands of equations and hundreds of PEs is not feasible with this approach. Instead of attempting to recover structures with heuristics, we propose to preserve the connections as they were modeled so as to minimize communication cost.

# 4. PHASE 1: MAPPING EQUATIONS TO VIRTUAL PEs

Given the specification of a physical model that enumerates the physical model equations, a map must be built that groups equations into a structured virtual PE graph $G$ that maintains the structure of the physical model. Equations must first be partitioned to a structured virtual PE graph of unconstrained size. Second, the graph must be reduced in size via folding to fit into available resources of the *target platform*. The target platform, which is typically an FPGA but could be an ASIC, is the device that the circuit will be placed on. There are limited resources on the target platform, thus folding is necessary for physical models whose structured virtual PE graphs exceed the size of the target platform.

## 4.1 Partitioning equations

Let $G = (v, e)$, where $v = \{v_1, v_2 ... , v_n\}$ is a set of $n$ vertices and $e = \{e_1, e_2, ..., e_k\}$ is a set of $k$ edges between vertices in $v$. Let $E = \{E_1, E_2, ..., E_m\}$ be the set of equations defined in the specification of the physical model. The set of vertices $v$ represent virtual PEs, which may have equations from $E$ allocated to them. The set of edges $e$ represent communication channels between virtual PEs. If an edge $e_i = (v, u)$ exists, then there exists dependencies between the equations hosted in $v$ and $u$. The graph $G$ and its nodes and edges are defined by the structure of the physical model; a three-level binary-tree shaped Weibel lung model thus would have a graph that contains:

$G_v = \{v1, v2, v3, v4, v5, v6, v7\}$

$G_e = \{(v1,v2),(v1,v3),(v2,4),(v2,v5),(v3,v6),(v3,v7)\})$

Each equation $E_i$ can be allocated to a vertex $v_i$ in $G$ according to a surjective mapping function $f : E \rightarrow G_v$. The function $f$ depends on the structure of $G$, and maps groups of equations that represent the same physical element, e.g., a lung branch or atrial cell, to a single vertex. The result of applying the map function $f$ to each equation yields a structured virtual PE graph $G$ which maintains the basic structure of the physical model, and where each vertex (virtual PE) contains equations that represent some physical element of the physical model.

## 4.2 Folding

A physical model may be very large – a Weibel model with 11 generations contains 4000 differential equations. In order to meet the physical constraints of using a real platform when mapping virtual PEs to physical PEs, the virtual PE graph $G$ must first be scaled down. We perform *graph folding* on $G$ by applying a homomorphic folding function $\varphi$ that maps the larger graph to a smaller, more compact version $G'$ while preserving the structure of $G$. In particular, $\varphi$ maps $G$ to $G'$, where the size $n$ of the vertex set of $G'$ is less than or equal to the number of supportable PEs in the target platform $S$; $\varphi : G \rightarrow G' \mid G'_n < S$. $\varphi$ must also maintain the topology of $G$ in $G'$ by either maintaining an existing edge of

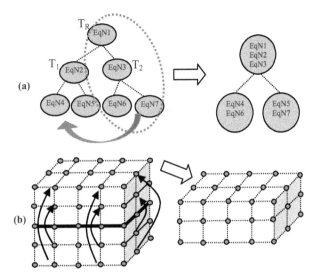

**Figure 3: Contraction of the PE dependency graph by folding: (a) binary tree (b) 3-dimensional mesh.**

$G$ in $G'$, or by merging the equations of vertex $a \in G$ into vertex $b \in G'$ such that the length of any edge connected to the merged vertices is constant. Informally, structures that are symmetric can generally be folded by cutting the graph into two subgraphs, and merging vertices that share the same position in each subgraph. Folding of graphs has been previously explored in graph theory literature [1][7][26]. Aleliunas [1] and Ellis [7] utilized folding techniques in order reduce the aspect ratio of rectangular graphs into forms that could be embedded onto a two-dimensional grid. Other work has developed algorithms for folding strongly balanced hypertrees in order to embed them into hypercube structures [26].

The exact definition of $\varphi$ depends on the physical model structure. Different physical models can reuse the same folding functions as long as their structures match, thus a folding function for each structure type must be identified. A potential pitfall of folding is that structured virtual PE graph sizes tended to be reduced by halves, potentially creating a situation where almost half of the physical PE regions of the target platform are empty. One solution is to simply manually merge the final few virtual PEs if the size constraint of the target platform is only slightly less than the size of the structured virtual PE graph. The following section provides examples that target binary tree physical models, describing the mapping function $f$ and folding function $\varphi$ which result in the generation of a structured virtual PE graph.

## 4.3 Lung model example

A small Weibel lung model with three generations of bifurcating airways is structured as a binary tree with $2^3-1 = 7$ branches, or fourteen interdependent differential equations for computing the pressure and volume of each branch. Let the set of equations $E$ in the specification of the physical model be ordered such that the first $l$ equations compute the volume and pressure of the root node, the next $l$ equations compute the left child of the root, followed by $l$ equations for the right child of the root, and so on. Equations can thus be initially partitioned to vertices in $G$ via $f(e_i) = i\ /\ l$. The left side of Figure 3(a) shows a representative structured PE graph, where EqNx represents the equations allocated to each node.

Consider if the target platform for the three-generation Weibel lung model is an FPGA that contains only enough resources for three PEs. Since each vertex in the graph represents a virtual PE that must eventually be physically placed, an excess of four PEs will not fit into the device. The graph can be folded as shown in the right side of Figure 3(a), by merging nodes in such a way as to maintain the graph structure. Let $T_R$ be the root of the graph $G$, and $T_1$ and $T_2$ be the subtrees whose roots are the left and right children of $T_R$, respectively. We fold $T_2$ into $T_1$ by traversing down each subtree simultaneously, and moving any equations within the current node of $T_2$ into the equivalent node of $T_1$. The root node $T_R$ is also merged into the root node of $T_1$, otherwise $T_R$ would contain only a single child. This method maintains the adjacency of vertices in $T_2$ within $T_1$, as long as each subtree is symmetrical. Non-symmetrical structures can still be folded imperfectly by merging the vertices in $T_2$ that have no corresponding vertex in $T_1$ such that a minimum of additional edge length is required.

## 5. PHASE 2: MAPPING VIRTUAL PEs TO PHYSICAL PEs

Once a structured graph of virtual PEs has been created, each virtual PE must be mapped to a physical location on the target platform. This mapping must consider both the average and maximum distances between PEs to reduce congestion and critical paths introduced via inter-PE communication channels. The simple solution to this problem is to let a commercial synthesis tool flatten the design hierarchy, and run heuristic algorithms to select an appropriate placement. However, a circuit that contains hundreds of PEs is sufficiently complex such that modern tools cannot find good solutions without having additional constraints specified. Our approach defines a two-dimensional grid of physical PE regions on a target FPGA platform. Each physical PE region in the grid contains just enough resources to implement a single PE. Physical PE regions are defined at specific locations to create a two-dimensional grid that can be addressed using a XY Cartesian coordinate system. Whether or not the physical PE region actually contains a physical PE depends on the subsequent mapping. Virtual PEs can be mapped to physical PE regions on the grid using either structure-specific graph embedding techniques that place a guest graph into a host graph algorithmically, or by a generic simulated annealing approach with custom cost functions to reduce wire length.

## 5.1 FPGA platform two-dimensional grid

When performing place and route operations on large PE networks using commercial tools (Xilinx ISE 13.4) and a flattened netlist, we noticed that the critical path most often manifests between memories or logic components that belong to the same PE. Each PE in our design requires two memories (BRAMs), one multiplier (DSP), and approximately 250 lookup-tables (LUTs). We expected that communication channels between different PEs would be the primary cause of delay. Because of the complexity of large PE networks, the tools are not able to always place components of the same PE nearby each other. This problem can be addressed via the use of placement constraints during synthesis and place and route.

We first utilize Relationally Placed Macros (RPMs) to establish relative distances between PE memories. RPMs have been shown to provide faster circuit designs, even with modern tools [20]. On Xilinx FPGAs, a Cartesian coordinate system is used to specify the locations of components like DSPs and BRAMs (Figure 4). BRAM and DSP modules are physically located in homogeneous

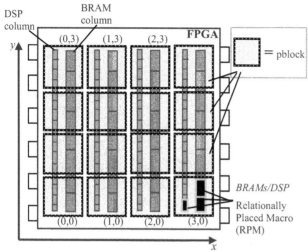

DSP column | BRAM column | FPGA | = pblock

BRAMs/DSP
Relationally Placed Macro (RPM)

**Figure 4: A 4x4 grid of physical PEs on a FPGA. Physical PEs are constrained to specific areas using pblocks.**

columns that stretch the height of the FPGA. We create an RPM for a PE using the Xilinx RLOC constraint by specifying that the offset between its instruction and data memories should be X=0, Y=1, and that the offset between the instruction memory and the DSP should be exactly X=-4, Y=0. The RPM thus ensures that PE memories are placed in neighboring BRAMs within the same BRAM column, and that the related DSP module is in the closest available location in a neighboring DSP column.

RPMs are useful for ensuring the close locality of BRAM and DSP modules that belong to the same PE, but we still must constrain each PE to specific physical PE regions on the target platform. We utilize the Xilinx AREA_GROUP constraint during place and route to place PEs into physical PE regions. A selection of physical components of the FPGA (BRAM, DSPs, and slices) is first grouped into a *pblock*. We use the Xilinx PlanAhead tool to manually create pblocks in a grid structure. Each Pblock contains enough resources for a PE: two BRAMs, multiple DSPs, and more than 300 LUTs. The PEs in the design netlist can then be constrained via the AREA_GROUP constraint to a specific pblock region. The use of pblocks not only designates an exact location to place a PE, but also helps the place and route tools by requiring that the components in a PE hierarchy be placed within the pblock area. Since the area of the pblock is roughly what is required of a PE, the resulting PE implementation is densely packed and optimized. The use of placement constraints helps to shift the circuit critical path from internal PE connections to PE network communication channels.

We target a Xilinx XC6VSX475T. The Virtex6 platform contains approximately 297K LUTs, 2K DSP units, and 1K Block RAM (36KB each) memories. The grid size that can be constructed is 14x39, yielding a maximum of 504 PEs. For the vast majority of physical models, 500 PEs is sufficient for much faster than real-time simulation speeds. We note that our approach is not limited to one specific tool, platform or vendor; all FPGAs consist of a regular, reconfigurable fabric and most vendors allow blocks of resources to be grouped to create uniform structures. We consider only the specifically denoted FPGA and vendor (Xilinx) above to ease the discussion.

## 5.2 Graph embedding based placement

Physical models that exhibit common structures are able to take advantage of graph embedding techniques during physical placement. *Graph embedding* is the process of mapping a guest

graph of architecture *g* onto a host graph of a different architecture *h*. Graph embedding has studied for at least 30 years by mathematical theorists, and many optimal solutions have been found for the embedding of structures like trees and meshes onto grids and hypercubes [6][15][24]. The typical metric that graph embedding algorithms are evaluated by is *maximum dilation*, or the maximum number of nodes that a wire may need to pass through to be completed. Since in physical model-solving PE networks the communication channels are point-to-point between PEs, the dilation is always exactly one. We thus alter the metric's definition slightly to be the maximum wire length between any two PEs. A second important metric is the *average dilation*, or the average wire length of all communication channels in the circuit.

By taking advantage of the research on graph embedding techniques to map virtual PEs to physical PEs on the target platform, the resulting physical placement can achieve smaller maximum and average dilation in the circuit. Smaller maximum dilation implies a reduction in the critical path, since once a PE has been constrained using RPMs and pblocks the longest wires for any complex network is typically connected between different PEs (as opposed to internal PE connections). Lower average dilation means that less routing resources will be required, which typically results in faster circuits [28]. In the next sections, we first define the graph embedding problem. We then show how to utilize a graph embedding technique called H-tree construction to embed a binary tree structured physical model into a 2D grid of PEs.

### 5.2.1 *Graph embedding*

The graph embedding problem relates to the general mapping problem [3], where computational tasks must be placed onto a host architecture such that communication between PEs is minimized. Let $G_T = (V_T, E_T)$ be the guest graph, where $G_T$ is the structured virtual PE graph (see section 4). Let $G_H = (V_H, E_H)$, where $G_H$ is a graph that represents the physical PE layout. $V_H$ is a set of all the physical PE regions, and $E_H$ is initially empty because no connections exist until virtual PEs are placed. An embedding of $G_T$ onto $G_H$ is a result of applying an injective mapping function $\psi_V : V_T \rightarrow V_H$ to every vertex in $G_T$. Once the vertex mapping has been completed and a placement is created, then an additional mapping $\psi_E : E_T \rightarrow E_H$ can be inferred automatically by creating an edge $e = (u,v) \in E_H$ for every edge $p = (l,k) \in E_T$ where $\psi_V^{-1}(l) = u$ and $\psi_V^{-1}(k) = v$.

The quality of the graph embedding is denoted by the average and maximum dilation of the result of applying $\psi_V$ and $\psi_E$. Since dilation in the context of PE networks on FPGAs with point-to-point communication is wire length, we use a basic Euclidean distance measure $D = sqrt( (y2-y1)^2 + (x2-x1)^2 )$. While possible to measure dilation using specific FPGA routing architecture characteristics [10], at a macro level the simple distance between physical grid locations will suffice.

### 5.2.2 *Example: Binary tree embedding onto 2D grid*

Embedded binary trees onto two-dimensional grids is a thoroughly researched area [6][14][24]. It has been proven that the graph embedding of a binary tree onto optimally-sized square grids have an $O(sqrt(n))$ maximum dilation, where *n* is the number of generations of the tree. We utilize the H-tree construction technique that is used in VLSI for the layout of tree architectures onto optimally sized square hosts [23][30]. H-tree construction creates an H-fractal tree shaped liked that of Figure 5, where each subsequent branch of the tree alternates between

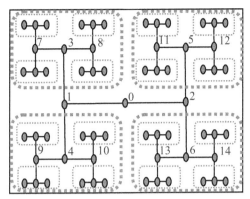

**Figure 5: Six level binary-tree placed on a square 2-dimensional mesh. Dashed boxes indicate recursive splits into subtrees.**

horizontal and vertical tracks and wire length is halved. This process is done by splitting the graph recursively into four subtrees until leaf nodes can be placed. Where each split occurs, a track is used to host the root of the split and its two children, which are the roots of the actual 4 subtrees. In Figure 5, the tree is labeled by breadth-first ordering, such that the root is '0', the left child is '1', the right child is '2', and so on. Leaf nodes are not labeled for figure clarity. The thick dashed boxes represent the subtrees of the first recursive split; the row of vertices '0', '1', and '2' have a horizontal track allocated to them. The thin dashed boxes represent the subtrees created by a second recursive split of each of the first four subtrees. Additional horizontal tracks are added for the three relevant parent nodes of each split subtree. Following the second split, leaf nodes can be placed nearby their parents.

For optimally-sized square grids, the method demonstrated in Figure 5 produces optimal results (in terms of dilation). However, for rectangular-shaped grids such as the 14x39 PE grid available on our target FPGA, H-tree construction can not be immediately applied without some modifications. For example, the number of vertical tracks required for a 7-generation tree using the H-tree method is 31, or more than twice the number of available columns in the FPGA PE grid. We can take advantage of the fact that our FPGA can route wires between PEs diagonally, as opposed to the strict row-column ordering of previous H-tree considerations [14]. Also, since the width of the target is the limiting factor to the number of possible recursive splits, it's not possible to maintain the nice H-fractal shape of the graph embedding in a rectangular grid. We therefore define a base case for the bottom k-generations of a tree that can no longer maintain H-fractal shape, such that an optimal placement of lower generations and leaf nodes can be completed.

To embed the tree, we first perform placement via recursive splits down to the leaves of the tree, than perform compaction and reordering of rows to further minimize maximum wire length.

1. Separate the grid into 4 quadrants to host the initial split of the tree.

2. Place the root node $M_0$ and its children $L_0$, $R_0$ in the center row of the grid. $M_0$ is placed in a column in the center of the grid. $L_0$ and $R_0$ are placed in a middle column of the neighboring upper and lower quadrants

3. Place each child of $L_0$ and $R_0$ onto the same vertical track as its parent, and onto the center row of a quadrant (Figure 6a).

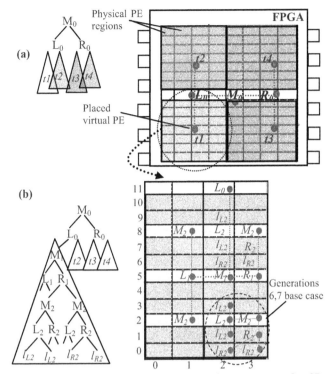

**Figure 6: Embedding 7-level binary tree into a rectangular 2D grid: (a) Initial split of 4 subtrees (not to scale), (b) Two additional recursive splits. White rows host root and children of a split branch. For clarity, not all branches are shown.**

4. Recursively split each subtree by placing the children of the subtree's root on the same row, and allocating additional rows to host new subtrees (Figure 6b).

5. At generation N-1, utilize a known placement to place the final levels (non-fractal shape).

The process described in the steps above can be seen in Figure 6. The binary tree is split into four subtrees and assigned to a quadrant of the grid. The blue lines mark connections between physical PE regions that contain a mapped virtual PE, which are marked with blue dots. The graph embedding follows the H-tree fractal shape design until the grid becomes too narrow to maintain the shape when placing the final two generations of the tree. At that point, a base case known placement is utilized to place the remaining virtual PEs into physical PE regions with minimal wire lengths. Note that rows four and ten contain no mapped virtual PEs, which unnecessarily inflates the maximum wire length. A simple greedy algorithm can be used to compact the graph embedding by moving the row with the longest wire until no improvement can be made.

## 5.3 Simulated annealing based placement

This section provides a general method for mapping a structured virtual PE graph to physical PEs by using a simulated annealing approach. Such a general method can be useful when a physical model has no obvious structure for which a graph embedding algorithm could be used, such as an unbalanced or asymmetrical tree [8]. Simulated annealing also yields useful comparisons to the graph embedding approach by providing reasonable PE placements. We define a cost function that considers FPGA architectural features, critical path length, and wire congestion; it is shown experimentally that our cost function correlates linearly

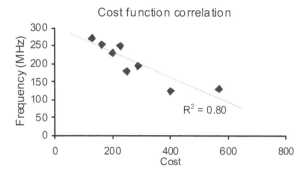

Figure 7: Simulated annealing cost function correlates with resulting circuit frequency. A variety of different physical models are represented.

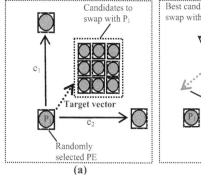
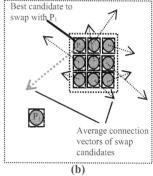

Figure 8: The neighbor function picks two PEs (P1,P2) by randomly selecting P1, (a) finding candidates for P2 by averaging P1's connections (e1, e2), and (b) picking P2 based on the distance between P1 and a candidate's average connection vector endpoint.

with resulting circuit frequency. We also present a neighbor function that swaps PEs using vectors based on the placement of connected PEs. Our neighbor function provides faster convergence and results in lower cost placements than performing random swaps of PEs.

### 5.3.1 Cost function

The cost function of the simulated annealing based placement approach is defined as:

$$Cost = w1*Sum + w2*Max + w3*Gaps$$

*Sum* is the total of all the wire lengths in the design. By minimizing the sum of the wire lengths, the wire congestion in the design is reduced, which impacts critical path timing less. *Max* is the maximum wire length in the design. Minimizing *Max* is the key goal during simulated annealing, because it will likely represent the critical path in the circuit. *Gaps* is the number of wires that cross an area on the FPGA that must be routed through or around. For example, on most Xilinx Virtex 6 chips there is a large gap in the middle for monitoring or programming components and where user design logic can not be placed (see Figure 11). Wires through such gaps incur extra routing delays and thus we strive to reduce the amount of those types of connections. The constants *w1*, *w2*, and *w3* are weighting coefficients that can be used as tuning knobs for the algorithm. Typical values of *w1*, *w2*, and *w3* are 0.1, 10, and 1 respectively. *w2* is the most critical parameter, and should be selected based on the total number of wires in the design. If there are many wires, the *w1*Sum* factor may be very high, and the maximum wire length M*ax* factor may not contribute much to the cost of the current solution – in such cases *w2* should be increased to offset this effect. Figure 7 shows a linear regression representing how the cost function relates to the resulting circuit frequency of a PE network placed using simulated annealing.

### 5.3.2 Neighbor function

The neighbor function in a simulated annealing algorithm moves the current state of the design in order to explore the solution space of the problem. The neighbor function presented here attempts to cluster connected PEs together, hopefully reducing wire lengths in the process. A random physical PE region $P_1$ that contains a mapped virtual PE $V$ is first selected to be moved. Each connection $e = (P_1,P_p)$ in $V$ is evaluated, where $P_p$ is the physical PE region of the virtual PE connected to $V$. A vector $v = (r,\theta)$ is built such that $r = sqrt(dx^2 + dy^2)$ and $\theta = tan^{-1}(dy/dx)$, where $dx$ and $dy$ are the differences in the x and y coordinates between $P_1$ and $P_p$. An average of all the connection vectors yields a target

vector that identifies a physical PE region that would reduce the average wire length of the connections to the PE if the virtual PE were placed there. If the target physical PE region does not have a virtual PE mapped, than the virtual PE is moved onto the target physical PE region. If the target physical PE region does have a virtual PE mapped, than an evaluation of the target physical PE region and each of its neighbors in the grid takes place to determine the best candidate for a swap. The target physical PE region and its neighbors have their connections' vectors averaged in turn. The region that has an average connection vector endpoint closest to $P_1$ is selected to be swapped. If any of the neighbors do not contain mapped virtual PEs, than the empty neighbor is automatically selected to be swapped. Figure 8 shows how the neighbor function works. A random PE $P_1$ is first selected. An average of the two connections of $P_1$, $e_1$ and $e_2$, yields a target vector that denotes an area of the platform where $P_1$ should be placed to minimize the wire lengths of $e_1$ and $e_2$. Each candidate physical PE region in the area has its connections averaged (Figure 8b). The candidate physical PE region that has an average connection vector closest to $P_1$ is in the top left, thus a swap would occur with the top left PE ($P_2$) and $P_1$.

Figure 9 shows the convergence of the design cost towards a final solution for 50K iterations of the simulated annealing algorithm while implementing a neuron model utilizing 256 PEs. Using our custom neighbor function, the resulting cost is 50% less than given by the random alternative.

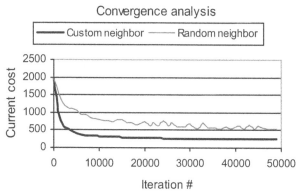

Figure 9: Convergence of custom neighbor function compared to random swaps.

### 5.3.3 *Annealing temperature schedule*

The cooling schedule used during simulated annealing can cause dramatic differences in the obtained solution [18]. To verify that we chose the correct schedule for this problem, we have experimented with linear, geometric, and exponential type cooling schedule functions. We found that both linear and geometric schedules produce a solution with a similar cost for a given physical model, while the exponential schedule ($\alpha = 0.99$) yields a solution that is highly dependent on the initial random placement and does not generally produce a good result. This is due to the quickly decaying nature of the exponential function, which makes it difficult to escape local minima in the solution space. All experiments in this paper utilize a geometric cooling schedule.

## 6. EXPERIMENTS

To evaluate graph embedding as a technique for accelerating physical model simulations on FPGAs, we implemented a number of physical models of varying size on a Xilinx XC6VSX475T-2ff1156 FPGA. The physical models include a Weibel lung that is structured as a binary tree, a one-dimensional neuron array, and a two-dimensional grid of neurons. Each physical model is implemented using both 256 and 500 PEs. We use Xilinx ISE 13.4 software to synthesize and implement VHDL descriptions of the PE networks for all experiments, with flags '-ol high' and '-xe normal' to encourage the tool to work hard at achieving timing closure. Note that to implement the 11-generation Weibel model, we use 500 physical PEs. Recall that the target platform is constrained to 504 physical PEs. We fold the Weibel model to a structured virtual PE graph of 512 nodes, and then manually merge a few of the leafs until the size constraint is met. The alternative is to continue folding the structured virtual PE graph until the size constraint is met, which would result in 256 virtual PEs and almost 50% of the available resources unutilized.

For each physical model, we implemented three methods of placement for the PE networks. The first method utilizes the compiler from previous work [11] to partition the physical model equations to PEs and generate a custom communication network. No constraints are used to map the PEs to specific physical PE regions; we rely on the Xilinx tools to place and route PEs onto the target platform. The second method first creates a structured graph of virtual PEs, folds it to fit FPGA platform constraints, and then utilizes the simulated annealing approach of section 5.3 to map virtual PEs to physical regions. For the simulated annealing algorithm in all cases we utilize a geometric cooling schedule, and

let the algorithm run for 50K iterations to reach a steady state. The weighting constants ($w1,w2,w3$) are (0.08,10,1). The third method creates a structured virtual PE graph of the physical model, folds it to fit the FPGA target platform size constraint, and then uses a graph embedding algorithm specific to the selected physical model. The Weibel model uses a H-tree graph embedding as described previously. The one-dimensional neuron model is a linear array of 6400 neurons, thus the graph embedding that is used places PEs into rows and connects the rows at the edges to form a Hamiltonian path amongst all PEs. The two-dimensional neuron model consists of a two-dimensional 64x64 mesh of neurons, where each neuron is connected to at most 4 neighbors. The graph embedding for the two-dimensional neuron model is a direct mapping onto the two-dimensional grid of FPGA physical regions, after folding the original physical model.

## 6.1 Results

Figure 10 shows the resulting circuit frequencies of implementing PE networks on an FPGA with the above three techniques. The 'NoPhys_XlnxPlcmt' columns do not use physical placement constraints. 'Phys_SimAnnlPlcmt' columns use simulated annealing to map virtual PEs to physical PE regions. 'Phys_EmbedPlcmt' uses an embedding approach appropriate to the implemented model. For the same model, all three approaches use the same RTL description of the circuit. The graph embedding approach is almost always able to produce a circuit that tops 300 MHz. The ceiling for the circuit frequency in a PE network is approximately 310 MHz for the selected platform. The ceiling can be determined by implementing a circuit with a single PE and evaluating the critical path of the internal datapath. It is not possible for a network of PEs to go faster than the ceiling, and any decrease in performance can be attributed to critical paths introduced by inter-PE connections. The graph embedding approach is typically able to minimize the critical path length and thus provide placements that allow the circuit to approach the frequency ceiling. The only embedding example that could not reach the ceiling of 310 MHz is the 11-generation Weibel lung model using 500 PEs. Because the two-dimensional grid of the physical PE regions is narrow, an optimal embedding of the tree cannot occur. Wire lengths between successive generations are much longer, resulting in longer critical path delays.

Some data points of the method using no physical placement constraints are marked 'N/A'. This indicates that the Xilinx tools were not able to place and route the design due to high

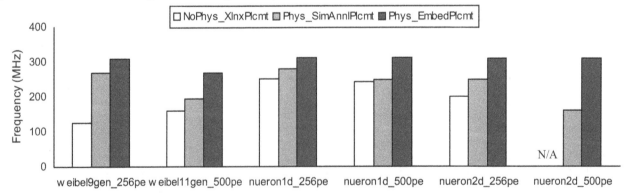

**Figure 10: Frequencies of PE network implementations simulating a Weibel lung and 1D/2D neuron networks. Each PE network was placed with (i) no physical region constraints, (ii) physical regions selected by simulated annealing, and (iii) physical regions selected by embedding the model structure onto the FPGA grid. Points marked 'N/A' could not be routed because of high complexity. (i), (ii), and (iii) all use the same RTL description during synthesis, but (ii) and (iii) use region constraints.**

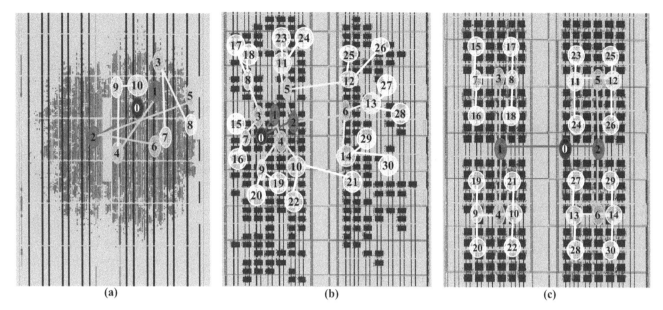

(a)                                   (b)                                   (c)

**Figure 11: Different placements of a 256 PE Weibel lung model. The virtual PEs of the physical model are labeled in breadth-first order, where 0 is the root. Dark nodes are closer to the root. (a) Unconstrained placement of PEs performed by Xilinx tools. (b) PEs mapped to physical PE regions by simulated annealing. (c) PEs mapped to physical PE regions via a graph embedding algorithm. Empty (lighter) space in the circuits could be used to implement other logic, such as tracing or debug support.**

congestion. The compiler that partitioned the equations and created the communication network could not adequately reduce the data dependencies between PEs for these large physical models, resulting in an overwhelming number of wires in the network. Note that the designs are routable if we use either a simulated annealing or graph embedding approach, which indicates that graph embedding or a simulating annealing approach enable implementation of physical models on an FPGA that previously could not be implemented on the FPGA.

## 6.2 A look inside the FPGA

Figure 11 shows a graphical depiction of the placement of the first few generations of a nine generation Weibel model on 256 PEs, as captured by the Xilinx PlanAhead tool. An overlay of nodes and connections shows where virtual PEs have been mapped onto the FPGA. Figure 11(a) shows how Xilinx ISE implements the PE network in the absence of additional constraints that map to specific physical regions. Due to the complexity of the circuit, the resources of a single PE can be spread over a wide area, thus we have marked only the approximate central location of the first four generations of the left subtree of the graph. Note that if we do not specify placement constraints, the tool places PEs at non-optimal locations such that the wire distances between PEs can be very long. For example, the wires between node two and its children five and six span more than halfway across the entire design.

Figure 11(b) depicts a typical result of using the simulated annealing algorithm. Each black block indicates where a virtual PE was mapped to a physical PE location. An empty space in the grid means that no virtual PE was mapped to the grid at that physical region. The effect of the simulated annealing algorithm can be seen by evaluating the placement of the virtual PEs onto the grid. Nodes that share connections tend to be grouped together, while overall the tree tends to expand outward from the center of the grid. Leaf nodes are grouped towards the outside of the grid. Figure 11(c) shows an embedding of the tree onto the host grid using the graph embedding approach. Recall that the center of many common (Xilinx) FPGAs contains immutable

logic, and thus minimization of the routing across the center is desired. The embedding requires only a single wire across the gap, at the second generation of the tree.

We also measured the static and dynamic power of each case using the Xilinx XPower Analyzer. The unconstrained placement uses approximately 20% less power on average than both the simulated annealing and embedding constrained placement approaches.

## 7. CONCLUSION

We presented an approach for fast physical model simulation on FPGAs that makes use of the physical model's structure to improve performance. The approach's first phase maps physical model equations to a structured virtual PE graph and groups related equations. The approach's second phase maps the structured virtual PE graph to a two-dimensional grid of FPGA physical regions by using either a graph embedding or simulated annealing technique. The graph embedding and simulated annealing techniques provide 65% and 35% average increases in circuit frequencies, respectively, compared to placements that do not map to specific physical regions.

## 8. ACKNOWLEDGEMENTS

This work was supported in part by the National Science Foundation (CNS1016792, CPS1136146), the Semiconductor Research Corporation (GRC 2143.001), and a U.S. Department of Education GAANN fellowship.

## 9. REFERENCES

[1]  Aleliunas, R., and Rosenberg, A.L. 1982. On Embedding Rectangular Grids in Square Grids. Computers, IEEE Transactions on , vol.C-31, no.9, pp.907-913, Sept. 1982.

[2]  Banerjee, P., Sur-Kolay, S., Bishnu, A., Das, S., Nandy, and S.C., Bhattacharjee, S. 2009. FPGA placement using space-filling curves: Theory meets practice. ACM Trans. Embed. Comput. Syst. vol. 9, no. 2, Oct. 2009.

[3] Berman, F., and Snyder, L. 1987. On mapping parallel algorithms into parallel architectures, Journal of Parallel and Distributed Computing, vol. 4, no.5, Oct. 1987, pp 439-458.

[4] Bhatelé, A., and Kalé, L.V. 2008. Benefits of Topology Aware Mapping for Mesh Interconnects. Parallel Processing Letters, vol.18, no.4, pp.549-566, 2008.

[5] Bokhari, S.H. 1981. On the Mapping Problem. Computers, IEEE Transactions on , vol.C-30, no.3, pp. 207-214, March 1981.

[6] Chen, W.K., and Stallmann, M. 1995. On embedding binary trees into hypercubes. J. Parallel Distrib. Comput. 24, 2 (February 1995), 132-138.

[7] Ellis, J.A. 1991. Embedding Rectangular Grids Into Square Grids. IEEE Transactions on Computers, pp. 46-52, Jan. 1991.

[8] Gabryś, E., Rybaczuk, M.,and Kędzia, A. 2005. Fractal models of circulatory system. Symmetrical and asymmetrical approach comparison, Chaos, Solitons Fractals, vol. 24, no. 3, May 2005, pp 707-715.

[9] Gholkar, A., Isaacs, A., and Arya, H. 2004. Hardware-In-Loop Simulator for Mini Aerial Vehicle, Sixth Real- Time Linux Workshop, NTU, Singapore, Nov. 2004.

[10] Gopalakrishnan, P., Li, X., and Pileggi, L. 2006. Architecture-aware FPGA placement using metric embedding. In Proceedings of the 43rd annual Design Automation Conference (DAC '06). ACM, New York, NY, USA, pp. 460-465.

[11] Huang, C., Vahid, F., and Givargis, T. 2011. A Custom FPGA Processor for Physical Model Ordinary Differential Equation Solving. Embedded Systems Letters, IEEE , vol.3, no.4, pp.113-116, Dec. 2011.

[12] Huang, C., Miller, B., Vahid, F., and Givargis, T. 2012. Synthesis of custom networks of heterogeneous processing elements for complex physical system emulation. In Proceedings of the eighth IEEE/ACM/IFIP international conference on Hardware/software codesign and system synthesis (CODES+ISSS '12). ACM, New York, NY, USA, pp. 215-224.

[13] Jiang, Z., Pajic, M., and Mangharam, R. 2011. Model-Based Closed-Loop Testing of Implantable Pacemakers. Cyber-Physical Systems (ICCPS), 2011 IEEE/ACM International Conference on, pp.131-140, April 2011.

[14] Lee, S.K., and Choi, H.A. 1996. Embedding of complete binary trees into meshes with row-column routing. Parallel and Distributed Systems, IEEE Transactions on , vol.7, no.5, pp.493-497, May 1996.

[15] Matic, S. 1990. Emulation of hypercube architecture on nearest-neighbor mesh-connected processing elements. Computers, IEEE Transactions on , vol.39, no.5, pp.698-700, May 1990.

[16] Miller, B., Vahid, F., and Givargis, T. 2012. Digital mockups for the testing of a medical ventilator. In Proceedings of the 2nd ACM SIGHIT International Health Informatics Symposium (IHI '12). ACM, New York, NY, USA, pp. 859-862.

[17] Motuk, E., Woods, R., and Bilbao, S. 2005. Implementation of finite difference schemes for the wave equation on FPGA. ICASSP.

[18] Nourani, Y., and Andresen, B. 1998. A comparison of simulated annealing cooling strategies. Journal of Physics A: Mathematical and General, vol. 31, no. 41, 1998.

[19] de Pimentel, J.C.G., and Tirat-Gefen, Y.G. 2006. Hardware Acceleration for Real Time Simulation of Physiological Systems. Engineering in Medicine and Biology Society, 2006. EMBS '06. 28th Annual International Conference of the IEEE , vol., no., pp. 218-223, Aug. 2006.

[20] Singh, S. 2011. The RLOC is dead - long live the RLOC. In Proceedings of the 19th ACM/SIGDA international symposium on Field programmable gate arrays (FPGA '11). ACM, New York, NY, USA, pp. 185-188.

[21] Terman, D., Ahn, S., Wang, X., and Just, W. 2008. Reducing neuronal networks to discrete dynamics, Physica D: Nonlinear Phenomena, vol. 237, no. 3, March 2008.

[22] Tagkopoulos, I., Zukowski, C., Cavelier, G., and Anastassiou, D. 2003. A custom FPGA for the simulation of gene regulatory networks. In Proceedings of the 13th ACM Great Lakes symposium on VLSI (GLSVLSI '03). ACM, New York, NY, USA, pp. 132-135.

[23] Ullma, J.D. 1984. Computational Aspects of VLSI. W. H. Freeman & Co., New York, NY, USA.

[24] Ullman, S., and Narahari, B. 1990. Mapping binary precedence trees to hypercubes and meshes. Parallel and Distributed Processing, 1990. Proceedings of the Second IEEE Symposium on , pp. 838-841, Dec. 1990.

[25] van Meurs, WL. 2011. Modeling and Simulation in Biomedical Engineering: Applications in Cardiorespiratory Physiology. McGraw-Hill Professional.

[26] Wagner, A.S. 1991. Embedding all binary trees in the hypercube. Parallel and Distributed Processing, Proceedings of the Third IEEE Symposium on , pp. 104-111, Dec 1991.

[27] Weibel, E.R. 1963. Morphometry of the Human Lung. Berlin, Germany: Springer-Verlag 1963.

[28] Xilinx, 2010. Inc. Virtex-6 FPGA Routing Optimization Design Techniques. http://www.xilinx.com/support/documentation/white_papers/wp311.pdf

[29] Zhang, H., Holden, A.V., and Boyett, M.R. 2001. Gradient model versus mosaic model of the sinoatrial node. Circulation. vol. 103, pp. 584-588.

[30] Zienicke, P. 1990. Embeddings of Treelike Graphs into 2-Dimensional Meshes. In Proceedings of the 16th International Workshop on Graph-Theoretic Concepts in Computer Science (WG '90). London, UK, pp. 182-192.

# Area-Efficient Near-Associative Memories on FPGAs

Udit Dhawan
udit@seas.upenn.edu

André DeHon
andre@acm.org

Department of Electrical and Systems Engineering
University of Pennsylvania
200 S. 33rd St.
Philadelphia, PA 19104

## ABSTRACT

Associative memories can map sparsely used keys to values with low latency but can incur heavy area overheads. The lack of customized hardware for associative memories in today's mainstream FPGAs exacerbates the overhead cost of building these memories using the fixed address match BRAMs. In this paper, we develop a new, FPGA-friendly, memory architecture based on a multiple hash scheme that is able to achieve near-associative performance (less than 5% of evictions due to conflicts) without the area overheads of a fully associative memory on FPGAs. Using the proposed architecture as a 64KB L1 data cache, we show that it is able to achieve near-associative miss-rates while consuming 6-7× less FPGA memory resources for a set of benchmark programs from the SPEC2006 suite than fully associative memories generated by the Xilinx Coregen tool. Benefits increase with match width, allowing area reduction up to 100×. At the same time, the new architecture has lower latency than the fully associative memory—3.7 ns for a 1024-entry flat version or 6.1 ns for an area-efficient version compared to 8.8 ns for a fully associative memory for a 64b key.

## Categories and Subject Descriptors

B.3.2 [**Memory Structures**]: Design Styles—*Associative Memories*; B.7.1 [**Integrated Circuits**]: Types and Design Styles—*Gate Arrays*; E.2 [**Data**]: Data Storage Representations—*Hash-table representations*

## General Terms

Algorithms, Design, Performance

## Keywords

FPGA; BRAM; Associative Memory; CAM; Cache; Hashing

## 1. INTRODUCTION

With increasing use of high frequency soft processors on FPGAs (*e.g.*, [26, 12]) and an increasing use of FPGAs for processor emulation (*e.g.*, [22, 21, 20, 13]), we need to be able to implement high-performance memory sub-systems on FPGAs (such as caches and TLBs). However, FPGAs are notoriously poor at supporting the associative memories that are often needed in high-performance processors. For example, a recent work [21] observed:

> "Lesson 2: *The major challenges when mapping ASIC-style RTL for a CMP system on an FPGA are highly associative memory structures...*"

The Content-Addressable Memories (CAMs) needed to implement associative memories cannot be built efficiently out of LUTs and the hardwired SRAM blocks provided in modern, mainstream FPGAs (*e.g.* Xilinx BRAM, Altera M4K). While Xilinx Coregen can produce parameterized CAMs [23], they can have enormous overheads. For example, on a recent Xilinx Virtex 6 device with 36Kbit Block RAMs (BRAMs), a 512-entry CAM with a 40-bit key requires 64 BRAMs to perform the match, despite the fact that 512, 64-bit entries can be stored in a single BRAM. That is, *the overhead for implementing the match portion for the fully associative memory on this FPGA is* 64× *the stored memory capacity*. The overheads increase with the match width. [25] shows that fully associative memories implemented on the Stratix architecture have comparably high overheads.

We show how to implement maps with substantially less overhead in comparison to a fully associative memory using BRAMs. We achieve these savings, in part, by implementing memories that are only **statistically** guaranteed to be conflict free. As such, we call them near-associative memories. Specifically, we use a multiple hash scheme [1, 14] based on a generalization of [7] that can be efficiently implemented on top of BRAMs. We further develop efficient replacement policies exploiting the power of choice [1, 14, 16, 11]. This allows us to reduce the conflict miss probability to below 0.03% for the above 512-entry CAM while using only 12 total BRAMs.

Our novel contributions include:

- Customization of the table-based Perfect Hash scheme [7] for efficient implementation on FPGAs (Sec. 3.2)
- FPGA-customized memory architecture that can be tuned to trade-off BRAM usage with conflict miss rate (Sec. 3)
- Analytic derivation of optimal sparsity factor (Sec. 3.7)
- Analytic characterization of capacity (Sec. 3.5) and miss rate (Sec. 3.4), showing that the architecture can achieve very low (≈ 0.05%) conflict miss rates with substantially fewer BRAMs than Xilinx Coregen-style associative memories

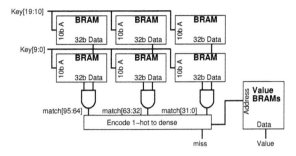

**Figure 1: Fully Associative Memory using BRAMs (20b match, 96-entry example shown)**

- Identification of a family of replacement policies and characterization of their performance, area, and cycle time implications (Sec. 4)
- Empirical quantitative comparison of the area and performance of our new memory organization against fully associative and set-associative memories (Sec. 5)

## 2. BACKGROUND
### 2.1 Associative Memories

An associative memory provides a mapping between a match key and a data value. The set of match keys can be sparse compared to the universe of potential keys. An associative memory of capacity $M$ can hold any $M$ entries; as long as the capacity is not exceeded, there are no conflicts among stored key-value pairs in an associative memory. If the system does need to store a new key-value pair when the memory is at capacity, the memory controller is free to choose any existing key-value pair for replacement, typically based on a policy such as least-recently used (LRU), least-recently inserted (LRI), or least-frequently used (LFU).

However, this freedom comes at a high area and energy cost, since the hardware needs to perform programmable, parallel matches in the entire memory against the incoming key. As a result, fully associative memories are typically only feasible for shallow memories with small keys such as translation look-aside buffers. Nevertheless, the use of fully associative memories or content-addressable memories (CAMs) can be crucial to enhance performance in many applications like network routing [15] and dictionary lookups for pattern matching and data compression/decompression [5].

### 2.2 Fully Associative Memories on FPGAs

Building fully associative memories or CAMs on modern, mainstream FPGAs is expensive because the memory resources present on these devices do not naturally support the structures needed to implement a fully associative memory. In a custom implementation, a CAM address-match cell is programmable so it can match against any key. However, in an ordinary SRAM array, the address-match cell is fixed. Since FPGAs only contain ordinary SRAM blocks, CAMs must be built out of logic and these embedded SRAMs (*e.g.*, BRAMs), as shown in Fig. 1.

In order to evaluate how area-inefficient building CAMs on FPGAs using SRAM blocks can be, we created custom CAMs the way Xilinx Coregen program suggests [23] for a fully associative memory for a Virtex 6 FPGA (xc6vlx240t-2 device) [24]. This device contains 416, 36Kbit Block RAMs, which can be organized as $18 \times 2048$, $36 \times 1024$ or $72 \times 512$ memories (where there is a parity bit for each byte stored).

In order to build an $m$-wide, $n$-deep CAM on a Virtex FPGA, Coregen organizes it as a matrix with $2^m$ rows (a row each for all the *possible* match keys) and $n$ columns (a column for each of the locations for an associated value). Each matrix cell is a single bit where, for each possible match key, a 1 in a cell means that the data is at the location specified by that column, otherwise, it is not. Using such an organization, one can fit a 10-bit wide, 32-entry deep CAM match unit in a single BRAM (using a $36 \times 1024$ configuration) [23]. In order to build deeper CAMs, one can use multiple BRAMs and send in the same 10 bits to be matched to each BRAM. This requires $\lceil \frac{n}{32} \rceil$ BRAMs, where $n$ is the depth of the CAM. Building this further, if the data to be matched is wider than 10 bits, then we can use multiple 10-bit match BRAM sets and build a final AND-tree to see if there was a complete match or not. This means that the total number of BRAMs needed to build the match unit for a $m$-wide, $n$-deep CAM using this organization is:

$$\# \text{ BRAMs} = \left\lceil \frac{m}{10} \right\rceil \times \left\lceil \frac{n}{32} \right\rceil \qquad (1)$$

Now, let us assume that we are building a fully associative memory for storing 64-bit wide data values associated with 64-bit match keys. Table 1 shows the number of BRAMs needed to implement this memory for different depths. We observe that, for a memory deeper than 1024 entries, we run out of the BRAMs available on the device (shown in red italics text). Consequently, we would like to know how to build maps much more compactly than the normal fully associative memory design, especially when the key-width is large or a high capacity is needed.

**Table 1: BRAMs consumed for a Fully Associative Memory with 64b match key and 64b data values**

| Depth | BRAMs consumed for Match Unit | Data | Total BRAMs consumed |
|---|---|---|---|
| 256 | 56 | 1 | 57 |
| 512 | 112 | 1 | 113 |
| 1024 | 224 | 2 | 226 |
| *2048* | *448* | *4* | *452* |

## 3. A NEAR-ASSOCIATIVE MEMORY

The Coregen-style associative memories are inefficient for three reasons: (1) they demand dense storage of 10b match subfields—which typically means sparse storage of keys since we must allocate space for *potential* keys rather than present keys, (2) they demand sparse (one-hot) encoding of results, (3) they demand re-encoding of the one-hot results into a dense address and indirection to retrieve the actual data value. Ideally, we would like to be able to do almost the opposite: (1) densely store only present key-values pairs, (2) densely store results, (3) directly retrieve the data from a single memory lookup. Taking these as our targets, we create a hash-based memory system with an efficient implementation around BRAMs, called the Dynamic Multi-Hash Cache Architecture or dMHC, that can yield near-associative performance.

### 3.1 Basic Approach

Ideally, we would like to be able to compute a simple function of all the bits of the key, get the address where the data value is stored, and fetch the stored value in a single memory

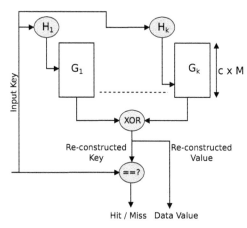

**Figure 2: A Generic dMHC(k,c)**

lookup. A direct-mapped cache works roughly like this, except it can have high conflict rates since many keys will map to a single memory location. Similarly, a typical hash table functions in a similar manner, but stores many data values linked together in the same location; finding the intended value from the slot can sometimes take many memory operations or considerable hardware. If we make the hash table very sparse, we can reduce the probability of conflicts, and hence expected number of key-value pairs mapped in a single hash slot, at the expense of a much larger table.

Instead, we build on an idea that comes from Bloom Filters [3], Multihash Tables [1, 14], and Perfect Hash functions [7]: *use multiple orthogonal hashes.* Bloom Filters determine set membership, with a possibility of having false positives, by hashing the input key with $k$ independent hash functions and setting (reading) a 1-bit memory indexed by each of hash function. On a set membership test (read), the bits are AND'ed together. If any bits are not set, that's a demonstration that the key in question is not in the set. If all the bits are set, either the key is in the set or we have a false-positive due to the fact that multiple keys happened to have set all the hash bits associated with this key.

We define the *sparsity factor*, $c$, as the ratio of the depth of the memory tables to the number of values stored in the tables. If the hash functions are independent and map all keys to random memory entries, then the probability of a key getting a false hit in any memory is less than $\frac{1}{c}$. The probability of a false hit in **all** $k$ memories is less than $c^{-k}$, which can be made small by increasing $c$ or $k$—we'll see how to best do this later in Sec. 3.7.

As originally defined, the Bloom Filter only identifies set membership, but we want to store (and retrieve) a value as well. We can extend the idea by storing the associated data value in the memory along with the single presence bit. Now, AND'ing the presence bits tells us if we have the value. However, we cannot AND the values and get the right result. Instead we will show in the following sections that we can reasonably XOR the values to retrieve the appropriate result. In many applications, we will want to know when a false-positive has occurred. To do that, we will further need to store the key in the memories along with the data value, like we store the address in a direct-mapped memory to know when we actually have a cache hit.

## 3.2  Hardware Organization

The top-level hardware organization of our dMHC architecture is shown in Fig. 2. We use $k$ mutually orthogonal hash functions, $H_1$ to $H_k$, and a programmable lookup table called a G table for each hash function. These G tables are used to store the key-value pairs. Each of the G tables is made $c\times$ deeper (*i.e.*, made sparse) than the total capacity (number of entries) in the memory, where $c$ is an integer (a power of 2 in our implementations). In the rest of the paper, we refer to a generic instance of our architecture as dMHC(k,c) with $k$ hash functions and a sparsity factor of $c$.

For an input key $D$, we divide it into $p = \lceil |D|/n \rceil$ equal parts, $n$ being the number of bits in the final hash value ($n = \log_2(c \times M)$), where $M$ is the total number of entries in the memory). Our family of orthogonal hash functions look like the expression shown in Eq. (2):

$$H_i(D) = \text{XOR}(\phi_{i,1}(D_1), \dots \phi_{i,p}(D_p), P) \qquad (2)$$

Here $P$ is an arbitrary $n$-bit prime number, and $\phi_i(x)$ is a bit permutation function such as bit-reversal and pairwise bit swap. For $H_1$, we can use the identity function: $\phi_{1,j}(x) = x$. For $H_i, i > 1$, we might set $\phi_{i,j}(x) = \text{rotate}(x, r(i, j))$, where $r(i, j)$ is different for every value of $j$ within a given $i$. This family of hash functions was shown to possess the properties of uniform randomness and good local dispersion in [18]. These properties make it highly unlikely for similar keys to have the same hashed values and be stored in the same locations. At the same time, these hash functions allow a simple FPGA implementation (Table 2).

The G tables store the key-value pairs in a distributed form. Each key-value pair is mapped into $k$ G table entries that can later be combined together to form the original key-value pair. We use XOR for this purpose. Traditional hash tables and set-associative caches demand that we compare the input key to the stored keys in each of the $k$ slots (ways) and use the comparison result to select the appropriate entry. By storing the values this way, we reduce the latency to recover the key-value pair. As shown in the Fig. 2, the G table outputs are fed to an XOR-reduce tree to re-construct the key-value pair from the $k$ pieces read off the G tables. In [7], modulo arithmetic is used both for the hash functions and for combining the G table outputs. We replace modulo arithmetic with XORs to make these computations more efficient for LUT-based implementation. The change to XOR's forces us to use power-of-two G tables and $M$ entries.

## 3.3  Access Operation

Here we explain the operation of our memory for a read access (write access is similar) for a dMHC(k,c) instance. The memory receives a read operation along with the key to be looked up. First, we compute $k$ hash values on the key to get $h_i$ ($i$ in $1...k$). Each $h_i$ is an index into the G table $G_i$ and from each table we read the key field $key_i$ ($= G_i[h_i].key$) and the value field $val_i$ ($= G_i[h_i].val$) stored at that index. Then, we can re-construct the stored key and the value as:

$$key = \text{XOR}_1^k(key_i) \qquad (3)$$

$$val = \text{XOR}_1^k(val_i) \qquad (4)$$

Next, we compare the re-constructed key against the input key to check if they both match. In case they match, the key-value pair is present in the memory and we can return the data value at the same time; otherwise, the key-value pair is not in the memory and we get a miss. In case of a miss, we then yield to a memory controller to service the miss, which we explain later in the Sec. 4.

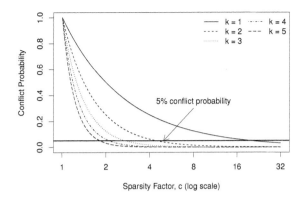

Figure 3: Conflict Probabilities

## 3.4 Conflict Probability Analysis

Now that we have described the hardware architecture and operation of our dMHC architecture, we present an analytical characterization on a parameterized dMHC(k,c) instance to show how we can reduce the conflict probability to arbitrarily small values.

In the dMHC architecture, there is a conflict when all the $G_i$ table entries that an input key hashes into are in use by one or more key-value pairs already present in the memory. The probability of an input key colliding with the present key-value pairs in a single G table is approximately:

$$P_{collide} < \frac{\text{Capacity}}{\text{G Table Depth}} = \frac{|M|}{|G|} = \frac{1}{c} \quad (5)$$

Since all the hash functions are mutually orthogonal, the probability that an input key collides in all the hash functions is:

$$P_{k-collide} < (P_{collide})^k \propto \frac{1}{c^k} \quad (6)$$

This suggests that by choosing high values of parameters $k$ and $c$, we can make the probability $P_{k-collide}$ arbitrarily small. Consequently, the common case is that new key-value pairs do not have a complete collision and can be inserted easily.

We can further define the conflict miss ratio as:

$$P_{conflict\_miss} = \frac{\text{Conflict Eviction Count}}{\text{Total Misses}} \quad (7)$$

$P_{conflict\_miss}$ is zero for a fully associative memory. Fig. 3 plots Eq. (6) to show how the conflict miss probability falls as a function of the sparsity factor, $c$ for a particular number of hash functions, $k$.

## 3.5 dMHC Area Model

In order to achieve near-associativity, dMHC could require high values of the $k$ and $c$ parameters. In order quantify the FPGA resources consumed by a generic dMHC instance and compare them with those consumed by a fully associative memory, we develop an FPGA area model for a dMHC(k,c) design. In a dMHC design, BRAMs are consumed by the G tables used for storing the different pieces of the key-value pairs (we also need to store the original key-value pairs as we will explain later in Sec. 4, but we skip that for the time being). For simplicity of our area model, we assume that all the BRAMs are used in a $36 \times 1024$ configuration, giving us an effective data width of 32 bits per BRAM entry. Also,

we assume that there are $M$ entries in the memory, $w_k$ is the key width and $w_v$ is the data value width. The number of BRAMs consumed by a generic dMHC(k,c) instance for implementing the match portion of the memory can then be expressed as:

$$BRAM_{dmhc\_match} = k \times \left\lceil \frac{w_k + w_v}{32} \right\rceil \times \left\lceil \frac{cM}{1024} \right\rceil \quad (8)$$

dMHC needs to perform logic computation in form of hash function computations, XOR-reduce on the G table outputs and the final match on the key. The number of LUTs needed for these are expressed in Table 2.

Table 2: 6-LUTs consumed by dMHC(k,c)

| Hash Functions and XOR-reduce | Key Match |
|---|---|
| $k \times \log_2(cM) \times \left\lceil \left( \left\lceil \frac{w_k}{\log_2(cM)} \right\rceil + 1 \right) / 6 \right\rceil$ $+ (w_k + w_v) \times \left\lceil \frac{k}{6} \right\rceil$ | $\left\lceil \frac{w_k}{3} \right\rceil$ $+ \left\lceil \frac{\left\lceil \frac{w_k}{3} \right\rceil}{5} \right\rceil$ |

Since BRAMs are scarcer than LUTs, we can understand most of the benefits by comparing BRAM usage for a fully associative memory's match and the G tables in a generic dMHC(k,c) design. Revising Eq. 1 to use the same parameters as our dMHC(k,c) area model:

$$BRAM_{fully\_assoc\_match} = \left\lceil \frac{w_k}{10} \right\rceil \times \left\lceil \frac{M}{32} \right\rceil \quad (9)$$

Taking the ratio of these BRAM counts, we get:

$$\frac{BRAM_{dmhc\_match}}{BRAM_{fully\_assoc\_match}} = \frac{k \times \left\lceil \frac{w_k + w_v}{32} \right\rceil \times \left\lceil \frac{cM}{1024} \right\rceil}{\left( \left\lceil \frac{w_k}{10} \right\rceil \times \left\lceil \frac{M}{32} \right\rceil \right)}$$

$$\approx \frac{kc}{100} \times \frac{w_k + w_v}{w_k} \quad (10)$$

In case $w_v \approx w_k$, we can reduce the above expression to:

$$\frac{BRAM_{dmhc\_match}}{BRAM_{fully\_assoc\_match}} \approx \frac{kc}{50} \quad (11)$$

From this we can observe that, in case $k = 4, c = 2$ suffices, *the dMHC(4,2) match unit uses less than one-sixth the BRAMs of the fully associative memory (for $w_k \approx w_v$).*

## 3.6 Reducing G-Table Width

The G table architecture as described in the previous sections provides the same functionality as the exhaustive search in a fully associative memory's matrix, albeit with a low (configurable in $k$ and $c$) conflict rate. Each entry in our G tables is comprised of a $w_k$-bit wide *key* field and a $w_v$-bit wide *value* field. This could directly translate into a very wide G table whenever the key is wide and/or the data value is wide. On top of this, our architecture has to store these fields $k$ times for $k$ hash functions. This is primarily because, given an input key, we are trying to match the key as well as fetch the data value in a single BRAM cycle as shown in Fig. 2. For the rest of the paper, we refer to this design as the Flat dMHC design.

In the ideal case, we would like to only keep a single copy all the key-value pairs (instead of $k$ copies). We can modify the Flat dMHC architecture to do just that. The simple idea is that we store all the key-value pairs only once in a single table and only store their address information in the G tables. Then, given a key, we can fetch these $k$ G table entries and XOR them together to get the exact memory

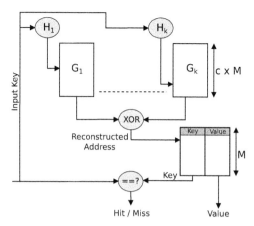

**Figure 4: A Two-Level dMHC(k,c)**

location of the key in the first BRAM cycle. Then, in the second BRAM cycle, we can fetch the key-value pair from that location and perform the match on the key to rule out a false-positive. The resulting dMHC architecture is shown in the Fig. 4. As we can see in the figure, this new design results in a 2 BRAM cycle access, hence, we call it the 2-level dMHC. The two cycle access with a level of indirection is similar to the perfect hash design in [7].

For a dMHC with $M$ entries, the addresses are of the order $\log_2(M)$. Therefore, the BRAM consumption for the G tables falls from $O((w_k + w_v) \times M)$ in case of the Flat dMHC to $O(M \log_2(M))$ for the 2-level dMHC for any $(k,c)$. This can result in significant reduction in BRAM consumption for the G tables as the 2-level dMHC G table widths are independent of the widths of the key-value pairs.

Modifying Eq. (8) for the 2-level dMHC design, we get:

$$BRAM_{dmhc\_match\_2level} = k \times \left\lceil \frac{\log_2(M)}{32} \right\rceil \times \left\lceil \frac{cM}{1024} \right\rceil \quad (12)$$

Taking the ratio of the BRAMs consumed for the match unit in the 2-level dMHC against the fully associative match, we get:

$$\frac{BRAM_{dmhc\_match\_2level}}{BRAM_{fully\_assoc\_match}} = \frac{k \times \left\lceil \frac{\log_2(M)}{32} \right\rceil \times \left\lceil \frac{cM}{1024} \right\rceil}{\left( \left\lceil \frac{w_k}{10} \right\rceil \times \left\lceil \frac{M}{32} \right\rceil \right)}$$
$$\approx \frac{kc}{100} \times \frac{\log_2(M)}{w_k} \quad (13)$$

In comparison to the Flat dMHC design, the 2-level dMHC design provides additional BRAM savings as long as $\log_2(M) < 2w_k$. In a typical case, where $w_k$ is 64-bits, we save BRAMs as long as our capacity is less than $2^{128}$ entries, which is much larger than one would expect to see in practice. Now, *for the 2-level dMHC with $w_k = 64$ bits, a dMHC(4,2) with 1024 entries would consume $\frac{1}{80}^{th}$ of the BRAMs consumed by the fully associative memory — roughly 14× less than the flat dMHC design.*

### 3.6.1 *A Performance-Area Hybrid dMHC*

The Flat dMHC gives us a single BRAM cycle latency but consumes a large number of BRAMs. The 2-level dMHC consumes significantly fewer BRAMs, but, results in a two BRAM cycle access. Even for the latency sensitive cases, there could be two cases: (1) where we need to know if the key-value is present in the memory as soon as possible, or,

(2) where we need the data value quickly, and we can confirm the presence in the memory later (*e.g.* in a processor pipeline where we can squash the operation in later pipeline stages). It is possible to modify our 2-level dMHC to achieve both these cases. For (1), we can simply add the key fields back into the G tables. This will allow us to reconstruct the key in the first BRAM cycle and signal the rest of the system if it is found in the memory or not. For (2), we need to add the data value fields in the G tables and then we can simply reconstruct the value in the first BRAM cycle.

### 3.7  Minimum Area to Achieve Miss-Rate

Let us assume a dMHC of $M$ entries with $w_k$-wide keys and $w_v$-wide data values. Ideally, there may be multiple ways to achieve a particular conflict rate since there could be multiple $(k,c)$-pairs that achieve the same conflict miss probability (see Eq. (6)). Thus, it should be possible to choose the BRAM-optimal dMHC configuration to achieve a given conflict miss probability for a given memory capacity.

Since the parameter $c$ should be a power of 2, let $c = 2^g$. Also, from Eq. (6), we have:

$$P_{conflict} \approx \frac{1}{c^k} = 2^{-kg} \quad (14)$$

In order to achieve an arbitrarily low conflict probability, we can equate the above expression to a low value, say,

$$2^{-kg} = 2^{-n} \text{ or, } kg = n \quad (15)$$

For example, $n = 16$ gives a conflict miss probability of 1 in 65536. With $n = 16$, we have the options in implementing a dMHC with $(g = 1, k = 16)$ to $(g = 16, k = 1)$. We can make this decision based on the number of BRAMs consumed for each of the above configurations. For this we only consider the number of BRAMs consumed by the match unit (i.e., G tables). We start with Eq. 8. Since, the G table width ($w_k + w_v$ in the flat case in Eq. 8 or $\log_2(M)$ in the 2-level case) is independent of $k$ and $c$, we can replace it with a constant $\alpha$. As we will see, the final result is independent of $\alpha$, so the conclusion here holds for all dMHC variants.

$$BRAM_{dmhc\_match}(k,c) = \alpha \times k \times \left\lceil \frac{cM}{1024} \right\rceil$$

Now, $k = \frac{n}{g} = \frac{n}{\log_2(c)}$. Therefore,

$$BRAM_{dmhc\_match}(c) \approx \alpha` \times \frac{ncM}{\log_2(c)} \quad (16)$$

Taking derivative of Eq. 16 w.r.t $c$, we see that it is minimized for $c = e$ (=2.718). Since we demand that $c$ be a power of 2, that suggests the best choice is to always set $c$ to 2 or 4. Later in Sec. 5, we experimentally show that $c = 2$ is sufficient to achieve a near-associative performance.

## 4.  dMHC **MEMORY MANAGEMENT**

To manage an $M$-deep dMHC dynamically, holding at most $M$ match values at a time, we will need to delete and insert values in the memory and occasionally relocate values.

- If we are at capacity, we need to select an entry and remove it from the memory. This involves some cleanup of state (Sec. 4.3).
- Once we have space, we need to insert the new entry into the memory.

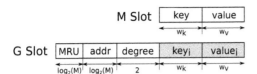

**Figure 5: G and M slot compositions for a dMHC with capacity $M$, $w_k$-wide keys and $w_v$-wide values. The shaded fields in the G slots are only present in the Flat dMHC design (MRU: Most Recent User)**

1. most of time $(1 - (1 - e^{-\frac{1}{c}})^k)$, this simply means writing values into memories (Sec. 4.4).

2. a small fraction of the time $(< c^{-k})$, the new entry will conflict with all $k$ existing entries.

   (a) In most conflict cases $(> 1 - (2c^2(e^{\frac{1}{c}} - 1))^{-k})$ one or more of the conflicting G-table users will only be used by a single, existing entry (Sec. 4.5). By removing one of these entries, we can insert the new entry.

   (b) We can then try to re-insert the entry we just removed. With probability $> 1 - c^{k-1}$, we can re-insert this entry without conflict (Sec. 4.5).

   (c) If it conflicts, we continue removing and re-inserting entries with similar probability of success. As a result, we can almost always eventually accommodate all the entries in the memory (Sec. 4.6).

The remainder of this section describes the details of the state and operations needed to implement our management algorithm.

## 4.1 Table Composition

We refer to each entry in a G table as a G slot, and the number of key-value pairs using a particular G slot as its degree. The table with the original key-value pairs is the M table, and we refer to each entry in there as an M slot. Fig. 5 shows the composition of each G slot and M slot. The remainder of this section explains the rationale and use for each of the subcomponents of these table entries.

## 4.2 Servicing Misses in dMHC

In the dMHC architecture, like in an associative memory or any cache, a miss occurs when the input data is not found in the memory. In the dMHC architecture, we could have a compulsory miss, capacity miss or a conflict miss (on the other hand, an associative memory has no conflict misses). Upon a miss, in order to insert the new key-value pair into the memory, the first step is to find space in the memory for insertion. For a capacity $M$ dMHC we cannot hold more than $M$ key-value pairs at a given time. If there are less than $M$ key-value pairs stored in the memory, then we have empty slots for inserting the new key-value pair. However, if we are already at capacity, we need to evict a key-value pair in order to accommodate the incoming key-value pair.

There exist many eviction policies such as Least Recently Used (LRU) and Least Frequently Used (LFU). For our dMHC architecture, we use the Least Recently Inserted (LRI) policy. In most cases LRI policy performs as well as the LRU policy but requires less state to be maintained (LRU requires keeping age for each entry, where as LRI can be implemented simply as a single global counter). In Sec. 4.5 we further highlight the advantage of using the LRI policy in the dMHC architecture.

## 4.3 Clean-up on Eviction

As explained in Sec. 3, each key-value pair is stored by assigning suitable values to the G slots hashed into by the key. Moreover, the conflict probability computation in Eq. 6 assumed that, for a maximum of $M$ key-value pairs in the memory, no more than $M$ G slots (out of a total of $c \times M$) are being used in the G tables. Assuming uniformly distributed hash functions, the used G slots are uniformly distributed. When we are evicting a key-value pair, if we do not cleanup the G slots being used by the evicted key-value pair, then we could potentially end up in a situation where there are more than $M$ G slots in use in one or more G tables, which would increase the conflict probability computed in Eq. 6. Therefore it is necessary to free up the G slots that are not being used for storing the key-value pairs present in the memory in order to continue reaping the benefits of the low probability as given by Eq. (6). Cleaning up a G slot simply requires resetting its contents to all zeros. At the same time, it is possible, albeit with a low probability, that a G slot used by the evicted key-value pair was being used by another key-value pair still present in the memory. In that case, we do not want to reset the contents of that G slot, because it would render that other key-value pair unreachable, effectively evicting it from the memory.

In order to solve this problem, we store the *degree* of each G slot along with the key-value information. This is the same basic solution used to allow deletion in counting Bloom filters [8]. Now, we can only reset those G slots that have a degree *one*, as they were being used exclusively by the evicted key-value pair. We also decrement the degree of all other G slots, as now they are being used by one less key-value pair. For an $M$-deep dMHC, the maximum degree of a G slot could be $M$, adding $\log_2(M)$ bits to the G slot. However, with a high sparsity factor and uniformly random hash functions, the maximum expected value of the degree is low. For example, at any given time, with proper cleanup, probability of all G slots being used by two or more key-value pairs is close to $(2c^2(e^{\frac{1}{c}} - 1))^{-k}$, which is 0.14% for a dMHC(4,2). In order to corroborate this analytical result, we also simulated a dMHC(4,2) for a set of SPEC2006 benchmark programs and recorded the degree of G slots for each eviction. For k=4, c=2, M=1024, the average degree is 1.01, and the probability the degree is 2 or greater is less than 0.007%. Consequently, we can get away with using a small number of bits in the G slot for keeping track of its degree (2 bits in our current implementation). Although uncommon, the degree of a G slot can overflow the maximum of three in our designs. The only consequence of this, is that we may end up freeing the slot prematurely, forcing us to take a miss to refill the slot.

## 4.4 Inserting data into dMHC

Once we have free space in our memory, we can go ahead and insert the new key-value pair. The new key hashes into $k$ G slots. With a high probability of $1 - (1 - e^{-\frac{1}{c}})^k$ (0.976 for a dMHC(4,2)), the G slots hashed into by the new key will not all be in use by the key-value pairs already present in the memory. In other words, with a high probability we can find at least one degree zero G slot which is not being used to store any key-value pair. Then, we can assign that G slot suitable values (all the fields) such that all the $k$ G slots can now reproduce the original key-value pair for the Flat dMHC design or the location in the memory for the 2-level dMHC design. This requires the same XOR calculations as shown in Eq. (4). At the same time, we increment the degree of all the G slots used by the new key-value pair.

## 4.5 Resolving Conflicts in dMHC

With a probability roughly equal to $(1 - e^{-\frac{1}{c}})^k$ (0.024 for a dMHC(4,2) design), all the G slots hashed into by the incoming key will be in use by one or more key-value pairs already present in the memory. In that case, we will have to re-assign the fields in at least one G slot in order to accommodate the new key-value pair. Since all of these G slots are being used by other key-value pairs, re-assigning their values will render the associated key-value pairs unreachable, effectively evicting them from the memory due to this newly created conflict (we call them being victimized). Nevertheless, in order to be able to insert a new key-value pair, we must re-assign values in at least one G slot.

Mathematically, whenever such a conflict occurs, we can find a G slot that is being used by only a single key-value pair with a probability greater than $1 - (2c^2(e^{\frac{1}{c}} - 1))^{-k}$ (0.9986 for dMHC(4,2)). Once we are able to locate a G slot that has a degree of one, we can re-assign its fields such that the new fields, along with the fields in the other $k - 1$ G slots, correspond to the newly inserted key-value pair.

By re-assigning the G slot fields we victimize one or more existing key-value pairs, one in the most common case. However, since each key-value pair is stored using $k$, G slots, it might be possible to re-insert a victimized key-value pair by modifying the fields in another of its remaining $(k - 1)$ G slots. Continuing the idea of Eq. (6), with a probability of $1 - c^{1-k}$, we can re-insert this entry by modifying a G slot which is being used only by this key-value pair. Here the conflict probability is $c^{1-k}$ rather than $c^{-k}$ because we know it will conflict with the newly inserted entry that caused the this key-value pair to be victimized in the first place. However, with a very low probability $((2c^2(e^{\frac{1}{c}} - 1))^{-k})$, we create another conflict (when the G slot chosen to re-insert the victimized key-value pair has a degree greater than one). In that case, we continue removing and re-inserting entries with similar probability of success. As a result, we can almost always eventually accommodate all the entries in the memory, resulting in a generalized *N-hop Repair* strategy, where at each hop we re-insert a victimized key-value pair. This is equivalent to moving a hash entry to accommodate an insertion (*c.f.* [11]).

In order to be able to evict and re-insert the key-value pairs, we need to store all the original key-value pairs as well; this allows us to recompute the hash values and the new values to be assigned to the G slot fields. The 2-level dMHC is already storing these key-value pairs, but this forces us to add an M table for the Flat dMHC. Furthermore, to repair the victimized key-value pair, we need the address of the M slot it is stored in. Therefore, we add another $\log_2(M)$ bits to a G slot giving us the address of that key-value pair that used this G slot most recently. This way we only repair the key-value pair that was accessed most recently using this G slot (we do not expect this G slot to be used by more than one key-value pairs in the most common case).

When we do victimize more than one key-value pairs (less than 0.14% of the time for dMHC(4,2)) two things go bad – (a)

since we only re-insert one of the victimized key-value-pairs, we lose memory capacity by letting the other victimized key-value pairs stay in the memory even though they cannot be accessed anymore, and (b) the G slots storing information for these key-value pairs are not cleaned up as explained in the Sec. 4.3, affecting the conflict miss probability. However, since the LRI policy chooses the M slot to be evicted in a periodic manner, we will eventually be able to evict these stale key-value pairs and also cleanup their G slots.

---

**Function** LDVN(K, N)
// $K$ is the input key
$h_i \leftarrow H_i(K)$ for $1 \leq i \leq k$
$key \leftarrow \text{XOR}(G_i[h_i].key...G_k[h_k].key)$
$val \leftarrow \text{XOR}(G_i[h_i].val...G_k[h_k].val)$
$m \leftarrow \text{XOR}(G_i[h_i].addr...G_k[h_k].addr)$
**if** $key==K$ **then**
    $G_i[h_i].m \leftarrow m$ for $1 \leq i \leq k$
    **return** $val$   // hit
**else**
    $new\_m \leftarrow m\_slot\_counter$
    $h_i' \leftarrow H_i(\text{M}[new\_m].key)$ for $1 \leq i \leq k$
    $\text{cleanup}(G_i[h_i'])$ for $1 \leq i \leq k$
    **if** *there is an unused* $h_i$ **then**
        use $h_i$ to store $K$ at M[$new\_m$]
    **else**
        choose $i$ s.t. $\deg(G_i[h_i]) = $
            $\text{min\_deg}(G_1[h_1]...G_k[h_k])$
        re-assign $G_i[h_i].\{key, val, addr\}$ to store $K$ at M[$new\_m$]
        $victim\_m \leftarrow G_i[h_i].m$
        LDV($victim\_m$, $i$, N);
    **end**
    $G_i[h_i].m \leftarrow new\_m$ for $1 \leq i \leq k$
    $m\_slot\_counter ++$ // *LRI replacement of* M *slots*
    **return** dMHC_$miss$
**end**
**EndFunction**

**Function** LDV($m\_slot$, $j$, N)
**if** $N = 0$ **then**
    **return** 0  //no more hops
**else**
    $h_i \leftarrow H_i(\text{M}[m\_slot].key)$ for $1 \leq i \leq k$
    choose $i \neq j$ s.t. $\deg(G_i[h_i]) = $
        $\text{min\_deg}(G_1[h_1]...G_k[h_k])$
    re-assign $G_i[h_i].\{key, val, addr\}$ to store M[$m\_slot$].key at M[$m\_slot$]
    $victim\_m \leftarrow G_i[h_i].m$
    $G_i[h_i].m \leftarrow m\_slot$
    **return** LDV($victim\_m$, $i$, $N - 1$)
**end**
**EndFunction**

**Algorithm 1:** Pseudocode for Lowest Degree Victim with N-hop Repair Policy

## 4.6 Lowest Degree Victim with N-hop Repair

Generalizing the strategy above, this brings us to the Lowest Degree Victimization policy for inserting new key-value pairs in case of a conflict: to resolve a conflict, we reassign the G slot with the lowest degree which would victimize the

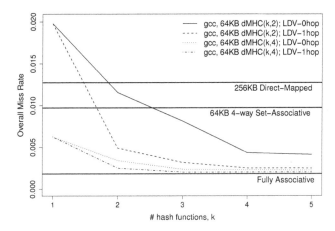

Figure 6: Miss-Rates for a 64KB dMHC for gcc

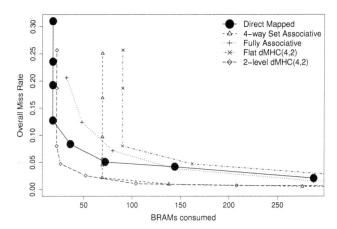

Figure 7: BRAMs v/s Miss-Rates for gcc

least number of M slots. Algorithm 1 shows the complete algorithm for dMHC memory management.

# 5. PERFORMANCE COMPARISON

## 5.1 Case Study: L1 Data Cache Miss-Rates

Fully associative memories would make for high performance L1 data (or instruction) caches for a processor, albeit with heavy area overheads. The large overhead is why we do not see them as on-chip caches in a commodity processor. Our analytical model shows that the dMHC architecture can achieve a near-associative memory performance at much lower BRAM consumption (Sec. 3). To validate our theoretical performance and area predictions, we modeled the dMHC as an L1 data cache and performed address trace-driven simulations on a small set of eight benchmark programs from the SPEC2006 Benchmark Suite [9] using traces from a 64-bit x86-simulator [2] simulating each benchmark for 100M cycles. Memory reference counts for the address traces used in the present work are highlighted in Table 3 (column I).

In order to perform a direct comparison, we also simulated a fully associative memory and several set-associative caches for the same benchmarks. Fig. 6 shows how the overall miss-rate varies for our architecture with respect to the parameters $k$ and $c$ for the benchmark gcc for a 64KB L1 dMHC cache with a block size of 8, 64b data values. (miss-rate is same for both Flat and 2-level dMHC designs). The figure also shows the miss-rate achieved with a fully associative memory of same capacity as the dMHC, a direct-mapped cache with four times the capacity and a 4-way set-associative cache of same capacity. As suggested by our analytical model, increasing the values of $k$ and/or $c$ reduces the number of conflicts (thereby reducing the overall miss-rate), approaching the miss-rate achieved by a fully associative memory of the same capacity at high values. Moreover, some dMHC configurations perform better than a bigger direct-mapped cache and a set-associative cache of same capacity. Also, the 1-hop repair strategy outperforms the 0-hop strategy for the same dMHC configurations. In Sec. 5.3, we compare the BRAM consumption for these caches.

## 5.2 Hardware Implementation

We implemented the proposed dMHC architecture (both Flat and 2-level designs) in Bluespec SystemVerilog [4] hard-

ware description language. Our tool[1] can generate a parameterized dMHC instance to target a particular conflict miss-rate or BRAM budget. Using the Bluespec compiler we generate Verilog HDL code which we then synthesize using Xilinx ISE 13.2 toolchain. We also implemented the 0-hop and 1-hop LDV policies for memory management directly in Bluespec as low level control FSMs. In order to reduce the miss-service latency in the memory controller, we have implemented both the policies as parallel as possible.

## 5.3 Case Study: L1 Data Cache BRAMs

Table 3 shows the BRAM usage ratio for eight SPEC2006 benchmarks for a 64KB L1 data cache. For each benchmark, we identify a dMHC instance that uses the least number of BRAMs while achieving a near-associative miss rate (that is, less than 5% of misses are due to conflicts). In each row we indicate the conflict ratio (as defined in Eq. (7)) and the most BRAM-efficient dMHC configuration achieving that. For each chosen configuration, we also report the fully associative to dMHC BRAM usage ratio (Flat and 2-level both with LDV-1hop policy). From the data in Table 3, we observe that a dMHC(4,2) configuration with 1-hop repair policy is able to achieve desirable conflict ratios in most of the cases.

Results from Table 3 show that our architecture is able to achieve a near-associative performance for a dMHC(4,2) configuration. However, it is also necessary to compare the BRAM cost of these designs. In order to achieve that, we extend our simulations by integrating the achieved miss-rates with the BRAM consumption for our designs as well as other caches. For this we ran simulations varying the size of all the caches from 1KB to the point where we saturate all the BRAMs available on the xc6vlx240t-2 device, and for each cache size, we record the miss-rate achieved and the number of BRAMs consumed. Fig. 7 shows how the miss-rate falls when we increase the capacity of these caches in terms of BRAMs. For any type of cache, increasing the number of BRAMs increases capacity, and therefore reduces misses. From Fig. 7, we can establish that the 2-level dMHC design is able to yield the lowest miss-rate per unit BRAM consumption across a large range of cache sizes.

Furthermore, dMHC architecture is able to achieve higher BRAM savings as the match width is increased. Fig. 9 shows

---

[1] http://ic.ese.upenn.edu/distributions/dmhc_fpga2013

**Table 3: Fully Associative to dMHC BRAM Ratio for a 64KB L1-Cache for SPEC2006 Benchmarks**

| Benchmark (Mem instrs) | Conf. Ratio (%) | dMHC config (k,c) | Flat BRAM Ratio | 2-level BRAM Ratio |
|---|---|---|---|---|
| art (19.9M) | 2.6 | (4,2) | 0.9 | 6.0 |
| gcc (15.7M) | 3.2 | (4,2) | 0.9 | 6.0 |
| go (35.5M) | 3.8 | (4,2) | 0.9 | 6.0 |
| hmmer (41.9M) | 1.4 | (3,2) | 1.2 | 6.5 |
| libq (30.2M) | 0.04 | (2,2) | 1.7 | 7.2 |
| mcf (32.2M) | 2.8 | (4,2) | 0.9 | 6.0 |
| sjeng (26.9M) | 4.9 | (4,2) | 0.9 | 6.0 |
| sphinx3 (33.1M) | 4.6 | (3,2) | 1.2 | 6.5 |

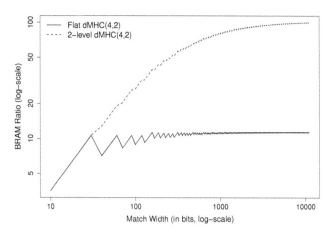

Figure 9: Fully Associative Memory to dMHC(4,2) BRAM usage ratio

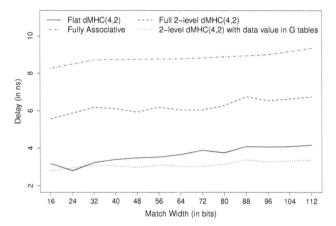

Figure 8: dMHC vs Fully Associative delays for a 1024-entry memory holding 64b values

the BRAM savings for the Flat as well as the 2-level dMHC designs over the Coregen-style fully associative memory, all of depth 1024 entries. For the Flat variant, the saving ratio saturates at about 11× where as the 2-level variant is able to save upto 100× over the fully associative memory.

## 5.4 dMHC Timing

Another disadvantage of the Coregen-style fully associative memory is the low frequency of operation. Reviewing Fig. 1, a fully associative memory with capacity $M$ has an $M$-bit, 1-hot to $\log_2(M)$-bit dense encoder in the critical path resulting in a high latency, even when $M$ is moderately high (say 1024). By storing the address information in the compact form ($\log_2(M)$ for a capacity of $M$), dMHC avoids such a slow path. In order to compare the timing performance of the dMHC architecture with the fully associative memory, we created 1024-entry dMHC and fully associative memory designs with 64b values and varying key-widths from 16b to 120b. These designs were then placed and routed using Xilinx ISE 13.2 for a Virtex 6 (xc6vlx240t-2) device. Fig. 8 shows the best-case latency achieved for these designs against the key-widths (these are the delays between providing the match key and receiving the corresponding data value out). Along with different BRAM footprints, the Flat and the 2-level dMHC designs have slightly different critical paths. Apart from that, the 2-level dMHC

requires 2 BRAM cycles to fetch the data value in the most general case. Using the 2-level dMHC variant where we store the data values in the G tables, we can achieve a much lower (single BRAM cycle) latency in the most common hit case.

## 6. RELATED WORK

Seznec [17] introduced a cache based on the multiple hash idea. He showed that using a cache with multiple physical ways, where each way is indexed by a different hash function, called a skewed-associative cache, resulted in a lower miss-rate than a regular direct-mapped or a set-associative cache. He further showed that a 2-way skewed-associative cache has a miss-rate close to a regular 4-way set-associative cache, however with the hardware complexity of a 2-way set-associative cache. Once we have a design that has choice, we can further reduce the conflicts by moving entries in the cache when conflicts arise [11]. Sanchez's Z-Cache extended the skewed-associative caches by introducing smart replacement policies that try to reduce the miss-rates by exploiting moves to expand the pool of eviction candidates and then choosing a suitable cache block to be evicted [16]. In the Z-Cache, there is *always* a conflict on insertion, and the question is which present entry should be removed. In most cases the dMHC has no conflict on insertion. Furthermore, since we keep track of sharing degrees, we can greedily search along a single conflicting entry for replacements, whereas the Z-Cache must expand a tree of exponentially increasing candidates. Since the Z-Cache is set associative, it demands a comparison and mux selection in the critical path after memory lookup, whereas our Flat dMHC produces the candidate result after a single memory lookup.

Bloomier filters [6] extend Bloom filters by giving the exact pattern that matched along with the set membership. These have been effectively used in applications such as accelarating virus detection using FPGA hardware [10], however setting up a Bloomier filter requires some level of preprocessing making it much more suitable for use where static support is involved. Our design has some similarity to Song's multiple hash function counting Bloom Filter [19]. However, note that Song only uses the hash function to determine the size of hash buckets that are stored off chip—particularly to avoid off-chip lookups on most cases and minimize lookups in others. Furthermore, our management logic is simpler and suitable to direct hardware implementation.

## 7. CONCLUSIONS

We have introduced the dMHC memory architecture that achieves nearly associative memory performance. Furthermore, we have shown how it can be parameterized (capacity, k, c, flat/2-level/hybrid, 0-hop/1-hop) and tuned so we can engineer the BRAM usage, conflict miss rate, and access latency of the memory. We showed that dMHC instances use their BRAMs more effectively than traditional alternatives (fully associative, set-associative, direct-mapped) achieving lower miss rates than the alternatives over a larger range of BRAM budgets (Sec. 5.3). Furthermore, we've shown that the dMHC implementations have lower access latency (Fig. 8). The dMHC should be in any FPGA application or reconfigurable computing designer's arsenal of building blocks.

## 8. ACKNOWLEDGMENTS

This material is based upon work supported by the DARPA CRASH program through the United States Air Force Research Laboratory (AFRL) under Contract No. FA8650-10-C-7090. The views expressed are those of the authors and do not reflect the official policy or position of the Department of Defense or the U.S. Government.

## 9. REFERENCES

[1] Y. Azar, A. Z. Border, A. R. Karlin, and E. Upfal. Balanced allocation. In *Proc. ACM STOC*, pages 593–602, 1994. 1, 3.1

[2] S. Battle, A. D. Hilton, M. Hempstead, and A. Roth. Flexible register management using reference counting. In *Proc. Intl. Symp. on High-Perf. Comp. Arch.*, pages 273–284. IEEE, 2012. 5.1

[3] B. H. Bloom. Space/time trade-offs in hash coding with allowable errors. *CACM*, 13(7):422–426, July 1970. 3.1

[4] Bluespec, Inc. Bluespec SystemVerilog. 5.2

[5] S. Bunton and G. Borriello. Practical dictionary management for hardware data compression. *CACM*, 35(1):95–104, 1992. 2.1

[6] B. Chazelle, J. Kilian, R. Rubinfeld, and A. Tal. The bloomier filter: an efficient data structure for static support lookup tables. In *Proc. ACM-SIAM SODA*, SODA '04, pages 30–39, Philadelphia, PA, USA, 2004. Society for Industrial and Applied Mathematics. 6

[7] Z. J. Czech, G. Havas, and B. S. Majewski. An optimal algorithm for generating minimal perfect hash functions. *Information Processing Letters*, 43(5):257–264, 1992. 1, 3.1, 3.2, 3.6

[8] L. Fan, P. Cao, J. Almeida, and A. Z. Border. Sumary cache: A scalable wide-area web cache sharing protocol. *IEEE/ACM Trans. Networking*, 8(3):281–293, 2000. 4.3

[9] J. L. Henning. SPEC CPU2006 benchmark descriptions. *SIGARCH Comput. Archit. News*, 34(4):1–17, September 2006. 5.1

[10] J. Ho and G. Lemieux. PERG: A scalable FPGA-based pattern-matching engine with consolidated bloomier filters. In *ICFPT*, pages 73–80, December 2008. 6

[11] A. Kirsch and M. Mitzenmacher. The power of one move: Hashing schemes for hardware. *IEEE/ACM Trans. Networking*, 18(6):1752–1765, 2010. 1, 4.5, 6

[12] C. E. LaForest and G. Steffan. Octavo: an FPGA-centric processor family. In *FPGA*, pages 97–106, 2012. 1

[13] S.-L. L. Lu, P. Yiannacouras, T. Suh, R. Kassa, and M. Konow. A desktop computer with a reconfigurable Pentium. *ACM Tr. Reconfig. Tech. and Sys.*, 1(1), March 2008. 1

[14] M. Mitzenmacher. Studying balanced allocation with differential equations. *Combinatorics, Probability, and Computing*, 8(5):473–482, 1999. 1, 3.1

[15] J. Naous, D. Erickson, G. A. Covington, G. Appenzeller, and N. McKeown. Implementing an OpenFlow switch on the NetFPGA platform. In *Proc. ACM/IEEE Symp. ANCS*, pages 1–9, 2008. 2.1

[16] D. Sanchez and C. Kozyrakis. The ZCache: Decoupling ways and associativity. In *MICRO*, pages 196–207, 2010. 1, 6

[17] A. Seznec. A case for two-way skewed-associative caches. In *ISCA*, pages 169–178, 1993. 6

[18] A. Seznec and F. Bodin. Skewed-associative caches. In *PARLE*, pages 304–316, 1993. 3.2

[19] H. Song, S. Dharmapurikar, J. Turner, and J. Lockwood. Fast hash table lookup using extended bloom filter: an aid to network processing. In *Proceedings of the Conference on Applications, technologies, architectures, and protocols for computer communications*, pages 181–192, 2005. 6

[20] J. Wawrzynek, D. Patterson, M. Oskin, S.-L. Lu, C. Kozyrakis, J. C. Hoe, D. Chiou, and K. Asanović. RAMP: Research accelerator for multiple processors. *IEEE Micro*, 27(2):46–57, 2007. 1

[21] S. Wee, J. Casper, N. Njoroge, Y. Tesylar, D. Ge, C. Kozyrakis, and K. Olukotun. A practical FPGA based framework for novel CMP research. In *FPGA*, pages 116–125, 2007. 1

[22] R. Wunderlich and J. C. Hoe. In-system FPGA prototyping of an Itanium microarchitecture. In *ICCD*, pages 288–294, 2004. 1

[23] Xilinx, Inc., 2100 Logic Drive, San Jose, CA 95124. *Parameterizable Content-Addressable Memory*, March 2011. XAPP 1151 <http://www.xilinx.com/support/documentation/application_notes/xapp1151_Param_CAM.pdf>. 1, 2.2

[24] Xilinx, Inc., 2100 Logic Drive, San Jose, CA 95124. *Virtex-6 FPGA Data Sheet: DC and Switching Characteristics*, September 2011. DS512 <http://www.xilinx.com/support/documentation/data_sheets/ds152.pdf>. 2.2

[25] P. Yiannacouras and J. Rose. A parameterized automatic cache generator for FPGAs. In *ICFPT*, pages 324–327, 2003. 1

[26] P. Yiannacouras, J. G. Steffan, and J. Rose. Exploration and customization of FPGA-based soft processors. *IEEE Trans. Computer-Aided Design*, 26(2):266–277, 2007 2007. 1

# Dynafuse: Dynamic Dependence Analysis for FPGA Pipeline Fusion and Locality Optimizations

Jeremy Fowers, Greg Stitt
University of Florida
Department of Electrical and Computer Engineering
Gainesville, FL 32611
{jfowers, gstitt}@ufl.edu

## ABSTRACT

Although high-level synthesis improves FPGA productivity by enabling designers to use high-level code, the resulting performance is often significantly worse than register-transfer-level designs. One cause of such limited optimization is that high-level synthesis tools are restricted by multiple possible dependencies due to the undecidability of alias analysis. In this paper, we introduce the *Dynafuse* optimization, which analyzes dependencies dynamically to resolve aliases and enable runtime circuit optimizations. To resolve aliases, Dynafuse provides a specialized software data structure that dynamically determines definition-use chains between FPGA functions. In addition, Dynafuse statically creates a reconfigurable overlay network that uses detected dependencies to dynamically adjust connections between functions and memories in order to fuse pipelines and exploit data locality. Experimental results show that Dynafuse sped up two existing FPGA applications by 1.6-1.8x when exploiting locality and by 3-5x when fusing pipelines. Furthermore, the speedup from pipeline fusion increases linearly with the number of fused functions, which suggests larger applications will experience larger improvements.

## Categories and Subject Descriptors

B.5.2. [**Register-Transfer-Level Implementation**]: Design Aids—*Optimization*

## Keywords

FPGA, high-level synthesis, pipeline fusion

## 1. INTRODUCTION

High-level synthesis (HLS) [3][5][6][18][34][37][38] combined with hardware/software partitioning [9][31] is a widely studied approach for improving FPGA productivity that enables designers to specify FPGA-accelerated applications using high-level code. Previous approaches include specialized synthesis and partitioning for a variety of systems including SoCs [6][33], tightly coupled single-board embedded systems [30], and also loosely coupled systems with FPGAs and microprocessors implemented on different boards (e.g., PCIe) [18].

Although recent HLS studies have made numerous advances, one limitation is that current approaches are generally unaware of many runtime data dependencies between FPGA-implemented functions, which prevents important optimizations. For example, Figure 1(a) illustrates typical behavior of a synthesized application using example code consisting of two FPGA-implemented functions: *F1()* and *F2()*. Upon reaching this code (step 1), the application executes *F1()* on the FPGA by first transferring input array *A* from CPU memory to FPGA memory. The FPGA then executes *F1()* and writes the output array *B* to FPGA memory. Finally, the CPU transfers *B* back to the CPU memory. The application then executes other code and later (step 2) repeats this process for *F2()* by transferring *B* back to the FPGA memory, executing *F2()* on the FPGA, and transferring the results *C* back to the CPU.

Ideally, as shown in Figure 1(b), HLS could have exploited the temporal locality of *B* within FPGA memory and eliminated the repeated transfer of *B* between the CPU and FPGA to achieve a speedup of 1.5x for this example. However, with only static knowledge of possible dependencies, current HLS approaches cannot guarantee data coherency because an alias in software may change the CPU copy of *B* before *F2()*. Most importantly, knowledge of dependencies potentially enables HLS to fuse function pipelines [24] as shown in Figure 1(c), providing a significant performance improvement that almost completely hides the execution time of *F2()*, with an overall speedup of 2x compared to the original accelerated design.

As opposed to being an oversight, previous HLS approaches do not fully analyze function dependencies due to the undecidable alias analysis problem [1][2][26][28]. Even for approaches that restrict aliases, statically determining all possible dependencies is difficult due to a large potential number of function call combinations. In this paper, we address this problem by introducing the *Dynafuse* optimization, which complements existing high-level synthesis approaches by using a specialized software data structure to track function dependencies at runtime, thereby resolving all potential aliases. Dynafuse combines this analysis with a dynamically reconfigurable network of function pipelines that uses the detected dependencies to perform dynamic pipeline fusion while also exploiting detected locality to minimize inter-device communication as shown in Figure 1 (b-c). Experimental results for two applications show that Dynafuse achieves speedup from 3-5x compared to FPGA implementations without Dynafuse. Furthermore, the results show that speedup increases linearly with the number of fused functions, which suggests larger applications will experience larger improvements. Even without pipeline fusion, exploiting the temporal locality of FPGA data improved performance by 1.6-1.8x.

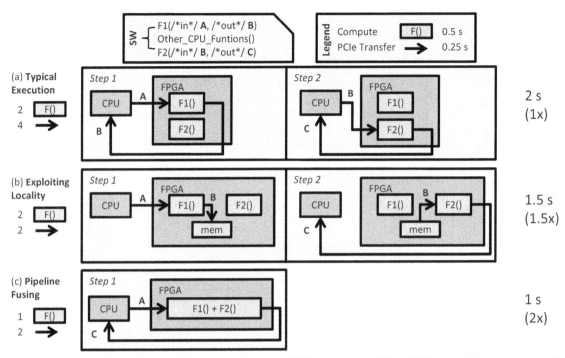

**Figure 1:** Execution of a sample application with two inter-dependent FPGA functions, F1() and F2(), with (a) a typical execution where output is returned to the CPU after every function call, (b) Dynafuse exploiting the temporal locality of FPGA outputs to save 2 PCIe transfers, and (c) Dynafuse fusing F1() and F2() into a single pipeline to create a 2x speedup.

Envisioned usage scenarios for Dynafuse include integration with existing HLS tools to provide synthesized FPGA functions for fusion, while using Dynafuse data structures in the high-level code to determine function dependencies. Alternatively, Dynafuse could be integrated with any FPGA-based hardware/software partitioning approach (e.g., [9][31][36]) that uses either custom or library-provided FPGA functions.

## 2. PREVIOUS WORK

Many static tests are used to determine when instruction- and data-level parallelism are possible by ensuring that dependencies do not exist between two functions [26], such as the constant test [26], Greatest Common Denominator [1], Banerjee's tests [2], and the Omega test [28]. These tests assume that dependencies exist between all functions and then attempt to prove independence whenever possible. Dynafuse complements these approaches by accurately determining when pipeline parallelism is possible by dynamically proving uninterrupted dependencies between specific functions.

High-level synthesis (HLS) techniques based on C code often require the designer to code explicit parallelism [11][12][20][22][25][35] and/or restrict important elements of C such as pointers, dynamic memory allocation, and recursion [11][22][24][25][26][32][35] to more effectively extract parallelism from sequential code. When used as a stand-alone optimization for existing FPGA accelerators (e.g., IP libraries), Dynafuse differs from these approaches by being almost completely transparent and imposing fewer coding restrictions upon designers. Additionally, Dynafuse benefits from existing HLS techniques because they can be used to create the pipelined FPGA functions that Dynafuse relies on.

Single-assignment C [24] and Spark [15] apply pipeline fusion (referred to as loop fusion in their papers) at compile time to create speedup. Both approaches prevent aliases and simplify

dependence analysis by banning pointers. Additionally, Single-assignment C uses single-static-assignment (SSA) form to make use-definition chains explicit. Dynafuse differs from these approaches by performing the pipeline fusion at runtime, which imposes fewer coding restrictions.

Gordon [13] uses a stream-processing model to parallelize software on many-cored CPUs and applies software pipeline fusion to create parallelism. Actors, the abstraction that carry out computation, can only communicate by explicitly passing messages through software FIFOs; therefore all inter-actor dependencies are declared by the designer. Dynafuse transparently detects inter-function dependencies without any explicit dependence information from the designer.

SpC [29] performs high-level synthesis without restricting pointers; however, it does not allow dynamic memory allocation. SpC resolves aliases at compile time by generating wires and memories in hardware such that any circuit whose input is made ambiguous by a pointer is capable of receiving values from all potential sources. Dynafuse allows for dynamic memory allocation and does not require additional hardware to respect potential aliases.

Devos [8] uses the polyhedral model [3] to profile applications for data locality and perform loop transformations, including loop fusion, at compile time. This work differs from Dynafuse by analyzing every one of the billions of memory accesses in the application, whereas Dynafuse only analyses dependencies between FPGA functions. As a result, Dynafuse has many orders-of magnitude fewer inputs, allowing it to determine data locality and dependencies at runtime without a profiling step.

Warp processing [33] dynamically decompiles and profiles software applications to identify and synthesize kernel functions into FPGA functions at runtime. Warp processing and Dynafuse are similar in their transparency and ability to optimize at runtime, but warp processing does not dynamically resolve dependencies and instead uses binary synthesis with traditional alias analysis techniques to create a fixed circuit. Dynafuse could complement warp processing by exploiting detected dependencies to fuse synthesized functions.

Wernsing [36] and Greco [14] both use libraries of FPGA functions to speed up existing applications. Dynafuse can further optimize these applications by fusing their pipelined FPGA functions and eliminating unnecessary transfers between the FPGA and CPU.

# 3. DYNAFUSE OVERVIEW

This section overviews the goals of the Dynafuse dynamic dependence analysis and the corresponding optimizations enabled by such analysis. The approach for realizing these optimizations is presented in Section 4. Although the paper is presented in the context of high-level synthesis, the approach is also applicable to any situation where a designer performs hardware/software partitioning for FPGA accelerators (e.g., [9][31][36]). We evaluate the optimizations for loosely coupled (PCIe) FPGA accelerators, although the approach could be applied to more tightly coupled accelerators, in which case locality exploitation would provide smaller improvements. For simplicity, we refer to all FPGA-implemented code as functions, although the approach could potentially apply to any granularity (loops, blocks, etc.).

## 3.1 Dynamic Dependence Analysis

To enable the proposed optimizations, Dynafuse requires knowledge of runtime dependencies for FPGA-implemented functions. Static dependence analysis has been studied for decades in order to extract parallelism and enable optimizations [1][2][26][28], but the undecidability of alias analysis complicates the problem by creating additional dependencies that prevent many optimizations. For example, as shown in Figure 2, static analysis may determine a function is dependent on multiple possible operations based on the existence or non-existence of an alias. In this example, *f4()* could potentially depend on *f1(), f2(), or f3()* depending on whether or not the *a, b,* and *c* pointers are aliases of each other. In the case where there are not aliases, *f1(), f2(),* and *f3()* can execute in parallel, and *f4()* can be fused with *f1()*. However, because static analysis can only detect possible dependencies, compilers and synthesis generally must make conservative assumptions (e.g., executing all functions sequentially or not fusing functions) to ensure correctness.

Dynamic dependence analysis overcomes the limitations of static analysis by resolving aliases at runtime to determine actual

```
void f(int *a, int *b, int *c) {
    ...
    *a = f1();
    *b = f2();
    *c = f3();
    f4(a);
}
```

**Figure 2.** Sample code demonstrating how aliases complicate static dependence analysis, where *f4()* may depend on *f1(), f2(), or f3()*, depending on whether or not *b* or *c* are aliases of *a*.

dependencies. Although a complete runtime analysis of all data dependencies would have prohibitive overhead [3], the proposed optimizations only require knowledge of definition-use and use-definition dependencies for inputs and outputs of FPGA-

implemented functions. With this restriction, our goal for dynamic dependence analysis is defined as follows:

*At the beginning of an FPGA-implemented function call, determine if the defining operation for every function input (i.e., definition-use chain) is an output from another FPGA-implemented function.*

To address this problem, Dynafuse uses specialized data structures combined with a delayed, access-triggered execution model, as described in Section 4.1.

Note that dynamic dependence analysis is not necessarily required to enable the proposed optimizations. If a high-level synthesis tool performs global, inter-procedural, flow-sensitive alias analysis [16], then in some cases the tool will identify all points-to possibilities for each pointer. However, this global analysis is likely infeasible for large applications and, more importantly, is still unable to determine which of these many possibilities will define a function input at runtime. Profiling the application can help identify which dependencies are the most likely to define a function input, but does not show how runtime dependencies change for different inputs. High-level synthesis could potentially create circuits for all combinations of possible function input definitions and then enable the appropriate circuit based on runtime conditions. However, such an approach could have significant overhead due to the many possible definitions and points-to possibilities. Furthermore, high-level synthesis is unlikely to fuse functions that are called in different branches or at different levels of the call hierarchy due to the need for a global definition-use analysis, which is further complicated by the many points-to possibilities. We are unaware of any tool, compiler, or previous study that performs such a thorough analysis. Dynafuse simplifies the definition-use analysis by waiting to determine actual runtime dependencies and then dynamically creating the appropriate pipeline. This dynamic analysis allows for two or more dependent functions to be fused regardless of the number of possible definitions and call locations.

## 3.2 Dependence-Enabled Optimizations

After dynamically determining dependencies between FPGA-implemented functions, Dynafuse dynamically applies three circuit optimizations: pipeline fusion, locality exploitation, and accelerator clustering.

### 3.2.1 Dynamic Pipeline Fusion

Pipeline fusion is a common optimization in digital circuits that creates a single pipeline from multiple pipelined functions. For example, Figure 1(a-b) illustrated FPGA execution of multiple separate pipelines, where *F1()* executed first on the FPGA, then transferred results to a memory (either on the microprocessor or FPGA) and then started executing *F2()*. In this case, the execution time of the application was the sum of the execution times of *F1(), F2(),* plus all data transfers. By fusing the pipelines of these functions, the resulting circuit increases the depth of parallelism, allowing *F1(), F2(),* and data transfers to occur in parallel using streaming. This fusion essentially hides the execution time of all but one of the functions, while also eliminating the transferring of intermediate results to memory (assuming no other region of code uses those intermediate results). With fused pipelines, an application only transfers the initial input and final output over PCIe (see Figure 1(b)), which can save N*2-2 transfers, where N is the number of fused functions in the pipeline.

```
void main()
{
        //Create Arrays
        CoherentArray<int> input(/*size*/ 50);
        CoherentArray<int> inter(/*size*/ 50);
        CoherentArray<int> output(/*size*/ 50);
        //Initialize input
        for(int i = 0; i < 50; i++) {
            input[i] = rand(); }
        //f1() on FPGA
        //inter is not retrieved at function return
        FPGA_f1(/*in*/input, /*out*/inter);
        //f2() on FPGA
        //output is not retrieved at function return
        FPGA_f2(/*in*/inter, /*out*/output);
        //Print results
        //All of output retrieved at first loop iteration
        for(int i = 0; i < 50; i++) {
            printf("Output %d: %d", i, output[i]); }
}
```

**Figure 3.** Example application demonstrating the syntax for declaring, referencing, reading, and writing coherent arrays.

Although pipeline fusion is not new, applicability of this optimization has been limited due to the difficulty of determining dependencies between all function I/O. By dynamically tracking dependencies, Dynafuse can determine function inputs defined by other FPGA functions at the beginning of each function call. Detecting these definitions at runtime with traditional pipeline fusion does not help because previous approaches create the circuit for the fused pipelines at compile time. To overcome this limitation, our approach synthesizes a *fusion network* on the FPGA that enables dynamically reconfigurable connections between function pipelines at runtime. Therefore, Dynafuse allows synthesized accelerators to execute independently or to be fused at runtime after detecting appropriate dependencies. Section 4.2.1 describes the details of this fusion network.

### 3.2.2 Locality Exploitation

As shown in Figure 1(a), a common bottleneck with FPGA accelerators is slow communication between the FPGA and microprocessor, especially for loosely coupled systems. This problem is worsened by unnecessary transfers that result from a high-level synthesis tool lacking the ability to fully analyze use-definition chains for function inputs. By determining these chains, as overviewed in Section 3.1, Dynafuse can dynamically analyze temporal locality of data used by FPGA-implemented functions. For the example in Figure 1(a), Dynafuse would detect that array *B* is defined by *F1()* and then used only by *F2()*. By leaving the *B* array in FPGA memory, *locality exploitation* enables potential pipeline fusion while also greatly reducing communication times for functions where pipeline fusion is unavailable.

Locality exploitation is enabled by the same techniques as dynamic dependence analysis, which is described in Section 4.1.

### 3.2.3 Accelerator Clustering

One requirement for pipeline fusion to be possible is that high-level synthesis must implement all accelerators in the same bitfile. Even when not using pipeline fusion, functions exhibiting temporal locality can be combined into the same bitfile to prevent time-consuming FPGA reconfigurations. To enable such optimization, our approach performs *accelerator clustering*, which we informally define as the following optimization problem:

*Given a set of FPGA-implemented functions, cluster the functions into one or more bitfiles such that overall execution time is minimized.*

For a single bitfile, accelerator clustering is similar to traditional hardware/software partitioning, with the additional requirement for considering the effects of pipeline fusion. Consideration of multiple bitfiles greatly increases the solution space due to all possible combinations of bitfiles, where functions may be replicated in multiple bitfiles to reduce reconfiguration frequency.

Because accelerator clustering is challenging enough for an entire study, in this paper we focus on a heuristic that is sufficient for pipeline fusion. We defer the investigation of a more general solution to future work.

## 4. DYNAFUSE APPROACH

This section describes how Dynafuse achieves the described optimizations using specialized software data structures (Section 4.1) combined with a dynamically configurable overlay network (Section 4.2).

### 4.1 Software Data Structures

Dynafuse uses specialized software data structures to perform dependence analysis for FPGA functions, to guarantee coherency of FPGA and CPU memories, and to control dynamic optimizations for the FPGA accelerators. Dynafuse achieves such functionality with two data structures, *coherent arrays* and the *FPGA function queue*, as described in the following sections.

### 4.1.1 Coherent Arrays

One significant challenge with reducing inter-device data transfers is guaranteeing data coherency. An ideal approach would analyze definition-use chains for a completed FPGA function and then transfer the output data to the devices corresponding to each use. In this case, if another FPGA function used output data from a previous FPGA function, the application would avoid an unnecessary transfer back and forth from the CPU. However, this optimization requires that software does not use the data in between the two FPGA functions, which can be difficult to detect statically due to aliases. For this optimization to be possible, Dynafuse needs to dynamically detect any software accesses to data stored in FPGA memories.

To solve this problem, Dynafuse uses a specialized array data structure, referred to as a coherent array, for any data shared by both software code and FPGA accelerators. The coherent array wraps a standard array with locality information and automatic coherency management, while providing an interface that enables the array to detect any access, even in the case of aliases. As shown in Figure 3, a coherent array provides the same software interface as a standard array by using an overloaded array reference [] operator. Coherent arrays also provide a specialized *coherent pointer* (not shown) that can be dereferenced like a standard pointer. The key difference from traditional arrays is that coherent arrays force all aliases to use coherent pointers, so that the array is aware of all accesses.

Coherent arrays track the *active location* of array data, which we define as the memory, either on the FPGA or CPU, that is up-to-date with the most recent changes. When software accesses a

| (a) # | Code | Xfers |
|---|---|---|
| 1 | int A[] | |
| 2 | int B[] | |
| 3 | int C[] | |
| 4 | FPGA_f1(/*in*/ A, /*out*/ B) | A in, **B out** |
| 5 | FPGA_f2(/*in*/ B, /*out*/ C) | **B in**, C out |
| 6 | File.write(C) | |

| (b) # | Code | Coherent Array Active Location | | | Xfers |
|---|---|---|---|---|---|
| | | A | B | C | |
| 1 | CoherentArray<int> A | CPU | - | - | |
| 2 | CoherentArray<int> B | CPU | CPU | - | |
| 3 | CoherentArray<int> C | CPU | CPU | CPU | |
| 4 | FPGA_f1(/*in*/ A, /*out*/ B) | FPGA | FPGA | CPU | A in |
| 5 | FPGA_f2(/*in*/ B, /*out*/ C) | FPGA | FPGA | FPGA | |
| 6 | File.write(C) | FPGA | FPGA | CPU | C out |

**Figure 4.** Application execution with (a) standard arrays, which performs unnecessary PCIe transfers of array *B* in lines 4 and 5, and (b) coherent arrays, which track active locations to avoid these transfers.

| # | Code | FPGA Function Queue Contents | Pipelines Executing |
|---|---|---|---|
| 1 | f1(/*in*/ A, /*out*/ B) | [A⇒f1⇒B] | None |
| 2 | f2(/*in*/ B, /*out*/ C) | [A⇒f1⇒B⇒f2⇒C] | None |
| 3 | f3(/*in*/ X, /*out*/ Y) | [A⇒f1⇒B⇒f2⇒C],[X⇒f3⇒Y] | None |
| 4 | File.write(C); | [X⇒f3⇒Y] | [f1⇒f2] |
| 5 | File.write(Y); | Empty | [f3] |

**Figure 5.** Example application with 3 FPGA functions. The first two are interdependent and the third is unrelated. All 3 functions are delayed and placed in the queue. The queue detects the definition-use chain between f1 and f2 and fuses them into a pipeline during the access-triggered execution in line 4. Access triggered execution occurs for f3 in line 5.

coherent array, either with the [] operator or by dereferencing a coherent pointer, the coherent array checks the active location of the data before returning or modifying the corresponding value. If the active location is on the CPU then the coherent array simply returns or modifies the array data from the requested index, or from the corresponding pointer location.

Figure 4 compares execution using traditional arrays and coherent arrays. With traditional arrays (Figure 4(a)), the application transfers every input and output array to/from the FPGA for each function. Figure 4(b) shows application behavior with coherent arrays. The active location of a coherent array always starts in CPU memory (lines 1-3). When software provides a coherent array as input data or output storage for an FPGA function, the coherent array changes the active location to FPGA memory. When used as an FPGA function input, the coherent array automatically transfers the array data over PCIe to FPGA memory (lines 4-5). When software accesses a coherent array whose active location is on the FPGA, the coherent array transfers the data over PCIe to CPU memory (line 6) and in the case of a write changes the active location to the CPU.

As shown in Figure 4, coherent arrays enable data used by FPGA functions to stay in FPGA memories until software changes the data. Such functionality exploits temporal locality of data across FPGA functions, which improves performance by eliminating unnecessary PCIe transfers.

One limitation of the coherent array is software performance overhead compared to a standard array. For example, when using coherent arrays for computationally intensive software functions, the [] operator overloading caused a 60% execution time overhead. Fortunately, in most situations involving an FPGA co-processor, time-critical functions are implemented on the FPGA, in which case software simply initializes the coherent array with minimal overhead. However, for situations where such overhead is prohibitive, coherent arrays provide a getPointer() function that

returns a standard pointer to the data, after ensuring the data is in CPU memory. With this pointer, the software code can use standard arrays without the overhead of the coherent array. Such functionality is appropriate for expert designers who know when aliases cannot possibly cause coherency problems.

An additional limitation is that coherent arrays do not detect software accesses to data until they happen. Given static knowledge of dependencies, an approach could potentially prefetch FPGA outputs, making them available to software sooner. Dynafuse and static analysis are therefore complementary and could be combined.

### 4.1.2 FPGA Function Queue

To dynamically fuse pipelines, Dynafuse must be able to determine definition-use chains for all data defined by previously executed FPGA functions. Traditionally, compilers would perform this analysis statically by creating and analyzing a control/data flow graph or similar structure. However, such analysis can have a prohibitive overhead when performed at runtime. To simplify the problem, Dynafuse uses a data structure called the FPGA function queue, which tracks the execution and dependencies of all FPGA-implemented functions.

Unlike traditional software execution, whenever software reaches an FPGA-implemented function, the function is not immediately executed on the FPGA. Instead, software adds the function to the FPGA function queue, as in Figure 5 lines 1-3. For the example in the figure, this process continues for three FPGA function calls. When software attempts to access a coherent array defined by a function in the queue, as in Figure 5 line 4, the queue starts the execution of the corresponding functions on the FPGA to produce the requested data. We refer to this execution model as *delayed, access-triggered execution*. Although delaying the execution of FPGA-implemented functions seems counter-intuitive, this delay is necessary to dynamically determine a series of functions that can be fused into a single FPGA pipeline. If each function executed immediately, there would be no opportunities for fusion.

When a function is added to the FPGA function queue, the queue performs definition-use analysis based on the coherent array parameters to each function in the queue. If one pipelined function defines a coherent array, and a later pipelined function uses that array, then Dynafuse can fuse the pipelines of the two functions. By analyzing the entire queue, the FPGA function queue can determine a chain of dependent functions that can be fused. For the example in Figure 5, definition-use analysis determines that *f1()* and *f2()* can be fused, while *f3()* is independent. After determining fusible functions, the FPGA

205

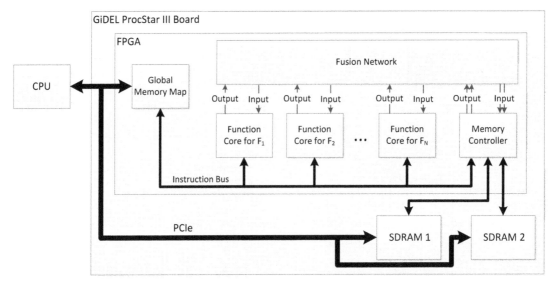

**Figure 6.** Overview of the loosely coupled FPGA architecture for a fusion network with $N$ function cores.

function queue generates a set of instructions to configure the fusion network (see Section 4.2) on the FPGA to implement the appropriate fusion. These instructions specify the memory containing the initial input, the memory that will hold the final output, the input source for each function core, and the runtime arguments for each function core.

The FPGA function queue allows software to call functions in a completely transparent, serial manner, and yet benefit from enhanced deep parallelism. The queue requires no preprocessing of code and is independent of data-dependent control flow that may make static analysis of function orderings difficult.

One limitation of the FPGA function queue is that delaying FPGA execution could in rare cases have significant overhead. For example, consider an FPGA function *F1()* followed by an independent, time-consuming software function *F2()*, followed by more software *F3()* that uses the output of *F1()*. In this case, *F1()* could have executed in parallel with *F2()*, but with Dynafuse, *F1()* is not triggered until *F3()* executes. However, such a situation is rare and a designer could easily optimize the code to prevent this situation. We could also trivially add an option that immediately executes a given function for such situations.

## 4.2 FPGA Circuit Architecture

The overall FPGA circuit architecture used by Dynafuse is shown in Figure 6. The architecture combines a memory-mapped communication interface (referred to as the Global Memory Map, GMM) and memory controller with a series of function cores (FCs) that represent accelerator circuits for different functions, along with additional logic that connects the circuits to the rest of the architecture. The purpose of this architecture is to accept instructions from the FPGA function queue (Section 4.1.2) that specify how to fuse the function cores according to the dynamic dependence analysis.

The following sections describe the details of the fusion network (Section 4.2.1) in addition to accelerator clustering (Section 4.2.2), which determines which function cores are included in a bitfile and the size of the corresponding fusion network.

### 4.2.1 Fusion Network

Although the FPGA function queue detects which FPGA functions can exploit pipeline fusion, the synthesized circuit must

support this fusion. Previous pipeline fusion optimizations apply fusion at compile time by creating fixed connections between function pipelines. Dynamic pipeline fusion requires reconfigurable connections between pipelines (i.e., function cores), which we implement using an overlay network referred to as the *fusion network*, shown in detail in Figure 7.

Each function core contains the pipeline for one FPGA function and a memory-mapped interface for receiving instructions from the GMM. The number of function cores varies depending on the number of FPGA-implemented functions and the number of expected fused pipeline instances determined during high-level synthesis. The architecture connects the function cores to the GMM by a bus and to each other using the fusion network. Currently, as shown in Figure 7, the fusion network provides a fully connected network between function cores using a series of multiplexers to allow any function to receive input and control signals from any other function core that outputs values with the

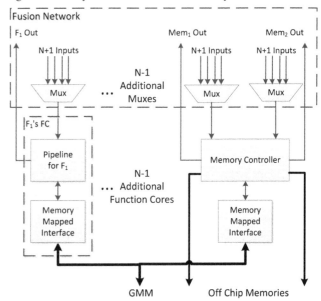

**Figure 7.** Zoomed in view of the all-to-all fusion network with $N$ function cores (only function core 1 is shown) and the memory controller.

same bit width. For example, a function core that takes 16-bit input will be networked to every function core with 16-bit output. The bit-width restriction saves routing logic and prevents incompatible functions from being networked together. Note that Figure 7 shows a fusion network where all functions have identical bit-widths for simplicity. Additionally, all function cores follow a template for top-level signals that ensures correct control flow through the fusion network.

Each interface to the FPGA's off-chip memories is treated as a function core that can operate on any bit width, and connected to the fusion network to provide input data and output storage to the network. Although a fully connected fusion network will not scale to large numbers of function cores, most FPGA applications do not implement numerous functions in the same bitfile. In our 5-function image segmentation example (see Section 5.1) the fusion network uses only 142 LUTs, which is only 0.7% of the total logic for the application. For very large applications, Dynafuse could potentially improve scalability with a packet- or circuit-switched overlay (e.g., [7][19]).

Instructions provided by the CPU to the GMM reconfigure the fusion network to use a specific memory as input, to create a pipeline of any number of function cores in any order as specified by the FPGA function queue, and then to use a specific memory to store the output. The CPU provides runtime arguments (i.e., inputs not in coherent arrays) for each function core using the GMM bus. Configuring the fusion network generally only takes a few extra cycles, depending on the pipeline size and number of arguments, compared to execution without Dynafuse.

Overhead of the fusion network depends on the number of function cores, the output width of each core, and how many cores have compatible bit widths. A few wide pipeline outputs will create more overhead than many pipelines with less output width. The 5-function image segmentation example in Section 5.1 uses pipelines with output widths of 32, 32, 1, 1, and 32 bits and uses 142 LUTs for the fusion network, while the 3-funciton FFT averaging example has pipelines of width 64, 64, and 64 bits and uses 191 LUTs.

### 4.2.2 Accelerator Clustering

To perform accelerator clustering, Dynafuse profiles the application by executing all functions in software, while also inserting the functions into the FPGA function queue for further analysis. This initial profile (Figure 8(a)) allows accelerator clustering to determine software execution times for each function. In addition, by analyzing the dependencies in the FPGA function queue, accelerator clustering predicts potential opportunities for pipeline fusion. Although FPGA performance could be estimated using numerous existing techniques [17][27], we currently use a heuristic that physically measures performance for certain input sizes, and then interpolates performance for all inputs. Appropriate performance estimation heuristics depend greatly on the intended usage. The chosen heuristic is appropriate for situations where bitfiles exist for individual functions (e.g., core libraries). When using Dynafuse in high-level synthesis tools, analytic estimations [17][27] would be more appropriate.

Accelerator clustering initially evaluates all possible combinations of bitfile configurations (Figure 8(b)). For K FPGA functions in the profile, Dynafuse considers placing K functions on K bitfiles (Figure 8(b) #1), combining K functions into fewer than K bitfiles (Figure 8(b) #2), placing K functions on one bitfile (Figure 8(b) #3), and also running some or all functions on the

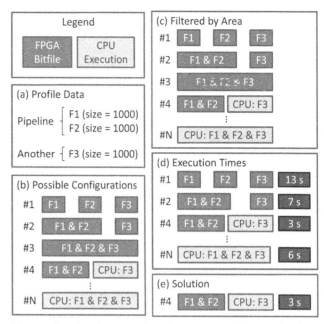

**Figure 8.** Accelerator clustering steps: (a) profile from application code, (b) generated configurations of bitfiles, (c) configurations with resource-constraint violating bitfiles eliminated, (d) execution times for each configuration, (e) fastest configuration. In this example only 2 functions fit on the FPGA.

CPU instead of the FPGA (Figure 8(b) #4 and #N). Next, Dynafuse eliminates those configurations that violate resource constraints of the targeted FPGA (Figure 8(c)). Like performance estimation, accelerator clustering can potentially use any type of area estimation [21] depending on the intended context. For the purposes of this paper, area estimation simply adds the number of resources for each FPGA-implemented function (e.g., LUTs, DSPs, block RAM). After eliminating bitfiles that violate area constraints, accelerator clustering estimates the performance of each bitfile possibility, shown in Figure 8(d), by using the collected software execution times, the estimated FPGA executions times, and the reconfiguration times of the targeted FPGA. Accelerator clustering identifies the bitfile combination with the lowest total execution time see Figure 8(e), which provides the information necessary for high-level synthesis or similar tools to generate the corresponding fusion network.

This accelerator clustering heuristic always produces the fastest possible configuration, assuming the estimations are perfectly accurate. However, the heuristic has exponential time complexity, which makes it impractical for large applications. For example, an application with 20 functions has 100,000 possible configurations. For larger applications, accelerator clustering uses branch-and-bound to prune bitfile combinations where reconfiguration times outweigh the CPU-only (no FPGA) execution time. Numerous other optimization problem heuristics (e.g., simulated annealing) could also be used to effectively reduce the solution space. In our experience, we have found that most high-performance FPGA applications consist of a small number of computationally intensive functions. Therefore, branch-and-bound was practical for our purposes. A complete investigation of accelerator clustering for different use cases is planned for future work.

## 4.3  Limitations

One limitation of Dynafuse is that the analysis is currently limited to the granularity of functions. However, we do not believe this is a significant limitation because many applications encapsulate FPGA execution using a function that hides communication and synchronization routines. Hardware/software partitioning could potentially enable the use of any granularity by simply wrapping any regions partitioned to hardware inside a function.

One current limitation is that Dynafuse performs definition-use analysis on entire coherent arrays. In other words, Dynafuse does not distinguish between definitions or uses of individual array elements and the entire array. This simplification requires that the entire array must always be transferred between memories. We could potentially extend the definition-use analysis to handle individual array elements, but in our experience, most FPGA-implemented functions tend to use the entire array.

Another limitation is that Dynafuse requires the high-level code to use coherent arrays when interacting with FPGA-implemented functions. Although this requirement does require a designer to modify the source code, the use of overloaded operators requires minimal the changes and the resulting Dynafuse optimizations impose no other restrictions on coding style.

## 5.  EXPERIMENTAL RESULTS

In this section, we discuss the experimental setup (Section 5.1) and present results (Section 5.2) that show the performance benefits of Dynafuse compared to both typical FPGA implementations and to software execution.

### 5.1  Experimental Setup

The targeted FPGA was a Stratix III E260 FPGA on a GiDEL PROCStar III board. This board was placed in a PCIe x8 slot of a Linux node with a 2.27 GHz quad-core Xeon E5520 processor and 6 GB of RAM, which executed all software functions.

We evaluated Dynafuse using two detailed application case studies. The first application performed image segmentation, with functionality similar to the FPGA datapath described in [22], applied to 1920x1080 32-bit color images. The application consisted of 5 functions in sequence: RGB to HSV color space conversion (32-bit input and output), HSV value threshold filtering (32-bit input, binary output), morphological erosion (3x3 structuring element, binary input and output), morphological dilation (3x3 structuring element, binary input and output), and Sobel edge detection (two convolutions with 3x3 impulse response, binary input and 32-bit output).

The second case study performed a frequency-domain averaging filter. This study combined 3 functions: Fast Fourier Transform (FFT), dot product (frequency-domain input times averaging impulse response), and Inverse Fast Fourier Transform (IFFT). All 3 FFT Averaging kernel functions have complex floating-point (32 bits each for real and imaginary values, 64 bits total) input and output widths. The FFT and IFFT functions perform transforms of size 8192, which was the largest that could be accommodated by the resources on the targeted FPGA.

The original C++ source code for both applications involved pointer operations combined with control constructs that resulted in multiple possible function input definitions. Every FPGA function was preceded by pointer operations that initialized data and API calls that transferred data to the FPGA and started execution. Every FPGA call was followed by a loop that waits for FPGA execution to finish, in addition to an if statement to check for errors or exceptions. These control statements created additional dependencies for all later operations. Therefore, for each sequence of function calls, the number of possible input definitions increased for every call. Although these applications could potentially be rewritten to simplify dependencies, dynamic dependence analysis is a more transparent approach that imposes fewer restrictions on high-level coding style.

For each function, we created a software version in C++ and a fully pipelined FPGA version in VHDL. We designed the FPGA functions to both fit into the fusion network (Section 4.2.1) and to operate as standalone accelerators. The functions for FFT and IFFT for the CPU and FPGA are based on FFTW 3.3.2 and Altera's FFT v9.1 IP, respectively, and the rest are coded by hand. The pipelines for erosion, dilation, and edge detection are based on previous FPGA architectures for sliding-window applications (e.g., [10]). We compiled all software functions with g++ 4.4.6 using –O3 optimizations.

The VHDL for the system architecture (see Figure 6) was automatically generated by accelerator clustering, which selected the appropriate function cores from a library (based on a profile of the application software, see Section 4.2.2) and stitched them together with a fusion network. We then synthesized all FPGA implementations using Quartus 9.1.

### 5.2  Results

For each case study, we performed 5 separate tests using different optimizations, as shown in Figure 9. The first 2 tests show the performance of each function running in software and on the FPGA without any Dynafuse optimizations applied. The following 3 tests incrementally add the 3 Dynafuse optimizations, starting with accelerator clustering, then locality exploitation, and finally pipeline fusion. All FPGA times include related software initialization, communication, and coherency management.

For both examples, the area constraints of the FPGA allowed accelerator clustering to create bitfiles that included all respective functions. These individual bitfiles eliminated the need for reconfiguration, which provided a significant 26-935x speedup over using the FPGA with no optimizations. However, these improvements are not unique to Dynafuse; most HLS tools share multiple accelerators in a single bitfile. Therefore, speedups for the remaining optimizations use the accelerator-clustered results as the baseline to represent a fairer comparison with existing HLS tools. However, there are FPGA tools that do not automatically combine function circuits into a single bitfile [36]. We included the accelerator clustering results to show the bottleneck caused by reconfiguration times in applications with multiple bitfiles. Clearly, at least on loosely coupled FPGAs, combining accelerators into one bitfile is essential for good performance.

The locality exploiting optimization eliminated one PCIe transfer for the first and last functions and all PCIe transfers for the intermediate functions. This optimization gave image segmentation 1.59x application speedup over accelerator clustering alone by speeding up individual function calls by as much as 1.9x. FFT averaging experienced 1.75x application speedup and up to 2.8x speedup per function. In general, the locality optimizations reduced N*2-2 PCIe transfers, where N was the number of FPGA functions (5 for image segmentation and 3 for the frequency-domain averaging filter).

Legend: AC = Accelerator Clustering, LE = Locality Exploitation, PF = Pipeline Fusion

(a)

| Device | Optimization | | | Function Execution Time (s) | | | | | Total (s) | Speedup (vs) | |
|---|---|---|---|---|---|---|---|---|---|---|---|
| | AC | LE | PF | Convert | Threshold | Erode | Dilate | Edge | | CPU | AC |
| CPU | - | - | - | 0.065 | 0.023 | 0.031 | 0.021 | 0.036 | 0.176 | 1 | 1.13 |
| FPGA | - | - | - | 1.04 | 1.04 | 1.04 | 1.04 | 1.04 | 5.2 | 0.03 | 0.04 |
| FPGA | ✓ | - | - | 0.04 | 0.04 | 0.04 | 0.04 | 0.04 | 0.2 | 0.88 | 1 |
| FPGA | ✓ | ✓ | - | 0.03 | 0.021 | 0.022 | 0.022 | 0.031 | 0.126 | 1.4 | 1.59 |
| FPGA | ✓ | ✓ | ✓ | - | - | - | - | - | 0.04 | 4.4 | 5 |

(b)

| Device | Optimization | | | Function Execution Time (s) | | | Total (s) | Speedup (vs) | |
|---|---|---|---|---|---|---|---|---|---|
| | AC | LE | PF | FFT | Averaging | IFFT | | CPU | AC |
| CPU | - | - | - | 0.00018 | 0.00018 | 0.0004 | 0.00076 | 1 | 5.52 |
| FPGA | - | - | - | 1.31 | 1.31 | 1.31 | 3.93 | 0.0001 | 0.001 |
| FPGA | ✓ | - | - | 0.0014 | 0.0014 | 0.0014 | 0.0042 | 0.18 | 1 |
| FPGA | ✓ | ✓ | - | 0.001 | 0.0005 | 0.0009 | 0.0024 | 0.32 | 1.75 |
| FPGA | ✓ | ✓ | ✓ | - | - | - | 0.0014 | 0.54 | 3 |

**Figure 9.** Dynafuse results for (a) image segmentation and (b) FFT averaging filter. Results are given for the CPU and the FPGA with 0-3 optimizations applied. Speedup for total execution time is given against both CPU and accelerator-clustered FPGA circuits.

Lastly, pipeline fusion was able to execute all of the FPGA functions concurrently in each application. Fusing the 5 pipelines from image segmentation created a 5x application speedup over accelerator clustering. Fusing the 3 pipelines from FFT averaging created a 3x application speedup over accelerator clustering. In general, fusing N pipelined functions with Dynafuse creates N times speedup over executing each function individually.

Software execution times are provided in first rows of Figure 9(a) and (b) as a baseline for comparing FPGA performance. The relative performance of the FPGA improves significantly as each optimization is added. Image segmentation is 4.4x faster on the FPGA than the CPU with pipeline fusion applied, as opposed to 1.1x slower with accelerator clustering only. FFT averaging is 5.5x slower than the CPU with accelerator clustering only, and 1.8x slower with pipeline fusion. We did not expect the FPGA implementations of FFT averaging to outperform the highly optimized FFTW software implementation, although the results show that Dynafuse provides significant speedup for FFT averaging in common situations where a fast quad-core x86 CPU is not available (e.g., embedded systems).

## 6. CONCLUSIONS

This paper introduces the Dynafuse optimization for FPGA-accelerated applications using high-level synthesis. Dynafuse eliminates limitations of static dependence analysis by dynamically tracking dependencies of FPGA-implemented functions. Dynafuse combines this dependence analysis with a dynamically reconfigurable network of FPGA-accelerator functions that enables locality optimizations and dynamic pipeline fusion for functions with appropriate dependencies. Unlike previous approaches that restrict pointer usage to prevent aliases, Dynafuse resolves aliases dynamically to determine actual

dependencies and enable further optimization, while imposing fewer coding restrictions.

Experimental results demonstrate that pipeline fusion reduces the execution time of an arbitrary number of pipelined FPGA functions down to the execution time for a single function. Fusion created 5x speedup for an image-segmentation application with 5 pipelined FPGA functions and 3x speedup for an FFT-averaging application with 3 functions. The results also show that N*2-2 data transfers between the FPGA and CPU can be eliminated for chains of N inter-dependent FPGA functions, resulting in up to 1.75x application speedup.

Future work will include more in-depth heuristics for accelerator clustering. In addition, we plan to expand Dynafuse to automatically execute functions in parallel on different devices when the dynamic analysis shows there are no dependencies between the functions.

## 7. ACKNOWLEDGEMENTS

This work was supported by the National Science Foundation grant CNS-0914474.

## 8. REFERENCES

[1]   U. Banerjee. An introduction to a formal theory of dependence analysis. *The Journal of Supercomputing*, 2:133–149, 1988.

[2]   U. Banerjee, R. Eigenmann, A. Nicolau, and D. Padua. Automatic program parallelization. *Proceedings of the IEEE*, 81(2):211 –243, Feb 1993.

[3]   P. Brisk, A.K. Verma, and P. Ienne. "Optimal polynomial-time interprocedural register allocation for high-level synthesis and ASIP design." In*Computer-Aided Design, 2007. ICCAD 2007. IEEE/ACM International Conference on*, pp. 172-179. IEEE, 2007.

[4] K. Beyls and E. D'Hollander. Discovery of locality-improving refactorings by reuse path analysis. In M. Gerndt and D. Kranzlmüller, editors, *High Performance Computing and Communications*, volume 4208 of *Lecture Notes in Computer Science*, pages 220–229. Springer Berlin / Heidelberg, 2006.

[5] A. Canis, J. Choi, M. Aldham, V. Zhang, A. Kammoona, J.H. Anderson, S. Brown, and T. Czajkowski. "LegUp: high-level synthesis for FPGA-based processor/accelerator systems." In*Proceedings of the 19th ACM/SIGDA international symposium on Field programmable gate arrays*, pp. 33-36. ACM, 2011.

[6] J. Cong. A new generation of C-based synthesis tool and domain specific computing, in Proc. *IEEE Int. SoC Conf.*, vol. 6507, Newport Beach, CA, USA, Sept. 2008, pp. 386–386.

[7] J. Coole, G. Stitt. Intermediate fabrics: Virtual architectures for circuit portability and fast placement and routing, *Hardware/Software Codesign and System Synthesis (CODES+ISSS), 2010 IEEE/ACM/IFIP International Conference on* , vol., no., pages 13-22, 24-29 Oct. 2010

[8] H. Devos, K. Beyls, M. Christiaens, J. Van Campenhout, E. D'Hollander, and D. Stroobandt. Finding and applying loop transformations for generating optimized fpga implementations. In P. Stenström, editor, *Transactions on High-Performance Embedded Architectures and Compilers I*, volume 4050 of *Lecture Notes in Computer Science*, pages 159–178. Springer Berlin / Heidelberg, 2007.

[9] P. Eles, Z. Peng, K. Kuchinski, and A. Doboli, System level hardware/software partitioning based on simulated annealing and tabu search*, Des. Autom. Embed. Syst.*, vol. 2, no. 1, pp. 5–32, Jan. 1997.

[10] J. Fowers, G. Brown, P. Cooke, and G. Stitt, A performance and energy comparison of FPGAs, GPUs, and multicores for sliding-window applications, *FPGA*, pp. 47–56, 2012.

[11] M. Fujita and H. Nakamura. The standard specc language. In *Proceedings of the 14th international symposium on Systems synthesis*, ISSS '01, pages 81–86, New York, NY, USA, 2001. ACM.

[12] D. Galloway. The transmogrifier c hardware description language and compiler for fpgas. In *IEEE Symposuim on FPGAs for Custom Computing Machines*, pages 136–144, 1995.

[13] M. I. Gordon, W. Thies, and S. Amarasinghe. Exploiting coarse-grained task, data, and pipeline parallelism in stream programs. *SIGPLAN Not.*, 41(11):151–162, Oct 2006.

[14] J. Greco, G. Cieslewski, A. Jacobs, I. Troxel, and A. George. Hardware/software interface for high-performance space computing with fpga coprocessors. In *Aerospace Conference, 2006 IEEE*.

[15] S. Gupta, R. K. Gupta, N. D. Dutt, and A. Nicolau. Coordinated parallelizing compiler optimizations and high-level synthesis. *ACM Trans. Des. Autom. Electron. Syst.*, 9(4):441–470, Oct 2004.

[16] M. Hind, M. Burke, P. Carini, and J. Choi. "Interprocedural pointer alias analysis." *ACM Transactions on Programming Languages and Systems (TOPLAS)* 21, no. 4 (1999): 848-894.

[17] B. Holland, K. Nagarajan, and A. D. George, Rat: Rc amenability test for rapid performance prediction. *ACM Trans. Reconfigurable Technol. Syst.*, vol. 1, no. 4, pp. 1–31, 2009.

[18] Impulse Accelerated Technologies, Impulse C, 2003. http://impulseaccelerated.com.

[19] N. Kapre, N. Mehta, M. deLorimier, R. Rubin, H. Barnor, M. J. Wilson, M. Wrighton, and A. DeHon, Packet-switched vs. time-multiplexed FPGA overlay networks. In *Proceedings of the IEEE Symposium on Field-Programmable Custom Computing Machine*s, 2006.

[20] D. C. Ku and G. De Micheli. Hardware c - a language for hardware design. Technical report, Defense Technical Information Center OAI-PMH Repository [http://stinet.dtic.mil/oai/oai] (United States), 1998.

[21] D. Kulkarni,W. A. Najjar, R. Rinker, and F. J. Kurdahi, Fast area estimation to support compiler optimizations in FPGA-based

reconfigurable systems, in FCCM '02: Proceedings of the 10th Annual IEEE Symposium on Field-Programmable Custom Computing Machines. Washington, DC, USA: IEEE Computer Society, 2002, p. 239.

[22] F. Lin, X. Dong, B. M. Chen, K.-Y. Lum, and T. H. Lee, A robust realtime embedded vision system on an unmanned rotorcraft for ground target following. *IEEE Transactions on Industrial Electronics*, vol. 59, pp. 1038–1049, February 2012.

[23] S. Loo, B. Wells, N. Freije, and J. Kulick. Handel-c for rapid prototyping of vlsi coprocessors for real time systems. In *System Theory, 2002. Proceedings of the Thirty-Fourth Southeastern Symposium on*, pages 6 – 10, 2002.

[24] W. Najjar, W. Bohm, B. Draper, J. Hammes, R. Rinker, J. Beveridge, M. Chawathe, and C. Ross. High-level language abstraction for reconfigurable computing. *Computer*, 36(8):63 – 69, Aug 2003.

[25] P. Panda. Systemc - a modeling platform supporting multiple design abstractions. In *System Synthesis, 2001. Proceedings. The 14th International Symposium on*, pages 75 – 80, 2001.

[26] P. Petersen and D. Padua. Static and dynamic evaluation of data dependence analysis techniques. *Parallel and Distributed Systems, IEEE Transactions on*, 7(11):1121 – 1132, Nov 1996.

[27] W. Pfeiffer and N. J. Wright, Modeling and predicting application performance on parallel computers using hpc challenge benchmarks. In *22nd IEEE International Parallel and Distributed Processing Symposium*, Hyatt Regency Hotel, Miami, FL, 2008, 2008.

[28] W. Pugh. The omega test: a fast and practical integer programming algorithm for dependence analysis. In *Proceedings of the 1991 ACM/IEEE conference on Supercomputing*, Supercomputing '91, pages 4–13, New York, NY, USA, 1991. ACM.

[29] L. Semeria and G. De Micheli. Spc: synthesis of pointers in c application of pointer analysis to the behavioral synthesis from c. In *Computer-Aided Design, 1998. ICCAD 98. Digest of Technical Papers. 1998 IEEE/ACM International Conference on*, pages 340 – 346, Nov 1998.

[30] SRC Computers, SRC Carte Programming Environment, 2012. http://www.srccomp.com/techpubs/carte.asp.

[31] G. Stitt, R. Lysecky, F. Vahid. Dynamic Hardware/Software Partitioning: A First Approach. Design Automation Conference (DAC), 2003.

[32] C. Stroud, R. Munoz, and D. Pierce. Behavioral model synthesis with cones. *Design Test of Computers, IEEE*, 5(3):22 –30, June 1988.

[33] F. Vahid, G. Stitt, and R. Lysecky. Warp processing: Dynamic translation of binaries to fpga circuits. *Computer*, 41(7):40 –46, July 2008.

[34] J. Villarreal, A. Park, W. Najjar, and R. Halstead. Designing modular hardware accelerators in c with roccc 2.0. In *Field-Programmable Custom Computing Machines, Annual IEEE Symposium on*, pages 127–134, Los Alamitos, CA, USA, 2010. IEEE Computer Society.

[35] K. Wakabayashi. C-based synthesis experiences with a behavior synthesizer, "cyber". In *Design, Automation and Test in Europe Conference and Exhibition 1999. Proceedings*, pages 390 –393, March 1999.

[36] J. R. Wernsing and G. Stitt. Elastic computing: A portable optimization framework for hybrid computers. *Parallel Comput.*, 38(8):438–464, Aug 2012.

[37] Xilinx Inc. AutoESL high-level synthesis tool. 2011. http://www.xilinx.com/tools/autoesl.htm.

[38] Xilinx Inc. Vivado high-level synthesis. 2012. http://www.xilinx.com/products/design-tools/vivado/integration/esl-design/hls/index.htm.

# A Remote Memory Access Infrastructure for Global Address Space Programming Models in FPGAs

Ruediger Willenberg
Dept. of Electrical & Computer Engineering
University of Toronto
Toronto, Ontario, Canada
willenbe@eecg.toronto.edu

Paul Chow
Dept. of Electrical & Computer Engineering
University of Toronto
Toronto, Ontario, Canada
pc@eecg.toronto.edu

## ABSTRACT

We are proposing a shared-memory communication infrastructure that provides a common parallel programming interface for FPGA and CPU components in a heterogeneous system. Our intent is to ease the integration of reconfigurable hardware into parallel programming models like Partitioned Global Address Space (PGAS). For this purpose, we introduce a remote memory access component based on Active Messages that implements the core API of the Berkeley GASNet communication library, and a simple controller that manages communication and synchronization for custom FPGA cores. We demonstrate how these components deliver a simple and easily configurable communication mechanism between distributed memories in a multi-FPGA system with processors as well as custom hardware nodes.

## Categories and Subject Descriptors

C.0 [**Computer Systems Organization**]: General—*Hardware/Software interfaces*; C.1.3 [**Computer Systems Organization**]: Processor Architectures—*Adaptable Architectures*; D.1.3 [**Software**]: Programming Techniques—*Parallel Programming*

## General Terms

Design Performance Languages

## Keywords

Parallel Programming Models; FPGA; PGAS; RDMA

## 1. MOTIVATION

High-Performance Reconfigurable Computing (HPRC) systems present two main challenges to application programmers: What parallel programming model to use, and how to incorporate reconfigurable hardware into a software application.

The first problem, inherent to all distributed computing, is what model of the existing hardware and memory distribution to present to the application programmer. This has implications for how to distribute and communicate data across the system, how to synchronize computations, and for how explicitly the programmer has to consider the physical makeup of the system. On the one end, *Shared Memory* presents a unified address space to the programmer, similar to the one found on a single host. On the other end, *Distributed Memory* only lets the programmer access the local memory, and all data exchange with other nodes happens explicitly through communication called *Message Passing*. The shared memory model is easy to program, but often leads to inefficient code, since the compiler cannot sufficiently reason about data access and communication patterns. The distributed model can produce very efficient implementations, but is very cumbersome to program.

The second problem involves the fact that most high-performance application programmers understand software and CPU-based systems, but not reconfigurable hardware. Part of that problem is being attacked by emerging tools to translate high-level language CPU code into Register-Transfer Language, with mixed results so far. However, besides an automatic synthesis path, applications also require an infrastructure for communication between software and hardware computation nodes, the equivalent of a communication API between CPU hosts. Preferably, this infrastructure should be independent from specific FPGA platforms, given the multitude of concepts and products that connect FPGAs with CPU-based host systems.

Both problems presented above point to the larger issue of increasing software and hardware complexity. Performance and efficiency are still the most common metrics for computing systems, but *productivity*, as measured by the required effort to design, debug and maintain high-performance computing applications, has been recognized as essential to continued progress towards exascale systems [17].

In our opinion, a unified programming model and API for all components in a heterogeneous system (see Figure 1) is crucial to keeping applications maintainable and scalable. Furthermore, the prototyping of algorithms in software and the subsequent migration to hardware accelerators is facilitated by such a common API.

In this paper, we will present our vision of a C++-based application design process that is based on the *Partitioned Global Address Space* model (PGAS). As our main contribution, we introduce an FPGA communication infrastructure compatible to GASNet[12], an existing PGAS communica-

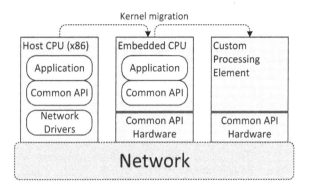

**Figure 1: Example for a multiple-platform system with unified parallel API: Host CPU, embedded FPGA processor and custom FPGA component**

tion API that maps well to FPGA as well as software components. This way, we enable cross-platform communication as well as easier software-hardware migration. The two main building blocks of this infrastructure are:

1. GAScore (Global Address Space core), a component that manages the remote memory communication for embedded processors and dedicated hardware processing elements. GAScore implements a GASNet-based API for embedded processors and custom hardware cores.

2. PAMS (Programmable Active Message Sequencer), a small communication controller that manages messaging, synchronization and GAScore access for custom hardware cores.

This paper is organized as follows: In Section 2, we give a bit of background on parallel programming models and the GASNet library on which our work is based. Section 3 introduces the hardware cores we developed in detail, and Section 4 explains the software stack that we plan to build on top of these components. Section 5 examines current system performance. Related work is referenced in Section 6. Section 7 elaborates on our next steps, and Section 8 concludes.

## 2. BACKGROUND

While our presented work is centered on implementation of a hardware communication core, it is important to understand the larger agenda that justifies this effort. Therefore, we will briefly introduce the parallel programming model that our hardware accommodates. We will also give a quick overview of the GASNet communication API that our design closely models.

### 2.1 Partitioned Global Address Space model

The two basic memory models for distributed parallel programming are called *shared memory* and *distributed memory* (better known by its practical implementation, *message-passing*). Shared memory assumes on the application level that all memory locations in the distributed system are directly accessible in a single address space. Accesses to physically remote memories need to be implemented by a runtime library. This library also needs to manage memory consistency and coherency. While the opacity of physical mem-

ory distribution eases programming of applications with this model, it can lead to inefficient data distribution and synchronization overhead. The most popular implementation of shared-memory parallel programming is the language and compiler extension *OpenMP*[5].

In distributed memory models, no direct access to remote memory is possible. Data needs to be communicated through the passing of messages, which will then be correctly related to local memory by the local process. Communication is implicitly two-sided, with both sender and receiver having to call functions for a transfer to be initiated. Message-passing can be fine-tuned for efficiency, but is more complex to implement. Furthermore, with the increasing size of computing clusters, the two-sided communication approach becomes a bottleneck for scalability. The dominant standard for message-passing is the *Message Passing Interface*[4] (MPI).

*Partitioned Global Address Space* (PGAS) offers a tradeoff between the two models described above. Every location in shared memory is directly accessible by any processing node. However, PGAS languages and libraries offer an explicit distinction between local and shared memory. Remote memory accesses are one-sided: When the memory of a remote node is accessed, no implicit synchronisation with the computation process on that node is happening. This is different from message-passing, where communication is always two-sided[1]. As a consequence of these attributes, PGAS offers the following advantages:

- Programmers have better awareness of the cost of a memory operation.

- The explicit designation of remote memory enables a relaxed use of consistency and coherency, and therefore avoids redundant synchronization overhead.

- One-sided access allows better scalability on large systems.

Languages that implement this programming model include the dialects Unified Parallel C (UPC)[8], Co-Array Fortran (CAF)[1] and the Java-based Titanium[7], as well as the newly designed parallel idioms Chapel[13] and X10[14]. SHMEM[6] and Global Arrays[20] are application libraries making use of the PGAS model.

### 2.2 GASNet communication library

*GASNet* (Global Address Space Networking) has been specified as a remote communication library for the Berkeley UPC and Titanium languages. Its API structure acknowledges, but does not require, the capabilities of *Remote Direct Memory Access* (RDMA) networking hardware like *Infiniband*[3]. GASNet's *Core API* is based on the principle of *Active Messages*[23]. Active messages are essentially asynchronous remote procedure calls. They are initiated by calling a *Request* function. The call defines the source address to copy from, the number of bytes to copy and the target address on the remote node. Besides payload data, an active message always includes a handler code and handler arguments. The handler code specifies which function to call on the remote target when the message arrives, and the arguments are handed to that function. Handler functions can fulfill synchronization purposes, process the arrived data in some way or initiate replies. An active message request does

---

[1]MPI 2.0 has heavily constrained one-sided Remote Memory Access support, but this is not part of the message-passing paradigm. For a detailed critique of its limitations, see [11].

not require an answer. However, if an answer is required, for example in a remote memory read, a handler function is allowed to initiate exactly one *Reply* message, which can only go back to the requesting node. These constraints safeguard against deadlocks.

Core API Active Messages are limited to packet sizes that can be easily supported by network hardware. The GAS-Net *Extended API* offers transfer functions for unlimited sizes and several types of barrier synchronization. It can be implemented entirely through Core API calls. However, sophisticated RDMA networking hardware can directly support Extended API functions.

# 3. SYSTEM OVERVIEW

In general, parallel programming models and APIs can be accommodated to a variety of infrastructures, so consequently MPI can be run on top of GASNet as well as GASNet can be run on top of MPI. Both of them are being able to communicate over regular TCP/IP-based networking stacks or Remote DMA hardware like Infiniband. However, each of these translations through software stacks costs performance. We have therefore concluded that dedicated hardware support for our chosen API GASNet is essential to maintain low latency, a crucial metric for parallel systems. Consequently, our main communication component uses a control API very close to GASNet and directly implements its Active Message capability for memory-to-memory transfers.

## 3.1 GAScore structure and use

The *GAScore* (Global Address Space core) is an implementation of GASNet functionality in hardware form. Processing nodes in FPGA systems that use GAScore are composed as shown in Figure 2. A computing element in the form of an embedded processor or a hardware processing engine is connected to one port of a dual-ported local memory (BlockRAM). The second memory port is connected to the GAScore. The GAScore is connected to the on-chip network.

The computing element is connected to the GAScore with four Fast Simplex Links (FSLs), essentially Xilinx-specific 32-bit-wide FIFOs. Figure 3 takes a closer look at the internal structure of the GAScore and illustrates the purpose of the four connections in receiving and transmitting Active Messages.

If an Active Message packet arrives from the on-chip network (see lower right corner of Figure 3), it is processed by the *Receive* unit. If the message holds a data payload, that payload is first written to the intended memory location specified in the message parameters. Because of the previously described deadlock-avoidance constraints, the receiving processing node never learns the sender's node address. Instead, the source node address is written into a *Token buffer*, which returns a token code as a key to the stored node address. The token and further parameters and arguments are transmitted over FSL 1 to the computing element, thereby calling the intended *handler function*. Whenever the handler function completes, it returns the token through FSL 2 and the Token buffer can free the stored source node address.

The computing element can request the sending of Active Messages by writing any message parameters and handler function arguments over FSL 3. Unless the request is for a short message without payload, the *Transmit* unit reads

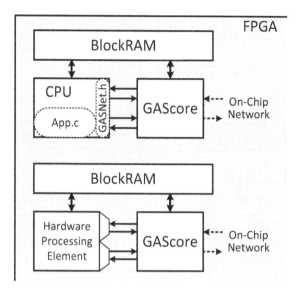

Figure 2: On-chip GAScore configurations

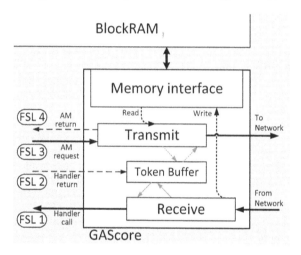

Figure 3: Internal GAScore structure

data from memory. This data, message parameters and handler function arguments are combined into an Active Message to be sent out over the network. A message can either be a new request, or it can be a handler function's reply to a prior request, as in the case of a remote read. In the first case, the computing node includes a destination node with the parameters. In the second case, the handler function includes the priorly received token. The token is used to look up the destination address in the Token Buffer. When the message has been sent, the GAScore signals the completion of the message request over FSL 4. This informs the computing element that the data to be transmitted has been read, and that the related memory area can now be freely operated on again.

While the data flow between computing node and GAScore could be multiplexed into two links, transmission and reception have explicitly been kept independent so that no deadlocks can occur. The only shared components are the Token Buffer, which needs no locking, and the memory bus, which is shared round-robin between reads and writes.

Table 1: GAScore synthesis statistics, Xilinx XC5VLX155T-1

| Resource | # | % |
|----------|------|------|
| Registers | 760 | 0.78 |
| LUTs | 1336 | 1.37 |
| BRAMs | 2 | 0.47 |

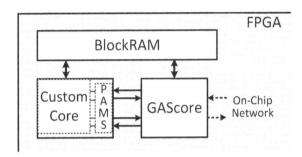

Figure 4: GAScore configuration with custom core and PAMS

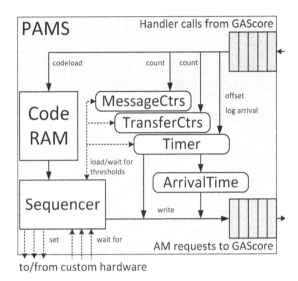

Figure 5: PAMS overview

Table 1 shows the resource utilization at a maximum clock speed of 142.6MHz, projected by synthesis for a GAScore with BRAM interface on a Xilinx XC5VLX155T-1. While synthesis numbers are not as reliable as final implementation numbers, we can see that a single GAScore uses a very small amount of chip resources.

## 3.2 Programmable Active Message Sequencer

For the Xilinx Microblaze embedded processor, a GAS-Net Core API library implementation has been developed that translates to and from the GAScore FSL channels (see Figure 2). Because the parameter format and GAScore functionality have been so closely modeled on the GASNet specification, translation is very simple and efficient. We are convinced that the code can be easily adapted to other embedded processor architectures.

On the other hand, custom hardware cores can implement their own mechanisms to send Active Message requests to the GAScore and process Handler function calls. However, this would be fairly redundant work for different computation cores, and individual implementations would make incompatibilites more likely.

Instead, we have developed a small application-specific controller that executes a limited set of machine code instructions, called the *Programmable Active Message Sequencer* (PAMS), to control the GAScore communication and synchronize it with core computations. Figure 4 shows a custom core/GAScore combination with the PAMS. A structural overview of the PAMS can be seen in Figure 5. The sequencer has the following features:

- PAMS code can be loaded and re-loaded into the sequencer instruction RAM through specialized Active Messages.
- Message counters (MessageCtrs) can be configured to count messages of a specific handler code and indicate when a threshold is reached. This is useful, for example, for barriers.
- Transfer counters (TransferCtrs) can be configured to count the data that messages of a specific handler code

have written into memory. They also have a configurable threshold. This is useful for *soft* barriers, where synchronization is achieved by having received the expected amount of data from other nodes.

- The sequencer can wait for a specific timer threshold. This is especially useful for programming benchmarks.
- The timer can be modified by a particular offset, which is useful when multiple FPGAs did not come out of reset in the same cycle.
- When a message has arrived, the current timer is copied into the *ArrivalTime* register. The value can be polled by sending a special message whose handler code does not trigger the copying.
- The sequencer can set control outputs to the custom hardware and wait on control inputs from the custom hardware.
- All possible wait conditions can be configured into one wait instruction, so that execution continues as soon as all conditions are met.
- Finally, the sequencer can write Active Message requests to GAScore that include attached arguments from code, from the timer or from the *ArrivalTime* register.

Figure 6 shows pseudocode for implementing a simple barrier in a 16-node system, as benchmarked in Section 5.2. There are two different code versions, one for node 0 and one for all the other nodes. For benchmarking purposes, all nodes are primed to start at a predefined time. All nodes except 0 send a *barrier_call* message to node 0, and then wait for a *barrier_done* message. Node 0 waits for 15 *barrier_call* messages (assuming a 16-node system) and then sends one *barrier_done* to every node. Each node automatically logs the arrival time of the last message in their *ArrivalTime* register, so that it can later be read for benchmarking purposes.

All benchmarks in this paper were realized through corresponding configuration of the sequencers in each core. The PAMS could also be used to implement the GASNet Extended API mentioned in Section 2.

```
/* node 0 */
set_timer_threshold(STARTTIME);
wait_for_timer();
set_msg_ctr0(barrier_call,15);
wait_for_msg_ctr0();
send_AM(barrier_done,1);
send_AM(barrier_done,2);
send_AM(barrier_done,3);
            [...]
send_AM(barrier_done,13);
send_AM(barrier_done,14);
send_AM(barrier_done,15);

/* node 1-15 */
set_timer_threshold(STARTTIME);
wait_for_timer();
send_AM(barrier_call,0);
set_msg_ctr0(barrier_done,1);
wait_for_msg_ctr0();
```

**Figure 6: Example PAMS code**

Table 2: PAMS synthesis statistics, Xilinx XC5VLX155T-1

| Resource | # | % |
|---|---|---|
| Registers | 943 | 0.97 |
| LUTs | 1035 | 1.06 |
| BRAM18s | 1 | 0.24 |

Table 2 shows the resource utilization at a maximum clock speed of 136.2MHz, projected by synthesis for a PAMS with four control inputs and four control outputs on a Xilinx XC5VLX155T-1. As was the case with the GAScore, we can see that a single PAMS uses a very small amount of logic resources.

### 3.3 On- and Off-chip Networking

A system of several GAScore-equipped computing nodes on one FPGA is pictured in Figure 7. In this example, two nodes use an embedded processor and two nodes use a hardware processing element (PE). Each GAScore connects to an on-chip network of *NetIfs*. NetIfs are simple FSL-based cut-through routers originally introduced for use by an on-chip MPI system in [21]. The NetIfs are arranged in a fully connected network. The feasibility of such fully-connected networks with FPGA routing resources has been examined in [22]; however, other topologies are under consideration for larger FPGAs where routing fabric does not increase proportionally with logic area.

Off-chip connections through other network and peripheral interfaces can be implemented through bridge components that can connect to NetIfs. In Figure 7, two Off-Chip Communication Controllers (OCCC) manage external data transfer to two different directions. Depending on the OCCC, communication can, for example, happen over board-level connections, optical or copper-based networks or PCI host buses. The choice of external interface does not influence GAScore functionality since its communication model is implemented on top of the physical network layer.

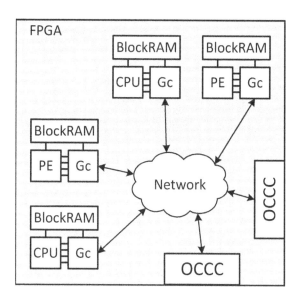

**Figure 7: Four-node system with Off-Chip Communication Controllers**

### 3.4 Portability

As explained in Section 3.2, GASNet software only needs a lightweight interface layer to control the GAScore component because its Active Message requests and Handler calls use the same parameters as the corresponding C functions. For the same reason, FPGA communication with host architectures running GASNet will be straightforward. The challenge is reduced to implementing bridges between host hardware and FPGA NetIfs, something which has already been successfully demonstrated in previous work[21].

A further advantage of this compatibility is the possibility to prototype code on a host architecture and then easily migrate it to an embedded processor. When CPU computation is translated into a pure hardware implementation at some point, the patterns of data movement and synchronization can be easily preserved.

### 4. SOFTWARE STACK AND CODE GENERATION PROCESS

Figure 8 illustrates the software stack that we envision on top of our component infrastructure. GASNet serves as the basic communication layer between all components. On top of the GASNet library sits a C++ library currently under development that unites proven PGAS and heterogeneity concepts from existing languages and libraries. Its main features are:

- Complex data classes for multi-dimensional arrays, etc.
- Location and node subset classes that allow modeling of heterogeneous systems
- Data layout types to control platform-specific data distribution independently from the data class itself

Applications can be written in C++ to run with the PGAS library. However, many scientists use Domain-Specific Languages (DSLs) that enable more productive and efficient modeling of problems in their specific area. We envision our C++ library to also be a suitable runtime environment

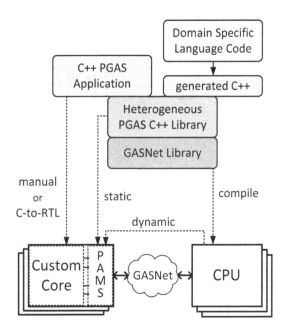

Figure 8: PGAS software stack and code/binary generation

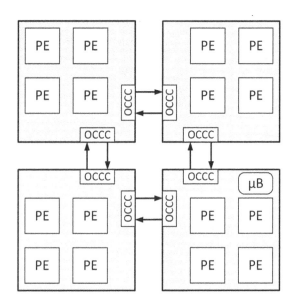

Figure 9: BEE3 quad-FPGA system with 16 hardware processing elements (PE) and one MicroBlaze processor($\mu$B) for configuration and benchmarking purposes

for C++ code that was automatically generated from DSL code.

For debugging purposes, an application should always be able to execute correctly (though possibly inefficiently) after compilation to a pure multi-CPU environment running GASNet. Based on profiling, the application designer can decide which functions should be migrated to hardware. Performance-critical functions can then be translated into FPGA hardware, either manually by a skilled hardware designer or through High-Level Synthesis (HLS/"C-to-gates") tools.

The communication and synchronization patterns that the PAMS needs to run for the new hardware kernel can be generated automatically by the library, either statically at compile time or, if required, dynamically at runtime. The ability to re-program the PAMS through GASNet enables dynamically changed control patterns at any time.

Since our C++ library is still in a very early design stage, all evaluations and benchmarks of our hardware components so far have been done just with the GASNet library and hand-written PAMS code.

## 5. PERFORMANCE EVALUATION

For a parallel computation system, it is imperative to keep the cost of remote data accesses as low as possible, so that exchange of data with other computation nodes does not carry an excessive penalty. Therefore, our main concern in evaluating our component is that remote data can be read and written with relatively low latency. Furthermore, we measure the maximum latency of two types of barriers, since barrier latency is performance-critical for many real-world applications. Given foreseeable contention for shared networking resources, a second aspect we investigate is how much overhead single data transfers incur, and therefore how efficiently the available network bandwidth can be used.

We have deliberately not included any application benchmarks in our evaluation. At this stage of development, it is important to understand the exact performance of this first implementation of our memory-to-memory transfer core using the NetIf infrastructure. Any application benchmark would be defined by the quality of a custom hardware core implementation, as well as the network bandwidth and congestion that is characteristic to this specific topology and board hardware (In fact, these characteristics *do* strongly affect our barrier benchmarks). We would not be able to draw definitive conclusions on whether our component or another influence is the impediment to better performance.

### 5.1 Test system

As a testbed, a demonstration system is implemented on a BEE3[16] multi-FPGA board. The BEE3 holds four Xilinx XC5VLX155T FPGAs. They are connected in a bidirectional ring with 32-bit-wide communication at 100MT/s in each direction. The system is clocked at 100MHz.

A single FPGA holds four hardware computation nodes and one Microblaze processor, each connected to 64Kbytes of BlockRAM and one GAScore. All four GAScores, as well as two off-chip communication controllers for both ring directions, are connected to one NetIf each, resulting in a fully-connected topology of seven NetIfs as illustrated in Figure 7. Figure 9 shows the complete system, with the four FPGAs building a network of 17 computation nodes. Nodes 0-15 are identical hardware processing elements (PE). Node 16 is the Microblaze processor ($\mu$B) in the fourth FPGA; the other three Microblaze processors are not utilized in the system. The Microblaze is used to program the PAMS in each processing element, poll the other nodes for any benchmark results and output the results through a RS232 UART.

Table 3 shows the implementation results for one chip with four hardware nodes and one MicroBlaze processor, using Xilinx Platform Studio 10.1.03.

**Table 3: Test system implementation results, Xilinx XC5VLX155T-1**

| Resource | # | % |
|---|---|---|
| Registers | 11160 | 11 |
| LUTs | 18651 | 19 |
| Slices | 8058 | 33 |
| BRAMs | 98 | 46 |

**Table 4: Short message latencies between nodes**

| Ring distance | 1-way (us) | 2-way (us) |
|---|---|---|
| 0 | 0.17 | 0.35 |
| 1 | 0.24 | 0.49 |
| 2 | 0.31 | 0.63 |

**Table 5: Single-word memory transfer latencies**

| Ring distance | 1-way (us) remote write | 2-way (us) remote read |
|---|---|---|
| 0 | 0.29 | 0.47 |
| 1 | 0.36 | 0.61 |
| 2 | 0.43 | 0.75 |

The system could be run at up to 138MHz with the same resource use. Clearly a decidedly larger system could be implemented on each FPGA. However, because of the fully connected topology, routing resources are expected to run out before logic does.

## 5.2 Latency results

Initially, we tested how long a single short message between two nodes takes from sending to receive completion. Because nodes inside an FPGA are fully connected and we tested without any congestion, results do not differ depending on which node inside the same FPGA was used for a measurement. This applies to all congestion-free measurements. Consequently, latency only differs with varying off-chip distances, which is why for a 4-chip ring we get values for 0, 1 and 2 FPGA hops. The latency for a short message varies between 170ns for an on-chip message to 310ns for a 2-hop message, equivalent to 17 and 31 clock cycles. A 2-way or "ping-pong" message takes only slightly more than double the time, since our PAMS allows very quick turnaround.

Next, we determined how long the smallest possible transfer from memory to memory takes, equivalent to remotely writing a datum. Latency increases by 12 cycles or 120us. This is only partially due to memory access latency: To ensure correctness, the GAScore only sends the handler call to the computing element when the memory has been completely written. This is in contrast to short messages, where parameters are transmitted onwards in cut-through style before the network packet has completely arrived. The latency for the equivalent of a remote read can be easily predicted since this is a combination of a short request and a long reply, and therefore only adds the previous 12-cycle delay to one side of the original 2-way latency.

For barrier latency, we first evaluated a straightforward implementation where all nodes send a barrier request to node 0; after receiving all 15 requests, node 0 sends *bar-*

**Table 6: Simple barrier latency (us)**

| Latency to node 0 | 0.87 us |
|---|---|
| Latency for all | 1.96 us |

**Table 7: "Staggered" barrier latency (us)**

| Latency to node 0 | 0.62 us |
|---|---|
| Latency for all | 1.48 us |

*rier_done* signals back to all other nodes. Table 6 shows how long it takes for all messages to reach node 0 (which is when the first node is done with the barrier) and how long it takes for all nodes to be notified about the completed barrier.

Contrary to the previous measurements, for the barrier the off-chip connections become a bottleneck where several messages contend for the same channel that can only transmit one message at a time.

To alleviate the bottleneck, our second measurement uses a staggered or tree-based barrier: Every node sends their barrier request to an on-chip node that functions as a hub. Only those hub nodes connect off-chip to node 0. Node 0 sends the *barrier_done* message back to the hub nodes, who distribute it to their on-chip neighbors. As all presented benchmarks, this change is implemented just through reprogramming the PAMS in each node, no hardware changes are necessary.

Table 7 shows the results. They are not dramatically better for two reasons: First, the three hub requests to node 0 from off-chip contend with the three local requests on the first chip, for which node 0 is the hub. Node 0 therefore still receives six of the previous 15 requests. Secondly, the off-chip non-hub nodes now have a longer communication latency for each single request, since they have to go through two nodes instead of one.

## 5.3 Bandwidth results

We further examined the transfer times for memory-to-memory operations of different sizes to determine how big the impact of latency is on effective bandwidth. Figure 10 shows that we reach about half of the optimum bandwidth at transfer sizes between 64 and 256 bytes, but that bandwidth for smaller transfer sizes suffers decidedly. These results are problematic, since PGAS enables user applications to commonly read and write single words of remote data, something that is heavily penalized here in terms of throughput. Almost any network infrastructure allows network saturation on large data packets, however ours clearly needs improvement on small amounts of data.

## 5.4 Discussion

It is clear from our latency numbers that a custom implementation of a memory-to-memory transfer could do in a few cycles what our communication infrastructure does in 17 or more cycles. Part of this disadvantage is a trade-off for a programming model that is easier to manage. This becomes clear as soon as the remote memory access happens across the board to another chip: Considerable effort is necessary to integrate a chip-to-chip interface into the communication. To the GAScore user, communication to an on-chip neighbor or any off-chip location is completely identical and does

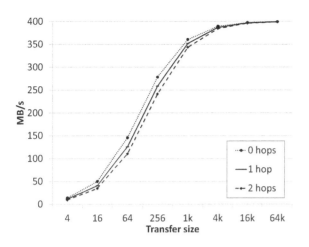

**Figure 10: Effective bandwidth depending on transfer size**

not introduce additional complexity. Furthermore, systems of dozens or hundreds of nodes stay easily manageable.

However, there is certainly room for improvement in the GAScore performance. A major bottleneck is introduced by serializing Active Message requests and Handler calls through the 32-bit FSLs. This is unavoidable when using a MicroBlaze processor, however a custom hardware core could quite well transmit all the parameters in parallel. In fact, we are considering moving the complete PAMS into the GAScore to minimize the delay in receiving, processing and sending Active Messages. The GAScore would in that case only connect through control bits to custom hardware cores. We will examine if this approach would introduce other disadvantages. Similarly, latency as well as bandwidth on the NetIf side could be improved significantly by extending from a 32-bit to a 128-bit network, something that TMD-MPI has already done.

A positive side effect of our benchmarks has been to demonstrate how the introduction of the Programmable Active Message Sequencer has helped testing productivity. In our early attempts at evaluation, every benchmark had to be hardcoded into custom logic and resulted in another place-and-route run. With the PAMS, small modifications and experiments with different sequences (e.g. the second barrier benchmark) can be implemented with a simple bitstream update. We are planning to further ease development of communication patterns by writing a PAMS/GASNet emulator.

## 6. RELATED WORK

Substantive prior work has been done to connect on-chip memory resources more smoothly with each other and with off-chip resources. CoRAM as introduced by Chung et al.[15] is an on-FPGA infrastructure to abstract external memory interfaces from hardware processing cores. CoRAMs are instances of on-chip memory that can be directly accessed by the processing unit on one port. A second port is connected to finite state machines that execute so-called *control threads*, which manage transfer of data to and from off-chip RAM. The processing core is therefore completely abstracted from the external memory interface. The use of

different control threads enables the on-chip RAM to function as scratchpad memories, caches or FIFOs. CoRAM does not focus on communication with remote memories, and does not take distributed programming models into consideration. It is principally intended to provide an abstraction to external memory.

The approach of having a similar, migration-conducive API for software and hardware components has been successfully used by Saldana et al.[21]. TMD-MPI is a library that implements a subset of the MPI standard to enable message passing between FPGA and CPU components. It has successfully demonstrated a common communication model for the simulation of molecular dynamics. Its downsides are the ones incumbent to any message-passing system: The need for low-level transfer management, two-sided communication and its scalability limits, the inefficiencies of indirect communication to remote memories and, finally, the impediments to dynamic memory accesses and the use of linked data structures.

Hthreads [10] is a hybrid shared-memory programming model that focuses on implementing FPGA hardware in the form of real-time operating system threads, with most of the properties of software, but adding real concurrency. Hthreads focuses on components sharing buses with each other in single-chip processor systems, and lacks a scalable programming model for multi-node systems.

VForce [19] extends VSIPL++, an established C++ high-performance computing and signal processing library, to use reconfigurable hardware for select library functions. VForce supports runtime binding so that the same application code can run on systems with and without supporting reconfigurable hardware. We expect our heterogeneous PGAS C++ library to behave in a similar fashion, however with a focus on PGAS coding concepts and (optionally) more explicit awareness of heterogeneity for the application programmer. Furthermore, VForce seems to focus on heterogeneity in a single node, while scalability across larger systems and networks is integral to our architecture.

On the PGAS side, SHMEM+ [9] is an extended version of the established SHMEM library that uses the concept of *multilevel PGAS* as defined by its authors: Every processing node has multiple levels of main memory, e.g. CPU main memory as well as an FPGA accelerator's main memory, which are accessed differently by SHMEM+. For node-to-node transfers GASNet is used, for transfers to a local or remote FPGA a vendor-specific interface has to be accessed by the local CPU. The SHMEM+ authors exclude on-chip memory from being remotely accessible, concluding that it is only useful for caching purposes. We think that there are classes of applications with small, latency-critical datasets, and therefore provide this access, especially since the exchangable memory component in our GAScore means there is no added cost to it.

El-Ghazawi et al.[18] examine two different approaches to use FPGAs with Unified Parallel C: In the library approach, a core library of FPGA bitstreams for specific functionalities exists. Function cores can be explicitly loaded into the FPGA. An asynchronous function call transfers data for processing into the FPGA, a later completion wait transfers the processed data back into CPU-accessible memory. The second approach uses a C-to-RTL synthesis of selected portions of the UPC code: A parser identifies *upc_forall*-statements that can be well parallelized in hardware and splits their compilation off to Impulse-C[2]; corresponding data transfers to and from the FPGA are inserted into the CPU code.

The common concern with the two PGAS solutions is that they leave the CPU(s) in charge of all communication management, while the FPGA remains in a classic, passive accelerator role. Truly efficient one-sided communication as embraced by PGAS is therefore not available, and FPGA capabilities are underutilized.

## 7. FUTURE WORK

Our most urgent work lies in improving latency as discussed in section 5.4. We are optimistic that we can improve performance significantly with the suggested changes.

In the short term, we plan to extend the GAScore memory interface to off-chip DRAM to open the system to a larger set of applications and data set sizes. A common multi-ported memory controller supports eight ports, so that four processing nodes with one processing element and one GAScore each could access a DRAM module.

For many applications on distributed arrays, built-in strided and scatter-gather accesses would be beneficial and could minimize the workload portion that a processing element needs to spent on initiating data transfers.

Our long term intentions are focused on the software stack described in Section 4. GAScore and the Programmable Active Message Sequencer are laying the groundwork for this by creating a common interface for processors and hardware cores. We plan to examine how to best model heterogeneity in a high-level language PGAS implementation and how to best migrate performance-critical kernels into logic.

## 8. CONCLUSION

We introduced a remote memory communication engine, GAScore, which can be easily interfaced by embedded processors as well as hardware engines on FPGAs. Furthermore, we introduced PAMS, a communication controller that simplifies using custom hardware cores with GASNet. Compatibility to a popular shared memory networking library, GASNet, assures easy integration with host-based parallel programming solutions and enables development of heterogeneous computing applications. We discussed how these low-level components fit into a larger approach for computing application development.

Our evaluation and results have shown us two things: First, there is room for improvement in the achieved latency for messages and data transfers. We have several ideas on how to optimize performance and improve those results. Secondly, we succeeded in providing an easy-to-use set of components for remote memory access. Especially the flexibility added through the Programmable Active Message Sequencer facilitates easier integration of custom hardware into a shared-memory-based parallel processing system. The ability to change communication and control patterns without a complete implementation run boosts design productivity. Like GAScore, PAMS delivers its functionality on a very low area budget.

At this point, our components provide the envisioned low-level functionality, but for a competitive system we need to markedly improve performance. Furthermore, we need to add the necessary software and hardware components to extend the existing infrastructure into a truly productive, heterogeneous, parallel programming environment.

## 9. ACKNOWLEDGEMENTS

We thank the CMC, NSERC and Xilinx for supporting our research. Special thanks to Manuel Saldaña of Arches Computing Systems for his BEE3 compile scripts and the NetIf infrastructure.

## 10. REFERENCES

[1] Co-Array Fortran. http://www.co-array.org/.
[2] Impulse C. http://www.impulseaccelerated.com/.
[3] Infiniband trade association. http://www.infinibandta.org/.
[4] Message passing interface forum. http://www.mpi-forum.org/.
[5] OpenMP application programming interface version 3.1. http://www.openmp.org/mp-documents/OpenMP3.1.pdf.
[6] OpenSHMEM application programming interface. http://openshmem.org/.
[7] Titanium. http://titanium.cs.berkeley.edu/.
[8] Unified parallel C. http://upc.gwu.org/.
[9] V. Aggarwal, A. D. George, C. Yoon, K. Yalamanchili, and H. Lam. SHMEM+: A multilevel-PGAS programming model for reconfigurable supercomputing. *ACM Trans. Reconfigurable Technol. Syst.*, 4(3):26:1–26:24, Aug. 2011.
[10] E. Anderson, J. Agron, W. Peck, J. Stevens, F. Baijot, E. Komp, R. Sass, and D. Andrews. Enabling a uniform programming model across the software/hardware boundary. In *Field-Programmable Custom Computing Machines, 2006. FCCM '06. 14th Annual IEEE Symposium on*, pages 89 –98, april 2006.
[11] D. Bonachea and J. Duell. Problems with using mpi 1.1 and 2.0 as compilation targets for parallel language implementations. *Int. J. High Perform. Comput. Netw.*, 1(1-3):91–99, Aug. 2004.
[12] D. Bonachea and J. Jeong. GASNet: A portable high-performance communication layer for global address-space languages. Cs258 parallel computer architecture project report, University of California Berkeley, Spring 2002.
[13] D. Callahan, B. L. Chamberlain, and H. P. Zima. The cascade high productivity language. In *in Ninth International Workshop on High-Level Parallel Programming Models and Supportive Environments (HIPS 04)*, pages 52–60, 2004.
[14] P. Charles, C. Grothoff, V. Saraswat, C. Donawa, A. Kielstra, K. Ebcioglu, C. von Praun, and V. Sarkar. X10: an object-oriented approach to non-uniform cluster computing. In *Proceedings of the 20th annual ACM SIGPLAN conference on Object-oriented programming, systems, languages, and applications*, OOPSLA '05, pages 519–538, New York, NY, USA, 2005. ACM.
[15] E. S. Chung, J. C. Hoe, and K. Mai. CoRAM: an in-fabric memory architecture for FPGA-based computing. In *Proceedings of the 19th ACM/SIGDA international symposium on Field programmable gate arrays*, FPGA '11, pages 97–106, New York, NY, USA, 2011. ACM.
[16] J. Davis, C. Thacker, and C. Chang. BEE3:

Revitalizing computer architecture research. Technical report msr-tr-2009-45, Microsoft Research, April 2009.

[17] J. Dongarra, R. Graybill, W. Harrod, R. Lucas, E. Lusk, P. Luszczek, J. McMahon, A. Snavely, J. Vetter, K. Yelick, S. R. Alam, R. Campbell, L. Carrington, T.-Y. Chen, O. Khalili, J. S. Meredith, and M. Tikir. *DARPA's HPCS Program: History, Models, Tools, Languages*, volume Volume 72, pages 1–100. Elsevier, 2008.

[18] T. El-Ghazawi, O. Serres, S. Bahra, M. Huang, and E. El-Araby. Parallel programming of high-performance reconfigurable computing systems with Unified Parallel C. In *Proceedings of Reconfigurable Systems Summer Institute*, 2008.

[19] N. Moore, A. Conti, M. Leeser, and L. King. Writing portable applications that dynamically bind at run time to reconfigurable hardware. In *Field-Programmable Custom Computing Machines, 2007. FCCM 2007. 15th Annual IEEE Symposium on*, pages 229 –238, april 2007.

[20] J. Nieplocha, R. Harrison, and R. Littlefield. Global arrays: a portable *shared-memory* programming model for distributed memory computers. In *Supercomputing '94. Proceedings*, pages 340 –349, 816, nov 1994.

[21] M. Saldaña, A. Patel, C. Madill, D. Nunes, D. Wang, P. Chow, R. Wittig, H. Styles, and A. Putnam. MPI as a programming model for high-performance reconfigurable computers. *ACM Trans. Reconfigurable Technol. Syst.*, 3(4):22:1–22:29, Nov. 2010.

[22] M. Saldaña, L. Shannon, and P. Chow. The routability of multiprocessor network topologies in FPGAs. In *Proceedings of the 2006 International Workshop on System-level Interconnect Prediction*, SLIP '06, pages 49–56, New York, NY, USA, 2006. ACM.

[23] T. von Eicken, D. E. Culler, S. C. Goldstein, and K. E. Schauser. Active messages: a mechanism for integrated communication and computation. In *Proceedings of the 19th Annual International Symposium on Computer Architecture*, ISCA '92, pages 256–266, New York, NY, USA, 1992. ACM.

# C-to-CoRAM: Compiling Perfect Loop Nests to the Portable CoRAM Abstraction

Gabriel Weisz
Computer Science Department
Carnegie Mellon University
Pittsburgh, PA, USA
gweisz@cs.cmu.edu

James C. Hoe
Electrical & Computer Engineering Department
Carnegie Mellon University
Pittsburgh, PA, USA
jhoe@ece.cmu.edu

## ABSTRACT

This paper presents initial work on developing a C compiler for the CoRAM FPGA computing abstraction. The presented effort focuses on compiling fixed-bound perfect loop nests that operate on large data sets in external DRAM. As required by the CoRAM abstraction, the compiler partitions source code into two separate implementation components: (1) hardware kernel pipelines to be mapped onto the reconfigurable logic fabric; and (2) control threads that express, in a C-like language, the sequencing and coordination of data transfers between the hardware kernels and external DRAM. The compiler performs optimizations to increase parallelism and use DRAM bandwidth efficiently. It can target different FPGA platforms that support the CoRAM abstraction, either natively in a future FPGA or in soft-logic on today's devices. The CoRAM abstraction provides a convenient high-level compilation target to simplify the task of design optimization and system generation. The compiler is evaluated using three test programs (matrix-matrix multiplication, $k$-nearest neighbor, and 2D convolution) on the Xilinx ML605 and the Altera DE4. Results show that our compiler is able to target the different platforms and effectively exploit their dissimilar capacities and features. Depending on the application, the compiler-generated implementations achieve performance ranging from a factor of 4 slower to a factor of 2 faster relative to hand-designed implementations, as measured on actual hardware.

## Categories and Subject Descriptors

B.5.2 [**Hardware**]: REGISTER-TRANSFER-LEVEL IMPLEMENTATION:Automatic synthesis; Optimization

## General Terms

Design

## Keywords

FPGA computing, High-level Synthesis, Loop optimization, Data reuse

## 1. INTRODUCTION

**Motivations.** Modern FPGAs are capable and efficient computing devices in a wide range of application areas ([9], [20], [11], and [15]), but have failed to achieve widespread use. A major obstacle to the adoption of FPGAs for computing is the high degree of difficulty associated with developing FPGA applications. Prior work such as CoRAM [10], LEAP [1] and VirtualRC [17] have approached this problem from the architectural side by virtualizing an FPGA's external memory and I/O interfaces. Such approaches save development time by avoiding repeated effort in infrastructure development and enabling portability of completed applications. What cannot be solved through architecture and abstraction is the inherent difficulty in manually mapping algorithms to hardware datapaths that target the FPGA's reconfigurable fabric.

Verilog and VHDL, the prevailing design languages for targeting FPGAs, follow a hardware-centric paradigm that requires a designer to directly manage highly concurrent, fine-grained operations with per-cycle coordination. Algorithmic and application experts prefer to operate at a much higher level of abstraction, and would rather use sequential languages such as C. As we will discuss in Section 2, there has been much research and development on compilers that can automatically generate hardware designs for FPGAs from C and other programming languages.

**Compiling Perfect Loop Nests for an FPGA.** This paper presents work on developing a C compiler that can produce a complete FPGA-based implementation from perfect loop nests with fixed bounds. Perfect loop nests are those in which all computation occurs within the innermost loop body. The innermost loop body can access large data sets residing in off-chip DRAM, using both array and indirect pointer references. This class of programs includes many important scientific and numerical applications. As they typically exhibit a high degree of inherent parallelism and predictable data access patterns, these programs are well suited for implementation on an FPGA. Moreover, others have worked on transforming non-perfect loop nests into perfect loop nests [21].

Unlike previous C-to-gates and C-to-FPGA compilers, our work focuses primarily on achieving efficient use of off-chip DRAM memory bandwidth and on-chip SRAM buffers. We use ROCCC (Riverside Optimizing Compiler for Configurable Computing [23]) to generate streaming hardware kernel pipelines corresponding to the innermost loop body. Our compiler seeks to saturate these kernel pipelines by managing the flow of the input and output data streams between the kernel pipelines and external DRAM. Our compiler, built on top of LLVM [24], analyzes the memory references in a loop nest for dependencies and access patterns. The compiler then introduces optimizations to increase parallelism, coalesce memory accesses, infer data reuse, and support efficiently strided memory accesses.

**CoRAM Compilation Target.** Unlike previous C-to-FPGA compilers, our compiler does not directly target the bare FPGA fabric. Instead, we target the CoRAM FPGA computing abstraction. Figure 1 presents a conceptual depiction that demonstates how the CoRAM abstraction enforces a separation of concerns between processing and data movements. Under the CoRAM abstraction, applications are partitioned into kernel pipelines, which implement computation, and control threads, which sequence control flow and data transfers. A kernel pipeline performs a specific task each time it is invoked, interacting solely with attached CoRAM SRAM buffers and control threads. Section 3 discusses the CoRAM abstraction in more detail.

Targeting the virtualized CoRAM abstraction allows our compiler to create implementations for any supported FPGA platform, either natively in future FPGAs or using soft-logic on today's devices. In this paper, we tested our compiler using the Xilinx ML605 and Altera DE4 platforms. On these platforms, the CoRAM abstraction is supported by a soft-logic microarchitectural implementation. The CoRAM abstraction greatly simplifies our compilation task because control flow and the management and optimization of memory data movements are easily expressible in CoRAM control threads. The CoRAM abstraction also serves to mask even non-trivial platform differences, such as the number of DDR memory channels. Our evaluation shows that our compiler can not only transparently support different FPGA platforms, but can also effectively optimize our test programs (matrix-matrix multiplication, $k$-nearest neighbor, and 2D convolution) for the characteristics of the different targets. On these test programs, our compiler produced implementations comparable to hand-designed implementations in performance, ranging from a factor of 4 slower to a factor of 2 faster.

**Overview.** The remainder of this paper is organized as follows. Sections 2 and 3 provide background on prior art in C-to-hardware compilation and the CoRAM abstraction. Section 4 presents the design and implementation of our compiler. Section 5 presents our evaluations. Finally, section 6 concludes and identifies future extensions.

## 2. RELATED WORK

### 2.1 C-to-Hardware Compilers

There is extensive prior and current work, both commercial and academic, on compiling from high-level software programming languages to hardware implementations. We provide a brief survey of the most closely related projects in the field of C-to-hardware compilation.

ROCCC [23], Impulse-C [25], Handel-C [26] and Catapult-C [27] are all examples of C-to-hardware compilers for generating hardware kernels. Loop nests are among the key program structures exploited by these tools for parallelism and performance. A common feature is that users can annotate loops for pipelining or unrolling optimizations. These tools do not provide integrated end-to-end support for off-chip DRAM access; the generated kernels interface with on-chip

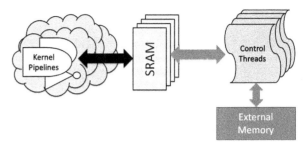

*Figure 1:* CoRAM Abstraction Concept.

SRAMs or assume a streaming data interface that relies on external logic to provide input data and handle output data. Our work uses ROCCC to generate streaming pipelined implementations of hardware kernels from the innermost loop body of the loop nest. Xilinx Vivado [28] (formerly AutoESL) is a Xilinx-specific tool that compiles C code to hardware kernels that can utilize on-chip BRAMs for interfaces.

Compared to the aforementioned work, the applicability of our compiler is limited to perfect loop nests. However, our compiler produces complete, optimized implementations that can interact with large data sets residing in DRAM. Altera C2H [29] does produce accelerators with pipelined memory accesses as a part of the Altera NIOS framework, but does not automatically perform optimizations to exploit data reuse and/or interchange loops to increase parallelism.

LegUp [8] represents a different class of hardware compilers for building hybrid hardware/software embedded systems. Their focus is on starting with a software-only implementation, and reaching greater performance and/or power/energy efficiency through the addition of hardware accelerators of hot program sections.

Our example programs are implemented from C source code (Listings 2, 3, 4, and 5). It would be possible to use existing C-to-gates tools such as the ones described above to implement them on an FPGA, but some work would be required (through the introduction of source code annotations at the very least) in order to create high performance parallel implementations that implement reuse-optimized data transfers between external DRAM and block memories.

### 2.2 Loop Nest Optimizations

Loop Nest Optimizations are also well studied in the literature. Polyhedral analysis is the state-of-the-art technology for automatic pipelining and parallelization of loop nests [18]. It defines an *iteration vector* that encodes how variables change within the loop nest. Optimizations are constructed as affine transformations of these iteration vectors [5].

Diniz and Park [14] describe compiler analyses using the polyhedral model to find data reuse and reordering. Alias, Pasca, and Plesco [2] use polyhedral analysis to tile and parallelize applications for implementation on an FPGA. Bayliss and Constantinides [6] use the polyhedral model to optimize the memory accesses of an application and create hardware for address generation. Cong, et al. [13] investigated a broad set of mechanisms, including loop interchange, for optimizing data reuse, buffer sizes, and memory bandwidth.

The papers referenced above have a strong focus on specific optimizations. The goal of our work is not to contribute new loop nest optimizations but to employ them—extensively leveraging the analysis infrastructure built into

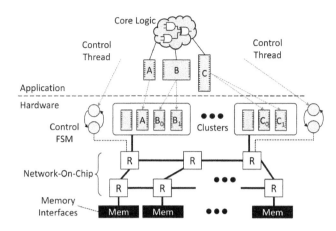

*Figure 2:* CoRAM Microarchitectural Sketch (figure from [12]).

LLVM [24]—in order to efficiently support C-to-hardware compilation for the CoRAM abstraction [10]. Our current capabilities (presented in Section 4) do not require polyhedral analysis. Extensions to incorporate polyhedral analysis would allow us to automatically introduce memory blocking transformations and set block sizes. The test programs used in this paper (Listings 2, 3, 4, and 5) are explicitly blocked by hand at the source code level. A polyhedral framework, such as LLVM's Polly [16] project, provides a path to incorporating these analyses and optimizations.

## 3. CORAM TARGET ABSTRACTION

Our compiler targets the CoRAM abstraction, which provides a convenient virtualization of the communication and control infrastructure that connects in-fabric kernel pipelines to external memory (DRAM). Figure 1 offers a conceptual depiction of the CoRAM abstraction. Kernel pipelines are localized in space and in time, and perform a specific task each time they are invoked, interacting solely with attached SRAM buffers and control threads.

The application developer uses a C-based language (with pointer support) to define a set of control threads that dynamically manage the contents of the SRAMs and coordinate the invocation of the kernel pipelines. This separation of concerns between processing and data movement allows for a high-level virtualized execution environment that simplifies an application's development and improves the application's portability and scalability.

A fully CoRAM-compliant FPGA would implement the underlying mechanisms for data transport between kernel pipelines and external memory with native, hardwired datapaths. This abstraction layer, akin to an ISA for processors, enables application-level compatibility across different FPGA families and device generations.

Figure 2 offers a microarchitectural sketch of a possible datapath implementing the CoRAM abstraction. This design can be scaled to up to thousands of CoRAM clusters, depending on the capacity of the FPGA [12]. CoRAM SRAM blocks, like embedded SRAMs in modern FPGAs, are arranged into columns and organized into clusters. A cluster is a group of CoRAM blocks attached to the same network-on-chip endpoint. Grouping blocks together into clusters reduces the number of network endpoints needed, and provides a mechanism to compose several CoRAMs into larger blocks (with a customizable aspect ratio), but limits available band-

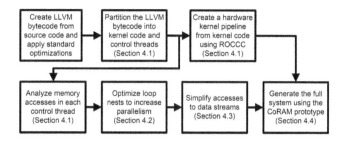

*Figure 3:* Generating an FPGA system from source code.

width due to the shared network endpoint. Each cluster is managed by an attached Control Unit, which is responsible for executing the control threads that run within the cluster. Control threads in the CoRAM programming abstraction can be realized by direct synthesis into reconfigurable logic as finite state machines, or can be executed on dedicated microcontrollers. In addition to native CoRAM constructs, a customizable library of "personality" extensions, layered on top of the basic CoRAM SRAM blocks and APIs, implement FIFO queues, caches, and similar structures.

While no FPGA available today natively supports the CoRAM abstraction, it is available for off-the-shelf Xilinx and Altera FPGA platforms (ML605 and DE4, respectively), supported by soft-logic implementations of the necessary mechanisms [22]. The implementations include a network-on-chip that uses CONNECT [19], control threads that are compiled into state machines, and CoRAM blocks that are mapped on top of conventional block SRAMs. More details are available in our prior work [10] and publicly available prototype [22].

## 4. COMPILER IMPLEMENTATION

Our current compiler can only handle perfect loop nests with fixed loop bounds. Although limited, perfect loop nests appear extensively in scientific and numerical kernels, and others have worked on transforming non-perfect loop nests into perfect loop nests [21].

Our compiler is implemented as a compiler pass for the LLVM compiler infrastructure [24]. It operates on LLVM bytecode instructions using built-in facilities for program analyses and manipulation. The programmer is presented with the familiar "make" build process that automates the flow from C source code to a complete FPGA design.

Figure 3 shows the steps that create an FPGA system from software source code. These steps are:

• Creating LLVM bytecode from source code (and applying standard optimizations).

• Partitioning the LLVM bytecode into kernel code and control threads (Section 4.1).

• Applying ROCCC to kernel code in order to generate kernel pipelines (Section 4.1).

• Analyzing memory accesses to discover data access patterns (Section 4.1).

• Optimizing control thread loop nests (Section 4.2).

• Simplifying data streams (Section 4.3).

• Producing the complete system using the CoRAM Design Generator (Section 4.4).

We continue with a detailed discussion of the important steps in the implementation process.

```
1 Returns True if the instruction is a
    kernel instruction; otherwise False
2 Bool IsKernel(Instruction i)
3  If  i is a store
4    return True
5  Else if i is a non-loop branch
6    return True
7  Else if i is a loop branch
8    return False
9  Else
10   For each Instruction u that consumes
       the value produced by i
11     If u uses i as a load/store address OR
12       IsKernel(u) == False
13       return False
14   return True            // catch all
```

*Listing 1:* Classification Algorithm.

## 4.1 Kernel Extraction and Synthesis

The CoRAM abstraction requires a separation between the processing kernel – the portion of the application actually performing computation – and the code implementing data transfers and control flow. This separation is achieved by classifying bytecode instructions as computing or non-computing bytecode instructions and extracting the computing bytecode instructions.

Listing 1 gives simplified pseudo code of the decision function IsKernel( ) that decides whether or not each of the bytecode instructions in the innermost loop body belongs to the processing kernel. In essence, a bytecode instruction is a part of the processing kernel only if its entire subtree of dependent bytecode instructions all belong to the processing kernel. Caching the categorization of previously processed instructions ensures that each bytecode instruction is only visited once; the runtime is therefore linear in the number of bytecode instructions.

The bytecode instructions that are flagged as belonging to the processing kernel are re-emitted as a C function. Load and store bytecode instructions in the emitted function are used as placeholders for creating input and output queues during hardware mapping. The addresses used by these bytecode instructions, retained in the original loop nest, are used in later optimization phases. The compiler can recognize memory addresses that are used as accumulation variables (first read and then written to in the loop body) and pair them for special processing. Separate control threads are created for each input and output variable, which simplifies later optimizations.

The processing kernel is compiled by ROCCC [23] into a hardware kernel pipeline, with streaming input and output interfaces replacing load/store bytecode instructions. Each input and output streaming buffer is mapped to distinct CoRAM memory blocks and managed by a different control thread. In Section 4.2 we will explain optimizations that increase processing throughput by instantiating multiple concurrent kernel pipelines and/or increasing the size of kernel pipeline through unrolling.

Figure 4 offers a generic system containing multiple parallel kernel pipelines that receive data from CoRAM FIFO personalities that implement input streaming buffers (A and B). The CoRAM personalities in the figure have been composed with additional logic to create "Reuse Buffers" that implement a data reuse pattern detected by the compiler

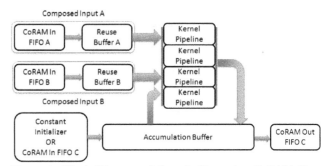

*Figure 4:* Block Diagram of Generic Streaming CoRAM Kernel Pipelines with associated CoRAM Personalities and Reuse Buffers.

(discussed in Section 4.3). Bandwidth requirements are also reduced, as after recognizing an accumulation variable, the compiler has introduced an Accumulation Buffer that removes the need for explicit synchronization between read and write threads, and an Initializer to avoid reading data initialized by a constant from DRAM (C).

The compiler produces optimized control threads to fill the input buffers as quickly as possible. Without data-dependence stalls, each hardware kernel pipeline can issue one loop iteration every cycle. The outputs of an iteration are produced in-order after the pipeline delay. The control threads must obey data dependencies and will stall an input data stream if it depends on the output of in-flight iterations.

LLVM's Scalar Evolution framework is used to analyze the memory accesses in loop in each control thread, to infer information that is used in later optimizations. Each variable used as an address is analyzed, and its progression at each loop is flagged as exhibiting one of the following patterns:

- Unchanging: same address across iterations.
- Stride-1: consecutive data items across iterations.
- Computable: non-consecutive data items following an analyzable progression, such as stride-permutation and indirect accesses.
- Undetermined progression.

## 4.2 Loop Optimizations

The ROCCC generated kernel pipelines can only be saturated if there are no data dependencies across iterations of the innermost loop. When the kernel pipeline is replicated for higher performance, even greater parallelism is required to achieve peak computational throughput. We apply one of two optimizations to obtain the necessary parallelism.

**Loop Interchange.** The default mechanism used for increasing parallelism is interchanging loops. This is a classic loop nest transformation. We move loops at which an accumulation occurs outwards in the loop nest. Selecting an appropriate loop ordering requires a balance between creating potential parallelism and minimizing on chip buffering—too little parallelism causes pipeline stalls; too much parallelism may require excessively large on-chip buffers.

Our compiler follows a simple heuristic for reordering that works especially well when the loop nest has been blocked for better memory locality. We select one or more consecutive loops at which the output variable is accumulated, and move these loops outward until (1) encountering another accumulating loop; (2) reaching the top of the loop nest; or (3) reaching a user-specified threshold in the amount of output data that must be buffered. The intent of this strategy is that the user may match the CoRAM block size to the application block size.

Reordering loops without taking into account data patterns might convert sequential memory accesses into strided accesses. Section 4.3 will show how our compiler can transpose strided data in transit, allowing these accesses to be supported with little performance penalty.

**Loop Unrolling.** The user may choose to fully unroll the innermost loop instead of interchanging loops. Unrolling the innermost loop creates a new function that cascades instances of the baseline processing kernel. As the entire loop has been unrolled, it no longer can contain a loop-carried dependency, although the resulting hardware may contain an input for an accumulation at another loop. The cascaded kernel pipeline created by ROCCC reads each input, with the exception of the accumulated variable, for each instance of the baseline kernel pipeline. The accumulated variable is read once and passed between the cascaded instances. Our compiler can optionally attempt to balance the unrolled function's dataflow graph in order to minimize long paths (and the corresponding pipeline depth). Balancing may be disabled if the order of the operations must be preserved, such as when implementing certain floating-point kernels.

**Trade-off.** The decision to unroll or interchange loops is currently left to the user. This decision affects both the amount of data that is buffered and the organization of the streaming data buffers. An implementation that interchanges loops will likely implement a larger number of discrete kernel pipelines (with a shorter pipeline depth) than one that unrolls the innermost loop. This reduces the required number of pipeline buffers, but increases the number of kernel pipelines and accumulated values (one per kernel pipeline) that must be buffered. Different realizations of matrix-matrix multiplication are presented in Section 5.1.1, where our results show that loop interchange produces a smaller design. In contrast, Section 5.2 presents code for which loop unrolling produces a smaller design.

## 4.3  Simplifying Data Streams

The compiler next optimizes the loop nest of each control thread to coalesce memory accesses, infer data reuse, and simplify the loop nest. Each kernel pipeline receives the same data that it would receive without optimization, allowing each control thread to be processed independently.

Figure 5 illustrates four transformations from the perspective of an input data stream. Output data is optimized similarly. The patterns are inferred from information gathered earlier in the workflow (See Figure 3), and may span multiple loops. In each illustration, the top portion shows a pattern that is repeated in the original full data stream (flowing left to right). Elements of the data stream are labeled with their addresses. The bottom portion shows the reduced data stream as actually fetched from external DRAM, and how the original data stream is recreated. The various patterns are processed as follows:

**(a) Repeat:** The addressing pattern comprises repeated memory reads of the same address (A), either over the innermost loop or multiple consecutive inner loop levels. The control thread's loop is replaced by a single memory read request, and a buffer reproduces the original stream. In addition to repeating a single address, any of the following patterns may be repeated to reuse larger blocks.

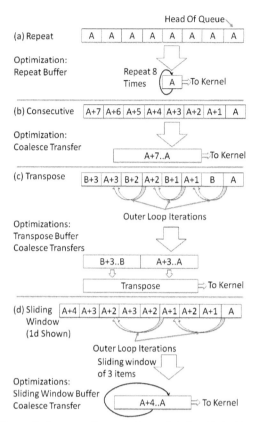

*Figure 5:* Access patterns and associated optimizations.

**(b) Consecutive:** The addressing pattern contains n stride-1 accesses of data items starting at A, such as when visiting successive elements of an array. The loop for generating the n consecutive reads is replaced by a single burst read request of size n. The underlying CoRAM-based streaming buffer is not altered as the same elements pass through it.

**(c) Transpose:** The addressing pattern corresponds to a strided memory read loop, such as when visiting the elements of a sub-block of a row-major 2D array in column order. The control threads generate burst read requests for required rows of the sub-block and buffer the entire sub-block. A stride-permutation personality reorders the stream on the fly to recreate the original strided data stream. The control thread's loop nest is reduced by implementing burst reads of entire sub-block rows. Strides need not be fixed, and may depend on indirect accesses (as in Listing 3).

**(d) Sliding Window:** The pattern corresponds to n successive reads to consecutive addresses starting at A, followed by another n successive reads from consecutive addresses starting at A+1, and so on. This "sliding window" pattern is common in filters. The control thread generates a simple burst read from consecutive memory locations starting at A. A special CoRAM personality buffers all of the data in the sliding window in block memory, and ensures that the data is delivered in the correct order. As in (b) above, inner loop nests for generating this complex pattern are completely simplified away with a single burst read request. The figure presents a one dimensional sliding window, but the compiler also supports two dimensional sliding windows. Data items within a row are routed to parallel kernel pipelines by multiplexers and interleaved across rows.

225

| Platform | Xilinx ML605 | Terasic DE4 |
|---|---|---|
| FPGA | Xilinx LX240T [30] | Altera EP4SGX530[31] |
| Logic Cells (Overhead (%)) | 241,152 33% | 531,200 30 % |
| Block Memory (Overhead (%)) | 14,976 KB 13% | 27,376 KB 18% |
| DSPs | 768 | 1,024 |
| DRAM Bandwidth | 6.4 GB/s | 12.8 GB/s |
| DRAM Capacity | 512 MB | 2 GB |
| PCI Express | x8 | x8 |
| UART Speed | 500 KBits/s | 115 KBits/s |

*Table 1:* Parameters for test platforms. "Overhead" includes the memory controllers, network-on-chip, among other components.

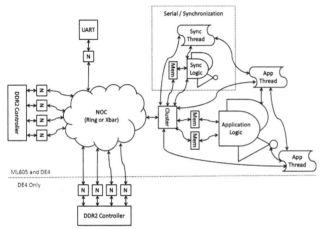

*Figure 6:* Complete design resulting from compilations.

## 4.4 FPGA Design Generation

The compiler backend produces the FPGA implementation by invoking the CoRAM Design Generator with: (1) the ROCCC-generated VHDL kernel pipelines; (2) The control threads; and (3) the required CoRAM personalities. Basic CoRAM personalities such as streaming data buffers already exist in the CoRAM personality library. A one-time effort was necessary to build reuse buffer CoRAM personalities that support repeated data, transposed data, and sliding windows.

The CoRAM Design Generator creates a single FPGA design containing: (1) the kernel pipelines; (2) the FSMs compiled from the control threads; and (3) the soft-logic implementation of the CoRAM architecture (including the underlying platform-specific on-chip communication, external memory modules, and I/O modules). This FPGA design is processed by platform-specific synthesis tools that create a bitstream for programming onto a device. The CoRAM Design Generator also generates RTL models for simulation-only studies that allows flexibly specifying the parameters of hypothetical FPGA target platforms (see Section 5.1.4).

The CoRAM Design Generator currently supports the Xilinx ML605 and Altera DE4 platforms. Table 1 summarizes the most salient characteristics of the two platforms. The two rows in Table 1 labeled "Overhead" indicate resources consumed by the soft-logic CoRAM implementation without an attached user design. This is not a pure overhead as, even in hand-crafted designs, kernel pipelines must be supported by non zero-cost infrastructure for communicating with DRAM and I/O.

Figure 6 offers a block diagram of the complete FPGA design. Most of the details shown in the figure, aside from control threads, hardware kernels, and CoRAM personalities, are below the CoRAM abstraction and handled by the CoRAM Design Generator.

The figure shows memory controllers connected to a soft-logic network-on-chip through multiple network endpoints (labeled "N"), which avoids bottlenecking the available memory bandwidth. The network-on-chip can (interchangeably) implement a variety of topologies, including the ring and crossbar networks used in the evaluation, which vary in logic cost and provided bandwidth. On the Altera DE4 with two memory controllers, the global address space is interleaved between the two channels at 256-byte boundaries. We elect to use a single CoRAM cluster to service all of user logic generated by our compiler. The cluster connects multiple CoRAM blocks and the associated control threads to the network-on-chip—one block and thread per memory variable in the innermost loop body. Communication channels between the control threads and the hardware kernel pipelines are automatically inserted to support synchronization, including a staging mechanism (labeled "Serial/Synchronization"), which allows the host computer to communicate with the FPGA platform for data transfers and to collect performance results.

Switching between ML605 or DE4 targets is trivial - a configuration file specifies the number of memory controllers (and associated network endpoints) to instantiate, and the CoRAM Design Generator provides wrappers for floating point IP cores and scripts to invoke device specific bitstream generation tools.

## 5. EVALUATIONS

We evaluate our compiler on three code examples: single precision matrix-matrix multiply, $k$-nearest neighbor, and two dimensional single precision convolution (actual source code included in Listings 2, 3, 4, and 5). We use standard "blocked" implementations of these algorithms. For example, in Listing 2, the 3 outer loops correspond to the familiar triple-loop in standard matrix-matrix multiplication, except in a blocked implementation. Multiply-accumulate operations are performed on sub-matrix tiles (thus the inner 3 loops) and not on individual elements. By buffering and operating on the data tiles on chip, blocking algorithms increase the number of times a data value fetched from memory is reused.[1] All experiments run kernel pipelines, reuse buffers, and other components at 100MHz, the highest clock speed currently supported by the CoRAM prototype.

### 5.1 Matrix-Matrix Multiply

Listing 2 gives the source code for matrix-matrix multiplication (MMM) used to evaluate our compiler. In order to work with the current compiler, the matrix sizes (separate SIZE_I, SIZE_J, SIZE_K to allow for non-square matrices), and block sizes (separate BI, BJ, BK to allow for non-square blocking) must be fixed at compile-time. SIZE_I, SIZE_J, SIZE_K must be multiples of BI, BJ, BK, respectively.

The innermost loop (line 8) in this baseline MMM implementation has a loop-carried dependency through the accumulation of C[i*SIZE_I+j], preventing parallel or overlapped

---

[1]While not a part of the current work, polyhedral techniques[7] could automatically create blocking structures.

```
1 void mmm(float *A,float *B,float *C,
    unsigned SIZE_I,unsigned SIZE_J,
    unsigned SIZE_K) {
2   unsigned i,j,k,i0,j0,k0;
3   for(i0=0;i0<SIZE_I;i0+=BI)
4    for(j0=0;j0<SIZE_J;j0+=BJ)
5     for(k0=0;k0<SIZE_K;k0+=BK)
6      for(i=i0;i<i0+BI;i++)
7       for(j=j0;j<j0+BJ;j++)
8        for(k=k0;k<k0+BK;k++)
9         C[i*SIZE_I+j]+=A[i*SIZE_I+k] *
          B[k*SIZE_K+j];
```

*Listing 2:* Blocked MMM Source Code.

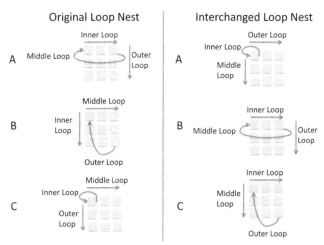

*Figure 7:* MMM variable progressions.

executions of the loop body. As discussed in Section 4.2, either loop interchange or loop unrolling must be applied to achieve hardware concurrency. Figure 7 examines the data access patterns of A, B, and C within the innermost three loops, for both before and after the loop interchange. In the bottom left, which presents the accesses pattern of the accumulation variable C, the figure shows that the same matrix element is read and written by all iterations of the innermost loop, creating a loop-carried dependency. After interchange, the invariant access is now at the outer loop, and the inner and the middle loop iterations are no longer data dependent, and can be executed in parallel or be pipelined.

In experiments that implement parallel kernel pipelines, each data stream is distributed "round robin" among them, and Reuse Buffers in front of the kernel pipelines allow them to issue a computation each cycle. The arrangement of kernel pipelines and Reuse Buffers as presented in Figure 4.

The inner loop at line 8 in the original code may be unrolled rather than interchanged via a user specified compiler flag. For experiments in Section 5.1.1 that implement loop unrolling, the data access patterns that follow those on the left side of Figure 7. The middle and outer loops provide the data independent iterations to the pipelined kernel based on the fully unrolled inner loop. The inner loop's loop-carried dependencies caused by the memory variable C become signals that pass from pipeline stage to pipeline stage; only the final accumulated value of C from the final stage is written to memory. The arrangement of kernel pipelines and reuse buffers is once again as depicted in Figure 4, except that there is only one kernel pipeline that accepts multiple data items from each input data stream. There is a singular ac-

| # | Opt | BI,BJ | %LC/MEM/DSP | GFlop/sec(%) |
|---|-----|-------|-------------|--------------|
| 1 | I | 64, 64 | 84 / 32 / 41 | 12.6 (98) |
| 2 | U | 64, 64 | 83 / 92 / 41 | 12.6 (98) |
| 3 | I | 32, 128 | 82 / 32 / 41 | 10.4 (81) |
| 4 | U | 32, 128 | 83 / 92 / 41 | 10.4 (81) |
| 5 | I | 32, 64 | 83 / 32 / 41 | 8.6 (67) |
| 6 | U | 32, 64 | 81 / 92 / 41 | 8.6 (67) |
| 7 | I | 128, 64 | 86 / 33 / 41 | 12.7 (99) |
| 8 | U | 128, 64 | 86 / 92 / 41 | 12.6 (98) |

*Table 2:* ML605 Block size experiments configurations. For all trials, square matrices of size 1024 are used. For the Optimization column, "I"=Interchange and "U"=Unroll.

cumulated value for each computation that feeds back into the kernel pipeline across blocks.

### 5.1.1 Block Sizing and Loop Optimizations

The first experiments examine the effects of different block sizes in combination with different loop optimizations. Our goal is to demonstrate the range of possible outcomes enabled by the rapid exploration of design options through our compiler. We use a block size of 64-by-64 as the baseline on square 1024-by-1024 MMM. We then consider non-square blocks that are twice, half and the same size as the baseline block size. For each choice of block size, we apply either the loop interchange or the loop unrolling optimization, and create kernel pipelines containing 64 single precision floating-point adders and 64 single precision floating-point multipliers. When synthesized for the LX240T on the Xilinx ML605, ROCCC-generated pipelines at 100MHz yield a theoretical peak performance of 12.8 GFlop/sec.

Table 2 reports the measured performance on the Xilinx ML605 for all combinations of 4 block sizes (indicated by columns **BI** and **BJ**) and the 2 loop optimizations (indicated by column **Opt**: Interchange or Unrolling). The fourth column indicates resource utilization in terms of the percentage of the LX240T's Logic Cells (**LC**), Block Ram (**MEM**), and DSP Blocks (**DSP**) used by each design (as reported by ISE 13.4). Execution times are measured using a hardware counter that counts clock cycles from when computation has started (input arrays A and B starting in DRAM) to when computation has finished (output array C completely written to DRAM). The column **GFlop/sec** reports the absolute performance in GFlop/sec and the percentage of the 12.8 GFlop/sec peak attained.

Rows **1** and **2** show that square blocks are effective, as both experiments achieve over 98% of peak performance; the loop interchanging optimization results in less BRAM usage. The results in the remaining rows show that poor choices of block sizes can indeed negatively impact performance. Rows **3** and **4** show that a rectangular 32-by-128 blocking (the same size as the baseline square 64-by-64 blocking) leads to a drop in performance (only 81% of the peak performance). Halving the block size to 32-by-64 (rows **5** and **6**) further hurts performance even more (down to 67% of peak performance). Doubling the block size to 64-by-128 (rows **7** and **8**) provides minimal performance improvements.

As a point of reference, the best performing implementation of MMM on the Xilinx ML605 we could find was Bao, et al. [4]. Their hand-tuned design uses a systolic array of 2x2 multiply-accumulators connected by a ring network, and implements 32 processing elements running at 200 MHz. They achieve 50.4 GFlop/sec on MMM of size

```
1 void mmm_indirect(unsigned **base,
    unsigned SIZE_I,unsigned SIZE_J,
    unsigned SIZE_K) {
2   unsigned i,j,k,i0,j0,k0;
3   float **A=(float **)base[0];
4   float **B=(float **)base[1];
5   float **C=(float **)base[2];
6   for(i0=0;i0<SIZE_I;i0+=BS_I)
7    for(j0=0;j0<SIZE_J;j0+=BS_J)
8     for(k0=0;k0<SIZE_K;k0+=BS_K)
9      for(i=i0;i<i0+BS_I;i++)
10      for(j=j0;j<j0+BS_J;j++)
11       for(k=k0;k<k0+BS_K;k++)
12        C[i][j]+=A[i][k]*B[k][j];
```

*Listing 3:* Blocked MMM with Indirection.

| # | Kern | Net | % LC/MEM/DSP | GFlop/sec |
|---|------|-----|--------------|-----------|
| **9** | 64 | Ring | 97 / 28 / 25 | 12.6 |
| **10** | 128 | Xbar | 96 / 38 / 50 | 25.4 |

*Table 3:* MMM Experiments on the DE4. In these trials, square matrices of size 1024 and blocks sized to the number of kernels.

2048-by-2048.[2] Their carefully hand-tuned MMM is 4 times faster (2x from higher frequency and 2x from better logic packing). However, our design is automatically produced from C source code by a compiler that can handle perfect loop nests and can flexibly re-target any CoRAM supported platform.

### 5.1.2  Indirection

Support for indirect memory references is evaluated using another common matrix-matrix multiplication implementation (Listing 3) with indirect row-major 2D matrices. We also load the base address of each matrix from memory.

The hardware generated by this program has the same basic structure as the one generated for Listings 2, since the real differences manifest mostly in the control threads. The implementation of this program does require an instance of the CoRAM Load-Store personality for each control thread, which allows the control threads to directly access DRAM in order to dereference pointers. In the other examples, control threads only make requests to transfer data between DRAM and the streaming buffers, and do not examine the memory data values themselves. The Load-Store personality supports memory reads and writes by the control threads, and includes a scratchpad for caching dereferenced values.

In general, memory indirections can introduce a significant performance overhead. In this particular example, the indirections are infrequent and readily amortized with the help of the scratchpad. We achieved 98% of the peak performance of the kernel pipelines on the Xilinx ML605, using the same configuration as Row **1** of Table 2.

### 5.1.3  Network and Memory Controllers

We recompiled the unmodified MMM program in Listing 2 for the Altera DE4 platform to test our claims of portability and scalability. The EP4SGX530 FPGA on the Altera DE4 provides twice the logic capacity as the LX240T on the ML605, and twice the DRAM bandwidth through two independent DDR controllers. These differences are transparent to the programmer, who requests two memory controllers

| Parameter | Kintex-7 XC7K70T [32] | Virtex-7 XC7V2000T[32] |
|-----------|------------------------|-------------------------|
| Logic Cells | 65,600 | 1,954,560 |
| Block Ram | 4,860KB | 46,512KB |
| DSP | 240 | 2,160 |
| Mem Controllers | 1 | 4 |
| Kernels Used | 8 | 512 |
| Data Size | 128 | 1024 |
| Block Size | 16 | 512 |
| GFlop/sec | 1.44 | 93.6 |

*Table 4:* Simulations targeting Xilinx 7-series chips.

from the CoRAM Design Generator ("NUM_MC=2") and invokes a (provided) DE4 bitstream generation script.

Row **9** in Table 3 reports the synthesis and performance results achieved by simply recompiling the best-performing configuration on the Xilinx ML605 (Row **1** of Table 2, 64-by-64 block, 64 parallel kernel pipelines). The resulting design reached the same performance as on the Xilinx ML605, approximately 98% of the theoretical peak performance of the kernel pipeline (also synthesized to 100 MHz on the DE4).

With the extra capacity of the DE4's EP4SGX530, we can instantiate a larger number (128) of parallel kernel pipelines than on the Xilinx ML605, and do so by setting "MAXKERNELS=128" and similarly redefining the constant that sets the block size. Through the CoRAM Design Generator, we also selected the higher-performance crossbar network-on-chip topology to deliver DE4's dual DDR memory bandwidth and service the larger number of kernels. As row **10** in Table 3 reports, we can easily double performance by re-tuning to the greater capacity of the Altera DE4 platform.

### 5.1.4  Scaling

To further demonstrate portability and scalability, we compile the MMM code for hypothetical FPGA platforms sized to mimic the smallest and largest of Xilinx's Virtex-7 parts. We conservatively assume the kernel pipelines run at the same 100 MHz as in the earlier experiments. The assumed FPGA configuration and the performance results are shown in Table 4. The results show that our compiler is able to produce designs to take up the available level of logic resources of the two FPGAs and produce a commensurate level of performance for the logic resources consumed. In the small extreme (which mimics the small Kintex FPGA), we found the overhead of the CoRAM infrastructure to be nearly $\frac{2}{3}$ of the available logic resources,[3] and we only fit 8 kernels. In the large extreme, the compiler scaled up the design and performance as expected. We assume that the large FPGA will be fitted with four DDR channels.

## 5.2  $k$-Nearest Neighbor

The second example in our evaluation is the $k$-Nearest Neighbor ($k$-NN) algorithm (Listing 4). This algorithm finds the $k$ best matches for each input vector (called a *target descriptor*) among a larger set of *reference descriptors*. We use the square of Euclidean distance metric to compare 128 element vectors of single byte integers.

In the example code, we block the iteration over target descriptors into two loops (lines 2 and 4) to increase data

---

[2]As both designs overlap computation with communication, and we report throughput rather than absolute computation time, the difference in matrix sizes is irrelevant.

[3]As previously discussed, this is not pure overhead, as even hand-crafted designs require infrastructure for buffering and communication.

```
1 void match(unsigned char *target,
    unsigned char *ref, void *out,
    unsigned Sz, unsigned TSz,
    unsigned RSz, unsigned Ni) {
2  for (unsigned bi=0;bi<TSz;bi+=BSz) {
3   for(unsigned ri=0;ri<RSz;ri++) {
4    for(unsigned li=bi;li<bi+BSz;li++) {
5     unsigned cur=0;
6     for(unsigned i=0;i<Sz;i++) {
7      short val=(short)target[li*Sz+i]-
8      (short)ref[ri*Sz+i];
9      unsigned short v=val*val;
10     cur+=v;
11     }
12    StoreMin(out,cur,Ni,RSz,BSz,TSz)⁴;
```

*Listing 4: k-Nearest Neighbor Source Code.*

| # | MC | Depth | % LC/MEM/DSP | %Eff |
|---|----|-------|--------------|------|
| **11** | 2 | 8 | 80 / 33 / 100 | 73 |
| **12** | 1 | 16 | 83 / 25 / 100 | 90 |

*Table 5: k-NN Experiments. "Depth" indicates the number of target descriptors buffered per kernel, and "%Eff" indicates the percentage of peak performance achieved.*

reuse and locality. The loop at line 3 iterates over all reference descriptors. The evaluation is based on finding k=2 nearest neighbors, a common scenario in vision algorithms, where a much further second nearest neighbor indicates a strong match. As in MMM, our compiler can generate kernel pipelines based on either loop unrolling or loop interchange (Section 4.2). We have found that in this application, interchanging loops (to support a large number of parallel kernel pipelines) is not cost effective due to excessive buffering requirements. Therefore, we focus on loop unrolling (lines 6-10) to create a large kernel, which is then replicated 8 times for parallel processing. We target the Altera DE4 platform for this evaluation, and can make a direct comparison against a high-quality hand designed implementation that we are using in an internal research project.

Table 5 presents our experimental configurations and results. Row **11** reports an implementation that uses two memory controllers. We were only able to successfully implement on-chip buffers that were 8 target descriptors deep, and consequently achieved only 73% of the potential throughput. The implementation reported in Row **12** has removed one memory controller, which has freed enough resources to double the buffer size. This halved the number of times that the "ri" loop (line 4) was executed, which effectively halves the bandwidth requirements. The result is that the implementation in Row **12** is able to reach 90% of the unrolled kernel pipeline's peak throughput. In comparison, our hand designed implementation can pack in 16 kernels on the EP4SGX530 on the Altera DE4, and achieve twice the performance over our compiler-generated implementation.

## 5.3 Two Dimensional Convolution

Listing 5 shows our final example, a direct two-dimensional convolution. In our evaluations (using a 2048-by-2048 data set, and 32-by-32 blocks), we focus on small convolution sizes (5-by-5 and 13-by-13) because larger convolutions are

---

[4]This example has a non-perfect loop nest due to the reduction step (implemented via macro StoreMin on line 12). Our compiler instantiates special hardware for known reductions. The rest of the loop nest is compiled as described.

```
1 void calc_2d_filter(float *IN,
    float *OUT, float *FILTER, unsigned Sz,
    unsigned BSz, unsigned FSize) {
2  unsigned starti,startj,i,j,ii,jj;
3  for (starti=0;starti<Sz;starti+=BSz)
4   for(startj=0;startj<Sz;startj+=BSz)
5    for(i=starti;i<starti+BSz;i++)
6     for(j=startj;j<startj+BSz;j++)
7      for(ii=0;ii<FSz;ii++)
8       for(jj=0;jj<FSz;jj++)
9        OUT[i*Sz+j]+=IN[(i+ii)*(Sz+FSz-1)
          +j+jj]*FILTER[ii*FSz+jj];
```

*Listing 5: Blocked Two Dimensional Convolution.*

| # | Filter Size | % LC/MEM/DSP | GFlop/sec (%) |
|---|-------------|--------------|---------------|
| **13** | 5 | 58 / 24 / 22 | 4.4 (69) |
| **14** | 13 | 60 / 26/ 22 | 6.398 (99.9) |

*Table 6: 2D Convolution Experiments.*

more commonly implemented with the help of Fast Fourier Transforms. As with the previous examples, the loop-based implementation has been blocked for data locality.

In this example, the compiler applies the loop interchange optimization to the two inner-most loops (which were causing a loop-carried dependency in the loop body), and moves them above the two loops originally at lines 5 and 6. When processing the IN buffer, the compiler detects two sequential accesses due to loop variables j and jj, with a computable access pattern between them and outside them due to loop variables i and ii. The compiler uses this information to infer a two dimensional sliding window buffer, which is instantiated along with a buffer to store the entirety of FILTER, which has a very significant effect on performance.

Our results are shown in Table 6. The compiler generated design fits 32 kernel pipelines onto the LX240T of the ML605. The system with 5-by-5 filters achieves 4.4 GFlop/sec, or 69% of the theoretical peak throughput on 5-by-5 filters. For 13-by-13 filters, increased data reuse allows nearly 100% of the kernel pipeline's theoretical peak throughput (6.4GFlop/sec) to be reached.

As a reference, Bao, et al. [4] (also compared to for MMM in Section 5.1.1) report a hand-tuned implementation of a 2048-by-2048 two-dimensional convolution with a filter size of 5-by-5. Their design, like ours, contains 32 processing elements. However, they only report 2.04 GFlop/sec of sustained performance. We suspect their lower performance is due to differences in the exploitation of data reuse.

## 6. CONCLUSIONS AND FUTURE WORK

We have presented a compiler that creates full FPGA implementations of perfect loop nests directly from software source code. Three test programs and two real world platforms demonstrate the efficacy of the compiler, and achieve performance ranging from a factor of 4 slower to a factor of 2 faster than hand designed implementations. This demonstrates that our compiler is a promising step towards enabling FPGA design creation by software developers without hardware design skills.

We are considering several enhancements to our compiler:

- Allowing imperfect loop nests to support more programs.

- Including polyhedral analyses to support better optimizations and allow the compiler to create a blocked computation structure.

- Targeting platforms that contain multiple FPGAs and very different memory interfaces, such as Convey's[3].

**Acknowledgements:** Funding for this work was provided in part by NSF CCF-1012851 and by Altera. We thank Eric Chung, Michael Papamichael, and Yu Wang for technical assistance, the individuals that assisted with proofreading, and the anonymous reviewers. We thank Xilinx and Altera for their FPGA and tool donations. We thank Bluespec for their tool donations and support.

# 7. REFERENCES

[1] Michael Adler, Kermin E. Fleming, Angshuman Parashar, Michael Pellauer, and Joel Emer. Leap Scratchpads: Automatic Memory and Cache Management for Reconfigurable Logic. In *Proceedings of the 19th ACM/SIGDA International Symposium on Field Programmable Gate Arrays*, FPGA '11, pages 25–28, New York, NY, USA, 2011. ACM.

[2] Christophe Alias, Bogdan Pasca, and Alexandru Plesco. FPGA-Specific Synthesis of Loop-Nests With Pipelined Computational Cores. *Microprocessors and Microsystems*, June 2012.

[3] J.D. Bakos. High-Performance Heterogeneous Computing with the Convey HC-1. *Computing in Science Engineering*, 12(6):80 –87, nov.-dec. 2010.

[4] Wenqi Bao, Jiang Jiang, Yuzhuo Fu, and Qing Sun. A Reconfigurable Macro-Pipelined Systolic Accelerator Architecture. In *FPT*, pages 1–6, 2011.

[5] Cedric Bastoul. Code Generation in the Polyhedral Model Is Easier Than You Think. In *Proceedings of the 13th International Conference on Parallel Architectures and Compilation Techniques*, PACT '04, pages 7–16, Washington, DC, USA, 2004. IEEE Computer Society.

[6] Samuel Bayliss and George A. Constantinides. Optimizing SDRAM bandwidth for Custom FPGA Loop Accelerators. In *Proceedings of the ACM/SIGDA International Symposium on Field Programmable Gate Arrays*, FPGA '12, pages 195–204, New York, NY, USA, 2012. ACM.

[7] Uday Bondhugula, Albert Hartono, J. Ramanujam, and P. Sadayappan. A Practical Automatic Polyhedral Parallelizer and Locality Optimizer. In *Proceedings of the 2008 ACM SIGPLAN Conference on Programming Language Design and Implementation*, PLDI '08, pages 101–113, New York, NY, USA, 2008. ACM.

[8] Andrew Canis, Jongsok Choi, Mark Aldham, Victor Zhang, Ahmed Kammoona, Jason H. Anderson, Stephen Brown, and Tomasz Czajkowski. LegUp: High-Level Synthesis for FPGA-Based Processor/Accelerator Systems. In *Proceedings of the 19th ACM/SIGDA international symposium on Field programmable gate arrays*, FPGA '11, pages 33–36, New York, NY, USA, 2011. ACM.

[9] Shuai Che, Jie Li, Jeremy W. Sheaffer, Kevin Skadron, and John Lach. Accelerating Compute-Intensive Applications with GPUs and FPGAs. In *Proceedings of the 2008 Symposium on Application Specific Processors*, SASP '08, pages 101–107, Washington, DC, USA, 2008. IEEE Computer Society.

[10] Eric S. Chung, James C. Hoe, and Ken Mai. CoRAM: An In-Fabric Memory Architecture for FPGA-Based Computing. In *Proceedings of the 19th ACM/SIGDA International Symposium on Field Programmable Gate Arrays*, FPGA '11, pages 97–106, New York, NY, USA, 2011. ACM.

[11] Eric S. Chung, Peter A. Milder, James C. Hoe, and Ken Mai. Single-Chip Heterogeneous Computing : Does the Future Include Custom Logic , FPGAs , and GPGPUs? *International Symposium on Microarchitecture (MICRO-43), Atlanta, GA, 2010*, pages 225–236, 2010.

[12] Eric S. Chung, Michael K. Papamichael, Gabriel Weisz, James C. Hoe, and Ken Mai. Prototype and evaluation of the CoRAM Memory Architecture for FPGA-Based Computing. In *Proceedings of the ACM/SIGDA International Symposium on Field Programmable Gate Arrays*, FPGA '12, pages 139–142, New York, NY, USA, 2012. ACM.

[13] Jason Cong, Peng Zhang, and Yi Zou. Combined Loop Transformation and Hierarchy Allocation for Data Reuse Optimization. In *Proceedings of the International Conference on Computer-Aided Design*, ICCAD '11, pages 185–192, Piscataway, NJ, USA, 2011. IEEE Press.

[14] Pedro C. Diniz and Joonseok Park. Data Reorganization Engines for the Next Generation of System-on-a-Chip FPGAs. In *Proceedings of the 2002 ACM/SIGDA Tenth International Symposium on Field-Programmable Gate Arrays*, FPGA '02, pages 237–244, New York, NY, USA, 2002. ACM.

[15] Jeremy Fowers, Greg Brown, Patrick Cooke, and Greg Stitt. A Performance and Energy Comparison of FPGAs, GPUs, and Multicores for Sliding-Window Applications. In *Proceedings of the ACM/SIGDA International Symposium on Field Programmable Gate Arrays*, FPGA '12, pages 47–56, New York, NY, USA, 2012. ACM.

[16] Tobias Grosser, Hongbin Zheng, Raghesh A, Andreas Simbürger, Armin Grösslinger, and Louis-Noël Pouchet. Polly - Polyhedral Optimization in LLVM . In *First International Workshop on Polyhedral Compilation Techniques (IMPACT'11)*, Chamonix, France, April 2011.

[17] Robert Kirchgessner, Greg Stitt, Alan George, and Herman Lam. VirtualRC: A Virtual FPGA Platform for Applications and Tools Portability. In *Proceedings of the ACM/SIGDA International Symposium on Field Programmable Gate Arrays*, FPGA '12, pages 205–208, New York, NY, USA, 2012. ACM.

[18] Christian Lengauer. Loop parallelization in the polytope model. In *Proceedings of the 4th International Conference on Concurrency Theory*, CONCUR '93, pages 398–416, London, UK, UK, 1993. Springer-Verlag.

[19] Michael K. Papamichael and James C. Hoe. CONNECT: Re-examining Conventional Wisdom for Designing NOCS in the Context of FPGAs. In *Proceedings of the ACM/SIGDA International Symposium on Field Programmable Gate Arrays*, FPGA '12, pages 37–46, New York, NY, USA, 2012. ACM.

[20] David Barrie Thomas, Lee Howes, and Wayne Luk. A Comparison of CPUs, GPUs, FPGAs, and Massively Parallel Processor Arrays for Random Number Generation. In *Proceedings of the ACM/SIGDA International Symposium on Field Programmable Gate Arrays*, FPGA '09, pages 63–72, New York, NY, USA, 2009. ACM.

[21] Jingling Xue. On Loop Restructuring by Converting Imperfect to Perfect Loop Nests. In *IEEE Second International Conference on Algorithms and Architectures for Parallel Processing, 1996. ICAPP '96.*, pages 421 –429, jun 1996.

[22] www.ece.cmu.edu/~coram.

[23] www.jacquardcomputing.com/roccc/.

[24] http://www.llvm.org/.

[25] www.impulseaccelerated.com/products.htm.

[26] www.mentor.com/products/fpga/handel-c/.

[27] www.mentor.com/esl/catapult/overview.

[28] www.xilinx.com/products/design-tools/vivado/index.htm.

[29] www.altera.com/devices/processor/nios2/tools/c2h/ni2-c2h.html.

[30] www.xilinx.com/support/documentation/data_sheets/ds150.pdf.

[31] www.altera.com/literature/hb/stratix-iv/stratix4_handbook.pdf.

[32] www.xilinx.com/support/documentation/data_sheets/ds180_7Series_Overview.pdf.

# Architecture Support for Custom Instructions with Memory Operations

Jason Cong
cong@cs.ucla.edu

Karthik Gururaj
karthikg@cs.ucla.edu

Department of Computer Science, University of California Los Angeles

## ABSTRACT

Customized instructions (CIs) implemented using custom functional units (CFUs) have been proposed as a way of improving performance and energy efficiency of software while minimizing cost of designing and verifying accelerators from scratch. However, previous work allows CIs to only communicate with the processor through registers or with limited memory operations. In this work we propose an architecture that allows CIs to seamlessly execute memory operations without any special synchronization operations to guarantee program order of instructions. Our results show that our architecture can provide 24% energy savings with 14% performance improvement for 2-issue and 4-issue superscalar processor cores.

**Categories and Subject Descriptors:** C.1.0 [Processor Architectures]: General

**Keywords:** ASIP, Custom instructions, Speculation.

## 1. INTRODUCTION

Instruction-set customizations have been proposed in [1, 3, 6, 4, 10, 9] which allow certain patterns of operations to be executed efficiently on CFUs added to the processor pipeline. Integration of CFUs with a superscalar pipeline provides additional opportunities : typical superscalar processors have hardware for speculatively executing instructions and rolling back and recovering to a correct state when there is mis-speculation. In our work we propose an architecture for integrating CFUs with the superscalar pipeline such that the CFUs can perform memory operations without depending on the compiler to synchronize accesses with the rest of the program.

## 2. RELATED WORK AND OUR CONTRIBUTIONS

In [18, 4, 10, 9, 17, 12], the CFUs read (write) their inputs (outputs) directly from (to) the register file of the processor and cannot access memory. However, since the CFU cannot

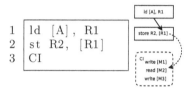

```
1   ld  [A] , R1
2   st  R2, [R1]
3   CI
```

**Figure 1: Memory ordering example**

access memory, the size of the computation pattern that can be implemented on a CFU is constrained. The primary problem with allowing CFUs to launch memory operations is to ensure that memory is updated and read in a consistent fashion with respect to other in-flight memory instructions in the superscalar pipeline. In the GARP [13], VEAL [8] and OneChip [7] systems, the compiler needs to insert some special instructions to ensure all preceding memory operations have completed before launching the custom instruction. Systems with architecturally visible storage (AVS) [5, 14] also depend on the compiler for synchronization.

In this paper, our goal is to design an architecture such that custom instructions (CIs) with memory operations can execute seamlessly along with other instructions in the processor pipeline without any special synchronization operations. More precisely, we present an architecture for integrating CFUs with the processor pipeline with the following properties: (1) CFUs can launch memory operations to directly access the L1 D-cache of the processor. (2) *No synchronization instructions need to be inserted before/after the CI*; this greatly reduces the burden on the compiler especially for applications with operations whose memory address cannot be determined beforehand. Our proposed microarchitecture ensures the correct ordering among the different memory operations.

## 3. CHALLENGES AND OUR PROPOSED SOLUTION FOR SUPPORTING MEMORY OPERATIONS IN CFUS

*Note*: For a more detailed explanation of our architecture, additional results and analysis, we refer the reader to our technical report [11].

In this section we explain the issues associated when CFUs connected to an out-of-order (OoO) core are allowed to launch memory operations directly and propose modifications in the compilation flow and underlying microarchitecture of the core to support such CFUs.

*Lifetime of a CI*: A CI is essentially a set of operations grouped together by the compiler to be executed as a single instruction. The primary inputs for a CI always come from the registers of the processor; all input registers must be ready before a CI is ready to execute. Once a CI starts executing, it can issue a series of memory operations into the processor's pipeline. Outputs of the CI can write to the processor's registers or memory.

## 3.1 Issue 1: Maintaining program order for memory operations

Consider the simple example in Figure 1. The CI to be executed launches three memory operations: a read from location $M2$ and writes to $M1$ and $M3$. For previous work [7, 14], the CI needs to at least wait until the addresses of *all* preceding memory operations are computed before proceeding; this is enforced by inserting synchronization instructions before the CI. We overcome this limitation by modifying the core's microarchitecture. The key difference of our approach is that we make the memory operations launched by a CI ***visible to the OoO processor's pipeline in program order***. In the decode stage of the pipeline, in which program order is still maintained, the CI in Figure 1 will launch three memory operations (which we call *mem-rops*) into the dispatch stage. In the dispatch stage, each operation is assigned a tag representing its program order. The OoO pipeline will assign one entry for the store and three entries for the CI in the LSQ. Even if the store instruction's address is computed after the CI begins execution, the LSQ will check whether any successive operations have an address conflict. In the case of a conflict, the OoO pipeline will ensure that the CI is squashed and a pipeline flush occurs.

## 3.2 Issue 2: Ordering of memory operations within a CI

For the CI in Figure 1, assume that the first write operation to address $M1$ and the read operation reading from $M2$ overlap/conflict. In the case of normal memory instructions, if the read executes before the write, the read will be squashed and re-executed in the OoO pipeline. However, the instruction stream of the program contains only the CI and not the individual memory operations. Re-execution will need to begin from the CI, but the same conflict will occur again. To overcome this problem, we place a constraint during the CI compilation phase: the compiler cannot cluster a memory operation in a CI if there is a preceding memory write operation within the CI which may cause a conflict. The compiler uses alias analysis (possibly in a conservative way) to satisfy this constraint. Memory dependences between different CIs are handled as described in Section 3.1.

## 3.3 Issue 3: Possible partial commit to memory

For the CI in Figure 1, assume that the first write operation to address $M1$ commits and updates memory. However, after this commit, it is determined that the write operation to $M3$ fails because of a TLB translation fault. This would leave the memory in an inconsistent state since the write to address $M1$ was committed. We overcome this problem by delaying the commit of all write memory operations launched by the CI until the successful completion of the CI (no TLB faults). The compiler inserts additional instructions that are executed in case a CI causes a TLB fault.

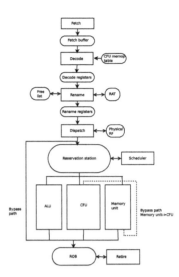

**Figure 2: Layout of the processor pipeline with tightly integrated CFU**

## 3.4 Issue 4: Handling a variable number of memory operations

Since CIs can span multiple basic blocks in the program, the number of memory operations launched by a CI could vary across executions and need not be deterministic before the CI starts executing. This issue is solved by launching the maximum number of memory operations that a CI can execute during the decode stage. In the case where a particular memory operation is not executed, the CI supplies a 'dummy' address for these operations, effectively turning them into nops.

## 4. DETAILS OF PROPOSED ARCHITECTURE

Figure 2 shows the basic layout of how our reconfigurable CFU units interact with the rest of the processor pipeline. We will briefly explain each component of this interaction.

## 4.1 Decode stage

Since the number of ports of the register file (and other components in the microarchitecture of a superscalar processor such as the RAT, free list, reservation station) is limited, we split a complex CI into multiple simple operations which we call *rops* (similar to the micro-ops in x86 processors). *Sreg-rops* only read from registers, *dreg-rops* only write to registers and *mem-rops* read/write from/to memory.

The opcode of the CI is used to determine the number and type (read/write) of *mem-rops* that the CI will launch. We introduce a SRAM table called *CFU memop table* to store the mapping between the CI opcode and the number of memory operations launched by the CI. This is a programmable table which is filled up when a new application is launched.

## 4.2 Dispatch stage

The dispatch stage is the last stage in the pipeline where instructions are processed in order (apart from the commit stage). Each instruction is assigned a *sequence id* or *SID* which represents the program order. The main job of the dispatch stage is to perform resource allocation – i.e., create entries in the ROB (and assigning *SIDs*) for each instruction/*rop*, the reservation station and in the LSQ for memory instructions/*rops*. Since *mem-rops* get their address (and data) operands directly from the CIs (and not the register file), each entry in the reservation table needs to be expanded to accommodate this information. We analyzed that for a modern superscalar processor with 256 physical registers and a 128-entry ROB, where CIs can have at most 16 *mem-rops*, the area of the reservation station in the baseline processor would be 0.17 mm$^2$, while the modified reservation station would occupy 0.21 mm$^2$ at the 45 nm node (from McPAT [15]).

## 4.3 Scheduler and execute stage

A CI is ready to execute when all the *sreg-rops* issued by it are ready. The scheduler decides which CFU to assign to a particular CI. Once the CFU has obtained all its register operands, it begins execution. When a memory operation is encountered, the CFU computes the address (and possibly data) for the operation and sends it over the bypass path to forward it to the *mem-rop* waiting in the RS.

The *mem-rop*, using the address obtained from the CFU, proceeds with the memory operation in a manner identical to load/store instructions. Assuming there are no conflicts in the LSQ or TLB misses, the memory operation completes and waits in the ROB for retirement. If the *mem-rop* is a memory read operation, the read value is forwarded to the CFU over the bypass paths.

The CFU completes execution and forwards the results to *dreg-rops* waiting in the RS after which the *dreg-rops* wait in the ROB for retirement.

## 4.4 Retire stage

Unlike store instructions, write memory *mem-rops* launched by CIs are allowed to update memory only when all the *rops* launched by the CI have retired because of reasons explained in Section 3.3.

## 5. RESULTS

We use the LLVM compiler framework [2] to analyze and extract CIs from the SPEC integer 2006 benchmark suite. Our baseline core is a 2-issue superscalar core with tightly integrated CFUs. Our chip is a tiled CMP system where each tile could be a core or a reconfigurable fabric tile with 2000 slices and 150 DSP blocks (density based on Virtex-6 numbers). We assume a 5-cycle, pipelined link between the FPGA fabric and core pipeline.

We use the AutoESL HLS tool for synthesizing our CFUs and Xilinx XPower for energy numbers for the FPGA. We use Wisconsin's GEMS simulation infrastructure [16] to model the performance of our system and McPAT [15] to estimate energy of the processor core. Our cores and the CFUs run at different frequencies – the core runs at 2 GHz while the frequency of the CFU is provided by Xilinx ISE. To keep the interface logic as simple as possible, the CFU is operated at a clock period which is an integer multiple of the CPU clock period. For five of our benchmarks, the CFUs selected by our compiler pass could operate at 200 MHz (1 FPGA cycle = 10 core cycles) while for the other two benchmarks, the CFUs operated at 125 MHz (1 FPGA cycle = 16 core cycles).

Table 1 shows the performance when the CFUs are pipelined. The initiation interval of pipelining varies between 1 and 3 FPGA cycles (as determined by AutoPilot). With pipelin-

ing, we begin to see significant performance improvements – an average of around 14%. The key point in our approach is to compare the performance of a 2-issue core augmented with CFUs (column 2) with a 4-issue core (column 5). *Our architecture can beat the performance of a 4-issue core when using a 2-issue core and CFUs.* For benchmarks with significant ILP (*libquantum, hmmer, sjeng, h264*), the speed-up is reasonable. Benchmarks such as *mcf*, which have a large working set, see very little improvement – mainly because they are limited by cache misses.

Table 2 shows the energy consumption (normalized to the 2-issue core). Here, we see that having CFUs provides significant energy savings. On the average, we see a 24% energy reduction. Of the total energy savings, we observe that 41% of the total energy savings in our system comes from the reduced number of accesses to the I-cache, instruction buffer and decode logic, 32% comes from reduced energy consumption of the ALUs (since many arithmetic operations are performed in the FPGA now) and register files. The remaining 27% is distributed among the reservation station, rename logic and ROB.

## 6. CONCLUSIONS

In this paper we present an architecture by which CIs can launch memory operations and execute speculatively when integrated with a superscalar processor pipeline. Our approach does not need any synchronization or detailed memory analysis by the compiler. Our experiments show that even for pointer-heavy benchmarks, our approach can provide an average of 24% energy savings and 14% performance improvement over software-only implementations.

## 7. ACKNOWLEDGMENT

The authors acknowledge the support of the GSRC, one of six research centers funded under the FCRP, a SRC entity and Xilinx.

## 8. REFERENCES

[1] Altera NIOS-II processor. http://www.altera.com/devices/processor/nios2/ni2-index.html.

[2] The LLVM compilation infrastructure. http://llvm.org.

[3] Xtensa customizable processor. http://www.tensilica.com/products/xtensa-customizable.

[4] K. Atasu, C. Ozturan, G. Dundar, O. Mencer, and W. Luk. Chips: Custom hardware instruction processor synthesis. *Computer-Aided Design of Integrated Circuits and Systems, IEEE Transactions on*, 27(3):528 –541, march 2008.

[5] P. Biswas, N. D. Dutt, L. Pozzi, and P. Ienne. Introduction of architecturally visible storage in instruction set extensions. *Computer-Aided Design of Integrated Circuits and Systems, IEEE Transactions on*, 26(3):435 –446, march 2007.

[6] P. Brisk, A. Kaplan, and M. Sarrafzadeh. Area-efficient instruction set synthesis for reconfigurable system-on-chip designs. In *Design Automation Conference, 2004. Proceedings. 41st*, pages 395 –400, july 2004.

[7] J. E. Carrillo and P. Chow. The effect of reconfigurable units in superscalar processors. In *Proceedings of the*

**Table 1: Normalized performance (#cycles elapsed) with pipelined CFUs on FPGAs**

|  | 2-issue/128 entries | | 2-issue/256 entries | | 4-issue/128 entries | | 4-issue/256 entries | |
|---|---|---|---|---|---|---|---|---|
|  | baseline | CFU | baseline | CFU | baseline | CFU | baseline | CFU |
| bzip2 | 1.000 | 0.924 | 0.999 | 0.924 | 0.958 | 0.885 | 0.956 | 0.884 |
| libquantum | 1.000 | 0.703 | 1.000 | 0.703 | 0.653 | 0.459 | 0.653 | 0.459 |
| hmmer | 1.000 | 0.781 | 1.000 | 0.781 | 0.775 | 0.605 | 0.775 | 0.605 |
| mcf | 1.000 | 0.938 | 1.000 | 0.938 | 0.973 | 0.913 | 0.973 | 0.913 |
| gobmk | 1.000 | 0.940 | 0.999 | 0.940 | 0.982 | 0.924 | 0.981 | 0.923 |
| h264 | 1.000 | 0.802 | 0.998 | 0.801 | 0.765 | 0.613 | 0.763 | 0.612 |
| sjeng | 1.000 | 0.899 | 0.999 | 0.898 | 0.895 | 0.805 | 0.894 | 0.804 |
| Average | 1.000 | 0.855 | 0.999 | 0.855 | 0.857 | 0.743 | 0.857 | 0.743 |
| Improvement(%) | - | 14.460 | - | 14.461 | - | 13.277 | - | 13.278 |

**Table 2: Normalized total energy consumption with pipelined CFUs on FPGAs**

|  | 2-issue/128 entries | | 2-issue/256 entries | | 4-issue/128 entries | | 4-issue/256 entries | |
|---|---|---|---|---|---|---|---|---|
|  | baseline | CFU | baseline | CFU | baseline | CFU | baseline | CFU |
| bzip2 | 1.000 | 0.736 | 1.046 | 0.806 | 1.367 | 1.027 | 1.452 | 1.098 |
| libquantum | 1.000 | 0.746 | 1.058 | 0.809 | 1.044 | 0.787 | 1.141 | 0.825 |
| hmmer | 1.000 | 0.726 | 1.094 | 0.816 | 1.079 | 0.798 | 1.291 | 1.007 |
| mcf | 1.000 | 0.748 | 1.060 | 0.836 | 1.035 | 0.800 | 1.123 | 0.876 |
| gobmk | 1.000 | 0.734 | 1.011 | 0.788 | 1.391 | 1.060 | 1.412 | 1.102 |
| h264 | 1.000 | 0.782 | 1.051 | 0.757 | 1.137 | 0.881 | 1.224 | 0.923 |
| sjeng | 1.000 | 0.731 | 1.029 | 0.769 | 1.290 | 0.992 | 1.343 | 1.001 |
| Average | 1.000 | 0.743 | 1.050 | 0.797 | 1.192 | 0.907 | 1.284 | 0.976 |
| Improvement(%) | 0.000 | 25.672 | 0.000 | 24.075 | 0.000 | 23.942 | 0.000 | 23.948 |

*2001 ACM/SIGDA ninth international symposium on Field programmable gate arrays*, FPGA '01, pages 141–150, New York, NY, USA, 2001. ACM.

[8] N. Clark, A. Hormati, and S. Mahlke. Veal: Virtualized execution accelerator for loops. In *Computer Architecture, 2008. ISCA '08. 35th International Symposium on*, pages 389 –400, june 2008.

[9] N. Clark, M. Kudlur, H. Park, S. Mahlke, and K. Flautner. Application-specific processing on a general-purpose core via transparent instruction set customization. In *Microarchitecture, 2004. MICRO-37 2004. 37th International Symposium on*, pages 30 – 40, dec. 2004.

[10] J. Cong, Y. Fan, G. Han, and Z. Zhang. Application-specific instruction generation for configurable processor architectures. In *Proceedings of the 2004 ACM/SIGDA 12th international symposium on Field programmable gate arrays*, FPGA '04, pages 183–189, New York, NY, USA, 2004. ACM.

[11] J. Cong and K. Gururaj. Architecture support for custom instructions with memory operations. Technical Report 120019, University of California Los Angeles, November 2012.

[12] Q. Dinh, D. Chen, and M. D. F. Wong. Efficient asip design for configurable processors with fine-grained resource sharing. In *Proceedings of the 16th international ACM/SIGDA symposium on Field programmable gate arrays*, FPGA '08, pages 99–106, New York, NY, USA, 2008. ACM.

[13] J. Hauser and J. Wawrzynek. Garp: a MIPS processor with a reconfigurable coprocessor. In *FPGAs for Custom Computing Machines, 1997. Proceedings., The 5th Annual IEEE Symposium on*, pages 12 –21, apr 1997.

[14] T. Kluter, S. Burri, P. Brisk, E. Charbon, and P. Ienne. Virtual ways: Efficient coherence for architecturally visible storage in automatic instruction set extensions. In *HiPEAC*, volume 5952 of *Lecture Notes in Computer Science*, pages 126–140. Springer, 2010.

[15] S. Li, J. H. Ahn, R. D. Strong, J. B. Brockman, D. M. Tullsen, and N. P. Jouppi. Mcpat: an integrated power, area, and timing modeling framework for multicore and manycore architectures. In *Proceedings of the 42nd Annual IEEE/ACM International Symposium on Microarchitecture*, MICRO 42, pages 469–480, New York, NY, USA, 2009. ACM.

[16] M. M. K. Martin, D. J. Sorin, B. M. Beckmann, M. R. Marty, M. Xu, A. R. Alameldeen, K. E. Moore, M. D. Hill, and D. A. Wood. Multifacet's general execution-driven multiprocessor simulator (gems) toolset. *SIGARCH Comput. Archit. News*, 33:92–99, November 2005.

[17] L. Pozzi and P. Ienne. Exploiting pipelining to relax register-file port constraints of instruction-set extensions. In *Proceedings of the 2005 international conference on Compilers, architectures and synthesis for embedded systems*, CASES '05, pages 2–10, New York, NY, USA, 2005. ACM.

[18] Z. Ye, A. Moshovos, S. Hauck, and P. Banerjee. Chimaera: a high-performance architecture with a tightly-coupled reconfigurable functional unit. In *Computer Architecture, 2000. Proceedings of the 27th International Symposium on*, pages 225 –235, june 2000.

# An FPGA Based Parallel Architecture for Music Melody Matching

Hao Wang and Jyh-Charn Liu
Department of Computer Science and Engineering
Texas A&M University
College Station, TX 77840
{haowang, liu}@cse.tamu.edu

## ABSTRACT

We propose an FPGA-based high performance parallel architecture for music retrieval through singing. The database consists of monophonic MIDI files which are modeled into strings, and the user sung query is modeled as a set of regular expressions (regexp), with consideration of possible key transpositions and tempo variations to tolerate imperfectly sung queries. An approximate regexp matching algorithm is developed to calculate the similarity between a regexp and a string, using edit distance as the metrics. The algorithm supports user sung queries starting anywhere in the database song, not necessarily from the beginning. Using the proposed formal models and algorithms, the similarity between the user sung query and each song in the database can be evaluated and the top-10 most similar results will be reported.

We designed the approximate regexp matching algorithm in such way that all terms of the regexp can execute concurrently, which perfectly fits the massive parallelism provided by FPGA. The FPGA implemented *melody matching engine* (*MME*) is a parameterized modular architecture that can be reconfigured to implement different regexps by simply updating their parameter registers, and can therefore avoid the time-consuming code re-synthesis. MME also includes an on-board DDR2 memory to store the database, so that they can be read in to calculate edit distances locally on the board. This way, each MME forms a self-contained system and multiple MMEs can be clustered to increase parallel processing power, with virtually no overhead. MME is evaluated using the query corpus of ThinkIT with 355 sung files and database of 5563 MIDI files. It achieves a top-10 hit rate of 90.7% and a runtime of 19.4 seconds, averaging 54.6 milliseconds for a single query. MME achieves significant speedup over software-based systems while providing the same level of flexibility.

## Categories and Subject Descriptors

C.1.4 [**Processor Architectures**]: Parallel Architectures
F.1.1 [**Computation by Abstract Devices**]: Automata
H.5.5 [**Information Interfaces and Presentation**]: Sound and Music Computing

## General Terms

Algorithms, Design, Languages.

## Keywords

Music information retrieval, FPGA, Regular expression

## 1. INTRODUCTION

Nowadays, music is much more accessible in a digital file format than a physical copy. With the ever-growing disk space, people can easily store thousands of songs on their personal computers, and most internet media providers maintain a music database with millions of songs. The large scale of music database makes its efficient and effective retrieval more and more challenging. The traditional way to organize music files is to use auxiliary text metadata such as song title and artist name, so that well-developed string matching algorithms can be employed to efficiently retrieve the desired song given its exact metadata. However, such systems would provide poor user experience or even fail if the user forgets the exact metadata. Under such circumstances, support of *query by humming* [1] will be invaluable for a music information retrieval (MIR) system, where the music is retrieved not by its auxiliary metadata but by its acoustic content. This content-based music retrieval technique has become more and more appealing because melody is the natural and unique signature of a music piece, and retrieval by singing the melody is considered a lot more user-friendly than inputting its non-semantically-related text metadata.

Many content-based MIR systems [2][3][4] have been developed to meet the emerging needs of query by humming. The traditional way of melody matching was to model both database music pieces and the user sung query as character sequences and then apply string matching algorithms. Some researchers have developed methods for modeling [5][6] and retrieval [7] of polyphonic music, but many more are focusing on monophonic ones, because for polyphonic music it is very hard to clearly define the next character in the sequence, as there may be multiple channels of sounds simultaneously on. In the context of monophonic music retrieval, the most commonly used format to store database music files are MIDI [8], which represents music in its score level. A typical MIDI file is composed of sequential note events specified with a pitch, onset time, and duration. The user sung queries are also captured as monophonic WAV files, whose pitch sequence along the time axis can be acquired by fundamental frequency estimators, based on either time domain autocorrelation methods [9][10][11] or frequency domain cepstrum analysis approaches [12].

There are two major directions to discretize the database and user query into digital formats for their matching of each other, namely note-based and frame-based methods. The prior one attracts considerable research efforts because users naturally sing a music piece in notes, and notes are also the fundamental building blocks of MIDI files. Signatures can be extracted as strings [13], n-grams [16][17][18] or hidden Markov chains [19][20], and similarity between user query and database files can be calculated by approximate string matching algorithms [14][15] or in a probabilistic manner. Most systems of this category depend on accurate note segmentation [21] from the pitch sequence of a user query, which is sensitive to noises and therefore limits the system's retrieval accuracy. This leads many other researchers to focus on matching the user query and database files directly at the frame level, where the pitches of both sides are sampled into a time series and their edit distance [22] is calculated by approximate string matching algorithms. This way, the rhythm information is encoded in the frame sequence, and no explicit note segmentation is required. For this reason, frame-based systems can usually achieve better retrieval accuracy than note-based systems. However, their finer-grain time resolution results in larger database and user query, and therefore have a longer run time.

Several research efforts have been proposed to improve performance of frame-based systems, such as recursive alignment [26], score-level fusion of multiple classifiers [27], and hierarchical filtering [28]. A hybrid system is proposed in [29] where note-based methods are first used to filter out most unlikely database candidates, and the rest are compared to user input using frame-based methods. An evaluation method and testbed for content-based MIR systems is proposed in [30], and various types of retrieval techniques are evaluated and compared in [31].

No matter which direction a MIR system follows, the tolerance of key transpositions and tempo variations between the user sung query and its original melody is essential for its proper functioning, because few users can sing songs perfectly in their original keys and rhythms. Key transpositions can be taken care of by shifting the query to have the same average pitch as the database song [28], or by interval coding [17] where the differences between adjacent pitches, rather than their absolute values, are used for matching. To compensate rhythm variations, linear scaling [23] and dynamic time warping (DTW) [24][25] are commonly used to stretch/shrink the user query. Linear scaling tunes the user query faster or slower at certain preset ratios, while DTW allows finer grain continuous alignments within a tempo variation range.

In this paper, we adopted the frame-based method to parse both music database and user sung query into frame sequences. The database is modeled as strings and the user query is modeled as a set of regular expressions (regexp) to tolerate both key transposition and tempo variation. We also developed an approximate regexp matching algorithm to calculate the edit distance between a regexp and a string. The algorithm supports *overlapped matching*, where a character of the string needs to be treated not only as the "next" symbol for any on-going matching processes, but also as the "beginning" symbol of a substring for a new matching process. This way, user sung queries can start anywhere in the database song, not necessarily from the beginning. After the edit distances between the user sung query

and each database song are calculated, the top-10 most similar ones will be reported as the retrieval result.

The regexp model of user query and its corresponding matching algorithm are such designed that the regexp is composed of modular terms sharing the same architecture, and all of its terms can run in parallel. This fits the intrinsic massive parallelism of FPGA architecture perfectly and therefore achieves significant speed up compared to traditional software-based solutions. The FPGA implementation of the system is named the *melody matching engine* (*MME*), which is a parameterized modular architecture that can be reconfigured to implement different regexps by simply updating its parameter registers, and can therefore avoid the time-consuming code re-synthesis encountered by traditional FPGA designs. Our experiments show that MME can achieve up to 1135X speedup over software-based systems, while attaining a high top-10 hit rate of 90.7%. This clearly shows the effectiveness and efficiency of the proposed models, algorithm, and system.

The rest of paper is organized as follows. Section 2 introduces the modeling of database and user sung query. Section 3 discusses the approximate regexp matching algorithm. We describe the implementation details of the system in section 4. The system is evaluated in section 5, and the paper is concluded in section 6.

## 2. SYSTEM MODELING

The database music pieces are stored as MIDI files, and the user sung queries are captured by the microphone as WAV files. In order to evaluate their similarity, both sides are re-represented using the same underlying frame structure. Each frame is associated with a pitch value and all frames have the same time duration. This way, both database and user query are parsed into frame sequences, which are further modeled as strings and regexps in subsections 2.1 and 2.2, respectively.

## 2.1 Modeling of MIDI File

MIDI (Musical Instrument Digital Interface) is an industrial specification of commands for electronic musical instruments and peripheral devices to interface with each other. A MIDI command can specify a note event such as pitch and onset time, a control signal such as pitch bend and audio panning, or a clock signal such as tempo. A MID file (file extension .mid) is a stream of MIDI commands coded in binary format which is playable by a music player to generate the acoustic effects perceivable by an end user. MID files are more like musical scores rather than recorded music performances such as MP3 files, which makes them very compact in size and easily distributable via the Internet.

The database we used in this study are all monophonic MID files, which only contain very basic tempo information and note events. The notes are non-overlapping with each other, meaning that a note can begin only after a previous note has ended. The database MID files are parsed by MIDICSV [32] to extract musical information into comma separated values (CSV) text files. To illustrate this process, we show the famous "Happy Birthday to You" song in both professional sheet format and CSV format. We first show its musical score [42] in Figure 1 as follows.

**Figure 1. Musical Score of "Happy Birthday to You"**

The corresponding CSV version of the same song is listed in Table 1, where the left column is the timeline in clock pulses, the middle column contains the events, and the right column are the events' corresponding values. The first two rows are setup parameters specifying that a quarter note spans 480 clock pulses and lasts 600,000 microseconds, i.e., a clock pulse occurs every 1250 microseconds. With this information we can convert the timeline from clock pulses to seconds. In the rest of rows, a Note_on event signifies the onset of a note with its pitch specified in the value field, and a Note_off event denotes the end of a note.

**Table 1. CSV version of "Happy Birthday to You"**

| Time | Event | Value |
|------|-------|-------|
| 0 | Header | 480 |
| 0 | Tempo | 600000 |
| 960 | Note_on | 60 |
| 1320 | Note_off | |
| 1320 | Note_on | 60 |
| 1440 | Note_off | |
| 1440 | Note_on | 62 |
| 1920 | Note_off | |
| 1920 | Note_on | 60 |
| 2400 | Note_off | |
| 2400 | Note_on | 65 |
| 2880 | Note_off | |
| 2880 | Note_on | 64 |
| 3840 | Note_off | |

MIDI standards specify a pitch range from 0 to 127, i.e., the same range of ASCII values of characters. Therefore, when parsing the MID file into frame sequence, we can use characters to represent the frame's pitch values. As for the time duration of one frame, we choose the value of $l$ milliseconds to balance the resultant database size and retrieval accuracy. As will become clear later, too short a frame length will result in a larger database, while too long a frame length will be unable to capture all essential musical information. An appropriate value for $l$ will be determined in the experiments of subsection 5.2.

With the above frame settings, the database MID file can be represented as a string, where each character lasts $l$ milliseconds with the pitch being its ASCII value. For example, if $l$ is 100 milliseconds, the "Happy Birthday to You" song can be converted into the following string

$S_{ll}$: <<<<<<<>>>>><<<<<AAAAAA@@@@@@@@@@@@@ (1)

The silent parts of the MIDI files, if any, are removed because they do not carry meaningful music information. This way, all essential music information of the entire MID files database are converted into a set of database MID strings. To ease the later processing of key transpositions of user queries, the database MID strings are all shifted to have the average pitch of 60.

## 2.2 Modeling of User Query

The user sung queries are recorded by microphone, which converts the continuous analog signal into a discrete digital format stored as WAV files (file extension .wav). The query corpus data used in this study are all monophonic files sampled at 8000 Hz. The musical sounds are comprised of periodic signals, which have different frequencies for different pitches. To extract pitch values from such signals, we need a pitch detector which estimates the fundamental frequency ($f_0$) of the signal at each point of the timeline to get its dominant pitch. As this part is more involved with signal processing and is beyond the scope of this study, we directly adopted the autocorrelation-based YIN algorithm [10] as the pitch detector, whose MATLAB source code is publically accessible at [33]. YIN generates $f_0$ estimation for each sample point of the input WAV file, which can then be converted to a pitch value using the following formula:

$$p = 69 + 12 \times log_2(\frac{f_0}{440 \ Hz}) \qquad (2)$$

where $A_4$ (440 Hz, the A note above middle C) is assigned with pitch number 69 and an octave is evenly divided into 12 semitones. We use the aperiodicity measurement generated by YIN algorithm to identify voiced sounds, and all silent parts are filtered out as we do to the database MID files. As the final output, we get an array of pitch values, with each array element lasting 125 microseconds, i.e., inverse of the sample rate of the WAV file. To match the frame settings of database MID strings, we re-write the pitch array into a frame sequence using the same frame length $l$, generating a string of user query, denoted as $S_u$.

It is noteworthy that the users will seldom sing the query in the same key and tempo as its original melody. However, even with key transpositions and tempo variations, a user sung query may still be perceived by other users as similar to its original melody, if they share roughly the same "pitch contour". Therefore, a robust content-based MIR system needs to retrieve user sung queries in a transposition and tempo invariant manner.

Although a pitch sequence can be made transposition-invariant by interval coding [17], it has the disadvantage of assessing only a minor penalty for a transposition in the middle of melody, which however will usually be perceived as a major change. An alternative is to pitch-shift the user query string $S_u$ to $S_u^i$, where $S_u^i$ has an average pitch of $i$ so that it has the same average pitch as the melody to be matched. Recall that in subsection 2.1 we shift all database MID strings to have the average pitch of 60, and therefore by shifting $S_u$ to $S_u^{60}$ we can have a user query with the same average pitch 60 as all database MID files. However, as the user will typically sing only a portion of the melody, and there is a good chance that the local average of user sung portion differs from the global average of the complete melody, we compensate their possible difference by further shifting $S_u^{60}$ up and down by up to $k$. This way, we generate a total of $2k+1$ copies $\{S_u^{60-k}, ..., S_u^{60+k}\}$ of user query strings. With the average-pitch variation threshold $k$ being sufficiently large, it is safe to claim that one of the $2k+1$ variants of user query will align well with its matched portion of the original melody. However, too big a value $k$ will result in an unnecessarily large search space which translates to a long processing time. An appropriate value of $k$ will be tuned in the experiments of subsection 5.2 to cover adequate search space while not wasting processing power.

For analysis of tempo variations, we extract notes from the pitch array as the analysis object, because users naturally sing the query in a note-by-note basis and they will usually change the rhythm of all notes during the recording. Although it seems opposite to the claimed frame-based method, keep in mind that the concept of note is utilized here solely for the purpose of formal discussion, and in implementations the underlying structure is still frames.

To reconstruct notes from a pitch array, adjacent elements with the same pitch value are assembled together as one note, which is then represented as a character class with constraint repetition (CCR). The term CCR is originally proposed in [34] to re-write regexps into a modular format suitable for implementation on FPGA. Character class is a set of acceptable characters, and constraint repetition is a quantifier defining the number of repetitions that a character class can be matched. There are three types of constraint repetitions, namely $\{x\}$ (matching exactly $x$ times), $\{x,y\}$ (matching no less than $x$ times and no more than $y$ times) and $\{x,\}$ (matching at least $x$ times). In the context of this paper, the CCR representation of a user sung note would have a character class of only one character, and a constraint repetition of type $\{x\}$. The entire user sung query of $n$ notes can be modeled as a regexp composed of $n$ CCR terms as follows.

$$R = p_1\{x_1\} \cdot p_2\{x_2\} \cdot \ldots \cdot p_n\{x_n\} \qquad (3)$$

where $p_i$ is the character corresponding to the pitch value of note $i$, $\{x_i\}$ is the constraint repetition of note $i$, and '$\cdot$' is the concatenation operator. This way, the user query string $S_u$ can be rewritten as the following CCR based regexp, if the user sings exactly the same as the sheet music of Figure 1 and $S_u = S_H$:

$$R_u : <\{7\} \cdot >\{6\} \cdot <\{6\} \cdot A\{6\} \cdot @\{12\} \qquad (4)$$

With the user sung note modeled as CCR, its variation in tempo can be tolerated by expanding the constraint repetition from type $\{x\}$ to type $\{x, y\}$, so that instead of matching the database MID note of exactly the same duration, it can now match a note of any duration within the specified tolerable range. For a CCR note with constraint repetition $\{x\}$, empirical results suggest that expansion to $\{y, 4y\}$ would cover most tempo variations and lead to the best matching accuracy, where $y = \lceil 0.6x \rceil$ and "$\lceil \rceil$" denotes the ceiling function. This way, the original $R_u$ can be relaxed in tempo as follows:

$$R_u' = <\{5,20\} \cdot >\{4,16\} \cdot <\{4,16\} \cdot A\{4,16\} \cdot @\{8,32\} \quad (5)$$

The CCR model of note is advantageous over linear scaling in the aspect that each note is treated individually so that local rhythm distortion can be tolerated and will not always lead to high global dissimilarity.

With key transposition and tempo variation considered together, a user query can be modeled as a set of CCR based regexps using the process shown in equation (6), so that both variations in key and tempo can be tolerated, leading to a robust MIR system.

$$\textit{User query} \xrightarrow{\textit{digitize}} S_u \xrightarrow{\textit{key transpositions}} \{S_u^{60-k}, \ldots, S_u^{60+k}\}$$
$$\xrightarrow{\textit{tempo variations}} \{R_u^{60-k}, \ldots, R_u^{60+k}\} \qquad (6)$$

# 3. THE APPROXIMATE REGEXP MATCHING ALGORITHM

With the aforementioned string model of database music and regexp model of user sung query, we can design a regexp matching algorithm for melody matching, with consideration of the following two points.

Firstly, the user will usually only sing the portion of melody that he or she is familiar with as the query, which can start anywhere in the original melody. Therefore, when matching against the query regexp, the database MID string needs not to be matched in its entirety, and the presence of a matching substring should be sufficient to assert the matching. This is referred to as *overlapped matching*, where each character of the input string needs to be treated not only as the "next symbol" for any on-going matching processes, but also as the "beginning symbol" of a substring for a new matching process. Secondly, the user query may not exactly match the database melody even after key transposition and tempo variation, because noises are always inevitable. Therefore we need an approximate matching algorithm to measure the degree of dissimilarity introduced by noises and imperfect singing, rather than the traditional exact matching algorithms which only generate a yes or no matching signal.

Taking the above-mentioned points into account, in this section we introduce an approximate regexp matching algorithm (named AREM) in the overlapping matching context, which can evaluate the similarity between the user query regexp and the database MID string, using edit distance as the similarity measure. Its sequential version is first discussed in subsection 3.1, which is then parallelized in subsection 3.2 to fit the FPGA architecture for acceleration.

## 3.1 Sequential Version of AREM

The term *edit distance*, previously known as *Levenshtein distance* [22], has been widely applied in quantitative analysis of similarity. In overlapped matching context, the edit distance between a string and a regexp is defined as the least cost of edits needed to convert any of its substrings to exactly match the regexp. Unless otherwise specified, all "edit distance" terms used later in this section are referred in the overlapped matching context. In its traditional definition, edits include insertion of a new character, deletion of an existing character, or substitution of a non-matching character to a matching one, and each edit has its associated edit cost. However, in design of the approximate regexp matching algorithm for a content-based MIR system, we only allow substitution edits and we exclude insertion and deletion edits. This is justified because the database MID strings and user query regexp only carry essential music melody information, which we claim should not be deleted or inserted to make a matching. The edit cost associated with substitution edits is defined as the ASCII value difference between the acceptable character and the actual input character, and the match of the two is regarded as a substitution with no cost. This way, more penalties will be assessed as the user sung query deviates more from its original melody, and no cost will be incurred if the melody is sung perfectly.

We will elaborate the approximate regexp matching algorithm in the rest of this section, and the following notations are introduced to facilitate the discussion. Consider a database MID string of $m$ characters $S_m = \{c_1, \ldots, c_m\}$ where $c_k$ is the $k^{th}$ input character and it is processed at cycle $k$. Let $S_k$ denote the substring $\{c_1, \ldots, c_k\}$ of $S_m$. The query regexp of $n$ notes is rewritten into CCR format $R_n = CCR_1 \cdot \ldots \cdot CCR_n$, where each $CCR_i$ is called a state which represents the progress that $R_n$ has been matched up to, and it is in the format of $p_i\{y_i, 4y_i\}$ as introduced in subsection 2.2. Recall that although CCR is a note representation, its underlying structures are still frames. For its frame-level analysis, we decompose state $CCR_i$ into sub-states of $CCR_i^0 \bullet \ldots \bullet CCR_i^{4y_i}$, where each sub-state is a frame and $CCR_i^j$ denotes the sub-state that $p_i$ has been matched $j$ times. The sub-states of $CCR_i$ can be divided into three groups by the matching progress they represent. $CCR_i^0$ is the *initial* sub-state where the matching process just starts for $CCR_i$, $CCR_i^{y_i} \bullet \ldots \bullet CCR_i^{4y_i}$ are the *qualifying* sub-states where the matching process has satisfied the constraint repetition and is ready to move forward to $CCR_{i+1}$, and $CCR_i^1 \bullet \ldots \bullet CCR_i^{y_i-1}$ are the *non-qualifying* sub-states where the matching process is still making its way towards qualifying sub-states. Note that $CCR_i^0$ does not contain any music information and it only serves as an interaction method between adjacent CCRs. Let $R_i^j$ denote the sub-regexp that starts with $CCR_1^0$ and ends at $CCR_i^j$. Each $CCR_i^j$ carries two counters $ed_{i,j,k-1}$ and $ed_{i,j,k}$ to store its edit distance values of previous cycle $k-1$ and current cycle $k$, respectively, where $ed_{i,j,k}$ denotes the edit distance between $S_k$ and $R_i^j$.

With the above sub-state model of query regexp and its corresponding notations, we can draw the state transition diagram between $CCR_1$ and $CCR_2$ in Figure 2. Although only the first two CCRs of $R_n$ are shown, the same transition diagram is applicable to all other adjacent CCRs.

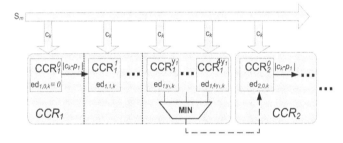

**Figure 2. State transition diagram**

Sub-state $CCR_1^0$ is the initial sub-state of the whole regexp, and its edit distance counter is set to be constant zero to support overlapped matching, i.e., the following equation:

$$ed_{1,0,k} = 0 \text{ for all } k. \tag{7}$$

This way, $CCR_1^0$ serves as a brand new starting point for any substring of $S_m$ starting at any input character.

Each input character $c_k$ is broadcasted to all sub-states at cycle $k$, triggering an intra-state substitution edit transition and incurring an edit cost, which is denoted by the labeled solid arrow. The edit distance counters of sub-states are updated accordingly by the following equation:

$$ed_{i,j,k} = ed_{i,j-1,k-1} + |c_k - p_i|, \ 1 \leq j \leq 4y_i \tag{8}$$

The optimality of equation (8) can be proven by a simple induction analysis. The *MIN* function then selects the minimum one from all qualifying sub-states and propagates it to the initial sub-state of its successor $CCR_{i+1}$ via an inter-state transition (denoted as dotted arrow), i.e., the following equation:

$$ed_{i+1,0,k} = min (ed_{i,y_i,k} , \ldots, ed_{i,4y_i,k}), 1 \leq i \leq n-1 \tag{9}$$

This way, $CCR_{i+1}$ will base its processing on the best result of the past, and therefore the basis of the induction analysis for $CCR_{i+1}$ holds. Combined together, equation (8) and (9) guarantee the optimality of all calculated edit distance values, and hence the correctness of the proposed algorithm shown in Figure 3. To improve the readability of the pseudo-code, we introduce the following two variables:

$$curr\_min_{i,k} = min (ed_{i,y_i,k} , \ldots, ed_{i,4y_i,k}), \text{ and} \tag{10}$$

$$overall\_min_{i,k} = min(curr\_min_{i,1}, \ldots, curr\_min_{i,k}). \tag{11}$$

The semantic meaning of these two variables can be better illustrated in the case of $i = n$, i.e., the final CCR of $R_n$. At cycle $k$, different substrings ending with $c_k$ may make different matching progress towards the end of $R_n$, and those that successfully propagated to qualifying sub-states of $CCR_n$ can claim an approximate match with their associated edit costs, i.e., $ed_{n,y_n,k}$, ..., or $ed_{n,4y_n,k}$. Among them, the minimum one is selected as $curr\_min_{n,k}$ and the minimum of $curr\_min_{n,k}$ over all $k$ cycles are selected as $overall\_min_{n,k}$, which by definition is the edit distance between $R_n$ and $S_k$ in overlapped matching mode, because it is the minimum chosen from all possible substrings of $S_k$. The semantic meaning of the two variables for cases of $i < n$ can then be understood in a similar way, by regarding $CCR_i$ as the final CCR of regexp $R_i$. Finally, $overall\_min_{n,m}$ is the edit distance between user query regexp $R_n$ and database MID string $S_m$.

| | |
|---|---|
| (1) | $ed_{1,0,0} = 0$ ; //By equation (7) |
| (2) | All other $ed_{i,j,0} = SYS\_MAX$; // The maximum value |
| (3) | //allowed in the system |
| (4) | $overall\_ed_{i,0} = SYS\_MAX$     for $1 \leq i \leq n$; |
| (5) | foreach ($c_k$ of $S_m$)   { |
| (6) |      $ed_{1,0,k} = 0$;                //By equation (7) |
| (7) |      for ($i = 1$; $i \leq n$; $i$++) {    //Iterate through CCRs |
| (8) |          for($j = 1$; $j \leq 4y_i$; $j$++) { //Iterate through sub-states |
| (9) |              $ed_{i,j,k} = ed_{i,j-1,k-1} + |c_k - p_i|$; // By equation (8) |
| (10) |          } |
| (11) |          $curr\_min_{i,k} = min (ed_{i,y_i,k} , \ldots, ed_{i,4y_i,k})$; |
| (12) |          $overall\_min_{i,k} = min(overall\_min_{i,k-1}, curr\_min_{i,k})$; |
| (13) |          for($j = 0$; $j \leq 4y_i$; $j$++) { //Store current cycle ed |
| (14) |              $ed_{i,j,k-1} = ed_{i,j,k}$;    // to previous cycle ed, for |
| (15) |          }                  //use of next cycle |
| (16) |          if ($i < n$) |
| (17) |              $ed_{i+1,0,k} = curr\_min_{i,k}$ ; //By equation (9) |
| (18) |      } |
| (19) | } |
| (20) | Report $overall\_min_{n,m}$ as the edit distance |

**Figure 3. Pseudo Code of AREM algorithm**

### 3.2 Parallelization of AREM

Note from line (9) of Figure 3 that the edit distance value of a sub-state at cycle $k$ is solely dependent on its direct predecessor sub-state's edit distance values at cycle $k-1$, and the input character $c_k$. Because $c_k$ is broadcasted to all sub-states, they can update their edit distance values concurrently, a favorable manner for FPGA implementation using Verilog non-blocking assignments. However, several other issues have to be taken into account before the algorithm is implemented in FPGA for hardware acceleration. Firstly, different CCRs may have different constraint repetitions, and therefore the *MIN* function at line (11) may have different number of inputs. This leads to different execution path and time for CCRs, which makes their synchronization very difficult. Secondly, when the FPGA needs to implement a new user query, its regexp structures need to be reflected in the hardware description language (HDL) code as new logic functions, due to the changes in the number of sub-states and the way to loop through them. This translates to rerun of the synthesis, map, place and route process of the entire system for each new user query, which usually takes hours of time to finish. As such, the wait time for the end user is intolerable.

We can solve both problems by restructuring the CCR based regexp into a modular format, where all CCRs have the same constraint repetition. This way, all CCRs will have the same number of sub-states, and they can share the same MIN and loop functions. Recall that $CCR_i$ is in the format of $p_i\{y_i,4y_i\}$, where the upper bound of the constraint repetition is always four times the lower bound. Therefore, we propose to use $p_i\{1,4\}$ as an atomic and modular building block. This way, we can break the original "molecule" CCR into a sequence of "atom" CCRs denoted as ACCR. All ACCRs share the same architecture and logic functions, and they are only different in the acceptable characters, which however can be stored in registers.

This leads to a modular, parameterized design where the parameters (acceptable characters) of ACCRs can be rapidly updated to implement a new regexp, without modifying their underlying logic functions. The time-consuming reconfiguration process can therefore be avoided by pre-implementing a system of ACCR modules at a one-time cost, a tremendous value for time-sensitive scenarios such as the MIR system.

# 4. IMPLEMENTATION

In this section we will describe the co-design details of a software/hardware system consisting of a frontend PC and a backend FPGA. The PC generates the database MID strings and converts the user sung query to an ACCR-based regexp, as described in previous sections. The FPGA implements the *melody matching engine* (*MME*), a modular architecture composed of pre-implemented ACCRs. The database MID strings are transferred to the FPGA's onboard DDR2 memory, and the query regexp can be implemented by MME through fast parameter updates. This way, the most computation-intensive works, i.e., calculations of edit distances between regexp and strings, are offloaded to FPGA for hardware acceleration. The calculated results are returned back to PC, and the 10 MIDI files with top-10 smallest edit distances are reported to the user as the retrieved songs. Details of the FPGA implementation and its integration with PC end are discussed in subsection 4.1 and 4.2, respectively.

## 4.1 FPGA End

A major design goal when designing MME is the reconfiguration time to implement a new user query, because the response time for an end user includes both regexp-updating and regexp-matching time. This is different from traditional FPGA designs where the objective is usually timing performance. For this matter, we developed a modular architecture for MME to support fast reconfiguration, where an ACCR engine is designed in subsection 4.1.1 as the general implementation of an arbitrary ACCR term, and an array of ACCR engines is pre-implemented to

accommodate an arbitrary ACCR-based regexp. To eliminate the confusion when discussing the relationship between the algorithm and its implementation, we use *ACCR term* to denote its regexp model, and *ACCR engine* to denote its hardware implementation.

### 4.1.1 ACCR Engine

An $ACCR_i$ engine implements the behavior of an $ACCR_i$ term, which is in the form of $p_i\{1,4\}$. Its internal architecture is illustrated in Figure 4, which contains five edit distance registers to store $ed_{i,0,k}$, ... , and $ed_{i,4,k}$, respectively, a *curr_min$_i$* register to store the minimum of edit distances at the current cycle, and a *overall_min$_i$* register to store the minimum of *curr_min$_i$* over all cycles. These registers store runtime variables which will be dynamically updated as the matching proceeds. In addition, $ACCR_i$ engine also contains static parameter registers $p_i$ to store its acceptable character, $i$ to store its index in the query regexp $R_n$, and $n$ to store the number of ACCR terms in $R_n$. The latter two parameters together determine if $ACCR_i$ engine is implementing the final $ACCR_n$ term, and accordingly it should either report its *curr_min$_i$* to its successor for future processing, or report its *overall_min$_i$* as the final result. Beyond these registers, $ACCR_i$ also contains functional units, such as a subtractor to calculate the substitution edit cost, four adders to implement equation (8), and a comparator tree to implement the *MIN* function of equation (9). The MIN function is implemented in combinational logic so that the *curr_min$_i$* can be calculated at the same cycle after ($ed_{i,1,k}$, ... , $ed_{i,4,k}$) are updated. It will then be propagated to $ed_{i+1,0,k}$ of its successor $ACCR_{i+1}$ for further processing from the next cycle on. This way, $ACCR_i$ will update its edit distance registers, finish the MIN function, and propagates *curr_min$_i$* to its successor in a single cycle time, so that at the next cycle all ACCR engines can process the input character in parallel.

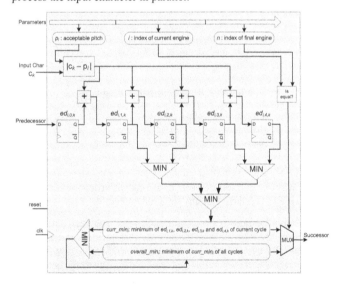

**Figure 4. Architecture of ACCR$_i$ engine**

Note that the edit distance counters $ed_{i,0,k-1}$ , ... , $ed_{i,3,k-1}$ (which store edit distance values of last cycle) are essential for line (9) of Figure 3, because otherwise an edit distance value will be updated by its predecessor sub-state before its old value is used to update its successor sub-state, i.e., a race condition. However, they can be safely removed in the $ACCR_i$ engine, because edit distance values are stored in flip-flops and can be updated by non-blocking assignments in parallel, without race conditions.

The ACCR$_i$ engine reads its parameter configurations from a register file, implemented in Block RAM (BRAM), using $i$ as the address. All ACCR engines will be reset after receiving an input character of '\n', the delimiter of database MID strings, so that MME can start matching a new melody.

### 4.1.2 Melody Matching Engine

With its general and modular design, we can pre-implement an array of $t$ ACCR engines to build a modular melody matching engine (MME) as shown in Figure 5. An appropriate value for MME size $t$ will be determined later in subsection 5.2.

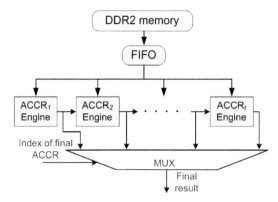

**Figure 5. Architecture of MME**

The database MID strings are stored in high-density on-board DDR2 memory for fast access, and each character is broadcasted to all ACCR engines for parallel processing. The database MID strings are read in sequence, in which mode the DDR2 memory can achieve peak throughput as this access pattern does not have command conflicts or bank conflicts. The DDR2 memory controller works at a clock frequency different from that of the ACCR engines, and we used a FIFO to address the meta-stability issue [35] caused by signal transitions across different clock domains.

The MME architecture can accommodate query regexps of different lengths, because all ACCR engines share the same architecture and they are all capable of implementing the final ACCR$_n$ term of R$_n$. A multiplexer is employed to locate the final ACCR$_n$ engine and take the appropriate *overall_min$_n$* value as final result, using $n$ as the selection signal.

A problem naturally arises for regexps of more than $t$ ACCR terms, which exceeds the capacity of MME. In such circumstances, we will sort the CCR terms of the regexp in ascending order by their constraint repetition, before we break the CCR-based regexp into ACCR sequence. CCR terms with smaller constraint repetitions (which represent user sung notes with shorter durations) will be trimmed off until the resultant regexp contains no more than $t$ ACCRs. This is justified by the fact that short notes of the user query are more likely to be noises or irregular sounds, and therefore carry less essential musical information than longer notes do.

The proposed MME is a modular architecture, where all ACCR engines work concurrently in parallel to provide substantial speedup compared to software implementations, while at the same time they can be easily and rapidly reconfigured by reading new parameters from on-chip Block RAM. This way, MME can achieve both hardware-level speed and software-level flexibility.

## 4.2 Integration with PC End

The PC side is responsible for all frontend works, including user interface, database MID string generation, and user query parsing. The flow diagram of the integrated software/hardware system is shown in Figure 6, where the right hand side bounded by dotted box is implemented in FPGA, while all other steps are running on the PC. We adopted SIRC (Simple Interface for Reconfigurable Computing) [36] as the communication framework between PC and FPGA. SIRC is developed by Microsoft as an attempt to ease the usage of the raw Ethernet functionality provided by the FPGA board, and it frees researchers from the burdens of building low level software drivers and hardware interface logics, so that they can focus more on the high level system functions. On the hardware side, it utilizes on-chip BRAM to implement three fast buffers, namely the input buffer to store the input data transferred from PC, the parameter buffer to store MME's parameter configurations, and the output buffer to store the calculated results. SIRC provides a set of hardware application programming interfaces (API) to read data from and write data to these buffers. MME starts processing after receiving the *start* signal from PC, and it triggers a *done* signal after finishing processing. On the software side, SIRC also provides a set of APIs to send data to input buffer and parameter buffers, retrieve data from output buffer, send *start* command, and detect *done* signal.

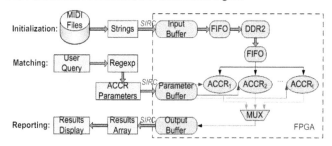

**Figure 6. System flow chart**

In the initialization phase, the database MIDI files are processed as discussed in subsection 2.1, and the resultant strings are downloaded into the input buffer in multiple batches, because the input buffer is not big enough to accommodate the entire database. All batches are further transferred to DDR2 memory and reassembled back there as a whole. SIRC hardware API and DDR2 memory controller work at different clock frequencies and the resultant meta-stability issue is addressed by using a FIFO.

In the matching phase, the user sung query is parsed into a regexp of $n$ ACCR terms as discussed in subsection 2.2 and 3.2, and the parameters of each ACCR$_i$ term including its acceptable pitch $p_i$, index $i$, and the index of the final ACCR term $n$ are encapsulated into a packet and sent over to the parameter buffer. MME will read parameters to update each ACCR engine, start processing the database MID strings, and finally write edit distance results into the output buffer.

In the reporting phase, edit distance results stored in the output buffer are retrieved by PC, and the MIDI songs with top-10 minimum edit distances are reported to the user as the retrieval results, i.e., they are the 10 most possible songs that the user has sung.

Through the high speed Gigabit Ethernet, MME can update its database music rapidly, and a new user query (typically several hundred bytes) can be downloaded and implemented in almost real time. By storing the database locally, MME forms a self-contained system and its communication with PC is minimized. Therefore MME is a highly-scalable architecture, and many FPGAs can be easily clustered together to serve multiple user queries simultaneously, with virtually no overhead.

# 5. EXPERIMENTS

We conducted experiments in this section to evaluate the performance of the proposed system in terms of both accuracy and speed. The PC end software runs on an Intel Xeon quad core CPU working at 2.8 GHz with 16GB of DDR3 memory, and the FPGA end is implemented on the popular XUPV5 evaluation board with Virtex 5 LX110T (69120 registers and LUTs) FPGA chip and 256 MB DDR2 memory. Synthesis results will be discussed in subsection 5.1 to show the FPGA device utilization of MME. We then tune the parameters in subsection 5.2 to determine the appropriate values for frame length $l$, average-pitch variation threshold $k$, and MME size $t$. Finally, accuracy and speed performance of the proposed system are given and compared with related works in subsection 5.3.

## 5.1 Synthesis Results

The Verilog codes of ACCR engine and MME are synthesized, mapped, placed and routed by Xilinx ISE design suite 10.1, and the reports show that each ACCR engine utilizes 57 slice registers and 159 slice LUTs and can run at 100MHz. With the SIRC hardware interface and DDR2 memory controller altogether utilizing around 4% of the chip area, the Virtex 5 LX110T device can implement a total of 300 ACCR engines at an occupancy ratio of 87%.

The time spent on each step of the implementation process is reported in Table 2, from which we can see that the total implementation time of the FPGA end takes around 9 hours to finish. Although newer versions of the ISE software are able to utilize multiple cores to do the mapping, placing and routing works, it still requires hours of time to finish. The implementation time can become even longer if the design approaches the chip's capacity, or if the developer wants to push the performance to its limit.

**Table 2. Implementation time of MME**

| Implementation Step | Run Time |
| --- | --- |
| Synthesis | 19 minutes |
| Map | 2 hours and 15 minutes |
| Place & Route | 6 hours and 19 minutes |

The time-consuming implementation process is inevitable for reconfiguration of traditional FPGA designs, where the HDL source codes need to be modified to reflect the design changes. However, this re-compilation of source code can be circumvented for MME due to its parameterized modular design, and it can be reconfigured to implement a new regexp by simply updating its parameter registers. This is a tremendous value for application scenarios where the functions to be implemented on FPGA regularly change, a category that content-based MIR systems fall into exactly.

## 5.2 Parameters Tuning

In this subsection we tune the previously defined variables, i.e., frame length $l$, average-pitch variation threshold $k$, and MME size $t$, to achieve the best retrieval accuracy. The retrieval accuracy is tested using ThinkIT's corpus [37] which includes 355 WAV files as user queries and 106 ground truth MIDI files. We further include 5463 MIDI files from the Essen [38] collection as noises, generating a database of 5569 MIDI files. The user sung queries may start anywhere in their original melodies, not necessarily from the beginning. We used the top-10 hit rate as the accuracy metric, where the user query is said to be successfully retrieved if its original melody is in the reported top-10 most similar MIDI files, and the top-10 hit rate is counted as the percentage of successfully retrieved queries over all 355 user queries.

We first tune the average-pitch variation threshold $k$, with the frame length $l$ set to 20 milliseconds (sufficiently small to capture most music information of the user query) and the MME size $t$ set to include all 300 ACCR engines (sufficiently large to accommodate most user query regexps). The retrieval accuracy increases along with $k$ as shown in Figure 7, due to the increasing regexp search space. However, the accuracy improvement becomes negligible when $k$ is increased beyond 4, implying that the search space is saturated. Therefore, we determine the value of $k$ to be 4, so that the search space is properly bounded while still guaranteeing high retrieval accuracy.

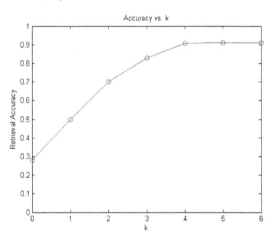

**Figure 7. Average-pitch Variation Threshold vs. Accuracy**

We then conducted experiments to study how frame length parameter $l$ affects the retrieval accuracy, and the results are shown in Figure 8. Generally speaking, a smaller frame length is more favorable than a bigger one, because the prior one is capable of capturing more musical details while the latter one may miss some essential musical information, especially for fast-rhythm melodies with many short notes. The downside of short frame length is the bigger resultant database size, and hence longer retrieval time. We can observe from Figure 8 that retrieval accuracy will not be further improved for frame lengths under 100 milliseconds, because they are beyond the shortest note distinguishable by the end user. Therefore, we chose 100 milliseconds as the frame length, so that we can minimize the database size to improve retrieval speed while at the same time retaining high retrieval accuracy.

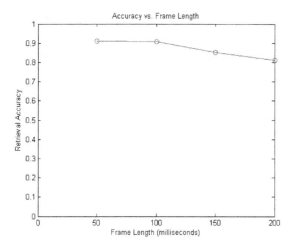

**Figure 8. Frame Length vs. Accuracy**

Finally, in most cases the user singing query is around 10 seconds including the silent parts. With the frame length set to 100 milliseconds, the resultant query regexp will contain around 100 ACCR terms, and therefore we set the MME size to 100. When the user query is too long to fit MME, it will be trimmed using the strategy discussed in subsection 4.1.2. This way, the 300 ACCR engines implemented on FPGA can be grouped into 3 MMEs running in parallel, each of which can implement one query regexp variant. With average-pitch variation threshold set to 4, all the 9 variants of the user query can be processed in 3 rounds.

## 5.3 Performance Evaluation and Comparison

We then tested the system performance using the parameters determined in the previous subsection. To summarize, the database of 5569 MID files are converted into strings stored in a plaintext file of 1.62 Megabytes, and each user query is parsed and average-pitch shifted into 9 regexp variants, each of which contains no more than 100 ACCR terms. On the FPGA side, 3 MMEs run in parallel, and it takes 3 rounds to finish processing of all 9 variants of the user query. Through the high speed Gigabit Ethernet, the database can be downloaded onto FPGA in less than 15 milliseconds, and the user query regexp parameters (several hundred bytes) can be transferred to the parameter buffer in almost real time. We then feed the query regexps of all 355 user sung WAV files into the MMEs for retrieval, and the total runtime for all queries as well as the average runtime for each query are listed in Table 3.

**Table 3. Retrieval Time**

|  | Total | Average |
|---|---|---|
| runtime | 19.4 seconds | 54.6 milliseconds |

Theoretically, for each user query the system needs to process a total of $1.62 \times 3 = 4.86$ Megabytes worth of data, which can be done in 48.6 milliseconds as the MME works at 100 MHz. This is very close to the actual performance shown in Table 3, which additionally includes the parameters downloading and results reporting phases.

We then compare the performance of the proposed system with related works selected from Music Information Retrieval Evaluation eXchange (MIREX) [39]. MIREX is a platform for researchers to present their state-of-the-art music retrieval related algorithms, and also a framework for formal evaluation of such algorithms. We selected several competitive algorithms from past sessions and compare their retrieval accuracy (top-10 hit rate) and runtime with MME in Table 4. Speedups of MME compared to these algorithms are also listed in the rightmost column.

**Table 4. Performance Comparison**

| Method | Platform | Runtime | Accuracy | Speedup |
|---|---|---|---|---|
| CSJ2 [40] | Dual Intel Xeon Quad Core @ 2.0 GHz with 24 GB memory | 210 minutes | 86% | 649X |
| HAFR1 [41] | Dual AMD Opteron Quad Core @ 2.0 GHz with 32 GB memory | 247 minutes | 80.6% | 764X |
| YF2 [41] | Intel Core 2 Quad Core @ 2.40GHz with 8GB memory | 367 minutes | 90.4% | 1135X |
| MME | XUPV5 FPGA @ 100MHz with 256 MB memory | 19.4 seconds | 90.7% | 1X |

The most accurate solution reported in MIREX is proposed by Yeh and Fang [41] using a partial linear scaling method. It achieves retrieval accuracy of 90.4%, similar to that of MME but 1135X times slower. As can be seen from Table 4, all software based systems need tens of seconds for the retrieval of one user query, which is an unacceptable response time for real world MIR systems. In contrast, the proposed FPGA-based MME can return the retrieval result in just 50 milliseconds.

## 6. CONCLUSION

In this paper we proposed an FPGA-based parallel architecture for fast content-based music melody matching. The database MIDI files are modeled into strings and the user sung query is modeled as regexp composed of ACCR terms. We designed an approximate matching algorithm to calculate the edit distance between an ACCR-based regexp and an input string, where the ACCR terms can run in parallel. The algorithm is implemented in FPGA as a melody matching engine (MME) for hardware acceleration. MME is a modular architecture composed of ACCR engines, each of which implements the functionality of an ACCR term. This way, MME can implement a new user query by simple updating the ACCR engines' parameters, avoiding the time-consuming re-implementation of the source code. The relatively self-contained structure of MME makes it highly-scalable, and multiple FPGA can be easily clustered together to achieve more parallel processing power. Our experiments show that the proposed modeling can accurately capture the musical essence of both database melodies and user queries, and achieves a top-10 hit rate of 90.7%. Moreover, MME can process a user query in just 54.6 milliseconds, a significant speedup compared to software-based solutions. In conclusion, MME is a highly efficient, flexible, and scalable content-based MIR system.

## 7. REFERENCES

[1] http://en.wikipedia.org/wiki/Query_by_humming

[2] M. A. Casey, R. Veltkamp, M. Goto, M. Leman, C. Rhodes, and M. Slaney, "Content-Based Music Information Retrieval: Current Directions and Future Challenges", Proceedings of the IEEE, 2008.

[3] R. Typke, F. Wiering, and R. C. Veltkamp, "A Survey of Music Information Retrieval Systems", ISMIR 2005.

[4] N. Orio, "Music Retrieval: A Tutorial and Review", Foundations and Trends® in Information Retrieval, Vol. 1, No. 1, pp 1-90, 2006.

[5] J. Pickens, "Feature Selection for Polyphonic Music Retrieval", SIGIR 2001.

[6] J. Pickens, "Harmonic Models for Polyphonic Music Retrieval", CIKM 2002.

[7] S. Doraisamy and S. M. R üger, "An Approach Towards a Polyphonic Music Retrieval System", ISMIR 2001.

[8] http://en.wikipedia.org/wiki/MIDI

[9] L. R. Rabiner, "On the Use of Autocorrelation Analysis for Pitch Detection", IEEE Transactions on Acoustics, Speech, and Signal Processing, Vol. ASSP-25, No. 1, 1977

[10] A. d. Cheveigne´ and H. Kawahara, "YIN, a Fundamental Frequency Estimator for Speech and Music", The Journal of the Acoustical Society of America, 2002

[11] P. McLeod and G. Wyvill, "A Smart Way to Find Pitch", ICMC 2005.

[12] A. M. Noll, "Cepstrum Pitch Determination," Journal of the Acoustical Society of America, Vol. 41, No. 2, 1967

[13] A. Ghias, J. Logan, D. Chamberlin, and B. Smith, "Query By Humming: Musical Information Retrieval In an Audio Database", Proc of ACM Multimedia, 1995

[14] C.-C. Liu, J.-L. Hsu, and A. L.P. Chen, "An Approximate String Matching Algorithm for Content-Based Music Data Retrieval", ICMCS 1999.

[15] K. Lemström, "String Matching Techniques for Music Retrieval", PhD thesis, University of Helsinki, 2000

[16] Y.-H. Tseng, "Content-Based Retrieval for Music Collections", SIGIR 1999.

[17] S. Downie and M. Nelson, "Evaluation of a Simple and Effective Music Information Retrieval System", SIGIR 2000.

[18] B. Cui, H. V. Jagadish, B. C. Ooi, and K.-L. Tan, "Compacting Music Signatures for Efficient Music Retrieval", EDBT 2008.

[19] J. Shifrin, B. Pardo, C. Meek, and W. Birmingham, "HMM-Based Musical Query Retrieval," JCDL 2002.

[20] E. Unal, S. S. Narayanan, and E. Chew, "A Statistical Approach to Retrieval under User-dependent Uncertainty in Query-by-Humming Systems", MIR2004.

[21] N. H. Adams, M. A. Bartsch, and G. H. Wakefield, "Note Segmentation and Quantization for Music Information Retrieval", IEEE Transactions on Audio, Speech, and Language Processing, Vol. 14, No. 1, 2006

[22] Levenshtein VI. "Binary codes capable of correcting deletions, insertions, and reversals". *Soviet Physics Doklady*, 10: 707–10, 1966.

[23] J.-S. Jang, H.-R. Lee, and M.-Y. Kao, "Content-based Music Retrieval Using Linear Scaling and Branch-and-bound Tree Search", ICME 2001.

[24] P. Senin, "Dynamic Time Warping Algorithm Review", University of Hawaii at Manoa, Tech. Rep., 2008.

[25] Y. Zhu and D. Shasha, "Warping Indexes with Envelope Transforms for Query by Humming", SIGMOD 2003.

[26] X. Wu, M. Li, J. Liu, J. Yang, and Y. Yan, "A Top-down Approach to Melody Match in Pitch Contour for Query by Humming", ISCSLP 2006.

[27] G. P. Nam, T. T. T. Luong, H. H. Nam, K. R. Park, and S.-J. Park, "Intelligent Query by Humming System Based on Score Level Fusion of Multiple Classifiers", EURASIP Journal on Advances in Signal Processing, 2011.

[28] J.-S. Jang and H.-R. Lee, "Hierarchical Filtering Method for Content-based Music Retrieval via Acoustic Input", ACM Multimedia, 2001.

[29] L. Wang, S. Huang, S. Hu, J. Liang, and B. Xu, "An Efficient Method for Query by Humming System Based on Multi-Similarity Measurement Fusion", ICALIP 2008.

[30] R. B. Dannenberg, W. P. Birmingham, G. Tzanetakis, C. Meek, N. Hu, and B. Pardo, "The MUSART Testbed for Query-By-Humming Evaluation", ISMIR 2003.

[31] N. Hu and R. B. Dannenberg, "A Comparison of Melodic Database Retrieval Techniques Using Sung Queries", JCDL 2002.

[32] http://www.fourmilab.ch/webtools/midicsv/

[33] http://audition.ens.fr/adc/sw/yin.zip

[34] H. Wang, S. Pu, G. Knezek, and J.-C. Liu, "MIN-MAX: A Counter Based Algorithm for Regular Expression Matching", IEEE Transactions on Parallel and Distributed Systems, January 2013.

[35] Altera white paper, "Understanding Metastability in FPGAs", http://www.altera.com/literature/wp/wp-01082-quartus-ii-metastability.pdf

[36] K. Eguro, "SIRC: An Extensible Reconfigurable Computing Communication API", FCCM 2010.

[37] http://mirlab.org/dataSet/public/IOACAS_QBH_Coprus1.rar

[38] http://www.esac-data.org/

[39] http://www.music-ir.org/mirex/wiki/MIREX_HOME

[40] http://www.music-ir.org/mirex/wiki/2009:Query-by-Singing/Humming_Results

[41] http://www.music-ir.org/mirex/wiki/2010:Query-by-Singing/Humming_Results

[42] http://www.music-for-music-teachers.com/happy-birthday.html

# An FPGA Memcached Appliance

**Sai Rahul Chalamalasetti**
University of Massachusetts Lowell[§]
Hewlett Packard[‡]
Sairahul.Chalamalasetti@hp.com

**Alvin AuYoung**
Hewlett Packard Labs[†]
Alvin.Auyoung@hp.com

**Kevin Lim**
Hewlett Packard Labs[†]
Kevin.Lim2@hp.com

**Parthasarathy Ranganathan**
Hewlett Packard Labs[†]
Partha.Ranganathan@hp.com

**Mitch Wright**
Hewlett Packard[‡]
Mitch.Wright@hp.com

**Martin Margala**
University of Massachusetts Lowell[§]
Martin_Margala@uml.edu

## ABSTRACT

Providing low-latency access to large amounts of data is one of the foremost requirements for many web services. To address these needs, systems such as Memcached have been created which provide a distributed, all in-memory key-value store. These systems are critical and often deployed across hundreds or thousands of servers. However, these systems are not well matched for commodity servers, as they require significant CPU resources to achieve reasonable network bandwidth, yet the core Memcached functions do not benefit from the high performance of standard server CPUs.

In this paper, we demonstrate the design of an FPGA-based Memcached appliance. We take Memcached, a complex software system, and implement its core functionality on an FPGA. By leveraging the FPGA's design and utilizing its customizable logic to create a specialized appliance we are able to tightly integrate networking, compute, and memory. This integration allows us to overcome many of the bottlenecks found in standard servers. Our design provides performance on-par with baseline servers, but consumes only 9% of the power of the baseline. Scaled out, we see benefits at the data center level, substantially improving the performance-per-dollar while improving energy efficiency by 3.2X to 10.9X.

## Categories and Subject Descriptors

B.5.1 [**Design**]: Styles; D.3.2 [**Programming Languages**]: Java

## General Terms

Algorithms, Performance, Design

## Keywords

Memcached appliance; FPGA; Low Power; Energy Efficiency; Data Centers

## 1. INTRODUCTION

Today's web services generate an unprecedented amount of structured and unstructured data. Because service providers derive tremendous value from obtaining fast access to such data, it is critical to have the right infrastructure for data storage and retrieval. Scale-out technologies and key-value stores, such as Memcached, have become the de facto standard for deploying such infrastructure, as most of the largest content-serving systems rely on the ability to scale quickly in response to increasing client traffic and data generation.

One of the most fundamental aspects to Memcached is its all in-memory design. By solely utilizing memory, Memcached provides substantially lower latency data access than other comparable storage systems. This low-latency performance is critical for interactive web applications, evidenced by web service providers such as Facebook and Zynga dedicating an entire tier of servers to Memcached. More broadly, Memcached is representative of a growing shift towards scale-out, in-memory applications; including MonetDB, VoltDB, and HANA.

Memcached posts unique challenges to existing servers due to its architecture. Memcached is created to be a key-value cache that stores key-value pairs in a distributed hash table. Its goal is to provide a fast caching layer in-between a web server and its backend storage (e.g., a database running MySQL). It is geared towards caching small values and keys, often on the order of 200 bytes or smaller. Thus Memcached clients generate many small requests to the server, placing importance on the server's ability to handle and generate responses to many small packets. Despite the small key and value sizes, often each server has 10's to 100's of GB of memory, placing an importance on large memory capacities. On the other hand, Memcached is designed as a very simple cache which offers minimal functionality on its data, and thus does little computation.

Based on the Memcached characteristics, alternate architectures can offer benefits for both performance and efficiency. There has been some prior work looking at alternate CPU and GPU architectures for Memcached, showing promise [1]. Unlike prior work, we address the bottlenecks by designing a system that more fundamentally addresses Memcached requirements of tightly integrated networking and memory coupled with light compute: we instead utilize an FPGA to implement a Memcached appliance. We leverage the FPGA to provide specialized logic to implement the base functionality of the Memcached server, consisting of accepting requests, finding the requested key-value pair, and performing the requested get or set operation.

To convert the Memcached software to an FPGA implementation we address several challenges, including handling high network rates, variable length keys and values, and dynamic memory allocation. We show that an implementation is feasible, and through its integration and specialization achieves comparable peak performance to a standard server while consuming only 9% of its power. At datacenter scale, an FPGA Memcached appliance can provide up to 5.9X performance-per-TCO-$ improvement versus existing servers by providing high performance, low power alternatives.

Sai Rahul Chalamalasetti worked on this research project while he was a summer intern in Hewlett Packard.

[§]1 University Avenue, Lowell, MA, USA, [†] 11445 Compaq Center West Drive, Houston, TX

[‡] 1501 Page Mill Road, Palo Alto, CA

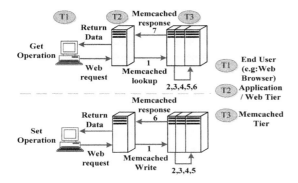

Figure 1: Memcached architectural diagram and use case

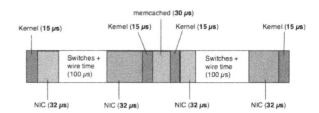

Figure 2: Latency bottleneck analysis on a standard server [6]

The rest of the paper is organized as follows. Section 2 provides a background on the Memcached software and key bottlenecks. Section 3 provides motivation behind implementing Memcached on an FPGA. Section 4 goes into our detailed Memcached appliance design description. Section 5 provides an evaluation of the performance and power of the appliance, and its impact at the datacenter level. Section 6 discusses future work, and Section 7 discusses related work. Section 8 concludes the paper.

## 2. BACKGROUND

### 2.1 Memcached overview

Memcached is an in-memory distributed data cache primarily used at the application-layer of a Web stack. Many large and well-known content-serving systems such as Facebook, Google App Server, Twitter, Flickr, Zynga, and Wikipedia rely on Memcached to alleviate the load on their back-end databases and provide clients with low-latency and high-throughput access to content.

Given its critical role in so many Web 2.0 infrastructures, Memcached is an important application to consider in the class of Web 2.0 workloads. A typical deployment places a cluster of Memcached servers in between the Web (or application) tier and back-end database. The Memcached servers are used by the Web tier to cache popular objects, such as pre-processed text, images, session state, or page counters, which would have otherwise been retrieved from the database directly, possibly via disk I/O. Based on public and inferred numbers, Memcached clusters can vary in size from as small as 30 physical machines to thousands of machines with a significant memory footprint.

A Memcached cluster provides a lightweight, distributed *hash table* for storing small objects (up to 1 MB), exposing a simple set/get interface. Each object's key is used to determine which individual Memcached server within the cluster will store the object. Typically, a hash function is chosen to balance keys evenly across the cluster [2]. Individual Memcached servers do not communicate with each other, as each server is responsible for its own independent range of keys. Because the servers do not interact, the performance of a single Memcached server can be used to generalize the behavior of an entire cluster.

Due to its simplicity, Memcached is the de facto standard for distributed caching, and is used extensively. In fact, it plays such a critical role in Web infrastructures that larger deployments, such as those of Zynga and Facebook, dedicate physical servers to run *only* Memcached [3,4]. Therefore designing better performing and more cost-effective servers for Memcached workloads can offer significant benefits.

### 2.2 Memcached architecture in-depth

Figure 1 illustrates the Memcached architecture and how it is used in web infrastructures. Memcached provides a simple set of commands for accessing data, with the two most dominant commands being get and set [5]; other commands, for example, include add, increment, and compare and swap. Gets and sets have ratios of up to 30:1 gets:sets seen in real world deployments [5]. Below we review the access paths for get and set commands.

**Get:** A get will retrieve the value associated with the user-specified key, if it is located in the Memcached server. If it is not found, it is up to the user to determine where to obtain the proper value. (Typically a miss will then lead to a database lookup and/or recomputation to determine the appropriate value.) A requesting client first determines which Memcached server to access. A key, which can potentially be an ASCII string up to 250 characters long, is sent to the server in a message including the command (get), the key length, and any optional message flags.

A get performs the following steps: 1. The request is received at the network interface and is sent to the CPU. 2. The Memcached server will read the data out of the request packet to identify the key. 3. The server performs a hash on the key value to translate the key into a fixed 32 bit value. 4. The value is used to index into a hash table that stores the key-value pairs. 5. If the key is found, its value data is accessed and prepared to be sent back to the client in a response message. 6. The entry corresponding to the key is also promoted in a doubly linked list that is used to perform least recently used (LRU) replacement if the Memcached server is full. 7. The server either sends out a reply to the client with the key-value pair, or a message indicating that the key was not found.

**Set:** A set will write the specified key-value pair into the Memcached server's storage. Values are typically small objects, often a few hundred bytes large. To handle memory management, Memcached uses *slab allocation*. In slab allocation, Memcached allocates a large chunk of memory and breaks it up into smaller segments of a fixed size according to the slab class' size. This method of allocation reduces the overhead of dynamically allocating and deallocating many small objects. Memory is therefore handled in fixed sizes, with values stored in the smallest slab class that will accommodate the size of value. (Thus there may be some internal fragmentation per object.) When storing a new value, the LRU list for the slab class is checked to see if the last element can be evicted. If there are no free segments within a slab class, a new slab is allocated if there is free memory.

A set performs the following steps: 1. The request is received at the network interface and is sent to the CPU. 2. The server will read the data from the packet to identify the key, value, flags, and total message size. 3. The server then requests a slot from the correct slab memory class to store the key-value pair. The item is promoted to the most recently used position of the slab's LRU list. 4. After copying the data into the slab element, the server performs a hash on the key to determine the hash bucket to store the data. 5. The data is written to the head of the hash bucket. 6. A reply is sent back to the client to indicate the request is completed.

## 2.3 Bottlenecks

As described in the previous section, Memcached servers primarily handle network requests, perform hash table lookups, and access data. This design implies that network latency is quite important, as is providing fast access to memory. Figure 2 shows previously profiled [6] Memcached latency breakdowns on modern servers. To gain additional insight into Memcached performance, we performed similar tests using stress test clients that send a mixture of 40:1 gets:sets, trying to achieve the maximum throughput possible.

**Performance:** Both the prior analysis and our performance analysis show that there is significant time spent in the networking stack, and in calculating the hash values of the keys. In general the CPU shows poor utilization (low IPC), despite thousands of requests per second being processed, and spends most of its time processing work other than the core Memcached functions.

The results highlight some of the key bottlenecks present in current Memcached systems. Most of the network processing, for example TCP/UDP, is carried out in the software stack. In a Memcached application, requests initiate from web application servers. Due to its architecture with many small, cached objects, multiple web application servers will generate millions of requests, which results in the Memcached server spending most of its processing time to handle and keep track of the requests. For example, a study from RAMCloud research by Stanford [6] has shown the distribution of latencies over the whole Memcached packet processing, where 64 $\mu s$ is spent for transferring packet from Network Interface Card, 30 $\mu s$ on the Linux software stack, and merely 30$\mu s$ on the Memcached software. To measure network latency numbers specifically for UDP, we carried out a test between two servers, with one acting as client, and another as the Memcached server. Our tests showed that the NIC plus Linux UDP processing took 25$\mu s$ for sending, and another 25$\mu s$ for responding back to client. Both results confirm that network processing is a major bottleneck for Memcached servers.

**Power:** Our measured baseline server has two Intel Xeon CPUs (12 cores total) with 64 GB of DRAM. It consumes 258W of total power, of which 190W of power is distributed between the two CPUs in the system. The rest of 64W and 8W is consumed by DRAM memory, and 1GbE Ethernet NIC. Compared to the total system utilization, the CPU consumes a disproportionate amount of power. It is therefore one of the biggest challenges to achieving better energy efficiency for Memcached servers.

**Low-power systems:** While low power Atom or ARM systems may seem like an ideal alternative, our experiments with an Atom-based system showed it only achieved 8-12% of the performance of the Xeon system, largely due to its inability to handle the high network rates. As the overall performance-energy efficiency is lower than our baseline system, we only consider our Xeon server in the rest of the paper.

## 3. UTILIZING FPGAS FOR MEMCACHED
## 3.1 Opportunities for an FPGA appliance

Based on the discussion in the previous section, it is apparent that existing servers are not well matched for Memcached. Instead we consider alternate architectures that can have both better performance and better energy efficiency than existing servers. We specifically design an FPGA Memcached appliance where the networking, compute, and memory are tightly integrated and software overhead is removed. By appliance we refer to a system

that specifically performs the Memcached protocol, as opposed to a general purpose server.

An FPGA has several advantages versus a traditional CPU; one of the foremost is power consumption. It is difficult to reduce CPU power as static power of processors is growing as transistors become smaller. The millions of transistors required to implement multiple cores in a general purpose processor affect the total power consumption of the system, and based on our Memcached analysis, do not provide significant performance benefits. Another drawback of traditional CPUs is their high frequency of operation (2-3 GHz), which is directly proportional to dynamic power consumption. Conversely, an FPGA can be customized for the application being run, providing high performance without needing general purpose processors or high clock frequencies.

FPGAs also offer a means to reduce the network latency. The study from Stanford on latencies of transferring packets from network to Memcached software illustrated that 50% and 25% of total processing time is spent on NIC transfer and the software stack, respectively. Thus network processing latency is currently a significant bottleneck. One option is to replace the software stack functionality in hardware by using Offload Engines (OEs), such as TCP/IP or UDP OE. However, a solution of directly augmenting OEs to a NIC card would only increase performance by 25%. An efficient hardware interface to server CPUs is needed to address the major portion of NIC interface latency.

In our approach, we propose to bring the main Memcached application *closer* to the NIC and OE so that we can decrease the 75% network-related latency that CPU systems suffer. We map the NIC, OE and Memcached application running all together on a single FPGA. Since, FPGAs are traditionally used for networking applications, such as switches, routers, and flow control, etc., we leverage the FPGA devices and network connections on our FPGA board. Due to the maturity of FPGA devices in networking applications, Ethernet IPs to communicate with the MAC and read Ethernet frames are readily available.

## 3.2 Key Implementation Challenges

Despite FPGAs providing many solutions to problems that are encountered by contemporary CPU systems, a direct replacement of CPU system with a standalone FPGA is a cumbersome task. One main reason is the use of high level programming languages and tool chains for CPU systems which are designed to ease programming burden and quickly allow users to check the operation of the written application. On the other hand, FPGAs are mainly programmable through hardware description languages (such as VHDL/Verilog), which take a longer time to design and test on the board. Even though many alternatives such as C to gates, Impulse C, Mitrion-C, etc. have been proposed, they do not effectively optimize the algorithm to be mapped on the hardware. Therefore implementing applications in an FPGA must be done on relatively mature software that has wide-spread adoption to justify the programming overhead.

Apart from programming support, the other challenge of porting software code written for CPUs to FPGAs is the direct portability of software algorithms to FPGA hardware. Therefore, alternative, FPGA-friendly solutions have to be devised and implemented. For example, Memcached uses Least Recently Used (LRU) replacement policy to select data to be replaced when its capacity is full. These LRU lists are maintained using a doubly linked list, a structure that is not efficiently implementable on hardware or FPGAs. Therefore, an alternative replacement algorithm must be used in our designs. There are several other similar algorithm challenges faced throughout the Memcached appliance, such as

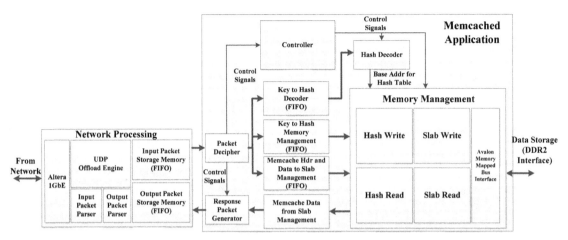

Figure 3: Overall FPGA Memcached appliance architecture

handling the variable length data sizes normally handled by dynamic slab allocation. Doing dynamic memory allocation of varying sizes is difficult in hardware, and thus we designed the system to enable the user to specify at run time the number of slabs to use, and utilize power of 2 sizes for the slab classes.

Lastly, FPGAs do not achieve the multi-GHz frequency of a general purpose processor. Thus any designs implemented on an FPGA must be carefully programmed to take advantage of the parallelism and support for complex operations that FPGAs offer.

## 4. FPGA MEMCACHED DESIGN DETAILS

### 4.1 FPGA Appliance Overview

The proposed system shown in Figure 3 depicts the block level diagram of our FPGA-based standalone Memcached appliance architecture. Our design consists of two main blocks: a networking block and a Memcached application block, along with an Altera TSE MAC for Ethernet interface, and a DDR2 memory controller interface to store cache data in DRAM modules. Our current design is implemented on an Altera Terasic DE-4 board.

The Memcached system transfers command and data between machines through an Ethernet interface. Hence, in our system initially the command or data packets received on 1Gbit Ethernet port are forwarded to a MAC IP module. The data from the MAC is then transferred to the network *offload engine* (OE), which parses through the input packet flow to detect relevant packets, and transmits required Memcached command and data to later stages by extracting packet header and user data information. The offload engine module is also used to generate the response packets with the data from the Memcached appliance. After the received packet is available from the OE, the data is stored on the FPGA internal memory in a FIFO so that continuous requests from multiple application clients will not be discarded while a prior user command request is being processed.

Subsequent to the OE receiving the network packet and placing it in the FIFO, an *input packet parser* module is then used to read the packet data to distinguish between different operations, for example get and set. Because the Memcached packet format in the Ethernet packet varies with the type of operation, the parser module is used to extract the relevant data needed to complete the requested operation. The parser signals the main controller to start executing the user command when the complete packet data is parsed and stored.

Following the packet parser, the controller signals and monitors the hash decoder and memory management modules in tandem depending on the received command. The hash decoder performs a hash on the key sent by the client and determines the specific address of the requested item in the hash table. Once the address for a specific hash table location is determined, the controller will perform the respective operation depending on the read or write request from the client. The memory management module is responsible for allocating memory to items as they are written to the Memcached storage, or reading data from memory for get operations. In particular Memcached uses slab allocation, which allocates memory in large chunks based on fixed, pre-defined sizes, to help speed allocation of many small (often <1 KB) objects. The memory management either finds items to replace or allocates new memory on writes, if available.

Any data that needs to be sent back to the client is written into a response packet, which is then handled by an *output packet parser* module. In the case of set operations, these responses are a simple "complete" message, and in the case of get operations that do not find a key, they are a simple "miss" message.

#### 4.1.1 Limitations

Our Memcached appliance is currently in the early prototype stage as we add more functionality. In terms of application limitations, whereas the baseline Memcached software supports multiple commands [7], we only support the two most common ones, get and set. There are very modest logic requirements to support these operations (shown in 5.2.1), and we expect there would only be minor additional logic to support the other operations as well.

Similarly while the software supports variable length keys, we currently support a fixed 64 byte key size, which is a common size according to previous studies [5]. While most of our modules are designed to accommodate variable length keys, and our memory system supports up to 256 byte keys, there are several of our state machines and serializing logic that need to be modified to support variable length keys. We plan to fix these shortcomings in the near future. While our appliance takes in and stores all of the flags and fields from full set and get messages, we currently do not consider the extra fields, mainly time stamp during Memcached operation. In the Memcached software, the time stamp is not used to proactively remove expired items, and thus we expect it is feasible to support the time stamps in our design.

Regarding networking limitations, we currently use a UDP interface to our Memcached appliance, as opposed to the more ubiquitous TCP interface. This limitation is due to only UDP OEs being available in the public domain; once TCP OEs are available, we will modify our design to use those. As Memcached read operations (i.e., gets) are sometimes used with UDP in actual large deployments [8, 9], we expect the drawbacks to be minimal. While UDP does not guarantee reliable transmission, and therefore may be unsuitable to be deployed, we believe our early prototype system is suitable to measure performance and power consumption of memcached appliance on FPGA.

## 4.2 Network Processing

### 4.2.1 Network Offload Engine

To implement the network Offload Engine we use a UDP OE [10] to extract packet data and header information. The UDP OE communicates with the MAC to read the data transferred to it, and parse for Ethernet IP information. The UDP OE checks the Ethernet IP information, such as IP address, and MAC to confirm that packet is destined for the appliance. It also checks if the input packet is a UDP packet, and stores the Ethernet packet header information in registers (e.g., IP address, source port, destination port). After the packet header information is registered, the OE routes the data from the MAC directly to the core on the other end by signaling that new data is available. In a similar manner, to transfer data onto the network, the module transmitting the data initially passes Ethernet packet information to the UDP OE. The OE checks if the data being sent has a valid IP address, and proceeds to send the data to the Altera MAC by assembling the Ethernet packet header field along with the data.

### 4.2.2 Packet Parser and Storage

Memcached command packets generally include command information and key(s), which are stored in the Ethernet data field. Additional data may also be included based on the command; for example, set commands will also include the value to store. As data is being extracted by the OE it is sent to an *input packet parser* that separates out the Ethernet header packet information (source network IP address, source port) and data, and places them into the *input packet storage memory*. This memory consists of two FIFOs, implemented in on-chip MRAM blocks. One FIFO contains the entire Memcached request, and the other FIFO contains only request Ethernet packet header information. The header FIFO is only written once when the complete packet is saved to the input packet FIFO, and has a special header padded to it indicating the packet is valid. By writing the packets to a FIFO, the appliance is able to buffer incoming packets while the Memcached backend is in use.

Apart from routing the input UDP packets to the FIFO, the packet storage memory module also takes care of overflow conditions of the FIFO when the FIFO memory is full and any new packet request or ongoing packet request that is being stored has to be discarded. Since the size of memory on FPGA is limited—normally on the order of a few MBs—the size of the input packet FIFO is designed to be only 512 KB. Challenges with dropped packets can potentially be overcome by storing the data on off-chip QDR-II SRAM modules that are common with network processing-oriented FPGA boards. However due to the unavailability of low latency QDR-II SRAM memory blocks on the DE-4 board, we are instead using an Altera FIFO IP based buffer in our current design.

### 4.2.3 Request Response Handling

The UDP OE is also used to send out responses to Memcached requests. The responses are formed by the Memcached application block with Ethernet packet header and Memcached packet data (key, value). The responses are placed into *output packet storage memory*, which consists of output packet FIFOs analogous to the input packet FIFOs. The *output packet parser* monitors the header FIFO, waiting for a response to be fully generated. Once completed, it is sent to the UDP OE which handles forming a UDP packet and sending it to the network.

## 4.3 Memcached Application

### 4.3.1 Packet Decipher

After analyzing the structure of Memcached packets [11], we observed that not all request packets have the same data fields. Hence, the *packet decipher* module analyzes the received Memcached request, and stores respective field information for further command processing. The Memcached command packet can be distinguished as two types: request or response packet. Irrespective of request or response packet, the Memcached packet consists of a header field, which includes data such as the opcode, the key length, and total data length. After the header field, the packet format varies depending on the type of operation (set or get). For example, set operations carry data to be stored in the hash table, and thus user data in conjunction with the key are concatenated after the header field. In a similar manner, for a get operation the client sends a packet with basic header field, and a key to index the hash table.

Once the packet decipher module detects data in the input header FIFO, it checks for the special header padding to confirm if the complete packet is available. If the header indicates an error (due to an overflow), the module removes the invalid data from the input header and packet FIFOs. After confirmation of data availability in the input packet FIFO, the decipher module ensures the packet is a Memcached request. Then the rest of the header field information is stored into corresponding field registers so other modules can access them to complete the requested operation. The rest of the packet data is stored into FIFO memory modules so that they can be routed to *memory management* to eventually be saved into DRAM. We use three different FIFO memory modules to store the data before memory management processes it. The key data is needed for both the *hash decoder* and memory management. However the decoder uses a 96-bit data interface, thus two different FIFO's are used to route key data. The third FIFO is used to store user data, which is used primarily for set operations where data has to be stored into DRAM.

### 4.3.2 Response Generator

Any data retrieved for a get command is sent to a FIFO which stores data prior to the *response packet generator*. The response packet generator assembles the data with the command header. It sends the information to the output packet storage memory, which is processed and sent to the UDP OE. However, when the requested key cannot be found a miss response packet is generated. A set command will lead to the default Memcached set response that it has completed the request.

### 4.3.3 Memcached Controller

As shown in Figure 3, the controller coordinates the hash decoder and hash and slab memory management to perform the requested command. The controller first directs the hash decoder to perform a hash on the key to determine the hash table address. Once the decoder signals the controller that it has completed, the controller then signals the hash or slab memory management module to perform either get or set operations. For example, during get operations once the hash value is ready the hash memory management performs a lookup on the hash table address. Once the value is retrieved, the controller has the data placed into a FIFO in preparation for the response packet generator. If the data

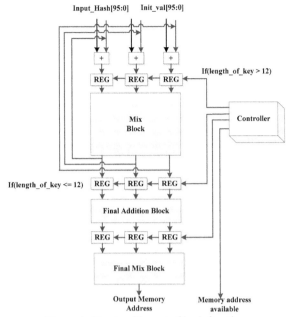

Figure 4: Structural layout of hash function

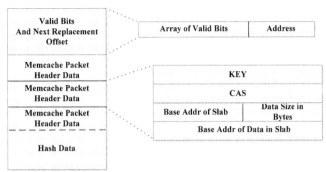

Figure 5: Layout of hash bucket data structure

is not found in the hash bucket, the controller has the response packet generator generate a miss response.

For sets, the controller first commands the slab memory management to store the data item. Once the data is written, the address is recorded and passed to the hash memory manager. The hash decoder performs a hash of the key to determine the hash table location that the new key-value pair should be stored in, and the hash memory manager writes it into the appropriate entry. Once completed the controller instructs the response packet generator to reply to the client with a completion message.

In addition to coordination, the controller also takes of system startup configuration operations, such as creation of slabs, and cleaning DRAM. Since metadata is stored along with Memcached data in DRAM, any invalid data in the DRAM could disrupt operation of the system. Therefore memory cleaning is performed before system is made available.

### 4.3.4 Hash Decoder

The Memcached application uses a hash table data structure to store and lookup its data, providing fast, constant time access. The hash table is indexed using the key data, which can be a variable number of bytes. The key data is passed through a hash function to generate a 32 bit index value. The Memcached software already uses an efficient hash decoding scheme [12] that can operate on variable length input keys. Thus we used the already implemented function and tried to port an efficient hardware module that replicates its functionality.

The hash decoder is customized to accept inputs of three 32 bit segments (12 bytes or 96 bits) of the input key distributed over three internal variables a, b and c (each 32 bits). Initially, the hash algorithm accumulates the first set of 12 byte key segments with a constant, so that the mix module has an initial state. After the combine state is processed the input variables are passed to the mix state. At this point the counter, *length_of_key* decrements by 12 bytes for each iteration of combine and mix module execution. After each iteration the hash decoder compares the length_of_key counter to check if the remaining hash key length is greater than 12. If the remaining length is less than or equal to 12, the intermediate key will be routed to the final addition block, which

takes care of the combine functionality for key lengths less than or equal to 12. The internal variables a, b and c are then computed with the final addition/combine block. The variables are passed to the final mix data path to post process the internal states so that the final constant hash value is computed.

The main challenges of directly porting a pipelined version of the software algorithm are the throughput and resource utilization. The direct pipelined implementation of the software hash function to hardware resulted in 6 clock cycles (cc) of latency in the mix module, and 7 cc of latency in final mix state. Hence, for commonly seen key sizes of 60 bytes [5], the latency is about 34 cc, resulting in poor overall performance. Hence, a design space throughput exploration was performed to identify a design that best balanced both hash latency and overall module frequency. From the study we concluded the ideal hash decoder implementation has the mix block take 3 cc, and the final block take 4 cc of latency.

### 4.3.5 Memory Management

The DRAM-based memory for the Memcached appliance is categorized into two memory sections, one as hash memory, and another as slab memory. The slabs accommodate variable sizes to store different sized user data. As explained in Section 4.3.3, in our system the controller creates slabs depending on user inputs, such as the number of slabs, and amount of bytes to allocate to the slabs. After the slab memory has been reserved, the remaining DRAM capacity is then assigned to be used as hash memory.

### 4.3.5.1 Hash Memory Data Structure

The layout for the hash data is shown in Figure 5. The hash table stores entries with only the data needed to provide fast lookups for key-value pairs, including the key, base address of value, and size of value. While the hash table entries include the key, they do not directly include the value data, which is instead handled by the slab memory management. To access the hash memory for read and write operations, we use the *hash read* and *hash write* sub-modules respectively.

The hash table consists of buckets which hold multiple hash entries; the buckets allow multiple items which map onto the same index to be present in the hash table. When a key is looked up in the hash table, the entries in the hash bucket are iterated over to compare each of their keys, and Compare and Swap (CAS) to the one being searched for. The 32 bit hash value is masked with the value (number of hash buckets – 1) to determine the final index value. Our appliance has a fixed number of entries (4) per hash bucket, unlike the software, which does not have a limit to hash bucket length.

The other two fields of slab address storage information, such as *base address of slab, data size stored in slab, and base address of*

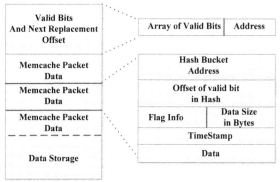

Figure 6: Layout of slab data structure

*data item in slab* are used for get or set operations. More detail on the use of these fields will be explained in the following sections on get and set operation. In addition to lists in the hash bucket, the *valid bit* field is used to assist in the data eviction policy when all lists in the bucket are utilized. Our implemented replacement policy will be explained in more depth in Section 4.3.5.3.

**Write Management:** The controller first signals to the hash write sub-module that the hash value is available. The hash write module reads valid bits field from the indexed bucket, starting at the *next replacement offset* to check for empty entries in the bucket. If there are no empty entries, a replacement policy is performed to evict a data item, and allocate the entry to the new data write request. After the offset for hash entry is determined, the hash write sub-module writes the key, and in parallel signals the slab write management module to start writing the data (stored in the data FIFO) into the allocated slab memory. Once the data is written, the slab write sub-module acknowledges the hash write with the base address of slab, base address of data stored, and size of data stored in slab. The hash write module uses this information to complete its write operation, and signals to the controller that the set operation is completed.

**Read Management:** The 32-bit hash values from different keys will potentially alias to the same hash bucket, which is why each bucket has multiple entries. Hence, the hash read sub-module is responsible for finding the entry with the matching key in the hash bucket (if one exists). Once the address to a hash bucket is available, the hash read sub-module reads the key information from individual entries sequentially to compare with the packet's key. If they match, the base slab address of data and size of data are passed to the slab read sub-module to read data from DRAM. However, if the keys do not match, a new data read request will be passed to the controller to access the next entry. If a miss occurs with all 4 entries stored in the hash bucket, the hash read sub-module signals the controller that it is a get miss.

### 4.3.5.2 Slab Memory Data Structure
The slabs are used to store the main Memcached packet information, including any *flags*, the *data size*, any *time stamps*, and the data itself. Keys from the command, and their corresponding slab base address information are only stored within the hash table memory. Similar to hash bucket entries, each slab data item stores *hash base address* information, and the *location of the entry in the hash bucket*. In addition to slab data, the slabs store *valid bit* information to assist in data replacement policy. There are *slab write* and *slab read* sub-modules that write and read data from slab memory, respectively.

**Write Management:** While the key is stored in a hash bucket entry, the hash write sub-module requests the appropriate slab base address given the associated data size. The slab write sub-module then reads the valid bits, and the *next replacement offset* to find an empty slot within the slab to store the input data. If none is found, data must be evicted from the slab using a replacement policy. Once a slot is available, the slab write sub-module starts writing the header information, and data stored in the header and data storage FIFO.

In the case where data was evicted, the slab write sub-module also clears the data's corresponding valid bit in its hash bucket, indicating that the item has been evicted.

**Read Management:** The slab read sub-module is responsible for reading data from the slab slot after the hash read sub-module transfers the base address of the data and offset. The data retrieved from the slab slot is stored into a response FIFO which the response packet generator uses to generate a get response packet.

### 4.3.5.3 Replacement policy
As Memcached provides caching of data, it must eventually evict items as its capacity becomes full. As described above, there are two scenarios where the capacity is full: either the hash bucket has no free entries, or the slab class has no free entries. In both cases we use round robin replacement to select the entry to evict. While an LRU policy would potentially provide greater eviction accuracy (the software uses an LRU policy), it is difficult to implement efficiently in hardware for the multi-GB DRAM sizes used in the appliance. Hence, we use pseudo-round robin replacement policy where the next data item after the latest written data item is considered for replacement when all the data items in hash or slab are full. To augment round robin and make it more effective, we also keep track of the valid bits within the hash buckets and slab classes. These valid bits are first checked to see if there are any entries that are invalid (for example, they have expired or they have been deleted). Any invalid entries are used first before evicting currently valid entries.

When items are evicted from either a hash bucket or a slab class, their corresponding slab or hash entry must be evicted as well. Thus each hash entry has the base address of the slab entry, and each slab entry has a pointer to the hash entry. These are used to invalidate the corresponding entries.

### 4.3.5.4 Metadata storage requirements
Our design requires a few extra bytes of metadata not required in the original design. These include a 32 byte array of valid bits per hash bucket. Per slab, there is a 32 byte counter, and a variable number of valid bits based on the size of the elements in the slab. Assuming a 128 MB slab, this metadata overhead is about 256KB. There is some additional data required for storing addresses for the hash bucket and hash offset, as well as slab base address, for slab entries and hash entries respectively. We utilize unused bits in the data words that store the CAS value and flag values to store these addresses, avoiding additional metadata overhead.

## 5. EVALUATION
### 5.1 Methodology
To test our proposed FPGA Memcached appliance, we mapped the design on a DE-4 development board [13] with an Altera Stratix IV 530 FPGA. The board is interfaced with two 4GB DDR2 memory modules, four 1GbE ports, and standalone power supply of 12V, and 3.3V. The Stratix IV 530 FPGA used on the DE-4 development board has total resources of 424K logic cells, and 21Mb of memory to map user functionality. While 8 GB of total memory may be considered small for a Memcached server, this capacity was due to the limitations of readily available

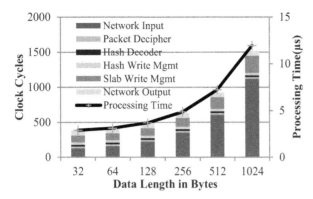

Figure 7: Set Operation Clock Cycle Distribution

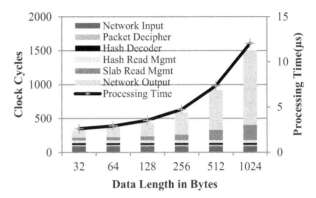

Figure 8: Get operation clock cycle distribution

memory controller IP, which has limited addressing range, and the development board design, which only supports SODIMMs. We anticipate newer FPGA boards to support larger capacities that would be more amenable for Memcached servers.

We implemented our Memcached appliance using a holistic approach of integrating our design with other Altera IPs. The Altera IPs used in our implementation are the Altera Triple Speed Ethernet IP to communicate with 1GbE port, and the DDR2 memory controller to interface with SODIMM memory modules. After the design is programmed onto the FPGA, an Altera system console is used to program the appliance's IP and load slab memory registers prior to use.

We test our appliance using a microbenchmark that uses the binary protocol format [11], and generates packets with different data sizes. The various data sizes we tested are 10, 32, 64, 128, 512, and 1024 bytes. However, we kept the key length constant at 64 bytes. The microbenchmark generates a stream of commands (get, set). The initial accesses are interleaved to populate the cache, but otherwise are streams of only one operation.

## 5.2 Detailed Analysis

### 5.2.1 Hardware Resource Utilization

The current appliance design operates at 125MHz, and has a total resource utilization of 7% of the logic, and 16% of the memory bit resources on the DE-4's Stratix IV 530 FPGA (including all of the Altera cores). A more detailed illustration of resource utilization for individual components is shown in Table 1. While the application uses a large amount of memory, its logic requirements are not very high, as it is composed mostly of state machines. Most of the logic utilized by the design is for the Altera cores.

The basic Memcached design (FPGA$_1$) only occupies a small fraction of the total FPGA resources. Thus we mapped a second instance of the Memcached appliance (FPGA$_2$) onto the FPGA, interfaced to the second memory controller, SODIMM, and ethernet port. Thus each instance is independent. While it reduces the memory capacity per instance, it doubles the throughput; as each instance will cache a smaller range of keys, we do not expect it to negatively affect the hit rate. We used the dual Memcached mapping on the FPGA to analyze the throughput impact due to multiple instances being mapped. Even with two Memcached appliances operating on the single FPGA, the operational frequency of both designs is still 125 MHz. Table 1 also shows the utilization results on the Stratix IV FPGA.

### 5.2.2 Memcached application analysis

We measured the performance of our proposed system on the FPGA board by running multiple test cases of varying user data size for the Memcached requests. Our results are shown in Figure

7 and Figure 8. We used counters on the FPGA to keep track of the number of clock cycles that each module of the appliance contributes to overall operation execution time. It can be seen from the latency figures that for the FPGA Memcached appliance, a majority of the time for a Memcached operation is spent on the network side and memory read/write operations.

**Set Operation:** The cycle breakdown of set operations is shown in Figure 7. As set operations must read in a packet with key and value data, the network input module responsible for transferring the packet to the Memcached application takes a significant amount of clock cycles. The network input time grows as data size is larger, growing at an almost linear rate from 512 B to 1024 B. The primary reason for the high network input clock cycles with larger data payloads is because the UDP OE we used has an 8-bit I/O interface. The rest of the appliance interfaces are 256-bit, thus data must be converted before being transferred from the OE to the rest of the appliance, resulting in sub-optimal performance. We expect that greater network bandwidths and a wider OE interface the network performance would greatly improve performance.

After the packet parser concatenates the packet, the Memcached packet decipher module is responsible to distinguish the Memcached packets, and store the data into intermediate FIFOs. Hence the packet decipher latency also varies with input packet size. Although the hash decoder is designed to function on variable length keys, we only send 64 byte keys, so the hash decoder latency is constant at 23 clock cycles.

The time spent in slab write management also varies with respect to input data size. As the size of the data increases the slab write sub-module must spend more clock cycles writing the data to DRAM. In contrast, the hash write management consumes a very small fraction of total execution time as the amount of data written is constant. After the data is written into memory, a response packet will be passed back to the client to confirm data write operation. Since the response packet consists of a basic Memcached header field, the network output module accounts for

Table 1: Hardware Resource Utilization

|  | Total Memcached Instances | | UDP OE | Packet Parser | Memcached Application |
|---|---|---|---|---|---|
|  | One | Two |  |  |  |
| Comb. ALU's | 21,044 | 42,478 | 1,501 | 154 | 8,593 |
| Logic Reg. | 22,517 | 45,164 | 1,342 | 238 | 6,447 |
| Mem (b) | 3.2M | 6.4M | 20,400 | 0 | 2.22M |
| DSP | 7 | 14 | 0 | 0 | 7 |

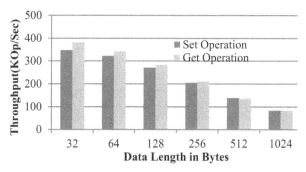

Figure 9: FPGA Memcached Performance

Table 2: Total Cost of Ownership comparison for 1000 CPU servers

| | CPU₁ | CPU₂ | FPGA₂ₐ | FPGA₂ᵦ | FPGA₃ₐ | FPGA₃ᵦ |
|---|---|---|---|---|---|---|
| **Space (T$/Y)** | 456 | 456 | 456 | 456 | 456 | 456 |
| **Power & Cooling (T$/Y)** | 2033 | 2033 | 593 | 296 | 593 | 296 |
| **Infrastructure Cost (M$/Y)** | 38 | 38 | 51 | 76 | 51 | 152 |
| **Total(M$/Y)** | 40.5 | 40.5 | 52 | 77 | 52 | 153 |
| **Perf/$ (Ops/s/$)** | **24.69** | **7.40** | **43.51** | **14.79** | **88.62** | **29.92** |
| **Perf (Mops/s)** | 1000 | 300 | 2262 | 2262 | 4608 | 4608 |

only a small portion of the total set operation clock cycles.

Overall we see that the FPGA performance is influenced by data sizes, and performs best with smaller data. As Memcached is often used with very small objects [5], we expect the appliance to fit well with potential use cases.

**Get Operation:** The get operation packet consists of a Memcached header field with a key to look up data in the cache. Therefore the size of the input packet is far smaller than in set operations. Unlike the set operation, the network input module only consumes a small fraction of total get operation execution time. Other modules that are responsible for only a small number of cycles are the hash decoder, and hash read management modules. The hash read management is only used to compare input key with key stored in memory and consumes only 42 clock cycles to read 64 byte key from memory, and compare it with input command key. During the actual data memory reads, the slab read sub-module consumes more clock cycles, and also increases as the data size read from memory increases. .

Similar to slab read management, the execution time of the network output module responsible to transmit data from the Memcached appliance to the client system increases by increasing the data size of the request.

## 5.3 Overall Appliance Performance

### 5.3.1 Throughput
Based on the clock cycles required for the get and set operations, we calculated the overall throughput of our appliance performing either gets or sets. The results are shown in Figure 9. We see that at 128B data sizes, the appliance achieves nearly 270KOps/s for gets and sets, which is comparable to baseline server results that we obtained. As the data size increases we see a drop off in performance due to the reasons described in the previous section. Based on our results, we found that having larger width interfaces to the OE would significantly benefit performance.

### 5.3.2 Power and Energy Efficiency
We measured the power consumption of our appliance through a current clamp on the input 12V power supply to accurately measure the power by deducting any AC/DC conversion losses.

Table 3: Power, Performance and Energy Efficiency Comparison

| System | Power Consum. (W) | Perf. (KOps/Sec) | Perf./W (KOps/Sec/W) |
|---|---|---|---|
| CPU₁ | 202 | 1000 | 4.95 |
| CPU₂ | 202 | 300 | 1.49 |
| FPGA₁ | 17.4 | 283 | 16.26 |
| FPGA₂ | 18.84 | 566 | 30.04 |

As shown in Table 3, we found that the whole appliance consumed only 17.4W (FPGA₁). When we mapped another Memcached appliance onto the FPGA, the power consumption only increased to 18.8W (FPGA₂), indicating there is significant benefit to maximizing the per-FPGA resource utilization.

Using the measured power consumption, along with the throughput achieved for get operations of 128B data sizes, we calculated the overall performance-per-Watt efficiency of our single and dual Memcached appliance designs. We also compared to two baseline servers: one that achieves 300K Ops/s (CPU₂), and one with optimistic performance of 1M Ops/s (CPU₁). In both cases we used a server with power based on our baseline server, which was a dual-socket Xeon, but reduced to 8 GB of memory to match the FPGA. Versus both of the baseline servers we see a 3.2X to 10.9X improvement in energy efficiency for the single Memcached appliance, and a 6.1X to 20.2X improvement for the dual Memcached appliance. The specialized implementation and low-power nature of the FPGA help to dramatically reduce the power consumption for our Memcached appliance.

## 5.4 Data Center Total Cost of Ownership
To compare performance and total cost of ownership (TCO), we used a cost model [14] that reflects monthly cost of operating a data center. We use similar cost factors considered by [15] to calculate TCO of a data center running a tier of 1000 Memcached servers. We assumed the baseline servers each had 64 GB of memory, and that the datacenter operator wanted to achieve that specific total cluster memory capacity.

Given that goal, we considered a cluster made up of the previous baseline servers CPU₁ and CPU₂. We also considered two different FPGA designs. One (FPGA₂), is based on the dual Memcached appliance design from before, with 16 GB of RAM, and using the performance achieved in the previous section. The second (FPGA₃) is a forward-looking higher-end design that also uses two Memcached appliances, but has 32 GB of RAM, and uses performance based on estimates with the OE I/O width bottlenecks removed. Each FPGA had two price points, A, which costs $1000, and B, which costs $3000. We expect higher end FPGAs to have costs closer to B, while lower end FPGAs or ones leveraging commodity pricing may cost closer to A.

Based on these systems, we calculated the overall TCO costs as space, power and cooling, and infrastructure costs, and estimated the overall Performance-per-TCO-$ (Ops/s/TCO-$) of the entire cluster. We see that a low cost FPGA (FPGA₂ₐ) is able to provide substantially higher perf/$ than CPU₂, due in part to its low cost, its low power, and relatively high performance. Even a high cost FPGA (FPAG₂ᵦ) can slightly improve perf/$. A higher performing, but more expensive solution (FPGA₃ᵦ), continues to show benefits even against optimistic server designs (CPU₁).

# 6. FUTURE WORK

Based on our analysis, we found that the performance is constrained through the network I/O interfaces for 10GbE Ethernet connections. The UDP OE design used has an I/O interface of 8-bit whose bandwidth saturates just over 1Gbps. Also, the Memcached appliance is designed to operate with 256-bit memory I/O and 32-bit memcached packet parsing; hence, glue logic is required to convert the network I/O interface from 8-bit to 32-bit, and 256-bit words for parser/response and memory I/O respectively, resulting in extra latency that increases with packet size. Modifications to the current UDP OE or implementing an efficient network OE with wider data width that could utilize the full potential of the 32-bit Altera 10GbE IP core would leverage next generation network connections (e.g. 10GbE).

Lastly, although the UDP protocol is used for get operations in some Memcached clusters, due to lack of reliable packet delivery, TCP is typically used for set operations. To allow our system to directly operate in conjunction to contemporary CPU based systems, we would like to incorporate TCP OE functionality in parallel to an optimized UDP OE.

# 7. RELATED WORK

Several related works have explored alternative architectures for Memcached servers. Work by Berezecki et al. [9] used a many-core Tilera processor to run Memcached, and they proposed software modifications to optimize the software to run on multiple cores. Their architecture improved performance, and they also noted that improved network processing was a significant reason for the advantages. In comparison, our design focuses on a specialized, low-power, highly integrated architecture.

Work by Hetherington et al. [1] explores using GPUs to perform certain portions of the Memcached software. They implement get operation lookups on a GPU, taking advantage of the GPU's parallelism to operate on multiple requests simultaneously. They find that GPUs can provide performance improvements, but a key limitation is moving data between the CPU and GPU. In contrast, our work addresses the significant network-related bottlenecks, and supports both get and set operations.

Work by Jose et al. [16] explores using high performance Infiniband RDMA fabrics for Memcached. They rearchitect the Memcached software to use their modified interface and RDMA transfers. They are able to significantly improve performance, also confirming our conclusions that network processing latency is the primary performance bottleneck. Our work addresses the whole Memcached stack, offering significantly lower power along with a high performance, standard Ethernet interface.

Other work by Atikoglu et al. [5] has examined and characterized a large scale Memcached deployment at Facebook. Their work serves as a motivation for much of our work, identifying key trends in the sizes of keys and data, and overall cluster usage.

# 8. CONCLUSION

The continued growth in web services that need to provide low-latency access to large amounts of data, in turn, motivate improved system designs for in-memory distributed data caches such as memcached. In this paper, we argue that the I/O-intensive nature of such workloads, requiring fast communication and DRAM data access, better matches accelerator-based systems compared to currently-used traditional general-purpose servers.

We propose an FPGA-based implementation of a Memcached appliance that tightly integrates networking and memory access with compute for improved performance and energy efficiency. Our design addresses important challenges specific to the memcached workload such as high network rates, variable-length keys, and dynamic memory allocation, and includes algorithms adapted to hardware-efficient algorithms. We prototyped our architecture on an Altera DE-4 development board. Our design consumes 9% of the power of a corresponding traditional baseline server, and provides significant energy efficiency improvements (3.2X to 10.9X). Additionally, at a data-center level, our approach enables significant total-cost-of-ownership improvements compared to traditional designs. Overall, our results argue for future systems for Memcached servers to be accelerators based, but also point to the broad promise of accelerator-based solutions in the emerging era of data-centric computing.

# 9. REFERENCES

[1] T. Hetherington, T. Rogers, L. Hsu, M. O'Connor, and T. Aamodt. 2012. Characterizing and evaluating a key-value store application on heterogeneous CPU-GPU systems. In *Proceedings of the 2012 IEEE International Symposium on Performance Analysis of Systems & Software*. IEEE Computer Society, Washington, DC, USA, 88-98.

[2] D. Karger, E. Lehman, T. Leighton, M. Levine, D. Lewin and R.Panigrahy. Consistent hashing and random trees: Distributed caching protocols for relieving hot spots on the World Wide Web.

[3] J. Sobel. Keeping Up (The Facebook Blog). http://blog.facebook.com/blog.php?post=7899307130, 2011.

[4] A. Arsikere. 2011. Building a scalable game server. http://code.zynga.com/2011/07/building-ascalable-game-server/

[5] B. Atikoglu, Y. Xu, E. Frachtenberg, S. Jiang, and M. Paleczny. 2012. Workload analysis of a large-scale key-value store. In *Proceedings of the 12th ACM SIGMETRICS/PERFORMANCE joint international conference on Measurement and Modeling of Computer Systems*. ACM, New York, NY, USA, 53-64.

[6] Low latency RPC in RAMCloud, forum.stanford.edu/events/.../2011plenaryRosenblum.pdf

[7] Memcached Commands http://code.google.com/p/memcached/wiki/NewCommands

[8] Scaling memcached at Facebook, http://www.facebook.com/note.php?note_id=39391378919

[9] M. Berezecki, E. Frachtenberg, M. Paleczny, and K. Steele. 2011. Many-core key-value store. In *Proceedings of the 2011 International Green Computing Conference and Workshops*. IEEE Computer Society, Washington, DC, USA, 1-8.

[10] UDP Offload Engine, http://www.opencores.org

[11] Memcached Command Binary Protocol. http://code.google.com/p/memcached/wiki/BinaryProtocolRevamped

[12] Memcached hash function. http://burtleburtle.net/bob/hash/doobs.html

[13] Terasic DE-4 Development board, www.terasic.com

[14] C. Patel and A. Shah. 2005. Cost model for planning, development and operation of a data center. *Hewlett-Packard Laboratories Technical Report*, 2005.

[15] S. Chalamalasetti, M. Margala, W. Vanderbauwhede, M. Wright, and P. Ranganathan. 2012. Evaluating FPGA-acceleration for real-time unstructured search. In *Proceedings of the 2012 IEEE International Symposium on Performance Analysis of Systems & Software*. IEEE Computer Society, Washington, DC, USA, 200-209.

[16] J. Jose, H. Subramoni, M. Luo, M. Zhang, J. Huang, M. Wasi-ur-Rahman, N. Islam, X. Ouyang, H. Wang, S. Sur, and D. K. Panda. 2011. Memcached Design on High Performance RDMA Capable Interconnects. In *Proceedings of the 2011 International Conference on Parallel Processing*. IEEE Computer Society, Washington, DC, USA, 743-752.

# High Throughput and Programmable Online Traffic Classifier on FPGA*

Da Tong, Lu Sun, Kiran Kumar Matam, Viktor Prasanna
Ming Hsieh Department of Electrical Engineering
University of Southern California
{datong, lusun, kmatam, prasanna}@usc.edu

## ABSTRACT

Machine learning (ML) algorithms have been shown to be effective in classifying the dynamic internet traffic today. Using additional features and sophisticated ML techniques can improve accuracy and can classify a broad range of application classes. Realizing such classifiers to meet high data rates is challenging. In this paper, we propose two architectures to realize complete online traffic classifier using flow-level features. First, we develop a traffic classifier based on C4.5 decision tree algorithm and Entropy-MDL discretization algorithm. It achieves an accuracy of 97.92% when classifying a traffic trace consisting of eight application classes. Next, we accelerate our classifier using two architectures on FPGA. One architecture stores the classifier in on-chip distributed RAM. It is designed to sustain a high throughput. The other architecture stores the classifier in block RAM. It is designed to operate with small hardware footprint and thus built at low hardware cost. Experimental results show that our high throughput architecture can sustain a throughput of 550 Gbps assuming 40 Byte packet size. Our low cost architecture demonstrates a 22% better resource efficiency than the high throughput design. It can be easily replicated to achieve 449 Gbps while supporting 160 input traffic streams concurrently. Both architectures are parameterizable and programmable to support any binary-tree-based traffic classifier. We develop a tool which allows users to easily map a binary-tree-based classifier to hardware. The tool takes a classifier as input and automatically generates the Verilog code for the corresponding hardware architecture.

## Categories and Subject Descriptors

C.1.3 [**Computer Systems Organization**]: PROCESSOR ARCHITECTURES—*Adaptable architectures*

*This work was partially supported by the US NSF under grant CCF-1116781.

## General Terms

Algorithms, Design, Performance

## Keywords

Traffic classification, machine learning, C4.5 decision tree, discretization, FPGA acceleration, high throughput, programmable, low cost

## 1. INTRODUCTION

Traffic classification forms basis for many important network management tasks such as flow prioritization, traffic shaping/policing, and diagnostic policing. Accurate traffic classification also benefits network security in dynamic access control and intrusion detection. In addition to being an essential part in network operations, traffic classification also contributes to the planning of future network architecture [13, 5, 21].

Existing traffic classifiers fall into four categories: (1) *port number* based schemes classify traffic based on well-known transport layer port numbers; (2) *deep packet inspection* (DPI) examines the traffic payload against a set of known signatures; (3) *heuristic* based techniques [10, 11] classify traffic based on connection patterns; and (4) *machine learning* based techniques exploit statistical properties of traffic. However, port number based approaches are no longer reliable because applications today tend to use dynamic port numbers for connections. DPI techniques [18, 16] can reach extremely high accuracy; but they cannot cope with encrypted traffic. Heuristic based approaches suffer from low accuracy and large memory requirement to store the connection patterns. On the other hand, machine learning based traffic classification has drawn a lot of attention in the research community recently [3, 1, 13]. It demonstrates not only high accuracy but also robustness to today's dynamic internet traffic. However, realizing such classifiers to meet high data rates is challenging. Hardware acceleration for these classifiers is required to achieve online classification.

In this paper, we propose two architectures to realize complete online traffic classifier using *flow-level* features. These two architectures use distributed RAM and block RAM respectively. We conduct detailed experiments to evaluate the performance of these architectures in terms of throughput, resource efficiency and scalability on a state-of-art FPGA device.

Our contributions in this work are:

- We conduct extensive experiments to identify a feature set that achieves high accuracy. Our classifier built upon this flow-level feature set can achieve an overall accuracy of 97.92% in classifying a traffic trace consisting of eight application classes.

- We propose complete hardware solution to machine learning based traffic classifier. Our architectures not only realize online traffic classification, but also perform online discretization which is an essential step in any machine learning based technique.

- To the best of our knowledge, our high throughput architecture is the first FPGA design for 400+ Gbps online traffic classification using *flow-level* features. Implementation results on a state-of-the-art FPGA show that our high throughput design can achieve a throughput of 550 Gbps. On the other hand, our low cost design demonstrates a 22% better resource efficiency than the high throughput design. It can be easily replicated to achieve 449 Gbps while supporting 160 input traffic streams concurrently.

- Both architectures are parameterizable and programmable to support any binary-tree-based traffic classifier.

The rest of the paper is organized as following. Section 2 gives the background and related work in traffic classification. Section 3 discusses the methodology to select a high accuracy feature set. Section 4 describes the C4.5 decision tree based classifier. Section 5 presents the two hardware architectures to accelerate the classifier. Section 6 evaluates our prototype implementation on FPGA. Section 7 concludes the paper.

## 2. RELATED WORK

### 2.1 C4.5 based Traffic Classification

Machine learning based techniques classify internet traffic based on statistical properties of traffic flows [3, 1, 13]. Among existing machine learning approaches, C4.5 algorithm has been recognized as one of the most accurate algorithms for traffic classification.

[1] evaluates the effectiveness of machine learning algorithms in classifying encrypted traffic. They study five Algorithms AdaBoost, Support Vector Machine(SVM), Naive Bayesian, RIPPER, and C4.5 Algorithm. They use a set of 22 features, including packet-level features (e.g. packet sizes) and flow-level features (e.g. packet inter-arrival time), to build the machine learning classifiers. They show that C4.5 decision tree Algorithm gives the best accuracy among all the considered techniques. They achieve over 83% accuracy in identifying SSH traffic and over 97.8% accuracy in identifying Skype traffic.

[13] investigates the discriminative power of nine flow-level feature sets. They show that features such as packet size, port number and their related statistics always give the highest accuracy. This observation holds for all the four machine learning Algorithms they evaluate, i.e., Naive Bayes, SVM, k-Nearest-Neighbour(kNN), and C4.5 decision tree. They claim that C4.5 Algorithm gives the highest accuracy using any feature set. They also show that discretization is a necessary preprocessing step in traffic classification. The accuracy of machine learning Algorithms can be greatly improved by using discretized training dataset.

[2] shows that Skype traffic can be accurately classified without investigating packet payload. They evaluate two classifiers built from AdaBoost and C4.5 using ten flow-level features. AdaBoost classifier achieves an accuracy of 97% when classifying UDP Skype traffic and 94% accuracy when classifying TCP Skype traffic. The C4.5 classifier can achieve an accuracy of 98% and 94% respectively.

### 2.2 FPGA based Traffic Classifier

In order to accelerate the machine learning based traffic classifier, several works have been proposed to implement the classifiers in hardware.

In [14], an FPGA based architecture is presented to improve the classification performance of C4.5 decision tree classifier. They reduce the number of memory accesses during the search by efficiently storing the classifier on hardware. Memory accesses are parallelized to further improve the performance. They analytically show that their architecture reduces the number of memory accesses in the worst case from 26 to 5. However, no FPGA implementation results of the architecture are presented in their paper.

[9] proposes an FPGA based architecture to realize an accurate and high throughput classification of multimedia traffic using simple *packet-level* features. Their classifier is built upon k-Nearest-Neighbor Algorithm and trained using three packet-level features (port number, packet size, and protocol). Their classifier achieves high accuracy when the number of training data exceeds $10K$. The place and route result of their hardware implementation shows that they achieve a throughput of 40 Gbps. As they consider only three simple packet-level features, their architecture is restricted to classifiers with small number of application classes. It cannot handle general classifier using flow-level features.

[15] proposes a hardware architecture on NetFPGA for decision tree based classifier. Their architecture is fully parameterizable in terms of throughput, number of features, tree depth and maximum number of nodes with in a tree level. So their architecture can support any general decision tree based classifier. Several optimizations on storage of the tree structure are proposed to improve latency and lower hardware cost. Although their paper presents a programmable implementation of a decision tree based classifier, their experimental results show that the clock rate they achieve is around 67 MHz only. This clock rate is not sufficient to perform online traffic classification.

We are not aware of any prior work that realizes a complete flow-level online traffic classifier. None of the previous works propose a hardware solution for discretizaion, which is an essential step in traffic classification. In this paper, we first develop a highly accurate classifier using flow-level features. We then propose two architectures to enable online discretization and classification. Both architectures are programmable with respect to the structure of the classifier, i.e., number of features, number of nodes in each level, number of application classes, and so on. They are flexible to support any binary-tree-based classifier.

## 3. CONSTRUCTION OF FEATURE SET

One of the challenge in building a machine learning based traffic classifier is to choose the appropriate set of features. Appropriate feature set is the set of features which are effective in classifying the targeted applications from each other.

Table 1: **Application Protocols in Our Traffic Traces**

| Application Protocol | Description |
|---|---|
| HTTP | Hypertext Transfer Protocol |
| MSN | MSN Messenger by Microsoft |
| P2PTV | P2P live streaming applications |
| QQ_IM | QQ Instant Messenger by Tencent |
| Skype | Skype voice calls and video calls |
| Skype_IM | Skype Instant Messenger |
| Thunder | P2P service by Thunder Networks |
| Yahoo_IM | Yahoo Instant Messenger |

In this section we discuss the methodology for identifying the feature set.

## 3.1 Dataset

Our dataset is built from two sources: a general traffic trace provided by a major network vendor and Tstat [19], a publicly available labeled traffic trace. Unlike many previous works targeting at only one or two application classes, our dataset consists of eight application classes as listed in Table 1. These classes include Peer-to-peer (P2P) applications and Instance Messaging (IM) applications, which cannot be accurately classified using traditional port number or DPI based classification schemes. Each application class in the dataset consists of 700 traffic flows. This dataset is used as both training set and testing set in our experiments.

## 3.2 Feature Selection

### 3.2.1 Candidate Features

Unlike many previous works which focus only on accuracy, the features in our work must be feasible in an online traffic classifier. Therefore we consider the following criteria when selecting the candidate features for the classifier.

- High Accuracy: The overall accuracy is the weighted average of *true positive rate* of all application classes. *true positive rate* is the fraction of traffic flows correctly classified for an application class.
- Early Classification: It is important to decide the class of the traffic flow by looking at only the first few initial packets. Therefore features characterizing a complete flow, such as duration, are not acceptable.
- Low Cost: it requires high computation power to calculate statistical features from traffic flows. This limits the usage of these features in online traffic classifiers where features need to be computed very fast. So we constrain our selections to a set of low cost features. They are avg/min/max/variance of features.

In order to achieve high accuracy in classifying a traffic trace consisting of broad application classes, our work uses flow-level features as opposed to packet-level features used in many other works. A flow is defined as a series of packets that share the same five tuple information: protocol, source port number, destination port number, source IP address and destination IP address. We first identify eight candidate features which meet the above criteria. These features have been shown to be the most effective features for machine learning based traffic classification [13, 2, 21, 1, 4, 3, 5]. They are

- *Protocol*: the protocol associated with the flow.
- *Src. Port Number*: the source port number associated with the flow.

Table 2: **Candidate Feature Sets**

| Feature Set | Classic Features | | | Sizes of First N Packets | Packets size statistics | | | |
|---|---|---|---|---|---|---|---|---|
| | Protocol | Src. Port No. | Dst. Port No. | | Avg. Packet Size (byte) | Max. Packet Size (byte) | Min. Packet Size (byte) | Var. of Packet Size |
| Set A | × | × | × | | | | | |
| Set B | × | × | × | × | | | | |
| Set C | × | × | × | | × | × | × | |
| Set D | × | × | × | | × | × | × | × |
| Set E | × | × | × | × | × | × | × | |
| Set F | × | × | × | × | × | × | × | × |

- *Dest. Port Number*: the destination port number associated with the flow.
- *Sizes of First N Packets*: sizes of the first $N$ packets in the flow.
- *Avg. Packet Size*: average packet size of the first $N$ packets in the flow.
- *Max. Packet Size*: maximum packet size among the first $N$ packets in the flow.
- *Min. Packet Size*: minimum packet size among the first $N$ packets in the flow.
- *Var. of Packet Size*: variance of sizes of the first $N$ packets in the flow.

We group the above features into six sets as shown in Table 2. Each feature set in the table is a different combination of the above features. In this paper, we refer *Protocol, Src. Port Number* and *Dest. Port Number* as classic features; *Avg/Max/Min/Var Packet Size* as statistical features. The statistical features listed above comes from first $N$ packets in the flow. Next, we will identify the best value of $N$ and the appropriate set of features for our classifier.

### 3.2.2 Methodology

We conduct extensive experiments to identify the value of $N$ and the appropriate feature set for our classifier. Each feature set is evaluated using the same machine learning Algorithm (i.e., C4.5 Algorithm) and dataset. We apply the commonly used 10-fold cross validation technique [12] which breaks the dataset into 10 equally sized sets. In this technique, we perform 10 iterations; during each iteration, 9 sets are used as training sets and 1 set is used as testing set. The training sets are used to build the classifier and the testing set is used to evaluate the accuracy of the classifier. The overall accuracy of a feature set is computed by taking the average accuracy over 10 such iterations.

All training and testing data are discretized in the experiments. Discretization is the process of converting continuous feature values into discrete feature values. It is known that discretization can help to create more accurate machine learning classifiers. Previous literature [13] has also shown that this fact holds true when applying machine learning Algorithms to traffic classification. We adopt Entropy-MDL [6], the most commonly used discretization Algorithm, to convert feature values into discrete values.

### 3.2.3 Emperically Optimized Feature Set

In this section we use the methodology discussed in Section 3.2.2 to identify a set of features that achieves the highest accuracy. We denote this emperically optimized feature set (EOFS). Note that, our methodology explores a limited design space using the available training data.

Figure 1 shows the overall accuracy achieved by each feature set. It can be observed that Feature Set C and Feature Set D achieve the highest accuracy among all feature sets.

## Figure 1: Overall Accuracy of Each Feature Set

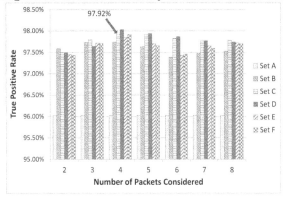

Figure 1: Overall Accuracy of Each Feature Set

## Table 3: Confusion Matrix for Classic Feature Set

| | HTTP | MSN | P2PTV | QQ_IM | Skype | Skype_IM | Thun. | Yahoo_IM |
|---|---|---|---|---|---|---|---|---|
| HTTP | 100.00 | 0.00 | 0.00 | 0.00 | 0.00 | 0.00 | 0.00 | 0.00 |
| MSN | 0.00 | 99.95 | 0.05 | 0.00 | 0.00 | 0.00 | 0.00 | 0.00 |
| P2PTV | 0.24 | 0.19 | 98.00 | 0.00 | 1.09 | 0.00 | 0.05 | 0.43 |
| QQ_IM | 0.39 | 0.00 | 0.00 | 99.59 | 0.00 | 0.00 | 0.03 | 0.00 |
| Skype | 0.00 | 0.00 | 1.15 | 0.00 | 94.55 | 0.05 | 4.25 | 0.00 |
| Skype_IM | 0.00 | 0.00 | 0.00 | 0.00 | 0.00 | 100.00 | 0.00 | 0.00 |
| Thunder | 0.00 | 0.00 | 0.12 | 0.00 | 8.00 | 0.02 | 91.85 | 0.00 |
| Yahoo_IM | 0.00 | 0.07 | 0.00 | 0.00 | 0.00 | 0.00 | 0.00 | 99.93 |

## Table 4: Confusion Matrix for EOFS

| | HTTP | MSN | P2PTV | QQ_IM | Skype | Skype_IM | Thun. | Yahoo_IM |
|---|---|---|---|---|---|---|---|---|
| HTTP | 99.90 | 0.00 | 0.10 | 0.00 | 0.00 | 0.00 | 0.00 | 0.00 |
| MSN | 0.02 | 99.93 | 0.00 | 0.00 | 0.00 | 0.00 | 0.00 | 0.05 |
| P2PTV | 0.28 | 0.00 | 99.19 | 0.02 | 0.40 | 0.00 | 0.09 | 0.00 |
| QQ_IM | 0.28 | 0.00 | 0.00 | 99.64 | 0.00 | 0.03 | 0.05 | 0.00 |
| Skype | 0.00 | 0.00 | 0.34 | 0.05 | 98.78 | 0.07 | 0.76 | 0.00 |
| Skype_IM | 0.00 | 0.00 | 0.00 | 0.02 | 0.05 | 99.93 | 0.00 | 0.00 |
| Thunder | 0.00 | 0.00 | 0.02 | 0.07 | 1.60 | 0.02 | 98.28 | 0.00 |
| Yahoo_IM | 0.00 | 0.09 | 0.00 | 0.00 | 0.00 | 0.00 | 0.00 | 99.91 |

Feature Set C and Feature Set D differs only by one feature, i.e. variance of packet size. Computing variance requires more hardware resources; therefore, Feature Set C is favored over Feature Set D.

From Figure 1 it can also be observed that maximum overall accuracy is reached when using features from the first 4 packets in a flow. Having fewer than 4 or more packets in the feature set decreases the overall accuracy. This is because our traffic trace includes P2P and IM flows whose first 3-4 packets in a flow are used for initial connection establishment. Thus the values and statistical properties of the first few packets are essential in classifying these traffic flows.

To conclude, Feature Set C is our EOFS and it is computed from first 4 packets in a traffic flow. It achieves an overall accuracy of 97.92%.

### 3.2.4 Pitfalls of Classic Feature Set

Our evaluation also demonstrates that the classic feature set (i.e., *Protocol*, *Src.PortNumber*, and *Dest.PortNumber*) used in traditional machine learning based traffic classification scheme is not sufficient in classifying a general traffic trace where P2P traffic exists. Although the overall accuracy achieved by the classic feature set reaches 96.0%, it cannot distinguish different classes of P2P traffic from each other.

Table 3 and Table 4 show the confusion matrices of classic feature set and our EOFS. The confusion matrix shows the fraction of traffic flows from an application class that are classified as other application classes. Each row index represents the actual application class; each column index represents the predicted application class. For example, in Table 1, 0.24% of P2PTV traffic is classified as HTTP traffic.

It can be observed from Table 3 that the major pitfall of classic feature set is that it cannot distinguish P2P traffic from each other. For example, 8% of the Thunder traffic has been falsely classified as Skype; 4.25% and 1.15% of the Skype traffic has been falsely classified as Thunder and P2PTV respectively. This directly degrades the overall accuracy of classic feature set shown in Figure 1.

On the other hand, our EOFS can classify both P2P and non-P2P traffic with high accuracy. According to Table 4, in the worst case, only 0.76% of Skype traffic is falsely classified as Thunder traffic; only 1.60% of Thunder traffic is falsely classified as Skype traffic. We can expect that our EOFS outperforms the traditional classic feature set in a real world setting where more number of classes from P2P exist.

## 4. C4.5 CLASSIFIER

As mentioned in Section 3, our traffic classifier is built upon C4.5 decision tree Algorithm. C4.5 Algorithm is a well-known machine learning algorithm proposed by Quinlan [17]. C4.5 based classifiers have demonstrated high true positive rate with different target applications, test traces, and experiment setups [1] [2] [20]. This section presents in detail how we apply C4.5 Algorithm to build our classifier. It consists of two steps: input discretization and classifier construction. Note that the constructed discretizer and the C4.5 classifier are implemented in hardware.

### 4.1 Discretization

In Section 3, we identify Feature Set C, i.e., {source port number, destination port number, average packet size, max packet size, and min packet size}, as the feature set for our classifier. We first discretize all numerical values of these features in the sample traffic flows before using them as training data to build the classifier. We adopted Entropy-MDL [6], the most commonly used discretization Algorithm, to convert these feature values into discrete values.

### 4.2 Building the C4.5 Classifier

The training data used in our work are the feature vectors extracted from labeled traffic flows. A feature vector consists of the discretized values of the six features in our feature set and a label indicating the application class associated with the flow.

We extracted in total 5600 training samples from our dataset into WEKA [7], an existing machine learning software. The 5600 training samples consist of 700 samples from each of the application classes in Table 1.

The classifier generated by the C4.5 Algorithm is essentially a binary decision tree. It can be characterized by leaf nodes and non-leaf nodes. Each leaf node in the decision tree is an application class. When an input feature vector arrives at a leaf node, it is classified as the application class associated with the leaf node. Each non-leaf node is a decision node which has a comparison key, a left child node and a right child node. The comparison key has a value and a feature type. When an input feature vector arrives at a non-leaf node, it is compared against the key at the node. If the feature value equals the key, the input feature vector

**Figure 2: An Example of C4.5 Decision Tree Based Classifier**

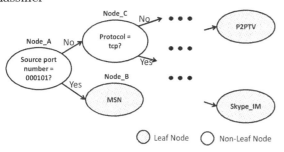

will be passed to the left child node; otherwise, it will be passed to the right child node.

Figure 2 shows a simple example of a C4.5 decision tree classifier. In this example, $Node\_A$ is a non-leaf node, its key has a value of 000101 for feature type 'source port number'. $Node\_B$ is its left child node and $Node\_C$ is its right child node. $Node\_B$ is a leaf node; any input feature vector that arrives at $Node\_B$ will be classified as application class of MSN.

## 4.3 Classification Algorithm

Once the C4.5 classifier is built, the classification of any test feature vector from a traffic flow consists of two phases: discretization and classification. The feature vectors in the test traffic flows are converted to discrete vectors during the discretization phase. During the classification phase, the discretized feature vectors traverse the C4.5 classifier until they reach a leaf node.

Let $q$ denote an instance of test traffic flow. Our goal is to classify $q$ into an application class. Let $F[i]$ denote the raw feature value of feature type $i$. Then, $q$ has a raw feature vector consisting of six feature values $\{F[0], F[1], F[2], F[3], F[4], F[5]\}$, i.e., {protocol, source port, destination port, avg. packet size, max. packet size, and min. packet size}. Let $\{D[0], D[1], D[2], D[3], D[4], D[5]\}$ denote the output discrete values from the discretization phase. These values are passed as an input feature vector into the classification phase. The detailed Algorithms involved in the discretization phase and the classification phase are shown in Algorithm 1 and Algorithm 2.

## 5. ARCHITECTURE

The proposed classification Algorithm in the previous section is highly desirable for hardware implementation. In this section, we propose a high throughput architecture and a low cost architecture to realize online classification of traffic flows in hardware. The high throughput architecture adopts a pipelined design and takes advantage of the on-chip distributed RAM to achieve high performance. The low cost design minimizes the usage of hardware resources by reusing the hardware components.

As stated in Section 4, an input traffic flow is represented by a feature vector consisting of raw values of its features, i.e., protocol, source port number, destination port number, avg. packet size, max. packet size, and min. packet size. First, it is passed through the discretizer which outputs a discrete feature vector. This discrete feature vector will then traverse the C4.5 tree classifier until it reaches a leaf node.

---

**Algorithm 1** Phase 1: Discretization for each feature

1: Let $d_1, d_2, ..., d_{n-1}$ divide $[0, \infty]$ continuous space in to n intervals. Let $i_1$ denote $[0, d_1), i_2$ denote $[d_1, d_2)$, $i_3$ denote $[d_2, d_3),...,i_{n-1}$ denote $[d_{n-2}, d_{n-1})$, and $i_n$ denote $[d_{n-1}, \infty]$. Let $c_1, c_2, ...c_n$ denote the corresponding discretized values for $i_1, i_2, ..., i_n$.
2: $F$ is the given input feature value for which we need to identify the discretized value.
3: $D$ is the output discretized value for $F$.
4: Let $High = n, Low = 1$
5: **while** true **do**
6:     $Mid = (High + Low)/2$
7:     **if** $High=Low$ **then**
8:         $D=c_{High}$, break
9:     **end if**
10:    **if** $F < d_{Mid}$ **then**
11:        $High=Mid$
12:    **else**
13:        $Low=Mid + 1$
14:    **end if**
15: **end while**

---

**Algorithm 2** Phase 2: Classification

1: Let $current\_node$ be the node which is currently accessed.
2: Let $value$ denote the value of the key stored at $current\_node$. $value$ is an application class in leaf nodes.
3: For non-leaf nodes, let $feature$ denote the type of the key stored in the node. Since there are six features involved in the classifier, $feature$ is an integer between 0 and 5.
4: Initialize $current\_node = root\ node$.
5: **while** $current\_node \neq leaf\ node$ **do**
6:     **if** $D[feature] = value$ **then**
7:         $current\_node = left\ child\ node$.
8:     **else**
9:         $current\_node = right\ child\ node$
10:    **end if**
11: **end while**
12: $q = value\ at\ current\_node$.

---

## 5.1 Performance Metrics

This paper considers the following factors when constructing the classifier on hardware:

- *Throughput* is measured as the number of bits classified per second. The minimum raw *throughput* can be computed as the product of number of flows classified per second, minimum packet size (i.e., 40 Bytes), and number of packets needed in a traffic flow to extract features (i.e., 4 packets).

- *Resource Efficiency* is measured as amount of hardware resources per unit of throughput. On a FPGA device, the amount of hardware resources is represented by number of occupied slices. For a block RAM, we assume the hardware resources it consumes equals the number of slices of the same size. On a Virtext-6 FPGA, each slice contains four 6-input Look-Up Tables and each block RAM provides 18 Kb of memory. Therefore, one block RAM is equated to 72 slices. Since block RAM is highly optimized in terms of area, we multiply the number of slices it consumes with a

**Figure 4: Mapping from Discretizer to Hardware**

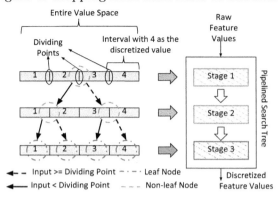

**Figure 5: Example of Memory Structure**

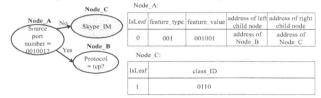

factor of 1/35. This is because it is observed that FPGA on average consumes 35 times more area than an ASIC platform which is highly optimized for area [8]. Therefore, the hardware resources consumed by one block RAM equals (72 slices) × *percentage of block RAM occupied* × 1/35.

## 5.2 High Throughput Design

The mapping of the C4.5 classifier to hardware is shown in Figure 3. The classifier consists of a discretizer and a C4.5 tree classifier. Both components can be mapped to hardware as a binary tree. Each level of the binary tree corresponds to a stage in the hardware. All stages are pipelined to achieve high throughput. Each stage consists of a processing element and a distributed RAM. The distributed RAM stores all the nodes of the corresponding level in the tree. When a feature vector arrives at a node in the stage, the node is retrieved from the corresponding distributed RAM. Based on the content in the retrieved node, the processing element will decide the address of the node to be accessed by the feature vector in the next stage.

### 5.2.1 Discretizer

The discretization phase described in Section 4.3 can be realized by a binary search tree in hardware. Let $n-1$ dividing points divide the continuous space of the input values in to $n$ intervals. The midpoint among the dividing points is stored at the root node of the binary search tree. All the intervals less than this dividing point are stored in the left subtree of the root node and remaining intervals in the right subtree of the root node. The left subtree and right subtree are recursively defined in the same way. Each leaf node stores the end points of an interval. Each level in the binary search tree is mapped to a pipeline stage in the hardware architecture. So the input value of a feature is discretized by traversing the binary search tree in a pipeline manner. An example on mapping of the discretizer to hardware architecture is illustrated in Figure 4.

In our architecture, all the tree nodes are stored in distributed RAM. Each stage of the pipeline consists of a distributed RAM and a processing element (PE). In the distributed RAM, the nodes of the corresponding level in the tree are stored. The PE decides whether the feature vector traverses to the left or right child node.

### 5.2.2 Programmable Memory Organization

Nodes of a stage are stored in the distributed RAM attached to it. One memory word stores one node. Therefore, the number of entries in each distributed RAM equals the number of nodes in that level of the tree. In the discretizer, the memory word storing a node consists of the value of the dividing point and the addresses of its child nodes. In the C4.5 tree classifier, the memory word storing a leaf node consists of *class_ID* associated with the node and a 1-bit mask indicating whether it is a leaf node. The memory word storing a non-leaf node consists of the same 1-bit mask, the type of feature associated with the key in the node, the value of the key, and the addresses of its child nodes.

Figure 5 gives an example of memory structure for a leaf node and a non-leaf node in a C4.5 tree classifier. *Node_A* is a non-leaf node which has a feature value of 001001. Its key type is source port number. In our classifier, this feature type is identified as 001. *Node_C* is a leaf node which is associated with the Skype_IM application class. In our classifier, this application class is identified by *class_ID* of 0110.

The structure of the memory storing the C4.5 tree classifier is fully parameterized. Number of memory words in the memory attached to a stage is parameterized with number of nodes in the corresponding tree level. Width of a memory word (i.e., number of bits representing a memory word) is the sum of widths of *feature_type*, *feature_value*, and addresses of child nodes. These widths are parameterized and can be determined from the structure of the C4.5 tree classifier. Number of feature types in the classifier determines the width of *feature_type*; range of discretized feature values determines the width of *feature_value*; number of child nodes in the next tree level determines the address width of child nodes. For a memory word storing a leaf node, number of applications classes in the classifier determines the width of *class_ID*.

These parameterizations enable the programmability of our architecture. Any binary-tree-based classifier can be mapped to our architecture by specifying the parameters mentioned above. Users can generate the memory structure suitable for their classifier by programming the parameters. Once the memory structure is generated, the classifier can be loaded into memory accordingly.

### 5.2.3 Processing Element in C4.5 Classifier

Figure 6 shows the high level architecture of processing element in each stage. The processing element takes as input a feature vector, a *class_ID*, and the address of the node to be accessed. A node is first retrieved from the distributed RAM attached to the stage based on the input address. If a leaf node is retrieved, feature vector will be classified by assigning the value in leaf node to *class_ID*. If a non-leaf node is retrieved, the input feature vector will be compared against the key in the node. The address of the node to

**Figure 3: Mapping from Decision Tree to Hardware**

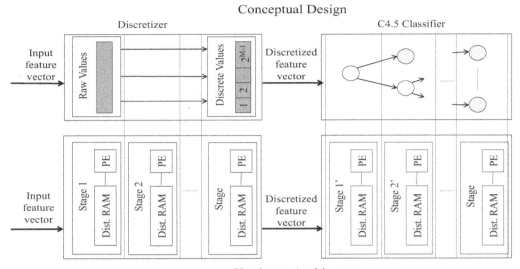

Conceptual Design

Hardware Architecture

◯ (shaded) Leaf Node    ◯ Non-Leaf Node

**Figure 6: Architecture of Processing Element**

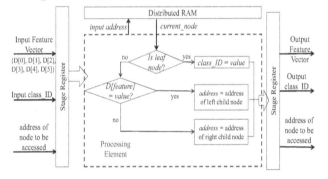

**Figure 7: Overall Architecture of Low Cost Design**

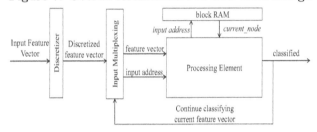

be accessed in the next stage will be decided based on the comparison result.

## 5.3 Low Cost Design

In addition to the high throughput architecture, we also propose an architecture which can be built at low hardware cost. This architecture is designed to operate with small hardware footprint. It stores the classifier in a block RAM. In contrast to the high throughput design where each level of the decision tree and discretizer is mapped to a separate Processing Element attached with a distributed RAM, the low cost design allows all levels of C4.5 tree classifier to share the same Processing Element and memory.

Figure 7 shows the overall architecture of the low cost design. The architecture consists of four components: Discretizer, Input Multiplexer, block RAM, and Processing Element. All tree nodes in the classifier are stored in block RAM. Since a block RAM is dual ported, our architecture can support two input traffic streams concurrently.

When an input feature vector comes in, it first goes through Discretizer. Then, it traverses the decision tree by iteratively going through Input Multiplexing, block RAM and Processing Element until it is classified.

The architecture is at low hardware cost in the sense that the logic it consumes does not grow with the size of the C4.5

tree classifier. In contrast to the high throughput architecture where each level of the classifier consumes one Processing Element, this architecture uses only one Processing Element and Input Multiplexer regardless of the size and number of levels of the classifier. Due to the low cost nature of this architecture, it can be duplicated to support multiple input traffic streams. Impact of number of input traffic streams on the throughput and resource usage of this architecture will be evaluated later in Section 6.3. The components in this architecture are described below.

### 5.3.1 Input Multiplexer

The component decides whether a feature vector should continue traversing the C4.5 tree classifier or a new input feature vector should be loaded. Figure 8 shows the detailed architecture of the input multiplexing component. After a new input feature vector is loaded, it will pass the new vector to the next stage along with the address of the root node of the tree. When continuing on classifying the current feature vector, it will pass this current vector to the next stage along with the address of the child node to be accessed in the next stage. The current feature vector and the address of the child node are provided by the feature comparison unit.

### 5.3.2 Block RAM and Processing Element

This component retrieves the child node to be accessed from block RAM. The memory organization is defined in

**Figure 8: Architecture of Input Multiplexer**

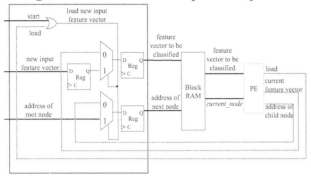

Input Multiplexer

the same way as in our high throughput design. The dual port block RAM can support two accesses concurrently.

The Processing Element logic is similar to that in our high throughput design with slight modification to fit into the low cost architecture. In addition to performing the logic mentioned in our previous design, the Processing Element in this low cost design also outputs a control signal. This control signal is passed to Input Multiplexer and is enabled when a feature vector reaches a leaf node. The Input Multiplexer will load a new input feature vector when this signal is enabled.

### 5.3.3 Low Cost Discretizer

The low cost discretizer stores all tree nodes in one block RAM and makes usage of one processing element only. The input raw feature vector iteratively goes through the processing element until it is eventually discretized. Its architecture looks very similar to the low cost architecture of the C4.5 tree classifier described above.

## 5.4 Architecture Generation Tool

In our design, the operation of the PE does not depend on the classifier structure. However as explained in Section 5.2.2, width of memory words, number of memory words, and number of the levels of pipeline stages depend on the classifier. We parameterize these variables in our memory design. So our designs are programmable to support different binary tree based classifiers.

Our architecture generation tool facilitates users in generating the Verilog code. The tool accepts binary tree based classifier as input to our tool and generates Verilog source code. The tool consists of three modules: `Tree processor`, `Code generator`, and `Classifier memory generator`. The binary tree based classifier which is to mapped on to the hardware is given as input to the `Tree processor` module. Based on the binary tree based classifier, `Tree processor` module computes the tree parameters and passes them to the `Code generator` module. The parameters include 1) Number of feature types, 2) Number of levels in the tree, 3) Number of nodes in each level, and 4) Number of application types. Based on these tree parameters the `Code generator` module computes the design parameters and generates the verilog source code. The design parameters are 1) number of bits required by the fields in the memory word (feature_type, feature_value, class_ID, and the left and right pointers in the node), the number of levels of pipeline for the high throughput design.

**Figure 9: Architecture generation tool**

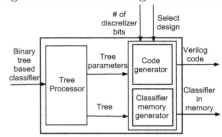

The binary tree based classifier is passed from the `Tree processor` module to the `Classifier memory generator` module which generates the tree in to memory. The generated tree is stored level by level. In each level the number of nodes in the level and the corresponding nodes are stored. The nodes are stored as explained in Section 5.2.2. Users can also select the number of output discretizer bits and the design to use among our two designs. The architecture of our tool is shown in Figure 9.

## 6. EXPERIMENTAL RESULTS

We implement both high throughput architecture and low cost architecture on FPGA. Our target device is Virtex-6 XC6LX670 with -2 speed grade. All results are post place and route results using Xilinx ISE 14.2.

Our architecture consists of a discretizer and a C4.5 classifier. Both the components are parameterized. The parameters for the discretizer are

- *width of raw feature value*: this is the number of bits representing the raw feature values. It is also the width of the memory word where a non-leaf node in the discretizer is stored.
- *width of discretized feature value*: this is the width of the memory word where a leaf node in the discretizer is stored. It also determines the height of the complete binary tree.

The parameters for the C4.5 classifier are

- *number of levels in the tree*: this determines the number of stages in the architecture. The classifier built from C4.5 algorithm using the feature set we identify has 43 levels.
- *number of nodes in each level*: this determines the number of memory words needed in each tree level. This number varies from 1 to 5 in the classifier we build from Section 4.

We evaluate the impact of these parameters on the throughput and resource consumption. In our experiments on discretizer, *width of raw feature value* varies from 16 to 48 bits and *width of discretized value* from 4 to 8 bits. We vary the total number of nodes in the C4.5 classifier from 32 to 1024 and the number of levels from 6 to 48. Also, we assume a bottleneck level having 25% of the total number of nodes in the classifier. The remaining nodes are equally distributed among other levels of the tree. In addition, we evaluate the scalability of the low cost design by replicating it to support multiple input traffic streams. We also compare the resource efficiency of the high throughput design and the low cost design.

Table 5: Performance of Discretizer

| High Throughput Design | | | | Low Cost Design | | | |
|---|---|---|---|---|---|---|---|
| Clock Rate (MHz) | | | | Clock Rate (MHz) | | | |
| | 4 bits | 6 bits | 8 bits | | 4 bits | 6 bits | 8 bits |
| 48 bits | 396 | 402 | 235 | 48 bits | 343 | 372 | 376 |
| 32 bits | 440 | 410 | 252 | 32 bits | 357 | 405 | 305 |
| 16 bits | 611 | 593 | 323 | 16 bits | 378 | 409 | 410 |

| # of Occupied Slices | | | | # of Occupied Slices | | | |
|---|---|---|---|---|---|---|---|
| | 4 bits | 6 bits | 8 bits | | 4 bits | 6 bits | 8 bits |
| 48 bits | 191 | 301 | 379 | 48 bits | 83 | 102 | 152 |
| 32 bits | 121 | 186 | 256 | 32 bits | 59 | 74 | 109 |
| 16 bits | 70 | 108 | 148 | 16 bits | 31 | 44 | 64 |

| Resource efficiency (slices/Gbps) | | | | Resource efficiency (slices/Gbps) | | | |
|---|---|---|---|---|---|---|---|
| | 4 bits | 6 bits | 8 bits | | 4 bits | 6 bits | 8 bits |
| 48 bits | 0.19 | 0.29 | 0.63 | 48 bits | 1.09 | 1.69 | 2.41 |
| 32 bits | 0.11 | 0.18 | 0.40 | 32 bits | 0.75 | 1.13 | 2.16 |
| 16 bits | 0.04 | 0.07 | 0.18 | 16 bits | 0.37 | 0.67 | 0.93 |

Table 6: Performance of Low Cost C4.5 Classifier

| Total # of Nodes | # of Tree Levels | Max # of nodes per level | Clock Rate (MHz) | Throughput (Gbps) | # of Occupied Slices | Resource efficiency (slices/Gbps) |
|---|---|---|---|---|---|---|
| 1024 | 48 | 256 | 334 | 5.94 | 125 | 21.01 |
| 512 | 24 | 128 | 321 | 11.41 | 117 | 10.22 |
| 256 | 24 | 64 | 308 | 10.95 | 136 | 12.38 |
| 128 | 12 | 32 | 358 | 25.46 | 121 | 4.77 |
| 64 | 12 | 16 | 338 | 24.04 | 117 | 4.87 |
| 32 | 6 | 8 | 340 | 48.36 | 125 | 2.59 |

## 6.1 Performance of proposed C4.5 classifier

In this experiment, we evaluate the performance of our 43-level classifier implementation using our two architecture designs. This classifier is generated by running C4.5 Algorithm on our dataset using EOFS identified in Section 3.2.3. Each level of this C4.5 classifier has no more than 6 nodes.

Our high throughput design achieves a clock rate of 215 MHz. In each clock cycle two flows are classified since the distributed RAM is dual ported. As we classify the flows using the first 4 data packets, assuming 40 bytes packet size, the throughput is 550 Gbps. We observe that number of occupied slices is 6429.

The low cost design achieves a clock rate of 308 MHz. It processes two input traffic streams concurrently since block RAM is dual ported. In the worst case each input feature vector traverses through the 43 tree levels. In our architecture, operation in each tree level takes 3 clock cycles. Therefore 129 cycles are needed to classify a flow in the worst case. Assuming 4 packets per flow and 40 bytes packet size, the throughput will be 6 Gbps. The number of occupied slices is 135 in addition to the block RAM.

## 6.2 Scalability of discretizer / C4.5 traffic classifier

The clock rate and resource usage of the discretizer using both the designs are shown in Table 5. The row index represents width of raw feature values while the column index represents the width of discretized feature values.

The results show that both high throughput design and low cost design sustain high clock rate. However, since low cost design takes multiple cycles to discretize a value, its throughput is lower than the high throughput design. The low cost design consumes much fewer slices than high throughput design since it has only one processing element and one memory block. In our results, cost of block RAM is converted to number of slices by the calculation described in Section 5.1. We will discuss resource efficiency of both the designs in Section 6.4.

Table 7 shows the performance of high throughput design w.r.t. the total number of nodes and number of levels in the classifier. It achieves a throughput of 460.8 Gbps when realizing a 48-level classifier with 1024 nodes and a through-

put of 947.2 Gbps when realizing a 6-level classifier with 32 nodes.

Table 6 shows the performance of low cost design. It achieves 5.94 Gbps when realizing a 48-level classifier with 1024 nodes. We observe that the low cost design sustains a high clock rate even when we scale to large number of tree nodes. Since the number of clock cycles is linearly proportional to the number of levels in the tree to classify a flow, the throughput will drop when the number of levels of the tree increases. On the other hand, the resource usage of low cost design remains nearly the same for tree structures of different sizes.

Our low cost design can be easily replicated to support multiple input traffic streams. Its performance when processing multiple streams concurrently is shown in Table 8. High clock rate is maintained as the number of threads grow from 4 to 160. The resource usage increases linearly when the number of threads increases. Yet the resource efficiency remains the same. The results in Table 6 and Table 8 show that the low cost design is highly scalable w.r.t size of the classifier and number of input traffic streams.

Table 7: Performance of High Throughput C4.5 Classifier

| Total # of Nodes | # of Tree Levels | Max # of nodes per level | Clock Rate (MHz) | Throughput (Gbps) | # of Occupied Slices | Resource efficiency (slices/Gbps) |
|---|---|---|---|---|---|---|
| 1024 | 48 | 256 | 180 | 460.8 | 12429 | 26.93 |
| 512 | 24 | 128 | 206 | 527.36 | 6916 | 13.15 |
| 256 | 24 | 64 | 234 | 599.04 | 4360 | 7.28 |
| 128 | 12 | 32 | 260 | 665.6 | 2266 | 3.41 |
| 64 | 12 | 16 | 342 | 875.52 | 1328 | 1.52 |
| 32 | 6 | 8 | 370 | 947.2 | 673 | 0.71 |

## 6.3 Comparison between Two Architectures

To compare the two designs, we use resource efficiency defined in Section 5.1 as the metric. The comparison between the resource efficiency of both the designs is shown in Fig-

Table 8: Performance of Multi-Stream Low Cost C4.5 Classifier

| Total # of Threads | # of Nodes | # of Tree Levels | Clock Rate (MHz) | Throughput (Gbps) | # of Occupied Slices | Resource efficiency (slice/Gbps) |
|---|---|---|---|---|---|---|
| 4 | 1024 | 48 | 329 | 11.70 | 330 | 28.21 |
| 8 | 1024 | 48 | 326 | 23.24 | 619 | 26.61 |
| 16 | 1024 | 48 | 348 | 49.50 | 1240 | 25.03 |
| 32 | 1024 | 48 | 330 | 94.03 | 2465 | 26.22 |
| 64 | 1024 | 48 | 330 | 187.75 | 4741 | 25.25 |
| 160 | 1024 | 48 | 315 | 449 | 11708 | 26.06 |

**Figure 10: Comparison of resource efficiency of high throughput and low cost designs**

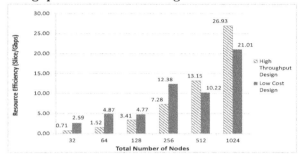

ure 10. We can observe that when the size of the classifier is small, the resource efficiency of high throughput design is better than the low cost design. The same trend can be observed in Table 5. Since the discretizer is small, the high throughput design has better resource efficiency than the low cost design. However the resource efficiency of low cost design increases at a slower rate than the high throughput design. From the 32 node classifier to the 1024 node classifier, the resource usage of the low cost design stays almost the same, while the resource usage high throughput design increases by nearly 19 times. Therefore when the classifier is large, the low cost design outperforms the high throughput design in terms of resource efficiency. As shown in Figure 10 when the classifier has 1024 nodes, the resource efficiency of low cost design is 1.22 times better than the high throughput design.

## 7. CONCLUSION

In this paper, we proposed a high throughput architecture and a low cost architecture to realize complete online flow-level traffic classifier. We constructed a C4.5 classifier based on an emperically optimized feature set we identify. The classifier model achieved 97.92% overall accuracy in classifying 8 application protocols including classic, P2P, and instant messaging applications. Our high throughput architecture accelerated this classifier to 550 Gbps and our low cost architecture accelerated it to 6 Gbps. Both architectures were programmable to support any binary-tree-based classifier. To the best of our knowledge, ours is the first work which achieves high accuracy and high throughput at the same time. We also evaluated the performance of the two architectures w.r.t. the resource requirement of the classifier. We observed that our high throughput design outperformed the low cost design in both throughput and resource efficiency when realizing small-scale classifiers. On the other hand, the resource efficiency of our low cost architecture remained the same regardless of the number of input traffic streams. Thus it could be replicated to offer comparable throughput as our high throughput design with constant resource efficiency. This result contradicted with the common opinion that distributed RAM based design was always favored over block RAM design. In the future, we will study the tradeoffs between performance and cost of the two architectures. We will also explore the potential of our work in a broader scope of high speed classification problems.

## 8. REFERENCES

[1] R. Alshammari and A. N. Zincir-Heywood. Machine learning based encrypted traffic classification: identifying ssh and skype. In *the proc. of CISDA*, pages 289–296, 2009.

[2] D. Angevine and A. Zincir-Heywood. A preliminary investigation of skype traffic classification using a minimalist feature set. In *the proc. of ARES*, pages 1075–1079, 2008.

[3] L. Bernaille, R. Teixeira, I. Akodkenou, A. Soule, and K. Salamatian. Traffic classification on the fly. *ACM SIGCOMM Computer Communication Review*, 36:23–26, April 2006.

[4] D. Bonfiglio, M. Mellia, M. Meo, D. Rossi, and P. Tofanelli. Revealing skype traffic: when randomness plays with you. In *the proc. of SIGCOMM*, pages 37–48, 2007.

[5] J. Erman, M. Arlitt, and A. Mahanti. Traffic classification using clustering algorithms. In *the proc. of MineNet*, pages 281–286, 2006.

[6] U. M. Fayyad and K. B. Irani. Multi-interval discretization of continuous valued attributes for classification learning. In *the proc. of IJCAI*, pages 1022–1027, 1993.

[7] M. Hall, E. Frank, G. Holmes, B. Pfahringer, P. Reutemann, and I. H. Witten. The weka data mining software: an update. *SIGKDD Explor. Newsl.*, 11(1):10–18, Nov. 2009.

[8] M.-H. Ho, Y.-Q. Ai, T. C.-P. Chau, S. C. L. Yuen, C.-S. Choy, P. H. W. Leong, and K.-P. Pun. Architecture and design flow for a highly efficient structured asic. *VLSI*, PP(99):1, 2012.

[9] W. Jiang and M. Gokhale. Real-time classification of multimedia traffic using fpga. In *the proc. of FPL*, 2010.

[10] T. Karagiannis, A. Broido, M. Faloutsos, and K. Claffy. Transport layer identification of p2p traffic. In *the proc. of IMC*, 2004.

[11] T. Karagiannis, K. Papagiannaki, and M. Faloutsos. Blinc: multilevel traffic classification in the dark. In *the proc. of SIGCOMM*, 2005.

[12] R. Kohavi. A study of cross-validation and bootstrap for accuracy estimation and model selection. In *the proc. of IJCAI*, pages 1137–1143. Morgan Kaufmann, 1995.

[13] Y.-s. Lim, H.-c. Kim, J. Jeong, C.-k. Kim, T. T. Kwon, and Y. Choi. Internet traffic classification demystified: on the sources of the discriminative power. In *the Proc. of ACM Co-NEXT*, '10, pages 9:1–9:12, 2010.

[14] Y. Luo, K. Xiang, and S. Li. Acceleration of decision tree searching for ip traffic classification. In *the proc. of ANCS*, 2008.

[15] A. Monemi, R. Zarei, M. Marsono, and M. Khalil-Hani. Parameterizable decision tree classifier on netfpga. *Advances in Intelligent Systems and Computing*, 182:119–128, 2013.

[16] A. W. Moore and K. Papagiannaki. Toward the accurate identification of network applications. *LNCS*, 3431/2005:41–54, 2005.

[17] J. R. Quinlan. *C4.5: programs for machine learning*. Morgan Kaufmann Publishers Inc., 1993.

[18] S. Sen, O. Spatscheck, and D. Wang. Accurate, scalable innetwork identification of p2p traffic using application signatures. In *the proc. of WWW*, 2004.

[19] T. Traces. http://tstat.tlc.polito.it/traces.shtml.

[20] N. Williams, S. Zander, and G. Armitage. A preliminary performance comparison of five machine learning algorithms for practical ip traffic flow classification. *SIGCOMM Comput. Commun. Rev.*, 36(5):5–16, 2006.

[21] S. Zander, T. Nguyen, and G. Armitage. Automated traffic classification and application identification using machine learning. In *the proc. of LCN*, pages 250 – 257, 2005.

# Poster Session 1

## FPGA Bitstream Compression and Decompression Using LZ and Golomb Coding

Jinsong Mao, Hao Zhou, Haijiang Ye, Jinmei Lai
*Fudan University*
Contact: jmlai@fudan.edu.cn

In this paper we propose an optimized bitstream compression algorithm based on LZ and a novel architecture of decompressor, the proposed algorithm improves the Compression Ratio by fully utilizing the regularity of configuration bits of CLB (Configurable Logic Box) in FPGA and using the variable length Golomb coding method. The experimental results show that the Optimized method can improve the Compression Ratio of LZSS by 32.3% for bitstream with high regularity and 10.3% for bitstream with low regularity, and our approach shows a higher flexibility than the BMC+RLE arithmetic when compressing the bitstream with high regularity for various FPGA. Moreover, we design a two-buffer-window decompressor to download the compressed bitstreams. In order to increase the throughput of the proposed decompressor, we design a multi-stage data selector in it. The post-simulation of the decompressor shows that its throughput is up to 9280 Mbps under 65nm CMOS process. And that is 4352Mbps when verified on a Virtex-5 FPGA. This project is supported by the National HighTechnology Research and Development (863) Thematic Program of China, No. 2012AA012001.

**ACM Categories & Descriptors:** E.4: Data Compaction and Compression; B.2.4: High-Speed Arithmetic;

**Keywords:** FPGA Bitstream, Compression, Decompression, LZ, Golomb Coding.

## Indirect Connection Aware Attraction for FPGA Clustering

Meng Yang, *State Key Lab of ASIC, Fudan University*
Jiarong Tong, *State Key Lab of ASIC, Fudan University*
A.E.A. Almaini, *Edinburgh Napier University*
Contact: mengyang@fudan.edu.cn

Indirect connection aware attraction clustering algorithm is proposed for clustered field programmable gate array architecture model to achieve simultaneously optimization of several performance metrics. A new cost function considers the attraction of the subsequent Basic Logic Elements (BLEs) to the selected cluster, the number of the used pins already in the cluster, as well as critical path delay. The attractions of which BLEs are directly and indirectly connected to the selected cluster are taken into account. As a result, more external nets are absorbed into clusters, less number of pins per cluster and fewer clusters are required.

Hence, smaller channel width is required for routing and speed of the design is improved. Performance comparisons are carried out in details with respect to state-of-the-art clustering techniques interconnect resource aware clustering (iRAC) and many-objective clustering (MO-Pack). Results show that the proposed algorithm outperforms these two clustering approaches with achievements of 38.8% and 42.2% respectively in terms of channel widths and 40.1% and 44.8% respectively in terms of number of external nets but with no critical path and area overhead.

**ACM Categories & Descriptors:** B.7.1 Types and Design Styles; B.7.2 Design Aids

**Keywords:** Field-programmable gate arrays; FPGAs; computer aided design; optimization; clustering

## Towards Automatic Customization of Interconnect and Memory in the CoRAM Abstraction

Eric S. Chung, *Microsoft Research*
Michael K. Papamichael, *Carnegie Mellon University*
Contact: erchung@microsoft.com

When developing applications to run on FPGAs, we tend to expend great effort on crafting the custom hardware acceleration datapath---but blindly turn to the FPGA vendor tool/library to provide default solutions for on-chip interconnect and external interfaces. This often leads to ineffective communication- or memory-bound implementations since the design and tuning of the default general-purpose solutions necessarily makes design compromises for generality. This is counterproductive as the FPGA's flexible reconfigurability should afford us great opportunities for performance gain and cost reduction through extensive application-specific customization of the interconnect and interface IPs.

This work presents a compiler that generates custom interconnect topology and connectivity with appropriately scaled capacity to support an application's exact communication requirements at a minimized cost. More specifically, the compiler analyzes an application developed for the CoRAM abstraction [1,2] for its connectivity and bandwidth requirements between the hardware processing kernels and external DRAM banks. The result is an extremely fine-tuned custom-topology soft-logic network-on-chip interconnect, which is enabled by the CONNECT NoC framework [3].

We perform an extensive evaluation that benchmarks two applications against the standard CoRAM implementation flow that relies on a fixed generically-tuned general-purpose soft-logic network-on-chip. Our RTL-driven evaluation shows a large opportunity for area reduction and improved efficiency (up by 48%) without any impact on application performance.

**ACM Categories & Descriptors:** C.0 [**Computer System Organization**]: System Architectures

**Keywords:** FPGA computing, memory architecture, Network-on-Chip

# A Latency-Optimized Hybrid Network for Clustering FPGAs

Trevor Bunker, *University of California, San Diego*
Steven Swanson, *University of California, San Diego*
Contact: tbunker@eng.ucsd.edu

The data-intensive applications that will shape computing in the coming decades require scalable architectures that incorporate scalable data and compute resources and can support unstructured (e.g., logs) and semi-structured (e.g., large graph, XML) data sets. To explore the suitability of FPGAs for these computations, we are constructing an FPGA-based system with a memory capacity of 512 GB from a collection of 32 Virtex-5 FPGAs spread across 8 enclosures. This poster describes the system's interconnect that combines inter-enclosure high-speed serial links and wide, single-ended intra-enclosure on-board traces with a network topology that optimizes for latency and bandwidth for small packets. The network uses a multi-level radix-12 router optimized for the asymmetry between the inter- and intra-enclosure links. The system has a peak theoretical bisection bandwidth of 247.2 Gb/s and a total switching capacity of 2.13 Tb/s. Under random traffic, the network sustains an aggregate throughput of 354.3 Gb/s. The channel transceivers and router consume 22% of the FPGAs' Block RAMs and 33% of their FPGA Slices.

**ACM Categories & Descriptors:** B.4.3 Interconnections (Subsystems); B.5.1 Design; C.2.1 Network Architecture and Design

**Keywords:** FPGA; High-Radix Router; Low Latency Network; High-Speed Serial; Data-Intensive Applications

# Genome Sequencing Using MapReduce on FPGA with Multiple Hardware Accelerators

Chao Wang, *University of Sci. and Tech. of China*
Xi Li, *University of Sci. and Tech. of China*
Xuehai Zhou, *University of Sci. and Tech. of China*
Jim Martin, *Clemson University*
Ray C.C. Cheung, *City University of HongKong*
Contact: saintwc@mail.ustc.edu.cn

The genome sequencing problem with short reads is an emerging field with seemingly limitless possibilities for advances in numerous scientific research and application domains. It has been the hot topic during the past few years. Growing with the data population and the ease to access for personal users, how to shorten the response interval for short read mapping at a large scale computing domain is extremely important. In this paper we propose a novel FPGA-based acceleration solution with Map-Reduce framework on multiple hardware acceleration engines. The combination of hardware accelerators and Map-Reduce execution flow could greatly expedite the task of aligning short length reads to a known reference genome. Our approach is based on preprocessing the reference genomes and iterative jobs for aligning the continuous incoming reads. The read-mapping algorithm is modeled after the creditable RMAP software approach. Furthermore, theoretical speedup analysis on a MapReduce programming platform is presented, which

demonstrates that our proposed architecture has efficient potential to reduce the average waiting time for large scale short reads applications.

**ACM Categories & Descriptors:** C.1.3 Other Architecture Styles

**Keywords:** Short reads; genome sequencing; FPGA; MapReduce

# Hardware Implemented Real-Time Operating System

Soon Ee Ong, Siaw Chen Lee, *Altera Corporation*
Noohul Basheer Zain Ali, *Universiti Teknologi Petronas*
Contact: sclee@altera.com

Real-Time Operating System (RTOS) usually implemented as software component at fundamental layer of embedded system which consumes computing time and memory resources. This will introduce extra overhead and latency to the system. In addition to this, the software layer of RTOS also indirectly raises the complexity of system software. Shifting RTOS from software to hardware is an inspiring idea to abstract RTOS layer out from the embedded system software framework. It has the advantages of helping to reduce the system software complexity, as well as improves the system performance by reducing overhead and latency of RTOS. This paper presented a **S**imple and **E**fficient hardware implemented Real-Time **O**perating **S**ystem (SEOS) architected for high portability and scalability. SEOS operates at co-processor level as an independent hardware component. It contains all essential OS services needed for embedded system design. This includes kernel scheduler, inter-task communication and synchronization (i.e. mutex, semaphore, mailbox), timer and IRQ handler. The application software interfaces with SEOS through a set of standard Application Programming Interface (API). Furthermore, SEOS is also equipped with Generic Bus Interface and Interconnect Bridge to enable effortless OS porting across different processor platforms. These innovative approaches have made SEOS to be plug-and-play in nature. Our test result shows that SEOS is having performance improvement over commercial software based RTOS, μC/OS-II, in several areas. SEOS consumes 31.6% less overhead in context switching, improves task level interrupt latency by 83.5%, shorten inter-task communication latency by 71.9% and significantly improves on performance jitter.

**ACM Categories & Descriptors:** C.m Miscellaneous

**Keywords:** Real-Time Operating System, RTOS, hardware implemented RTOS, SEOS

# Hybrid Masking using Intra-Masking Dual-Rail Memory on LUT for SCA-Resistant AES Implementation on FPGA

Anh-Tuan Hoang, *Ritsumeikan University, Japan*
Takeshi Fujino, *Ritsumeikan University, Japan*
Contact: anh-tuan@fc.ritsumei.ac.jp

In current countermeasure design trends against Different Power Analysis (DPA), security at gate level is required in addition to the security algorithm. Several Dual-rail pre-charge logics (DPL) have been proposed to achieve this goal. Designs using ASIC can attain this goal owing to its backend design restrictions on placement and routing. However, implementing these designs on Field Programmable Gate Array (FPGA) without information leakage is still a problem because of the difficulty involved in the restrictions on placement and routing on FPGA.

This paper describes our novel Hybrid Masking implementations using Intra-Masking Dual-rail Memory (IMDRM) approach for Side-channel-resistant AES. The hybrid masking scheme includes an additive mask and a multiplicative mask. The additive masking scheme utilizes a dual-rail memory, in which all unsafe nodes, such as unmasking and masking, the dual-rail memory and buses are packed into a single LUT. This makes them balanced and independent of the placement and routing tools. The multiplicative masking scheme is then applied over the additive masked values. It removes the joint-leakage, which is caused by the joint processing of the masks and the masked values inside the dual-rail memory. The design is independent of the cryptographic algorithm and persistent with SCA attacks even after 1,000,000 traces. It also occupied smaller hardware size than most other advanced SCA resistant implementations such as the Wave Dynamic Differential Logic, the Masked Dual-Rail Pre-charge Logic, and the Intra-Masking Dual-Rail Memory.

**ACM Categories & Descriptors:** B.7.1 [Hardware]: Integrated circuits – Algorithms implemented in hardware

**Keywords:** Side-Channel Attack, Differential Power Analysis (DPA), Masking, Dual-Rail Memory, Intra-Masking Dual-Rail Memory on LUT, Hybrid masking, SCA Resistance, AES, Field Programmable Gate Array (FPGA)

# FPGA-based Acceleration of Cascaded Support Vector Machines for Embedded Applications

Christos Kyrkou, *University of Cyprus*
Christos-Savvas Bouganis, *London Imperial College*
Theocharis Theocharides, *University of Cyprus*
Contact: ckyrkou@gmail.com

Support Vector Machines (SVMs) are considered one of the most popular classification algorithms yielding high accuracy rates. However, SVMs often require processing a large number of support vectors, making the classification process computationally demanding, and hence it is challenging to meet real-time processing constraints imposed by many embedded applications. In order to improve SVM classification times the cascade classification scheme has been proposed. However, even in this case real-time performance is still challenging to achieve without exploiting the throughput and processing requirements of each cascade stage. Hence the design of an FPGA-based accelerator for cascaded SVM processing is proposed; in addition to a hardware reduction method in order to reduce the implementation requirements of the cascade SVM leading to significant resource savings. The accelerator was implemented on a Virtex 5 FPGA platform and evaluated using face detection as the target application on 640×480 resolution images. It was compared against FPGA implementations of the same cascade processing architecture but without using the reduction method, and a single parallel SVM classifier. The accelerator is capable an average performance of 70 frames-per-second, achieving a speed-up of 5× over the single parallel SVM classifier. Furthermore, the hardware reduction method results in the utilization of 43% less FPGA LUT resources, with only 0.7% reduction in classification accuracy.

**ACM Categories & Descriptors:** B.2.1 [**Arithmetic and Logic Structures**]: Design Styles—*pipeline, parallel*; B.7.1 [**Integrated Circuits**]: Types and Design Styles—*Gate arrays, Algorithms implemented in hardware*; C.3 [**Special-Purpose and Application-Based Systems**]: Real-time and embedded systems

**Keywords:** FPGA, Parallel Architecture, Cascaded Classifiers, Support Vector Machines, Hardware Adaptation.

# Precision Fault Injection Method Based on Correspondence Between Configuration Bitstream and Architecture

Zhou Jing, Chen Lei, Wang Shuo
*Beijing Microelectronics Technology Institute*
Contact: plbabygirl@126.com

SRAM-based FPGAs are increasingly being used; however they are susceptible to SEUs. To emulate the effects of SEUs, a variety of fault injection techniques have been studied. As fault injection process helps little to SEU mechanism study. For further study, a novel Automated Precision Fault Injection System (APFIS) has been developed by Beijing Microelectronics Technology Institute (BMTI), which is engaged in the design, test, package, failure analysis of the Large-scale integration (LSI) and Very Large Scale Integration (VLSI). However, the APFIS is not precise enough. As a result, a more accurate precision fault injection method is studied in this paper. The Automated Precision Fault Injection System-II (APFIS-II) based on this method is made. As early Xilinx devices are still used in special applications without such useful tools, which allowing users to optimize their design conveniently. In this paper, APFIS-II is implemented with Virtex device to improve the reliability of system which contains early devices. The detailed information about the FPGA architecture and configuration bitstream is analyzed. After that, the correspondence between the FPGA resources on-chip and the configuration bitstream is drawn. According to the corresponding relationship, the bitstream is divided into several segments. By APFIS-II, faults are accurately injected into a certain segment instead of the entire bitstream. As a result, faults are able to be injected into a certain resource on-chip. Through this method, the fault injection process is more effective and more targeted, which helps a lot to the study of SEU mechanism and the mitigation techniques.

**ACM Categories & Descriptors:** C.4 Precision Fault Injection; Performance of Systems – fault tolerance

**Keywords:** FPGA, SEU, fault injection, configuration bitstream Decode.

# Custom Instruction Generation and Mapping for Reconfigurable Instruction Set Processors

Chao Wang, Xi Li
*University of Science and Technology of China*
Huizhen Zhang, *Huaqiao University, China*
Jinsong Ji, Xuehai Zhou
*University of Science and Technology of China*
Contact: saintwc@mail.ustc.edu.cn

Reconfigurable instruction set processors (RISP) is an emerging research field for state-of-the-art adaptive systems. However, it still poses significant challenges to generate and map the custom instructions to the original codes. This paper proposes a generation and mapping scheme to extend custom instructions for adaptive RISP. First a target function blocks (basic blocks) are generated from a dynamic profiler. Then the selected hot spot will be considered as a custom instruction and implemented in reconfigurable hardware logic units. With respect to the instruction selection, an instruction generator is utilized to provide a mapping mechanism from hot blocks to hardware implementations, using data flow analysis, instruction clustering, subgraph enumerating and subgraph merging techniques. Finally the original executable files are recompiled and regenerated by a customized GCC compiler. To demonstrate the effectiveness and performance of the framework, a prototype instruction generator has been implemented to verify the correctness and efficiency of the mapping mechanism.

**ACM Categories & Descriptors:** C.0 Instruction Set Design

**Keywords:** Reconfigurable instruction set processors; dynamic profiling; code mapping; custom instruction generation

# High Performance Architecture for Object Detection in Streamed Video

Pavel Zemčík, Roman Juránek, Petr Musil,
Martin Musil, Michal Hradiš
*FIT, Brno University of Technology*
Contact: ijuranek@fit.vutbr.cz

Object detection is one of the key tasks in computer vision. It is computationally intensive and it is reasonable to accelerate it in hardware. The possible benefits of the acceleration are reduction of the computational load of the host computer system, increase of the overall performance of the applications, and reduction of the power consumption. We present novel architecture for multi-scale object detection in video streams. The architecture uses scanning window classifiers produced by WaldBoost learning algorithm, and simple image features. It employs small image buffer for data under processing, and on-the-fly scaling units to enable detection of object in multiple scales. The whole processing chain is pipelined and thus more image windows are processed in parallel. We implemented the engine in Spartan 6 FPGA and we show that it can process 640×480 pixel video streams at over 160 frames per second without the need of external memory. The design takes only a fraction of resources, compared to similar state of the art approaches.

**ACM Categories & Descriptors:** B.8.2 Performance Analysis and Design Aids; I.4.8 Scene Analysis

**Keywords:** Object Detection; WaldBoost; Local Rank Functions; Local Binary Patterns; FPGA, Stream Processing

# Poster Session 2

## Automatic Multidimensional Memory Partitioning for FPGA-Based Accelerators

Yuxin Wang, *Peking University, Beijing, China*
Peng Li, *Peking University, Beijing, China*
Peng Zhang, *University of California, Los Angeles*
Chen Zhang, *Peking University, Beijing, China*
Jason Cong, *University of California, Los Angeles and UCLA/PKU Joint Research Institute, USA*
Contact: featherxinxin@gmail.com

With the increase of data processing throughput in reconfigurable computing, data parallelism is now crucial for the performance of FPGA-based accelerators. However, most of the data parallelism optimizations are still performed manually by experienced hardware designers. Memory partitioning is widely adopted to efficiently increase the memory bandwidth by using multiple memory banks and reducing data access conflict. Previous methods for memory partitioning mainly focused on one-dimensional arrays. As a consequence, designers must flatten a multidimensional array to fit those methodologies, but it makes the partition related to the dimensional width of the array. In this work we propose an automatic memory partitioning scheme for multidimensional arrays to provide high data throughput of on-chip memories for the loop pipelining in high-level synthesis. Linear transformation is applied to optimize the layout of the data elements in the memory banks, with the partition unrelated to the dimensional width. Two transformation vectors are used to map the original data element onto different banks and different inner bank offsets. The vector for the optimal bank mapping is decided by non-conflict access constraint. In addition, a memory padding technique is proposed to find a vector for inner bank offset with a trade-off between practicality and optimality. We use six benchmarks with different access patterns to prove our idea. Compared to the previous one-dimensional partitioning work, the experimental results show that our approach saves up to 21% of block RAMs, 19% in slices, and 46% in DSPs.

**ACM Categories & Descriptors:** B.5.2: Design Aids–*automatic synthesis*;

**Keywords:** High-Level Synthesis, Memory Partitioning, Memory Padding, Linear Transformation

## A Novel Multithread Routing Method for FPGAs

Chun Zhu, Qiuli Li, Jian Wang, Jinmei Lai*
*Fudan University*
Contact: jmlai@fudan.edu.cn

We propose a platform-independent multithread routing method for FPGAs including two aspects: single high fanout net is routed parallel within itself and several low fanout nets are

routed parallel between themselves. Routing for high fanout nets usually takes considerable time because of the large physical area surrounded by bounding boxes to traverse and tens of terminals to connect. Therefore, one high fanout net is partitioned into several subnets with fewer terminals and smaller bounding boxes to be routed in parallel. However, low fanout nets with intrinsic small bounding boxes and few terminals could hardly be divided. Instead, low fanout nets whose bounding boxes are not overlapping with each other are routed concurrently. A new graph, named bounding box graph, was utilized to facilitate the process of selecting several nets to be routed concurrently. In this graph, one vertex stands for a corresponding net and one edge between two connected vertex means that the two represented nets have their bounding boxes overlapped. Several strategies are introduced to balance the load among threads and ensure the deterministic results. The routing times scale down with increasing number of threads. On a 4-core processor, this technique improves the run-time by ~1.9 × with routing quality degrading by no more than 2.3%.

**ACM Categories & Descriptors:** B.7.1 Types and Design Styles; B.7.2 Design Aids; D.1.3 Concurrent Programming

**Keywords:** FPGA routing; multithread; high fanout nets; low fanout nets; bounding box graph; platform-independent

## FPGA Meta-data Management System for Accelerating Implementation Time with Incremental Compilation

Andrew Love, Peter Athanas
*Virginia Polytechnic Institute and State University*
Contact: arlove@vt.edu

The paper presents a mechanism whereby data representing FPGA components to be used in a back-end acceleration flow can be automatically captured, retrieved, and assembled. The FPGA components can be pre-compiled into a very low-level format, such as a bitstream or hard-macro, which is then represented by the meta-data file. The meta-data file maintains the full design information, including mapping between physical and logical primitives, routing and resource utilization. Pre-compiling the components reduces the amount of time required for design assembly, while using meta-data stores required component information for incorporation into a full design. High-level meta-data is also created from a full design for assembly purposes, containing each of the required components. Additionally, information representing design net-lists are automatically obtained and fetched, describing the inter-component connection structure. The high-level meta-data supplies a logical-level description of the connection structure, while the component meta-data contains a mapping of this logical information into physical locations. The FPGA back-end acceleration flow leverages this full design information to obtain significant average speed-up of 15-40x in compilation time over the standard flow.

**ACM Categories & Descriptors:** H.3.6 [Library Automation]; E.1 [Data]: Data Structures – records

**Keywords:** FPGA; back-end acceleration; meta-data

## Achieving Modular Dynamic Partial Reconfiguration with a Difference-Based Flow

Sezer Gören, *Yeditepe University*
Yusuf Turk, *Yeditepe University*
Ozgur Ozkurt, *Vestek R&D*
Abdullah Yildiz, *Yeditepe University*
H. Fatih Ugurdag, *Ozyegin University*
Contact: sgoren@cse.yeditepe.edu.tr

Dynamic Partial Reconfiguration (DPR) of Xilinx FPGAs in cases where there is significant logic difference between subsequent configurations is made possible by Xilinx module-based PR flow. Xilinx supports this flow only for high-end FPGAs and requires paid license, without which Xilinx PlanAhead software disables the related knobs and features. This poster presents a unique methodology (called DPR-LD) that enables DPR of low-end and high-end Xilinx FPGAs and requires no paid license. DPR-LD stands for DPR for Large Differences. DPR-LD uses the free Xilinx difference-based bit file generation software (bitgen), which normally is meant only for small differences between subsequent configurations. DPR-LD can be realized through either FPGA Editor or PlanAhead. Our FPGA Editor flow requires several physical constraints to ensure contention-free implementation of static and dynamic modules. We use implementation, floorplanning, and placement constraints to partition the design into several physical regions (one per module) for mapping, packing, placement, and routing. In order to avoid routing of a module to cross over another module, "fortress block"s are used to isolate the modules from each other. However, fortress blocks lead to wasted FPGA resources. On the other hand, in our PlanAhead flow, the physical constraints are entered via a GUI, and the corresponding actual physical constraints are generated automatically and without wasting FPGA resources. To evaluate the two approaches, a proof-of-concept application with a single dynamic region was implemented using both flows. In addition, a multiple dynamic region design was implemented with our PlanAhead flow.

**ACM Categories & Descriptors:** C.4 [Computer Systems Organization]: Performance of Systems—Modeling techniques

**Keywords:** Dynamic Partial Reconfiguration

## A Novel Run-time Auto-reconfigurable FPGA Architecture for Fast Fault Recovery with Backward Compatibility

Hasan Baig and Jeong-A Lee, *Computer Systems Lab, Chosun University, Gwangju, South Korea*
Contact: hasan.baig@hotmail.com

A self-repairing fault-tolerant FPGA architecture is developed which is also compatible with existing island-style routing network. Due to this backward compatibility, the proposed architecture can not only be implemented easily in the existing FPGA devices but a new fault-tolerant FPGA device can also be fabricated utilizing the existing island-style routing architecture.

A generic fault-tolerant Computation Cell is developed which can be incorporated in existing FPGA CLB (Configurable Logic Block) having 8 LUTs at least. The proposed fault-tolerant FPGA architecture is comprised of Computation Tiles each of which consists of computation cells which are able to heal themselves from transient errors. Computation Tile also contains stem cells which help computation cells to recover from permanent errors all at once. This architecture is centrally controlled by an on-chip fault-tolerant core whose main responsibility is to define the healing priority when an error occurs in more than one of the computation tile at the same time. It also communicates with the external PC software which identifies the faulty tile and reconfigures it through dynamic partial reconfiguration. The robust operation of a proposed architecture is implemented and verified on XILINX Virtex-5 FPGA device. From our proposed fault-tolerant scheme of utilizing the existing routing strategies together with partial reconfiguration of stem cells we achieved a number of benefits, including a fast fault recovery and avoidance of using complicated routing strategies, as compared to recently developed fault-tolerant FPGA architectures.

**ACM Categories & Descriptors:** B.8.1 Reliability, Testing and Fault-Tolerance

**Keywords:** Fault-tolerance; FPGA; Partial Reconfiguration; Self-Reconfiguration; Self-repair; Stem cell; System Biology

## Hardware Acceleration of TEA and XTEA Algorithms on FPGA, GPU and Multi-Core Processors

Vivek Venugopal, Devu Manikantan Shila
*United Technologies Research Center*
Contact: vivek@vivekvenugopal.net

Field programmable gate arrays (FPGA) are extensively used for rapid prototyping in embedded system applications. While hardware acceleration can be done via specialized processors like a Graphical Processing Unit (GPU), they can also be accomplished with FPGAs for more specialized scenarios. GPUs essentially consist of massively parallel cores and have high memory bandwidth; FPGAs, on the other hand, provide flexibility in terms of customizable I/O and computational resources. In this paper, we explore the usage of GPUs and FPGAs as cryptographic co-processors in streaming dataflow systems with huge rate of data inhalation. Two classic lightweight encryption algorithms, Tiny Encryption Algorithm (TEA) and Extended Tiny Encryption Algorithm (XTEA), are targeted for implementation on GPUs and FPGAs. The GPU implementations of TEA and XTEA in this study depict a maximum speedup of 13x over CPU based implementation. The pipelined FPGA implementation is able to realize a throughput of 6-9x more than the GPU for small plaintext sizes.

**ACM Categories & Descriptors:** B.5 Register-Transfer-Level Implementation;

**Keywords:** Tiny Encryption Algorithm; cryptography; field programmable gate arrays; parallel processing; graphics processing units

# A Novel FPGA Design Framework with VLSI Post-routing Performance Analysis

Qian Zhao, Kazuki Inoue, Motoki Amagasaki, Masahiro Iida, Morihiro Kuga, and Toshinori Sueyoshi, *Kumamoto University*
Contact: cho@arch.cs.kumamoto-u.ac.jp

The most widely used open-source field-programmable gate array (FPGA) placement and routing tool is VPR, which can define the target FPGA, perform placement and routing, and report area and timing information. However, it cannot be used in FPGA IP design efficiently for two reasons. First, for most newly developed FPGA architectures, VPR cannot support them directly. Modifying the C-coded VPR for using it to evaluate a number of new architectures requires a long time. Second, the accuracy of the VPR performance results is not enough for the evaluation of a complete synthesizable FPGA IP in the design that targets the productions of LSI. We propose a FPGA design framework that in particular improves FPGA IP design efficiency. A novel FPGA routing tool is developed in this framework, namely EasyRouter. EasyRouter is developed using the C# language. When an object-oriented programming method is used, the source codes are fewer and easier manage compared to VPR, which shortens the development time. By using simple HDL templates, EasyRouter can automatically generate entire chip HDL codes and the configuration bitstream. With these files, the FPGA IP can be evaluated with commercial VLSI CADs with high accuracy and reliability.

**ACM Categories & Descriptors:** B.5.2 Design Aids

**Keywords:** FPGA; CAD; Routing

# An FPGA-Based Transient Error Simulator for Evaluating Resilient System Designs

Chia-Hsiang Chen, Shiming Song, Zhengya Zhang
*University of Michigan, Ann Arbor*
Contact: uchchen@umich.edu

Error-resilient designs have become more important with the continued device scaling. One critical challenge of designing error-resilient systems is the lack of tools to quickly and accurately evaluate the effectiveness and performance of such systems. We propose an FPGA-based transient error simulator to accelerate transient error simulations incorporating accurate datapath delay models and realistic error models. Compared to conventional digital error simulators, the FPGA-based transient error simulator operates at a finer time step and captures intricate interactions between errors and datapath under different circuit-level error detection and correction techniques. The error simulator is constructed using configurable datapath delay model and error model, making it general-purpose and widely applicable.

We demonstrate the capability of this simulator in the evaluation of two popular error-resilient design techniques, pre-edge and post-edge detection and correction, using a synthesized CORDIC processor and an Alpha processor that operate under soft error, coupling noise and voltage droop models. The proposed error simulator uncovers insights to guide practical designs, including the choice of checking window in pre-edge designs and the optimal operating frequency in post-edge designs. The FPGA-based transient simulation will complement circuit simulation and system emulation for resilient system designs.

**ACM Categories & Descriptors:** B.8 Performance and Reliability; I.6 Simulation and Modeling

**Keywords:** Reliability; Error-Resilient Design; Error Detection and Correction; Transient Simulation; FPGA-Based Simulation

# Acceleration of the Long Read Mapping on a PC-FPGA Architecture

Peng Chen, Chao Wang, Xi Li, Xuehai Zhou
*University of Science and Technology of China*
Contact: blueardour@gmail.com

The genome sequence alignment, whereby ultra scale of sequence reads should be compared to an enormous long reference, has been one central challenge to the biologists for a long period. For recent years, new sequencing technology makes it possible to generate longer reads (sequences of genome fragments) which seem more valuable for the life science research. It has been foreseen that long genome reads (length longer than 200 base pairs) will dominate the field in the near future. Unfortunately, most of the state-of-art aligners nowadays are optimized and only applicable for the short read mapping while present long read aligners are still not satisfying at the aspect of speed. In this paper, we propose a novel PC-FPGA hybrid system to improve the performance of the long read mapping. The BWA-SW algorithm is chosen as the alignment approach and by accelerating the bottleneck of the algorithm, our solution could archive a significant improvement in term of speed. Experiments demonstrate that the described system is as accurate as the BWA-SW aligner and about 1.41-2.73 times faster than it for reads with lengths ranging from 500bp to 2000bp.

**ACM Categories & Descriptors:** C.1.3 Computer System Organization; Processor Architectures; Other Architecture Styles, Heterogeneous (hybrid) systems

**Keywords:** Sequence alignment; long read mapping; BWA-SW; hardware acceleration; FPGA

# Poster Session 3

## Effect of Fixed-Point Arithmetic on Deep Belief Networks

Jingfei Jiang, Rongdong Hu
*National University of Defence Technology*
Mikel Luján, *University of Manchester*
Contact: jingfeijiang@nudt.edu.cn

Deep Belief Networks (DBNs) are state-of-the-art learning algorithms building on a subset of neural networks, Restricted Boltzmann Machine (RBM). DBNs are computationally intensive posing the question of whether DBNs can be FPGA accelerated. Fixed-point arithmetic can have an important influence on the execution time and prediction accuracy of a DBN. Previous studies have focused only on customized RBM accelerators with a fixed data-width. Our results experiments demonstrate that variable data-widths can obtain similar performance levels. We can also observe that the most suitable data-widths for different types of DBN are not unique or fixed. From this we conclude that a DBN accelerator should support various data-widths rather than only fixed one as done in previous work. The processing performance of DBN accelerators in FPGA is almost always constrained not by the capacity of the processing units, but by their on-chip RAM capacity and speed. We propose an efficient memory sub-system combining junction and padding methods to reduce bandwidth usage for DBN accelerators, which shows that supporting various data-widths is not as difficult as it may sound. The cost is only little in hardware terms and does not affect the critical path. We design a generation tool to help users reconfiguring the memory sub-system with arbitrary data-width flexibly. Our tool can also be used as an advanced IP core generator above FPGA memory controller supporting parallel memory access in irregular data-width for other applications.

**ACM Categories & Descriptors:** C.3 [Special-purpose and application-based systems]: neural network processing systems

**Keywords:** Deep belief network; Fixed-Point Arithmetic; Memory Subsystem

## A Memory-efficient Hardware Architecture for Real-time Feature Detection of the SIFT Algorithm

Wenjuan Deng, Yiqun Zhu, *University of Nottingham*
Contact: eexwd2@nottingham.ac.uk

The SIFT (Scale Invariant Feature Transform) is a most popular image processing algorithm that has been widely used in solving image matching related problems. However, SIFT is of high computational complexity and large memory requirement that prevent it from being applied to applications that are unable to offer large on-chip memory. Based on the analysis of the memory requirement of SIFT feature detection, a novel memory access strategy is proposed to reduce the hardware memory usage. In addition, to achieve real-time performance of high resolution video streams, dedicated hardware architecture with multi-pixel based processing scheme has been developed. Compared with conventional designs, our design achieves hardware memory reduction of at least 58.8%.

**ACM Categories & Descriptors:** B. Hardware; B.5 Register-transfer-level implementation; B.5.1 Design; Subjects: Styles

**Keywords:** FPGA, Hardware Architecture, Memory Reduction, SIFT, Feature Detection

## Exploiting Algorithmic-Level Memory Parallelism in Distributed Logic-Memory Architecture through Hardware-Assisted Dynamic Graph

Bai Yu, Abigail Fuentes, Mike Riera, Mingjie Lin
*University of Central Florida*
Contact: mingjie@eecs.ucf.edu

Emerging FPGA device, integrated with abundant RAM blocks and high-performance processor cores, offers an unprecedented opportunity to effectively implement single-chip distributed logic-memory (DLM) architectures. Being "memory-centric", the DLM architecture can significantly improve the overall performance and energy efficiency of many memory-intensive embedded applications, especially those that exhibit irregular array data access patterns at algorithmic level. However, implementing DLM architecture poses unique challenges to an FPGA designer in terms of 1) organizing and partitioning diverse on-chip memory resources, and 2) orchestrating effective data transmission between on-chip and off-chip memory. In this paper, we offer our solutions to both of these challenges. Specifically, 1) we propose a stochastic memory partitioning scheme based on the well-known simulated annealing algorithm. It obtains memory partitioning solutions that promote parallelized memory accesses by exploring large solution space; 2) we augment the proposed DLM architecture with a reconfigure hardware graph that can dynamically compute precedence relationship between memory partitions, thus effectively exploiting algorithmic level memory parallelism on a per-application basis.

We evaluate the effectiveness of our approach (A3) against two other DLM architecture synthesizing methods: an algorithmic-centric reconfigurable computing architectures with a single monolithic memory (A1) and the heterogeneous distributed architectures synthesized according to (A2). All experiments have been conducted with a Virtex-5 (XCV5LX155T-2) FPGA. On average, our experimental results show that our proposed A3 architecture outperforms A2 and A1 by 34% and 250%, respectively. Within the performance improvement of A3 over A2, more than 70% improvement comes from the hardware graph-based memory scheduling.

**ACM Categories & Descriptors:** D.1.3 Concurrent Programming; D.3.2 Language Classifications

**Keywords:** FPGA, memory parallelism, algorithmic level, dynamic graph.

## FPGA-Based HPC Application Design for Non-Experts

David Uliana, Krzysztof Kepa, Peter Athanas
*Virginia Tech*
Contact: duliana@vt.edu

This paper presents bFlow, an FPGA development framework for the rapid prototyping and implementation of hardware accelerators for hybrid computing platforms. This framework makes use of an abstracted, graphical front-end usable by those without computer engineering backgrounds, as well as an accelerated back-end that speeds up compilation times, increasing turns-per-day. bFlow's performance, usability, and application to the acceleration of big-data life-science problems verified by participants of the NSF-funded Summer Institute organised by the Virginia Bioinformatics Institute (VBI). In less than two weeks, a group of four non-computer science/computer engineering participants made modifications to a reference Smith-Waterman implementation, adding functionality and scaling throughput by a factor of four to 600 million base pairs per second.

**ACM Categories & Descriptors:** B.6.3 Design Aids; B.8.2 Performance Analysis and Design Aids

**Keywords:** Big-data, Bioinformatics, Convey HC-1, Co-processor, Design Productivity, Field-programmable Gate Arrays, Heterogeneous computing

## AutoMapper - An Automated Tool for Optimal Hardware Resource Allocation for Networking Applications on FPGA

Swapnil Haria, *Birla Institute of Technology & Science, Pilani*
Viktor Prasanna, *University of Southern California*
Contact: swapnilster@gmail.com

It has now become imperative for routers to support complicated lookup schemes, based on the specific function of the networking hardware. It is no longer possible to ensure an optimal resource utilization using manual organization techniques due to the increasing complexity of lookup schemes, as well as the large number of potential implementation choices. We have developed an automated tool, AutoMapper, which can map lookup schemes onto a particular target architecture optimally, thereby providing a superior alternative to the time-consuming and resource inefficient technique of manual conversion. It is based on an Integer Linear Programming (ILP) formulation that is able to allocate the limited hardware resources for a single lookup scheme, while optimizing any of the three performance metrics of latency, throughput or power consumption. Accurate formulation of the objective function and the constraint equations guarantee optimality in terms of the chosen performance metric. We demonstrate the operation of the developed tool, by successfully mapping complex real world lookup schemes onto a state-of-the art FPGA device, with execution times being under a second on a dual-core computer with 4 GB of RAM, running at 2.40 GHz.

**ACM Categories & Descriptors:** C.2.1 Network Architecture and Design

**Keywords:** Resource Allocation; Networking; High-level Tool

## Performance and Toolchain of a Combined GPU/FPGA Desktop

Bruno da Silva, *Erasmus University College, Brussels*
An Braeken, *Erasmus University College, Brussels*
Erik H. D'Hollander, *Ghent University, Ghent, Belgium*
Abdellah Touhafi, *Erasmus University College,Brussels*
Jan G. Cornelis, *Free University of Brussels, Belgium*
Jan Lemeire, *Free University of Brussels, Belgium*
Contact: dhollander@elis.ugent.be

Low-power, high-performance computing nowadays relies on accelerator cards to speed up the calculations. Combining the power of GPUs with the flexibility of FPGAs enlarges the scope of problems that can be accelerated [2, 3]. We describe the performance analysis of a desktop equipped with a GPU Tesla 2050 and an FPGA Virtex-6 LX240T. First, the balance between the I/O and the raw peak performance is depicted using the roofline model [4]. Next, the performance of a number of image processing algorithms is measured and the results are mapped onto the roofline graph. This allows to compare the GPU and the FPGA and also to optimize the algorithms for both accelerators. A programming toolchain is implemented, consisting of OpenCL for the GPU and several High-Level Synthesis compilers for the FPGA. Our results show that the HLS compilers outperform handwritten code and offer a performance comparable to the GPU. In addition the FPGA compilers reduce the development time by an order of magnitude, at the expense of an increased resource consumption. The roofline model also shows that both accelerators are equally limited by the input/output bandwidth to the host. A well-tuned accelerator-based codesign, identifying the parallelism, the computation and data patterns of different classes of algorithms, will enable to maximize the performance of the combined GPU/FPGA system [1].

**ACM Categories & Descriptors:** C.1.3 Processor Architectures: Heterogeneous (hybrid) systems —Performance; D.1.3 Program-ming Techniques: Parallel programming—High-level synthesis

**Keywords:** Performance; OpenCL; FPGA; GPU; accelerators; programming toolchain; HLS compilers

## Hardware Description and Synthesis of Control-Intensive Reconfigurable Dataflow Architectures

Marc-Andre Daigneault, Jean Pierre David
*Ecole Polytechnique de Montreal*
Contact: marc-andre.daigneault@polymtl.ca

Field-Programmable-Gate-Arrays are used increasingly to speed up applications in various fields of science. But as modern digital designs integrate hundreds of interconnected processing and memory units, the need for a higher level of abstraction to handle their descriptions is indisputable. This paper presents a beyond-RTL concurrent hardware description language that combines both Finite-State Machine (FSM) and constraint programming paradigms. At the featured level of abstraction, the user describes dynamic connections between data sources and sinks that may not always be ready to send or receive data tokens. The high-level description methodology enables a comprehensible description of behaviors such as data transfer synchronization, exclusivity, priority and constrained scheduling by the means of logical-implication rules constraining the data transfers authorizations. Dynamically connecting resources with potential combinatorial dependencies may lead to instability or deadlock. Such situations are automatically detected and fixed by the proposed compiler that generates a dedicated control-circuit optimizing the number of transfers that can be authorized at each clock cycle. The proposed design automation methodology is applied to the problem of deeply-pipelined vector reduction. A pipelined floating point accumulator and a matrix multiplication circuits are described with a few lines of code and automatically compiled into an FPGA. Results show that the synthesis results are comparable to those obtained with hand-written RTL but with much lower effort and time.

**ACM Categories & Descriptors:** B.6.3 Design Aids; J.6 Computer-Aided Engineering

**Keywords:** High-Level Synthesis; Hardware Description Language, Cyclic Combinatorial Relations; Dataflow Architectures; Streaming Interfaces;

# Automating Resource Optimisation in Reconfigurable Design

Xinyu Niu, Thomas C. P. Chau, Qiwei Jin,
Wayne Luk, *Imperial College London*
Qiang Liu, *Tianjin University*
Contact: niushin@gmail.com

A design approach is proposed to automatically identify and exploit run-time reconfiguration opportunities while optimising resource utilisation. We introduce Configuration Data Flow Graph, a hierarchical graph structure enabling reconfigurable designs to be synthesised in three steps: function analysis, configuration organisation, and run-time solution generation. Three applications, based on barrier option pricing, particle filter, and reverse time migration are used in evaluating the proposed approach. The run-time solutions approximate the theoretical performance by eliminating idle functions, and are 1.61 to 2.19 times faster than optimised static designs. FPGA designs developed with the proposed approach are up to 28.8 times faster than optimised CPU reference designs and 1.55 times faster than optimised GPU designs.

**ACM Categories & Descriptors: B.5.2 [Register-Transfer-Level Implementation]:** Design aids—Optimization; **C.0 [Computer System Organization]:** System architectures

**Keywords:** Run-time reconfiguration, Reconfigurable computing

# Poster Session 4

## Low Power FPGA Design Using Post-silicon Device Aging

Sheng Wei, Jason Xin Zheng, Miodrag Potkonjak
*University of California, Los Angeles*
Contact: shengwei@cs.ucla.edu

The impact of process variation (PV) in deep submicron CMOS technologies has raised major concerns for energy optimization efforts in FPGAs. We have developed a post-silicon leakage energy optimization scheme that raises the threshold voltage (by way of negative bias temperature instability (NBTI) aging) of the components that are either unused or not on the critical timing paths, thereby reducing the total leakage energy consumption. In order to obtain the input vectors for aging only the targeted transistors, we map the problem of minimizing leakage energy under timing constraints to an instance of the satisfiability (SAT) problem. We implemented low power designs targeting Xilinx Spartan6 FPGAs and analyzed the potential leakage power savings over a set of ITC99 and Opencores benchmarks. The analysis of the experimental results shows a substantial amount of potential leakage energy reduction with very small performance degradation.

**ACM Categories & Descriptors:** B.7.m [Hardware]: Integrated Circuits—Miscellaneous

**Keywords:** Low power; negative bias temperature instability; process variation

## Circuit Optimizations to Minimize Energy in the Global Interconnect of a Low-Power FPGA

Oluseyi Ayorinde, Benton H. Calhoun
*University of Virginia*
Contact: oaa4bj@virginia.edu

This work compares circuit and architecture choices in the global interconnect of an FPGA in order to find the minimum energy design for low voltage operation. We look at switch box topology, number of repeaters, receiver circuit topology, and dynamic voltage selection, all with the intent of minimizing energy consumption. We find the optimal choices are a pass gate switch box, employing a dual-VDD scheme with boosted gate voltages, a custom receiver circuit as both the final receiver in the global interconnect path and the repeaters. The results show that using these circuit choices lowers delay by up to 63% and energy by up to 87% from the standard FPGA circuit choices. This work also identifies the optimal VDD choices to maximize performance under energy constraints or vice versa.

**ACM Categories & Descriptors:** B.7.1 Types and Design Styles – *Gate arrays;* B.7.2 Design Aids – *Simulation*

**Keywords:** Circuit Optimization; FPGA; Global Interconnect; Sub-threshold FPGA; Dynamic Voltage Scaling; Dual-VDD Implementation

## Efficient System-Level Mapping from Streaming Applications to FPGAs

Jason Cong, Muhuan Huang, Peng Zhang
*University of California, Los Angeles*
Contact: mhhuang@cs.ucla.edu

Streaming processing is an important computation model that represents many applications in various domains such as video processing, signal processing and wireless communication. FPGA is a natural platform for streaming applications because the task-level pipelined parallelism can be efficiently implemented on FPGA by its customizable communication and memory architecture. In this paper we propose an efficient design space exploration algorithm to map kernels of streaming applications onto FPGAs. We aim at finding the most area-efficient selections of hardware modules from the implementation library while satisfying the system performance requirement. In particular, we consider both module selection and replication techniques. Design metrics are formulated in our high-level model based on these two techniques. In addition, we extend the analytic formulations in previous work by supporting complex stream graph structures like feedback loops. The proposed iterative exploration algorithm is based on the system of difference constraint (SDC) and thus can be solved in polynomial time. Compared to previous mainstream ILP-based solutions, our proposed algorithm is scalable and practical in large systems. Both the ILP formulation and our proposed iterative exploration mechanism are applied to a set of streaming applications from StreamIt benchmarks and also to one real example MPEG-4 decoder. Experiments demonstrate that our design space exploration algorithm can efficiently find a feasible solution with an average 5.7% area overhead.

**ACM Categories & Descriptors:** B.6.3 Design Aids

**Keywords:** Module Selection; Module Replication; Scheduling; SDC; Streaming; Throughput

## Defect Recovery in Nanodevice-Based Programmable Interconnects

Jason Cong, *University of California, Los Angeles*
Bingjun Xiao, *University of California, Los Angeles*
Contact: xiao@cs.ucla.edu

This work focuses on defect tolerance for nanodevice-based programmable interconnects of FPGAs. A single nanodevice can function as a routing switch in place of a pass transistor and its six-transistor SRAM cell in conventional FPGAs. Defects of nanodevices in programmable interconnects are manifested as losses of configurability and can be categorized into stuck-open defect and stuck-closed defect. First, we show that the stuck-closed defects of nanodevices have a much higher impact than the stuck-open defects. Instead of simply avoiding the stuck-closed defects, we recover them by treating them as shorting constraints in the routing. We develop a scalable algorithm to perform timing-driven routing under these extra constraints. We extend the idea of the resource negotiation to balance the goals of timing and routability under shorting constraints. We also develop several techniques to guide the router to map the shorting clusters to those nets with more shared paths for better utilization of routing resources while automatically balancing it with circuit performance. We also enhance the placement algorithm to recover logic blocks which become virtually unusable due to shorted pins. Simulation results show that at the up-to-date level of nanodevice defects ($10^8$–$10^{11}$x higher than CMOS), compared to the simple avoidance method, our approach reduces the degradation of resource usage by 87%, improves the routability by 37%, and reduce the degradation of circuit performance by 36%, at a negligible overhead of tool runtime.

**ACM Categories & Descriptors:** B.7.3 Reliability and Testing; B.7.2 Design Aids

**Keywords:** nanodevice; defect tolerance; programmable interconnects; route; placement;

## A High-Performance, Low-Energy FPGA Accelerator for Correntropy-Based Feature Tracking

Patrick Cooke, Jeremy Fowers, *University of Florida*
Lee Hunt, *Prioria, Inc.*
Greg Stitt, *University of Florida*

Computer-vision and signal-processing applications often require feature tracking to identify and track the motion of different objects (features) across a sequence of images. Numerous algorithms have been proposed, but common measures of similarity for real-time usage are either based on correlation, mean-squared error, or sum of absolute differences, which are not robust enough for safety-critical applications. To improve robustness, a recent feature-tracking algorithm called C-Flow uses correntropy from Information Theoretic Learning to significantly improve signal-to-noise ratio. In this presentation, we present an FPGA accelerator for C-Flow that is typically 3.6-8.5x faster than a GPU and show that the FPGA is the only device capable of real-time usage for large features. Furthermore, we show the FPGA accelerator is more appropriate for embedded usage, with energy consumption that is 2.5-22x less than the GPU.

**ACM Categories & Descriptors:** C.3 [**Special-purpose and Application-based Systems**]: Real-time and embedded systems

**Keywords:** FPGA, GPU, feature tracking, correntropy, optical flow.

## Scalable High-throughput Architecture for Large Balanced Tree Structures on FPGA

Yun Qu, *University of Southern California*
Viktor Prasanna, *University of Southern California*
Contact: yunqu@usc.edu

Architectures for tree structures on FPGAs as well as ASICs have been proposed over the years. The exponential growth in the memory size with respect to the tree levels restricts the scalability of these architectures due to limited on-chip memory.

For large trees, off-chip memory has to be used. We propose a pipeline architecture on FPGA for large balanced tree structures which achieves both scalability and high throughput. In the proposed architecture, each tree level is mapped onto a single or multiple Processing Elements (PEs) using dual-port distributed RAM, dual-port block RAM and off-chip RAM. We parameterize the pipeline architecture and optimize the performance with respect to scalability and throughput. The resulting architecture for the search tree is dual-threaded and deeply pipelined. It can accept two search requests per clock cycle and operates at a high clock rate of 280MHz. Post place-and-route results show that, by using only 17% of the logic resources and 9% of the BRAM available on a state-of-the-art FPGA, our dual-thread pipelined search tree can perform 560 million search operations per second in a tree containing 512K 64-bit keys.

**ACM Categories & Descriptors:** C.1.4 Parallel Architectures; C.3 Special-purpose and Application-based Systems

**Keywords:** Tree; FPGA; Scalable; High-throughput

## Co-simulation framework of SystemC SoC Virtual Prototype and Custom Logic

Nick Ni, Yi Peng, *Altera Corporation*
Contact: nni@altera.com

To address the increasing demand of System-on-Chip (SoC) for high performance applications and IP programmability, specialized SoC with custom logic is developed in a single chip or multi-chip system. Like any other SoC platforms, early software development before hardware availability using a Virtual Prototype (VP) is essential. However, the existing RTL for custom logic makes it non-trivial to simulate the entire system with software models written in high-level language (i.e. SystemC/C/C++). In this paper, we describe our unique virtual prototyping framework called "FPGA-In-the-Loop (FIL)" to enable co-simulation of software models in the VP and custom logic running in the FPGA at native speed. This platform enables designers to start early software development and integration of the entire hardware platform without needing to develop software models for custom logic. More importantly, our contributions lie in overcoming two of the biggest challenges in such co-simulation systems; 1) the communication channel performance bottleneck and 2) software-visible asynchronous signal timing correctness (i.e. interrupt). Our framework was able to 1) optimize communications between the VP and FPGA to achieve up to 872 Mbps effective throughput and 2) guarantee software-visible asynchronous signal delivery timing (i.e. interrupts) between the two simulation domains. Finally, we implemented our framework on a commercial hybrid platform with SoC and FPGA to demonstrate the complete embedded Linux stack communicating with custom video/touchscreen IPs running in the FPGA.

**ACM Categories & Descriptors:** B.1.2 [**Hardware**]: Control Structures and Microprogramming – *simulation*

**Keywords:** Virtual Platform, Virtual Prototype, SystemC, TLM, Custom Logic, FPGA, SoC, Embedded Software and Co-simulation

# Rectification of Advanced Microprocessors without Changing Routing on FPGAs

Satoshi Jo, Amir Masoud Gharehbaghi,
Takeshi Matsumoto, Masahiro Fujita
*The University of Tokyo*
Contact: amir@cad.t.u-tokyo.ac.jp

We propose a method for rectification of bugs in microprocessors that are implemented on FPGAs, by only changing the configuration of LUTs, without any modification to the routing. Therefore, correcting the bugs does not require resynthesis, which can be very long for complex microprocessors due to possible timing closure problems. As the structure of the circuit is preserved, correcting the bugs does not affect the timings of the circuit. In design phase, we may add additional LUTs to the original circuit, so that we can use them in the correction phase. After a bug is found, we perform the following two tasks. Fist, we find the candidate control signals as well as the required change to correct their behavior. This is done by using symbolic simulation and equivalency checking between the formal specification and the erroneous formal model of the processor. Then, we try to map the corrected functionality into the existing LUT structure. This is done by a novel method that formulates the problem as a QBF (Quantified Boolean Formula) problem, and solves it by repeatedly applying normal SAT solvers instead of QBF solvers under a CEGAR (Counter Example Guided Abstraction Refinement) paradigm. We show effectiveness of our method by correcting bugs in two complex out-of-order superscalar processors with two different timing error recovery mechanisms.

**ACM Categories & Descriptors:** B.8.1 Reliability, Testing, and Fault-Tolerance; B.7.2 Design Aids

**General Terms:** Algorithms; Verification

**Keywords:** Design Error Diagnosis; Design Error Rectification; QBF; CEGAR; FPGA; Formal Verification; Microprocessors

# Shadow AICs: Reaping the Benefits of And-Inverter Cones with Minimal Architectural Impact

Hadi Parandeh-Afshar, Grace Zgheib,
David Novo, Madhura Purnaprajna, Paolo Ienne
*Ecole Polytechnique Fédérale de Lausanne*
Contact: grace.zgheib@epfl.ch

Despite their many advantages, FPGAs are still inefficient. This inefficiency is mainly due to programmable routing networks; however, FPGA logic blocks also have their share of contribution. From the performance perspective, fewer hops in the routing network translates to a shorter critical path; and that requires large logic blocks capable of covering big portions of circuits. Recent work has shown that And-Inverter Cones (AICs) can considerably reduce the number of logic block levels compared to Look-Up Tables (LUTs). The best performance is achieved when both AICs and LUTs are used, but the AIC implementation requires radical changes in the FPGAs architecture.

In this paper, we use AICs as shadow logic for LUTs in LUT-clusters, which requires minimal architectural changes while exploiting the benefits of both AICs and LUTs. The basic idea is to reuse the input crossbar of LUT-clusters for the shadow AICs while combining both LUTs and AICs in the same cluster. We also propose changes in the AIC architecture to enhance mapping on AICs. Our experimental results indicate that the new cluster architecture can reduce the average circuit delay by 12% with respect to standard FPGA clusters. However, this performance gain comes at a price of 43% area overhead in terms of number of logic clusters.

Our results show that for a modest 6% increase in area, FPGA manufacturers can move towards next-generation FPGA logic elements. This transition would provide faster design options without major architectural changes.

**ACM Categories & Descriptors:** B.6.1 Design Styles; B.7.1 Types and Design Styles

**Keywords:** FPGA Logic Block; Technology Mapping; Shadow Logic; And-Inverter Cone

# Author Index

# Notes

www.ingramcontent.com/pod-product-compliance
Lightning Source LLC
Chambersburg PA
CBHW080356060326
40689CB00019B/4035